APPIAN

The Civil Wars

Translated with an Introduction by
JOHN CARTER

PENGUIN BOOKS

PENGUIN BOOKS

Published by the Penguin Group
Penguin Books Ltd, 27 Wrights Lane, London w8 5tz, England
Penguin Putnam Inc., 375 Hudson Street, New York, New York 10014, USA
Penguin Books Australia Ltd, Ringwood, Victoria, Australia
Penguin Books Canada Ltd, 10 Alcorn Avenue, Toronto, Ontario, Canada m4v 3b2
Penguin Books India (P) Ltd, 11, Community Centre, Panchsheel Park, New Delhi – 110 017, India
Penguin Books (NZ) Ltd, Private Bag 102902, NSMC, Auckland, New Zealand
Penguin Books (South Africa) (Pty) Ltd, 5 Watkins Street, Denver Ext 4, Johannesburg 2094, South Africa

Penguin Books Ltd, Registered Offices: Harmondsworth, Middlesex, England

This translation first published 1996

4

Copyright © John Carter, 1996
All rights reserved

The moral right of the translator has been asserted

Maps drawn by Nigel Andrews

Set in 9.5/12pt Monotype Bembo
Typeset by Datix International Limited, Bungay, Suffolk
Printed in England by Clays Ltd, St Ives plc

PENGUIN  CLASSICS

THE CIVIL WARS

APPIAN was born into the privileged Greek upper class of Alexandria, probably about AD 95. He rose to high office in his native city, and appears to have practised law at Rome, where he made the acquaintance of Fronto and pleaded in cases before the emperors Hadrian and Antoninus Pius. He composed his *Roman History* between *c.* AD 145 and 165, at the height of the period which Gibbon called 'the golden age of the Antonines'.

JOHN CARTER retired from a Senior Lectureship at Royal Holloway College, University of London, in 1992. He collaborated with Ian Scott-Kilvert on Cassius Dio's *The Roman History* (1987) for Penguin Classics, and other published work includes a history of Augustus' rise to power, *The Battle of Actium* (1970), and editions of Suetonius' life of Augustus, *Divus Augustus* (1982), and of Julius Caesar's own account of his war with Pompey, *Civil War* (2 vols., 1991 and 1993).

CONTENTS

The Civil Wars

ACKNOWLEDGEMENTS

This translation is dedicated to the memory of the late and kind Ian Scott-Kilvert, with whom I worked on Cassius Dio, *The Roman History: the Reign of Augustus* (Penguin Books, 1987). Without his suggestion that a new translation of Appian's *Civil Wars* was needed this version would never have been made. I can only hope that it succeeds in being a worthy companion to his translations of those other, better-regarded Greek writers on Roman affairs, Dio, Plutarch, and Polybius.

I should also like to thank Rosalind Thomas, Stephen Usher, Philip de Souza, and Paul Tweddle for constructive criticism and suggestions offered when the Introduction was in draft. Without their help this would undoubtedly have been worse in various ways, and I take sole responsibility for such faults as now remain. Dennis Napier was generous enough to read an early version of Book I. But my greatest debt is, as ever, to my wife both for her forbearance and support during the protracted birth of this book, and for her invaluable sense of what is and is not readable English.

John Carter

Bath
June 1995

INTRODUCTION

I. APPIAN AND HIS *ROMAN HISTORY*

a. *The Author and His Historical Context*

Appian concludes the Preface to his whole *Roman History*, of which the *Civil Wars* contained in the present volume is but a small part, with these words:

Who the author of this work is, many people know; I have myself given an indication, but to speak more plainly, I am Appian of Alexandria. I reached the highest distinction in my own country, and pleaded in cases at Rome before the emperors, until they promoted me to be one of their procurators. If anyone is keen to know more, there is a book of mine on the subject.

This is very nearly all we know of the author, since only a tiny fragment of the autobiography he refers to survives.[1] He must, however, have written his *Roman History* about the middle of the second century AD, because earlier in the Preface he observes that 'from the advent of the emperors to the present time is nearly two hundred years'. It is far from clear exactly what date he meant to indicate by the phrase 'the advent of the emperors' – perhaps Caesar's dictatorship (first in 49 BC), perhaps Philippi (42 BC), perhaps Actium (31 BC), perhaps even the constitutional settlement of 27 BC, but his expression is vague enough for this uncertainty not to matter. He also reckons a total of 900 years for the span of Roman history, which, given the traditional foundation date of Rome of 753 BC, leads to the same conclusion. Other evidence is provided by the fragment of autobiography mentioned above, which tells of Appian's providential escape from a party of Jews who were pursuing him in the Nile marshes at the time of the great Jewish revolt in AD 115–117. He can hardly have been less than twenty at the time, so it is unlikely that his date of birth should be placed much later than *c.* AD 95. This tallies with a letter written to Antoninus Pius (emperor AD 138–161) by Fronto, who was one of the most famous barristers of the day, and tutor to the emperor's adoptive son and successor Marcus

Aurelius. In this letter Fronto asks Pius, for at least the third time, to grant his old friend and fellow-practitioner Appian the rank of procurator, and explains that it is the honour in his old age that Appian covets, not the office or the pay. Fronto's letter is of unknown date, but seems most likely to belong to the years between AD 147 and 161.[2] Even in 147, Appian would have been over fifty, which by the standards of the ancient world certainly meant that he had entered old age, and he could well have been considerably older.

We have no idea when Appian died, but there exist two clues to the date he completed the *Roman History*. The first is his reference in Book I of the *Civil Wars* (ch. 38) to an administrative arrangement of Hadrian's which he notes was reversed by Pius — but he does not mention that Marcus Aurelius reinstated it, which we are told occurred in AD 163.[3] The second is a mention in the Preface of the Euphrates as the eastern boundary of the Empire, a fact which ceased to be true with Verus' Parthian expedition in AD 165.[4] The Preface, however, must surely have accompanied the first book or group of books of his projected history, as it did in Livy's case, and unless the whole work (improbably in view of its size) was published at the same time can only date the first part of it. All one can really say is that the most probable period of composition is between *c.* AD 145 and AD 165, and there is a reasonable probability that at least the first three-quarters of the *Roman History* had been published by AD 163. These decades are the apogee of what is often called the 'Golden Age' of the Antonines. Appian's optimism about the Roman imperial system (see IV*e* below) therefore hardly needs any other explanation.

The man himself, apart from what can be deduced from his *History*, remains otherwise hidden from us. We do not know whether the procuratorship he coveted and eventually won was honorary or real, and if the latter, where he exercised it. He must have been a member of the privileged Greek upper class of Alexandria (who hated, and were hated by, the Jews of that city), but what he means by 'the highest distinction in his own country' is not very clear. At this epoch talented and well-connected young men might well reach a prominent position in their own communities by the age of thirty or so, which would give ample time to make a second career at Rome. It has sometimes been thought that 'pleading cases before the emperors' (presumably Hadrian and Pius) refers to the activity of the counsel for the treasury (*advocatus fisci*). If that is so Appian has chosen a strangely oblique way of putting it, and we would not expect him to have had to depend on Fronto's intercession with Pius to be promoted procurator.[5] And it is equally obscure whether he wrote the *History* in Rome or in retirement at Alexandria.

b. *The* Roman History

Appian's Preface explains the nature and individuality of his account of Roman history. This is essentially a narrative of conquest and struggle, and therefore a narrative of war. This is not to say that he ignores the causes of war or the political and social conditions which brought it about in any particular case. But it is obvious that for Appian it is the fact that the Roman state became the most durable imperial power in history which constitutes and exemplifies the greatness and uniqueness of the Romans, and for him that aspect is to be seen and studied in the processes of conquest. Like his younger contemporary Aelius Aristides he wrote for a cultured Greek-speaking upper class of the eastern Mediterranean, who had long been not merely affected by Roman rule, but also deeply involved with its workings. Some of its members had already become Roman senators and even consuls, while many more, like Appian himself, had benefited from imperial patronage or served the Empire or its local representatives in one capacity or another. But although Rome had established a secure world-order, she remained a foreign power, her history and institutions generally little understood or appreciated by men who had been brought up on the Greek classics and did not subscribe to quite the same values as their political masters. For this audience and this story, the constitutional imprecision for which modern scholars are fond of berating Appian was unimportant.

Appian's fundamental idea is to paint a clearer picture of the relationship of the Romans to the various nations whom they brought under their sway 'in order to understand the weaknesses or endurance of peoples, as well as the virtues or good fortune of their conquerors, or any other factor which contributed to the result' (Preface, ch. 12). This leads him to break up his narrative in such a way that each book (or in the case of extended topics like the civil wars, groups of books) deals with the interaction of Rome and a particular ethnic group – Gauls, Syrians, Africans, and so on. None the less, he follows a fairly clear chronological scheme, placing the books in the order in which the various peoples first clashed with the Romans. This inevitably involved a certain separation of interlocking events. A good example is the Second Punic War, with its Spanish, Sicilian, and Italian theatres. Appian treats these in three separate books and restricts the term 'Hannibalic' to Hannibal's time in Italy.

The actual arrangement of the *Roman History* is known to us from Appian's own description in the Preface (chs. 14–15), from a notice in the Byzantine scholar Photius,[6] and from two other anonymous lists. From these it is possible to reconstruct the sequence and numbering of the books, as follows:

I	The Kings of Rome
II	Italy
III	The Samnites
IV	The Gauls
V	Sicily and the Islands
VI	Spain
VII	Hannibal
VIII	Carthage and Numidia (or Punic Wars)
IX	Macedonia and Illyria
X	Greece and Ionia
XI	Syria and Parthia
XII	The Mithridatic War
XIII–XVII	The Civil Wars I–V
XVIII–XXI	The Egyptian Wars I–IV
XXII	The Hundred Years
XXIII	Dacia
XXIV	The Arabian War

Of the list above, Books VI and VII, the first half of VIII, the second half of IX, the first half of XI, XII, and XIII–XVII have come down to us complete, as have excerpts from I–V and IX and fragments from XXIV and various unstated places. It is notable that the last three books find no mention in Appian's Preface, which speaks only of a single book after the wars of Augustus and Antonius (which he treated in the *Egyptian History*, see *Civil Wars* I.6), and that single book was intended to be descriptive of the present military and financial resources and dispositions of the Empire. It seems that he modified his original plan when he had reached the end of the Republic. Perhaps he realized that there was a least one major period of civil war under the Empire, the year AD 69, and that the additions made to the Empire by Augustus on the rivers Rhine and Danube and in Spain and the Alpine regions, by Claudius in Britain, and by Trajan in Dacia and Arabia, did not deserve to be passed over in silence. But we can only guess. There are also signs of a modification of the way in which he handled the civil wars themselves. The Preface (ch. 14) divides them into four periods, associated with the struggles of Marius against Sulla, Caesar against Pompeius, Antonius and Octavian against the murderers of Caesar, and finally Antonius and Octavian against each other. The first two periods correspond well enough with the first two books of the *Civil Wars*, but by the time Appian came to start that work he had decided, in accordance with the official Augustan view of the matter, that the final struggle between Antonius and Octavian (34–30 BC) was not a civil war and should be separately treated in his *Egyptian History* (see *Civil Wars* I.6). As a result he ended the *Civil Wars* in 35 BC with the defeat and death of Sextus Pompeius, and Books III–V cover both more and less than his preliminary description of their subject-matter. It appears that, like Livy before him and Dio Cassius after him, he could not resist the wealth of material at his disposal or the magnitude and pathos of the events of this period, and allowed his narrative to expand to a degree which he seems not to have envisaged when he wrote the Preface. If this view is correct, it would follow that Appian published the Preface (again, as noted above, like Livy) to accompany the first instalment (Books I–XII?) of his *Roman History*, and that even if, as some think,[7] the work may have remained unfinished at his death, substantial parts of it were published in his lifetime.

II. STRUCTURE AND CONTENT OF THE *CIVIL WARS*

a. The Place of the Civil Wars in the Scheme

Of his twenty-four books, Appian chose to devote no fewer than seven (the last three of the *Civil Wars* and all four of the *Egyptian History*) to the fourteen years between 44 and 30 BC, and a further two (the first two of the *Civil Wars*) to 133–44 BC. It is plain, then, how much importance he attached to the civil wars. On the face of it this seems somewhat paradoxical, since his stated aim is to examine the qualities of the Romans when compared with those of the other races against whom they fought in the process of building their Empire. However, another strand of thought is present in the general Preface to the *Roman History*. After alluding to, and listing, the vast resources of the Ptolemaic kings of Egypt in the first half of the third century BC, Appian remarks (sect. 10), 'Yet all these resources were wasted under their successors *through civil war, by which alone great empires are destroyed.*' Then a little later (sect. 14) he characterizes the internal discord and civil wars of the Romans as 'far more terrifying to them [*sc.* than their other wars]'. Put these together with his observation on Philippi that 'it was this battle above all that determined their constitution, which has not yet reverted to a republic' (*Civil Wars* IV.138), and it becomes evident that Appian regarded the civil wars, including the final struggle of Antonius and Octavian, as the last and greatest test of Roman character. He certainly tells the story of this terrible period in terms of a series of individuals; these stirred up, one after another, increasingly bitter conflicts as their desire for power became more and more unbridled, while monarchy – the ultimate end of this desire – consequently drew ever closer. It is also noticeable that in Book I, when tracing the beginning of the decline of the state into violence and narrating the conflict first of Italian against Roman and then of Roman against Roman in the wars of 90–82 BC, Appian again and again focuses sharply on the savagery, treachery, and lack of humanity of the participants. It is not so much the strategic or political logic of war as its horrors and its descending spiral of barbarity that he seems concerned to illustrate and make us understand. Facing the possible extinction of their greatness by the brutality, impiety, and extremism of these internecine struggles, the Romans none the less won through to a stable form of government and established their Empire on a footing of 'unity and monarchy' (*Civil Wars* I.6). After confronting and defeating, first their Italian neighbours, then the various peoples of the Mediterranean seaboard, their final enemies were themselves – as though an evil genius or foul shadow stood between them and the ultimate grasping of the prize for which they had toiled so many hundred years. That this is not an entirely fanciful notion is hinted at by the story Appian tells of Brutus, who when he was about to lead his army across from Asia to Europe to fight Antonius and Octavian saw an apparition which declared itself to be his evil *daimon* (spirit) and promised to appear again to him at Philippi.[8] It is true that Plutarch tells exactly the same story; but in his case it is incorporated into the narrative at the natural place, while Appian, by reserving it to almost the end of his extended final judgement on Brutus and Cassius after their deaths, gives it far more symbolic weight.

b. Structure and Contents of the Five Books

Book I opens with the Preface to the *Civil Wars* as a whole (chs. 1–6). Appian calls attention to the ever-increasing civil violence from the time of Tiberius Gracchus (133 BC), whom he identifies as the first Roman to be killed in a political disturbance, to the murderous events succeeding the death of Julius Caesar. The eventual triumph of Augustus over Antonius and Cleopatra brings a resolution, with the establishment of an authority that needed no form of election or authorization.

The central theme of the book's narrative is the civil war of Sulla and the Marians (chs. 55–102), which lasted, with intermissions, from 88 to 80 BC and had continuations in the shape of the revolt of Lepidus in 78–77 (ch. 107) and the campaigns of Metellus and Pompeius against the Marian general Sertorius and his successor Perperna in Spain until 73 (chs. 108–15). This war was itself a consequence of the preceding 'Social' or 'Marsic' War of 90–88 BC (chs. 39–54), in which the Italian allies of Rome rose against her, and whose result was to win full citizenship of Rome for all non-Roman inhabitants of Italy living south of the Po. This posed the problem of how to integrate the enormous mass of new citizens, who outnumbered the existing Romans, into the body politic, and stirred passions to such an extent that civil war erupted. The previous chapters of the book analyse the causes of the Social War. Appian presents it as a link in the chain of Rome's internal political squabbles, whose intensity and violence had escalated through a series of tribunates, starting with that of Tiberius Gracchus in 133 BC (chs. 7–20), and continuing with those of his brother Gaius in 123–122 BC (chs. 21–7), Appuleius Saturninus in 104–100 BC (chs. 28–33), and the younger Livius Drusus in 91 BC (chs. 34–8).

Book II covers the events of the years 63–44 BC. First we have a brief description of the conspiracy and military suppression of Catiline in 63 BC (chs. 1–7). Appian then gives us a fairly compressed account (chs. 7–31) of the so-called 'First Triumvirate'; this was a private compact between Pompeius, Caesar, and Crassus by which they dominated the state from Caesar's consulship in 59 BC until 53 BC, when the death of Crassus left Pompeius and Caesar to compete with each other for primacy. This section ends with the abortive negotiations of December 50 which led up to Caesar's crossing of the Rubicon early in January 49 BC. The war of Caesar and Pompeius of 49–48 BC follows, down to Pharsalus and the ignominious end of Pompeius in an Egyptian dinghy (chs. 32–87), then in quick succession the

Alexandrian, African, and Spanish campaigns (chs. 88–105), before we reach the very full account of the events which culminated in the murder and funeral of Caesar in March 44 BC (chs. 106–48). The book ends with a comparison of Alexander the Great and Caesar (chs. 149–54).[9]

Book III, unlike Books I and II, lacks any clearly dominating thread or climax, but its chief business is to follow the chequered relationship of Antonius and Octavian over the eighteen months separating the Ides of March from the formation of the 'Second Triumvirate'. The political and military developments after the murder of Caesar are complicated to explain and involve various chains of events in different places. It has to be said that Appian is not really up to the task, and there is a good deal of confusion in the first third of the book, with overlapping and in part duplicated presentation of the facts and a very insecure grasp of the chronology of certain key events between April and November 44 (see notes 3, 9, 28, 29, and 31 to Book III). Chs. 1–8 take the story of the dealings between Antonius, Brutus and Cassius, the senate, and Dolabella down to about June 44. Appian then turns back (chs. 9–24) to Caesar's heir, Octavian, and his arrival in Rome, his initial clash with Antonius, and his undercutting of Brutus' and Cassius' support. This covers March to July or so, and modulates (chs. 24–6) into a highly inaccurate account of the activities of Antonius, Brutus, Cassius, and Dolabella with respect to the eastern provinces. The section ends with the death of Trebonius in Asia at the hands of Dolabella (not earlier than December), before the narrative switches back (ch. 27) to Rome in late May. Thereafter things become clearer. Chs. 27–48 chart the growing distrust between Antonius and Octavian which leads to Octavian's raising of a private army, Antonius' decision to abandon Rome, and the desertion of two of his legions to Octavian in late November. The war of Mutina follows, January to April 43 (chs. 49–76), and then, after a brief reference to events in Syria and Macedonia (chs. 77–9), the book ends with Octavian's seizure of the consulship in August 43 (chs. 80–96) and the death of Decimus Brutus at the hands of an Alpine chief at around the same time (chs. 97–8). The theme of vengeance for the murder of Caesar, which is so important in the next book, closes this one: Decimus 'was the next of the murderers after Trebonius to pay the penalty'.

Book IV begins with the formation of the triumvirate between Antonius, Octavian, and Lepidus in November 43 BC (chs. 1–4). This leads directly to the savagery, endurance, and drama of the proscriptions, when lists were published of men eminent for their opposition to the triumvirs, or for their wealth, who were to be killed and have their property confiscated. Some of the results are vividly illustrated by Appian in the long, virtually free-standing, section which one might call 'Tales of the Proscriptions' (chs. 5–51). The remainder of the book leads inexorably on to the battles at Philippi in the autumn of 42 BC which constitute the first resolution of the sequence of events set off by the murder of Caesar. In the build-up to this, operations in two theatres of war only marginally connected with this main focus make their appearance, those in Africa (chs. 52–6) and Sicily (chs. 83–5), but they have far less weight in the narrative than the campaigns of Cassius and Brutus in Syria, Asia Minor, and Rhodes (chs. 57–82). Then Appian transfers both sets of opponents to Philippi (chs. 86–106), heightening the tension with a long speech from Cassius (chs. 90–100). The two battles (chs. 107–16, 117–31) follow, rounded off by an assessment of Brutus and Cassius (chs. 132–4) and a little final tidying-up (chs. 135–8).

Book V contains two main wars. The first is that of Perusia, conducted by Octavian against Antonius' brother Lucius and his supporters in Italy in the winter of 41–40 BC. The second is the far more protracted struggle of Octavian, in part against the wishes of Antonius, to subdue Sextus Pompeius and bring Sicily under his own control. This was eventually achieved in 36 BC, and according to Octavian terminated the civil wars (ch. 130) – a view Appian is happy to share (ch. 132), at least for the purposes of the overall scheme of the *Roman History*. After a couple of prefatory chapters Appian narrates the doings of Antonius in the east in the year after Philippi, and particularly the beginning of his relationship with Cleopatra (chs. 3–11). Then we return with Octavian to Italy and follow the escalation of general civilian discontent with triumviral rule which culminates in the movement led by Antonius' brother, the consul, against Octavian, the triumvir (chs. 12–29), and leads to war and to the epic siege and tragic end of the ancient Umbrian city of Perusia in the early spring of 40 BC (chs. 30–49). Potential war between Antonius and Octavian is headed off by their veterans and others, and the alliance reconsolidated at Brundisium in late 40 BC (chs. 50–66). The pair are then forced by public opinion to reach an agreement with Sextus Pompeius in 39 BC (chs. 67–74), before Antonius departs to Athens with Octavia for the winter of 39–38 BC (chs. 75–6). The rest of the book moves through Octavian's disastrous campaign of 38 BC against Sextus (chs. 77–92), and the coolness between Octavian and Antonius resolved at Tarentum in 37 BC (chs. 93–5), to the decisive naval battles of Mylae (chs. 96–108) and Naulochus (chs. 109–22) in 36 BC. Appian then describes Lepidus' ill-advised attempt to carry out a coup against Octavian (chs. 123–6) and Octavian's subsequent settlement of unrest among his soldiers, proclamation of the end of civil war, and acceptance of various honours (chs. 127–32). The book concludes (chs. 133–45) with the flight of Sextus to Asia in the hope of finding refuge with Antonius, and his failure and death some time in the first half of 35 BC.

III. THE HISTORIOGRAPHICAL CONTEXT

By the time that Appian came to write his *Roman History*, the Greek historical tradition was many centuries old. Starting in the middle of the fifth century with Herodotus, the 'Father of History', only a few years later it produced Thucydides, who might aptly be called the 'historian's historian'; and in these two are already to be found the germs of all later development. Both of course were driven by a passionate desire to understand the causes of the greatest events of their own age, and to set down that understanding for posterity. Both wrote masterpieces, and it would be a brave man who asserted that the one was a better historian than the other. But there the similarity ends. Where Herodotus is discursive, curious, and fond of stories and digressions, Thucydides is concentrated, austere, and single-minded in pursuit of the meaningful sequence of events. Herodotus' treatment is organic, Thucydides' strictly chronological. Herodotus offers a wonderful story, Thucydides believes history can instruct.

With some notable exceptions, later Greek historians tended to shy from the austerity of Thucydides and favour some of the more colourful aspects of Herodotus' writing. By the Hellenistic period history had come to fulfil some of the needs which fiction caters for in our own day. Readers liked tragic, sentimental, or improving stories, dramatic and unexpected turns of fortune, interesting and colourful digressions, a dash of the supernatural, descriptions of outlandish peoples, customs, and places, and plenty of lifelike and would-be authentic detail. A nice illustration of the sort of thing that appealed is provided by Cicero in a famous letter to his historian friend Lucceius, suggesting that he might take as his next subject Cicero's own experiences:

I fancy a work of moderate length could be made up, from the beginning of the [Catilinarian] plot to my return from exile . . . My experiences will give plenty of variety to your narrative, full of a certain kind of delectation to enthrall the minds of those who read when you are the writer. Nothing tends more to the reader's enjoyment than varieties of circumstance and vicissitudes of fortune. For myself, though far from desirable in the living, they will be pleasant in the reading; for there is something agreeable in the secure recollection of bygone unhappiness. For others, who went through no personal distress and painlessly survey misfortunes not their own, even the emotion of pity is enjoyable. Which of us is not affected pleasurably, along with a sentiment of compassion, at the story of the dying Epaminondas on the field of Mantinea, ordering the javelin to be plucked from his body only after he had been told in answer to his question that his shield was safe, so that even in the agony of his wound he could meet an honourable death with mind at ease?[10]

Elsewhere in the same letter Cicero even goes so far as to urge Lucceius to indulge in a little stretching of the literal truth in the interests of eulogy.

Such 'history' was a travesty of even the more naive characteristics of the Herodotean approach, and it must be precisely this romantic sensationalism against which Polybius had revolted a hundred years earlier.[11] He made a conscious return to Thucydidean standards of rational explanation, political relevance, and intellectual rigour in putting forward his account of 'how and under what system of government the Romans succeeded in less than fifty-three years in bringing under their rule almost the whole of the inhabited world, an achievement which is without parallel in human history'.[12] Polybius did not equal his model, perhaps because his insight into human character and motivation was not as keen as Thucydides', perhaps because he did not give his work the dramatic structure which Thucydides chose or was offered by the events he chronicled, perhaps because his writing does not have the strength and economy of Thucydides'; and he was a man of his age in including not only speeches (as all historians did; see IV*d* below), but also, in many of his narratives, elements of pathos and the portrayal of emotion. But he must be placed beside Thucydides in the seriousness of his approach and in the magnitude of his subject.

It would be far-fetched to pretend that Appian is a historian in the same class as Polybius or Thucydides, but equally it would be wrong to deny that he stands in their tradition, however inadequately. Consciously or unconsciously he recalls Thucydides' claim that the war he is about to chronicle was the greatest that the Greeks had ever fought, when he observes that 'no empire down to the present time ever reached such an extent or lasted so long',[13] and goes on, like Thucydides, to justify this assertion by historical comparisons. And is Polybius' *tyche* (fortune) so different a principle from Appian's *daimon* or *to daimonion* (Fate), which makes so emphatic an appearance at key moments in his story? It has long been taken for granted that Appian has no historical personality of his own and is a mere gatherer of other men's flowers; where his source is good, he is good, and vice versa. But let us give him credit for the legal sharpness he surely possessed, and assume that he had some sort of critical faculty, some powers of organization, some ability to select amongst the mass of material that was at his disposal. He is clearly not a romantic trifler. Only in the 'Tales of the Proscriptions' (IV. 5–51), and in some battle scenes, does he indulge a taste for dramatic and pathetic detail apparently for its own sake. He shows a sense of the economic realities underlying the upheavals of the late Republic, which is more than one can say of Cicero. He has a good understanding of the basic features of the political struggles of these years, as for example the analysis (at II.19) of the incipient breakdown of the system in the late fifties BC. The speeches of any substance which he gives to his characters at emphatic points in the narrative are designed not to display his rhetorical skill but to present arguments, attitudes, or interpretations which are important to the understanding of the events. A good instance is the speech of Antonius at III.33–8 which (though based on a seriously flawed account of the manoeuvrings for the control of the important provinces of Syria, Macedonia, and Gaul in the months following Caesar's death) is designed to make an overall case, against the thrust of Octavian's own memoirs, for his loyalty to the Caesarian cause and his success as consul in managing a very tricky political situation.

As to Appian's theme, it is certainly of high seriousness and one which no Roman of any epoch would have taken lightly. But it is here that Appian shows the influence of two other intellectual currents. One is the development of 'universal history', whose first practitioner is generally held to have been Ephorus, writing about the middle of the fourth century BC, only a few years before the conquests of Alexander brought into contact, and briefly unity, areas of the world which were far apart and had completely different languages, cultures, and political traditions. An exponent of this kind of history is Diodorus Siculus, writing in the middle of the first century BC. In his work, Rome figures little until the latest period. To a Greek, even one who came from Sicily, Roman power was not much more than a curiosity until the third century BC, and it was only during the second that it had really started to affect the Hellenic heartlands. But by

Appian's day, Rome had been unquestioned and unchallenged mistress of the whole Mediterranean world and of large areas beyond for a century and a half and possessed an empire the like of which had never been seen. That empire was, or had become by the mid-second century AD, unified in many ways. It also seemed to be stable and permanent, and it constituted, for those who lived within it, a kind of natural order or world on its own. Thus to write the history of its acquisition by the Romans was to write something that approached the universality of treatment aimed at by Diodorus and others.

The other current is a more exclusively Roman one, that of the compendious national history. The very first Roman to write history in Latin prose, namely the elder Cato in the first half of the second century BC, entitled his work 'Origins' (*Origines*) and certainly treated the early history (or what passed as such) of Rome and some other Italian states before passing on to more modern events. Octavian's contemporary, Livy, whose work is the only one of this type to survive, had several predecessors, upon whose shoulders there can be little doubt that he stood. In 143 books, of which only the first 45 (less 11–20) survive, Livy told the whole history of Rome, domestic and foreign, from the arrival of Aeneas in Latium to the consulship and early death of Augustus' stepson Drusus in 9 BC. The extant part of the work is suffused with patriotic pride and insistence upon the moral values which had brought Rome greatness. According to the notably pessimistic Preface, written very shortly after Octavian had succeeded in making himself sole master of the Roman state, the reason for the apparently unending civil discord of Livy's own times lay in the decay of the old virtues – such things as piety, endurance, self-control, and frugality. When Appian ascribes the success of the Romans in building their empire to 'virtue' (*arete*) and endurance,[14] he shows how much he has absorbed this Roman view of themselves and their history. But he resists the full moralistic interpretation of history by making these qualities secondary to good counsel and good luck – of which the first is resolutely rational and the second beyond human control, even if it may be determined at key moments by a supernatural power which turns out in the end to be beneficent for the world.

Appian was well aware that he had many predecessors, both Greek and Roman[15] (though in typical ancient fashion he does not name them: it would be interesting to know whether Livy's history was in fact so successful that it prevented anyone else ever attempting the same thing again). He therefore explains what it is that is distinctive about his work. First, it treats the relations of the Romans with their various adversaries people by people, or country by country, and it seems that this was a new approach to the writing of imperial history. Being less Rome-centred, it appeared to bring in something of the ethnographical appeal that was a popular element in historical writing, and it gave Appian the opportunity to indulge a geographical interest which is also noticeable at some points in the *Civil Wars* (for example, IV.105–6). Secondly, it compares the excellence (*arete*) of the Romans and their opponents, when matched in action against each other. In the *Civil Wars* Appian makes no specific comparisons between sides (Romans and non-Romans no longer being meaningful categories), but it is often clear enough from his narrative what conclusions we should draw (for example, III.69). The importance of good counsel (*euboulia*), which may legitimately be considered part of a broad definition of *arete*, is stressed in the narrative of the campaign of 48 BC in Greece, where Pompeius on several occasions is led to take fatally wrong decisions (see IV*a* below). And thirdly, he believes very definitely that the Roman Empire was the result of a deliberate enterprise of conquest: he belittles the 'Greek empire' whose hegemony was held successively by Athens, Sparta, and Boeotia in the fifth and fourth centuries on the grounds that 'their wars were waged not so much to acquire empire, as out of rivalry with each other; and the most glorious of them were fought to defend their own freedom against other attacking powers'.[16] This represents a truly imperial viewpoint, at odds with the older ideology of victory. According to the ideals of the Republic, in the eyes of the gods no war was justified except in self-defence, and Appian's disparagement of the Persian Wars certainly seems odd to any reader brought up with Livy's depiction of all Roman wars as fundamentally defensive in origin. It is clear that by Appian's day the existence and durability of the Roman Empire had given rise to the open acknowledgement of other attitudes, and to acceptance of the idea that the Empire was a Good Thing not just for Romans but for all.

IV. THE *CIVIL WARS*

a. Fate

Appian's explanation for the civil wars of the Republic lies in selfishness, lack of self-restraint, and lust for power; but he is equally concerned with the factors which determined the outcome and allowed the Romans (uniquely, in Appian's view) to do rather more than merely survive the terrible danger of such strife. Personal qualities, including leadership, intelligence, and determination, were very important. But above all there was a force at work that was beyond human control: fate (if one may so render the various terms, including God, that he uses for the idea).

Fate makes its appearance at a number of highly significant moments, underlining their importance. Before the death of Caesar, Appian relates the various things, including unpropitious omens, which came within a hair's breadth of revealing the plot to Caesar or causing him not to go into the senate-house, and comments, 'for Caesar had to suffer Caesar's fate' (II.116). Brutus reaches his suicide decision after the second battle at Philippi because his officers refuse to make the attempt to break through to his camp where there are still some other forces: 'at this point heaven unhinged them' (IV.131). The theme of fate is particularly marked in the narrative of the campaign in Greece in 48 BC which leads to Pharsalus. Pompeius, like Brutus and Cassius, is defeated not so much by his opponent as by fate, and Appian intersperses his comments as though he were a Greek tragic chorus. 'Such was Pompeius' rash misjudgement of the future course of events' (II.52), he says near the beginning; at a crucial moment in the siege of Dyrrachium, when Caesar could have been defeated, Labienus 'led astray by heaven' (II.62) persuaded Pompeius to pursue some unimportant fugitives; and before Pharsalus itself Pompeius acts foolishly and fate lays its hand upon him so that the enthusiasm of his army for battle sweeps him away – 'this was arranged by God to bring into being the imperial power that now embraces all' (II.71). There are other comments of the same type, but these will give an idea of Appian's treatment. Even Octavian, though ultimately successful, is not immune from the hand of fate: after defeating Sextus Pompeius he finds himself with a quite unexpected mutiny on his hands, on which Appian comments, 'As a result [of his success] he was full of pride; but heaven (to daimonion) showed its jealousy of his pride' (V.128).

The notion of 'divine harm' or 'malignant fate' (theoblabeia) is useful to Appian.[17] It enables him to approve of those who claimed to be fighting for the Republic and liberty, and at the same time to acknowledge that their defeat by an apparently less worthy cause was the inevitable order of things. There need be no contradiction between Appian's acceptance of Augustus as the final agent of fate in establishing monarchy, and a sometimes hostile portrayal of the process by which he reached power. To a man who held this view of history and believed in virtues of character as an explanation for success or failure, the precise details of chronology and political man-oeuvring are not of any great consequence so long as the main lines of the story are essentially accurate. He is notoriously careless over detail, as a glance at the notes to this translation will show; but his overall conception of the decline of the Roman state into violence, with its sombre highlights and the leitmotif of fate, is neither trivial nor inaccurate.

b. Emphasis

One of the most striking features of the *Civil Wars* is the weighting of the narrative in favour of certain conflicts rather than others. The most notable example is the lack of balance between the treatment accorded to the wars of Sulla and the Marians on the one hand and those of Caesar and the Pompeians on the other. Both lasted approximately the same space of time, both involved campaigns in Italy and in the provinces, both issued in dictat-orships. In both cases, further wars and civil struggle followed the death of the dictator. Both men decisively changed the face of Roman politics, and, by a paradox of the kind that the ancients seem to have enjoyed, the loser of the second conflict was the protégé of the winner of the first, while the winner of the second was a relative of the loser of the first. Yet Appian chose to treat Sulla and Marius much less fully, for reasons we can only guess at – perhaps the nature of his source material, perhaps the desire not to place a major climax too early in the work, perhaps a genuine feeling that Caesar really was a great deal more important than Sulla. Less immedi-ately striking, because the narrative simply sustains the level of detail reached at the end of Book II, but in reality much more of an anomaly, is the huge proportion of the work devoted to the mere two and a half years between the murder of Caesar and the triumph of his avengers on the field of Philippi. Again, within these two books we can see concentration first on the difficult formation of the alliance between Antonius and Octavian, and then on the fortunes of Brutus and Cassius, culminating at Philippi. Other matters are severely curtailed, for example the campaign of Brutus against Antonius' brother Gaius in Illyria–Macedonia (III.79), which even though it concerns Brutus has little bearing on the concentration of the Liberators' strength in Asia Minor and the build-up to the campaign of Philippi. It seems here that the dramatic shaping of the book has dictated its content, because on the face of it Brutus' confrontation with Gaius Antonius and other Roman troops is more relevant to the story of civil war than is the fully worked-up story of Cassius' encounter with the Rhodians and his old tutor Theodotus. The scale of the fifth book is more akin to that of the second, having patches of considerable detail and vividness interspersed with more summary narrative.

c. Chronology and Re-ordering of Material

Accurate chronology obviously requires a common system, or easily relatable systems, of recording dates. Somewhat less obviously, it requires a cultural habit of dating. While the Roman world in the time of which Appian writes possessed the first (more or less) in the shape of consular dates, it was to only a very limited degree that it possessed the second. Official documents, such as decrees of the senate and magisterial decisions, were dated; also private letters, because delays in delivery were quite unpredictable; and likewise legal instruments, such as contracts, for obvious reasons. But the precision that was necessary for administration, business, and some aspects of private life and civil law was not felt to be so necessary in other areas – amongst which, strangely enough, historical writing must be numbered. True to his character, Thucydides had attempted to cut through the fog of different local dating systems by ordering his narrative according to summers and winters, and one feels he would have gone further if he could. But critics of Thucydides, like Dionysius of Halicarnassus, attacked the rigidity of his method, claiming with some justice that it obscured as much as it revealed because it tended to separate events which formed a meaningful whole.

Stylistic considerations also came to act against chronological precision, in that an excess of detail was felt to interfere with the pleasure that a reader should derive from a unified, smoothly written account of the past. Here, as in many aspects of the literary culture of the ancient world, rhetorical training was the culprit. The painting of a convincing picture or the presentation of a persuasive argument, which was the aim of the orator and therefore the skill taught by the schools, elevated clever plausibility above tedious accuracy, and lifelike invention above honest ignorance. Hence a historian, or at least one who intended to win an audience (and it should be remembered that actual readings took place), needed to avoid intricate argument, excessive detail, and niggling precision – in other words what a modern writer would tend to relegate to footnotes. Such things should not be allowed to interrupt the flow of the narrative any more than should discussions of the merits of conflicting sources (which the capable writer will have resolved for himself as part of his preparation), or admissions that it is impossible to know exactly what happened at a particular point (since the schools taught the art of filling a vacuum with 'what was likely'). In the light of all this it is hardly surprising to find Appian saying, 'I thought it unnecessary to record the dates of everything, but I shall mention those of the most important events from time to time.'[18]

In fact by modern standards Appian keeps his promise only inadvertently, in that much of his narrative is anchored by the participation of so-and-so as consul, and the Romans of course dated years by the names of the consuls in office. More specific dates, such as Dio occasionally gives *honoris causa*, like the day of Augustus' death, are hard to find. What Appian seems to mean by 'dates' are the extremely sparse references to the 'international' dating system by Olympiads (used by Polybius) which appear in Book I (chs. 84, 99, 111) but not at all thereafter. Even these are vague in the extreme, since each Olympiad is a period of four years and Appian does not trouble to fix the year itself. But this vagueness is a consistent feature of Appianic narrative. For example, the only indications as to when the 'sedition' of Tiberius Gracchus took place are the remark in the preface to Book I that Sulla's domination of the state occurred about fifty years after the death of Gracchus, and the passing reference to the Sicilian slave war (but which?) as recent.[19]

Apart from this vagueness, there are also cases of straightforward muddle, like the misplacing of Cato's mission to Cyprus (II.23) or the chronological haze which surrounds the events of April to November 44 in Book III. Numerous errors of fact have been pointed out in the notes, and some are chronological. Mostly this seems to be a matter of carelessness, but other factors may be operative. Some of the material in the 'Tales of the Proscriptions' has been attracted from elsewhere, and although it may be out of place chronologically, there is an emotional and dramatic justification for its appearance here.[20] It has also been argued that Appian relocated the episode in which Brutus quoted Homer (IV.134) from Athens in the winter of 44–43 to Samos in the winter of 43–42, and postponed mentioning it until after Philippi, in order to enhance its dramatic effect.[21] The same is true of the story of the appearance of Caesar's ghost (see II*a* above). To sum up, although Appian's approach to chronology may seem slipshod, even unintelligent, there are reasons for it. These reasons may not weigh much with us, but they are an aspect of the difference between an ancient and a modern historian, and reflect what Appian thought was important.

d. Speeches and the Influence of Rhetoric

A feature of Appian's history that will immediately strike any reader who has not previously read any Greek or Latin historian is the presence of speeches. Some of these are elaborate, perhaps more so then the real situation would have called for. Most form pairs, either because they are genuine answers to each other, or because, although delivered at approximately the same time by different speakers to different audiences, they are reactions to the same circumstances (for example Antonius' speech to the senate and Brutus' on the Capitol, II.133–4, 137–41). A very few are isolated, like Cassius' speech at the Gulf of Melas in Book IV before the Liberators plunge into the campaign of Philippi. With the single exception of the proscription notice (IV.8–11), which possesses some of the characteristics of a speech in spite of the fact that Appian specifically claims it to be a translation of the triumviral edict, it is unlikely that any of these speeches reflect in more than the most general way what was actually said – if indeed anything at all was said. A rare chance to compare the historian's version with that actually delivered arises in the case of Cicero's speech in the senate at the beginning of 43 BC (III.52–3), the real version of which is the *Fifth Philippic*. This is not the place to compare the two in detail, but there is no sign that Appian made any use of the published speech. The one close match, the 'decimation' of the soldiers, is different in detail in Cicero, who speaks (inaccurately) of the slaughtering of centurions; and Appian entirely omits Cicero's main proposals, which are the politically significant part of the speech. On the other hand, the fact that Appian *reports*, rather than *composes*, what Antonius said in that most famous and inflammatory of speeches, his funeral oration for Caesar, is interesting because it is probable on other grounds that his account is fairly near the truth.

Why then are these speeches there? The answer is that by Appian's time they had become a compulsory ingredient of the genre of writing called history. It seems to have come naturally to the Greeks to present opposed views in dramatic or rhetorical shape. Their earliest literature, the epic of Homer, constantly dramatizes the action and conveys character and plot by means of speeches. It was probably impossible for Herodotus and Thucydides *not* to have used speeches, and in their works speeches serve to give emphasis, bring out contrasts, and act as vehicles for the revelation of motive, character, and cause. In the hands of Thucydides the speech became a full-blown tool of historical analysis, performing the function nowadays fulfilled by the historian commenting *in propria persona*. On occasion he even employed paired speeches delivered to different audiences, in which the second speaker, though he could not possibly have known the arguments of the first, nevertheless answers these arguments. And speeches had a further advantage, in that they entailed a change of style. The expository mode could give way, for a space, to the rhetorical, affording the reader the pleasure of a change, and allowing the writer, if he wished, to demonstrate his virtuosity in a different genre. Finally, speeches could be used not only for dramatic emphasis but also to mark moments of importance, heighten their significance, and put across interpretations of events for which the narrative provided no ready place. Good examples are the speech of Antonius to the military tribunes not long after Caesar's murder, which allows Appian to point out that Antonius had, or could have had, reasonable justification from a Caesarian point of view for his actions since that event (III.33–8); and the dialogue between Cocceius Nerva and Octavian at Brundisium in 40 BC, which is used to put the cases of the two triumvirs against each other (V.60–62).

All Appian is doing, then, is to work within a convention that was far too well established for him to spurn it. His speeches are well structured and perfectly competent, but they are not vehicles for any display of rhetorical virtuosity, for all that he had been a practising advocate in the courts for many years. But their distribution is interesting. In Book I there are none (if one excludes a nine-liner), and in Book V only four. Of the remaining eighteen, four are distributed between Pompeius and Caesar during the campaign of Pharsalus, while no fewer than fourteen fall between the murder of Caesar and the battle of Philippi, and confirm the dramatic focusing of the *Civil Wars* on this period. Appian displays other rhetorical traits in these parts of his work, such as the description of the state of mind of the two armies and their leaders at Pharsalus (II.77). Here he produces (though not in any frigid way) the kind of reflections on the tragedy and paradox of the imminent battle which we can be sure a connoisseur of the schools of rhetoric like the elder Seneca would have commended. Appian's version of the battle in fact differs quite widely from Caesar's own and conforms almost exactly, apart from the final elements, to the prescription preserved for us by the rhetorician Hermogenes: 'if we are describing a conflict, we shall first of all mention the preliminaries such as the generals' speeches, the dispositions on both sides, and their fears; next the attacks, the slaughter, and the dead; finally the victory trophy, the triumphal songs of the victors, the tears and enslavement of the victims'.[22] The whole tone of the account of the Pharsalus campaign is darkened by the idea that Pompeius is a doomed man, and it may not be unjust to see the entire episode as predominantly dramatic and tragic. There can also be very little doubt that the colourful but generic detail of the several sea-battles and naval disasters in Book V owes more to the urge to dramatize and provide excitement at key moments than to any eyewitness account. These episodes provide climaxes and dramatic reversals of fortune in a book where Sextus Pompeius is not a sympathetic or charismatic enough figure to take the part played by his father or by Brutus and Cassius in Books II–IV in resisting the tide of autocracy.

e. Appian's Historical Viewpoint

Although his account of the civil wars is sombre, Appian's overall view of the development of Roman history is optimistic. He has no doubt that the greatness of the Empire of the Romans surpasses that of all their predecessors, and that they deserve this Empire. They did not make the mistake of basing their power on the sea, like the Athenians and the Carthaginians, as Appian has the consul Censorinus explain (Book VIII, ch. 12). In the Preface (ch. 11) he says, 'Through the sufferings and dangers of seven hundred years they brought their empire to its present condition and achieved prosperity as a result of wise decisions.' And in the sub-preface to the *Civil Wars* he makes it still clearer that the Romans emerged from this time of trouble into 'harmony and monarchy' (see II*a* above). Such a view, as has been noted, is very different from the pessimism of Livy, and it is easy to explain why Appian held it. Ever since Augustus had laid down the main lines of imperial control and administration, change in the Empire had been slow and discreet. During Appian's own lifetime the problem of how power could be passed on at the death of an emperor seemed to have been solved by the device of adopting the chosen successor as a son. In the mid second century the frontiers seemed secure, and the days of conquest and strain over. There had been no real internal trouble since the palace killing of Domitian in AD 96, and apart from an army revolt a few years before that no serious fighting between citizens had occurred since the notorious year of the four emperors, AD 69. Economically, we can see that the Empire was starting to become a little arthritic. The independence and vigour of its cities were not what they had once been. However, a contemporary is not likely to have been aware of the trend, and there was nothing in the general conditions of the Roman world in Appian's day to cloud an expectation that things would remain good, or even get better. In short, change, with all its discomforts, seemed to have been halted and the mighty and permanent felicity of the Roman Empire to have taken its place. It must have been hard not to discern the hand of a beneficent providence in this. It is therefore quite unsurprising that Appian presents the Augustan Empire (for such it essentially still was in AD 150) as an inevitable and desirable outcome of the trauma and struggle from which it originated.

None the less, his attitude to monarchy remains somewhat ambiguous. There was a strand of ancient political philosophy which held that rule by a single good and wise individual was the best possible form of government, but Appian does not use this idea. For him, the contrast was not between such 'true' monarchy (desirable) and its perverted form, despotism, or 'tyranny' (undesirable), but between autocracy, of whatever kind, and democracy. He believes that it is natural for men to want to dominate others, and that this is one of the forces that brought the Republic down. The defining characteristic of civil wars or internal struggles (*Emphylia*, the title of these books) is, according to words he puts into Cassius' mouth (at IV. 69), precisely a struggle for personal power (*dynasteia*). The inexorable progression of the forms of such power enjoyed under the Roman Republic emerges quite clearly from his account: traditional constitutional dictatorship, Sulla's extended dictatorship, Pompeius' consulship without a colleague, Caesar's permanent dictatorship, and the triumvirate. They are all, in his view, species of monarchy, but represent not so much steps towards an ideal form of government as necessary remedies for a state of affairs that had become unmanageable. He describes Sulla as 'curing one ill [anarchy] with another [assumption of sole power]' (I.3). He approves of the peace and stability which had been brought about by Octavian's ultimate elimination of other sources of authority, but the language in which he describes the position won by the successful leader is cool: 'his [sc. Octavian–Augustus'] rule was strong and lasted a long time, and since he was fortunate in everything he did and was regarded with fear, he left a family dynasty to succeed him and enjoy a power similar to his own' (I.5). Appian's view of the democracy of the Republic has much the same characteristics. On a theoretical level he neither praises nor condemns it; but in practice, as operated under the conditions of the last century of the Republic, it proved unworkable and its defenders often craven, pigheaded, or incompetent. When he comes to sum up the achievement of Brutus and Cassius, he calls *demokratia* (the republic) 'a splendid but always profitless term' (IV.133). It could not withstand the currents of violence and ambition that swirled around it, and it is these, not any excellence or defects of the constitution, which Appian sets out to chart.

f. The Sources

Appian is the sole surviving continuous narrative source of any quality for the period 133–70 BC. In addition, he seems at intervals in the later books of the *Civil Wars*, particularly the last, to depend on accounts which differ from those that lie behind our other authorities. As a result, the question of his reliability is of considerable interest and there have been numerous attempts to identify the sources on which he relied. A persistent theory has seen the lost histories of Asinius Pollio as the bedrock of Books II–IV. Pollio served as an officer under Caesar, was with him at the crossing of the Rubicon, and fought at Pharsalus after managing to escape Curio's disaster in Africa in 49. It is certain that his history, which began at 60 BC, reached Philippi, but there is no agreement as to whether he recorded any events after 42 BC. Octavian's own autobiography covered the years 44–24 BC. Messalla Corvinus, a republican who transferred his loyalty to Antonius and finally to Octavian, becoming consul in 31 BC, wrote an account of the thirties BC which is likely to lie behind portions of Book V. Livy himself lived through these years, but this part of his history has not survived and it is not apparent to what extent, if any, Appian may have used it. Book I has defied all attempts to saddle it with a single coherent source, but we know of much first-hand evidence that was still available, for example the speeches of the two Gracchi, the memoirs of Sulla and Rutilius Rufus, and some histories. Some of the detail in Plutarch's *Life of Sulla*, presumably drawn from Sulla's memoirs, reappears in Appian, although we cannot tell whether he had it from Plutarch or not. One certainty is that his account of the conspiracy of Catiline is heavily in debt to Sallust's monograph, with significant parallels in substance and in detail: for instance the four names specified as 'leaders' by Appian at the opening of II.4 are clearly taken from

Sallust (*Cat.* 44.1), like the insignificant detail that Volturcius came from Croton, which occurs a sentence or two later in both accounts. In short, the inference is stronger here than in any other book that Appian used his sources eclectically.

Unfortunately, like most ancient authors, Appian hardly ever mentions an authority, and when he does we cannot be sure that he took more than the specifically acknowledged fact from that authority (for example III.77, the enigmatic Libo). Much of the scholarly discussion is also vitiated by an *a priori* assumption that Appian was little more than an excerptor, whose procedure was to follow a 'main source' for each main section of his work. On to this he might, on this view of his method, graft details taken from other relevant writers, or occasionally switch to another 'main source'. We can see that Livy did this with Polybius, rewriting, spicing up some details, and making occasional mistakes; but Livy, though a better writer, is a worse historian that Appian, and there is no proof that Appian proceeded in the same way. On the contrary, personal remarks and passages of analysis are embedded in the text in such a way as to suggest the opposite (see IV*a* above). Furthermore, the narrative is remarkably free of propagandistic bias (though Sulla fares badly), and where bias can be discerned it may be accompanied or followed by material displaying the opposite tendency.

Recent scholarship has therefore tended to discount the idea that Appian simply follows for long stretches the version of Pollio or any other authority. Along with this idea there also vanishes any misconceived hope of using Appian to arrive at the views of those lost historians. It is much safer to credit Appian with some critical intelligence and some familiarity with how a historian was supposed to go about his work.[23] That he did not uncritically reproduce his sources seems to be shown by the fact that he almost certainly impressed his own viewpoint and colouring on Octavian's report of the exchange of speeches between Lucius Antonius and himself after the fall of Perusia (V.45, n. 37). As Magnino has said:

it is not possible to think of a single source used as the basis of the picture, but of various sources, taken up at different moments of the story according to their depth of content and reliability of information. This will also serve to explain the lack of consistency in the tenor of the work as a whole, and the coexistence of pro-Antonian positions with others that are pro-Octavianic, or of nuances favourable to the senate besides others that are not, or of pro- and anti-monarchical attitudes together.[24]

Clearly, then, Appian was prepared to subordinate both detail and view-point of the sources he used to his own idea of what was important in his unfolding story. His views, like those of any other historian, were formed by the interaction of his own experience and understanding of the world with his reading and investigation. Several passages show that he tried to answer questions arising from his subject-matter, for example I.86, IV.19, V.21. We find extended comment or analysis, as at I.16, 104, II.19, 120, V.13, 17. There is the lengthy comparison of Caesar and Alexander (II.149–54) and full judgements on some other important figures such as Sulla, Brutus and Cassius (but not Pompeius Magnus). These, and other 'authorial' inter-ventions in the narrative, like those at I.85 or II.71, seem to be his own work. Broadly consistent with each other, they show that he had given some thought to the importance of leadership and to the nature of the revolution, or evolution, he was describing.

It appears that he saw the civil wars as a kind of tunnel of anarchy and violence through which the Romans had to go before their Empire could be established (see IV*d* above). This is why he picks on the violent episodes from 133 BC onwards, not attempting to relate them to each other or show how they might be products of other, common, problems, but as symptoms of the decline from a peaceful and law-abiding polity into the ultimate chaos of civil war. This surely is why he proportions the narrative as he does, and why (to answer a question raised above) he does not give more weight to the wars of Sulla and the Marians. What he needs for artistic purposes is a remorselessly darkening scenario, and to place too much deep gloom near the beginning would have marred the effect. The introductory book may be seen as a sort of prelude, in which the themes of conflict are paraded and given an outing, before being allowed to burst out in the full savagery of their development in Books II–IV. The idea of a kind of disease of violence (though the metaphor is not Appian's), which had gradually intensified after its first appearance in 133 BC, is indicated by Appian's comment on Sulla: '. . . such was the catastrophe to which their reckless-ness in political quarrelling had led them' (I.58). And this violence is itself the product of that lust for personal power which, by its destructive progress through various manifestations to arrive finally at the Augustan monarchy, gives a shape and a kind of inevitability to the *Civil Wars*. Appian, surely, composed this picture himself.

BIBLIOGRAPHICAL NOTE

The standard Greek text of Appian is that published by P. Viereck in the Teubner edition (2 vols., Leipzig, 1905: vol. II contains the *Civil Wars*, vol. I (revised Roos, 1936; Gabba, 1962) the rest). Viereck's text is reproduced (without any critical information at all) in the Loeb edition of the *Civil Wars* (vols. III and IV of *Appian's Roman History*, London and New York, 1913). This has a parallel translation into English by Horace White (originally published in 1889), which was revised for the Loeb by Iliff Robinson (1913), but unfortunately not brought into full agreement with Viereck's edition of the Greek. The present completely new and, it is hoped, more accurate translation also uses Viereck's text, with occasional departures where Viereck could not bring himself to correct nonsense or where subsequent scholarship has forced reconsideration. These departures are marked by an asterisk where they occur, and listed in the 'Notes on the Translation' below. There also exist very good and full commentaries in Italian (with a complete translation, in addition to the Greek text) by E. Gabba on Books I and V of the *Civil Wars* (Florence, 1958 (2nd ed., 1967) and 1970), and by D. Magnino on Book III (Florence, 1984). In English there is only a now rather outdated edition of Book I by J. L. Strachan-Davidson (London, 1902 (4th ed., 1969)), with pre-Viereck Greek text, brief commentary, and no translation. A concordance, *Concordantia in Appianum* (Alpha-Omega, Reihe A, CXXXIII.1), was published by Olms-Weidmann, Hildesheim–New York–Zürich, in 1993.

For basic facts and some guidance to Appian the reader has at his disposal reference works such as the *Oxford Classical Dictionary* and the *Oxford History of Classical Literature*, and books concerned with the ancient historiographical tradition as a whole, such as S. Usher's *The Historians of Greece and Rome* (London, 1969, reprinted 1985), which generally acknowledge Appian's existence without attempting more than a brief treatment. For those who wish to go further, there is, at last, a modern book-length study of Appian in English: Alain M. Gowing, *The Triumviral Narratives of Appian and Cassius Dio* (Ann Arbor, 1993). Although the formal coverage of this study is limited to Books III–V of the *Civil Wars*, much that Gowing says illuminates the work as a whole, and this is undoubtedly the book to which the English reader should first turn for a proper appreciation of Appian. For the remainder of the scholarly literature, see the very full bibliography in Gowing's book. Much of it is in French, German, or Italian. Notable here are: the general appraisal by E. Schwartz in *Paulys Realenzyklopädie*, vol. 2 (1896); E. Gabba's attempt to unravel the sources in his *Appiano e la Storia delle Guerre Civili* (Florence, 1956); the thesis of B. Goldmann, *Einheitlichkeit und Eigenständigkeit der Historia Romana des Appian* (Hildesheim, 1988), on whose conclusions parts of the present Introduction rest; Martin Hose's very full treatment of Appian's attitude to the characters, events, and political institutions of the past in *Erneuerung der Verganganheit: die Historiker im Imperium Romanum von Florus bis Cassius Dio* (Stuttgart and Leipzig, 1994); and the group of articles by K. Brodersen, I. Hahn, and others on Appian in *Aufstieg and Niedergang der römischen Welt, II: Prinzipät*, vol. 34.1 (ed. W. Haase and H. Temporini, Berlin and New York, 1993), pp. 339–554. For the broader topic of the relationship of historiography to rhetoric, and the implications of the view that for antiquity history was but a subspecies of rhetoric, see two excellent studies in English: T. P. Wiseman, *Clio's Cosmetics* (Leicester and Totowa, N.J., 1979), especially the first four chapters, and A. J. Woodman, *Rhetoric in Classical Historiography* (London and Sydney, 1988).

The sources for the late Republic in general, rather than Appian in particular, are well discussed by C. B. R. Pelling in two articles in the *Journal of Hellenic Studies*: 'Plutarch's method of work in the *Roman Lives*' (vol. 99, 1979, pp. 74–96) and 'Plutarch's adaptation of his source-material' (vol. 100, 1980, pp. 127–40). The fruit of these researches is summarized in the Introduction to his edition of Plutarch's *Life of Antony* (Cambridge, 1988).

Readers who wish to pursue the history of the period have an embarrassment of riches. The ancient literary source-material is plentiful, including Sallust, Cicero, Caesar, the Augustan poets, Plutarch, and Cassius Dio (to name only the most important); and modern scholars have devoted a great deal of effort to understanding the process which transformed the Republic into the Empire. For the Republic, the best short accounts are those of P. A. Brunt, *Social Conflicts in the Roman Republic* (London,

1971) and M. H. Crawford, *The Roman Republic* (London, 1978). An analysis of the crisis of the late Republic is given by M. Beard and M. Crawford, *Rome in the Late Republic* (London, 1985), while T. P. Wiseman (ed.), *Roman Political Life 90 BC–AD 69* (Exeter, 1985) is a useful brief introduction to its subject. C. Nicolet, *The World of the Citizen in Republican Rome* (trans. P. S. Falla, London, 1980, from the original French edition of 1976) is a comprehensive and fascinating treatment of the relation of the citizen to the state, accompanied by extensive quotation, in translation, of the source-material. G. Alföldy's *Social History of Rome* (1975, rev. ed., trans. D. Braund and F. Pollock, Routledge, 1988) is concise and up to date on social structures and problems. For an introduction to the archaeological picture, see T. W. Potter, *Roman Italy* (London, 1987), and on the Samnites and other Central Italian peoples, E. T. Salmon, *Samnium and the Samnites* (Cambridge, 1967) and Emma Dench, *From Barbarians to New Men: Greek, Roman, and Modern Perceptions of People from the Central Apennines* (Oxford, 1995). But two magisterial books are in a class of their own: P. A. Brunt, *The Fall of the Roman Republic and Related Essays* (Oxford, 1988), and Sir Ronald Syme's classic study of Augustus, *The Roman Revolution* (Oxford, 1939).

NOTES ON THE
TRANSLATION

(a) *Variations from Viereck's text* (see Bibliographical Note) occur at:

Book I, chs. 27 (124), 28 (125), 47 (204), 49 (212), 50 (216), 94 (434), 95 (444);

Book II, chs. 16 (59), 38 (151), 117 (491), 133 (557), 149 (624);

Book III, chs. 9 (32), 13 (46), 20 (76), 39 (161), 60 (248), 73 (298), 80 (327), 97 (401);

Book IV, chs. 5 (16), 18 (70), 53 (227), 58 (251), 74 (315), 80 (337), 88 (372), 120 (504), 128 (537);

Book V, chs. 109 (454), 111 (465), 117 (485), 129 (536).

All variations may be found in Viereck's own *apparatus criticus* or in Gabba's edition of Book I (see Bibliographical Note above), except for the transpositions at III.20 and IV.58 and the insertions at IV.88 and IV.128, for which I take full responsibility. (The bracketed numbers refer to the alternative system of reference by paragraph numbers, not used in this book.)

(b) *Proper names:* Appian converted Latin names to Greek forms. This translation restores them to their original Latin form. Where Greek names have a commonly used Latin form, e.g. Pharsalus, the Latin has been preferred, but many less well-known Greek place-names have been left as Greek. I have used a few traditional English equivalents (e.g. Rome, Athens, Rhodes), but not 'Pompey' or 'Antony' for Cn. Pompeius Magnus and M. Antonius.

Abbreviations and Symbols

b.	born
ch.	chapter
ed.	edited
n.	note
trans.	translated
*	indicates a variation from Viereck's text (see above)
<....>	enclose a supplement to, or a presumed gap in, the text

TABLE OF DATES

	Jan.–July	Campaign of Dyrrachium and Caesar's defeat (*c.* 7 July) (II.49–64)
	9 Aug.	Caesar decisively defeats Pompeius at Pharsalus (II.65–82)
	28 Sept.	Death of Pompeius, after his flight to Egypt (II.83–6)
	2 Oct.	Caesar arrives in Alexandria (II.88–9)
47	27 Mar.	Caesar victorious in Egypt (II.90)
	2 Aug.	Caesar defeats Pharnaces at Zela in Pontus (II.91)
	Sept.	Caesar returns to Rome (II.92–4)
	Dec.	Caesar crosses to Africa *(Tunisia)* (II.95)
46	6 Apr.	Caesar defeats Pompeians at Thapsus (II.96–7)
	9 Apr.	Suicide of Cato at Utica (II.98–100)
	Sept.	Caesar celebrates quadruple triumph in Rome (II.101–2)
	Nov.	Caesar leaves Rome for Spain (II.103)
45	17 Mar.	Caesar defeats Pompeius' sons at Munda *(south-east of Seville)* (II.104–5)
	Sept.?	Caesar arrives back in Rome, triumphs early October (II.106–10)
44	15 Mar.	Murder of Caesar, and aftermath (II.111–54)
	13 Apr.	Amatius, the pseudo-Marius, put to death (III.2)
	c. 14 Apr.	Brutus and Cassius move out of Rome (III.6–7)
	Apr. (end)	Arrival of Octavian in Rome (III.9–21)
	2 or 3 June	Passage of law conferring Cisalpine Gaul on Antonius in exchange for Macedonia (III.27–30)
	5 June	Corn commission granted to Brutus and Cassius (III.6)
	by 17 Sept.	Cyrene (or Bithynia?) and Crete granted to Cassius and Brutus respectively (III.8)
	Sept.	Plea by military tribunes to Antonius (III.31–9)
	after 25 Oct.	Dolabella leaves Rome for Syria, via Asia (III.24)
	Oct.–Nov.	Escalation of conflict between Antonius and Octavian (III.40–48).
	28 Nov.	Antonius leaves Rome, then besieges D. Brutus in Mutina (III.49)
	Dec.–Feb. (43)	Illegal occupation of Macedonia and Syria by Brutus and Cassius (III.78–9)
43	Jan. (mid)	Killing of Trebonius by Dolabella at Smyrna (III.25–6)
	Jan.–Apr.	War of Mutina, battles at Forum Gallorum (14 Apr.) and Mutina (21 Apr.); deaths of the consuls Hirtius and Pansa (III.50–77)

Apr.–Aug.?   Flight and death of D. Brutus (III.97–8)

Apr.–July   Gradual reconciliation of Antonius, Lepidus, Plancus, and Pollio (III.83–5)

July (end)   Cassius defeats Dolabella in Syria, starts to move against Egypt (IV.57–64)

19 Oct.   Octavian elected consul, after marching on Rome (III.80–82, 86–96)

27 Nov.   Triumvirs Antonius, Octavian and Lepidus enter office under Lex Titia (IV.2–3)

28 Nov. on   Proscriptions (IV.4–51)

Dec.   Sextus Pompeius gains control of Sicily (IV.83–5)

Dec.–Feb.? (42)   War in Africa between T. Sextius and Q. Cornificius (IV.53–6)

42 1 Jan.   *[Caesar deified]*

(first half)   Cassius attacks Rhodes (IV.65–74), Brutus the Lycians (IV.75–81)

June?–Oct.   Campaign of Philippi; battles on *c.* 1 Oct. and 23 Oct. (IV.86–137)

41   Antonius active in eastern provinces after wintering in Athens; spends next winter (41/40) in Alexandria with Cleopatra (V.4–11)

Relations between Octavian and the consul L. Antonius gradually worsen (V.12–29)

(autumn)   War breaks out in Italy. L. Antonius besieged in Perusia (V.30–37)

40 Jan. or Feb.   L. Antonius surrenders (V.38–51)

(spring)   M. Antonius returns to Italy, attacks Brundisium (V.52–9)

Sept.–Oct.   'Pact of Brundisium' between Octavian and Antonius (V.60–65)

39   Negotiations between Octavian, Antonius, and Sextus Pompeius, leading to Treaty of Puteoli (summer) (V.67–74)

38   Collapse of agreement between Sextus and triumvirs (IV.77)

Desertion of Menodorus to Octavian (V.78)

Abortive journey of Antonius to meet Octavian at Brundisium (V.79)

First campaign of Octavian against Sextus (V.80–92)

37	Treaty of Tarentum between Octavian and Antonius (summer); retrospective renewal of triumviral powers from 1 Jan. 37(?) (V.93–5)
36	Second campaign of Octavian against Sextus, defeat and flight of Sextus (V.96–132)
3 Sept.	Battle of Naulochus (V.118–21)
Sept.	Abortive challenge by Lepidus to Octavian's power (V.123–6)
35	Capture and death of Sextus in Bithynia (V.133–44)

The Civil Wars

BOOK I

1. At Rome, the common people and senate were frequently at odds with each other over the passing of laws and the cancellation of debts or the distribution of land, or during elections, but there was never any outbreak of civil violence. Only disagreements and legitimate quarrels took place, and they ended these with great restraint by making mutual concessions. On one occasion the people became involved in one of these quarrels when they were actually under arms for a campaign. However, they made no use of the weapons they had to hand, and instead hurried out to the hill which is called the Sacred Mount on account of this episode.[1] Even then they avoided violence, and created a magistracy, which they called the tribunate of the people, to defend their interests.[2] Its chief purpose was to ensure that the consuls, who were chosen from the senate, should not possess complete power over them in politics. As a result, from this time on the magistrates behaved in an increasingly more malevolent and quarrelsome way towards each other, and senate and people took sides as though they were scoring victories over each other while their magistrates strove to increase their powers.[3] In struggles of this sort Marcius Coriolanus was illegally banished, fled to the Volscians, and made war on his own country.[4]

2. Among these ancient troubles, this is the single example one can find of armed conflict – and that due to a deserter. No sword was ever brought into the assembly, and no Roman was ever killed by a Roman, until Tiberius Gracchus, while holding the office of tribune and in the act of proposing legislation, became the first man to die in civil unrest, and along with him a great number of people who had crowded together on the Capitol and were killed around the temple.[5] The disorders did not end even with this foul act; on each occasion when they occurred the Romans openly took sides against each other, and often carried daggers; from time to time some magistrate would be murdered in a temple, or in the assembly, or in the forum – a tribune or praetor or consul, or a candidate for these offices, or somebody otherwise distinguished. Undisciplined arrogance soon became the rule, along with a shameful contempt for law and justice. As the evil grew, open revolts took place against the government and large armies were led with violence against their native land by men who had been exiled, or condemned in the courts, or were feuding among themselves over some office or command. There were now many cases of individuals who would not relinquish power, and faction leaders who aspired to sole rule. Some refused to give up control of the armies entrusted to them by the people, and others even recruited foreigners on their own account, without public authority, to fight against their rivals. If one side took possession of Rome first, the other made war in theory against the rival faction, but in fact against their own country; they attacked it as though it were enemy soil, mercilessly slaughtered those who stood in their way, and proscribed,[6] banished, and confiscated the property of the rest, some of whom they even tortured horribly.[7]

3. No sort of atrocity was left undone until about fifty years after Gracchus one of these faction leaders, Cornelius Sulla, curing one ill with another, proclaimed himself sole master of the state for an indefinite period.[8] This post, called the dictatorship, to which an appointment might be made for six months at a time in the most serious emergencies, was one which the Romans had long since ceased to fill. Sulla however became dictator for life, technically by election, but in reality by force and necessity; none the less he was I think the first man not only to have the courage, when he had had enough of power, to lay down his monarchical office voluntarily and to add that he would give an account of his stewardship to his detractors, but also to be bold enough, when he was a private citizen, to go for some time to the forum in the sight of all, and return home unharmed: such was the effect that was still produced in onlookers, whether it was from fear of his government, or amazement that he had renounced power, or respect for his promise to undergo audit, or some feeling of goodwill towards him and a reflection that on balance his period of absolute rule had been for the good. Thus for a short while, in Sulla's lifetime, factional strife stopped and there was some compensation for the harm he had done.

4. But after Sulla similar disturbances flared up again until Gaius Caesar, who had enjoyed a long-term command in Gaul by decision of the people, was ordered by the senate to lay it down.[9] Caesar blamed not the senate, but Pompeius, who was hostile to him and had an army in Italy. He alleged that

Pompeius was plotting to deprive him of his command, and proposed either that each of them should retain his army as a safeguard against the hostility of the other, or that Pompeius should also give up the forces he had and become a private citizen obedient to the laws like himself. Neither proposal was accepted, so he moved from Gaul against Pompeius; he invaded his own country, put Pompeius to flight, followed him, won a splendid victory in a great battle in Thessaly,[10] and pursued him as he slipped away to Egypt. After Pompeius' murder at the hands of Egyptians, Caesar had some involvement in the affairs of Egypt and remained there until he had established the succession to the throne; he then returned to Rome. So he had decisively overcome, chiefly by force of arms, his greatest rival, who had acquired the name 'the Great' by his military exploits; and now that no one dared even to speak against him on any matter, he became the second Roman, following Sulla, to be appointed dictator for an indefinite period.[11] Again there was a complete lull in civil conflict, until he too, a man who had become strongly committed to the popular cause and highly experienced in the exercise of power, was murdered in the senate-house by Brutus and Cassius out of jealousy of his immense power and out of longing for the traditional constitution.[12] The people in fact missed him more than they had anyone else; they went round hunting for his killers, gave him a funeral in the middle of the forum, built a temple on the site of the pyre, and still sacrifice to him as a god.

5. After this, civil strife returned more intensely than ever and became of enormously increased importance. Murder, banishment, and capital proscription of large numbers both of senators and of the equestrian class[13] were of frequent occurrence. The faction leaders handed over enemies to each other and in so doing spared neither friends nor brothers; to so great an extent did hostility towards their rivals prevail over concern for their near and dear. And these three men, Antonius and Lepidus and the one who was formerly called Octavius,[14] but being a relative of Caesar's and adopted by him in his will was subsequently known as Caesar, proceeded to treat the government of Rome as their private property and divide it between themselves. After a short while they quarrelled over this division, as might be expected, and Octavian, who was superior in intelligence and experience, first deprived Lepidus of his portion, Africa, and then in the campaign of Actium took from Antonius his control of the area between Syria and the entrance to the Adriatic.[15] And in addition to these exploits, which were obviously impressive and astonished everyone, he also mounted a

naval expedition that led to the capture of Egypt, which was at that time the longest-lasting and strongest power since Alexander and the only one not then incorporated into the Roman empire as it is today.[16] As a result while he was still alive he became the first to be considered 'august' because of his achievements and be so called by the Romans. He could also, like Caesar and more powerfully than Caesar, declare himself ruler both of his own country and of all the nations subject to her, without further need of appointment or election or the pretence of it. His rule was strong and lasted a long time, and since he was fortunate in everything he did and was regarded with fear, he left a family dynasty to succeed him and enjoy a power similar to his own.

6. In this way the Roman state survived all kinds of civil disturbance to reach unity and monarchy; and I have collected together and composed an account of how this happened, both because it is a story well worth the attention of any who wish to contemplate limitless human ambition, terrible lust for power, indefatigable patience, and evil in ten thousand shapes, but particularly because it was necessary for me to write it in order to lead up to my Egyptian narrative, ending where that begins. For it was because of this civil war that Egypt was captured, Cleopatra being Antonius' ally.

By reason of its quantity, the material has been divided to run in this book from Sempronius Gracchus to Cornelius Sulla, and in the next to the death of Gaius Caesar.[17] The remaining books of the Civil Wars show how the triumvirs behaved towards each other and the Roman people, until the last and greatest trial of strength of the civil wars, Octavian's campaign at Actium against Antonius and his associate Cleopatra, which will form the beginning of the Egyptian narrative.[18]

7. As they subdued successive parts of Italy by war, the Romans confiscated a portion of the land and founded towns, or chose settlers from their own people to go to existing towns[19] – this being the alternative they devised to garrisons. In the case of the captured land which became theirs on each occasion, they distributed the cultivated area at once to settlers, or sold or leased it; but since they did not have time to allocate the very large quantity that was then lying uncultivated as a result of hostilities, they announced that this could for the moment be worked by anyone who wished at a rent of one tenth of the produce for arable land and one fifth for orchards.[20] Rents were also set for those who pastured larger and smaller beasts. This they did to increase the numbers of the people of Italy, whom they

considered exceptionally tough, so that they would have their kin to fight alongside them. But the result was the opposite. The rich gained possession of most of the undistributed land and after a while were confident that no one would take it back from them. They used persuasion or force to buy or seize property which adjoined their own, or any other smallholdings belonging to poor men, and came to operate great ranches instead of single farms. They employed slave hands and shepherds on these estates to avoid having free men dragged off the land to serve in the army, and they derived great profit from this form of ownership too, as the slaves had many children and no liability to military service and their numbers increased freely. For these reasons the powerful were becoming extremely rich, and the number of slaves in the country was reaching large proportions, while the Italian people were suffering from depopulation and a shortage of men, worn down as they were by poverty and taxes and military service.[21] And if they had any respite from these tribulations, they had no employment, because the land was owned by the rich who used slave farm workers instead of free men.[22]

8. Under these circumstances the Roman people became concerned that they might no longer have a ready supply of allies from Italy, and that their supremacy might be at risk from such large numbers of slaves. They did not consider reform, as it seemed neither easy nor altogether fair to take away from so many men so much property that they had held for so long, including their own trees and buildings and equipment, and eventually they reluctantly decided, on the proposal of the tribunes, that no one was to hold more than 500 *iugera* of this land, nor pasture on it more than one hundred larger or 500 smaller beasts.[23] In addition it was stipulated that a fixed number of free men should be employed, who would watch and report on what was being done. They embodied these provisions in a law, which they swore to observe, and laid down penalties, expecting that the remainder of the land would at once be sold in small parcels to the poor. But no notice was taken either of the laws or of the oaths; some who appeared to observe them made bogus transfers of land to their relations, while the majority completely ignored them. 9. At this point Tiberius Sempronius Gracchus, a man of noble birth, outstanding ambition, and formidable oratorical powers, and on all these counts very well known to everyone, became tribune and made a powerful speech about the people of Italy, saying that they were excellent fighters and related to the Romans by blood, but were declining slowly into poverty and depopulation and had

not even the hope of a remedy.[24] He expressed hostility to the slaves, because they made no military contribution and were never loyal to their masters, and blamed them for the recent calamity of the landowners in Sicily, which had been caused by slaves whose numbers had been swelled by the demands of agriculture, and for the war conducted by the Romans against them, which had been neither simple nor short but had dragged on with all sorts of dangerous twists of fortune.[25] So saying, he proposed to renew the law that no individual should hold more than 500 *iugera*, but modified its previous provisions by adding that children of occupiers could have half this amount. The remainder of the land was to be distributed to the poor by three elected commissioners, who were to rotate annually.

10. It was this provision which particularly disturbed the rich, because the commissioners would prevent them from ignoring the law as previously, and they would be unable to buy the land from those who received allotments, since Gracchus had foreseen this and was proposing to forbid sale. They gathered in groups, deploring their situation and supporting their case against the poor by pointing to the work they had put in over many years, their planting, their building. Some had bought land from their neighbours – were they to lose the money as well as the land? Some had family tombs on the land or said that holdings had been treated as fully owned and divided up on inheritance. Others claimed that their wives' dowries had been invested in such land, or that it had been given to their daughters as dowry, and moneylenders could show loans made on this security. In short, there was a babel of protest and lamentation. For their part, the poor made equal complaint, that they had been reduced from prosperity to abject poverty, and from that to childlessness, since they could not rear children. They listed the campaigns on which they had served to win this land, and were indignant at being deprived of access to common property, and at the same time they berated the rich for choosing slaves, who were always treacherous and malevolent and on that account exempt from military service, instead of free men and citizens and soldiers. While the two sides were thus complaining and attacking each other, another large group, composed of people from the colonies,[26] or from states enjoying equal political rights, or who had in some other way a share in this land, and had similar reasons for being afraid, came to Rome and gave their support to one side or the other. Emboldened by their numbers, they became rough and started a great many disturbances while they waited for the voting on the law, some being implacably opposed to its passing, others

intending to secure it at any price. Apart from their personal interest, they were goaded on by the desire to defeat their opponents, and made preparations against each other for the appointed day.

11. Now the idea of Gracchus' scheme was to secure not prosperity, but population; but he was carried away above all by the benefits of the plan, because he thought that nothing better or more splendid could possibly happen to Italy, and gave no consideration to the difficulties surrounding it. When the time for voting was imminent, he put forward many other attractive arguments at considerable length and finally asked whether it was not right for common property to be divided amongst all, and whether a citizen was not always a better man than a slave, a soldier more useful than a non-soldier, and one who had a share in the state more well-disposed to the public interest than one who had not. But he did not pursue the comparison long, as it was demeaning, and again turned to a rehearsal of their hopes and fears. He said that they had already forcibly seized a great deal of territory in war and hoped to win the rest of the inhabited world, but that at the present time everything was at stake: the question was whether through their strength in manpower they would gain possesssion of the remainder, or whether through their weakness and unpopularity they would be stripped by their enemies of even what they had. He exaggerated the glory and prosperity associated with one of these alternatives, and the danger and fear associated with the other. He encouraged the rich to bear these considerations in mind and if necessary make a special contribution of their own towards their hopes for the future by giving this land to men who would bring up children. They should not overlook greater matters while they squabbled about lesser, especially since they were receiving, as a reward for the labour they had expended, the unencumbered and special possession, secure for ever, without payment, of 500 *iugera* for each owner, plus half of this for each child in the case of those who had children.

Gracchus said a great deal along these lines, and stirred the poor and any others who were swayed by reason rather than by love of their possessions. He then ordered the clerk to read the law.   12. But Marcus Octavius, one of the other tribunes who had been primed by the landholders to stop the proceedings – and with the Romans the one who vetoes prevails – told the clerk to be silent. On this occasion Gracchus, after making a severe verbal attack on him, postponed the voting to the next meeting of the comitia < . . . > and having stationed a guard beside himself sufficient to tame Octavius even if he resisted, threatened the clerk and ordered him to read the law to the crowd. The clerk started to read but when Octavius forbade him he stopped. While the tribunes hurled abuse at each other and considerable disorder broke out among the crowd, the leading citizens requested the tribunes to refer their dispute to the senate. Gracchus seized on the suggestion because he thought the law found favour with all right-thinking people, and hurried to the senate-house. But when he was treated contemptuously there by the rich, as was possible in a small gathering, he hastened back to the forum and declared that he would put off to the ensuing *comitia* voting both on the law and on Octavius' holding of office, to decide whether a tribune who opposed the interests of the people should continue to hold his position. And so he did; for when Octavius, not in the least frightened, again objected, Gracchus proposed to take the vote on him first. When the first tribe voted that Octavius should lay down his office, Gracchus turned to him and begged him to change his mind. He would not, and Gracchus pressed on with the voting sequence. There were at that time thirty-five tribes, and the first seventeen had all angrily voted the same way. The eighteenth was about to cast the deciding vote when Gracchus again made an earnest attempt, in full view of the people, to persuade Octavius, who was at that moment pursuing a course of extreme risk, not to throw into chaos a project that was morally right and of the greatest utility to all Italy, nor to subvert such great enthusiasm on the part of the people, to whose wishes he ought to make some concession in his capacity of tribune, nor to look with indifference on the loss of his office by public condemnation. With these words he called on the gods to witness that it was with reluctance that he brought dishonour on a fellow-magistrate, and having failed to convince Octavius carried on with the vote. Octavius immediately became a private citizen and slipped away unnoticed.   **13.** In his place Quintus Mummius was chosen tribune, and the land law was passed.[27] The first men elected to carry out the distribution were Gracchus himself who proposed the law, his brother of the same name, and the proposer's father-in-law Appius Claudius, since the people had a real fear even now that the law might not be put into effect unless Gracchus himself, solidly supported by his kinsmen, initiated its operation.[28] Boasting over the law, Gracchus was escorted home by the crowd as though he were the founding father, not of one city, or of one clan, but of all the peoples of Italy. Then the victorious voters went home to the country, which they had left for the occasion, but the losers stayed in the city, still smarting and putting it about that Gracchus would be sorry, as soon as he became a private citizen, that he had committed an outrage against a sacred and inviolate office and had planted such seeds of discord in Italy.

14. It was now summer, when intending tribunes were declaring their candidacies; and the rich, as election day approached, were perfectly clearly supporting for office those who were most hostile to Gracchus. He feared that disaster was at hand if he did not become tribune for the next year also, and summoned the country people to come to vote. But they were busy with the harvest, and so under pressure from the short time still remaining before the day fixed for the election he resorted to the city population; he went round them in turn, begging each to choose him tribune for the following year because he was in danger on their account. When the voting took place, the first two tribes returned Gracchus. The rich protested that it was illegal for the same man to hold office in consecutive years.[29] As Rubrius, the tribune who had been chosen by lot to preside over this assembly, hesitated over the point, Mummius, the man who had been chosen to be tribune in place of Octavius, urged him to hand over the meeting to himself. But when Rubrius did so, the other tribunes demanded that the presidency be settled by lot, arguing that if Rubrius who had drawn it stood down, it reverted again to selection by lot from amongst all of them. On this point also there was heated argument, and Gracchus, getting the worst of it, first of all put off the voting till the next day and then, giving everything up for lost, put on mourning in spite of being still in office, and for the rest of the day led his son around the forum and presented him to everyone and asked them to protect him as though his own destruction at the hands of his enemies was imminent.[30]

15. The poor were overwhelmed with a feeling of great pity, along with some reflections: that as for themselves, they were no longer citizens equal under the law, but slaves to the power of the rich, and as for Gracchus, his great fear and suffering were a result of his concern for them. They escorted him home in a body that evening, lamenting and encouraging him to be optimistic about the next day. He took heart, gathered together his partisans before it was yet light, and after indicating a signal to be used if it was necessary to fight, occupied the temple and the centre of the assembly-place on the Capitoline, where the voting was to take place. When he was obstructed by the tribunes and the rich, who would not allow the voting procedure on the law to begin, he gave the signal. A shout suddenly came from those who were in the secret and violence at once broke out. Some of Gracchus' supporters acted as a bodyguard to protect him, while others

hitched up their clothing, snatched the rods and staves from the hands of the attendants, broke them in pieces, and drove the rich from the assembly. So great was the confusion and such the injuries that the tribunes deserted their places, the priests shut the temple, and large numbers of people ran wildly to escape. It was also erroneously alleged by some that Gracchus had deposed the other tribunes (a guess based on their invisibility), and by others that he was making himself tribune for the following year without election.

16. While this was happening the senate met in the temple of Fides. I am amazed that they never even thought of appointing a dictator, although they had often in crises of this sort found salvation in absolute power, and that the majority neither on that occasion, nor subsequently, so much as remembered this course of action which had proved most useful to their predecessors.[31] After taking their decisions, they went up to the Capitol. The first among them, leading the way, was the chief priest, as he is called, Cornelius Scipio Nasica; he shouted that those who wanted to save their country should follow him, and threw the hem of his toga over his head. This may have been to induce more of them to accompany him by the distinctiveness of his dress, or to fashion for the onlookers some symbol of war like a helmet, or to hide from the gods his shame at what he proposed to do.[32] When he came up to the sanctuary and rushed at the Gracchans, they gave way because they respected such a distinguished man and saw the senators following him; but the latter wrenched the staves from the very hands of the Gracchans, broke up the benches and other equipment which had been brought for an assembly, and struck and chased the Gracchans and drove them over the precipitous edges. In this rioting many of the Gracchans died, and Gracchus himself, trapped near the temple, was killed at the doorway beside the statues of the kings. All the bodies were thrown at night into the river.

17. Thus Gracchus, son of Gracchus who had been twice consul and of Cornelia, daughter of Scipio who had wrested supremacy from the Carthaginians, lost his life on the Capitol, while holding the office of tribune, as a result of an excellent scheme which he pushed forward by violent means.[33] And this foul crime, the first perpetrated in the public assembly, was not the last, but from time to time something similar would always occur. The city was divided between grief and rejoicing at the murder of Gracchus, one group mourning for themselves and for him and for the present situation, which they saw not as ordered political life, but as vio-

lence and the rule of force, the others thinking that everything they wished for had come about.

18. These events took place when Aristonicus was fighting the Romans for the control of Asia.[34] After the killing of Gracchus and the death of Appius Claudius, Fulvius Flaccus and Papirius Carbo were appointed in their places to allocate the land, along with the younger Gracchus.[35] Since the holders of the land did not bother to register it, the commissioners made a proclamation that accusations could be brought by informers. Immediately a large number of difficult cases arose. For when land of a different category which bordered on public land had been sold or distributed to the allies, in order to establish its dimensions the whole lot had to be investigated, and how it had been sold or distributed. Not all owners had kept their contracts of sale or titles of allotment, and such as were actually discovered were inconclusive. When it was re-surveyed some people were displaced to bare land from land that had been planted with trees and equipped with farm buildings, and others from cultivated land to land that was uncultivated or marshy or liable to flooding. Even in the beginning the division had never been done with any great accuracy, as this was territory seized by war. The proclamation that anyone who wished could work unallocated land encouraged many to cultivate what lay next to their own property and blur the distinction between the two, and the passage of time put everything on a fresh basis. Thus the injustice committed by the wealthy, though great, was hard to recognize; and what happened was in fact a general upheaval of people being transferred and settling down on land which had belonged to others.

19. All this then, and the haste with which judgements were given on these disputes, were more than the Italians could bear, and they chose Cornelius Scipio, who had sacked Carthage, to be spokesman for their grievances.[36] Because he had found them extremely supportive in the wars he was reluctant to ignore their request. So he went to the senate, and although he did not openly attack Gracchus' law because of the common people, he examined its problems in detail and proposed that the legal actions should be heard not by the land commissioners, since they were regarded as prejudiced by the litigants, but by others. He carried his point all the better because it seemed to be a fair one, and the consul Tuditanus was appointed to hear the cases.[37] However, after making a start on the task and realizing how difficult it was, Tuditanus led a campaign against the Illyrians and made this an excuse for not giving judgement; on the other hand the land commissioners were inactive, since nobody came before them to obtain judicial decisions. As a result the people began to be angry with Scipio and hate him, because they now saw this person, whom they had cherished to the point of arousing ill-will, on whose behalf they had put up much resistance to powerful men, and whom they had twice chosen consul unconstitutionally,[38] standing up against them in the interests of the Italians. When Scipio's enemies became aware of this, they proclaimed that he was completely set on undoing Gracchus' law and to this end intended an armed massacre.

20. The people listened to these allegations and were apprehensive, until Scipio was found dead, his body unmarked, with a notebook beside him which he had put to hand in the evening, intending to write that night a speech he was to give to a gathering of the public. Perhaps Cornelia, mother of the Gracchi, killed him, to prevent the repeal of Gracchus' law, assisted in the deed by her daughter Sempronia, who was married to Scipio but on account of her ugliness and childlessness neither was loved by, nor loved, him. Perhaps, as some think, he took his own life in the realization that he was incapable of carrying out what he had undertaken. There are some who say that slaves confessed under torture that strangers were brought into the back of the house at night who strangled him, and that those who discovered this shrank from publicizing it because the people were still angry with Scipio and pleased at his death. Scipio, anyway, was dead. He was not even accorded the honour of a public funeral, although he had contributed hugely to Rome's dominance of the world; thus does present anger outweigh past gratitude. But this episode, notable in itself, was no more than a subsidiary incident in the Gracchan disturbance.

21. Even after this those who were in possession of the land put off its distribution on various pretexts for a long time. There was a proposal that all the allies, who were making the most vocal opposition over the land, should be enrolled as Roman citizens, so that out of gratitude for the greater favour they would no longer quarrel about the land. The Italians gladly accepted this, preferring the citizenship to their estates. Their most important ally by far in this scheme was Fulvius Flaccus, who was simultaneously consul and one of the land commissioners;[39] but the senate resented the idea of giving their subjects political rights equal to their own, and so this attempt was abandoned and the populace, who had clung for so long to the

hope of land, were in despair. Being in this frame of mind, they welcomed the candidature for the tribunate of one of the land commissioners, Gaius Gracchus, the younger brother of the author of the law, who had kept quiet for a long time after the disaster to his brother. Since many of the senators thought little of him, he put himself forward for election as a tribune.[40] He was elected by a remarkable majority and immediately began to undermine the senate by making provision for the distribution to each citizen of a monthly grain ration, paid for from public funds – a practice never previously customary. Thus he quickly became the political leader of the people, with the support of Fulvius Flaccus. Immediately after this he was elected tribune for the following year also; for a law was already in existence that if there were not enough candidates the people could choose any Roman.[41]

22. In this way, then, Gaius Gracchus became tribune for the second time;[42] and exactly as he had the people in his pay, by another measure of this sort he became the leader of the equestrian class, whose status is intermediate between that of the senate and the people. He transferred the courts, which were suspect because of bribery, from the senators to the equestrians.[43] He particularly castigated the former for some recent cases, in which Aurelius Cotta and Salinator and yet a third, Manius Aquillius the governor of Asia, had been acquitted by the jurors although they had clearly indulged in bribery and the delegations which had been sent to give evidence against them were still in Rome and going round stirring up ill-feeling by broadcasting the details. Extremely ashamed of this, the senate did not oppose the law, and the people ratified it. In this way the courts were transferred from the senate to the equestrians. It is reported that when the law had only just been passed Gracchus said that with one blow he had laid low the senate, and as its effects unfolded the truth of his assertion became ever more apparent. For the fact that the equestrians sat in judgement on all the Romans and Italians,[44] and on the senators themselves, with the widest jurisdiction over property, civil rights, and exile, set them up as virtual rulers over the senators, who thus became no more than their subjects. At the elections the equestrians used to support the tribunes, and by getting in exchange from them whatever they wanted reached a point where the senators felt extremely threatened by them. Before long it came about that dominance in the state had been reversed, the senate possessing now only the prestige, but the equestrians the power. They went so far as not merely to exert influence, but openly and insultingly to abuse their power over the senators. They also took to accepting bribes, and having

once tasted huge profits themselves indulged in them even more disgracefully and greedily. They set paid accusers on the wealthy, and by agreement
amongst themselves and by the use of force did away with trials for bribery,[45] so that the practice of operating this kind of safeguard fell into complete disuse, and the judiciary law gave rise to another factional struggle,
which lasted a long time and was no less severe than those which preceded
it.

23. Gracchus also built long roads throughout Italy, putting a great
number of contractors and workmen in his debt, ready to do his bidding,
and he proposed the establishment of many colonies.[46] He wished to
confer on the Latins all the rights of Roman citizenship, arguing that the
senate could not decently refuse them to their kinsmen. To the other allies,
who were not allowed to cast a vote in the Roman assemblies, he proposed
to give this privilege in future, so that they could help him in the voting on
his laws.[47] The senate was particularly alarmed at this, and instructed the
consuls to make a proclamation that no non-voter should stay in Rome or
approach within five miles of the city during the period when these laws
were to be voted on. It prevailed on Livius Drusus, another one of the tribunes, to veto Gracchus' laws but not to tell the people his reasons (and
there was no obligation for reasons to be given). The senators also authorized Drusus to conciliate the people by proposing twelve colonies, which
so delighted them that they thought the laws put forward by Gracchus
were contemptible.

24. Having lost his pre-eminence as a popular leader, Gracchus sailed to
Africa. He was accompanied by Fulvius Flaccus, who had also been chosen
tribune, after his consulship, because of these projects.[48] It had been voted
to establish a colony in Africa, as the place had a reputation for fertility, and
these very men had been deliberately chosen to set it up, so that they
should be away from Rome for a little while and the senate might have
some rest from demagoguery. At the colony, they laid out the town on the
site where Carthage had once stood, brushing aside the fact that when
Scipio razed it he had uttered a solemn curse that it should be for ever
sheep-pasture.[49] They also made land allotments to 6,000 settlers instead of
to the lesser number that stood in the law, attempting thereby to win more
popularity with the people, and on their return to Rome they started to recruit the 6,000 from all over Italy. However, those who were still engaged
on the surveying in Africa reported that wolves had torn up and scattered
the boundary markers placed by Gracchus and Fulvius, and the augurs de-

clared that the settlement was ill-omened. The senate called an assembly, in which they intended to abrogate the law authorizing the colony. Gracchus and Fulvius, maddened by their impending failure here too, alleged that the senate had lied about the wolves. The boldest of the plebeians lent them their support, and brought daggers with them to the Capitol, where the assembly concerning the colony was going to take place.[50]

25. The people had already gathered and Fulvius had begun to speak about the business, when Gracchus arrived on the Capitol attended by a bodyguard of his sympathizers. Conscience-stricken by the extraordinary nature of his plans, he turned aside from the meeting of the assembly, entered the portico, and walked up and down waiting to see what would happen. Antyllus, who was one of the ordinary citizens who happened to be making a sacrifice in the portico, saw him in this disturbed state. He put his hand on him, whether because he had heard or suspected something, or was impelled for some other reason to speak to him, and implored him to spare his country. Gracchus became still more agitated and fearful, like a criminal caught in the act, and gave him a sharp look; and one of the party, without any signal having been made or any command given, but judging simply from the sharpness of Gracchus' look at Antyllus that the vital moment had already arrived, and thinking to gratify Gracchus by being the first to strike a blow, drew his dagger and killed Antyllus. A cry went up, and when the dead body was seen lying there in the middle of them the whole crowd poured down from the Capitol, fearing the same fate. Gracchus went into the forum, wanting to defend himself over what had happened. But no one would even meet him. They all turned aside from him as though he were polluted by blood. Gracchus and Fulvius, since they did not know what to do and through this premature act had lost the opportunity of carrying out their plans, hurried back to their houses. Their supporters accompanied them, but the rest of the populace filled the forum from midnight as though some disaster had occurred. The consul in the city, Opimius, ordered an armed force to assemble on the Capitol at dawn and sent mesengers to summon the senate. He himself took his place in the centre of things, at the temple of Castor and Pollux, and awaited developments.[51]

26. Such was the situation when the senate tried to summon Gracchus and Flaccus from their homes to the senate-house to defend themselves; but they had armed themselves and were hastening to the Aventine hill in

the hope that if they could seize it first the senate would come to some agreement with them. As they ran through the city they called the slaves to freedom, but none obeyed the call. With such support as they had they seized and fortified the temple of Diana. They also sent Quintus, Flaccus' son, to the senate to ask for reconciliation and the chance to live together in peace. The senate ordered them to put aside their weapons and come to the senate-house and say what they wanted, but otherwise to send no one else. When they sent Quintus with a second message, the consul Opimius arrested him because by the terms of the proclamation he no longer ranked as an ambassador. Opimius also sent his armed men into action against Gracchus and his followers. Gracchus fled with a single slave across the Pons Sublicius to some sacred spot on the other side of the river, and as he was on the point of arrest offered his throat to the slave. Flaccus took refuge in the workshop of a man he knew, and when the pursuers, not knowing which the house was, threatened to burn down the whole lane, the man who had taken him in was reluctant to betray his suppliant, but told someone else to do so. And so Flaccus was captured and put to death. The heads of Gracchus and Flaccus were taken to Opimius, who paid their weight in gold to the men who brought them. Their houses were looted by the mob, and their sympathizers were arrested by Opimius, who threw them into the gaol and gave orders for them to be strangled, although he agreed that Flaccus' son Quintus could choose his own mode of death. The consul then purified the city after the bloodshed, and the senate instructed him to erect a temple of Concord in the forum.

27. Such was the end of the civil unrest set in train by the younger Gracchus. Not long afterwards a law was passed permitting holders of the land, over which they were quarrelling, to sell it (for this had actually been forbidden by the elder Gracchus), and immediately the rich started to buy from the poor or find pretexts to evict them by force.[52] The situation continued to deteriorate for the poor, until Spurius Thorius,[53] as tribune, brought in a law which put an end to the process of allotting the land, and made it the property of its current holders, who were to pay a rent for it to the people, this money to be used for public distributions. This was indeed some consolation to the poor, thanks to the distributions, but it did nothing to increase the population. And once the Gracchan law, an admirable law which would have been of the greatest service had it been possible to enforce it, had been undermined by these tricks, another tribune very soon abolished the rents, and the people had been deprived of absolutely everything.[54] For this reason the numbers of both citizens and soldiers diminished still more, as did the returns from the public land, and the distributions, and legislation < . . . > * the court hearings coming to a standstill about fifteen years after Gracchus passed his law.[55]

28. At this same time the consul Caepio * pulled down the theatre which Lucius Cassius had begun, and indeed almost completed, because he believed that this too would be a cause of further disturbances, or that it was not in the public interest for Romans to become completely used to Greek luxuries.[56] As censor, Quintus Caecilius Metellus tried to demote Glaucia, a senator, and Appuleius Saturninus, who had already held the tribunate, for disgraceful conduct, but was unsuccessful because his colleague would not concur.[57] As a result Appuleius, to take revenge on Metellus, very soon put himself forward as a candidate for a second tribunate, waiting for the time when Glaucia was praetor and would preside over these tribunician elections.[58] But an aristocrat, Nonius, who was outspoken against Appuleius and abused Glaucia, was chosen for the office. Then Glaucia and Appuleius, who were afraid that if he became tribune he would turn the tables on them, set a gang of men to mob him as soon as he left the assembly on his way home, and stabbed him when he fled for refuge to an inn. Following this sorry and shocking episode, early in the morning, before the voters had had time to assemble, Glaucia and his supporters elected Appuleius to the tribunate. The fate of Nonius was hushed up for this reason, that Appuleius was to be tribune, and no one dared to call him further to account.

29. Metellus, too, they drove into exile, acting in alliance with Marius who was consul for the sixth time and was a secret enemy of his.[59] They all worked together like this: Appuleius brought forward a law to authorize land distribution in the region which the Romans now call Gaul;[60] this had been seized by the Cimbri, a Celtic people, but Marius had recently expelled them and appropriated the territory for Rome as it was no longer in Cimbric possession. There was a rider to this law, that if it were passed by the people, the senators were to swear within five days to observe its terms on pain of expulsion from the senate and a fine of twenty talents.[61] In this way they intended to safeguard themselves against those who disapproved of the law and take revenge on them, and particularly on Metellus, who was too proud to submit to the oath. This was the position with the law when Appuleius announced a day for the vote and sent messengers round to the rural population, in whom above all the coalition had confidence because these men had served as soldiers under Marius. But as the law gave the larger share of the land to the Italians, the city populace were discontented.[62]

30. Disorder broke out on the day appointed for the vote. The tribunes who attempted to veto the laws were violently attacked by Appuleius and had to leap off the platform, and the urban mob shouted that there had been thunder during the assembly (after which it is illegal for the Romans to pass any measure). Even so, Appuleius and his adherents persisted. Then the city folk hitched up their clothing, snatched whatever pieces of wood lay to hand, and scattered the rural voters. The latter were called together again by Appuleius, armed themselves with staves, and attacked the city dwellers and passed the law by violence. Straight after its passage, Marius, as consul, put it to the senate that they should consider the matter of the oath. Knowing that Metellus was a man of firm views, who stuck to what he thought or had previously said, he gave his own opinion first, but deceitfully, saying that he would never voluntarily swear this oath himself. When Metellus concurred with him in this pronouncement and all the others praised them, Marius dismissed the senate. Then late in the afternoon on the fifth day, which was the last set by the law for taking the oath, he hurriedly summoned them and said that he was afraid of the populace because they were so strongly in favour of the law, but he could see a clever way out, which was, to swear to obey the law in so far as it was a law. In this way they would trick the country people into dispersing now, and afterwards they would have no difficulty in showing that a law which was passed, against ancestral practice, by the use of violence and when thunder had been reported, was not a law at all.

31. This was his proposal; and finally, without waiting or allowing them a moment to think, as they were all dumb with consternation at the trick and at the little time that was now left, he rose and went to the temple of Saturn, where the oath had to be taken in front of the quaestors, and was the first to swear it, followed by his friends. All the others also swore, each afraid for himself, except for Metellus who alone did not take the oath but adhered fearlessly to his chosen course. On the next day, without delay, Appuleius sent his attendant for him and dragged him out of the senate-house. When the other tribunes came to his aid, Glaucia and Appuleius hurried to the country people and asserted that they would not get their land, nor would the law be put into effect, unless Metellus were exiled. They published the terms of a bill to banish him, adding that the consuls

were to make proclamation that no one should provide Metellus with fire or water or shelter,[63] and fixed a date for voting on this bill. The urban population were very angry and constantly escorted Metellus with daggers in their hands, but he thanked them, commended them for their views, and declared that he would not allow any danger to threaten his country on his account. And with these words he left Rome. Appuleius passed the bill into law and Marius made the proclamation it required.

32. This, then, was the manner in which Metellus, a man of the highest reputation, was exiled, and Appuleius then became tribune for a third time.[64] One of his colleagues was thought to be a fugitive slave; he claimed the elder Gracchus was his father, and because they missed Gracchus the people had supported him at the elections.[65] When the consular elections came on, Marcus Antonius was elected without dispute to one of the posts, but Glaucia and Memmius were rivals for the other.[66] Since Memmius had by far the better record, Glaucia and Appuleius were afraid of the result and sent men with clubs to attack him during the actual voting and beat him to death in full view of everyone. The assembly dispersed in uproar. Law, justice, and sense of shame had all disappeared. The people, resentful and angry, hurried to assemble the next day with the intention of killing Appuleius. He had collected another mob from the country and with Glaucia and the quaestor Gaius Saufeius seized the Capitol. When the senate resolved that they should be destroyed, Marius was displeased but nevertheless reluctantly armed some forces. As he was procrastinating, others cut the water supply to the sanctuary. Dying of thirst, Saufeius proposed that they burn the temple, but Glaucia and Appuleius, hoping that Marius would help them, surrendered first, and Saufeius followed their example. Everyone demanded that Marius kill them on the spot, but he imprisoned them in the senate-house as a more lawful course of action. The others, thinking this a mere pretext, tore the tiles off the senate-house and threw them at Appuleius and his followers until they had killed them, a quaestor and a tribune and a praetor, still wearing the insignia of office.

33. Not only were a large number of other people killed in this disturbance, but also another tribune, the reputed son of Gracchus, serving his first day in office.[67] For neither freedom, nor democracy, nor law, nor reputation, nor office, were of any help any longer to anybody when the holders of the tribunate, which had come into existence for the prevention of injustice and the protection of ordinary people, and was sacred and inviolate, both committed and suffered such wrongs. Now that Appuleius' party was

destroyed, senate and people clamoured for the recall of Metellus, but Publius Furius, a tribune, who was not of free birth but the son of an ex-slave, insolently resisted them and remained adamant even when Metellus' son Metellus pleaded with him in public, weeping and throwing himself at his feet. As a result of this scene, the son was in future called Pius, and Furius, when he was put on trial for this in the following year by the tribune Gaius Canuleius, was lynched by the people without being allowed a hearing.[68] Thus every year some horror would defile public life. Metellus was permitted to come back from exile, and they say the day was not long enough for him to greet all those who came to meet him at the gates. Such, then, were the results for the Romans of this third civil conflict, that of Appuleius, which came after the two associated with the Gracchi.

34. This was the state of affairs when the so-called Social War broke out, involving many of the peoples of Italy.[69] It began unexpectedly, rapidly became very serious, and caused enough apprehension to extinguish factional strife in Rome for some time. When it died down it too gave birth to other internal conflicts, and to faction leaders who were more powerful and employed against each other not legislative programmes, nor demagoguery, but whole armies. And for these reasons I have included it in this history, because it originated in the civil dissensions in Rome and it resulted in a much worse conflict of that type. Its beginnings were these: Fulvius Flaccus, when consul, was the first to give strong encouragement in a very open way to the Italians to aspire to Roman citizenship, so that they could be partners in empire instead of subjects.[70] Having introduced this policy, he would not be deflected from it, and was for this reason sent off by the senate to conduct a military campaign, in the course of which his consulship expired. Later he decided to become tribune and succeeded in obtaining the office along with the younger Gracchus, who was himself planning to introduce other measures of the same sort on behalf of Italy. And when both of them were killed, as I have previously explained, the inhabitants of Italy were still further provoked to anger; for they thought it wrong to be classed as subjects and not as partners, and wrong for Flaccus and Gracchus to have suffered this fate in a political struggle on their behalf.

35. After them came yet another tribune, Livius Drusus, who was of an extremely famous family.[71] At the request of the Italians he promised to put forward once again legislation on the subject of the citizenship, because this was what they most wanted, and they thought that by this single thing they

would immediately become masters instead of subjects. With this in mind, he won over the people and wooed them in advance with many colonial settlements in Italy and Sicily, which had been authorized some time previously but never set up.[72] He also tried by an impartial law to bring together the senate and the equestrians, who were very much at odds with each other at the time over jury service in the law courts. Obviously he could not restore the courts to the senate, but he dealt with each side by the following scheme. As the civil troubles had reduced the number of senators to hardly 300, his proposal was to add to the list the same number of equestrians, chosen by merit, and in future compose the juries from all of these.[73] He added a clause making them liable to prosecution for accepting bribes, a charge virtually unheard of because of the unchecked prevalence of the practice. Such was his scheme for dealing with the two groups, but it did not turn out at all as he expected. The senate resented so many men being added in bulk to its roll of members and transformed from equestrians to the highest in the land, thinking it not unlikely that when they had actually become senators they would form a faction to fight even more energetically on their own account against the existing senators.[74] The equestrians suspected that this favour meant that the courts would eventually be transferred from themselves to the senate alone, and because they had tasted huge gains and illicit power, were most unhappy with this thought.[75] In addition Drusus caused the whole body of the equestrians to become uncertain and suspicious of each other over who should be thought most worthy to be included among the 300, and the stronger candidates started to excite jealousy among the rest. Above all they were irritated by the reappearance of bribe-taking as a criminal offence, a charge which they thought had been completely eliminated by this time, so far as they were concerned.

36. In this way, although equestrians and senate were at odds with each other, they were united in their enmity towards Drusus, and only the common people were pleased with the colonies. And even the Italians, in whose interests chiefly Drusus was carrying out these schemes, were apprehensive about the colonial law because they expected that the land belonging to the Roman state which was still unallocated, and which was being farmed either clandestinely or after forcible seizure, would at once be taken from them, and that trouble would occur over their own land.[76] The Etruscans and Umbrians, who shared the same fears as the other Italians, were brought – it seems by the consuls – into the city, ostensibly to

complain, but in reality to destroy Drusus, and they openly opposed the law and waited for the day of voting in the assembly. Observing this, Drusus did not often go out, but made a practice of conducting business in his house in a poorly lit portico, and one evening as he was dismissing the crowd he suddenly cried out that he had been stabbed, and fell with the words still on his lips. A leather-worker's knife was discovered driven into his hip.

37. Thus Drusus too was killed during his tribunate. The equestrians seized on his political activity as a springboard from which to bring accusations against their opponents and persuaded a tribune, Quintus Varius,[77] to set up judicial proceedings against those persons assisting the Italians, openly or secretly, against the common weal; they hoped to bring all the powerful men into court immediately on a highly prejudicial charge and themselves to sit in judgement on them, and once these men were out of the way to exert a still more powerful grip on Rome. When the rest of the tribunes vetoed the proposal of the law, the equestrians formed a guard with swords in their hands and secured its passage; and when it was passed, their names at once appeared as accusers of the most prominent of the senators. Bestia did not even obey the summons but went into exile of his own accord to avoid surrendering himself into the hands of his enemies; Cotta came into court to answer the charge, but after making a proud defence of his political actions and openly abusing the equestrians, also left the city before the jury voted; Mummius Achaicus was disgracefully trapped by the equestrians, who promised to acquit him, was sentenced to exile, and spent the rest of his life on Delos.[78]   38. As this malice towards the aristocracy intensified, the ordinary people became distressed that so many men of such standing and achievement kept on being taken from them; and the Italians, learning of Drusus' fate and of the excuse for sending these men into exile, considered it intolerable for those who were politically active on their behalf to be treated in this way any longer, and as they saw no other method of realizing their hopes of gaining Roman citizenship, decided to secede from the Romans forthwith and make war on them to the best of their ability. They negotiated secretly among themselves to form a league for these purposes, and exchanged hostages as guarantees of good faith. For some time the Romans were unaware of these developments because of the judicial proceedings and factional strife in Rome, but when they found out they sent the most suitable of their own people out to each of the towns to discover unobtrusively what was going on. One of these men saw a youth being taken as a hostage from the town of Asculum to another

town and informed Servilius, the proconsul of the region (at that time, it appears, there were proconsuls of parts of Italy also – a practice which was in fact imitated and reintroduced long afterwards by the Roman emperor Hadrian, but did not long survive his death).[79] Servilius hurried somewhat hotheadedly to Asculum, issued dire threats to the people of the town, who were celebrating a festival, and was killed by them in the belief that their plans had already been detected. In addition they put to death Fonteius, his *legatus* (this being the title they use for senators who go out with provincial governors to assist them). Once these two had been killed, none of the other Romans was spared; the Asculans assaulted them, stabbed every one to death, and looted their property.

39. Now that the revolt had broken out, the neighbours of the Asculans all revealed their preparations together. These peoples were the Marsi, the Paeligni, the Vestini, and the Marrucini; they were followed by the Picentes, the Frentani, the Hirpini, the inhabitants of Pompeii and Venusia, the Iapyges, the Lucani and the Samnites (peoples which had a history of being troublesome to Rome), and all the other peoples, both inland and maritime, as you go from the river Liris, which people now seem to think is the Liternus, to the head of the Adriatic.[80] They sent representatives to Rome to complain that although they had worked with the Romans all along to build up their empire, they were not thought fit to share the citizenship of those they had helped; but the senate made an uncompromising reply, that if they were sorry for what they had done, they could send a deputation to ask for the citizenship, but not otherwise. Then the Italians, despairing of any other remedy, turned to making their preparations; in addition to the individual army of each state, there was another, federal, force of 100,000 horse and foot. Against them the Romans put into the field an equal number drawn from their own citizens and from the Italian peoples who were still allied with them.

40. On the Roman side the commanders were the consuls Sextus Iulius Caesar and Publius Rutilius Lupus;[81] both of them took the field for this great civil war while those who were left behind in Rome assumed responsibility for its defences, because the campaign lay within Italy and near the city. In view of the complexity of the war, and its many fronts, the Romans sent out as subordinates to the consuls the best commanders of the day: under Rutilius, there were Gnaeus Pompeius, who was the father of Pompeius nicknamed the Great, Quintus Caepio, Gaius Perperna, Gaius Marius, and Valerius Messalla;[82] and under Sextus Caesar, his own brother

Publius Lentulus, Titus Didius, Licinius Crassus, Cornelius Sulla, and in addition Marcellus.[83] They divided the country between them, holding their commands under the direction of the consuls, who visited them all, and the Romans kept sending them more men because they realized that this was a great conflict. On the Italian side there were separate commanders of the armies of each state, but the federal commanders-in-chief of the joint army and of the whole organization were Titus Lafrenius, Gaius Pontilius, Marius Egnatius, Quintus Poppaedius, Gaius Papius, Marcus Lamponius, Gaius Vidacilius, Herius Asinius, and Vettius Scato.[84] They divided up their army in a similar fashion and took up positions facing the Roman generals. Their successes and reverses were many, and, to summarize, the most notable of each were as follows.

41. Vettius Scato routed Sextus Iulius,[85] killing 2,000 of his men, and drove on against Aesernia, which supported the Romans. Lucius Scipio and Lucius Acilius, who were organizing the defence, fled disguised as slaves and eventually the enemy starved the town into submission. Marius Egnatius took Venafrum by treachery and slaughtered two Roman cohorts there. Publius Praesentius routed Perperna, who was at the head of 10,000 men, killed some 4,000, and captured the weapons of most of the remainder;[86] whereupon Rutilius the consul relieved Perperna of his command and gave the remnant of his army to Gaius Marius. Marcus Lamponius destroyed about 800 of Licinius Crassus' force and pursued the rest into Grumentum.

42. Gaius Papius had Nola betrayed to him and made an offer to the Romans in the town, who numbered 2,000, that if they changed their allegiance they could serve with him. Papius took into his army those who changed sides, but their leaders would not accept his offer and were taken prisoner and starved to death by him. He also captured Stabiae and Minervium and Salernum, which was a Roman colony, and enlisted the prisoners and slaves from these places.[87] When he burnt all the land encircling Nuceria, the neighbouring towns were panic-stricken and came over, and when he asked for forces they provided about 10,000 infantry and 1,000 cavalry. After this he took up a position menacing Acerrae. Sextus Caesar[88] reinforced his army with 10,000 Gaulish infantry and Numidian cavalry and infantry from Mauretania and marched to Acerrae; but Papius brought Oxyntas, the son of Jugurtha who had once ruled Numidia,[89] from Venusia, where he had been held under arrest by the Romans, dressed him in royal purple, and kept displaying him to the Numidians in Caesar's army.

When a large number of them deserted *en masse*, because Oxyntas was their own king, Caesar sent the rest of the Numidians back to Africa as unreliable. Papius then contemptuously engaged him, and had already broken down part of the fortifications of Caesar's camp, when Caesar sent out his cavalry by another gate and killed about 6,000 of Papius' men. Following this, Caesar broke camp and left Acerrae, while in Iapygia[90] Vidacilius won over Canusium and Venusia and many other towns. He took by siege some places that refused to join him, and dealt with the Romans in them by putting the prominent men to death and conscripting into his own army the common citizens and slaves.

43. On the Liris,[91] Rutilius the consul and Gaius Marius were constructing bridges to cross the river, not far from each other. Vettius Scato, who was encamped opposite them, but nearer to Marius, succeeded in setting an ambush by night in the ravines by Rutilius' bridge. At dawn, he allowed Rutilius to cross and then sprang the ambush, killing many of Rutilius' men on dry land and forcing many others into the river. In this battle Rutilius himself was wounded in the head by a missile and died shortly afterwards. At the other bridge Marius, realizing what had happened from the corpses being carried down by the river, thrust aside the force that stood in his way, crossed the river, took Scato's camp which had been left with a handful of defenders, and forced Scato not only to spend the night where he had won his victory but to decamp at dawn because he was short of supplies. When the bodies of Rutilius and many other aristocrats were brought for burial to Rome, the sight of the dead bodies of the consul and so many others proved grim and the resulting mourning lasted many days. After this the senate decreed that war casualties were to be buried where they died, so that the rest of the population should not be deterred from military service by what they saw. When they learnt of this, the enemy made the same regulation for themselves.

44. Rutilius had no successor in office for the rest of the year, because Sextus Caesar[92] did not have time to return to Rome to hold elections, and the senate assigned the command of his army to Gaius Marius and Quintus Caepio. Quintus Poppaedius, the commander opposing this Caepio, fled to him, posing as a deserter and bringing with him to hand over as a guarantee two slave babies whom he pretended were his sons and were dressed in purple-bordered clothes.[93] For proof of his good faith he also brought lumps of lead plated with gold and silver, and he pressed Caepio to bring his army and follow him with all speed, to capture his camp which was still

without a commander. Caepio obeyed and followed. When Poppaedius was near the ambush which had been prepared, he ran up a hill as though he were looking out for the enemy and gave his own men a signal. They emerged from cover and cut down Caepio and many of his men, whereupon the senate put the rest of his army under the command of Marius.

45. Sextus[94] Caesar, at the head of 30,000 foot and 5,000 horse, was unexpectedly set upon by Marius Egnatius while traversing a defile enclosed by cliffs.[95] He was forced back into the defile and retreated, being carried on a stretcher himself because he was ill, to a river over which there was a single bridge, where he lost the greater part of his force and the armour and weapons of the survivors. He escaped with difficulty to Teanum,[96] where he equipped as best he could the men he still had. Reinforcements quickly arrived, and he set out for Acerrae, which was still under siege from Papius. Here they encamped opposite each other, but neither of them was confident enough to undertake any manoeuvre against the other.

46. Cornelius Sulla and Gaius Marius were attacked by the Marsi, but thoroughly routed them, until they met an area of vineyard walls.[97] The Marsi climbed over the walls, suffering heavy losses, but Marius and Sulla decided not to follow. However, when Cornelius Sulla, whose camp was on the other side of the vineyards, saw what was happening, he met the Marsians as they ran out, and killed many of them, with the result that more than 6,000 were slaughtered and the arms of a much greater number captured by the Romans that day. But the Marsi, like wild beasts, became more enraged by their failure, armed themselves afresh, and made preparations to attack the Romans, who did not dare to make the first move or initiate battle. For the Marsi are an extremely warlike people, and this is reportedly the only occasion which furnished the Romans with a triumph over them, it being previously said that it was impossible to celebrate a triumph either over the Marsi or without them.

47. In the region around Mount Falernus, Gnaeus Pompeius was defeated and forced into Firmum by Vidacilius, Titus Lafrenius and Publius Ventidius,* who had joined forces for the purpose. While the other two departed for other objectives, Lafrenius besieged Pompeius, shut up in Firmum. Pompeius armed his survivors and refused battle, but when another army approached he sent Sulpicius round behind Lafrenius while he himself made a frontal attack on him. When battle had been joined and both sides were heavily engaged in the fighting, Sulpicius set fire to the enemy camp. On seeing this the enemy fled to Asculum in disarray and

without a general, as Lafrenius had fallen in battle, and Pompeius came up to the town and put it under siege.

48. Now Vidacilius had been born at Asculum, and came up quickly with eight legions because he feared for the town. He sent a message on ahead to the inhabitants that when they saw him approaching in the distance, they should make a sally against the besiegers so that the enemy had to fight on both fronts at once. The Asculans shrank from doing this, but even so Vidacilius broke through the middle of the enemy into the town with as many men as he could. He berated the people for their cowardice and disobedience, and in the belief that there was no longer any hope of saving the town put to death all his enemies who had for some time been at variance with him and had now from jealousy persuaded the ordinary people to disobey his message. He built a funeral pyre in the sanctuary and placed a couch on top of it; then he feasted beside it with his friends, and when the drinking was well under way took poison, laid himself down on the pyre, and ordered his friends to light it. Such was the end of Vidacilius, who thought it honourable to die for his country; but Sextus Caesar, who had been appointed proconsul by the senate on the expiry of his term of office,[98] attacked some 20,000 men of the enemy army while they were moving from one camp to another, killed about 8,000 of them, and captured the arms of many more. His siege of Asculum continued for a year, until as he was dying of disease he named Gaius Baebius as commander in his place.

49. Such were the operations which took place on the Adriatic side of Italy. When they heard of them, the peoples on the other side of Rome, the Etruscans and Umbrians and their neighbours, were all encouraged to revolt.[99] As a result the senate, who were afraid that it would be impossible to fight a war with enemies who encircled them, secured the coast from Cumae to Rome with garrisons of ex-slaves – then for the first time conscripted into the army because of the shortage of men[100] – and voted that the Italians who had still not seceded from the alliance should be Roman citizens, which was the single thing they all most strongly desired.* They made this decision known among the Etruscans, who gladly accepted the citizenship. By this concession the senate made the loyalists more loyal, the waverers less faint-hearted, and the enemy under arms less hostile because of the hope of something similar. However, the Romans did not enrol these new citizens in the thirty-five voting tribes which they currently had, in case they should outnumber the old citizens and carry the day at the elections, but distributed them among ten fresh tribes which voted after the others. Their vote was often useless, since the thirty-five were called on to vote first and formed the majority.[101] Either this was not noticed at first, or else the Italians were content, even so, with the arrangement; but later it was recognized, and became the cause of another round of civil strife.

50. The Adriatic peoples, as yet unaware of the Etruscan change of heart, sent 15,000 men by a long and difficult route to Etruria to fight alongside them. Gnaeus Pompeius, who was by this time consul, fell upon them and killed about 5,000 of them. The remainder fled home through trackless country and severe winter weather; <half survived by> * eating acorns, half perished. In the same winter, Porcius Cato, Pompeius' colleague, lost his life fighting against the Marsi, and Lucius Cluentius insolently took up a position only 600 yards away from Sulla's camp in the hills near Pompeii.[102] Unable to endure the insult, Sulla attacked Cluentius without waiting for his own foragers to come in, and retreated after getting the worst of it, but when he was given the assistance of his foragers he defeated Cluentius. The latter at first withdrew to another camp further away, but on receiving some Gaulish reinforcements approached Sulla again. As the armies came together a Gaul of huge size ran forward and challenged any Roman to single combat, but when a little Moor accepted the challenge and killed him, the Gauls were terrified and fled. Not even the rest of Cluentius' army stood their ground, now that their battle formation had been wrecked, and they fled in disarray to Nola. In the pursuit Sulla killed about 3,000 men as they fled, and because the Nolans were letting them in by a single gate to stop the enemy coming in with them, about 20,000 more died under the walls; among these was Cluentius, who fell fighting.

51. Sulla then moved to campaign against another people, the Hirpini, and attacked Aeclanum. The inhabitants, who expected the Lucanians to come to their help that very day, asked Sulla for time to consider their position. He spotted the trick, but gave them an hour and meanwhile piled bundles of firewood all round the town walls, which were made of wood. At the end of the hour, he started to set them on fire, and the inhabitants were terrified into surrendering the town. He looted it, saying that it had come over from compulsion not from sympathy, but spared the other towns as they joined him, until he had subdued the whole Hirpinian people. He then proceeded against the Samnites, avoiding the route where Mutilus, their general, was guarding the passes, and going by a different, roundabout way, which took them by surprise. He made a sudden attack

and killed a large number of his opponents; the survivors fl
directions, Mutilus himself being wounded and taking refuge
with a small force. Sulla destroyed Mutilus' camp, then moved
vianum, where the federal council of the rebels was located. This
three citadels, and while the inhabitants were intent on watchung Sulla
from one, he sent a force round with instructions to take whichever of the
other two strong points they could, and make a smoke signal if they succeeded. When the smoke arose, Sulla engaged the troops confronting him
and after fighting hard for three hours took the town.

52. These, then, were Sulla's successes that summer, and at the beginning
of winter he returned to Rome to stand for the consulship. Meanwhile
Gnaeus Pompeius subdued the Marsi and Marrucini and Vestini, while
Gaius Cosconius, another of the Roman commanders, attacked and burnt
Salapia, received the surrender of Cannae, and laid siege to Canusium. Here
the Samnites attacked him but he fought against them with great determination until after terrible slaughter on both sides he was worsted and
retreated to Cannae. Because there was a river between the two armies, the
Samnite general Trebatius challenged him either to cross it for a battle, or
to withdraw so that he himself could cross. Cosconius accordingly withdrew,
but fell on Trebatius as his army was crossing, defeated him in the battle,
and when he retreated in disorder towards the river slaughtered 15,000 of
his men; the remainder fled to Canusium with Trebatius. Cosconius then
overran the territories of Larinum, Venusia and Ausculum, and invaded the
Pedicoli, obtaining the surrender of that people in two days. 53. He was
succeeded in the command by Caecilius Metellus,[103] who attacked the
Iapygae and was victorious like Cosconius. Poppaedius, another of the
rebel generals, fell in this battle, and the survivors came over haphazardly to
Caecilius.

Such were the events in Italy during the course of the Social War, which
raged in full violence up to this point, when all the Italians became part of
the Roman state, with the temporary exception of the Lucanians and the
Samnites – and they too, I think, gained what they wanted at a later date. All
of them were enrolled in the tribes in the same way as those who had
become Roman citizens earlier, so that they should not outvote the old citizens by being mixed in with them and outnumbering them.[104]

54. At the same period, those who were involved in lending and borrowing money were quarrelling with each other in Rome: the lenders were
asking for interest on their loans, although there was an archaic law which

forbade lending at interest and prescribed a penalty for anyone who did so. It seems that the ancient Romans, like the Greeks, set their faces against lending at interest because it was worthy only of petty traders and was hard on the poor and gave rise to disputes and grudges – reasoning which influenced the Persians likewise to forbid borrowing on the grounds that it was conducive to deceit and lying. However, now that long-established custom had sanctioned the taking of interest, the one group demanded it as usual, and the other postponed payment on the excuse of war and civil unrest. Some even threatened that the lenders would pay the penalty of the law. The praetor Asellio, under whose jurisdiction the dispute fell, was unsuccessful in reconciling the parties and granted a trial in court, turning over to the jurors the problem of this conflict between law and custom.[105] But the lenders, exasperated that Asellio was giving the old law new vigour, killed him in the following way. He was making an offering to Castor and Pollux in the forum, with the people standing around him as usual at the ceremony. First a single stone was thrown at him, whereupon he cast aside the sacrificial bowl and ran towards the temple of Vesta. But his assailants got in front of him, prevented him entering the temple, and murdered him when he fled to an inn. Many of his pursuers believed him to have taken refuge with the Vestals and burst in on them, where it is sacrilege for a man to go. In this way Asellio, a praetor in office, in the act of making a libation, and wearing the holy gold-embroidered robe of a sacrificant, was murdered early in the day, in the middle of the forum, next to the sacred utensils. The senate made a proclamation that if anyone could succeed in proving anything about the murder of Asellio, he would receive, if a free citizen, a cash reward, if a slave, his freedom, and if an accomplice, pardon; but no one gave any information because the lenders covered everything up.

55. The murders and civil disturbances had so far been internal and sporadic; but after this the faction leaders struggled against each other with great armies in military fashion for the prize of their native land. The reasons why they embarked on this phase, immediately after the Social War, were as follows.

When Mithridates, King of Pontus and of certain other peoples, invaded Bithynia and Phrygia and the part of Asia which adjoins them, as I have described in the preceding volume, it fell to Sulla (who was consul, and still in Rome) to take command in Asia and conduct this war against Mithridates.[106] But Marius, thinking that the campaign would be straightforward

and extremely lucrative, coveted the command, and by making many
promises to the tribune Publius Sulpicius won him over as his ally in this
project. He also encouraged the newly enfranchised Italian citizens, who
were discriminated against in the voting procedure, to hope that they
would be distributed in all the tribes; he said nothing, however, about his
own needs, but said that he would deploy the goodwill of the Italians in
support of all he did. Sulpicius forthwith proposed a law on the subject,
which, if passed, would bring about everything that he and Marius wanted,
since the new citizens far outnumbered the old. But the latter realized this
and strenuously opposed the new citizens. They fought each other with
clubs and stones, and as the violence mounted the consuls, concerned because the day for voting on the law was imminent, proclaimed several days'
suspension of public business, as was done for the religious festivals, in order
to postpone the voting and give some intermission from the disorder.

56. Sulpicius, however, did not wait for the end of the period of suspension, but instructed his supporters to come to the forum with concealed
daggers and obey whatever orders he might give, even to attacking the consuls should that be necessary. When everything was ready, he condemned
the suspension of business as illegal and told the consuls Cornelius Sulla
and Quintus Pompeius to lift it immediately, so that he could proceed with
the voting on the laws. In the ensuing uproar those who had been previously prepared drew their daggers and threatened to kill the consuls as they
were contesting Sulpicius' demand, until Pompeius slipped away unobserved and Sulla withdrew on the pretext of consultation. Meanwhile
Pompeius' son, who was related to Sulla by marriage and was expressing his
views rather freely, was killed by Sulpicius' partisans while he was actually
speaking. Sulla reappeared, withdrew the suspension, and hurried to Capua
to the army there, intending to go across to Asia and take charge of the war
against Mithridates; for he was as yet unaware of any of the measures being
taken against him. Now that the suspension had been lifted and Sulla had
left Rome, Sulpicius passed the law and immediately elected Marius to the
command against Mithridates in place of Sulla – which was the reason why
all this had been done.

57. When Sulla discovered this, he decided to settle the matter by force
and summoned his army to a meeting, an army which was eagerly anticipating a profitable war against Mithridates and thought that Marius would
enlist other men in their place. Sulla spoke of the insulting violence offered
him by Sulpicius and Marius, and without making any other clear

accusation – for he was not bold enough to mention this kind of a war yet – encouraged them to be ready to obey orders. They grasped his meaning, and since they were nervous on their own account of missing the Mithridatic campaign, they found the plain words for what he had in mind and told him to take courage and lead them on Rome. Gratified, he immediately placed himself at the head of six legions. Except for one quaestor,[107] the officers of the army made off to Rome because they could not stomach leading an army against their own country. On the way, Sulla was met by a deputation who asked him why he was marching under arms against his native land, and he replied, 'To free her from her tyrants.' He said this a second and a third time to other deputations, but nevertheless announced that if they wished to assemble the senate and Marius and Sulpicius for a meeting with him on the Campus Martius, he would do whatever seemed best after consultation. As he approached Rome, his colleague Pompeius, who approved of his actions and was pleased at the turn of events, joined him, wishing to co-operate fully. Marius and Sulpicius, who needed a little time to make their preparations, sent another deputation on the pretence that this too represented the senate, to ask him to make camp no nearer than five miles from Rome until they had considered the situation. Sulla and Pompeius saw clearly the purpose of this request and promised to accede to it, but as soon as the deputation had left they followed. 58. Sulla himself occupied the Porta Esquilina and the adjoining walls with one legion, while Pompeius took the Porta Collina with another.[108] A third legion advanced on the Pons Sublicius, and a fourth remained in reserve outside the walls. With the others, Sulla entered the city, an enemy in appearance and in reality. For this reason the people living along his route opposed him by hurling missiles from the upper storeys, until he threatened to set fire to their houses. They then desisted, but Marius and Sulpicius went to confront him near the forum on the Esquiline with as many men as they had had time to arm, and there took place a struggle between political enemies which was the first conducted in Rome not under the guise of civil dissension, but nakedly as a war, complete with trumpets and military standards: such was the catastrophe to which their recklessness in political quarrelling had led them. Sulla's troops were being driven back, but he seized a standard and risked his life in the front line; this action immediately stayed their rout because of the awe in which they held their general and the dishonour they feared if they lost their standard. Sulla also summoned the reserves from his camp, and sent other forces round by the street known as the Subura, where they would be in a position to take the enemy in the rear. The Marians' resistance to the fresh troops was feeble, and because they were afraid of being encircled by the men coming round behind them, they called on the other townspeople who were still fighting from the buildings to come and help them, and proclaimed that any slaves who joined in the resistance would be given their freedom. But no one came to them, and in utter despair they fled at once out of the city, accompanied by those of the aristocracy who had supported them.

59. Sulla then made his way along the street called the Sacra Via,[109] and summarily punished in full public view some soldiers who had looted property along the way. He stationed guards at intervals across the city, and he and Pompeius passed the night in visiting each of the posts to ensure that nothing terrible happened, whether it was initiated by the terrified inhabitants or by the victorious army. When day came, they called the people to an assembly, expressed their regret that the state had for a long time been in the hands of demagogues, and said that they had acted as they had out of necessity. They proposed that no bill should be put to the people unless it had already been approved by the senate, a practice that once obtained but had long since been abandoned, and that voting should take place, not by tribes, but by centuries according to the constitution laid down by King Tullius.[110] They thought that these two measures would ensure that civil discord would not be caused either by a law being put to the people before it had been put to the senate, or by voting being controlled by the poor and hot-headed instead of by those who possessed property and good sense. They took many other powers away from the tribunate, which had become an office of great unconstitutional power, and they enrolled *en bloc* into the senate, which was very depleted in numbers at the time and therefore lacked authority, 300 new members chosen from the best-qualified citizens.[111] The measures which Sulpicius had passed after the consuls had suspended public business were all annulled as illegal.

60. In this way the episodes of civil strife escalated from rivalry and contentiousness to murder, and from murder to full-scale war; and this was the first army composed of Roman citizens to attack their own country as though it were a hostile power. From this point onwards their conflicts continued to be settled by military means and there were frequent attacks on Rome, and sieges, and every sort of incident of war, because nothing

remained, neither law, nor political institutions, nor patriotism, that could induce any sense of shame in the men of violence.

It had now been voted that because they had stirred up civil war, and fought against the consuls, and provoked slaves to revolt by offering them their freedom, Sulpicius, who was still tribune, and along with him Marius, who had held the consulship six times, his son Marius, Publius Cethegus, Junius Brutus, Gaius and Quintus Granius, Publius Albinovanus, Marcus Laetorius and those others who had fled with them from Rome, totalling about twelve, should be regarded as public enemies and that anyone could kill them with impunity or bring them before the consuls, and their property was to be forfeit. **61.** Agents were quickly sent out to hunt them down. Sulpicius they caught and killed, but Marius escaped and fled to Minturnae without a single companion or slave. As he rested in a dimly lit house, the magistrates of the town, who were in awe of the official proclamation but were reluctant to be the murderers of a man who had been six times consul and had a magnificent record of achievement, sent in a Gaul who was staying in the town to kill him with a sword. They say that the Gaul, as he approached Marius' straw mattress in the gloom, was gripped with fear as he imagined he saw fire and sparks flash from Marius' eyes; and when Marius himself, rising from his bed, thundered at him, 'Do you dare kill Gaius Marius?', the Gaul turned and rushed out of the door like a madman, shouting, 'I cannot kill Gaius Marius.' So the authorities, who even before this had been reluctant to act, were overwhelmed by a kind of religious fear and they recalled the prophecy from Marius' childhood, that he would hold seven consulships; for there is a story that when he was a boy seven eaglets landed in his lap and the interpreters declared that he would reach the highest office seven times. **62.** Remembering this, then, and believing that the Gaul's frenzy and terror were divinely inspired, the magistrates of Minturnae at once sent Marius out of the town to save himself as best he could. Well aware that he was being hunted by Sulla and that horsemen were pursuing him, he used byways to make for the coast and came to a hut, where he took some rest under a covering of leaves. Hearing a noise, he hid himself more deeply in the leaves; but as the noise became more distinct, he rushed to a boat moored nearby belonging to an old fisherman, overpowered the old man, and though a storm was raging cut the rope, hoisted the sail, and let chance take him where it would. He was carried to an island, and from it he crossed to Africa on a friendly ship which happened to pass by.[112] He was barred from Africa as a public enemy by the governor Sextilius and spent the winter afloat, just beyond the province, on the border with Numidia.[113] As they got to know of this, some of those who had been condemned with him sailed to join him while he was at sea there, namely Cethegus, Granius, Albinovanus, Laetorius and others, and his son Marius; after leaving Rome they had taken refuge with Hiempsal, the Numidian ruler, but had deserted his court because they were afraid they would be betrayed. These men were ready to overpower their own country by violence, exactly as Sulla had done, but as they lacked a military force they kept their eyes open for some opportunity.

63. In Rome, when Sulla, who was the first man to capture the city by force, and for whom perhaps monarchy was already a possibility, had dealt with his enemies, he renounced violence, sent his army ahead to Capua, and again exercised normal consular authority. After they had recovered from the fear of military force, the partisans of the exiles, who included many of the rich and a number of wealthy women, agitated for their return and spared neither effort nor expense to this end. They even plotted to kill the consuls since they believed it impossible for the exiles to return while the consuls were still alive. Sulla, of course, had the army which had been voted him for the war against Mithridates to keep him safe even after the expiry of his consulship, and the people took pity on the fears of Quintus Pompeius, the other consul, by decreeing that he should have charge of Italy and the other army that was operating there, which was currently under Gnaeus Pompeius.[114] When Gnaeus heard of this he was annoyed, but welcomed Quintus into his camp on arrival. On the next day, since he had no official position, he left Quintus for a short time when he was transacting some business, until the consul was killed by a mob of soldiers who surrounded him on the pretence of listening to him. The rest fled, but Gnaeus confronted the others, furious at the illegal killing of the consul; however, in spite of his displeasure he immediately took command of them.

64. When the news of Pompeius' murder reached Rome, Sulla immediately became afraid for himself and went about everywhere accompanied by his associates, whom he also kept with him at night. He did not, though, remain long in Rome, but departed to the army at Capua, and thence to Asia. The friends of the exiles, counting on the support of Cinna,[115] Sulla's successor as consul, stirred up the new citizens' interest in Marius' scheme for them to be distributed in all the tribes, so that they should not vote last and be completely powerless. This was a prelude to the return of Marius and his companions. When the old citizens forcibly opposed the proposal,

Cinna allied himself with the new citizens – allegedly laying out 300 talents in bribes – and the other consul Octavius allied himself with the old.[116] Cinna's followers, armed with concealed daggers, occupied the forum and shouted their demand to be distributed among all the tribes; but the sounder part of the crowd, also with daggers, were inclined to Octavius.[117] While the latter was still at home awaiting the outcome, it was reported that a majority of the tribunes had vetoed the proceedings, and the new citizens had rioted, going so far as to unsheathe their daggers in public and scale the rostra to threaten the obstructive tribunes. When he heard this, Octavius descended the Sacra Via with a close-packed mob, swept into the forum like a raging torrent, pushed his way through the middle of the crowd, and forced them apart. When he had overawed them, he drove Cinna away and reached the temple of Castor and Pollux.[118] His followers, attacking the new citizens without warning, killed a large number and pursued others to the city gates. **65.** Cinna, who was relying on the large numbers of the new citizens and expected to force his measures through, but saw the daring of the minority unexpectedly successful, ran through the city calling on the slaves to join him and earn their freedom. As no one rallied to him, he hurried out to the nearby towns which had only recently acquired membership of the Roman state – Tibur and Praeneste and everywhere as far as Nola – inciting them to rebellion and collecting money for the war. While he was busy with these activities and plans, his sympathizers Gaius Milonius, Quintus Sertorius, and another Gaius Marius fled to him from the senate.[119] For its part the senate decided that because Cinna had, when consul, deserted Rome in time of danger, and had promised slaves their freedom, he should no longer be regarded as either a consul or a Roman; and in his place they elected the priest of Jupiter, Lucius Merula. They say that this Flamen alone has the right to wear a cap all the time, while the others wear it only during religious ceremonies.[120] Cinna made his way to Capua, where there was another Roman army, and made overtures to its officers and the senators who lived there.[121] He appeared before them in the guise of consul, then laid aside the fasces as though he were a private citizen and addressed them tearfully: 'From you, fellow-citizens, I received this office: for the people elected me. But the senate has stripped me of it without reference to you. What I have suffered is my personal misfortune, but none the less I grieve for you. Why should we take any notice of the tribes at voting time? Why do we need you? How will you ever have any power in the assemblies or in the consular elections, if

you cannot guarantee the powers you bestow and if your decisions are annulled because the senate withholds approval?' **66**. After saying this to
rouse them, and pitying his own misfortune at length, he ripped his clothes,
jumped off the dais, and threw himself down among them, where he lay for
a long time. Finally, their resistance melted and they lifted him up and sat
him again on his official stool; picking up the fasces, they told him to take
heart, act as consul, and lead them wherever he wanted. Their officers immediately seized this chance of swearing the military oath to him, and each
administered it to his own subordinates. Cinna himself, now that his position was secure, hurried round the allied towns and roused them too, on
the grounds that it was largely in their interest that he had incurred disaster.
They contributed money and military forces, and he was joined by many
more people, including some of those who were influential at Rome, who
found political stability not to their taste.

While Cinna was thus occupied, the consuls Octavius and Merula fortified the city with ditches, made repairs to the walls, and placed artillery on
them; they sent for troops from the other towns that were still loyal to them
and from Cisalpine Gaul; and they summoned Gnaeus Pompeius, proconsul in command of military operations on the Adriatic side, to come
and help his country with all speed. **67**. On his arrival he encamped near
the Colline Gate, where Cinna confronted him and encamped opposite.
When he heard what had happened, Gaius Marius sailed back to Etruria,
accompanied by those who had been exiled with him and their slaves who
came from Rome to meet them, a total of about 500 men. Still dirty and
unshorn, he was a pitiable sight as he visited the towns.[122] He boasted of his
battles and victories over the Cimbri and his six consulships, and because
the promises he made about the method of voting, which passionately concerned them, carried conviction, he recruited 6,000 Etruscans and went to
join Cinna, who gladly accepted him as a partner in their present business.
When the armies were united, they took up positions on the Tiber in three
divisions: Cinna, accompanied by Carbo,[123] opposite Rome, Sertorius up-
stream of the city, and Marius downstream. The latter two controlled both
sides of the river and built bridges across it to interrupt the supply of food
to the city. Marius also took and sacked Ostia, while Cinna sent troops to
take Ariminum, to stop any military force reaching Rome from the conquered areas of Gaul. **68**. The consuls were apprehensive, and needed another army, but could not call on Sulla because he had already sailed for

Asia. They therefore ordered Caecilius Metellus, who was in charge of the operations against the Samnites which were all that was left of the Social War, to make peace with the Samnites on any terms he decently could and come to the aid of his beleaguered homeland. But Metellus would not agree to the Samnite demands, and when Marius heard of this he conceded them everything they were asking for from Metellus. In this way the Samnites too came to fight on Marius' side. Marius had also once done a favour to Appius Claudius, the military tribune in command of the defences of Rome on the Janiculum hill; he reminded Appius of this, and a gate was opened for him at dawn by which he entered the city. He let Cinna in, but they were immediately attacked and driven out by Octavius and Pompeius; and Pompeius' camp was struck several times by lightning, which caused the deaths of Pompeius and some other members of the aristocracy.

69. When Marius had gained control of the food supplies that came both up-river from the sea and down-river from the interior, he swiftly moved against the towns near Rome, where grain was stored for the population of Rome. He made sudden attacks on the garrisons and took Antium, Aricia, Lanuvium, and other places, some of them by treachery; and when he had secured his grip also on the supplies that came by land, he confidently proceeded directly against Rome along the so-called Appian Way before any other food could reach his opponents from elsewhere. He and Cinna and their subordinate commanders Carbo and Sertorius halted and made camp a dozen miles from the city, while Octavius and Crassus and Metellus took up a position near the Alban Hills and waited to see what would happen;[124] the latter were thought still to have the advantage in numbers and quality of troops, but were wary of putting their entire country at risk over-hastily in a single battle. Cinna sent heralds round the city to announce that slaves who deserted to him would be granted their freedom, and they immediately began to desert in droves. The senate was gravely disturbed, and in the expectation that the people would be uncontrollable if there was delay in providing food, changed its policy and sent a deputation to negotiate with Cinna. He asked them whether they approached him as consul or as a private citizen. They were unsure what to say and went back to Rome, but in the meantime many of the free citizens had joined the flight to Cinna, some because they were afraid of a famine, others because they had long been sympathizers but had been waiting to see which way things would go.   **70**. Cinna was already drawing humiliatingly close to the walls, and he encamped just out of missile range, while Octavius' party were still wondering what to do, terrified and unwilling to make any move against him because of the desertions and the negotiations. The senators were completely at a loss, but although they considered it hard that Lucius Merula, the priest of Jupiter, who had succeeded to Cinna, should be deprived of his office in spite of having committed no fault while holding it, under the pressure of the situation they unwillingly sent another deputation to Cinna, as consul. Because they no longer expected to obtain satisfactory terms, they simply asked him to swear not to perpetrate a massacre. He would not agree to be put on oath, but promised even so not to be the willing agent of any slaughter. He also gave orders that Octavius, who had gone round another way and entered the city by a different gate, should move away from the centre, because he could not guarantee Octavius' safety. Such was the answer Cinna made to the delegation, from high on his platform, behaving as consul; while Marius, standing beside the consular stool, said not a word but made it plain by the savagery of his expression what murder he would unleash. When the senate had accepted these terms, it summoned Cinna and Marius into the city, knowing that all this, though done in Cinna's name, was Marius' work. Then Marius smiled at them and remarked with bitter irony that exiles were not allowed to enter, and the tribunes at once carried a proposal to annul the sentence of exile passed on him and any others under Sulla.[125]

71. Cinna and Marius were received by a frightened population as they made their entry into Rome, and everything that belonged to those who in their view had opposed them was plundered without restraint. Octavius they had sworn not to harm, and the augurs and diviners had prophesied that he would remain safe, but his friends advised him to make his escape. He retorted that he would never leave the city while he was consul, but he did move from the centre and cross to the Janiculum with the nobility and a remnant of his army. Here he took his seat on his official stool, wearing the insignia of his office and surrounded by the rods and axes as befitted a consul. As Censorinus and some mounted men galloped towards him, his friends and the soldiers standing beside him again urged him to flee and brought him his horse, but he waited for death without even deigning to rise to his feet. Censorinus cut off his head and brought it to Cinna, and it was the first belonging to a consul to hang on the front of the rostra in the forum.[126] After him, the heads of the others who had been killed were hung up, and this foul practice, which began with Octavius, did not end there but extended to subsequent victims of political hostility. Straightaway

men went out to track down hostile members of the senate and the equestrian class; no account was taken of the latter once they had been put to death, but the heads of the senators were all displayed in front of the rostra. These events no longer aroused religious scruple, or human retribution, or fear of opprobrium; on the contrary, men turned to savage deeds, and from savage deeds to displays of sacrilege – merciless killing, decapitation of men already dead, and exhibition of the results to create fear or horror or a sacrilegious spectacle.

72. Those killed included Gaius and Lucius Iulius, who were brothers, Atilius Serranus, Publius Lentulus, Gaius Numitorius and Marcus Baebius, all caught in the street.[127] Crassus, who was in flight with his son, killed the boy before his pursuers could, but was himself killed by them.[128] The great speaker Marcus Antonius took refuge in a little place where the farmer who hid him and looked after him sent his slave to the inn to buy a better wine than usual. When the innkeeper wanted to know why on earth he was asking for a better wine, the slave whispered the reason to him and went home after making his purchase. The innkeeper hurried straight away to Marius to tell him, and when Marius heard it he was overjoyed and jumped up as if he intended to go and attend to the business in person, but he was restrained by his friends and a military tribune was sent who ordered some soldiers into the house. Antonius, who was a marvellous talker, charmed them by lengthy discussion, winning their sympathy and going into all sorts of wonderful detail, until the tribune, wondering what was happening, ran into the house himself. Discovering the soldiers hanging on Antonius' words, he killed him in mid-delivery and sent his head to Marius.[129]

73. Cornutus, who was hiding in a hut, was saved by his slaves in a clever way: coming across a corpse, they made a funeral pyre, and when the men who were tracking Cornutus down appeared, they set light to the pyre and said they were burning their master who had hanged himself.[130] In this way Cornutus was saved by his slaves; Quintus Ancharius, on the other hand, waited for Marius as he was going to sacrifice on the Capitol, hoping that the sanctity of the occasion would mollify him.[131] When Marius began the ceremony, Ancharius approached him and spoke to him, but Marius then and there, on the Capitol, ordered the bystanders to kill him. Ancharius' head, and those of Antonius and of the others who had been consuls or praetors, were displayed in the forum. No one was permitted to give any of the dead burial, and birds and dogs tore apart the bodies of such

distinguished men. There were many further unauthorized and uninvesti-
gated murders carried out by the rival parties, while other individuals were
banished, or had their property confiscated, or were stripped of office. The
laws passed under Sulla were also repealed. As for Sulla himself, all his
friends were put to death, his house was razed to the ground, his property
was declared forfeit, and he was proclaimed an enemy of the state; a search
was made for his wife and children, but they escaped. In short, the situation
brought unrelieved suffering of every kind.

74. In addition, to provide a show of legal authority after so many people
had been put to death without trial, hired accusers were put up against
Merula, the priest of Jupiter, out of resentment at the way he had succeeded
to the consulship, although he had done Cinna no wrong. Accusers were
also put up against Lutatius Catulus, Marius' colleague in the Cimbric war,
who had once been saved by Marius but had proved ungrateful and extremely bitter against him when he was driven into exile. These two were
being secretly watched, and when the day set for their trial came and they
were called to court (the procedure was for a summons to be issued four
times, at set intervals, after which an arrest could be made), Merula severed
his own veins, leaving a note beside him to say that when he cut them he
removed his cap (for it was a sin for a priest to die wearing it),[132] and Catulus deliberately suffocated himself by burning charcoal in a newly plastered
room that was still damp. Such were the deaths of Merula and Catulus. On
the other hand, the slaves who had deserted the city to join Cinna in accordance with the terms of his proclamation, and had been given their
freedom and then served in his army, were breaking into people's houses
and plundering them, and killing anyone they met; indeed some of them
even made a point of attacking their own masters. Cinna repeatedly ordered them to stop, but when he failed to secure their obedience he used a
large force of Gauls to surround them while it was still night and they were
off guard, and killed them all. Thus the slaves paid a fitting penalty for their
recurrent disloyalty to their masters.

75. For the next year Cinna, for the second time, and Marius, for the
seventh, were elected consuls;[133] in the case of the latter the prophecy of the
seven eaglets had come true, even after his flight and the proclamation that
anyone could kill him as an enemy of the state. He intended a series of drastic measures against Sulla, but died within a month of taking office. In his
place Cinna chose Valerius Flaccus, whom he sent to Asia, and when Flaccus too met his end picked Carbo to be his colleague.[134]

76. Sulla, who was in haste to return and deal with his enemies, accelerated all his operations against Mithridates, as I have already described. In less than three complete years he killed 160,000 men, recovered Greece, Macedonia, Ionia, Asia, and many other regions which Mithridates had occupied, stripped the king of his navy, and forced him to abandon these vast conquests for the confines of his inherited kingdom.[135] He then turned for home at the head of an army that was loyal, well trained, strong in numbers, and elated by its exploits. He also possessed plenty of ships, money, and equipment to meet any eventuality, and caused great alarm to his enemies. In fear of him, Cinna and Carbo accordingly sent agents all over Italy to collect money and armed forces and supplies of food, cultivated important people, and stirred up in particular the towns which had recently gained Roman citizenship, because it was on their account that they were in such danger. They set about a general programme of ship repair, sent for the fleet from Sicily, and mounted a guard on the coast; in fear and haste they too omitted no important preparation.

77. Sulla wrote arrogantly to the senate with a catalogue of his achievements, against Jugurtha in Numidia when he was a quaestor, in the Cimbric war when he was a deputy commander, in Cilicia when he was governor,[136] in the Social War, and as consul, but boasted above all about the recent Mithridatic campaign, listing for them all the many peoples which Mithridates had annexed but which he himself had won back for Rome; and he placed no less emphasis on the fact that he had welcomed men who had fled to him in desperation after being driven out of Rome by Cinna, and that he was helping them in their misfortunes. In return for these services, he said, his opponents had declared him an enemy of the state, razed his house to the ground, and killed his friends, while his wife and children had only just managed to make their escape to him. But he would soon be there to act in the interests of these refugees and the whole of Rome, and to exact vengeance from the perpetrators of these deeds. As for the other citizens, including the newly enfranchised, he would not hold any of them to blame for anything. When this letter was read, they were all terrified and sent a delegation to mediate between him and his enemies and announce that if he wanted assurances about his personal safety he should write forthwith to the senate; and Cinna and his associates were instructed not to levy troops until Sulla replied. This they promised to do, but as soon as the delegation left they immediately proclaimed themselves consuls for the following year so that they had no need to return hurriedly to

Rome to hold the elections. They then went round Italy raising an army, which they began to transport in detachments by sea to Dalmatia in the expectation of proceeding against Sulla from there.[137]

78. The first detachment crossed safely; but the second encountered a storm and any men who reached land immediately deserted and hurried home because they had no intention of fighting against fellow-Romans. When the rest heard this, they said that they too were no longer willing to cross to Dalmatia. Cinna, who was furious, summoned them to an assembly with the intention of cowing them, and they gathered angrily, quite ready to defend themselves. When one of the lictors who was clearing a path for Cinna struck a man who was in his way, another soldier hit the lictor. Cinna ordered his arrest, but everybody began to shout, stones were thrown at him, and those who were close to him went so far as to draw their daggers and stab him. Thus Cinna was another to die during his consulship. Although Carbo recalled from Dalmatia the men who had crossed, he was nervous about the current situation and did not return to Rome, in spite of an urgent appeal from the tribunes to conduct the election of a colleague for himself. When they threatened to deprive him of office, he came back and fixed a date for the consular election. The omens turned out unfavourably, and he announced another day, but that also was unlucky, because lightning struck the precincts of Luna and of Ceres, and the augurs put off the election until after the summer solstice. Thus Carbo remained sole consul.

79. The answer that Sulla made to the delegation from the senate was that although he could never be at peace himself with men who had committed such atrocities, he would not begrudge Rome the favour of sparing their lives; but as to their personal safety, he was the one who was in a better position to guarantee it permanently to them and to those who had sought his protection, since he had a loyal army. By this single remark he made it perfectly clear that he had no intention of disbanding his army but was already thinking of ruling as an autocrat. He also demanded from them full and complete restoration of his status, his property, his priesthood, and any other honours he had previously held, and sent back with the delegation representatives to deal with these matters. However, when they reached Brundisium and discovered that Cinna was dead and the city without an administration, they returned to Sulla with nothing achieved. Sulla himself, at the head of five Italian legions and 6,000 horse, to which he added other troops from the Peloponnese and Macedonia to a total of 40,000 men, sailed from the Piraeus to Patrae, and from Patrae to Brundisium, in 1,600 ships. The people of Brundisium made no resistance to his landing, for which he afterwards granted them an exemption from taxes which they still enjoy, and he set his army on the march inland.

80. Caecilius Metellus Pius had been appointed to take charge of the remnants of the Social War, but for fear of Marius and Cinna had not returned to Rome. He had awaited the outcome in Africa,[138] and now came to join Sulla, unbidden, accompanied by what allies he had, and still possessing the rank of proconsul (which is retained by its holders until they return to Rome). Metellus was followed by Gnaeus Pompeius, shortly to be known as Magnus, who was the son of the Pompeius who had been killed by lightning and was thought to have been hostile to Sulla;[139] but young Pompeius scotched this suspicion and came with a legion which he had collected in Picenum on the strength of his father's authority in the region. Not long afterwards he raised two further legions and became one of the most valuable of all Sulla's helpers; and for this reason Sulla held him in great respect, in spite of his extreme youth, and for him alone, so they say, rose to his feet when he entered the room. At the end of the war Sulla sent him to Africa to drive out Carbo's supporters and restore Hiempsal to the throne he had lost at the hands of the Numidians. Sulla even permitted Pompeius to celebrate a triumph over the Numidians, although he was under age and still only a member of the equestrian class.[140] As a result he became an important figure and was sent to Spain to fight Sertorius and afterwards to Pontus to fight Mithridates. Sulla was also joined by Cethegus, who had been one of his most bitter opponents, along with Cinna and Marius, and had been driven out of Rome with them;[141] he now threw himself on Sulla's mercy and offered his services in any capacity Sulla might wish.

81. As Sulla already had ample military forces and plenty of supporters from the nobility, he gave Pompeius and Cethegus posts as subordinate commanders, while he and Metellus as proconsuls took their places at the head of the army; for it seems that Sulla, like Metellus, having been appointed proconsul (against Mithridates), had not yet given up his rank in spite of being decreed an enemy of the state by Cinna. So Sulla advanced against his enemies with violent but hidden hatred, while the party in Rome were terrified, because they had a fair idea of Sulla's character and had fresh in their imaginations his previous assault and capture of the city; they also reflected on the decrees they had passed against him, and they saw

his house razed to the ground, his property forfeit, his friends put to death, and his family only just saved by escape. Judging that no middle course existed between victory and complete destruction, they rallied in their fear to the side of the consuls against Sulla, requesting contributions of men, food and money from outside Rome, and sparing neither effort nor commitment in their belief that they faced disaster.

82. Gaius Norbanus and Lucius Scipio, the current consuls, and with them Carbo, the consul of the previous year, who all shared an equal hatred of Sulla but were much more afraid than the others and were more deeply involved in what had been done, conscripted as effective an army as they could from Rome.[142] To it they added troops from Italy, and took the field against Sulla, dividing their forces, which at first numbered 200 cohorts of 500 men each,[143] but afterwards more. Public sympathy was overwhelmingly on the side of the consuls, since Sulla's action of marching against his own country appeared to be an act of war, while that of the consuls, even if it was undertaken in their own interest, had the cloak of patriotism. The majority of people, who were aware of the criminal nature of the deeds that had been done and thought that they also had reason to be afraid, cooperated with the consuls, since they well knew that Sulla intended not to punish or correct or overawe them, but to violate, kill, dispossess, and in short completely destroy them. Nor were they mistaken. The war brought disaster to them all – ten or twenty thousand of them dying in a single battle on several occasions, and 50,000 on both sides around Rome – and there was no horror that Sulla did not inflict on the survivors; whether individuals or communities, until he had made himself sole master of the whole Roman Empire for as long as he craved and wished it.

83. This seems indeed to have been foretold to them in this war by the divine power. Many unexplained attacks of panic were experienced all over Italy, both individually and collectively, and people remembered ancient, more terrifying, prophecies, and there were many portents: a mule foaled, a pregnant woman gave birth to a viper instead of a baby, and the god caused a great earthquake and knocked down some temples in Rome – and remember the Romans attach great weight to such things.[144] The temple on the Capitol, which had been built some 400 years previously by the kings, was burnt down for no reason that could be discovered. All these occurrences seemed to portend the great number of the dead, and the conquest of Italy and of the Romans themselves, and the capture of the city and the alteration of its constitution.

84. This war, then, began when Sulla arrived at Brundisium, in the 174th Olympiad;[145] but considering the scale of the operations and the enthusiasm with which the combatants pursued such a fight against their personal enemies, it did not last long by the standards of such great struggles. It was chiefly for this reason that their sufferings, concentrated by the zeal of the contending parties into a brief space of time, were greater and more painful. None the less it was three years, at least in Italy, before Sulla assumed power, and in Spain the war was prolonged even beyond his death.[146] In Italy the generals fought many battles, skirmishes, sieges, and every sort of military operation, both with whole armies and with parts of their forces, and all were notable. The greatest and most memorable, to be brief, were as follows.

The proconsuls' first battle was against Norbanus near Canusium, where Norbanus lost six thousand men to Sulla's seventy, and there were numerous wounded. Norbanus then moved to Capua.   85. While Sulla and Metellus were encamped near Teanum, Lucius Scipio confronted them with another army of poor morale who wanted peace. When they discovered this, Sulla's party sent a delegation to Scipio to discuss a settlement, although they neither wished nor hoped for such a thing, because they expected to be able to make his dispirited army mutiny. And this did in fact happen. Scipio, after receiving hostages for the parley, came down to the plain, and three representatives from each side conferred – it thus being impossible to know what was said. It appears that Scipio, who wanted to consult his colleague Norbanus about the proposals, sent Sertorius to brief him, and both armies remained inactive while they waited for the reply. But Sertorius, passing near Suessa, which had declared for Sulla, took the town, and Sulla made a protest to Scipio. The latter, whether because he was privy to the action or because he was at a loss for an answer in the face of this strange action by Sertorius, sent Sulla back his hostages. Scipio's army at once blamed the consuls for the senseless capture of Suessa during a truce and for sending back the hostages unasked, and they reached a secret arrangement with Sulla that they would go over to him if he came close. Directly he approached they deserted *en masse*, so that out of the whole army the only men he took prisoner were the consul Scipio and his son Lucius, still in their tent with no idea what to do. In my view, Scipio's ignorance of so wholesale an agreement shows a gross lack of generalship.

86. Failing to persuade Scipio and his son to change sides, Sulla sent

them away unharmed and despatched another delegation to Norbanus at Capua to seek an agreement, either because he was afraid of the greater part of Italy still standing by the consuls or because he was in fact scheming against Norbanus as he had against Scipio. But no one met him or even gave him an answer (Norbanus probably fearing he would be discredited in a similar way with his army), so Sulla broke camp and advanced, devastating all hostile territory, while Norbanus did the same elsewhere. Carbo hastened back to Rome and had Metellus and all the other senators who were with Sulla declared enemies of the state. It was also at this time that the Capitoline temple burnt down; some speculated that this was the work of Carbo, or of the consuls, or of Sulla's agents, but the truth was unclear and I am unable to arrive at any conclusion as to the cause, whatever it may have been, of this incident. Sertorius, who had some time previously been assigned the governorship of Spain, fled there after his capture of Suessa. Repulsed by the praetors who were already there, he became yet another man responsible for creating great trouble for the Romans at that time. And as the consuls' army constantly swelled with recruits from the major part of Italy, which was still loyal to them, and from neighbouring Cisalpine Gaul, not even Sulla could relax. He negotiated with as many of the Italians as he could, raising troops by offering friendship, threats, money, and hope of reward, until the rest of the summer had been consumed by both sides in these activities.

87. The consuls for the following year were Papirius Carbo, for the second time, and Marius, the nephew of the famous Marius, who was twenty-seven years old;[147] but a severe winter and much freezing weather kept all the forces apart. When spring came there was a tremendous battle on the river Aesis between Metellus and Carbo's general Carrinas.[148] This lasted from dawn until midday, when Carrinas was routed with the loss of a great number of men, and the whole region went over from the consuls to Metellus. Carbo came up with Metellus and kept him under blockade, until he heard that the other consul Marius had been defeated in a great battle at Praeneste, and withdrew to Ariminum with Pompeius hanging on his rear and causing difficulties. The defeat at Praeneste happened as follows: after Sulla had taken Setia, Marius, who was encamped nearby, withdrew a little, and when he reached the place called Sacriportus drew up his army for battle and fought vigorously. As the left wing began to give way, five cohorts of infantry and two of cavalry, not waiting for the rout to develop, threw away their standards all at the same time and deserted to Sulla.

This immediately set in train a terrible defeat for Marius. When his men all fled in exhaustion to Praeneste, with Sulla in hot pursuit, the people in the town let in the first arrivals, but in face of Sulla's attack shut the gates and hoisted Marius in with ropes. As a result another massacre took place beneath the walls, and Sulla took a large number of prisoners, of whom he put to death all the Samnites because they were always a thorn in the Roman flesh.

88. At approximately the same time Metellus likewise defeated the other army, that of Carbo, and on that occasion also five cohorts deserted to Metellus during the battle. Pompeius won a victory at Sena and looted the town.[149] Sulla shut Marius into Praeneste, dug ditches round the town, built a wall at some distance from it, and put Lucretius Ofella in charge of operations, intending to bring Marius to terms by battle instead of by famine. Since he saw no hope of escape, Marius hurried to eliminate his personal enemies before he died by sending instructions to Brutus, the urban praetor, to call a meeting of the senate, ostensibly for some other purpose, and kill Publius Antistius, another Papirius Carbo, Lucius Domitius, and Mucius Scaevola the Pontifex Maximus.[150] The first two of these were indeed murdered in the senate according to Marius' instructions, by assassins who had been brought into the senate-house. Domitius ran out, but was killed by the door, and they caught Scaevola just in front of the building. Their bodies were thrown into the Tiber, for it had now become usual not to bury the slain. Sulla sent his army in divisions by a variety of routes to surround Rome, giving them orders to seize the gates and if they were repulsed to move on Ostia. As they marched by, they were received with terror by the towns along the way, and when they approached Rome the city population opened the gates, both because they were suffering from famine and because they had grown accustomed to facing whatever current trouble was the worst.

89. When Sulla was informed of this, he came at once. He stationed his army outside the gates in the Campus Martius and himself entered the city, now that all the members of the opposite party had fled. He promptly confiscated their property and put it up for sale, and called the people to an assembly where he lamented the necessity for his present actions and told them to take heart because it would soon be a thing of the past and the Republic would be set on the right path. After attending to what he deemed urgent, and leaving some of his own men in charge of the city, he set out for Clusium, where the war, which continued, was at its most intense. The consuls had been reinforced in the meantime by some Celtiberian cavalry which had been sent back by the praetors in Spain, and when a cavalry engagement took place on the river Clanis Sulla killed about fifty of the enemy, and 270 of these Celtiberians deserted to him. Carbo put the remainder to death, either because he was provoked by the desertion of their fellow-nationals or because he feared they would follow suit. At the same time Sulla won a victory over his enemies at Saturnia with another division of his army, and Metellus, after sailing round to Ravenna, occupied the wheat-bearing plain which had been assigned to individual settlers.[151] Other Sullans entered Naples at night by treachery, killed all their enemies except for a few who escaped, and captured the city's triremes. At Clusium, there was a great battle between Sulla himself and Carbo; it lasted from early morning until evening, and as neither of them thought he had the advantage, they separated as night came on.   **90**. In the plain of Spoletium Pompeius and Crassus, both commanders of Sulla's, killed about 3,000 of Carbo's men and besieged Carrinas, the opposing general, until Carbo sent him another force. When he was told of this, Sulla lay in wait for them and killed about 2,000 of them on the march, but Carrinas in fact escaped by night in the heavy rain and darkness of a thunderstorm; the besiegers did indeed see something, but took little notice because of the downpour. Carbo heard that at Praeneste his colleague Marius was suffering from famine and sent Marcius to him with eight legions.[152] Pompeius ambushed and attacked them in a defile, routed them, and after killing a large number of them cut off the remainder on a hill. Marcius got away by leaving his watch fires burning, but his army blamed him for the ambush and became badly disaffected; one complete legion marched under its standards back to Ariminum without orders, but the others dispersed in small groups to their home towns, leaving their commander to return to Carbo with seven cohorts after this disaster. Marcus Lamponius from Lucania, Pontius Telesinus from Samnium, and Gutta from Capua were hurrying with 70,000 men to relieve Marius, but were blocked by Sulla in the pass which provided the only route. Marius himself, who already despaired of outside help, constructed a fort in the wide no-man's land, where he assembled soldiers and assault equipment and tried to force his way through Lucretius' lines. The attempt lasted several days, with varied fortune, but he had no success and was again shut into Praeneste.

91. At Faventia, at about the same time, Carbo and Norbanus reached Metellus' camp, after their day's march, not long before sunset. Although there was only an hour of daylight left and there were thick vineyards all around, hot-headedly and quite senselessly they formed their army up for battle in the hope of stampeding Metellus by the unexpectedness of the tactic. In this unsuitable spot and at this unsuitable hour they had the worst of it, and large numbers of their men became entangled in the vines and killed. The result was that about 10,000 were lost, 6,000 deserted and the rest dispersed, leaving only 1,000 who returned in good order to Arretium.*[153] When they heard the news, another legion of Lucanians which was coming up under Albinovanus went over to Metellus, in spite of the protests of their commander, who did not for the moment abandon his efforts, but continued on to join Norbanus;[154] however, a few days later he opened negotiations with Sulla, and on receiving a promise of immunity in return for some noteworthy exploit invited to dinner Norbanus and his generals – Gaius Antipater, Flavius Fimbria (brother of the man who committed suicide in Asia) and all the other commanders on Carbo's side who were there. When they arrived, he killed them all at table, except for Norbanus, who was the only one who did not come, and then fled to Sulla. This blow caused Ariminum and many of the other military camps in the area to go over to Sulla, and when the news reached Norbanus he took passage on a privately owned ship to Rhodes, because he no longer expected any of the friends who were with him to remain trustworthy or give him firm support in such a disastrous situation. Sulla later demanded his extradition, but while the Rhodians were still making up their minds Norbanus committed suicide in the middle of the town square.

92. Desperate to relieve Marius from siege, Carbo sent Damasippus with another two legions of soldiers to Praeneste, but they too were unable to get through the pass guarded by Sulla. The Gauls living between Ravenna and the Alps came over *en bloc* to Metellus, and Lucullus inflicted a defeat on other forces of Carbo's near Placentia. When Carbo heard this, although he still had 3,000 men at Clusium, together with two legions under Damasippus and others under Carrinas and Marcius, while a large force of Samnites, still in good heart, was managing to hold on for him at the pass, he despaired of the whole situation. Although he was still consul, he fled spinelessly with his entourage from Italy to Africa, hoping to bring it over to his side as a substitute for Italy.[155] As for those who were left behind, the army at Clusium lost 20,000 men after joining battle with Pompeius, and in the face of a disaster of such magnitude the remainder of this army broke up and slipped away to their home towns. Carrinas, Marcius, and Damasip-

pus marched on the pass with all the troops they had to join the Samnites in forcing a way through it if they possibly could. Even so, they failed in the attempt. They then turned towards Rome with the intention of taking it, as it was short of defenders and food, and made camp about twelve miles away, in the territory of Alba.

93. Alarmed for Rome, Sulla sent his cavalry ahead with all speed to harass his opponents on their march. He himself moved rapidly with his whole army to make camp at the Colline Gate, by the shrine of Venus, at about midday, when the enemy were already encamped round the city. A battle was fought at once, in the late afternoon, and although Sulla's right wing was victorious, his left was defeated and fled towards the gates. The men over military age who were on the walls, seeing the enemy running towards them along with their own men, operated the mechanism which lowered the gates. Many of the soldiers and many senators were crushed by the gates as they came down, and from fear and lack of any choice the others turned on the enemy. They fought all night and killed a great number, among them the generals Telesinus and Albinus, whose camps they captured. Lamponius the Lucanian, Marcius, Carrinas, and the other commanders of Carbo's party who were with them escaped. I believe the total death toll on both sides from this night's work amounted to 50,000, and Sulla massacred the 8,000 and more prisoners he took because most of them were Samnite. A day later Marcius and Carrinas were captured and brought to him, and even they were not spared, although they were Romans. Both were put to death and their heads sent to Praeneste for Lucretius to parade around the walls.

94. When the population of Praeneste saw this and discovered that Carbo's army had been totally destroyed and that he and Norbanus* had already left Italy and that Sulla's energy had brought the rest of Italy including Rome under his control, they surrendered the town to Lucretius; Marius descended into some underground tunnels and after a short interval committed suicide. Lucretius cut off Marius' head and sent it to Sulla, and Sulla, after placing it in front of the rostra in the middle of the forum, is reported to have mocked the consul's youth by saying: *First you learn to pull an oar, then you may take the helm.*[156]

When Lucretius took Praeneste, he killed some of the senators who had been officers under Marius immediately but kept the rest under guard. Sulla, on arrival, put the latter to death, and instructed the people in Praeneste to lay aside their weapons and go down, all of them, to the plain.

When they had done so he picked out the very few who could be of any use to him and ordered the rest to divide into three groups, Romans, Samnites, and Praenestines. When they had separated, he announced to the Romans that they too deserved death for what they had done, but pardoned them notwithstanding; all the others he slaughtered, though he allowed their wives and children to depart unharmed. He also sacked the town, which was particularly rich at that time.

So fell Praeneste; but another town, Norba, still resisted stubbornly until Aemilius Lepidus was admitted into it by treachery. Unbearably goaded by the treachery, some of the inhabitants then committed suicide, some killed each other by mutual agreement, and some actually hanged themselves; others barricaded the gates and set light to <*the houses* . . . > and a strong wind which fanned the flames caused such destruction to the town that not a single piece of booty was taken from it.   **95**. Such was the determination with which the inhabitants of Norba met their end.

When the people of Italy had been reduced by war and fire and massacre, Sulla's commanders went round stationing garrisons in suspect places. Pompeius was sent to Africa against Carbo and to Sicily against Carbo's followers. Sulla himself called the Romans to an assembly and after making a long and boastful speech about himself and issuing terrible threats to frighten them, concluded by saying that he would introduce a change which would be beneficial to the people, if they would obey him, but that he would spare none of his enemies the ultimate in torment, and would pursue with all his might the praetors and quaestors and military tribunes and anyone else who had co-operated with the enemy after the date when the consul Scipio failed to abide by his agreement with him.[157] With these words he immediately proscribed about forty senators and approximately 1,600 of the equestrian class. He seems to have been the first to publish a list of those he punished with death, and to add a statement detailing a prize for killers, rewards for informers, and penalties for concealment. Soon he added other senators' names to the list. Some of the proscribed were caught unawares and killed on the spot, in houses or streets or temple precincts, some were carried bodily to Sulla and hurled down at his feet, and some were dragged along the ground and trampled on, but no one who witnessed these horrors now uttered a word because everyone was terrified. Others were driven into exile and their* property confiscated. Agents hurried on the track of the fugitives from the city, searching everywhere and putting to death all those they captured.

96. There were also many cases of execution, exile and confiscation among the Italians who had complied in any way with the wishes of Carbo, Norbanus, Marius, or their subordinate commanders. On these grounds harsh verdicts were delivered and all sorts of charges laid, such as holding a command or serving in the army or contributing money or other aid or counsel generally against Sulla. Giving or receiving hospitality, friendship, or a loan constituted grounds for accusation, and there were actually cases of condemnation for showing sympathy or merely travelling in company with a suspect. Such accusations were particularly common against the wealthy. When charges against individuals ran short, Sulla turned on the towns and punished them too by pulling down their citadels or levelling their walls or imposing communal penalties or crushing them with enormous exactions; and on most of them he imposed settlements of his own soldiers, so that he would have garrisons up and down Italy, and transferred to them and shared out the land and buildings which had belonged to the Italians. This made them extremely loyal to him even after his death, for as their hold on this property lacked validity unless all his arrangements were valid, they supported him even after he had died.

Such being the situation in Italy, Carbo had meanwhile fled with many prominent men from Africa to Sicily, and thence to the island of Cossyra.[158] There they were arrested by men sent by Pompeius, who gave orders to the escort to kill the others without bringing them into his presence, but made Carbo, a man who had been three times consul, stand below him in chains while he ranted over him; he then put him to death and sent his head to Sulla.[159]

97. Now that his enemies had been completely dealt with as he wished, and all military opposition had been extinguished except for Sertorius, who was far away, Sulla sent Metellus out to fight the latter in Spain while he himself took sole charge of shaping all the political institutions of the state in the way he wanted. For there was no longer any talk of laws, or elections, or sortition, since everybody was quaking with fear and lying low or keeping silent.[160] A law was passed that all the arrangements Sulla had made as consul and proconsul should be ratified and not subject to investigation, and they erected a gilded equestrian statue of him in front of the rostra with the inscription 'Cornelius Sulla, Leader, Favoured of the Gods', – for that was what his flatterers used to call him in the light of his continued good fortune against his enemies, and something that started as flattery turned into a regular name.[161] I have come across an account which claimed that Sulla was described as 'the favourite of Venus' in this decree – which seems to me not unlikely, since he was also called Faustus, a name very near in meaning to 'auspicious' and 'favoured by Venus'.[162] There is also an oracle somewhere which was given him when he enquired about the future:

> Hearken to me, O Roman. Great power on the race of Aeneas,
> Cherishing them with her care, has Cypris conferred.[163] But be sure to
> Pay the immortals their dues every year. Nor forget you this precept:
> Bring gifts ever to Delphi. There is, as you climb from the sea
> Up to the Taurus snows, where named by its dwellers for Venus
> Stands lofty the Carian city,[164] a goddess, to whom if you humbly
> Offer an axe, you shall take for yourself o'ershadowing power.

Whichever of these names the Romans decreed when they put up the statue, they must have given them either in jest or because they wished to humour the man. However, he sent both a golden crown and an axe with this inscription:

> This offering mighty Sulla makes to thee,
> Fair Aphrodite, for I dreamed I saw
> Thee pass adorned with these among my host,
> And battle boldly, clad in Ares' gear.

98. Sulla was in fact an unelected king or tyrant who owed his position to violence and force of arms, but since he needed the pretence of appearing to have been elected, he engineered this too, in the following way. In ancient times, the Roman kings were chosen on merit; whenever a king died, a succession of senators held office for five days each, until the people approved another man as king. They called the five-day office-holder the *interrex*, because he was king for the time being. Now the outgoing consuls always conducted elections for their successors, and if by any mischance there was no consul, then too a temporary king was appointed to hold the elections. As there were no consuls after Carbo's death in Sicily and Marius' at Praeneste, Sulla went somewhere outside the city and told the senate to choose the so-called *interrex*. They chose Valerius Flaccus and expected him to set in train a consular election; but Sulla wrote instructing him to make known to the people that he, Sulla, thought it advantageous at the present moment that the city should have the magistracy they called

the dictatorship, which had been in abeyance for 400 years;[165] Flaccus also told them that whoever was elected should hold office not for a predetermined period, but until he had restored stability to Rome, Italy, and the whole Empire, which had been severely shaken by wars and factional strife. Common sense referred this view to Sulla himself, and there could be no doubt about it: at the end of his letter, Sulla was unable to restrain himself and revealed this too, that he thought that here also he could be of great service to the state.

99. These were Sulla's instructions; and the Romans unwillingly accepted this sham of an election as a token pretence of freedom and chose Sulla as despot with absolute power for as long as he wished. They neither followed legal voting procedure, nor imagined the matter to be in any way under their own control, but they had absolutely no other recourse. Even in the past the dictator's power had been despotic, but it was limited by its brief duration.[166] Now for the first time it became unlimited, and a true despotism. However, to give the word a fair sound they added this, that they were electing him dictator to make laws, of which he would be the sole arbiter, and to revise the constitution. In this way the Romans, who had had kings for more than 240 years, and after that had enjoyed democracy and annually elected consuls as their leaders for another 400 years, again had a taste of monarchy. This was at the time of the 175th Olympiad in Greece, when no Olympic contest took place except the sprint in the stadium, because Sulla had sent for the athletes and all the other shows to come to Rome to celebrate his achievements against Mithridates and the Italians.[167] The excuse he gave was the need for the masses to recover from their sufferings and enjoy some amusement.

100. In a show of observing the traditional constitution Sulla permitted the people to vote for consuls, and Marcus Tullius and Cornelius Dolabella were elected.[168] He himself, as dictator, was like a king over them: the axes were carried in front of him, twenty-four for a dictator, the same number that preceded the old kings,[169] and he surrounded himself with a large bodyguard. He repealed some laws and passed others, and he prohibited anyone from holding the praetorship before he had been quaestor, or holding the consulship before he had been praetor, or from holding the same office again before ten years had elapsed. He virtually abolished the tribunate of the people, enfeebling it and barring a tribune by law from holding any other office afterwards. For this reason those who laid claim to family or reputation avoided the office in future. I cannot say for sure whether it

was Sulla who took the tribunician elections from the people and gave them to the senate, which is the present position.[170] Because the senate had been much reduced in numbers by the civil disturbances and the wars, he enlarged it by adding to its membership about 300 from the most respected of the equestrians, taking a vote on each in the tribal assembly. He also freed and inserted into the list of citizens more than 10,000 of the youngest and strongest slaves of those who had been put to death, declaring them to be Romans and calling them Cornelii after himself, so that he could have 10,000 men from among the people to carry out his orders.[171] With the same object in view for Italy, he allotted (as I have said) to the twenty-three legions that had fought for him a large quantity of land belonging to the towns, some of which had never been distributed for cultivation and some of which was taken from them as a penalty.

101. He was so terrible and quick to anger in everything that he killed Quintus Lucretius Ofella in the open forum, although the latter had taken Praeneste for him and had set the seal on his own victory by bringing the siege of the consul Marius to a successful conclusion. Ofella had considered that although he was still only of equestrian status the scale of his achievement gave him the right, according to ancient custom, of becoming consul without previously holding the offices of quaestor and praetor, and he had canvassed the voters, refusing to change his mind in face of Sulla's prohibition and referral of the matter to the senate. After this, Sulla called the people to an assembly and said: 'Understand this, my friends, and hear it from my own lips: I killed Lucretius because he would not obey me.' And he told them a story: 'A farmer who was ploughing was being bitten by lice. Twice', he said, 'he let go of the plough and shook out his tunic; but when he was bitten again, he burnt the tunic so as not to keep wasting time. So I advise people who have been defeated twice not to ask for incineration the third time.' With these words, then, Sulla reinforced their terror, and ruled them as he pleased. He also celebrated a triumph for the Mithridatic war.[172] Some of them made fun of him and called his rule 'monarchy denied' because it was only the name of king that he kept back, while on the contrary others based their interpretation on what he had actually done and spoke of it as open despotism.

102. Such was the depth of the troubles which this war brought on the Romans themselves as well as on all the Italians. It also affected in a similar way all the peoples beyond Italy, who had recently been not only involved in wars against pirates and Mithridates and Sulla, but also worn down by

frequent demands for financial contributions, thanks to the bankruptcy of the treasury through the civil wars. For all the peoples and rulers who were allies of Rome, and all the city-states (not only those which paid tax, but also those which had entrusted themselves to Rome under treaties guaranteed by oath, and those which because of the help they provided or some other claim were autonomous and paid no contribution), were told to pay money and obey orders, and some of them were deprived of territory and ports which had been granted them by treaty.

Sulla also passed a decree that Alexander, son of the Alexander who had been king of Egypt, should be king in Alexandria. He had been brought up in Cos and handed over by the Coans to Mithridates, and then fled from Mithridates to Sulla, to whom he became close. The royal dynasty of Egypt lacked a male, and as the women of the royal family required a relative, Sulla hoped to make a substantial profit from this very rich kingdom. But after Alexander had reigned for nineteen days, proving a rather bad ruler for the Alexandrians in his reliance on Sulla, they brought him from the palace to the gymnasium and executed him.[173] This shows how little afraid they were of other powers, thanks to the size of their own kingdom and their immunity up to this point from troubles originating elsewhere.

103. The next year, although he was dictator, Sulla consented to hold the office of consul as well, with Metellus Pius as his colleague, in a show of preserving the outward appearance of republican government.[174] Perhaps this is the example followed even now by the Roman emperors, who when they announce the consuls in Rome, occasionally name themselves, thinking it quite acceptable to hold the consulship along with the supreme power. In the following year too the people pandered to Sulla and tried to elect him consul, but he would not have it; he returned as consuls Servilius Isauricus and Claudius Pulcher and himself voluntarily abdicated from the highest office, although there was no agitation for him to do so. And this seems to me another remarkable thing about Sulla, that he was the first and up to that time the only man to lay aside such great power without compulsion, in favour not of his children, like Ptolemy in Egypt and Ariobarzanes in Cappadocia and Seleucus in Syria, but of those who were the subjects of his despotism.[175] It is almost incredible that after forcing his way to power he should have recklessly and willingly put it aside when he had achieved mastery; and it is surprising, to say the least, that he was not afraid of having caused the death of more than 100,000 young men in this war, and of having killed personal enemies to the number of ninety senators and

about fifteen consuls, and 2,600 of the equestrian class, including those driven into exile. Their property had been confiscated and the bodies of many had been thrown out unburied, but Sulla proclaimed himself a private citizen, fearing neither the people at home nor the exiles abroad nor the towns which had been deprived of their citadels, defences, land, money, and immunity from taxation. 104. Such was the extent of his daring and good luck. It is reported that he said in the forum, when he was laying down his office, that he would also give an account of his actions, if anyone demanded it; and that when he had put aside the rods and axes, he dismissed his personal bodyguard and for some time continued to appear in public accompanied only by his friends, overawing even then the crowds of spectators. As he was on his way home one day a lad actually criticized him, and because no one drove him away grew confident and insulted Sulla all the way to his front door. Sulla, who was so quick to anger with men and communities of importance, patiently put up with the lad and as he entered his house, whether he understood the future or happened by chance to divine it, made only this reply, that this lad would prevent anyone else laying aside such power. And as it turned out this came true for the Romans not much later, because Gaius Caesar at no point renounced power. As for Sulla, I think he was someone who was vehement and effective in all he did, who desired to turn himself from a private citizen into an absolute ruler, and from an absolute ruler into a private citizen, and after this to live in rural isolation. I say this because he retired to his private estate at Cumae in Italy and there in the solitude enjoyed hunting and fishing, not because he was afraid of living in town as an ordinary citizen, nor again because he showed any feebleness in pursuing his aims; he was still at a vigorous stage of life, his health was excellent, and there were 120,000 men all over Italy who had recently served under him and received great rewards and quantities of land from him, and there were also ready in Rome the 10,000 Cornelii and the rest of the ordinary population who had taken his side and were grateful to him and still constituted a threat to his opponents, and all these felt that their own safety from retribution for what they had done in conjunction with Sulla lay in his continued survival. I believe that sated with war, sated with power, and sated with Rome, he finally fell in love with rural life.

105. Not long after Sulla's abdication, the Romans, after being saved from murder and despotism, had the flames of further civil conflict fanned

gradually into life. Quintus Catulus, one of Sulla's supporters, and Lepidus Aemilius, an opponent, who had become the consuls, were extremely hostile to each other and immediately began to disagree.[176] It was obvious that some fresh trouble would arise from this.

In the country, Sulla had a dream in which he seemed to see the divine spirit calling him; when day broke, he immediately told his friends about the dream and made his will in great haste, completing it that very day. After sealing it, he was attacked in the evening by a fever and died in the night, at the age of sixty, apparently living up to his soubriquet by being the most fortunate of men as regards not only his actual end but his entire life – if indeed it be considered good fortune to achieve everything one desires. Dissension at once broke out over him in the capital: some thought that his body ought to travel in solemn procession through Italy and be displayed in Rome in the forum and have the honour of a public funeral, but Lepidus and his party contested this. Catulus and the Sullans prevailed, and Sulla's corpse was carried through Italy to Rome in regal splendour on a gilded bier, followed by large numbers of trumpeters and horsemen and a throng of armed men on foot. Those who had served as soldiers under his command hurried under arms from every side to join the procession, and each as he arrived immediately assumed his place in military formation. A huge crowd of ordinary folk also gathered, such as had never been seen at any previous event. And at the head of the procession were carried the standards and the fasces which had accompanied him while he was alive and in power.

106. When the body had been carried as far as Rome, it was conveyed into the city in a procession of stupendous pomp. More than 2,000 hurriedly made golden crowns were carried past, these being gifts from the towns and from the legions which had served with Sulla and from his individual friends, and it is impossible to describe the lavishness of the other items that were sent to the funeral. Frightened by the assembled soldiery, all the priests and priestesses, in their separate colleges, and the whole senate, and the magistrates wearing their insignia of office, escorted the body. They were followed by another group consisting of the members of the equestrian class and all the soldiers who had served under Sulla's command, in their units. The latter had gathered enthusiastically, all hurrying to take part; they carried gilded standards and wore arms worked with silver, of the sort that are still in use for processions now. There was a vast number of trumpeters, alternating mournful with melting melodies. Sulla's praises

were chanted out, first by the senate and the equestrian order in turn, then by the soldiers, and then by the ordinary people, some genuinely regretting his loss, others even now as frightened of his army and his corpse as if he were still alive. As they gazed at the spectacle that was taking place and remembered what the man had done, they were overwhelmed, agreeing with their opponents that he had brought the latter the greatest good fortune but remained terrifying to themselves even in death. When the body had been placed on the speakers' platform in the forum, the finest orator of the day gave the funeral address, because Faustus, Sulla's son, was still very young; then some strong senators shouldered the bier and carried it to the Campus Martius, where only emperors are buried, and the equestrian order and the military galloped around the funeral pyre. 107. Such was Sulla's end.

As they came away from the pyre the consuls immediately began to quarrel and insult each other, and the sympathies of the city population were divided between them. In an attempt to win additional support, Lepidus promised to give the Italians back the land which Sulla had taken away from them. The senate, in fear of both, made them swear not to settle their dispute by armed force, but Lepidus, who had drawn Transalpine Gaul as his province, refused to return to hold the elections because he planned to use military force against Sulla's supporters the following year, without any fear of breaking his oath, as it was not considered to be binding beyond the end of his year of office.[177] The senate was not deceived, and recalled him; but equally aware why he had been recalled, he came accompanied by his entire army intending to enter the city with it. When he was stopped, he issued a call to arms, and a rival proclamation was made by Catulus. Lepidus was defeated in the battle which took place between them, not much beyond the Campus Martius, and after failing to hold out for very much longer sailed across to Sardinia where he died of a wasting disease. His army gradually disintegrated, disrupted by petty troubles, and Perperna[178] took the strongest part of it to Sertorius in Spain.

108. The remainder of the Sullan story concerns the struggle against Sertorius, which lasted eight years, and was never straightforward for the Romans. They were not fighting simply against the Spaniards, but here too against other Romans and against Sertorius, who had been chosen governor of Spain but when he was helping Carbo against Sulla had captured Suessa during a truce and gone as a fugitive to assume his command.[179] He

possessed troops from Italy itself, raised more from the Celtiberians, drove the praetors who were his predecessors out of Spain because from loyalty to Sulla they would not hand over their authority, and stoutly fought off Metellus, who had been sent against him by Sulla. He was well known for his nerve, and he conscripted a council of 300 from the friends who were with him, said they were the council of the Roman state, and called them the senate by way of insult to that body. It is probable that after the deaths of Sulla and subsequently Lepidus, and his acquisition of more Italian troops brought him by Lepidus' general Perperna, he would have marched on Italy if the senate had not become alarmed and sent another army and a second commander to Spain to join the first. This commander was Pompeius, who was still a young man but was famous for his exploits in Africa and in Italy itself under Sulla.   **109.** He climbed resolutely into the Alpine ranges, not by the route which was Hannibal's great achievement but by opening another near the sources of the Rhône and the Eridanus, which rise not far from each other in the Alps (the former flows through Transalpine Gaul to the Tyrrhenian Sea, the latter flows this side of the Alps to the Ionian Sea, changing its name from Eridanus to Po). When Pompeius reached Spain, Sertorius promptly cut to pieces a whole legion that had gone out to forage, together with its draught animals and camp attendants, and under Pompeius' very eyes plundered and destroyed the town of Lauron. A woman who had been taken at the siege clawed out the eyes of her captor when he went beyond the usual limits of ill-treatment, and when Sertorius heard about it he put to death the man's entire unit, although they were Roman, because they had become notorious for such high-handed behaviour.

110. The onset of winter then caused them to disengage, but with the arrival of spring they moved against each other, Metellus and Pompeius from the Pyrenees, where they had wintered, and Sertorius and Perperna from Lusitania.[180] They came to grips with each other near a town called Sucro. Although terrifying crashes of thunder and unnatural lightning came from a clear sky, these hardened soldiers remained undaunted and proceeded with the task of slaughtering each other until Metellus routed Perperna and sacked his camp, and Sertorius defeated Pompeius, who suffered a dangerous wound in the thigh from a spear. So concluded this encounter.

Sertorius had a white hind which was tame and allowed to roam. When she disappeared Sertorius thought it a bad omen and became depressed and did nothing, even in the face of taunts from the enemy about the hind. But when she was sighted running through the bushes Sertorius jumped up and immediately rained missiles on the enemy as though making the first-offerings to her at a sacrifice.

Soon afterwards Sertorius fought a great battle near Segontia which lasted from noon until night. He had the better of a cavalry battle with Pompeius and killed about 6,000 of his men with the loss of about half that number of his own, while on the same occasion Metellus killed about 5,000 of Perperna's. On the day after this battle Sertorius, reinforced with a large number of native troops, assaulted Metellus' camp unexpectedly in the late afternoon in a bold attempt to cut it off by a ditch, but Pompeius attacked him and forced him to desist from this insolence. These, then, were the events of this summer, and the armies again separated to go into winter quarters.

111. The following year (which fell within the 176th Olympiad) the Romans acquired two countries under the terms of wills, Bithynia on the death of Nicomedes and Cyrene on the death of Ptolemy, the Lagid king known as Apion.[181] Also various wars were raging: this one in Spain against Sertorius, one against Mithridates in the east, one against the pirates all over the Mediterranean, another in Crete against the Cretans, and the one in Italy against the gladiators, which also came on them suddenly and was equally intense. Although they were distracted by so many commitments, the Romans nevertheless sent out to Spain another two legions. Metellus and Pompeius added these to all the rest of their forces and descended with them from the Pyrenees to the river Ebro. Sertorius and Perperna came to meet them from Lusitania.

112. At this point many of Sertorius' men started to desert to Metellus, whereupon Sertorius in his anger began to inflict savage and barbarous punishments on many of them and became the target of their hatred. The soldiers particularly held it against him that he was accompanied everywhere by a guard of Celtiberians, not Romans, and that he had dismissed his Roman bodyguard and entrusted this duty to Celtiberians. The soldiers would not have tolerated the charge of being thought untrustworthy even if they had been campaigning against enemies of Rome; but they were above all resentful of the fact that they had been disloyal to their country because of Sertorius but were now regarded as disloyal by him also, and they thought it wrong that those who had stayed with him should be condemned because the others had deserted. The Celtiberians also took advan-

tage of the situation to insult the Romans because they could not be trusted. But they did not abandon Sertorius completely, because they needed
him: he was the most aggressive and successful soldier of the day. These
characteristics also caused the Celtiberians, because of his speed of action,
to call him Hannibal, whom they considered the most daring and cunning
of all the generals who had operated among them. Such was the state of
Sertorius' army when Metellus' subordinates made a series of rapid assaults
on towns he held and deported the male inhabitants to areas which were
subject to themselves. While Pompeius was besieging Palantia and was in-
serting balks of timber beneath the walls, which were of wood, Sertorius
appeared and raised the siege, but was too late to prevent the walls being set
on fire from beneath by Pompeius, who withdrew to join Metellus. Sertorius not only restored the fallen parts of the walls but also attacked a force
that was encamped near a place called Calagurris and killed 3,000 of them.
These were the events of this year in Spain.

113. The following year the Roman generals showed rather more confidence and contemptuously attacked the towns controlled by Sertorius.[182]
They detached much of his territory from him, and elated by their successes proceeded to move against further areas. Although no great battle
occurred, none the less, for a second time < . . . >, until in the subsequent
year Metellus and Pompeius launched another offensive with still less respect for their opponent. Sertorius on the other hand, under the influence
of some affliction sent from heaven, was glad to shirk the toil of administration and spent most of his time indulging himself and relaxing with
women, parties, and drinking. The result was that he suffered continual
defeat. He had also become not only quick to anger because he imagined
all kinds of disloyalties, but also savage in his punishments and suspicious of
everyone, so that Perperna, who had joined him voluntarily with a large
force after the revolt of Aemilius, feared for his life and laid a counter-plot
against him with ten accomplices. A number of these men were betrayed,
and although some were punished and some managed to escape, Perperna
surprisingly escaped detection; he therefore pressed on all the more urgently with his plan, and even though Sertorius went nowhere without his
bodyguard Perperna invited him to dinner, and when he had made Sertorius and the guards on duty in the dining-room drunk, killed them as the
meal came to an end.

114. The army immediately rose in tumultuous anger against Perperna,
as their feelings for Sertorius turned instantly from hatred to goodwill, in

accordance with the general tendency of men to desist from anger towards the dead when the source of irritation is no longer present, and to revert to compassion and recollection of their good qualities. Then they weighed up their present position. Although they lacked respect for Perperna because he held no magistracy, and thought that Sertorius' ability was the only thing that had saved them, both they and the natives who supported them (particularly the Lusitanians, thanks to Sertorius' great reliance on them) reluctantly declared for Perperna. But when Sertorius' will was opened and Perperna was named a legatee, their anger and hatred against him were roused still further, because he had committed such an unspeakable deed against a man who was not merely his commander and superior officer but also his friend and benefactor. They would actually have resorted to violence if Perperna had not bestirred himself to win over some with bribes and others with promises, while cowing yet others with threats and actually putting some to death to terrify the rest. He also went and addressed the civilian population, whipping up support like a popular politician and freeing those of their number who had been imprisoned by Sertorius; and to the Spaniards he gave back their hostages. By these methods they were brought under control and obeyed him as a commander (for in this he was reckoned the best after Sertorius), but even then they continued to resent him, because as he gained confidence he showed himself savage in inflicting punishment and put to death three of the Roman aristocrats who had accompanied him in his flight to Sertorius, along with his own nephew.

115. On Metellus' departure to other regions of Spain, because he thought it no longer unreasonable to leave Perperna to Pompeius, skirmishes and exploratory attacks took place over a period of days between Perperna and Pompeius, neither of whom deployed his full army. However, on the tenth day a great battle broke out, the reason being that they had decided to settle matters by a single encounter; Pompeius thought little of Perperna's generalship and Perperna, doubting that he would long enjoy the loyalty of his army, committed virtually his entire force to battle. Pompeius quickly gained the upper hand over a feeble commander and a demoralized army. In the general and undifferentiated rout, Perperna hid in some scrub, more afraid of his own side than of the enemy. He was captured by some cavalry and dragged to Pompeius, being cursed by his own people for murdering Sertorius, and shouting that he had plenty to reveal to Pompeius about the civil war in Rome – whether because this was really true or because he wanted to be brought unharmed to him. But Pompeius,

surely because he was afraid that Perperna would reveal something un-expected and start further trouble in Rome, sent orders to have him put to death before he set eyes on him. Pompeius was considered to have acted extremely prudently in the matter, and this was another feather in his cap. This was the end of the Spanish war, which coincided with the end of Sertorius' life and would surely not have been brought to such a swift and simple conclusion while he remained alive.

116. In Italy, at this same time, Spartacus, a Thracian who had once fought against the Romans and after being taken prisoner and sold had become a gladiator in a troop which was kept to provide entertainments at Capua, persuaded about seventy of his fellows to risk their lives for freedom rather than for exhibition as a spectacle. With them, he overpowered their guards and escaped. Then he equipped himself and his companions with staves and daggers seized from travellers and took refuge on Mount Vesuvius, where he allowed many runaway domestic slaves and some free farm hands to join him. With the gladiators Oenomaus and Crixus as his subordinates he plundered the nearby areas, and because he divided the spoils in equal shares his numbers quickly swelled. The first commander sent against him was Varinius Glaber, and the second Publius Valerius;[183] instead of legionary forces they had anyone they could quickly conscript on the way, because the Romans did not yet class the affair as a war, but as a kind of raid akin to piracy, and they were defeated when they attacked him. Spartacus himself actually captured Varinius' horse from under him; so nearly was a Roman general taken prisoner by a gladiator. After this, people flocked in still greater numbers to join Spartacus: his army now numbered 70,000 and he began to manufacture weapons and gather stores.

117. The government in Rome now despatched the consuls with two legions. Crixus, at the head of 3,000 men, was defeated and killed by one of them at Mount Garganus, with the loss of two-thirds of his force. Spartacus, who was eager to go through the Apennines to the Alpine regions, and then to Celtic lands from the Alps, was intercepted and prevented from escaping by the other consul, while his colleague conducted the pursuit. But Spartacus turned on each of them and defeated them separately.[184] In the aftermath they retreated in confusion, while Spartacus, first sacrificing 300 Roman prisoners to Crixus, made for Rome with 120,000 foot soldiers after burning the useless equipment and putting all the prisoners to death and slaughtering the draught animals to free himself of all encumbrances;

and although a large number of deserters approached him he refused to accept any of them. When the consuls made another stand in Picenum, there was a further great struggle and on that occasion also a great Roman defeat. Spartacus, however, changed his mind about marching on Rome because he was not yet a match for the defenders and his troops did not all have soldier's arms and equipment (no town had joined their cause, and they were all slaves, deserters and human flotsam). He seized the mountains around Thurii, together with the town itself, and then prevented traders bringing in gold and silver, barred his own men from acquiring any, and bought exclusively iron and bronze at good prices without harming those who brought them. As a result they had plenty of raw material and were well equipped and made frequent raiding expeditions. They again confronted the Romans in battle, defeated them, and on that occasion too returned to camp laden with booty.[185]

118. The war had now lasted three years and was causing the Romans great concern, although at the beginning it had been laughed at and regarded as trivial because it was against gladiators. When the appointment of other generals was proposed there was universal reluctance to stand, and no one put himself forward until Licinius Crassus, distinguished both for his family and his wealth, undertook to assume the post, and led six legions against Spartacus;[186] to these he added the two consular legions when he reached the front. He immediately punished the latter for their repeated defeats, making them draw lots for every tenth man to be put to death.[187] According to some, this was not what happened; instead, when he himself had suffered defeat after engaging the enemy with his whole force he had them all draw lots for the tenth place and put to death up to 4,000 men without being in the least deterred by their numbers. Whatever the truth, he established himself in the eyes of his men as more to be feared than a defeat at the hands of the enemy, and forthwith won a victory over 10,000 of Spartacus' men who were encamped separately somewhere. He killed two-thirds of them and marched confidently against Spartacus himself. After winning a brilliant victory, he pursued Spartacus as he fled towards the sea with the intention of sailing across to Sicily, overtook him, and walled him in with ditches, earthworks, and palisades. 119. Spartacus then tried to force his way out and reach the Samnite country, but Crassus killed almost 6,000 of his opponents at the beginning of the day and nearly as many more at evening, at the cost of three dead and seven wounded from the Roman army; so effective had their punishment been in altering their will

to win. Spartacus, who was waiting for some cavalry that were on their way to him, no longer went into battle with his full force, but conducted many separate harassing operations against his besiegers; he made sudden and repeated sorties against them, set fire to bundles of wood which he had thrown into the ditches, and made their work difficult. He crucified a Roman prisoner in no-man's land to demonstrate to his own troops the fate awaiting them if they were defeated. When the government at Rome heard of the siege and contemplated the dishonour they would incur from a protracted war with gladiators, they appointed Pompeius, who had recently arrived from Spain, to an additional command in the field, in the belief that the task of dealing with Spartacus was now substantial and difficult.   120. As a result of this appointment Crassus pressed on urgently with every means of attacking Spartacus, to stop Pompeius stealing his glory, while Spartacus, thinking to forestall Pompeius, invited Crassus to negotiate. When Crassus spurned the offer, Spartacus decided to make a desperate attempt, and with the cavalry which had by now arrived forced a way through the encircling fortifications with his whole army and retired towards Brundisium, with Crassus in pursuit. But when he discovered that Lucullus, who was on his way back from his victory over Mithridates,[188] was there, he despaired of everything and, at the head of a still large force, joined battle with Crassus. The fight was long, and bitterly contested, since so many tens of thousands of men had no other hope. Spartacus himself was wounded by a spear-thrust in the thigh, but went down on one knee, held his shield in front of him, and fought off his attackers until he and a great number of his followers were encircled and fell. The rest of his army was already in disorder and was cut down in huge numbers; consequently their losses were not easy to estimate (though the Romans lost about 1,000 men), and Spartacus' body was never found. Since there was still a very large number of fugitives from the battle in the mountains, Crassus proceeded against them. They formed themselves into four groups and kept up their resistance until there were only 6,000 survivors, who were taken prisoner and crucified all the way along the road from Rome to Capua.[189]

121. Crassus accomplished this in a space of six months and because of it immediately acquired a reputation to match that of Pompeius. He would not disband his army, because of Pompeius' refusal to do so, and they both announced their candidacy for the consulship. Crassus had held the praetorship, in accordance with Sulla's law, but Pompeius had held neither praetorship nor quaestorship and was only thirty-four years old; he had also

promised to restore to the tribunes many of their former powers.[190] They were elected, but even after this would not dismiss their armies and kept them near the city. They both made excuses, Pompeius claiming that he was waiting for Metellus' return to celebrate his Spanish triumph, Crassus saying that Pompeius ought to be the first to disband. The population of Rome, who discerned the seeds of fresh civil war and were afraid of a pair of armies encamped outside the city, begged the consuls, as they sat in state in the forum, to be reconciled with each other. At first they both refused, but when some persons gifted with divine inspiration foretold the most terrible consequences if the consuls continued to disagree, the crowd wailed, and in deep dejection, still remembering the disasters of the time of Sulla and Marius, made another appeal to them. Crassus relented first, stepped down from his seat and went over to Pompeius with his hand outstretched in reconciliation, whereupon Pompeius stood up and went quickly towards him. After they had grasped each other's hands there was general acclamation, and the assembly did not break up before the consuls had given official notice that they would dismiss their armies. Thus a dispute which threatened to develop into yet another serious internal conflict was firmly settled, and this point in the civil wars was reached approximately sixty years after the killing of Tiberius Gracchus.

BOOK II

1. After the period of Sulla's autocracy, and the subsequent activities of Sertorius and Perperna in Spain, the Romans became involved in further civil struggles of a similar kind. These culminated in the war between Gaius Caesar and Pompeius Magnus in which Pompeius was destroyed by Caesar, while Caesar was himself murdered in the senate-house by a group of men who thought he was behaving like a king. How this came about, and how Gaius and Pompeius were killed, is the subject of this second book of the civil wars.

Pompeius had recently cleared the sea of the pirates, of whom there were vast numbers everywhere, particularly at that time. Next he had subdued Mithridates, king of Pontus, and was in the course of making political arrangements for Mithridates' kingdom and for the other nations he had brought under Roman control in the east.[1] Caesar, on the other hand, was still a young man;[2] he spoke powerfully, was effective in action, and had unlimited daring and expectations. In pursuit of his ambition he was also prodigal beyond his means, so that at this period when he was aedile and praetor[3] he fell into debt and made himself the darling of the crowd, because the common people always approve of men who are generous with their money.[4]

2. Gaius Catilina,[5] who was well known for his distinguished reputation and illustrious birth, was an unstable character believed to have once killed his own son because he was in love with Aurelia Orestilla, who would not agree to marry someone who had a child. A sometime friend, follower and fanatical partisan of Sulla, he too had been driven into poverty by his ambition. Still courted by powerful men and women, he stood for the consulship in the hope of using it as a route to monarchical power.[6] Although he had great hopes of being elected, he was defeated because of this suspicion about him, and Cicero won the office in his place. Cicero was a most attractive speaker both informally and in public, but Catilina insulted those who voted for Cicero by mocking him; because of the obscurity of his birth, Catilina called him a 'new man' (this is a term they use for men who are prominent for their own achievements and not for those of their ancestors), and because of his non-metropolitan origins he called him '*inquilinus*', which means a lodger in someone else's house.[7] After this, Catilina turned completely away from political activity, because it was not at all a swift and sure way to absolute power, but was plagued by quarrelling and jealousy; he raised a great deal of money from a good number of women who hoped to lose their husbands in the uprising,[8] and together with some members of the senate and of the equestrian class formed a conspiracy, to which he also recruited ordinary Romans, foreigners, and slaves. His leading supporters were Cornelius Lentulus and Cethegus, who were praetors in Rome at the time.[9] He also sent men out across Italy to contact any of Sulla's soldiers who had spent the proceeds of their earlier violence and were keen for some sort of repetition; Gaius Manlius[10] went to Faesulae in Tuscany, others to Picenum and Apulia, and they inconspicuously gathered forces together for him.   3. None of this was yet known, when Fulvia, a distinguished woman, told Cicero about it: her lover Quintus Curius, a man who had been expelled from the senate for a catalogue of disgraceful behaviour and was thought a suitable member of this plot, empty-headedly strove to impress his loved one by asserting that he would soon be in a position of power. Rumours were in any case already rife about what was happening outside Rome. Cicero therefore stationed guards at intervals throughout the city and sent many of the leading men out to the suspect areas to keep an eye on what was taking place.[11] Catilina was nervous, in spite of the fact that no one yet dared to arrest him because of the lack of accurate information, and thought that delay would give rise to suspicion. He therefore pinned his hopes on rapid action. He sent his money on ahead of him to Faesulae, and after instructing his fellow-conspirators to kill Cicero and start fires in many different places in Rome on the same night, left the city to meet Gaius Manlius with the intention of collecting a second army immediately and making an attack while Rome was still alight.[12] So with the rods and axes blithely carried in front of him as though he were a proconsul he went to join Manlius, enlisting recruits on the way. As for Lentulus and the conspirators, they decided that once they knew that Catilina had reached Faesulae, Lentulus and Cethegus would wait at

Cicero's door in the morning carrying concealed daggers; when their rank secured them entry, they would talk about something or other to spin out the conversation in the courtyard, draw Cicero aside from the rest of the company, and kill him; then Lucius Bestia as tribune would immediately get criers to summon an assembly and accuse Cicero of being a coward, a warmonger, and a person who threw Rome into chaos when there was no crisis; and following Bestia's address to the people, that same night others would set the city alight in twelve places and loot the houses of the aristocracy and slaughter their owners.[13]

4. This was the plan formed by Lentulus, Cethegus, Statilius,[14] and Cassius,[15] the leaders of the rising, who then waited for the right moment; however, a delegation from the Allobroges, who had come to make a complaint against their own magistrates, <were in Rome and> were drawn into conspiring with Lentulus to arrange the revolt of Gaul against the Romans. With them Lentulus was sending to Catilina a man from Croton[16] called Volturcius, carrying an unsigned letter. But the Allobroges began to have doubts, and passed the information to Fabius Sanga, who was their patron in Rome as every community has its patron in the capital.[17] On hearing this from Sanga, Cicero arrested the Allobroges and Volturcius as they were leaving Rome and immediately brought them before the senate. They confessed to their compact with Lentulus' followers and when the latter were produced they maintained under cross-questioning that Lentulus had often said that there was a prophecy that Rome would have three Cornelii to rule her like kings, and of them Cinna and Sulla had already done so. 5. In the light of these words the senate stripped Lentulus of his magistracy and Cicero, after allocating the individual conspirators to the houses of the practors, immediately returned to the debate and took a vote on them. The senate-house was surrounded by uproar, as nothing was yet known for certain, and people were afraid of the conspirators. The slaves and freedmen of Lentulus and Cethegus collected a number of working men and came round by back streets to attack the houses of the praetors and rescue their masters. When he heard about this, Cicero ran out of the senate-house, stationed guards in the appropriate places, and returned to hurry on the debate. Silanus,[18] the consul-elect, spoke first (it is the Roman practice for the consul-elect to give his view first, I think because he will have to put into effect many of the decisions at issue and for this reason will treat each point with greater prudence and caution). Many of the speakers agreed with Silanus' view, that the men should be put to death. But when his turn

came to speak, Nero[19] argued that they should be kept in custody until Catilina had been destroyed by force and full information was available. **6**. Also Gaius Caesar – who enjoyed enormous popularity with the people and whom Cicero had therefore not been brave enough to challenge, although he was tainted with suspicion of complicity in the plot – proposed that Cicero should not inflict an irreversible punishment on distinguished men before their cases were argued and sentence passed; instead, he ought to distribute the accused around the towns of Italy, as he thought best, until Catilina had been suppressed and they could be brought back for trial. As this view appeared fair, the majority accepted it and completely changed their minds. However, Cato[20] then clearly revealed his suspicions of Caesar, and Cicero was apprehensive about the coming night and afraid that the crowd, which was in sympathy with the arrested men and was still waiting in suspense in the forum, in fear for itself and for the conspirators, would take some desperate action. These two persuaded the senate to condemn the accused without trial on the grounds that they had been caught red-handed. With the senate still in session Cicero conducted each of them from house to prison, and supervised their execution without informing the crowd. Then he made his appearance before the people in the forum and indicated that the conspirators' lives were over.[21] The members of the crowd dispersed, shuddering and giving thanks that they had escaped detection themselves. In this way the city recovered from the great fear which had hung over it that day. **7**. As for Catilina, he had by now armed about a quarter of the 20,000 men he had collected, and was withdrawing to Gaul to provide himself with further resources, when the other consul Antonius intercepted him at the foot of the Alps[22] and with little difficulty defeated a man who had impulsively embraced an enterprise to which he was unsuited and then without sufficient preparation put it to a still more impulsive trial of strength. Not that Catilina himself or any of the other aristocrats with him opted for flight; they died by charging into the enemy ranks.

Such was the end of Catilina's uprising, which nearly brought catastrophe on Rome. Cicero, who had been famous only for the force of his oratory, was much talked of as a man of action also. He was considered to have been without question the saviour of his disintegrating country, and thanks and praise of every description were heaped on him by the people's assembly. When Cato addressed him as the father of his country, everyone cheered. There is indeed a view that this complimentary title, which is still bestowed on emperors of our own day who seem to deserve it, started with

Cicero; for although these men are monarchs, it is voted to them not at the beginning of their reigns, along with their other titles, but later, and not by any means routinely, as a crowning testimonial to outstanding achievement.

8. Caesar had been chosen to go to Spain as praetor, but was detained for a while in Rome by his creditors as the debts he had incurred by his ambition far exceeded his assets.[23] This was when he is alleged to have said that he needed twenty-five million just to own nothing.[24] He came to whatever arrangements he could with those who were hounding him, and when he set foot in Spain, he paid no attention to municipal business or to hearing cases in court and so forth, because these matters were irrelevant to his plans. Instead, he gathered an army and attacked the remaining Spaniards piecemeal until he had brought Spain completely under Roman control and sent a great deal of money to the treasury in Rome. As a result the senate permitted him to triumph, and he was in the suburbs of Rome arranging the most splendid preparations for his triumphal procession at the time when candidacies for the consular elections were being declared. A candidate had to make his declaration in person, but if Caesar entered the city he could not go back out again and hold his triumphal procession.[25] As he was anxious for many reasons to press ahead and secure the office, and his procession was not ready, he sent a request to the senate to allow him to declare his candidacy in absence through his friends. He knew that although this was unconstitutional it had happened in previous cases. Cato opposed him and was filibustering the time away on the last day for the declaration of candidacies, when Caesar abandoned his triumph, hurried into the city, made his declaration to the magistrate, and waited for election day.

9. Meanwhile Pompeius, who had gained great prestige and power from his Mithridatic successes, wanted the senate to confirm the many grants he had made to kings and petty rulers and cities. A number of senators were jealous of this, and particularly Lucullus, Pompeius' predecessor in command against Mithridates, who was obstructing Pompeius and maintaining that he himself was responsible for the defeat of Mithridates because the king had been in a very weak state when he had left him to Pompeius. Lucullus was also being assisted by Crassus. So Pompeius, in his irritation, took Caesar into partnership and swore to help him win the consulship. Caesar at once made peace between him and Crassus. These three, the most powerful men in Rome, then pooled their interests. This coalition was treated in a volume by the Roman writer Varro, who called it 'The Beast with Three Heads'. The senate, who viewed them with suspicion, then elected Lucius Bibulus to be Caesar's colleague and oppose him.[26] 10. Straightaway there were disputes between them, and secret preparations were made to use armed force. Caesar, who was a good actor, addressed himself to Bibulus in the senate on the subject of co-operation, saying that they would damage the public interest if they fell out, and his sincerity proved convincing. He thus lulled Bibulus into unpreparedness and un-awareness of what was already going on, and after he had clandestinely got ready a large gang he introduced into the senate laws to better the condi-tion of the poor. One of these laws made distributions of land to the poor, and particularly of the very best land around Capua, which was leased out by the treasury; this was to go to fathers of three children, and made a vast crowd of people indebted to Caesar for the favour, as there suddenly ap-peared no less than 20,000 men, and these were only those who had three children each. When a large number of senators persisted in opposing the measure, Caesar pretended to be angry, saying that they were doing wrong, stormed out, and for the whole of the rest of the year refused to summon the senate but addressed the people from the rostra;[27] he asked Pompeius and Crassus in public for their opinion on the laws, and they supported them, and the people came to the voting carrying concealed daggers.   11. No one summoned the senate to meet, since it was unlawful for the other consul to do so,[28] so they gathered in Bibulus' house and although they took no action that matched Caesar's carefully planned use of force they considered that Bibulus should none the less put up some resistance to the laws and allow himself to be thought a loser rather than a quitter. Bibulus was persuaded, and burst into the forum while Caesar was still speaking. Scuffling and disorder broke out, and blows had already been exchanged when the men with daggers smashed Bibulus' fasces and insignia and wounded some of the tribunes who were with him. Undaunted, Bibulus bared his throat for the knife and at the top of his voice called on Caesar's friends to do the deed, saying, 'If I cannot persuade Caesar to do what is right, by dying like this I will lay the guilt and pollution at his door.' But he was reluctantly shepherded back to the nearby temple of Jupiter Stator by his friends. Cato, who was sent in next, pushed into the middle of the crowd like a young man and began to address them until he was lifted off his feet by Caesar's men and carried out. He gave them the slip and hurried back by a different way to the speakers' platform, where he abandoned as hopeless the idea of making a speech because no one would listen to him any longer, and rudely heckled Caesar until he was again picked up and thrown out, and Caesar secured approval for the laws.

12. In addition, Caesar made the people take an oath to regard the laws as permanently binding, and ordered the senate to do the same.[29] When Cato and many others resisted, Caesar proposed the death penalty for anyone who failed to swear, and the assembly confirmed this. The tribunes and everyone else were frightened into taking the oath forthwith, as further opposition was pointless when the law had been approved by the others.[30] One Vettius, an ordinary citizen, suddenly appeared in public with a drawn sword and maintained that he had been sent out by Bibulus, Cicero, and Cato to murder Caesar and Pompeius, and that he had been given his sword by Postumius, one of Bibulus' lictors.[31] From either side's viewpoint, the business was suspicious, and Caesar inflamed the feelings of the mob, but they postponed questioning Vettius until the next day. He was put under guard in the prison, but was murdered in the night. All kinds of speculations were rife, but Caesar persisted in alleging that this too had been done by those who were afraid of him, until the people agreed with him to protect those who had been the intended victims of the plot. Bibulus then abandoned everything, as though he were a private citizen, and did not emerge from his house for the whole of the rest of his magistracy.

13. For his part Caesar made no further investigations into the Vettius affair, now that he was the sole holder of political power. Apart from introducing laws to win the favour of the mob, he also confirmed all Pompeius' acts, as he had promised him. The equestrian class, whose status is intermediate between that of the people and that of the senate, were extremely influential on every question thanks to their wealth, the contracts they leased from the state for the collection of imposts and taxes due from the subject peoples, and the large number of highly committed staff they employed for this purpose. They had for some time been requesting the senate to remit part of the tax they had contracted for, but the senate kept postponing its response.[32] Caesar, who was by now bringing no business to the senate, but dealing only with the assembly, gave them a rebate of a third. Because they had received a favour which went far beyond what they had expected, they began to worship Caesar, and so by this one act of politics he acquired the support of another body of defenders, and one more powerful than the people. He also put on shows and wild-beast hunts beyond his

means, borrowing money for everything, and outdoing all previous performances in the lavishness of his preparations and the splendour of his gifts; in return for which he was appointed to govern Cisalpine and Transalpine Gaul for a period of five years and given four legions to command.[33]

14. Caesar realized that his absence from Rome would be prolonged, and that the resentment felt towards him would be all the greater because of the enormous favours he had granted. So he married his daughter to Pompeius (although she was engaged to Caepio),[34] in case Pompeius, in spite of being a friend, should envy the extent of his good fortune. He also placed the staunchest of his supporters in the magistracies of the coming year. He announced the election of Aulus Gabinius, one of his friends, as consul, and he himself married Calpurnia, the daughter of Gabinius' fellow-consul-elect Lucius Piso. This caused Cato to exclaim that political primacy was now procured by marriage-broking. As tribunes he chose Vatinius and Clodius Pulcher.[35] The latter had once been suspected of having sexual designs on Caesar's own wife when he was caught at a religious ceremony for women. Caesar himself, in spite of divorcing his wife, had taken no legal action against Clodius because of his great popularity with the people, but others prosecuted Clodius for sacrilege at the sacred ceremony and Cicero lent his support to the accusers.[36] Though called as a witness, Caesar did not denounce him, and now made him tribune as a way of plotting against Cicero, who was already blackening the compact of the three men to secure sole power. In this way their needs outweighed their grievances and they did a favour to one enemy in order to revenge themselves on another, and it seems that it was Clodius who first repaid Caesar by helping him to the Gallic command.[37]

15. Such were Caesar's actions as consul, and as soon as he laid this office down he immediately left Rome to take up the next. Clodius impeached Cicero for breach of the constitution because he had put Lentulus and Cethegus and their followers to death without trial. Although Cicero had displayed a most noble spirit of resolution in the affair itself, when it came to being prosecuted he collapsed; he put on miserable clothing and threw himself down covered in filth and squalor in front of those he met in the streets without even being ashamed of bothering people who knew nothing of the matter, so that thanks to his inappropriate behaviour he became a figure of fun instead of an object of pity.[38] Such was the state of cowardice he fell into over a single case which involved himself, a man who had all his life won a brilliant reputation in the cases of others; in like manner they say

Demosthenes the Athenian did not even wait for his case to be decided, but went into exile before the trial.[39] When Clodius even insulted him by interrupting his pleas in the street, Cicero abandoned all hope and like Demosthenes embraced exile voluntarily. A crowd of friends accompanied him out of the city, and the senate sent letters commending him to cities, kings and petty rulers. Clodius pulled down his town house and his country residences, and was so elated by this that he now compared himself to Pompeius, who was the most powerful man in Rome. 16. The latter, however, encouraged Milo, who was more audacious than Clodius and had succeeded* him in office, to hope for the consulship, and incited him to oppose Clodius; he also instructed him to put through a bill for Cicero's return, in the hope that when Cicero appeared he would be induced by his memory of what he had suffered to say no more about the current political scene, but would embroil Clodius in legal proceedings and other complications. And so Cicero, who had gone into exile because of Pompeius, returned home because of Pompeius, about sixteen months after his expulsion, and his town house and country residences were rebuilt at public expense. They say that when he was received at the gates in spectacular style by the entire population, the whole day was spent on greetings, as in the case of Demosthenes.

17. Caesar now had to his credit many brilliant achievements against the Gauls and the Britons, which I have described in my account of the Gauls, and came laden with riches to the part of Gaul which lies either side of the Po and borders on Italy, in order to give his army a short rest from continuous fighting. From here he sent generous gifts to a great many people in Rome, and the annual magistrates, other aristocrats, and all those who were going out to be provincial governors or army commanders came to meet him, individually. As a result he was surrounded by 120 lictors[40] and more than 200 senators, some repaying him for past favours, others trying to get hold of money, and still others wanting to procure some sort of advantage for themselves. All business now went through him, thanks to his large army, his financial strength, and his generous treatment of all. Pompeius and Crassus, his partners in power, also came to see him, and they jointly decided that Pompeius and Crassus should be consuls again and that Caesar should be voted another five years' governorship of the provinces he already held.[41] On these terms they separated. Domitius Ahenobarbus,[42] however, stood for the consulship against Pompeius, and when the appointed day came they both went down to the Campus for the election

while it was still dark. There was quarrelling and scuffling between the two sets of followers, until someone struck down Domitius' torch-bearer with a sword, following which they dispersed. Domitius himself was lucky to get safely back to his house, while some of Pompeius' clothing was carried home stained with blood; so close had both come to endangering their lives.

18. So Crassus and Pompeius were chosen consuls.[43] As they had promised, they voted Caesar his further five years, and at the allocation of the provinces and accompanying armies Pompeius chose Spain and Africa, but sent friends out to govern them while he remained in Rome, while Crassus took Syria and the nearby regions because he was keen to conduct a war against the Parthians which he thought would be simple, glorious, and profitable.[44] But there were many signs of ill-omen on his departure from the city; in particular the tribunes vetoed a war against the Parthians, who had done Rome no harm, and when Crassus would not yield, they pronounced a solemn public curse. Crassus paid no attention to this, and perished on Parthian territory along with his son of the same name and his army, of which not as many as 10,000 out of 100,000 escaped to Syria.[45] However, I will describe Crassus' disaster in the Parthian section of my work.[46] The Romans, who were in the grip of famine, chose Pompeius to oversee the corn supply and gave him twenty senators as assistants, as they had done in the case of the pirates.[47] By stationing them, as before, in the various provinces, he dealt with the problem, and soon filled Rome with plenty of grain, which raised his power and reputation to new heights.

19. It also happened that at this time Caesar's daughter, Pompeius' wife, died in pregnancy.[48] Now that the marriage connection was broken, everyone was afraid that Caesar and Pompeius, with their great armies, would very soon quarrel, particularly as the Republic had for some time been in a chaotic and unmanageable state. The magistrates were elected by violence or corruption, with criminal fanaticism and the use of stones or swords; the shameless offering and accepting of bribes now reached extreme levels, and the voters themselves came hired to the elections. There was even an instance of a stake of 800 talents deposited in connection with a consular election.[49] The consuls who were elected each year gave up hope of commanding armies and campaigning anywhere because they were shut out by the monopoly of power exercised by these three men; and the more degenerate among them made their profits instead from the treasury of the state and the election of their successors. For these reasons

honest men had altogether abandoned holding office, so that on one occasion the city was actually without magistrates for eight months because of
chaos of this sort, with Pompeius conniving at the situation because he
wanted to create the need for a dictatorship.[50] **20.** There was indeed a
widely aired view that the only cure for the present ills was a single holder
of power, and that someone ought to be chosen who was both influential
and tactful. By this they meant Pompeius, who possessed an adequate army,
seemed to have democratic leanings, and enjoyed the prestige to lead the
senate; he was also self-controlled and temperate in his private life, and
either was, or had the reputation of being, easily approachable. He professed
displeasure with this expectation, but in fact did all he could in secret to
bring it about and ignored the malfunctioning of the state and the subsequent lack of magistrates. Milo, who had helped him in the business with
Clodius and was popular with the people because of Cicero's return,
judged that in view of the present lack of magistrates it was a suitable
moment to run for the consulship. Pompeius however kept postponing the
elections[51] until Milo, depressed by Pompeius' disloyalty even to himself,
left the city for his home town of Lanuvium nineteen miles away (which
they say was the first city founded in Italy by Diomedes in his wanderings
after the fall of Troy). **21.** Clodius, who was returning on horseback from
a visit to his estates, met Milo at Bovillae, and the two of them, enemies as
they were, merely looked suspiciously at each other and passed by; but one
of Milo's slaves, whether by order or because he wanted to kill his master's
enemy, attacked Clodius and drove a dagger into the middle of his back.
Clodius, streaming with blood, was carried by his groom to the nearby inn,
where Milo and his slaves came after him and finished him off, if he was
not actually already dead. Milo claimed he had neither planned nor ordered
the murder, but as he was aware he was going to be accused of the worst, he
decided not to leave the job unfinished.[52] As the news of the event circulated in Rome, the stunned population stayed all night in the forum, and
in the morning Clodius' body was displayed on the rostra. It was then
snatched by Clodius' associates and some of the tribunes, and a crowd of
others along with them, and carried into the senate-house, either to do him
honour, because he was of senatorial family, or to reproach the senate for
their failure to act. The more reckless of the crowd heaped up the benches
and ceremonial seats of the senators to make him a funeral pyre, and its
flames consumed not only Clodius but also the senate-house and many
dwellings in the neighbourhood.

22. Milo was still so sure of himself that he was less concerned about the murder than annoyed by the honour paid to Clodius by his funeral. He therefore collected a mob of slaves and countrymen, distributed money to the city population, bought the support of a tribune, Marcus Caelius,[53] and returned with great bravado to Rome. As soon as he arrived, Caelius brought him into the forum to face the people he had bribed, as though they constituted an assembly. Caelius pretended that he was angry and was against allowing the trial to be put off, but hoped that if the crowd let Milo go he would be managing to sabotage the real trial. Milo said he had not planned the deed (arguing that he would not have set out to do this equipped with luggage-train and wife), and devoted the rest of his speech to attacking Clodius for being a thug and the friend of thugs who had gone so far as to burn the senate-house down over him; but while he was still speaking the rest of the tribunes and the part of the population which had not been bribed burst into the forum with weapons in their hands. Caelius and Milo escaped disguised as slaves, but there was great carnage among the others because the attackers made no further search for Milo's associates but killed anyone they met, Roman or foreigner indiscriminately, and particularly those who were conspicuous by their dress or their gold rings.[54] And because the government had broken down, the greater part of them, who were slaves, and armed when others were not, turned to wild looting under cover of the riot that had broken out. There was no crime they did not commit, and they even swept into private houses, going round and searching, they said, for Milo's associates but really for whatever they could easily steal. For many days they used Milo as their pretext for arson, stoning, and anything else they did.

23. The senate met in fear and looked to Pompeius to become dictator immediately, for the present situation seemed to them to need some such remedy. On the advice of Cato they chose him consul without a colleague, so that he could be in sole charge and have the power of a dictator, but still be accountable as a consul. He was the first consul to have two of the largest provinces[55] and an army and money and sole control of Rome by virtue of being consul without a colleague. To avoid being annoyed by the presence of Cato, he had it voted that Cato should annex Cyprus from King Ptolemy.[56] This was a measure already enacted by Clodius, because once when Clodius had been captured by pirates Ptolemy had been so mean that he had sent only two talents towards the ransom. Cato organized the administration of Cyprus after Ptolemy, on hearing of the decrees, had thrown his money into the sea and committed suicide. Pompeius proposed trials for other offences[57] and in particular for giving and receiving bribes (since he considered that this was the source of the malaise of the body politic and could be quickly cured), and laid down by law that anyone who wished could call a person to account for acts in the period between his own first consulship and the present.[58] This covered a little less than twenty years, during which time Caesar too had been consul. Caesar's friends suspected that Pompeius had gone back this far in order to insult and hurt Caesar, and urged him to remedy the present situation instead of raking up the past against so many distinguished men, among whom they named Caesar. As to Caesar, Pompeius was offended, saying that he was above suspicion and pointing out that his own second consulship lay within the period; and as to the great length of time, he said he had chosen it to facilitate proper reform of public life which had long been inflamed by the disease. **24.** With these words, he passed the law, and at once there was a mass of all kinds of court cases. To ensure that the jurors were not intimidated, he gave them his personal protection by stationing his soldiers around the court. The first to be condemned, in their absence, were Milo for the murder of Clodius, and Gabinius for flouting the law and for impiety, because he had invaded Egypt with his army in defiance of the Sibylline books and without legal authorization;[59] there followed Hypsaeus, Memmius, Sextus, and more after them, on charges of accepting bribes or distributing them to the mob.[60] When the crowd asked for the acquittal of Scaurus, Pompeius announced that they must accept the verdict; and when the people again shouted down the prosecution Pompeius' soldiers charged and there was some bloodshed. Consequently the people fell quiet, and Scaurus was found guilty.[61] All these men were condemned to exile, and Gabinius additionally to confiscation of his property. The senate warmly commended these actions and voted Pompeius two more legions and another period as proconsul of his provinces. Memmius had been found guilty of distributing bribes, but as Pompeius' law permitted him to escape sentence if he informed on another person, he summoned Pompeius' father-in-law Lucius Scipio[62] on a similar charge of bribery. When Pompeius responded to this by changing his clothing for that of a man on trial, many of the jurors also did likewise.[63] So Memmius took pity on the community and abandoned his prosecution.

25. Now that Pompeius had completed the reforms which required autocratic power, he made Scipio his colleague for the rest of the year. After

this others held the consular authority, but Pompeius exercised an un-
diminished degree of supervision and control; indeed at that time he was
the only person who mattered in Rome, as the senate strongly favoured
him, both because it resented Caesar for ignoring it during his own consulship, and because he had promptly tackled the unhealthy state of the Republic without being troublesome or oppressive to any of its members. The
exiles flocked to Caesar and advised him to beware of Pompeius because
the law against bribery was particularly aimed at himself.[64] Caesar reassured
them and spoke well of Pompeius, but persuaded the tribunes to propose a
law to permit him, Caesar, to stand *in absentia* for a second consulship. This
was passed without opposition while Pompeius was still consul. Caesar,
however, expected that the senate would make some move against him and
was afraid of becoming a private citizen at the mercy of his enemies.
Scheming, therefore, to retain power[65] until he was elected consul, he requested the senate to grant him a small extension of his existing governorship of Gaul, or of part of Gaul. When Marcellus,[66] Pompeius' successor as
consul, blocked this, Caesar is said to have replied to the person who
brought him the news by tapping the hilt of his sword and saying, 'This will
give me it.'

26. Caesar had established the town of Novum Comum at the foot of
the Alps and given it the Latin right, by which those inhabitants who hold
the chief magistracy every year become Roman citizens (for this is the
effect of being Latin).[67] One of them, who had held the office and was for
that reason considered to be Roman, was flogged by Marcellus for something or other in order to insult Caesar – for such a punishment was not
inflicted on Romans.[68] Furious with anger, Marcellus revealed his intention that the weals should be the mark of the non-Roman, and he told the
man to take them and show them to Caesar. Marcellus had already prefaced
this insulting piece of behaviour with a proposal to appoint governors to
succeed Caesar in his provinces before his time was up;[69] however, Pompeius stopped him with specious arguments and a show of goodwill, saying
that it was not right to humiliate a distinguished man who had rendered
much notable service to his country by slightly shortening his time, and
made it clear that Caesar ought to be relieved of his command immediately
his time ran out.[70] After this, bitter enemies of Caesar were elected to the
consulship for the following year, namely Aemilius Paullus and Claudius
Marcellus,[71] cousin of the previous Marcellus. Curio,[72] another passionate
enemy of Caesar's, who was very charming to the people and a most effect-

ive speaker, was to be tribune. Of these men, Caesar failed to bribe Claudius; but for 1,500 talents he bought Paullus' neutrality, and for still more Curio's co-operation, knowing that he was heavily burdened with debt. With the money Paullus erected a most beautiful building, the Basilica Paulli, for the benefit of the Roman population. 27. But Curio, to avoid being immediately detected in his change of allegiance, put forward a massive programme of road repair and construction, of which he himself would be in charge for a period of five years. He knew that none of this would actually happen, but hoped that Pompeius' associates would speak against it so that he would have a reason for turning against Pompeius. Things turned out as expected and he had his excuse for opposition, while Claudius proposed to send out successors to Caesar in his provinces, his time having indeed elapsed, and Paullus held his peace. Curio, apparently disagreeing with both parties, commended Claudius' motion, but by way of remedying a deficiency in it added a rider to the effect that Pompeius too should give up his provinces and army like Caesar; if this were done, he said, the Roman state would cease to be marred by fear and corruption. When a number of senators attacked this proposal on the grounds that it was unfair, since Pompeius' time had not expired, Curio revealed in clearer and blunter language his view that they ought not to send out successors to Caesar if they did not also impose them on Pompeius; his argument was that the mutual suspicion of the pair made any peace shaky unless they both went back to being private citizens. He said this knowing that Pompeius would not give up his authority. He was also aware that the people were not best pleased with Pompeius because of the bribery cases. As Curio's view was plausible, the people praised him for being the only person prepared to incur the enmity of both parties in a manner worthy of Rome, and on one occasion they even threw flowers as they escorted him home like an athlete participating in a hard and difficult contest; for at that stage no one thought that there was anything more dangerous than disagreeing with Pompeius.

28. Pompeius, who was lying sick elsewhere in Italy,[73] sent a clever letter to the senate, in which he praised Caesar's achievements and listed his own from the beginning, making the point that he had not deliberately sought his third consulship and the resulting provinces and army, but had been thought to deserve them when he had been called in to restore the state to health. As for the powers he claimed to have accepted unwillingly, 'I shall willingly', he said, 'surrender them to those who wish to take them back,

without waiting for my allotted time to expire.' The point of these words was to present a favourable picture of himself and arouse feeling against Caesar, who was refusing to surrender his command even when it was up. When he arrived in Rome Pompeius made other statements to similar effect and again promised to lay down his powers. As one who was Caesar's friend and kinsman, he asserted that Caesar too would be very happy to resign: his military campaigning had been arduous and had lasted for years against extremely warlike tribes, and now that he had made many additions to Roman territory he would come home to honours, thanksgivings and relaxation. He said this in the knowledge that successors to Caesar were about to be appointed while he himself would merely be bound by a promise. Curio exposed his manoeuvre by saying that what was needed was not a promise to resign his powers, but immediate resignation, nor should he deprive Caesar of his army before he himself also became a private citizen: in view of the private quarrel, it was no advantage either to Caesar or to the Roman people that such great powers should be exercised by a single person rather than be held by each of them as a safeguard against any threat to Rome from the other. Finally Curio came out into the open and mercilessly attacked Pompeius for aiming at absolute power which, given that he would not lay down his command now when he had Caesar to fear, he would never abandon. Curio's view was that if they did not comply both men should be decreed public enemies, and troops levied for use against them. By this proposal of course he very effectively concealed the fact that he had been bought by Caesar.   **29**. Pompeius was furious and made threats against him, and then immediately slipped out in extreme irritation to the suburbs.[74] The senate was now suspicious of both sides, but nevertheless thought Pompeius the more republican and disliked Caesar because he had ignored them during his consulship; and in fact they also thought it dangerous to dismiss the forces Pompeius commanded unless Caesar, who was outside the borders of the state and had greater ambitions, had first laid down his own command. The precisely opposite opinion was held by Curio, namely that they needed Caesar against Pompeius or else that both men should disarm simultaneously. Having failed to carry his point, he was in the act of dismissing the senate with nothing decided, as a tribune is entitled to do (and at this point Pompeius particularly regretted that he had restored the tribunate to its ancient competence after Sulla had reduced it to extreme weakness).[75] But as the meeting was breaking up, they passed just this one motion, that Caesar and Pompeius should each send one legion to Syria to garrison it because of Crassus' disaster. Pompeius craftily requested the return of the legion which he had recently lent to Caesar after a disaster suffered by two of Caesar's commanders, Titurius and Cotta.[76] Caesar, however, gave each man a present of 250 drachmae before he sent them off to Rome in company with another legion of his own.[77] As no threat appeared on the Syrian front these forces went into winter quarters at Capua. 30. The officers who had been sent by Pompeius to fetch them from Caesar spread a variety of anti-Caesarian reports and in addition maintained that his army, worn out by its lengthy labours and longing to be home, would come over to Pompeius when it had crossed the Alps. Such were their allegations, whether the reason was ignorance or bribery; in fact every single man was eager to serve Caesar to the limit of his endurance, because that is the soldier's code and because they had profited both from the ordinary spoils of war and from Caesar's additional generosity; for he gave freely, cultivating them for his own purposes, and although they realized what these purposes were they nevertheless stood by him. Pompeius, however, believed the reports and neither levied an army nor made any adequate preparations to counter a danger of this kind. In the senate each man was asked for his opinion. Claudius unscrupulously broke up the question and required them to state separately whether successors should be sent to Caesar and whether Pompeius should be stripped of his command. There was a majority against the latter proposal, and in favour of appointing successors to Caesar. Curio then put the question, whether they thought both of them should lay aside their powers, and twenty-two men voted against, but 370 preferred expediency to conflict and defected to Curio. Whereupon Claudius dismissed the senate, shouting, 'Have your way, be slaves to Caesar.' 31. An unfounded rumour then suddenly swept round that Caesar had crossed the Alps and was advancing on Rome. There was great commotion and general panic, and Claudius proposed that the legions at Capua should be mobilized against Caesar as an enemy of the state. When Curio opposed this on the grounds that the reports were untrue, Claudius retorted, 'If I am prevented by the vote of a public body from acting in the interests of the state, I shall act on my own authority as consul.'[78] With these words he hurried out of the senate to the suburbs,[79] accompanied by his fellow-consul, and proffered a sword to Pompeius, saying, 'I command you, I and my colleague here, to take the field against Caesar on behalf of our country; and for this purpose we grant you command of the forces which are now at Capua or elsewhere in Italy, and of any others you may wish to raise.' Pompeius accepted the responsibility, as it was an order from the consuls, but added, either to deceive or to produce the impression of acting correctly, 'If there is no better way.' Curio's authority did not extend outside the city (the tribunes not being allowed to go beyond the walls),[80] but he publicly deplored what had happened and demanded that the consuls should issue an edict that no one should yet comply with Pompeius' levy. But he had no success, and since his tribunate was on the point of expiry and he was in fear for his life and saw no further chance of helping Caesar, he made all speed to join him.

32. Shortly before this Caesar had crossed the sea from Britain[81] and gone by way of the Gauls on the Rhine to traverse the Alps with 5,000 infantry and 300 cavalry[82] and reach Ravenna, which bordered on Italy and was the last place in Caesar's province. He welcomed Curio warmly and confessed his gratitude for what had occurred, and weighed up the courses now open to him. Curio thought that he should assemble his whole army for a march on Rome, but Caesar still wanted to try for a settlement. He accordingly instructed his friends to agree on his behalf that he would give up his other provinces and military forces, and retain only two legions and Illyria with Cisalpine Gaul until he was elected consul. This seemed satisfactory to Pompeius, but the consuls were obstructive; so Caesar wrote to the senate, and Curio, after covering 270 miles in three days, delivered the letter to the new consuls as they entered the senate-house on the first day of the year.[83] It contained a solemn catalogue of Caesar's achievements from the beginning of his career, and the declaration that he was willing to lay down power at the same time as Pompeius, but if the latter continued in office he would not only refuse to resign but also come in haste to bring succour to his country and himself. On hearing this the senators all clamoured loudly, as though war had been declared, for Lucius Domitius to be Caesar's successor, and Domitius set out forthwith with 4,000 newly enrolled men.[84]

33. When Antonius and Cassius,[85] who had succeeded Curio as tribunes, supported Curio's policy, the senate, more partisan than ever, declared that its safety lay with Pompeius' army, while Caesar's was the enemy. The consuls Marcellus and Lentulus ordered Antonius and his followers to leave the chamber in case they came to some harm in spite of being tribunes. At this Antonius leapt up in fury from his seat with a great shout, and called upon the gods to witness against the consuls that violence was being done to the office of tribune, although this was sacred and in-

violable, and that he and his colleagues were being forcibly expelled for proposing a motion which they thought in the public interest, although they had caused no bloodshed or defilement. With these words he rushed out like a man possessed, prophesying war, slaughter, proscriptions, exile, confiscation of property and all the other ills they were about to suffer, and calling down solemn curses on those who were responsible. Curio and Cassius hurried out with him, because some soldiers of Pompeius' were already visible stationed round the senate-house. They left with great haste that very night to join Caesar, travelling secretly disguised as slaves in a hired vehicle. Caesar paraded them still dressed like this in front of his soldiers, whom he roused by saying that they, who had achieved so much, were now themselves considered enemies and that these important persons who had spoken up for them were being humiliatingly expelled.

34. Hostilities had now clearly begun and been declared on both sides, but the senate, thinking that Caesar's army would take some time to join him from Gaul and that he would never embark on such a great venture with only a small force, instructed Pompeius to conscript 130,000 Italians, particularly those whose previous military service had given them experience of war, and to enlist foreign troops of quality from the surrounding countries. They voted him the entire contents of the treasury as his warchest, and in addition their own private resources, if he should need them, to provide for the troops; and in their passionate frenzy to secure victory they demanded further contributions from the cities, requiring them with the greatest of urgency. As for Caesar, he had indeed sent for his army, but as he always exploited the dismay caused by his speed of execution and the fear engendered by his daring, rather than any strength created by his preparations, he decided to make the first move in this great war with his 5,000 men and forestall his enemies in occupying vital points in Italy.

35. He therefore sent his military tribunes ahead with a few of their boldest men, dressed in civilian clothing, to make their entry into Ariminum and suddenly seize the town – which lies within Italy and is the first town after you leave Gaul. In the evening he himself slipped out from dinner early, saying he felt unwell, and leaving his companions to go on eating climbed into a two-horse carriage and drove to Ariminum, followed at a distance by the cavalry. Coming at a fast pace to the river Rubicon, which is the frontier of Italy, he stopped and gazed at the stream, his resolve coming and going as he thought of all the troubles that would ensue if he

crossed this river under arms. By way of passing these reflections on to his companions, he said, 'If I refrain from this crossing, my friends, it will be the beginning of misfortune for me; but if I cross, it will be the beginning for all mankind.' And speaking like a man possessed, he crossed quickly, quoting the proverb 'Let the die be cast.' He resumed his fast pace from there, captured Ariminum at dawn, and continued his advance, stationing garrisons in strategic places and subduing all before him by force or generosity. In panic, people fled or migrated from all the little places, hurrying on in tears and disorder because they lacked any reliable information and believed Caesar to be driving forward with all his might at the head of a vast army.

36. When the consuls heard this news, they would not allow Pompeius a free hand to stabilize the situation in the light of his military experience, but urged him to leave Rome quickly and recruit in Italy, as if the city would very soon be captured. Because Caesar's invasion had taken place much sooner than they had expected, the remainder of the senate were frightened. They were still unprepared, and in panic they repented of having rejected Caesar's proposals: they only found them reasonable when fear had turned their partisanship into a readiness to take wise decisions. Many marvels and signs from heaven occurred: the sky seemed to rain blood, ancient statues of the gods sweated, several temples were struck by lightning, and a mule foaled; and there were many other prodigies which portended the destruction and permanent transformation of the constitution. By public proclamation prayers were offered up, as in times of crisis. The people, reminded of the sufferings of the time of Marius and Sulla, clamoured for Caesar and Pompeius to abandon the politics of personal power because this was the only way of stopping war, and Cicero urged that mediators be sent to Caesar.   37. The consuls opposed all proposals, which caused Favonius to mock Pompeius for something he had once said by calling on him to stamp his foot on the ground and produce armies from it. To which Pompeius replied, 'You will have them, if you will follow me and think it no disaster to abandon Rome, and even, if need be, Italy as well.' He explained that it was not in estates and houses that men's power and freedom lay, but that men, wherever they might be, had power and freedom always with them; when they took their revenge they would take their houses back as well. After making this point and issuing threats against those who were staying behind, if from concern for their estates or fixed assets they were found wanting in the struggle for their country, he quit the

senate and immediately left Rome for the army at Capua, followed by the consuls. For a long time the others could not decide what to do, and they spent the night talking together in the senate-house. At daybreak the majority none the less left the city and tried to catch up with Pompeius.

38. Caesar trapped and besieged in Corfinium his appointed successor as proconsul, Lucius Domitius, who had with him less than his full force of 4,000 men. Domitius attempted to escape, but was caught at the gate by inhabitants of the town and brought to Caesar.[86] As Domitius' army was inclined to join him, Caesar eagerly accepted them in order to encourage the other Pompeians to do likewise; Domitius himself he dismissed unharmed with his money, to go wherever he liked – hoping perhaps that he would stay with him out of gratitude, but not forbidding him to go to Pompeius. This all happened extremely quickly, and Pompeius moved rapidly from Capua to Luceria* and from there to Brundisium in order to cross the Adriatic to Epirus and make that his base for his war preparations. He wrote to every people, king, city, governor, and petty ruler asking them to contribute as speedily as possible what each could towards the war, which they promptly did. His own army was in Spain, ready to move wherever it might be needed.   39. He gave some of the legions he had with him at the time to the consuls to take across in advance to Epirus from Brundisium, and they sailed across at once without incident to Dyrrachium. (There are people who think that Dyrrachium and Epidamnus are the same, but they are mistaken, for this reason: Epidamnus, king of the non-Greek people of this region, founded a city by the sea and called it Epidamnus. Dyrrachus, his daughter's son – allegedly by Neptune – provided the city with a port and called it Dyrrachium. This Dyrrachus was attacked by his brothers, and Heracles, who was returning from Erytheia,[87] fought on his side in exchange for part of his territory. This is why the people of Dyrrachium reckon Heracles as their founder, because he shared their land, and though they do not exclude Dyrrachus they are prouder of Heracles because of his divinity. The story is that in this battle Dyrrachus' son Ionius was killed in error by Heracles, who gave his corpse a funeral and then threw it into the sea so that the sea might be named after him. Later the Briges,[88] returning from Phrygia, took possession of the area and of the city, and after them came the Taulantii, an Illyrian people, and after the Taulantii another Illyrian people, the Liburni, who had fast ships and plundered the surrounding regions. As a result the Romans term fast ships 'Liburnians', because these were the first they met. Some Liburni who had been expelled from

Dyrrachium called in the Corcyraeans, who were masters of the sea at the time, and drove out the Liburni. The Corcyraeans planted some settlers of their own among them, and so the port is considered to be Greek; but because they thought the name ill-omened, they changed it and called the port Epidamnus from the upper town, as did Thucydides. However, the old name has won, and Dyrrachium the place is called.)[89]

40. Some of Pompeius' army had sailed with the consuls to Dyrrachium, but he assembled the rest at Brundisium to wait for the return of the ships which had taken the consuls across. He beat off Caesar's attacks on the walls, and dug trenches in the streets,[90] until his fleet came back. He then put out to sea in the early evening, leaving his bravest men on the walls, who themselves sailed out with a fair wind when night fell. In this way Pompeius left Italy and crossed to Epirus with his entire army. Caesar was baffled as to which way to turn and from what point to start the campaign. He saw that support was flowing to Pompeius from all quarters, and he was afraid that Pompeius' army in Spain, which was large and well trained through long service, would attack him from the rear if he pursued Pompeius. So he decided to march to Spain and destroy it first, but divided his force into five. To protect Italy, he left one detachment in Brundisium, one in Hydruntum, and one in Tarentum. He sent another force under Quintus Valerius[91] to take possession of the grain-producing island of Sardinia, and Asinius Pollio to Sicily. Here Cato was in charge, and when Cato enquired whether it was from the senate or the people that he had authority to trespass in another man's sphere, Pollio replied, 'The master of Italy has sent me on this errand.' Cato answered to the effect that out of consideration for the provincials he would make no resistance, and sailed to Corcyra and thence to join Pompeius.

41. Caesar made haste to Rome, where with a variety of hopes and promises he reassured the people, who were terrified by the recollection of their sufferings at the hands of Sulla and Marius, and signalled his generosity towards his enemies by pointing out that he had captured and dismissed even Lucius Domitius unharmed and with his money. He broke open the locks on the state treasury and when Metellus,[92] one of the tribunes, tried to prevent him, threatened him with death. He also removed some of the untouchable money which is said to have been deposited a long time ago for use against the Gauls with a public curse against its disturbance for any reason other than the outbreak of a Gallic war. Caesar, however, claimed that he had himself neutralized the Gauls and released Rome from the

curse. He put Marcus Aemilius[93] in charge of the city and the tribune
Marcus Antonius in charge of Italy and its military forces. Overseas, he ap-
pointed Curio governor of Sicily in place of Cato, Quintus[94] governor of
Sardinia, sent Gaius Antonius[95] to Illyria, and entrusted Cisalpine Gaul to
Licinius Crassus.[96] He also gave orders for two fleets to be built as quickly as
possible, on the Adriatic and Tyrrhenian coasts, and appointed as admirals
Hortensius and Dolabella[97] while the ships were still under construction.

42. After strengthening Italy in this way to make it inaccessible to Pompeius, Caesar proceeded to Spain, where he met Pompeius' generals
Petreius and Afranius. In the first engagements against them, he had the
worst of it, but later they fought on nearly equal terms around the town of
Ilerda. Caesar made camp on some crags and obtained supplies by a bridge
over the river Sicoris. After a sudden flood had swept away the bridge,
Petreius' men killed a large number of Caesar's troops who were cut off on
the other side, and Caesar himself, along with the rest of his army, suffered
intense hardship from the difficult terrain, and hunger, and enemy action,
and the fact it was still winter. The operation was indistinguishable from a
siege, until with the arrival of summer Afranius and Petreius started to
march to the interior of Spain to recruit more soldiers. Caesar, always anticipating them, blocked off the passes with entrenchments, prevented
them from going on, and actually surrounded a detachment of theirs which
had been sent ahead to occupy a site for a camp. These raised their shields
above their heads, in token of surrender, but Caesar neither took them
prisoner nor put them to death; instead, he bid for popularity with his enemies everywhere by letting them go back safely to Afranius' army. As a
result there was constant fraternization between the camps and, among the
rank and file, talk of an understanding.   43. As for the senior officers, Afranius and others thought they should abandon Spain to Caesar and get
away unscathed to join Pompeius, but Petreius disagreed and raced through
the camp killing any of Caesar's men he could find fraternizing, and personally putting to death one of his own officers who tried to stop him.
Consequently the soldiers were still further angered by the grimness of
Petreius, and their sympathies turned towards Caesar and his generosity.
Then in a place where Caesar had prevented his opponents even from getting water, Petreius, who was at his wits' end, came with Afranius to negotiate with Caesar in full view of the two watching armies. The agreement
was that they for their part would abandon Spain to Caesar, while Caesar
would escort them unharmed to the river Var and allow them to make

their way from there to join Pompeius. When he reached the river Caesar called a meeting of those of them whose homes were in Rome or Italy and addressed them as follows: 'Enemies (I still use the word to make my point clearer to you), I did not kill either those of you who were sent ahead to seize a site for a camp and surrendered to me, or the rest of your army after I had blocked your access to water, in spite of the fact that Petreius had previously slaughtered some of my men who were cut off on the opposite bank of the Sicoris. If you feel any gratitude to me for these actions, let all Pompeius' soldiers know about them.' With these words he dismissed them, and appointed Quintus Cassius to govern Spain.

44. So much for Caesar's operations. In Africa, Attius Varus was the Pompeian commanding officer, and allied with him was the Numidian king Juba. On Caesar's side, Curio sailed from Sicily to attack them with two legions, twelve warships, and a large number of merchantmen. Putting in at Utica, he routed a few Numidian cavalry in a brief engagement near the town and consented to accept a salutation as *'Imperator'*[98] from his troops while their weapons were still in their hands. (It is a great honour for a general to be so saluted by his army, as though his men are certifying that he is a commander worthy of them; in the past this honour was accepted by generals for any great success, but I am informed that the qualification is now 10,000 enemy dead.) While Curio was still on his way across from Sicily, his opponents in Africa, expecting that his ambition would make him occupy Scipio's Camp because of the splendour of Scipio's great achievements,[99] poisoned the water. Nor were they disappointed, as Curio took up his position there and his troops immediately fell sick. When they drank the water, their vision became fogged and a deep torpid sleep ensued, which was followed by frequent vomiting and spasms affecting the whole body. Because of this Curio moved his camp alongside Utica itself, leading his army, weakened by ill-health, through a formidable and extensive marsh. When the news of Caesar's victory in Spain reached them, their morale recovered, and they were drawn up for battle in a restricted space by the sea. In the fierce fight which ensued, Curio lost one man to Varus' 600 dead and an even greater number of wounded. 45. On Juba's approach a false report swept ahead that because his kingdom was being pillaged by neighbouring peoples he had turned back at the river Bagradas, which was not far away, leaving his general Saburra at the river with a few troops. Curio believed this story, and in the middle of the morning, in the heat of

summer, took the best of his army by a sandy and waterless route to attack
Saburra. If there were any rivulets there in winter, they were dried up by
the heat of the sun, and the river was held by Saburra and by the king himself, who had not gone away. Thwarted, Curio took up a position on some
high ground, his men suffering from fatigue and thirst and the stifling heat.
When the enemy saw their condition, they crossed the river ready for
battle. Curio then descended quite senselessly and over-confidently at the
head of his enfeebled force, and was encircled by the Numidian cavalry. He
gave ground for a while, concentrating his men together, but when he got
into difficulties retreated again to the high ground. As defeat started to
loom, Asinius Pollio made his escape with a few men to the camp at Utica,
in case Varus concluded there had been a reverse over on the Bagradas and
attacked; for his part, Curio fell fighting without any thought for his own
safety, together with all the men who were with him, so that no one apart
from Pollio returned to Utica. This was how the battle on the Bagradas
ended, and Curio's head was cut off and brought to Juba.

46. In the camp at Utica, when the disaster became apparent, the admiral
Flamma at once sailed away with his fleet without picking up anyone who
was on shore; but Asinius took a small boat and went round the merchant
ships anchored off-shore asking them to sail further in and take the soldiers
on board. Some of them came in at night to do this, but under the press of
men trying to climb in the ships' boats sank, and the majority of the soldiers who were lifted off had valuables with them, for the sake of which the
merchants threw the men overboard. Such was the fate of those who
reached the ships, but those who remained ashore had similar experiences
during the course of the night. In the morning, they surrendered to Varus,
but Juba arrived, lined them up round the town wall and slaughtered them,
saying he was finishing off his victory, and taking no notice of even Varus'
protestations. In this way the two Roman legions which had sailed to
Africa with Curio were completely lost, along with their cavalry and light-
armed support and their camp attendants, and Juba returned to his own
territory in the belief that he had done Pompeius a very great service.

47. About this time Antonius was defeated in Illyria by Octavius, who
was Pompeius' commander operating against Dolabella.[100] Another part of
Caesar's army mutinied at Placentia, shouting at their officers that their dis-
charge was overdue and that they had not received the 500 denarii which
Caesar had promised them as a donative at Brundisium. On hearing this
Caesar hastened urgently from Massilia to Placentia and spoke to the still

mutinous troops as follows: 'You are as aware as I am of the speed with which I handle everything. If the war goes slowly, it is not our fault, but the fault of our enemies who have run away from us. In Gaul, you gained great profit from my leadership. You swore to follow me for the whole of this war, not simply a part of it, and now you abandon us in mid-course and mutiny against your officers and think it right to give orders to men from whom you ought to accept them. I call myself as a witness to the regard in which I have held you up to now; but I shall put into practice our ancient custom and have lots drawn for every tenth man to die in the Ninth legion, since the Ninth chiefly instigated the mutiny.' A cry of despair at once went up from the entire legion and when its officers fell to their knees and begged for mercy Caesar gradually and reluctantly gave way. He relented to the extent that only 120 men, thought to be the ringleaders, were to draw lots, of whom the twelve selected would be executed. Of these twelve it transpired that one had not even been in the camp when the mutiny occurred, and in his place Caesar put to death the centurion who had reported him.

48. In this way the mutiny at Placentia was brought to an end and Caesar went on to Rome, where the terrified people elected him dictator without any decree of the senate or any nomination from a magistrate.[101] Whether Caesar declined the office because it might cause resentment, or because he did not want it, he held it for only eleven days (as some believe) and proclaimed himself and Publius Isauricus[102] consuls for the following year. He appointed or changed provincial governors, making the decisions himself: Marcus Lepidus to Spain, Aulus Albinus to Sicily, Sextus Peducaeus to Sardinia, and Decimus Brutus to the newly conquered part of Gaul.[103] He distributed grain to the hungry city population and agreed to their request to let the exiles, apart from Milo, return. When they also asked for a cancellation of debts, because of the wars and upheavals and the consequent fall in the value of property put up for sale, instead of granting their demand he appointed valuers of what was for sale, and the debtors had to hand over this property to their creditors in lieu of cash. After taking these measures, at about the winter solstice he issued orders for his army to assemble at Brundisium and made his own departure in the Roman month of December without waiting for the imminent new year in spite of his office.[104] The people followed him, begging him to make peace with Pompeius, for it was plain that the victor would seize power for himself alone.

*

49. So Caesar set out, never relaxing his driving urgency, but all the while Pompeius had been building ships and collecting more money and an ever larger army. He captured forty of Caesar's ships in the Adriatic, and watched against his crossing; and when he put his army into training, he ran and rode with them and took the lead in endurance, allowing for his age, so that he gained their good will without any difficulty and they all flocked to see Pompeius' practice as though it was a show. At that time Caesar had ten legions of infantry and 10,000 Gallic cavalry, while Pompeius had five legions from Italy, with which he had crossed the Adriatic, together with their supporting cavalry, and two legions from the Parthian front, the survivors of Crassus' campaign, < . . . > and another group of those who had invaded Egypt with Gabinius,[105] making a total of eleven legions of Italian troops and about 7,000 cavalry. He had allied troops from Ionia, Macedonia, the Peloponnese, and Boeotia; also Cretan archers, Thracian slingers, and Pontic javelin-throwers; and for cavalry, there were some from Gaul, others from eastern Galatia, Commagenians sent by Antiochus, Cilicians, Cappadocians, a contingent from Lesser Armenia, Pamphylians, and Pisidians. He did not intend to use them all for battle, but for garrison duty, fortification work and other support for his Italian army, so that no Italian should be diverted from fighting. Such were his land forces, and he also had 600 warships complete with their crews, of which a hundred included Roman marines and were thought to be of particularly high quality, together with a large additional number of merchantmen and transports. There were many admirals for the squadrons, under the overall command of Marcus Bibulus.

50. When the preparations were complete, he called a meeting of the whole army together with the senators and members of the equestrian order who were with him, and addressed them thus: 'Men, the Athenians too abandoned their city when they were fighting for their freedom against the invader, because they thought a city consisted not in its buildings but in its men. Once they had taken this step they quickly recaptured their city and gave it greater renown. In the same way our own ancestors abandoned Rome in face of the invading Gauls, and Camillus hastened from Ardea to save it. Every sane man thinks his own country is wherever freedom is. It was with this in mind that we crossed from Italy and came here. We did not abandon our country; on the contrary, our purpose was to equip ourselves properly here on her behalf and protect her from someone who has long had designs on her and has bribed his way to the sudden capture of Italy.

This is a man you have decreed a public enemy, who at this very moment is despatching governors to your provinces and installing his appointees, some to control Rome, others Italy. Such is his effrontery in stripping the people of power. And if this is what he does when he is still at war and still apprehensive, and is (God willing) going to be brought to justice, is there any savagery or violence we can expect him to renounce when he wins? In addition, he has as his accomplices in treason men who have been bought with money acquired by him from your province of Gaul, men who prefer to be his slaves rather than enjoy equality with him.   51. However, I have not abandoned, and would not abandon, the struggle on your behalf and in your company. As general and soldier, I offer myself to you. I have never yet been defeated, and I pray that if I possess any experience and good luck in war, the gods will bring it all to bear on our present troubles. I pray too that I may be as auspicious a leader for our country now she is in danger as I was when she was enlarging her empire. We ought to draw encouragement both from the gods and from the arguments in favour of the war, which embody a just and splendid regard for the constitution of our fathers, and also from the extent of the resources we currently have, both naval and military. These are constantly growing and will be further increased when we go into action. Virtually all the peoples of the east and the Black Sea, Greek and non-Greek alike, are with us; and every king friendly to the Roman people or to me is making contributions of troops, weapons, provisions, or other supplies. Go then to your task with a spirit worthy of your country and yourselves and me; remember Caesar's violence and wrongdoing, and carry out your orders with alacrity.'   52. When he had finished, the entire army and the members of the senate who were with him – a numerous and very distinguished group – cheered and told him to lead them wherever he liked. Since it was still a bad time of year for weather and the coast lacked anchorages, he thought that Caesar would wait for the end of winter before sailing across, and that because he was consul he would use the time to deal with the business of his office. Pompeius therefore gave instructions to his admirals to keep watch at sea and distributed his army in winter quarters in Thessaly and Macedonia.

Such was Pompeius' rash misjudgement of the future course of events. Meanwhile Caesar, as I have said, hurried to Brundisium about the time of the winter solstice, judging that surprise would best strike terror into his enemies. He found neither provisions, nor equipment, nor a complete army gathered in Brundisium, but none the less he called an assembly of

those who were present and said: 53. 'Men, my partners in this great enterprise, I shall not be prevented from starting out either by the winter
season or by the slowness of other people or by lack of the appropriate
stores. In place of all these I think swiftness of action will serve. I believe
that we who are the first to gather here should first leave behind our slaves,
our pack-animals, our baggage, in fact everything necessary to ensure that
the ships we have here will accommodate us, and we should then embark
immediately, on our own, and make our crossing, in order to catch the
enemy off guard. Against the winter weather we can set our good fortune,
against our low numbers our daring, and against our lack of supplies our
enemies' abundance of them, which it is quite possible for us to seize as
soon as we land if we realize that failure will mean we have none of our
own. Let us attack their slaves and equipment and provisions while they are
passing the winter under cover. Let us attack while Pompeius imagines that
I am spending the winter like him or am occupied with consular pomp and
sacrificial ritual. You understand war, and I put it to you that the mightiest
weapon of war is surprise. It will also be the most signal honour for us to
pre-empt the glory of the events that are about to unfold, and to make
everything over on the other side secure before the arrival of the forces
which will directly follow us. Speaking for myself, at this critical moment
I would rather be afloat than making a speech, so that Pompeius, who imagines I am dealing with consular business in Rome, could set eyes on me;
as for you, although I know you are not difficult to convince, I none the
less await your answer.'

54. The whole army shouted enthusiastically for him to lead them on,
and he took five legions of infantry and 600 picked cavalry straight from
the speaker's platform down to the sea, where he had to ride at anchor because of rough weather. It was the winter solstice and to his distress and
frustration the wind kept preventing him from sailing for so long that he
was still in Brundisium on New Year's Day. Then two more legions arrived, and he embarked them too and put to sea in stormy weather, on
board merchantmen because the few warships he had were protecting Sardinia and Sicily. The gale carried him off course to the Ceraunian ranges,[106]
but he sent the ships back at once to fetch the rest of the army from
Brundisium and himself made his way by night along a rough, narrow path
to the town of Oricum with his force split into several parts because of the
difficulty of the terrain, and forming an easy object of attack if they had
been seen. At dawn his troops were with some difficulty reunited, and the

commander of the Oricum garrison, on being urged by those in the town not to resist the arrival of a Roman consul, handed over the keys to Caesar and stayed with him in a position of honour.[107] On the far side of Oricum Lucretius and Minucius,[108] who had eighteen warships guarding grain that was aboard transports, scuttled the transports to prevent Caesar capturing them, and made off to Dyrrachium. From Oricum Caesar pressed on to Apollonia, where the inhabitants welcomed him and the garrison commander Staberius fled. 55. Caesar assembled his army and reminded them that because of their speed of action they had, with some luck, survived the storm, made themselves masters, without warships, of a certain amount of the sea, taken Oricum and Apollonia without a blow, and were in occupation of enemy territory, just as he had said, while Pompeius was still unaware of the fact. 'If we can go on', he said, 'and take Dyrrachium, Pompeius' arsenal, before he arrives, we shall be in possession of all that they laboured throughout the summer to collect.' With these words he led them immediately on a forced march to Dyrrachium, without resting either by day or night. Pompeius, who had been alerted by this time, made a rival march from Macedonia, also with extreme haste, because he thought it of the utmost importance, as indeed it was, to protect his own supplies. He cut down the trees along the route to make the going difficult for Caesar, removed bridges over rivers, and burnt all the available food stocks. If either army saw flames or smoke or a cloud of dust in the distance, they assumed their opponents were responsible and were spurred to rivalry as though it were a race. They could find time for neither food nor sleep, and the eager, urgent shouts of the men who were leading them along with lights caused much disturbance and nervousness, as they believed the enemy drew ever nearer. From sheer exhaustion some threw away what they were carrying, or hid in ravines and were left behind, exchanging their terror of the enemy for instant rest.

56. These hardships were suffered by both armies, but none the less Pompeius reached Dyrrachium first and camped by the town. He sent ships and recaptured Oricum, and blockaded the coast more intensively with his fleet. Caesar made camp with the river Alor[109] lying between himself and Pompeius. Cavalry detachments crossed the river and clashed with each other individually, but the full armies did not engage because Pompeius was still training his recruits and Caesar was waiting for his troops from Brundisium. He judged that if they sailed across in merchant ships in the spring they would not elude Pompeius' triremes, which would put out to

the open sea in strength to maintain the blockade, but if they crossed in winter when the enemy were lying in wait among the islands, they might perhaps evade them or even force their way through because of the size of their ships and the strength of the wind. He therefore summoned them to come urgently. When they did not put to sea, he decided to go secretly across in person to his army, because he thought he was the only man who could easily make them sail. He told no one of his plan, but sent three slaves down to the river a mile and a half away to get a fast light boat ready with a first-rate skipper, pretending it was for a messenger of his.   **57**. Telling his companions to go on with the meal, he left the mess-tent on the pretext of being tired, put on ordinary clothes, and immediately mounted a carriage and drove to the boat in the guise of Caesar's messenger. He gave his subsequent commands through his slaves, remaining anonymous under his cloak in the darkness. Although there was a gale blowing, the slaves encouraged the skipper by saying that this very fact would give them the best chance of avoiding the nearby enemy. The skipper forced his way down the river under oars, but when he came to the mouth the wind and the rough sea were beating the current back. Urged on by the slaves, he made violent efforts, but as the ship failed to win any ground he grew tired and gave up. Then Caesar revealed himself and shouted to him, 'Be brave! Face the waves! Your cargo is Caesar and Caesar's luck.' The skipper and the rowers were amazed. They were all stirred to make a great effort and by brute force the ship began to leave the river. But the wind and the waves were always threatening to lift it and drive it on to the banks, until near dawn the crew became afraid that in daylight they would be visible to the enemy, and Caesar, angry with the malevolence of the divine power, permitted the ship to turn round and she ran up river before the strong wind. Some of them were astonished at Caesar's daring, but others criticized him for an exploit that did credit to a soldier but not to a general.   **58**. He realized he could not go unobserved a second time and ordered Postumius to make the crossing in his place and tell Gabinius to bring the army across the Adriatic without delay; and if Gabinius would not obey, to give the same message to Antonius, and thirdly to Calenus.[110] And if all three refused, there was another letter to the soldiers themselves, saying that all who wanted to should follow Postumius to the ships, put to sea, and come in to land wherever the wind took them without worrying about the ships because Caesar needed men, not ships. Thus Caesar abandoned calculation and put himself in the hands of chance.

Pompeius, who was eager to anticipate such developments, advanced ready for battle. Two of his soldiers, who were in the middle of the river trying to find out where it was easiest to cross, were killed by a single soldier of Caesar's who ran to attack them. Pompeius then broke camp because he thought this a bad omen, and everyone blamed him for missing an excellent opportunity.

59. When Postumius arrived in Brundisium after his crossing, Gabinius would not accept the orders and led volunteers by way of Illyria, without stopping anywhere. They were almost all killed by the Illyrians, and Caesar was too busy to take revenge.[111] Antonius embarked the others in the ships and sailed past Apollonia under full canvas in a strong wind. About midday the wind dropped and twenty of Pompeius' ships, which had put out to search the open water, sighted the enemy and gave chase. Because it was calm Antonius' men were afraid that the warships would hole or sink them with their rams. They made the appropriate preparations, and were already putting slings and missiles to use, when the wind suddenly burst on them more strongly than before. Their great sails unexpectedly filled with wind again and they sailed safely away. The warships were left labouring in the breaking waves and the wind and the big swell, and made vain efforts to prevent themselves being tossed on to a rocky and harbourless coast, after capturing two of Caesar's ships which had been driven on to a mudbank. Antonius reached harbour with the others at a place called Nymphaeum.

60. Caesar now had all his forces with him, as did Pompeius. They were encamped opposite each other, with numerous detachments of troops in forts along a line of hilltops.[112] Frequent clashes took place around each of these forts as the combatants dug fortifications to try and block each other in, and completion and construction of these continued on both sides under the most difficult conditions. In these clashes, Caesar's army was having the worst of it at one of the forts, when a centurion called Scaeva, who had been fighting spectacularly bravely, was hit in the eye by a javelin and sprang forward with a motion of his hand to indicate that he wished to say something. Silence fell, and he called out to one of Pompeius' centurions who was famous for his bravery, 'Save a man like yourself, save your friend, and send someone to lead me by the hand, as I am wounded.' Two soldiers ran forward thinking Scaeva was going to desert, but he killed one of them before the man realized the deception, and cut off the arm of the other at the shoulder. He did this because he despaired of saving either his own life or the fort. Shamed by this episode, the rest acquired fresh enthusi-

asm and the fort was saved. Its commander Minucius also suffered greatly. His shield is said to have been hit by 120 javelins, while his body was wounded in six places, and he too lost an eye. Caesar rewarded these men with many decorations.

In response to an offer of betrayal that had been made from Dyrrachium, he went as arranged by night with a few men to the gates and the shrine of Artemis < . . . >[113]

The same winter Scipio, Pompeius' father-in-law, brought him another army from Syria, and Gaius Calvisius,[114] who confronted him in Macedonia, was defeated with the loss of a legion, all but 800 men.

61. Caesar could get no supplies by sea because Pompeius enjoyed naval supremacy. Consequently his army was starving and made loaves from plants. Deserters brought loaves of this sort to Pompeius because they thought it would cheer him to see them, but he was not pleased, and said, 'Look at the kind of wild beasts we are up against!' Of necessity Caesar now gathered his whole army with the intention of forcing Pompeius to fight, even though he had no wish to. Pompeius, however, took possession of the majority of the forts, which had been left empty, and stayed quiet. Very annoyed at this, Caesar ventured on a difficult and surprising project, of walling in Pompeius' whole camp inside a continuous fortification stretching from the shore round to the shore. Even if he failed, he would win great renown from the attempt, for the circuit was 1,200 stades.[115] So he started on the enormous work, and Pompeius built counter-fortifications and counter-earthworks, so that they cancelled out each other's efforts. They had one great battle, in which Pompeius decisively routed Caesar's men, pursued them to their camp, captured a large number of their standards, and only just failed to take the eagle (which is the most august symbol of all for the Romans) when its bearer threw it over the defences to the men inside.[116] **62.** As the rout became obvious, Caesar brought up another force from the opposite direction, but this also was so terrified that when the men caught sight of Pompeius in the distance they failed either to maintain their present position at the gates, or go inside in an orderly manner, or obey commands. They turned round and fled, each where he could, impervious to shame or instructions or rational thought. Even though Caesar went round among them, cursing them and pointing out that Pompeius was still a long way away, they threw away the standards and took to their heels under his very eyes. Some looked impotently down at the ground, covered with shame and embarrassment, such was their confusion. One man actually inverted his standard and menaced his general with its butt-end. He was cut down by Caesar's bodyguard, but the troops streaming into the camp did not even man the defences. They abandoned everything, and left the ditch and bank unguarded. I think that if Pompeius had made a concerted attack on the fortification he would have taken it by superior force and finished the whole war by this single deed, if Labienus, led astray by heaven, had not urged him to turn on the fugitives. At the same moment Pompeius hesitated, perhaps because he suspected that the absence of defenders on the fortification was a trap, perhaps because he thought an attack was irrelevant as the war was already decided. So he turned to pursue the men outside. He killed many more of them, and in the two battles on that day he captured twenty-eight standards. He also lost his second chance of delivering the decisive blow. They say that even Caesar admitted this and said, 'Today my enemies would have finished the war if they had a commander who knew how to win a victory.'

63. Pompeius wrote to the kings and to all the cities exaggerating the extent of his victory, and believed that Caesar's army would immediately desert to him, because it was suffering from famine and demoralized by defeat, and particularly so its officers, because they feared retribution for their own mistakes. But they were divinely inspired to repent and feel ashamed of their failure, and when Caesar was lenient in his criticism and offered to pardon them they became still more angry with themselves and in a paradoxical reversal of attitude told him to make them draw lots according to the ancestral custom and put a tenth of them to death. When Caesar would not listen, their feelings of shame were reinforced. They agreed that they had done him wrong without good reason and clamoured for the standard-bearers to be put to death, alleging that they themselves would never have fled if the standards had not already been thrown away. But when Caesar would not consent even to this, and reluctantly punished a few men, such a wave of enthusiasm swept over them then and there in response to this self-restraint that they asked him to lead them immediately against the enemy. They pressed him with intense eagerness, pleading with him and promising to redeem their failure by winning a splendid victory. They turned to each other unprompted and swore an oath by individual companies, in front of Caesar himself, that they would not return from battle unless they were victorious. 64. His companions accordingly encouraged him to put such a change of heart and such eagerness on the part of the army to good use. However, to the rank and file he said that he

would lead them against the enemy when circumstances were more propitious, and told them not to forget their eagerness, and to his companions he made the point that he must first eradicate the fear of defeat that was widespread among the troops and destroy the surging confidence of the enemy. He further admitted that he had changed his mind about camping near Dyrrachium, where all Pompeius' supplies were, when the right course was to lure him elsewhere to suffer the same difficulties as themselves.

With these words he immediately set out for Apollonia, and from there retreated to Thessaly, slipping away under cover of night. Gomphi, a small town, shut him out, and in anger he took it and handed it over to his soldiers to sack. As one would expect of men who had been starving, they stuffed themselves endlessly with everything and became disgracefully drunk, particularly the Germans who were quite ridiculous when they were under the influence. I think that an attack by Pompeius then would have achieved a notable result, if out of contempt for Caesar he had not completely neglected to follow him until he encamped near Pharsalus after seven days' rapid marching. It is said that at Gomphi, among notable tragedies, there were to be seen, in a doctor's surgery, the corpses of the distinguished elders of the town with drinking-cups lying beside their unhurt bodies; twenty of them lay on the ground as if they had succumbed to drunkenness, and one, who had surely been giving them the poison, was sitting beside them on a chair, like a doctor.

65. When Caesar moved off, Pompeius called a council of war. Afranius thought he ought to shadow Caesar with his fleet, an arm in which he was far superior, and use their supremacy at sea to harass him, on the run and in difficulties as he was. Meanwhile Pompeius himself should rapidly lead the land forces to Italy, which was sympathetic to him and clear of enemy, and after making himself master of it and Gaul and Spain launch another attack on Caesar from a base in his own native land, the country which was the mistress of the world. But Pompeius disregarded this advice, which would have been the best, and listened to those who said that hunger would soon make Caesar's army desert to him, or that what remained to be done after the victory at Dyrrachium would give them little trouble. Also, the opposite course was highly disgraceful, to leave Caesar to run away and for the winner to run away just like the losers. Pompeius sided with the second view, out of respect particularly for the eastern peoples who had supported him, and from a wish not to risk any disaster to Lucius Scipio, who was still

in Macedonia. Intending to exploit his army's keenness for battle, he came up with Caesar and took up a position opposite him near Pharsalus, with nearly four miles between the camps.

66. Pompeius had supplies coming from every direction. The roads and harbours and strongpoints had been so organized beforehand that he had a continuous supply by land, and by sea every wind brought him something. Caesar, on the other hand, was suffering and had only what he could with difficulty find and seize. Even under these circumstances no one deserted him and his men longed with supernatural enthusiasm to come to grips with the enemy. They considered that their ten years' practice made them a great deal better at fighting than men who were still raw recruits, but that advancing age meant that they had less endurance for exhausting tasks of entrenchment, or circumvallation, or foraging. They were tired, and on the whole it seemed preferable to them to do something <*rather than*> perish by inaction and famine. Pompeius realized this and thought it risky to stake everything on a single engagement against men who were well trained and desperate and against Caesar's famous good luck. It would be more effective and less dangerous to wear them down through lack of supplies, as they were neither in control of productive territory, nor did they have the use of the sea, nor did they possess ships to make a speedy escape. On the basis of this excellent analysis he decided to conduct a war of attrition, and reduce his enemies from victims of hunger to victims of disease.   **67**. But he had around him a great number of senators of equal status to himself, and also the leading members of the equestrian order, and kings, and minor potentates. Some of them lacked experience; some were unreasonably elated by the successes at Dyrrachium; some also by their superiority in numbers; and some were thoroughly tired of the war and keen to put an unduly rapid end to it. They all urged Pompeius to fight, constantly drawing his attention to Caesar, who kept on forming up his army and offering battle; but from that very fact he drew the lesson for them, that Caesar was forced to do this because of his shortage of supplies, and precisely for this reason it was the right moment for them to do nothing, because Caesar was driven to act by necessity. All the troops protested against his decision, because they were over-elated by the events at Dyrrachium, and so did the men of rank, who mocked him for his love of office and said that he was deliberately delaying so that he could give orders to so many men of equal status to himself. They also called him King of Kings, and Agamemnon, because Agamemnon too had kings under his command in war. Pompeius therefore abandoned his own analysis and gave in to them, a victim of divine malice both on this occasion and on the others[117] throughout the war. Indeed, he was unnaturally slow and sluggish about everything, and prepared unwillingly for battle, to his own detriment and that of those who were misleading him.

68. That night, three legions of Caesar's were going out to forage. Caesar sent them out to bring in food in the belief that Pompeius was correct to hang back, and thinking that under no circumstances would the latter change his plan; but when he was informed of the preparations he was delighted at the pressure which he guessed the army had applied to Pompeius, and very quickly recalled all his own forces and made counter-preparations. He offered sacrifice in the depth of the night, invoking Mars and his own ancestress Venus (the Julian family is believed to descend, with an alteration in the name, from Aeneas and Aeneas' son Ilus)[118] and vowed, if he was successful, to make a thank-offering by building a temple to her in Rome as Bringer of Victory. When a meteor flashed across from Caesar's camp to Pompeius' and was extinguished, Pompeius' companions said something brilliant would accrue to them from the enemy, while Caesar said he would descend on and extinguish the Pompeian cause. The same night some of Pompeius' sacrificial animals escaped and were not recaptured, and a swarm of bees, which are a sluggish form of life, settled on the altar. A little before dawn a panic seized his army, and after going round himself and quieting it he fell into a deep sleep. When his companions roused him, he kept repeating that he had just dreamed he was dedicating a temple in Rome to Venus the Bringer of Victory.   **69.** Because they were ignorant of Caesar's prayer, Pompeius' friends and his whole army received this as welcome news. In other ways too they went into battle with unreasonable enthusiasm and contempt for the enemy as though victory was already won. Many of them had actually already adorned their tents with laurel, the symbol of victory, and their slaves were preparing a splendid banquet. Some were even quarrelling with each other over Caesar's high priesthood. Pompeius, with his experience of war, turned away and although his feelings of anger were justified he nevertheless concealed them and from hesitation and fear held his tongue, like a man no longer giving the orders, but receiving them and forced to act in every respect against his better judgement. Such was the extent of the despondency that overwhelmed this man, whose record was outstanding and who had enjoyed the best of fortune in every undertaking until that day. Perhaps it was because he had failed to convince them of his view of what needed to be done, and was gambling with the lives of so many men and with his own reputation for being hitherto undefeated. Or perhaps some more supernatural foreboding of the imminent disaster troubled him as he was about to be totally deprived of his great power that day. Anyway, after simply saying to his friends, 'Whichever side wins, today will see the start of terrible and unending troubles for Romans', he drew his forces up for battle. Some people believed that this extremely revealing remark slipped out under the influence of fear, and thought he would not have surrendered his supreme power even if he had been victorious.

70. As to the size of the army, there are various contradictory reports. I follow those Roman authorities who give the most plausible figures for the troops from Italy, whom they consider the decisive element;[119] they do not enumerate the allied element, or record their names, because they were foreigners and contributed little in the way of support. I think, then, that Caesar had 22,000 Italian troops, of whom about 1,000 were cavalry, and Pompeius more than double this number, of whom about 7,000 were cavalry. Thus in the view of the most reliable writers 70,000 men born in Italy joined battle with each other. Some put the total lower, at 60,000, others exaggerate and make them number 400,000. And of these some say that Pompeius outnumbered Caesar by half as much again, others that about two-thirds of all the combatants were his. Such is the extent of the disagreement over the true figure, but whatever the reality, each of the two commanders placed his chief hopes in his Italian troops. As to allied forces, Caesar had < . . . > Gallic cavalry and another contingent of horse from Transalpine Gaul; and also Greek light infantry from Dolopia, Acarnania, and Aetolia. This was the total of Caesar's allies, but Pompeius had all the peoples of the east in considerable strength, some fighting on horseback, others on foot, and from Greece there were the Spartans, commanded by their own kings,[120] and the rest of the Peloponnesians and the Boeotians with them. The Athenians, in spite of having announced that they were under the divine protection of Demeter and Persephone and would do no harm to either army, had also taken the field because they were attracted by the glory of participating in a war that was being fought for the mastery of the Roman state. 71. Apart from the Greeks, there were contingents from nearly all the peoples as you go in a circle along the coast towards the east: Thracians, Hellespontines, Bithynians, Phrygians, and Ionians; Lydians, Pamphylians, Pisidians, and Paphlagonians; the people of Cilicia, Syria, and

Phoenicia, the Jews and the neighbouring Arabs, Cypriots, Rhodians, Cretan slingers, and various other islanders. Also present were kings and petty rulers with their armies, Deiotarus the tetrarch of eastern Galatia and Ariarathes the king of Cappadocia. The Armenians from the near side of the Euphrates were commanded by Taxiles, those from beyond it by Megabates, deputizing for King Artapates,[121] and other lesser rulers shared in the effort. It is said that Pompeius was also reinforced by sixty ships from Egypt, sent by the king and queen, Cleopatra and her brother who was still a boy. But these did not fight with him, because neither did the rest of his fleet, which stayed inactive at Corcyra. I think it was particularly foolish of Pompeius to ignore his navy, where he was much superior. With it he could have completely deprived the enemy of imported supplies, but he engaged in an infantry battle against soldiers who boasted of their recent feats of endurance, and when it came to fighting behaved like wild beasts. It seems that although he was on his guard against them at Dyrrachium he was led astray by some heaven-sent madness, which could not have come at a better time for Caesar. Because of it Pompeius' army became thoughtlessly confident, overrode their commander, and turned to their task like men with no experience of war.

However, this was arranged by God to bring into being the imperial power that now embraces all. 72. At the time, both men assembled and encouraged their armies. Pompeius spoke to this effect: 'My fellow-soldiers, you are generals who have chosen the toil of battle, not subordinates who have it thrust upon them. I still wanted to wear Caesar down, but you yourselves have invited this contest. Like marshals of the battle, behave as the superior force to the inferior. Despise them as victors do the vanquished, as young men do the old, and as the unwearied do the exhausted. You have on your side all this strength, all these resources, and your consciousness of the cause. For we fight for freedom and for country, backed by the constitution, our glorious reputation, and so many men of both senatorial and equestrian rank, against one man who would pirate supreme power. Advance then, as you have been demanding. Advance with high hopes, picturing to yourselves their rout at Dyrrachium and the number of standards we captured on a single day as we defeated them.'

73. Such was Pompeius' speech. Caesar addressed his own men like this: 'My friends, we have already overcome the worst. We shall be fighting against men, instead of against hunger and want, and today will settle everything. Remember, I beg, the promise you made at Dyrrachium and the

oath you swore to each other, beneath my very eyes, that unless you were victorious you would not come back from battle. Men, here is the enemy we have come from the Pillars of Hercules to confront. Here are the people who have fled from Italy to escape us. For ten years we have striven manfully, we have brought numerous wars and countless battles to a successful conclusion, and we have subjected 400 Spanish, Gallic, and British peoples to our country's rule. For this, they tried to disband us without recognition, bereft of our triumph and our rewards. Neither by inviting them to do what is right, nor by obliging them, have I succeeded in changing their minds. You know the cases of those I have released unharmed in the hope that they would show us some fairness. Remember all these things today, and remember too, if you have any experience of it, my concern for you, my trust in you, and my generosity in rewarding you.   74. It is not difficult for veterans with a long record of endurance to get the better of raw recruits with no experience of war, especially when they are inclined to youthful insubordination and disobedience towards their commander, who I am informed is apprehensive and reluctant to join battle. The tide of his luck is past its flood, he has become hesitant and dilatory in everything, and he is no longer so much a giver as a taker of orders. And it is only to the Italians that even these considerations apply. You need not think about the allies, nor take any account of them; in short, you need not fight against them. They are slaves from Syria and Phrygia and Lydia, always ready to flee and always ready to be enslaved. I know well, as you shall soon see for yourselves, that not even Pompeius will trust them with a place in his line of battle.[122] I ask you to engage only with the Italian troops, even if the allies hang on your heels and harass you like a pack of dogs. When we have gained the day, let us spare the Italians because they are our kin, but instil fear into them them by destroying their allies. Most of all, though, I would like to be sure that you remember what you agreed, and have chosen total victory or death. As you go out to battle, pull down your own ramparts and fill in the ditch, so that if we fail to win we shall have nothing, while the enemy will see that we lack a camp and understand that necessity compels us to make our quarters in theirs.'

75. After saying this he nevertheless posted a guard of 2,000 of the oldest men on the tents. The others, as they went out, pulled down the earth bank in complete silence and filled up the ditch with it. When Pompeius saw this, he understood their act of daring, although others thought they were preparing for a retreat. He groaned inwardly to think that he and his men

were about to fight hand-to-hand with wild beasts in spite of possessing an effective drug against such beasts, namely hunger. But there was no going back now, as things were on a razor edge. So he left 4,000 Italians to guard his camp and drew up the rest between the town of Pharsalus and the river Enipeus, where Caesar was similarly marshalling his forces opposite. Each of them put the Italians in the centre, in three divisions slightly separated from each other, and the cavalry in squadrons on the wings.[123] Archers and slingers were interspersed everywhere among the troops. Such was the disposition of the legions, on which each of them pinned his chief hopes. The allies were ranged by themselves, as if for display. Pompeius' were noisy and polyglot, and from them he picked the Macedonians, Peloponnesians, Boeotians, and Athenians to station next to the block of legions, because he was convinced of their quietness and good discipline. He ordered the others, as Caesar guessed he would, to lie in wait in their units outside the main formation; then, when battle was joined, they were to outflank the enemy, pursue them while inflicting as much damage as they could, and sack Caesar's own camp, unprotected as it was by any ditch.

76. The commanders of Pompeius' main formation were his father-in-law Scipio in the centre, Domitius on the left, and Lentulus on the right; Afranius and Pompeius took overall responsibility for the army.[124] On Caesar's side the commanders were Sulla, Antonius, and Domitius,[125] and he himself took up his position on the right wing with the Tenth legion, as he usually did. When they saw this, the enemy redeployed the best of their cavalry against this wing to secure numerical superiority and if possible outflank it. Noting the manoeuvre, Caesar laid an ambush of 3,000 of his bravest infantry, whom he ordered to jump up when they saw the enemy coming round, leap in among them, and thrust their spears directly in the faces of their opponents. He said that young men who were inexperienced and still in the bloom of their youth would not be able to stand the danger to their faces. Such were the plans they devised against each other, while they moved round through their armies, dealing with urgent details and encouraging each man to be brave. They also issued passwords, Caesar 'Venus, Bringer of Victory', Pompeius 'Hercules the Unconquered'.

77. When they were quite ready, they waited like that for a long time in deep silence, still hanging back in hesitation and eyeing each other to see which of them would be the first to begin the battle. They were sorry for the ordinary soldiers, for never previously had such large Italian forces met on a single field, and they felt pity for the courage of two armies of

outstanding quality, particularly when they saw Italian lined up against Italian. As they stood on the brink of disaster, the ambition which blazed up and blinded both of them was extinguished and turned to fear. Cool reason purged them of their thirst for fame, estimated the danger, and assessed the cause – that it was through a struggle for supremacy that a pair of men were risking not simply becoming the lowest of the low if they were defeated, but losing their own lives, and that because of them this vast number of brave men were doing the same. They were struck by the thought that they had at one time been friends connected by marriage, who had often co-operated to secure status and power, but were now drawing their swords on each other and leading the men under their command into similar sacrilege, men who belonged to the same nation, city, tribe, or family; even brother did not fail to fight brother at that battle, for as you would expect when so many tens of thousands of men from a single nation attacked each other, extraordinary coincidences were numerous. Full of these thoughts, each of them was overwhelmed by a change of heart that could no longer be put into effect, and was reluctant to begin so great a gamble, knowing that he would become on that day either the most or the least significant person on earth. It is said that they both actually shed tears.

78. As they still hesitated and watched each other, the day was wearing on. All the Italian troops waited quietly, exactly in their places, but Pompeius noticed that his allied contingents were becoming disordered as a result of the delay and was afraid that they would initiate a collapse of discipline before fighting started. So he was the first to give the signal for battle, and Caesar sounded in answer. Immediately the trumpets, of which there were many in the different units of so large an army, roused the men with their high-pitched blasts, and the criers and officers hurried among them urging them on. They advanced proudly towards each other in amazement and in the profoundest silence, as they were used to war and had experienced many such encounters. And now, as they closed, first there were hails of arrows and stones, and the cavalry, who were a little in front of the infantry, engaged in skirmishes and charges against each other. Then as Pompeius' cavalry gained the upper hand they began to outflank the Tenth legion, whereupon Caesar signalled to the troops lying in ambush. They sprang to their feet and attacked the cavalry, striking upwards with their spears at the faces of the riders, who could not withstand either the fanaticism of their assailants or the thrusts directed at their eyes and faces, and retreated in disarray. Then Caesar's men, who had themselves feared being

outflanked, immediately began to encircle the enemy infantry on that wing, now that it was deprived of cavalry. **79**. When he was told of this, Pompeius instructed his infantry not to make any more rushes forward, or run out in front of the ranks, or throw their javelins, but to stand in their allotted positions with their weapons at the ready and repel the enemy hand-to-hand with their spears.[126] Some authorities approve of this tactic of his as excellent when an army is being outflanked, but Caesar condemns it in his letters. In his view the impact of the weapons is more forcible, when they are thrown, and the spirit of the men keener, when they charge; but if they stand still they lose heart, and because they are stationary, like targets, they are easy marks for their oncoming opponents. And so it proved, he says, in this case also, for he and the Tenth legion, after outflanking the troops of Pompeius' left, which was now bare of cavalry support, had nothing to fear from any quarter and hurled volleys of javelins at their sides until on attacking the disordered ranks they routed them and set victory in train. In the rest of the battle-line all manner of death and injury was still being inflicted. From such a great legionary army, engaged on such dreadful work, there rose not a cry nor a scream as men were wounded or killed, but only grunts and groans as they fell in perfect order where they had been stationed. Like the audience at a battle-spectacle, the allies were amazed at the discipline shown. Their wonder prevented them from finding the nerve to charge on to Caesar's tents, although these were guarded by a mere handful of the more elderly men, and they simply stood there astounded. **80**. When Pompeius' left wing crumbled, even then the legionaries retreated step by step still locked in battle, while the allies fled headlong, making no resistance and shouting 'We've lost.' They were the first to take their own tents and fortifications as though these belonged to an enemy, and they sacked and pillaged from them whatever they could carry away with them in their flight. By now the remainder of the Italian legionaries, who had seen the reverse in this part of the battlefield, were also in gradual retreat. At first they kept formation and continued to defend themselves as far as was possible; but when they were pressed by enemies who were fired by success, they turned to run. Caesar then made a particularly shrewd move to avoid another trial of strength and ensure that the result decided not an isolated battle, but the whole campaign. He sent heralds into the ranks all over the battlefield, who ordered the victors not to harm their fellow-countrymen, but attack only the allies. They also approached the defeated troops, urging them to stay where they were and not be afraid. As each man heard the message from his neighbour, he came to a halt, and this was now the distinguishing mark of Pompeius' legionaries, that they stood there unafraid, although otherwise, being Italians, they had similar equipment and spoke a similar language to their enemies. Caesar's men, sweeping through them, began to kill the allies, who were unable to resist, and the most tremendous carnage ensued.

81. When Pompeius saw the rout, he became deranged. He withdrew on foot to his camp and when he reached his tent sat there without uttering a word, as they say happened to Telamonian Ajax at the siege of Troy, the victim of heaven-sent madness in the midst of his enemies. As for the rest of his men, very few entered the camp, because Caesar's proclamation caused them to halt without fear, and when their enemies had run past they scattered group by group. As the day was nearing its end, Caesar ran frantically among his troops, begging them to make a further effort and take Pompeius' fortifications too, and pointing out to them that in the event of an enemy recovery they would be the victors of a single day, but if they took the enemy's camp, they would have settled the campaign by this one exploit. Accordingly, he stretched his hands out in entreaty to them and was the first to lead the charge. For their part, their limbs were tired, but their spirits were lifted by rational calculation and by their general's example. They were also buoyed up by their success so far and by the hope that they would take the defences of the camp and capture its considerable contents, and when men are hopeful, or favoured by good fortune, they pay little heed to weariness. So they attacked the camp too and set about the task with great contempt for the defenders. When Pompeius was informed, he only broke his strange silence to exclaim, 'So they're at our camp as well?', and with these words he changed his clothing, took horse with four companions, and rode without stopping until he reached Larisa at first light. Caesar, as he had threatened when exhorting his army, spent the night within Pompeius' fortifications; he himself dined on Pompeius' food, his whole army on that of Pompeius' men.[127]

82. The number of dead on either side, at least of Italians (for no enumeration at all was made of the allies, on account of their number and the low regard in which they were held), was thirty centurions and 200 (or according to others 1,200) legionaries from Caesar's army, and ten senators, including Lucius Domitius who had been appointed Caesar's successor in Gaul, and about forty distinguished members of the equestrian order from Pompeius'; as for the rest of his army, some inflate the casualties and put

them at 25,000, but Asinius Pollio, who was one of Caesar's subordinate officers in the battle, records that 6,000 Pompeian dead were found.

This was the result of the famous battle of Pharsalus. Caesar himself carried off from all the palm for bravery, in both first and second place, as everyone agrees, and alongside him the Tenth legion. In third place came Crassinius, a centurion. As Caesar was leaving camp for the battle, he asked Crassinius what he thought would happen, and in a loud voice Crassinius made the memorable reply, 'We shall win, Caesar, and whether I live or die I shall earn your approval today.' The army testified that he had switched from rank to rank like a man possessed and that his exploits were many and distinguished. When a search was made for him and he was found among the dead, Caesar adorned his body with the decorations of valour, buried him with them and made a special tomb for him near the mass grave.

83. Never slackening his pace, Pompeius made haste from Larisa to the sea, where after getting into a small boat he chanced to meet a ship that was sailing past, which took him to Mytilene. Here he picked up his wife Cornelia and embarked on four triremes, which had been sent him by the people of Tyre and Rhodes. He ignored Corcyra (once again) and Africa, where he had an intact fleet and another large army, and set off eastwards to the Parthian king, in the belief that through him he would win everything back, although he kept his intentions secret until he reluctantly admitted them to his companions when they were in Cilician waters. They told him to beware of the Parthian, who had recently been the target of Crassus' designs and was still furious after this business, and warned him against taking his beautiful wife Cornelia among foreigners who lacked self-control, especially as she had been married to Crassus.[128] When he proposed as second choices Egypt or Juba,[129] they rejected Juba as unworthy and agreed with him on Egypt, because it was close, and a great kingdom, and was still prosperous, and strong in ships, and food, and money; and its rulers, even if they were still children, were friends of Pompeius through their father.[130]

84. For these reasons Pompeius sailed to Egypt. Cleopatra, who shared the throne with her brother, had recently been ejected from Egypt and was gathering an army in Syria. Her brother Ptolemy was waiting for her attack at Mount Casius in Egypt, and by some divine chance the wind caused Pompeius to make his landfall there. Seeing a large army on shore he stopped his ship, and guessing, as was the case, that the king was there, sent a message about himself and mentioned his friendship with the king's father.

Ptolemy himself was about thirteen, and his guardians were Achillas, who had charge of the army, and the eunuch Pothinus, who had charge of the finances. They arranged a council to discuss what to do about Pompeius. One of those present was the rhetorician Theodotus of Samos, the king's tutor, who proposed an evil deed, namely that they should entrap and kill Pompeius to win Caesar's gratitude. His view was approved, and a wretched little boat, with some of the king's attendants on board, was sent out to Pompeius, as the water was shallow and difficult for large ships. Sempronius, a Roman who was then serving in the king's army but had once been under Pompeius' command, delivered greetings from the king to Pompeius and told him to take passage across to the boy as to a friend. At the same time as this was going on, the whole army was being drawn up along the beach as if to honour Pompeius, and the king could be seen quite plainly in the middle, wearing his purple robes.   **85**. Pompeius was suspicious of everything – the parade of the army, the meanness of the boat, and the fact that the king had neither come to meet him in person nor sent anyone important. Recalling to himself these lines from a play of Sophocles,[131]

> *The man who makes his journey to a despot's court*
> *Is but the despot's slave, however free he came,*

he stepped into the boat, becoming even more suspicious when no one said a word as they made the passage. Whether he recognized Sempronius because the latter was a Roman and had served under him, or whether he guessed it from the fact that he alone was standing up and that it was his military training which forbade him to sit beside a general, he turned to him and said, 'Don't I know you, fellow-soldier?' Sempronius then nodded assent, but when Pompeius turned away he immediately struck the first blow and then the others followed his example. Pompeius' wife and companions, who watched this from a distance, uttered cries of distress, and sailed hurriedly away as though they were escaping from an enemy country, stretching out their hands in prayer to the avenging gods of broken truces.   **86**. Pompeius' head was cut off by Pothinus' entourage, who kept it for Caesar in the belief that they would receive an enormous reward (although in fact he took appropriate vengeance on them for their terrible deed), and someone buried the rest of his body on the shore and erected a simple grave on which another hand inscribed:

RICH WAS THIS MAN IN TEMPLES
BUT POOR NOW IS HIS TOMB.[132]

In time this grave was entirely hidden by sand, but it and the bronze statues of Pompeius later erected at Mount Casius by his relatives, which had all been defaced and put away in the part of the sanctuary[133] not open to the public, were searched for and found in my time by the Roman emperor Hadrian when he was visiting Egypt.[134] He cleared Pompeius' grave for it to become famous again, and restored the images of the man himself.

Such then was the end of Pompeius' life. He was a man who had brought major wars to an end, had hugely benefited the Roman Empire, and had earned the name 'the Great' as a result. He had never previously lost a battle, but had been undefeated and attended by the greatest good fortune ever since his youth. Between the ages of twenty-three and fifty-eight he never ceased to exercise power in autocratic fashion, but because of the contrast with Caesar he enjoyed the reputation of governing democratically.

87. Lucius Scipio, Pompeius' father-in-law, and such other prominent men as had escaped from the battle at Pharsalus hastened to Corcyra to join Cato, who had been left in command of the rest of the land forces and 300 triremes. In this they displayed better judgement than Pompeius. The most distinguished of them shared out the fleet: Cassius[135] set off for the Black Sea, hoping to reach Pharnaces and make him rise against Caesar, while Scipio and Cato sailed for Africa, relying on Varus and his army and on the assistance of the Numidian king Juba. Pompeius,[136] Pompeius' elder son, together with Labienus and Scapula,[137] hurried to Spain, which they took as their area of responsibility, and here they instigated the revolt of the province against Caesar, raised another army from the Iberian and Celtiberian population and from slaves, and engaged in further preparations. These were the extensive forces still left from those that Pompeius had assembled, yet under the influence of divine madness he ignored them and fled. The group in Africa chose Cato to command them, but Cato would not consent because ex-consuls were present who outranked him, a person who had only held the praetorship in Rome. So Lucius Scipio assumed overall command, and there too a large army was assembled and trained. Thus in Africa and Spain two very considerable forces were being forged against Caesar.

88. Following his victory Caesar himself spent two days at Pharsalus, offering sacrifice and allowing his army to recuperate after the battle. Here he also discharged the Thessalians and granted them independence for having fought alongside him. In addition he gave the Athenians the pardon they requested, observing, 'How often is the glory of your ancestors going to save you from self-destruction?' On the third day, on receiving news of Pompeius' flight, he rode eastwards. He made the passage of the Hellespont in small boats because he was short of triremes, and was in the middle of crossing when Cassius appeared with his squadron of triremes, pressing on to reach Pharnaces. Although Cassius could have been successful with his numerous triremes against small boats, he was reduced to helplessness by fear of Caesar's celebrated, and at the time terrifying, good fortune and thought that Caesar was deliberately sailing to attack him. So he stretched out his hands, from a trireme to a small boat, and begged for forgiveness and surrendered his fleet. Such was the power of Caesar's reputation for success; for I can see no other explanation, and I think he never had a greater piece of luck at a desperate moment than when Cassius, the most aggressive of men, in command of seventy triremes, could not even bring himself to engage when he happened to catch Caesar unprepared. Yet this man who so cravenly surrendered to Caesar through fear alone when he chanced to meet him on the water later killed him in Rome when he had already become master of the state; and from this very fact it is plain that Cassius' fear on the present occasion was caused by the good fortune which favoured Caesar.[138]

89. When Caesar had crossed the Hellespont after this unlikely escape, the Ionians and Aeolians and all the other inhabitants of the great promontory (called collectively Lower Asia) sent him deputations of entreaty, and he granted them pardon. After discovering that Pompeius was bound for Egypt, he crossed to Rhodes but did not wait even there for his army which was on its way to him in separate detachments. With the men he had, he embarked on the triremes of Cassius and the Rhodians, and without revealing to anyone where he was sailing put to sea at dusk, having given instructions to the other helmsmen to follow the light on his own ship and, when daylight came, its flag. To his own helmsman, when they were well offshore, he gave the command to set course for Alexandria. After three days on the open sea he was at Alexandria, and was received by the king's ministers since the king was still at Mount Casius. At first, because he was accompanied by so few men, he pretended to be relaxed. He

received all and sundry in a friendly way, toured the city and admired its beauty, and stood in the crowd to listen to the philosophers. He therefore gained the goodwill and gratitude of the Alexandrians for not interfering with their affairs. 90. But after his army sailed in, he punished Pothinus and Achillas with death for their crime against Pompeius (Theodotus, who escaped, being later discovered in Asia and crucified by Cassius). When the Alexandrians rioted as a result, and the king's army came to attack him, there were various struggles around the palace and on the beaches beside it. While escaping from it, Caesar was forced into the sea and swam a long way underwater. The Alexandrians captured his cloak and hung it up as a trophy. Finally, there was a battle on the Nile between him and the king, which he won decisively. Nine months slipped away on this business, before he installed Cleopatra on the throne of Egypt in her brother's place. He made a voyage on the Nile to look at the country with a flotilla of 400 ships in the company of Cleopatra, and enjoyed himself with her in other ways as well. However, my Egyptian history will go into more detail about all this. Caesar could not bear to look at Pompeius' head when it was brought to him, but ordered it to be given burial, and a little shrine which was consecrated for it outside the city was given the name of the shrine of Nemesis. This was pulled down in my time by the Jews to meet some military need against the Roman emperor Trajan when he was eradicating them from Egypt.[139]

91. These were Caesar's actions in Alexandria, and he then moved quickly through Syria to confront Pharnaces. The latter had already accomplished a great deal: he had detached some territory from Roman control, had met Caesar's general Domitius in battle and won a notable victory,[140] and vastly encouraged by this had enslaved the population of the city of Amisus in Pontus, which supported the Romans, and castrated all the boys. Agitated by Caesar's approach, he repented and when Caesar was twenty-five miles away sent ambassadors to arrange peace, who took him a golden crown and foolishly offered him Pharnaces' daughter in marriage. When Caesar discovered what their gifts were, he advanced with his army and walked forward in conversation with the ambassadors until he reached the defences of Pharnaces' camp. Then he simply said, 'Is a man who has killed his father to escape justice, then?', leapt on to his horse, and as soon as the war-cry was uttered routed Pharnaces and killed a large number of his men, although accompanied by only about 1,000 cavalry who formed the vanguard with him. This was when he is reported to have said, 'Lucky

Pompeius! So these were the sort of enemies you met in your war against this man's father Mithridates, when you were reckoned great and called Great.' And his despatch to Rome about the battle ran: 'I came, I saw, I conquered.'[141]

92. After this Pharnaces was glad to take refuge in the Bosporan kingdom, which had been given him by Pompeius. Caesar, however, who had no time to waste on trifles when campaigns of such importance awaited him, proceeded to the province of Asia. On his way through it he made financial arrangements for the cities, which were labouring under the demands made by the tax contractors, as has been explained in my volume about Asia.[142] But when he discovered that there were riots in Rome and that Antonius, his Master of Horse,[143] had put the forum under military guard, he abandoned everything and hurried to Rome. When he arrived, the rioting in the city diminished, but other disturbances directed against him occurred in the army, because the men had not received what they had been promised after the victory at Pharsalus, and were also being illegally kept in service beyond their time. They all demanded to be discharged and sent home. He had announced a vague reward at Pharsalus, and some other vague amount to be paid when the war in Africa was over, and now sent a definite promise of another thousand drachmae each. However, they told him to make no more promises but give them the whole amount at once. They came close to killing Sallustius Crispus, the spokesman he sent, and would have done so if he had not escaped. When Caesar heard this, he took another legion, which had been watching Rome on Antonius' orders, and stationed it around his own house and at the ways out of the city, because he was afraid of looting. Everyone was frightened and advised him to take precautions against an attack by the army, but with supreme boldness he went to the soldiers on the Campus Martius, although they were still mutinous, and without warning appeared on a speaker's platform. 93. There was a great commotion as they converged, unarmed, and in their accustomed manner hailed him as 'Commander' on his sudden appearance in front of them. He told them to state what they wanted, but the same feelings of shock prevented them from daring even to mention the bounties to his face, and they shouted for something that seemed more reasonable, to be discharged from military service, in the hope that because he needed an army for the remaining campaigns he would say something about the bounties as well. Contrary to universal expectation, without the slightest hesitation he said, 'I discharge you.' They were all still more

amazed, and in the deep silence that ensued he added, 'And I shall give you everything I have promised, when I triumph with other troops.' This too appeared simultaneously unexpected and generous, and they immediately felt ashamed of appearing to have deliberately abandoned their commander when he was surrounded by so many enemies. They also reflected enviously how others would triumph in their place, and how they themselves would lose their share of the profits from Africa, which it was believed were going to be considerable, and would become enemies alike of both Caesar and his opponents. Apprehensive and at a loss, they quietened down even more, hoping that Caesar would make some concession and change his mind because of his current needs. He kept equally quiet, and when his companions begged him to say something else to the soldiers and not abandon with a few harsh words men who had been through many campaigns with him, he began his speech by addressing them as 'Citizens' and not as 'Soldiers' – a mark of men discharged from military service and now in civilian life.   94. They could bear it no longer and shouted that they repented, and pleaded to serve with him. As he was turning away and leaving the platform, some of them clamoured with greater urgency and pressed him to stay and punish the wrongdoers among their number. He lingered a little longer, neither going away nor coming back, pretending not to know what to do. However, he returned and declared that he would not punish any of them, but that he was pained that even the Tenth legion, which he had always particularly honoured, was involved in agitation of this sort. 'This legion alone', he said, 'I discharge from the army; but when I return from Africa, I will none the less give everything I have promised to it as well. And once our enemies are dealt with, I shall also give land to everyone – not in the style of Sulla, by taking property away from people and settling new owners alongside old and making them enemies of each other for ever, but by making distributions of publicly owned land, and of my own, and purchasing whatever else may be needed.' They all clapped and cheered, but the Tenth legion was deeply hurt because Caesar seemed implacable towards them alone, and they requested him to have lots drawn and punish some of their number with death. But as he had no need to rouse them any further now that they had truly repented, he made his peace with them all and immediately departed for the campaign in Africa.

95. He crossed the strait from Rhegium to Messana and reached

Lilybaeum. When he discovered that Cato, along with the 300 who had for a long time constituted a council of war and were called a senate, was at Utica guarding the war supplies with the fleet and part of the infantry, while their commander-in-chief Lucius Scipio and the best of their forces were encamped at Hadrumetum, he sailed against Scipio. He caught Scipio at a moment when he had gone to see Juba, and offered battle close beside Scipio's own camp in the belief that the absence of their commander afforded an excellent opportunity for coming to grips with the enemy. Labienus and Petreius, Scipio's subordinates, accepted the challenge and established a clear advantage over Caesar's forces. They routed them and pursued them arrogantly and contemptuously until Labienus, who was thrown when his horse was struck in the stomach, was picked up by his bodyguard, and Petreius, thinking that he had made a reliable test of the army and could secure victory when he pleased, abandoned the engagement with these words to his entourage: 'Let us not rob our commander Scipio of the victory.' It appeared to be another stroke of Caesar's luck, that when his enemies would apparently have secured victory the battle was suddenly called off by the winning side. In the retreat Caesar himself is said to have plunged in and turned round all the men <*he met*>, and with his own hand to have spun round and dragged to the front a fleeing bearer of one of the eagles, the most important standards; eventually Petreius disengaged and Caesar was glad to withdraw. Such was the result of Caesar's first battle in Africa.

96. It was expected that Scipio himself would appear with eight legions and 20,000 horse, the majority of them African, and a large number of light-armed infantry and about thirty elephants. With him would be king Juba at the head of a separate force of about 30,000 infantry, 20,000 Numidian horse, many javelin-throwers and another sixty elephants. Caesar's army were soon alarmed and began to be mutinous, thanks to the experience they had already had and their beliefs about the number and quality of their attackers, particularly the Numidian cavalry. They were also terrified by the prospect of fighting against elephants, to which they were unused. However, Bocchus, one of the two princes of Mauretania, seized Cirta, which was Juba's royal capital. On receipt of the news Juba, preferring to look after his personal interests, moved off with his own army and left only thirty elephants with Scipio. Caesar's army recovered its morale to such an extent that the Fifth legion asked to be deployed opposite the elephants and soundly defeated them (and as a result this legion bears elephants on its standards even now).   **97**. The fight was long and hard and fortune varied in every quarter of the battlefield, until the evening when Caesar just managed to secure victory and promptly destroyed Scipio's camp, not allowing even darkness to keep him from thorough exploitation and completion of his victory.[144] The enemy escaped in small groups wherever they could, and Scipio himself, the moment he had handed the command over to Afranius, fled by sea aboard twelve undecked ships.

His army had a combined strength of about 80,000 men, who had been trained for a long time and had been given confidence and courage by the previous battle; yet it, like Pompeius', was completely shattered in this way at the second encounter. Caesar's glory was magnified into an irresistible good fortune, and the losers no longer ascribed any credit to Caesar's character and ability, but put all their own mistakes down to his good luck. Surely this campaign, like the other, reached such a swift resolution because it collapsed through the misjudgement of the commanders, who failed either to wear Caesar down until he ran short of supplies, as he would in territory he did not control, or to carry their first victory through to conclusion.

98. The news reached Utica about three days later, and since Caesar was making directly for the town everyone fled. Cato restrained no one, and even provided ships for any prominent men who requested them. He himself stayed firmly at his post, and when the Uticans promised that they would ask for him to be spared even if they were not, he smiled and replied that he had no need of an accommodation with Caesar, and that Caesar was equally aware of the fact. He sealed all the valuables and handed over documentation for them all to the magistrates of Utica. In the evening he busied himself with a bath and dinner, and took his meal sitting down as had been his habit since the death of Pompeius.[145] His normal behaviour was unaltered, and he ate neither more nor less than usual. He talked with the others present about the people who had sailed off, asking whether the wind would be favourable for them and whether the interval before Caesar arrived in the morning was sufficient to allow them to make their escape. Even when he went to bed he made no change in his normal routine, except to embrace his son more warmly. When he discovered that his sword was not lying beside the bed in its usual place, he cried out that he was being betrayed to the enemy by his own household and asked what he was to use if attackers came in the night. When they begged him not to plan any action against his own life, but to sleep without his sword, he said more convincingly, 'If I have a mind to, can I not strangle myself with my clothing, or crush my head against the wall, or break my neck by hurling myself to the ground, or finish myself off by holding my breath?' With more in the same vein, he persuaded them to put his sword beside him, and when it was laid there he asked for Plato's work on the soul[146] and began to read. 99. When he had come to the end of Plato's dialogue, he supposed that the attendants at the door were asleep, and stabbed himself below the breastbone. His internal organs tumbled out, and the attendants heard a groan and came rushing in. The doctors replaced the organs, which were still undamaged, sewed up the cuts, and applied bandages. He regained consciousness, and again dissembled: he blamed himself for the feebleness of his blow, but expressed his gratitude to those who had saved him and said he needed to go to sleep. They then went away, taking his sword, and shut the door in the belief that he was quiet. But although he gave the impression that he was asleep, he silently tore the bandages off with his hands and undid the stitches of the injury. Like a wild animal, he enlarged the wound with his nails, opened up his stomach with his fingers, and tore his intestines out, until he died. He was about fifty years old, and is agreed to have been the most uncompromising of all men in his views, once they were formed on any matter, and to have distinguished what was just, or right, or good, on grounds not so much of convention but of high-minded argument. He had been married to Marcia, Philippus' daughter, from her girlhood and been very fond of her and sired sons by her; none the less he gave her to his friend Hortensius, who wanted children but happened not to have a fertile wife, until she conceived by him too, when he took her back into his household again as though he had made a loan.[147] Such was Cato's character, and the people of Utica gave him a splendid burial. Caesar, however, said that Cato had grudged him the opportunity for a fine gesture,[148] and when Cicero composed an encomium on him with the title *Cato*, Caesar responded with an attack which he called *Anticato*.

100. When Juba and Petreius discovered what had happened, they could see no prospect of escape or salvation for themselves and stabbed each other over their evening meal. Caesar made Juba's kingdom subject to Roman taxes and appointed Sallustius Crispus to govern it.[149] He pardoned the people of Utica and Cato's son, and when he caught Pompeius' daughter with two of her children in Utica sent them unharmed to young Pompeius.[150] Of the 300, he put to death any he found. The commander-in-chief Lucius Scipio was caught by a storm at sea and on meeting enemy

ships fought bravely until he was overpowered, when he committed suicide and threw himself into the sea. This also marked the end of Caesar's African campaign.

101. Caesar himself returned to Rome to celebrate four triumphs at once: one over Gaul, where he had brought many large tribes under Roman control and subdued others which had rebelled; a Pontic triumph over Pharnaces; an African triumph over the Africans who had supported Scipio, in which Juba's son, the writer Juba, was carried when he was only a baby; and also a kind of Egyptian triumph, between the Gallic and Pontic processions, for the naval battle on the Nile.[151] Although he was careful not to label anything in a triumph as belonging to Romans, because the civil wars were discreditable to himself and bad and ill-omened for the Romans, he none the less carried in procession in these triumphs twenty very varied pictures showing all the events and the persons involved – apart from Pompeius, whom alone he decided not to portray, since he was still much missed by all. The crowd, although they felt intimidated, groaned at the disasters to their own people, and particularly when they saw Lucius Scipio, the commander-in-chief, stabbing himself in the chest and throwing himself into the sea, and Petreius committing suicide at his meal, and Cato tearing himself apart like a wild animal. They were exultant over Achillas and Pothinus and laughed at the rout of Pharnaces.   102. It is said that money to the value of 65,000 talents was paraded in the triumphal processions, and also 2,822 golden crowns weighing 20,414 pounds. From this, immediately after the triumph, Caesar made distributions in excess of all his promises. To each soldier he gave 5,000 denarii, to each centurion double that amount, to each military tribune and prefect of cavalry double again, and to each member of the plebs one hundred denarii.[152] In addition, he put on various shows. There was horse-racing, and musical contests, and combats – one with a thousand footsoldiers opposing another thousand, another with 200 cavalry on each side, and another that was a mixed infantry and cavalry combat, as well as an elephant fight with twenty beasts a side and a naval battle with 4,000 oarsmen plus a thousand marines on each side to fight. He built the temple of Venus Genetrix, according to his vow on the eve of Pharsalus[153], and around the temple he laid out a precinct which he made into a square for the Romans, not a market-square but a place where people could meet to settle business, like the Persians who also had a square for those who wanted to obtain or learn about justice. He put beside the goddess a beautiful statue of Cleopatra, which is still there. He conducted a

census of the people and is said to have found the total to be half what it was before the war. This was the extent to which the rivalry of these men had dragged Rome down.

103. Caesar was now consul for the fourth time and marched to Spain to face young Pompeius.[154] This was the final campaign of the civil war, and had to be taken seriously. Those of the nobility who had made their escape from Africa had assembled there, and to them had come one force formed of soldiers surviving from Pharsalus and Africa itself, together with their leaders, and another composed of Iberians and Celtiberians, who are a brave people and always eager for battle. Also in service with Pompeius were a great crowd of slaves, who had been in training for four years and were ready to fight with the courage of despair. Pompeius was much misled by this and instead of avoiding battle, at once came to grips with Caesar when he arrived, although the older men, from their experience of the Pharsalus and Africa campaigns, advised him to wear Caesar down by delay and reduce him to want as he was operating in hostile territory. Caesar came from Rome in twenty-seven days, marching a very long way to attack an extremely powerful army. His own army were afraid, as never before, of the reputation of the enemy and of their numbers, training, and desperate attitude. 104. For this reason Caesar himself delayed until Pompeius came up to him somewhere as he was making a reconnaissance and accused him of cowardice. Unable to tolerate the insult, Caesar drew his forces up for battle outside the town of Corduba and on this occasion too he gave 'Venus' as the password,[155] while Pompeius on his side gave 'Piety'. As they were still advancing to engage each other, Caesar's army was seized by fear, and on top of that by a reluctance to fight. Caesar lifted up his hands to heaven and besought all the gods not to sully his glorious record with this one disaster. Then running up to the soldiers he appealed to them and abashed and encouraged them by removing his helmet. Even then they were still paralysed by fear, until he personally snatched a shield from one of them, said to the officers accompanying him, 'This will be the end of my life and of your campaigns', and ran far out in front of the line towards the enemy. He stopped only ten feet short of them, and 200 throwing-spears were hurled at him. Some of these he avoided, others he took on his shield. This made all the officers run forward and stand beside him, and the entire army attacked at the charge and fought all day, constantly winning and losing advantage in different parts of the field, until at evening they just

managed to secure victory. This is when Caesar is said to have remarked that he had often fought for victory, but that on this occasion he fought for his life as well.

105. After much slaughter the Pompeian army took refuge in Corduba. To stop the enemy escaping and preparing for another battle, Caesar gave his army orders to surround the town, and the men, exhausted from the day's events, piled up the bodies and equipment of the dead and thrust spears through them into the ground. Such was the wall beside which they made their bivouac. The next day the town was taken. Of the Pompeian officers, Scapula built a pyre and cremated himself, and the heads of Varus, Labienus, and other prominent men were brought to Caesar. Pompeius himself, accompanied by 150 cavalry, made his escape from the defeat to Carteia, where he had a fleet, and slipped into the dockyard like an ordinary civilian, carried in a litter. But when he saw that even the men here despaired of their safety, he became nervous of being betrayed and continued his flight on board a small boat. His foot became entangled in a rope, and a man severing the rope with a sword cut the sole of his foot instead. He sailed to some little place and was given attention, but was hunted from there too and fled by a difficult and thorny path which gave his wound no mercy. Eventually he sat down exhausted under a tree and when his pursuers set on him he was killed bravely resisting them. His head was brought to Caesar, who ordered someone to give it burial, and so this campaign too had unexpectedly been brought to an end by a single battle. The men who escaped from it were collected together by this Pompeius' younger brother (also called Pompeius but known by his first name, Sextus), who for the moment lay low and slipped from place to place, raiding.

106. Caesar had now brought the civil war to a complete end and he hurried back to Rome, honoured and feared like no man before him. For this reason every kind of superhuman honour was devised and heaped on him for his gratification: sacrificial ceremonies, contests,[156] and votive offerings in every sacred and public place, by tribe and among every people and in every kingdom friendly to Rome. Statues represented him in many different guises, and some of them showed him wearing a crown of oak leaves as the saviour of his country, an ancient honour paid by the saved to those who protected them. He was also entitled Father of His Country[157] and appointed dictator for life[158] and consul for ten years. His person was to be sacred and inviolate, he was to conduct business from a seat of ivory and

gold, and he was always to sacrifice clad in triumphal dress. Every year, on the anniversaries of his great battles, the priests and priestesses in Rome were to offer public prayer for him, and immediately on entering office the magistrates were to swear not to oppose Caesar's decisions. In honour of his birth they changed the name of the month Quintilis to Julius. Furthermore, they voted many temples to him as if he were a god, and one jointly to himself and Clemency, portrayed as greeting each other; thus they feared him as a master, but prayed that he would be merciful to them.   107. Some even proposed to call him king, until he heard of this and with threats forbade it himself, saying the name was evil after the curse laid on it by their ancestors. He dismissed from guard duty the praetorian cohorts which were still with him as a bodyguard after the war, and appeared with only his civilian attendants. When he was transacting business like this in front of the rostra, the senate, led by the consuls, and with every member wearing the appropriate garb, brought him the decree authorizing the honours mentioned above. He did indeed greet them, but he did not rise to his feet as they approached, nor when they waited in front of him, and thus provided another ground of suspicion to those who were accusing him of wishing for the royal title. He accepted the other honours, apart from the ten-year consulship, and announced that the consuls for the following year[159] would be himself and his Master of Horse Antonius. He appointed Lepidus, who was governor of Spain but was administering it through friends, to succeed Antonius as Master of Horse. He also recalled the exiles, except those whose crimes were unpardonable. He was reconciled with his personal enemies and before long appointed many of those who had fought against him to annual magistracies or provincial governorships or army commands. Much encouraged by this, the people hoped that he would also give them back democracy, just as Sulla had done, who had achieved a position of equal power. However, they were disappointed in this.

108. One of the people who were secretly fomenting the story about the kingship crowned a statue of Caesar with a laurel wreath bound with a white ribbon.[160] The tribunes Marullus and Caesetius discovered the perpetrator and held him in custody, maintaining that they were actually doing Caesar a favour because of his earlier threats against anyone who talked of monarchy. He took this with equanimity, and when he was hailed by others as king as he passed by the gates on his way from somewhere or other, and the people booed, he cleverly said to those who had saluted him,

'I'm not King, I'm Caesar', as though they had made a mistake over his name.[161] But Marullus and his associates again found out who had begun the demonstration, and instructed their attendants to bring the man officially before them for trial. Caesar's patience was exhausted, and in front of the senate he accused Marullus and his friends of laying an elaborate plot to misrepresent him as aiming at despotism, and concluded that they deserved death but that he would merely strip them of office and bar them from the senate-house. This episode particularly blackened him, as people thought he wanted the title, was responsible for these attempts to get it, and had become totally despotic: for the pretext for the punishment of Marullus and Caesetius concerned the title of king, while the office of tribune was sacred and inviolate by ancient law and oath.[162] Anger was inflamed by the fact that he did not even wait for the expiry of their term of office. 109. He noticed this himself and regretted what he had done, reflecting that this was the first occasion in time of peace, when he was not commanding in the field, that he had taken severe and unpalatable action. He is said to have told his friends to keep a watch on him, because he had given his enemies the hold they were looking for against him. When they enquired if he would agree to having the Spanish cohorts as his bodyguard again, he said, 'There is no worse fate than to be continuously protected; for that means you are in constant fear.' Even so, attempts to claim kingship for him did not stop. When he was watching the Lupercalia, seated on his golden chair in the forum in front of the rostra, Antonius, who was his fellow-consul and was on that occasion running naked and oiled, as is the custom of the priests of this festival, ran towards the rostra and put a diadem round his head.[163] When they saw this, a few people clapped but the majority booed, and Caesar threw away the diadem. Antonius replaced it, but Caesar again threw it away. While they were having this altercation with each other, the people remained quiet, nervous of which way the episode would end, but when Caesar carried his point they roared their delight and applauded him for not accepting the diadem.

110. Whether Caesar had abandoned hope, or was tired and wished to give up the attempt and its odium, or wanted to leave Rome to some of his enemies, or was hoping to cure his illness (he suffered from epileptic fits and sudden spasms, particularly when he was not busy), he was planning a great campaign against the Getae and the Parthians. He was pre-empting war with the Getae, who were a hardy and warlike people on the borders of the Empire, and exacting revenge from the Parthians for their breach of

faith towards Crassus. He was already sending sixteen legions and 10,000 cavalry ahead across the Adriatic. Another story was going the rounds, that there was a Sibylline prophecy that the Parthians would never submit to Rome unless a king were to march against them. As a result some had the nerve to say that as far as the Romans were concerned, he ought to be called their dictator or commander-in-chief or any other title they use as a substitute for 'king', but that in the case of the peoples subject to Rome he should openly be called king. This suggestion too he declined, and devoted his energies to hastening his departure because people in Rome were jealous of him.

III. Four days before he intended to depart, his enemies cut him down in the senate-house. They may have resented his success and his now excessive power, or maybe, as some alleged, they longed for the republic of their ancestors and were afraid (knowing him well) that he would conquer these nations as well and then indisputably become king. On reflection I am of the opinion that the plot did indeed originate over this additional title, although the difference it made was only of a word since in reality the dictator is exactly like a king. A pair of men in particular, both of whom had belonged to the party of Pompeius, took the initiative in forming the conspiracy. These were Marcus Brutus, surnamed Caepio, who was the son of that Brutus who had lost his life in the time of Sulla, and had found refuge with Caesar after the defeat at Pharsalus, and Gaius Cassius, the one who had surrendered his triremes to Caesar in the Hellespont. There was also Decimus Brutus Albinus, one of Caesar's most intimate associates.[164] All three had always acted in a manner that deserved the respect and trust they received from Caesar. He had placed matters of great importance in their hands, and on his departure for the campaign in Africa had given them military commands and put them in charge of Gaul – Decimus of Transalpine and Brutus of Cisalpine. 112. At the present time Brutus and Cassius were both about to be praetors in the city, but they were quarrelling with each other over the so-called urban praetorship, which has greater prestige than the others, either because they really were competing for the honour or in order to mount a pretence that they did not habitually act in concert over everything. When he made the decision between them, Caesar is supposed to have said to his companions that Cassius had right on his side, but he favoured Brutus; such was the kindness and honour he showed to the man in everything. It was even thought that Brutus was his son, because he was Cato's sister Servilia's lover when Brutus was born.[165]

For this reason, when victory was in his hands at Pharsalus, he is said to have told his officers to make every effort to save Brutus. Brutus may have been ungrateful; he may either not have known, or been sceptical, or ashamed, of his mother's lapse; he may have been excessively devoted to liberty and valued his country above all; or perhaps, being a descendant of that Brutus who had once expelled the kings, he was needled and shamed to do just this deed by the people (for on the statues of the elder Brutus, and on the judicial tribunal of the present one, there appeared many anonymous graffiti like 'Brutus, have you been bribed? Brutus, are you a corpse?' or 'Would you were with us now!' or 'Your descendants are not worthy of you' or 'You're no descendant of *his*'). Anyway, these and many other remarks of the same sort inflamed the young man to the act as if it were in his blood.

113. Rumours about the kingship became still more insistent. There was a meeting of the senate due to take place shortly, and Cassius took Brutus' arm and said, 'What are we going to do in the senate, if Caesar's clique propose to make him king?' Brutus replied that he would not be at the senate. When Cassius persisted in asking, 'But what if they summon us as praetors? What shall we do then, my good Brutus?' he replied, 'I shall defend my country to the death.' Then Cassius, embracing him, said, 'Is there a man among the nobility you would not win over with that sentiment? Or do you think it is the artisans and shopkeepers who write up slogans at your tribunal to shame you, and not the Roman aristocracy, who ask the other praetors for horse-races and beast-fights, but ask you for freedom as though it was a deed that was in your blood?' This was how they revealed to each other at that moment, for the first time, these thoughts which they had in fact been long pondering. Each of them then sounded out his own friends, and any associates of Caesar himself, if they knew them to be conspicuously brave. From their own acquaintances they gathered two brothers, Caecilius and Bucilianus, and in addition Rubrius Ruga, Quintus Ligarius, Marcus Spurius, Servius Galba, Sextius Naso, and Pontius Aquila – these all from their own associates, and from Caesar's the aforementioned Decimus, Gaius Casca, Trebonius, Tillius Cimber, and Minucius Basilus.[166] 114. When they thought there were enough of them, and judged it unnecessary to share their project further, they made a compact with each other, without taking oaths or making sacrifices. None of them backed out or betrayed the plot, and they looked for an occasion and a place to carry it out. Time was pressing, because Caesar was within four days of departing for his

campaigns and immediately acquiring a military guard. They had the senate-house in mind as a suitable spot, because they believed that the senators, even if they had not been forewarned, would eagerly associate themselves with the deed, as is said to have happened in the case of Romulus when he began to behave more like a despot than a king. They also thought that the deed, done like that earlier one in the senate-house, would appear to have been carried out, not as a piece of treachery, but on behalf of the community, and since it was an act performed in the common interest there would be no danger from Caesar's soldiers. Also the credit would remain with them, for it would be well known that they had initiated it. These were the considerations which made them fix unanimously on the senate-house, but they were divided over how to proceed. Some thought they should also make away with Antonius, Caesar's fellow-consul, who was the most powerful of his associates and enjoyed the highest esteem among the soldiers, but Brutus said that if they killed only Caesar they would win glory as tyrannicides for removing a king, but if they killed his associates they would be thought to have acted out of personal enmity as partisans of Pompeius. The conspirators found this point particularly persuasive, and waited for the impending meeting of the senate.

115. The day before the meeting, Caesar went to dinner with Lepidus, his Master of Horse. He brought Decimus Brutus Albinus to join in the drinking, and as they passed the cup round he put the question, 'What is the best sort of death for a human being?' Various views were expressed, but he himself thought a sudden death best of all. In this way he forecast his own fate and the subject of his conversation was what was to happen the next day. In the night, he lay in a heavy sleep as a result of the drink, and his wife Calpurnia, who had a dream in which she saw his body streaming with blood, tried to stop him leaving the house. When he offered sacrifice, the signs repeatedly proved ominous. He was actually on the point of sending Antonius to dismiss the senate, but Decimus, who was there, persuaded him not to lay himself open to the charge of disrespect but to go himself and dismiss it, and he was carried in a litter to do so. There was a performance taking place in Pompeius' theatre, and the senate was to meet in one of the rooms beside the theatre, as was the usual custom when the shows were on. From early in the morning Brutus and his associates had been in the colonnades in front of the theatre transacting business with any who needed them in their capacity as praetors,[167] but when they heard about the results of Caesar's sacrifices and the postponement of the meeting of the senate they

were completely at a loss. At this point, someone grasped Casca by the hand and said, 'You kept it from me, although I am your friend, but Brutus has told me.' Casca was conscience-stricken and thrown into sudden confusion, but the man smiled at him and said, 'Wherever will you get the money to stand for the aedileship?', whereupon Casca recovered. Brutus himself and Cassius were deep in thought talking to each other when a senator, Popillius Laenas, drew them towards him and said that he joined with them in praying for success for what they had in mind and encouraged them to make haste. They were disconcerted, but in their panic said nothing.

116. When Caesar was already being carried on his way, a member of his household who had learnt about the plot came running to reveal such information as he had acquired. He went to Calpurnia, and saying only that he needed Caesar on urgent business, waited for him to return from the senate, because he did not possess full information about the affair. Artemidorus, who had been Caesar's host on Cnidus, ran into the senate, but found him killed moments before. Someone else gave him a note about the conspiracy as he was sacrificing outside immediately before entering the hall where the senate was meeting, and this was found in his hand after his death. After he stepped out of the litter Laenas, the man who had shortly before prayed for success with Cassius and his companions, went up to him and talked privately with him in an animated fashion. At once some of the conspirators were perturbed by the sight and duration of the exchange, and they made signs to each other to commit suicide before being arrested; but as the conversation continued and they saw that Laenas was behaving like someone who was not revealing information so much as insistently requesting a favour, they breathed again, and when in addition they saw him embrace Caesar at the end, they recovered their courage. It is the custom for the magistrates to take the omens before entering the senate, and again Caesar's first sacrificial victim was without a heart or, according to others, without a head to the intestines.[168] When the soothsayer said this was a portent of death, Caesar laughed and said that much the same had happened to him in Spain when he was fighting Pompeius. The soothsayer replied that on that occasion also he had been in extreme danger, but now the portent was even more deadly. Caesar then told him to repeat the sacrifice, but even so none of the victims yielded good omens. Ashamed about wasting the time of the senate, and pressed by his enemies in their guise of friends, he spurned the sacred ritual and made his entrance: for Caesar had to suffer Caesar's fate.

How many sacrifices are made routinely?

117. The conspirators left Trebonius behind to detain Antonius in conversation outside the doors, and when Caesar had taken his ceremonial seat they crowded round him like friends, their daggers hidden. One of them, Tillius Cimber, approached him from the front and begged for his exiled brother's return. Caesar would not agree at all and wished to defer a decision. Cimber then took hold of Caesar's purple toga as though he was still pleading with him, and ripping the garment away pulled it from his neck,* shouting 'What are you waiting for, friends?' Casca, who was standing behind Caesar's head, aimed the first blow at his throat, but missed and wounded him in the chest. Caesar wrenched his toga out of Cimber's grasp, gripped Casca's hand, and as he sprang off the seat whirled round and pulled Casca after him with enormous force. While he was in this position one of the others drove a dagger into his side, stretched as it was in the action of twisting. Cassius also struck him in the face, Brutus in the thigh, and Bucilianus in the back, so that for a few moments Caesar kept turning from one to another of them with furious cries like a wild beast; but after Brutus' blow, <*whether* . . . > or giving up hope now, he wound himself in his toga and fell neatly at the foot of Pompeius' statue. Even then, after he had fallen, they went on savaging him until he had twenty-three wounds, and in the scuffle many of them struck each other with their daggers.

118. When the murderers had completed their foul deed, perpetrated in a sacred place against a man who was sacred and inviolate, people not only in the senate but all across Rome made an immediate rush to escape. Some senators were wounded and others lost their lives in the pandemonium. Many foreigners and ordinary inhabitants of Rome were also killed, the slaughter being unpremeditated and arising naturally from the breakdown of public order and from the ignorance of their attackers. The reason was that the gladiators, who had been armed from early in the morning in expectation of putting on a show, ran out of the theatre towards the screens of the senate-chamber, and out of terror the theatre emptied in a panic-stricken surge, and the goods displayed for sale were looted. Everybody barred their doors and prepared to defend themselves from their roofs.[169] Antonius concluded that the plot was against himself as well as Caesar, and prepared his house for a siege. Lepidus, the Master of Horse, who was in the forum when he heard what had happened, dashed across to the island in the Tiber where he had a legion and took them over to the Campus Martius to hold them in greater readiness for Antonius' orders, deferring to Antonius because the latter was closer to Caesar and also consul.[170] When they considered what to do, their impulse was to take revenge for what Caesar had suffered, but they feared that the senate would be on the side of the assassins and decided to await further developments. Caesar himself had no soldiers with him, because he did not like bodyguards, and his escort from his house to the senate had consisted simply of his lictors, most of the magistrates, and a further large throng made up of inhabitants of the capital, foreigners, and numerous slaves and ex-slaves. They had all fled at once, except for three slaves who stayed beside him and put his body into the litter, to carry home awkwardly (as three men would) the man who not long before had ruled both land and sea.

119. The murderers wanted to say something in the senate-chamber, but as no one stayed there they wound their togas around their left arms to serve as shields, and with their bloody swords in their hands ran shouting that they had destroyed a tyrant and a king. One of them carried a felt skullcap on a spear, as a symbol of freedom attained.[171] They urged the people to embrace the republic of their ancestors and reminded them of the first Brutus and the oath they had sworn at that time against the kings of long ago. They were quickly joined by some individuals with drawn swords who had had no part in the deed but were attempting to claim its glory, namely Lentulus Spinther, Favonius, Aquinus, Dolabella, Murcus, and Patiscus;[172] but instead of the glory, these men shared only the vengeance which was visited on the guilty. When the people did not rush to join them, the conspirators were at a loss and felt afraid. They still had confidence in the senate, for its members, even if they had at first taken to their heels as a result of the confusion and their own ignorance, were their relatives and friends and were equally oppressed by despotic rule. But they were suspicious of the ordinary people and of the many veteran soldiers of Caesar's who were in the city at the time; some of these were newly discharged and had been allocated to schemes of land settlement, others had already been settled in colonies but had come back to Rome to escort Caesar on his way when he left. In addition they were afraid of Lepidus and the forces under his command in the city, and also of how Antonius would behave as consul: they feared that he might ignore the senate, consult only the people,[173] and take some drastic action against themselves.

120. Such was their state of mind as they climbed to the Capitol accompanied by the gladiators. After consulting together they decided to distribute bribes to the ordinary people, hoping that when some of them started to approve of what had happened, the others would join in from love of freedom and from longing for the Republic. The conspirators still thought that the people were genuinely Roman, as they knew they had been in the time of the first Brutus when he overthrew the monarchy of that day. They failed to realize that they were expecting two contradictory things of the present population, that they should want to be free and at the same time take bribes. (The latter was the easier course, because the Republic has been rotten for a long time. The city masses are now thoroughly mixed with foreign blood, the freed slave has the same rights as a citizen, and those who are still slaves look no different from their masters, since apart from the senatorial dress the same clothes are worn by both slave and free; and the corn ration, which is supplied to the poor, but only in Rome, attracts the idle, destitute and hotheaded elements of the Italian population to the capital.) There was also a large number of discharged soldiers, who were no longer being sent back individually, as had once been the practice, to their homes, in case some of them had been involved in unjustifiable campaigns. Instead, they were going to go out and settle in large groups on land and property taken from others in contravention of justice. These men were now encamped in the sanctuaries and sacred precincts under a single stand-ard and a single officer appointed to supervise the new settlement. Since they were on the point of departure, they had already sold their possessions and were ready to be hired cheaply for any purpose.   121. It was therefore not difficult, from so many people like this, to assemble a crowd of sorts very quickly in the forum to hear Cassius' supporters. In spite of being bribed, they lacked the courage to approve what had happened, because they were afraid of Caesar's reputation and what action might be taken by the opposition, but they shouted for peace, as being in the interests of all, and repeatedly called upon the magistrates to pursue it. This was the device they thought of to secure the safety of the murderers, because there would be no peace without an amnesty. This was the mood of the crowd when the praetor Cinna, who was related to Caesar by marriage, was the first to appear in front of them.[174] He unexpectedly made his way in among them and threw off his praetor's insignia, despising it as the gift of a despot. He called Caesar a despot and the men who had killed him tyrannicides, and exalted the deed for its close similarity to that of their ancestors, and told them that the men who had done it were their benefactors, whom they should summon from the Capitol and load with honours. Such were Cinna's words, but his audience noticed that there were none who had not been bribed among their number, and would not summon the men, and they did no more than simply repeat their calls for peace.   **122**. Then Dolabella, a young man of some renown, who had been chosen by Caesar personally to hold the consulship for the remainder of the year once he himself had left Rome, after assuming consular dress and surrounding himself with the tokens of the office,[175] came forward and became the second speaker to abuse the man who had conferred these favours on him. He pretended that he had been privy to the plot and that it was only the deed he had, unwillingly, not shared – and some even allege that he proposed that the day should be observed as the birthday of Rome. At this the hired mob did indeed take heart, since a praetor and a consul were on their side, and they summoned Cassius and his associates from the temple precinct. The latter were delighted with Dolabella, and reckoned that they would have a man who was young and distinguished, and was consul, to oppose Antonius. None the less only Brutus and Cassius came down. Brutus' hand was still bleeding because he and Cassius had aimed blows at the same time against Caesar. When they appeared in front of the crowd, neither of them said anything self-deprecatory. They praised each other as though their actions had been indisputably honourable, congratulated the city, and made particular mention of Decimus for providing them with the gladiators at the critical moment. They incited the people to act like their ancestors when they had overthrown the kings – whose authority over them, unlike Caesar's, had derived not from violence but from legal election – and they advised them to recall both Sextus Pompeius (son of Pompeius Magnus, who had gone to war to defend the Republic against Caesar), who was still fighting against Caesar's commanders in Spain, and the tribunes Caesetius and Marullus, who were in exile after being stripped of office by Caesar.

123. So spoke Cassius and his supporters. They then went back up to the Capitol, because they had as yet no confidence in the gathering. Some of their close friends and relations, who were now able to reach the sanctuary for the first time, were chosen to form a delegation to meet Lepidus and Antonius on their behalf and discuss how to secure unity, plan for political freedom, and avert the disasters that would overtake their country if they failed to agree. The delegates did not commend what had occurred, because they were nervous in front of Caesar's friends, but they asked that it be accepted, now that it had happened. Compassion should be shown to the men who had done the deed and were motivated not by hatred but by sympathy for their country, and pity was due to Rome, already drained by continual civil strife and likely to lose even her remaining good men in the struggle that loomed ahead. It was wrong, they argued, for their opponents, if they felt hostility towards certain people, to quarrel bitterly with them when the state was in danger. It was far more ethical to settle their private differences along with those of the community or, if forgiveness was impossible, to put them off for the moment. **124**. Antonius and Lepidus wanted to avenge Caesar, either from friendship or the oath they had sworn, or because they coveted power and thought that things would be altogether more convenient for them if such a number of important men were quickly put out of the way. On the other hand they feared their opponents' friends and kinsmen and were nervous that the rest of the senate was swinging towards them. They were particularly afraid of Decimus, who had been appointed by Caesar to govern the part of Gaul which adjoined Italy and contained a large army.[176] They decided therefore to go on awaiting events, and devise a way, if they could, of bringing Decimus' army, which had become dispirited by incessant hardship, over to their own side. Antonius expressed their decision to the intermediaries thus: 'We shall take no action that stems from private enmity; but in view of the defilement, and of the oath we all swore to Caesar to protect his person or exact vengeance if anything should happen to him, loyalty to our oath would entail driving out the pollution and sharing our lives with a smaller number of men who are undefiled, rather than all being liable to the curse. But because you prefer the latter, we shall examine the matter with you in the senate and shall deem whatever course you may jointly approve to leave the community unpolluted.'

125. Such was the cautious answer Antonius made. The delegates thanked him and departed with high hopes for the whole business, being convinced that they would have the total co-operation of the senate. Antonius ordered the magistrates to post guards in the city during the hours of darkness, and to place their official seats at intervals in public and preside as though it were daytime. Everywhere in the city fires were lit, by whose light the associates of the murderers went hurrying round all night to the houses of the senators, pleading for them and for the republic of their ancestors. There were contrary visits from the leaders of the settlers, issuing threats if the grants of land, both those which had already been made and those which had been announced, were not honoured. By this time the least corrupt section of the populace, after discovering how few the conspirators were, were beginning to take heart; they were starting to remember Caesar, and were divided in their views. The same night Caesar's money and official papers were brought to Antonius, either because Caesar's wife transferred them in the belief that Antonius' house was a less dangerous place than her own at that moment, or in obedience to his orders.

126. While all this was taking place, an edict of Antonius' was proclaimed during the night, summoning the senate to meet before dawn in the temple of Tellus, which was very close to his house.[177] He was not confident enough either to go down to the senate-house, which lies at the foot of the Capitol,[178] because the other side had gladiators with them, or to bring troops into the city and provoke disturbance. None the less, Lepidus brought them in. As dawn approached the senators hastened to the senate-house, among them Cinna the praetor, who had reassumed the praetorian insignia which he had thrown aside on the previous day as the gift of a despot. When they saw him, some of the impartial citizenry and some of Caesar's veterans, who were angry with him because although he was related to Caesar he had been the first to slander him to the crowd, hurled stones at him and chased him. He took refuge in a house, but they fetched wood and were on the point of setting fire to it when Lepidus arrived with some soldiers and stopped them. This was the first free expression of opinion about Caesar, and it frightened the hired mob and his killers too.

127. In the senate, those who were untainted by sympathy for the act of violence, and resented it, were few, and the majority sought to help the murderers in various ways. First of all, they thought that the murderers could plausibly join them and sit with them, transformed from subjects of judgement to judges. Antonius made no attempt to block this resolution, knowing they would not come, and they did not. Next, to test the feeling of the senate, some of this majority brazenly gave the deed outright praise, calling its perpetrators tyrannicides and urging that they be given public honours. Others, demurring at granting honours, on the grounds that the murderers did not want them and had not been motivated by them, thought it fair simply to salute them as benefactors. Others again were against awarding such a title, and considered that their lives should simply be spared.

These were the tactics of some of them, on the lookout for the particular proposal the senate would accept first, and then gradually lay itself open to attack in other respects. The less corrupt abhorred the deed as an act of pollution, but were willing out of respect for great families to grant the murderers pardon; on the other hand they resented any further proposal to honour them as benefactors. Their opponents responded that saviours should not grudge the saved the best means of safety, and when someone said that to honour these men was to insult Caesar, they would not concede that the interests of the dead should prevail over those of the living. Another speaker argued powerfully that only one of the two propositions could stand: either they declared Caesar a tyrant or they granted the murderers immunity as an act of pity. This point was the only one their opponents would accept, and they asked to be allowed to vote on Caesar under oath, saying that if an unbiased judgement was wanted no one was to call the gods in witness against them for decrees they had been forced to pass when Caesar was already in power, none of which they had passed voluntarily or before they had come to fear for their own lives after the death of Pompeius and the subsequent death of thousands of others. **128**. Antonius, who was presiding over the debate and had been watching for his moment, observed a great deal being said that was neither incontestable nor unambiguous, and decided to upset their arguments by playing on their own fears and their concern for themselves. Knowing that a large number of the senators had themselves been appointed to future posts – magistracies in Rome, priesthoods, provincial governorships, and army commands (for in view of Caesar's impending departure for a long period of campaigning the appointments had been made up to five years ahead) – he called, as consul, for silence and said:

'Those who have asked for a vote on Caesar ought to be aware of this, that if he held legal office and was our elected leader all his acts and decisions remain valid; but if our decision is that he was an upstart who ruled by force, his body is cast out unburied beyond the borders of his country and all his acts are invalidated. To put the matter in a nutshell, his decisions have affected every part of the world, land and sea alike, and most of them will be complied with whether we like it or not, as I shall shortly demonstrate. I shall first put to you, then, something which is entirely under your own control, and also affects only yourselves, so that in dealing with a simple problem you may form some idea of the more difficult ones. Nearly all of us have either held office under Caesar, or are at this moment holding it as a result of his choice, or have been appointed to hold it in the future; for as you know he allocated us the city and annual magistracies and the provincial and army commands five years in advance. If, then, you are willing to resign these (and this is a sphere of decision that is particularly yours), this is the first question I think you should settle, and then I will put the rest.'

129. Such was the fuse Antonius lit, not under Caesar, but under the senators themselves, and he said no more. They all immediately leapt to their feet and started shouting and protesting against submitting themselves to further elections or to the popular choice instead of holding on firmly to what they had already got. Some were also agitated by being under age or by some other unacknowledged barrier to their election. The leader of these was none other than the consul Dolabella, who was obviously unable to become consul by legal election because he was only twenty-five.[179] There ensued a swift change from his previous day's pretence of having shared in the conspiracy. He heaped abuse on the majority, saying that if they decided to honour the murderers, they would be stigmatizing their own magistrates in order to secure a pretext for the safety of Cassius and his associates. But they held out to Dolabella and the others the hope that they would return them to the same magistracies, because the people would be grateful to them, and there would be no changes of office but only an election to put the transition from despotism on a more legal footing. This would also bring credit on office-holders for achieving the same honours under both despotic and democratic systems. While these words were still being spoken, some of the praetors laid their insignia aside to trick their opponents, as if they too, along with the others, intended to reassume them in a more constitutional fashion. But the trick was spotted by the others, who realized that they would no longer be in control of such an election.[180]

130. This was the situation, when Antonius and Lepidus emerged from the senate-house in response to the calls of a group of people which had been gathering for some time. When they were seen above the crowd, and silence had eventually been obtained over the shouts, someone yelled (whether spontaneously or prompted), 'Be careful they don't do it to you.' Whereupon Antonius undid a little of his tunic to show a breastplate underneath, provoking the spectators with the fact that it was not possible for even the consuls to be safe without armour. Some of them shouted that he should take revenge for what had been done, but the majority begged for peace. To the latter he said, 'This is what we are debating, how to have peace and make it last; for it is difficult to find a guarantee of it now, when hundreds of vows and solemn curses were useless even to Caesar.' Then he turned to the group who were clamouring for vengeance, commended them for choosing the course of greater piety and greater loyalty to their oath, and said, 'I would have lined up with you myself, and been the first to shout the same demand, if I had not been consul and bound to take account, not of justice, but of what is alleged to be expedient – for that is what those men inside urge on us. Of course this is why Caesar himself, who spared the Romans he captured in war because it was in the interests of the state, was killed by them.'

131. After this clever handling by Antonius of the different groups, those who favoured vengeance called on Lepidus to exact it. He was going to say something, when the distant section of the crowd asked him to come down into the forum so that they could all hear him. He went at once, thinking that the populace were already swinging his way, and when he reached the rostra he groaned and wept in full view for a long time. Eventually he recovered himself and said, 'I stood here yesterday with Caesar, on this spot, where I am now forced to ask what you want me to do about Caesar's murder.' Many of them shouted 'Avenge Caesar', but there was an answering shout from the hired part of the crowd: 'Peace for the city.' To the latter he replied, 'Of course. But what kind of peace do you mean? What oaths can make it safe? We took all the traditional oaths to Caesar and we trampled them underfoot, those of us who are supposed to be the flower of those who swore them.' Then he turned to those who wanted vengeance and said, 'Caesar, a truly sacred and worthy man, has gone from among us, but we hesitate to harm Rome for his survivors. Our senate is debating the question, and this is the opinion held by the majority.' When they again shouted 'Avenge him yourself', he replied, 'That is my desire, and my oath sanctions it even if I act alone. But you and I ought not to be alone in our desire, or alone in our resistance.'   **132.** So Lepidus too manoeuvred, and the hired men in the crowd, who knew that he was fond of honours, praised him and wanted to elect him to Caesar's priesthood.[181] He was pleased and asked them to be kind enough to remember it later, if they thought he deserved it. They then spoke much more freely because of the offer of the priesthood and pressed him to support peace, to which he replied, 'It is against the law of heaven, and against the law of men, but none the less I will do what you want.'

With these words Lepidus hurried into the senate-house, where all this time Dolabella had been holding forth in a disgraceful way about his office. Antonius, who was waiting in the meantime to see what the people would do, watched Dolabella with amusement, for they were at odds with each other. When he had had enough of the spectacle, and even the crowd had not done anything more hotheaded, he decided that on the one hand he had to spare the assassins' lives (concealing the fact that he had no choice, and pretending that he was sparing them as a mark of the profoundest goodwill), but on the other he would secure an agreement to ratify Caesar's acts and complete his projects.   133. He called for silence and spoke again: 'Gentlemen, my equals in rank, I expressed no view while you were debating the fate of our citizens who have broken the law; but to those who demand that we take a vote, not on them, but on Caesar, I have so far put forward for consideration only a single aspect of Caesar's activity, and that single aspect has, not without good reason, caused all this dispute. The reason is that if we resign our offices we will be admitting that we, numerous and important as we are, obtained them undeservedly. As for matters about which even simple information is difficult to obtain, cast your minds over them now and add them up city by city, province by province, king by king, and ruler by ruler. You know that virtually every area which Caesar brought under Roman control by force of arms, from the east to the west, was reorganized by him, and made more secure by regulations, favours and gifts. Which of these people do you think will accept our rule if they are stripped of what they received? Or perhaps you want to fill the world with wars because you think it right, in view of your country's extreme weakness, to spare the lives of men who have put themselves under a curse? I shall leave the more distant of these nations as yet more* matter for fear and foreboding, but what about people who are not merely our neighbours, but actually live in Italy alongside us? These are men who have received the rewards of their victory and have been settled by Caesar in large numbers together, under arms, in the same units in which they fought in the army. Many tens of thousands of them are still in Rome. What do you think they will do if we deprive them of the towns and lands they have been given or expect to be given? Last night in fact showed you what to expect on this score: when you were making your pleas on behalf of the law-breakers, the veterans were going round putting the opposite case and backing it with threats.   134. Do you think men who served in Caesar's army will stand and watch while his body is dragged in the dust, and broken, and thrown aside unburied (for these are the penalties prescribed for tyrants by the law)? Will they think they enjoy secure possession of the parts of Gaul and Britain they have taken when the man who gave them these is the victim of an atrocity? How will the populace here in Rome act? And the people of Italy? Gods and men will hate you if you insult the man who extended your sway to the Ocean and over unknown lands. Are we not more likely to be blamed and condemned for such extraordinary inconsistency, if we decide to honour the men who in front of the assembled senate and under the eyes of the gods struck down a consul in the senate-house and a sacrosanct individual in a sacred place? If we decide to dishonour the person who was honoured even by our enemies for his virtues? I warn you, then, to have no truck with any such proceedings, because they would be sacrilegious and exceed our powers; and I propose that we ratify all Caesar's acts and projects, and confer no praise of any kind on the law-breakers (for that would be neither just nor holy, nor consonant with the ratification of Caesar's acts), but spare their lives, if it be your wish, simply from pity, for the sake of their families and friends, provided that the latter agree on their behalf to accept this decision on the understanding that it is a favour.'

135. Antonius spoke with unusually deep intensity and urgency, and the resolution was passed. Everyone now calmed down and was well content that although there was to be no penalty exacted for Caesar's murder all his acts and decisions were to be valid 'in the public interest'. The friends of the pardoned men forced the addition of this phrase to protect them and show that practical needs, not justice, dictated the ratification, and Antonius yielded the point to them. When all this had been voted through, the leaders of the settlers asked for another decree, referring particularly to themselves and confirming their grants of land, to be passed in addition to the general one. Antonius did not refuse, thus revealing his fear to the senate, and the motion was passed together with another similar one concerning the men who were about to go out to colonies. In this way the session of the senate ended, and some individuals then gathered round Lucius Piso, to whom Caesar had entrusted his will,[182] and begged him not to reveal the contents of the will or give the body public burial, in case some fresh disturbance arose from this. When he would not agree to these demands, they threatened to bring an action against him for defrauding the Roman people of such a large sum of money which was now public property, thus again intimating that Caesar had been a despot. 136. Piso protested at the top of his voice and after asking the consuls to re-convene the senate, which had not yet dispersed, said, 'Those who claim to have eliminated one despot are already acting as so many despots over us in place of one. They are stopping me from burying the Pontifex Maximus, threatening me if I reveal the contents of the will, and confiscating his property as though he were a despot again. His acts which relate to them have been validated;

but what he left relating to himself they would invalidate – I refer not to Brutus and Cassius, but to the men who incited them to wreak this ruin. In the case of the funeral, the decision is properly yours; but in the case of the will, it is mine, and I will never betray what has been entrusted to me unless I am killed too.' Noise and anger erupted on all sides, particularly from those who in fact hoped that they would get something from the will, and a resolution was passed to make its contents public and to give Caesar a state funeral. This was agreed, and the senate dispersed.

137. When they learnt what had taken place, Brutus and Cassius issued a proclamation to the populace and requested them to come up to them on the Capitol. A large gathering quickly formed, and Brutus began: 'Citizens, we who met you yesterday in the forum now meet you here. We are not refugees looking either for sanctuary (since we have done no wrong) or for a strongpoint (since we entrust our own fate to you). But the violence and unexpectedness of what happened to Cinna have forced this course on us. I know that our enemies wrongly accuse us of perjury and blame us for the difficulty of obtaining a secure peace. What we have to say on these points we shall say in your presence, citizens, you who are to be our allies and enjoy your other democratic rights. After Gaius Caesar had marched from Gaul and taken up arms against his country, and Pompeius, the staunchest republican among you, suffered what he did, and then a great number of other fine Romans were driven to Africa and Spain and perished, with good reason Caesar felt afraid and established his despotism firmly; and when he asked for amnesty we granted it and swore to observe it. But if he had ordered us not simply to accept without protest what was over, but to agree to be slaves in the future, what would the men who are now plotting against us have said? In my opinion, being Romans they would have chosen to die a thousand times rather than consent under oath to serve as slaves. 138. Well then, if Caesar had gone no further in taking your liberty from you, we have broken our oath. But if he put back in your hands neither the magistracies of Rome nor the governorships of the provinces nor military commands nor priesthoods nor any other offices; if the senate was not consulted about anything, and the people never ratified anything; if, on the contrary, in every matter Caesar and his commands were all that counted, and unlike Sulla he was never sated with this abuse; and if Sulla destroyed his enemies but returned political rights to you, while Caesar on the eve of his departure for another long campaign has taken the elections away from you for five years ahead, what kind of freedom was this, when not so

much as a hope of it still glimmered? What about Caesetius and Marullus, the champions of the people? Were they not driven with insult from their sacrosanct and inviolate office? Ancestral law and oath enjoin that those who are still tribunes cannot so much as be brought to court. Yet Caesar banished them without even a trial. Which of us then has committed a crime against the inviolate? Is Caesar sacrosanct and inviolate, when we conferred this status on him not of our own free will, but under compulsion, and not before he had launched an armed attack on his native land and butchered so many good Romans? But did not our ancestors, on the other hand, take an oath, under a free constitution and without compulsion, to make the office of tribune sacrosanct and inviolate, and did they not call down curses if it should not always be so? And where did the revenues and accounts of the Empire go? Who opened the treasuries against our wishes? Who removed some of the untouchable and accursed money and threatened with death another tribune who tried to stop him?[183]

139. ' "But", they say, "what oath could now guarantee a lasting peace?" If there is no despot, there is no need of oaths. Our fathers never needed any. And if someone else covets despotic power, no Roman can be loyal or swear an oath in honesty to a despot. Still in the shadow of danger as we are, we proclaim and shall always proclaim these principles on behalf of our country. The proof is that although we enjoyed safe office with Caesar, we placed patriotism before office. Our opponents inflame you by making unfair allegations against us over the land settlements. Well, if any of you who have been given land, or are about to be given it, are here, please be good enough to identify yourselves.' 140. A large number did so, and he went on: 'You have done the right thing, gentlemen, to come here with the others. You are receiving due honour and reward from your country, and in return you must pay equal honour to her who sends you forth. The Roman people gave you to Caesar to fight the Gauls and the Britons, and your great deeds entitle you to enjoy honour and reward. But after he had bound you in advance by oath, he led you not only to attack Rome, which you did extremely unwillingly, but also to proceed against the noblest of your fellow-citizens in Africa, where you showed a similar reluctance. Now if this had been all you did, perhaps you would have felt ashamed to ask to be rewarded for deeds of this kind; but since neither envy, nor time, nor human forgetfulness will extinguish the memory of your exploits against the Gauls and the Britons, it is for these that you are receiving your rewards. In the past the Roman people used indeed to give their soldiers such

things, but they never took land from their own people or from the innocent, or allot land that was not theirs to other owners, or think that they
ought to respond by committing acts of injustice. When they overcame the
enemy, they did not even strip them of all their territory, but shared it with
them and settled the veterans on a part of it to watch over those they had
defeated. On occasion the conquered territory was insufficient, and then
they made extra allotments from public land or bought more. In this way
the Roman people settled you painlessly alongside all your enemies. On
the other hand, Sulla and Caesar, men who made armed attacks on their
native land as though it was enemy territory, and needed garrisons and
bodyguards in their very own country, neither sent you back home to your
own towns, nor bought land for you or distributed what had been owned
by individuals whose property was forfeit, nor gave rewards by way of consolation to those whose land was being taken, although they had plenty of
resources from the treasury and plenty from confiscations. On the contrary,
they treated Italy by the rules of war and robbery. They took their land,
houses, tombs, and sacred places away from the people of Italy – things we
do not even take from our foreign enemies, from whom we demand only a
tenth of the produce. 141. They distributed to you the property of
people of your own nation, the very people who enlisted you to serve
under Caesar against the Gauls, and escorted you forth, and on many occasions prayed to the gods by your spoils of victory. Furthermore, Sulla and
Caesar settled you on this land *en bloc,* under your standards and in military
order, unable to live in peace and always in fear of the expelled population,
because anyone who was homeless and had been deprived of his possessions was likely to prowl about and watch for the moment to ambush you.
This was the prime aim of the despots, not that you should receive land,
which of course they had means of providing from other sources, but that,
because you had enemies lying in wait for you, you should constitute a
strong and permanent defence of the power which had committed these
injustices in association with you. For it is crimes committed jointly, and
fear felt jointly, which make his bodyguard well disposed to a despot. And
this, for heaven's sake, they called "consolidated settlement", a process accompanied by the lamentations of your kindred and the uprooting of the
innocent. But while Sulla and Caesar deliberately made you enemies of
your countrymen for their own advantage, we, whose lives the current
leaders of our country claim to be sparing for compassionate reasons, confirm, and will confirm, as permanent these same grants of land to you, and

we call heaven to witness this. You retain, and will retain, what you have been given, and no man shall take it from you – not Brutus, not Cassius, not any of us here who have been the first to brave danger in the fight for your freedom. There is one single feature of the business which is open to criticism, but we shall put this right by a measure which will reconcile your countrymen to you and at the same time give you the greatest pleasure when you hear what it is: right from the start, we shall pay to those who are dispossessed the price of this land out of the public funds, so that you may own your allotments not merely with good title but also without incurring hostility.'

142. This was Brutus' speech. The whole audience, both as they still listened to him, and as they dispersed, approved it among themselves as very fair. They were full of admiration for him and his companions, because they seemed to be undaunted and very much on the side of the people. Their mood changed to one of goodwill and an intention to co-operate in the future. At daybreak the consuls summoned the population to an assembly, where the resolutions of the senate were read out and Cicero delivered a long speech in praise of the amnesty. The assembly was pleased and invited Cassius and his associates down from the sanctuary. The latter gave instructions that hostages should be sent up to them for that period, and the sons of Antonius and Lepidus were sent. When Brutus and his party were sighted, there was clapping and shouting and although the consuls wanted to say something the crowd would not allow it and said they should first shake the others by the hand and be reconciled with them. This was done, and the consuls' resolution was severely shaken by fear or jealousy that in other matters too these men were going to have the political advantage over them. 143. When the crowd saw Caesar's will being brought in, they immediately ordered it to be read. In it his sister's daughter's son Octavius was named his son by adoption, and to the people were bequeathed his gardens for general use, and also seventy-five denarii to every adult male Roman presently living in the city. The feelings of the people boiled up in anger again, because after previously hearing accusations of despotism they were now faced with the testamentary provisions of a public-spirited citizen. The most lamentable thing, they thought, was that Decimus Brutus was named as an adoptive son amongst the second heirs (it is a Roman habit to subjoin other names to those of the heirs, in case the latter should not take their share). At this, the disturbance became still worse. They thought it monstrous and sacrilegious that Decimus Brutus

should have plotted against Caesar when he had been named as a son. When Piso then brought Caesar's body into the forum a huge number of armed men gathered to guard it. It was laid with lavish pomp and cries of mourning on the rostra, whereupon wailing and lamentation arose again for a long time, and the armed men clashed their weapons, and very soon people began to change their minds about the amnesty. Then Antonius, seeing their state of mind, did not give up hope. He had been chosen to deliver the funeral oration as a consul for a consul, a friend for a friend, and a kinsman for a kinsman (being related to Caesar through his mother), and so he again pursued his tactic and spoke as follows:

144. 'It is not right, my fellow-citizens, for the funeral oration in praise of so great a man to be delivered by me, a single individual, instead of by his whole country. The honours that all of you alike, first senate and then people, decreed for him in admiration of his qualities when he was still alive, these I shall read aloud and regard my voice as being not mine, but yours.' He then read them out with a proud and thunderous expression on his face, emphasizing each with his voice and stressing particularly the terms with which they had sanctified him, calling him 'sacrosanct', 'inviolate', 'father of his country', 'benefactor', or 'leader', as they had done in no other case. As he came to each of these Antonius turned and made a gesture with his hand towards the body of Caesar, comparing the deed with the word. He also made a few brief comments on each, with a mixture of pity and indignation. Where the decree said 'Father of his country', he commented 'This is a proof of his mercy', and where it said 'Sacrosanct and inviolate' and 'Whoever shall take refuge with him shall also be unharmed', he said 'The victim is not some other person seeking refuge with him, but the sacrosanct and inviolate Caesar himself, who did not snatch these honours by force like a despot, indeed did not even ask for them. Evidently we are the most unfree of people because we give such things unasked to those who do not deserve them. But you, my loyal citizens, by showing him such honour at this moment, although he is no more, are defending us against the accusation of having lost our freedom.' **145.** And again he read out the oaths, by which they all undertook to protect Caesar and Caesar's person with all their might, and if anyone should conspire against him, those who failed to defend him were to be accursed. At this point he raised his voice very loud, stretched his hand out towards the Capitol, and said, 'O Jupiter, god of our ancestors, and ye other gods, for my own part I am prepared to defend Caesar according to my oath and the terms of the curse I called down on myself; but since it is the view of my equals that what we have decided will be for the best, I pray that it is for the best.' Noises of protest came from the senate at this remark, which was very plainly directed at them. Antonius calmed them down, saying by way of retractation, 'It seems, fellow-citizens, that what has happened is the work not of any man, but of some spirit. We must attend to the present instead of the past, because our future, and indeed our present, is poised on a knife-edge above great dangers and we risk being dragged back into our previous state of civil war, with the complete extinction of our city's remaining noble families. Let us then conduct this sacrosanct person to join the blest, and sing over him the customary hymn and dirge.'

146. So saying he hitched up his clothing like a man possessed, and girded himself so that he could easily use his hands.[184] He then stood close to the bier as though he were on stage, bending over it and straightening up again, and first of all chanted praise to Caesar as a heavenly deity, raising his hands in witness of Caesar's divine birth and at the same time rapidly reciting his campaigns and battles and victories, and the peoples he had brought under his country's rule, and the spoils he had sent home. He presented each as a marvel and constantly cried 'This man alone emerged victorious over all those who did battle with him.' 'And you', he said, 'were also the only man to avenge the violence offered to your country 300 years ago, by bringing to their knees the savage peoples who were the only ones ever to break in to Rome and set fire to it.' In this inspired frenzy he said much else, altering his voice from clarion-clear to dirge-like, grieving for Caesar as for a friend who had suffered injustice, weeping, and vowing that he desired to give his life for Caesar's. Then, swept very easily on to passionate emotion, he stripped the clothes from Caesar's body, raised them on a pole and waved them about, rent as they were by the stabs and befouled with the dictator's blood. At this the people, like a chorus, joined him in the most sorrowful lamentation and after this expression of emotion were again filled with anger. After the speech, other dirges accompanied by singing were chanted over the dead by choirs in the customary Roman manner, and they again recited his achievements and his fate. Somewhere in the lament Caesar himself was supposed to mention by name those of his enemies he had helped, and referring to his murderers said as if in wonder, 'To think that I actually saved the lives of these men who were to kill me.'[185] Then the people could stand it no longer. They considered it monstrous that all the murderers, who with the sole exception of Decimus had been

taken prisoner as partisans of Pompeius, had formed the conspiracy when instead of being punished they had been promoted to magistracies, provincial governorships, and military commands, and that Decimus had even been thought worthy of adoption as Caesar's son.

147. When the crowd were in this state, and near to violence, someone raised above the bier a wax effigy of Caesar – the body itself, lying on its back on the bier, not being visible. The effigy was turned in every direction by a mechanical device, and twenty-three wounds could be seen, savagely inflicted on every part of the body and on the face. This sight seemed so pitiful to the people that they could bear it no longer. Howling and lamenting, they surrounded the senate-house, where Caesar had been killed,[186] and burnt it down, and hurried about hunting for the murderers, who had slipped away some time previously. They were so maddened by anger and grief that because the tribune Cinna had the same name as the praetor Cinna who had made the speech against Caesar, they tore him to pieces like wild beasts without allowing him a word of explanation about the names, and no part of his body was recovered for burial. They began to set fire to the houses of the others, and in spite of desisting in face of their resistance and the pleas of their neighbours, threatened to come back with weapons the next day.

148. While the murderers escaped unobserved from the city, the people returned to Caesar's bier and started to carry it up to the Capitol, saying that it was a holy act to bury Caesar on sacred soil and place him with the gods. They were stopped by the priests and brought the bier back to the forum, where the ancient palace of the Roman kings stands. They collected together pieces of wood, and all the seating, of which there was a great quantity in the forum, and anything else of the same sort, and piled on top the trappings of the funeral procession, which were extremely lavish. Some of them threw on crowns and large numbers of military decorations of their own.[187] Then they lit the pyre and remained by it all night, on the spot where at first an altar was established, but there now stands a temple which was dedicated to Caesar himself after he was deemed to merit divine honours. It was his adopted son Octavius who, after changing his name to Caesar, following in his political footsteps, and greatly strengthening the empire, still supreme, which Caesar had founded, conferred on his father honours equal to those of the gods. Indeed, beginning with Caesar, the Romans still confer these honours today on each holder of the imperial power when he dies, provided he has not been a despot or a disgrace, in spite of the fact that previously when these men were alive they could not even bear to call them kings.

149. Thus Caesar died on the day they call the Ides of March, about the middle of Anthesterion, the day which the seer said he would not out-live.[188] In the morning Caesar made fun of him, and said, 'The Ides have come.' Unabashed, the seer replied, 'But not gone', and Caesar, ignoring not only the predictions of this sort given him with such confidence by the seer, but also the other portents I mentioned earlier, left the house and met his death. He was in the fifty-sixth year of his life, a man who was ex-tremely lucky in everything, gifted with a divine spark, disposed to great deeds, and fittingly compared with Alexander. They were both supremely ambitious, warlike, rapid in executing their decisions, careless of danger, un-sparing of their bodies, and believers not so much in strategy as in daring and good luck. One of them made a long journey across the desert in the hot season to the shrine of Ammon,[189] and when the sea was pushed back crossed the Pamphylian gulf by divine power, for heaven held back the deep for him until he passed, and it rained for him while he was on the march. In India he ventured on an unsailed sea. He also led the way up a scaling-ladder, leapt unaccompanied on to the enemy wall, and suffered thirteen wounds. He was never defeated and brought all his campaigns to an end after one or at most two pitched battles. In Europe he conquered much foreign territory and subdued the Greeks, who are a people ex-tremely difficult to govern and fond of their independence, and believe* that they had never obeyed anyone before him except Philip, and that for only a short time on the pretext that he was their leader in a war. As for Asia,[190] he overran virtually the whole of it. To sum up Alexander's luck and energy in a sentence, he conquered the lands that he saw, and died intent on tackling the rest.

150. In Caesar's case, the Adriatic yielded by becoming calm and navig-able in the middle of winter. He also crossed the western ocean in an un-precedented attempt to attack the Britons, and ordered his captains to wreck their ships by running them ashore on the British cliffs. He forced his way alone in a small boat at night against another stormy sea, when he ordered the captain to spread the sails and take courage not from the waves but from Caesar's good fortune.[191] On many occasions he was the only man to spring forward from a terrified mass of others and attack the enemy. The Gauls alone he faced thirty times in battle, finally conquering 400 of their tribes, who the Romans felt to be so menacing that in one of their laws concerning immunity from military service for priests and older men there was a clause 'unless the Gauls invade' – in which case priests and older men were to serve. In the Alexandrian war, when he was trapped by himself on a bridge and his life was in danger, he threw off his purple cloak and jumped into the sea. The enemy hunted for him, but he swam a long way under water without being seen, drawing breath only at intervals, until he approached a friendly ship, when he stretched out his hands, revealed himself, and was rescued. When he became involved in these civil wars, whether from fear, as he himself used to say, or from a desire for power, he came up against the best generals of his time and several great armies which were not composed of uncivilized peoples, as before, but of Romans at the peak of their success and fortune, and he too needed only one or two pitched battles in each case to defeat them. Not that his troops were unbeaten like Alexander's, since they were humiliated by the Gauls in the great disaster which overtook them when Cotta and Titurius were in command,[192] in Spain Petreius and Afranius had them hemmed in under virtual siege, at Dyrrachium and in Africa they were well and truly routed, and in Spain they were terrified of the younger Pompeius.[193] But Caesar himself was impossible to terrify and was victorious at the end of every campaign. By the use of force and the conferment of favour, and much more surely than Sulla and with a much stronger hand, he overcame the might of the Roman state, which already lorded it over land and sea from the far west to the river Euphrates, and he made himself king against the wishes of the Romans, even if he did not receive that title. And he died, like Alexander, planning fresh campaigns.

151. The pair of them had armies, too, which were equally enthusiastic and devoted to them and resembled wild beasts when it came to battle, but were frequently difficult to manage and made quarrelsome by the hardships they endured. When their leaders were dead, the soldiers mourned them, missed them, and granted them divine honours in a similar way. Both men were well formed in body and of fine appearance. Each traced his lineage back to Zeus, the one being a descendant of Aeacus and Heracles, the other of Anchises and Aphrodite. They were unusually ready to fight determined opponents, but very quick to offer settlement. They liked to pardon their captives, gave them help as well as pardon, and wanted nothing except simply to be supreme. To this extent they can be closely compared, but it was with unequal resources that they set out to seek power. Alexander

possessed a kingdom that had been firmly established under Philip, while Caesar was a private individual, from a noble and celebrated family, but very short of money.

152. Neither of them took any notice of omens which referred to them, nor showed any displeasure with the seers who prophesied their deaths. On more than one occasion the omens were similar and indicated a similar end for both. Twice each was confronted with a lobeless liver.[194] The first time it indicated extreme danger. In Alexander's case this was among the Oxy-dracae, when after he had climbed on to the enemy's wall at the head of his Macedonian troops the scaling-ladder broke, and he was left isolated on top. He leapt audaciously inwards towards the enemy, where he was badly beaten around the chest and neck with a massive club and was about to col-lapse, when the Macedonians, who had broken down the gates in panic, just managed to rescue him. In Caesar's case it happened in Spain, when his army was seized with terror when it was drawn up to face the younger Pompeius and would not engage the enemy. Caesar ran out in front of everyone into the space between the two armies and took 200 throwing-spears on his shield, until he too was rescued by his army, which was swept forward by shame and apprehension. Thus the first lobeless victim brought both of them into mortal danger, but the second brought death itself, as fol-lows. The seer Peithagoras told Apollodorus, who was afraid of Alexander and Hephaistion and was sacrificing, not to be afraid, because both of them would soon be out of the way.[195] When Hephaistion promptly died, Apol-lodorus was nervous that there might be some conspiracy against the king, and revealed the prophecy to him. Alexander, smiling, asked Peithagoras himself what the omen meant, and when Peithagoras replied that it meant his life was over, he smiled again and still thanked Apollodorus for his con-cern and the seer for his frankness. **153**. When Caesar was about to enter the senate for the last time, as I described not many pages back, the same omens appeared. He scoffed at them, saying they had been the same in Spain, and when the seer said that he had indeed been in danger on that occasion, and that the omen was now even more deadly, he made some concession to this forthrightness by repeating the sacrifice, until finally he became irritated by being delayed by the priests and went in to his death. And the same thing happened to Alexander, who was returning with his army from India to Babylon and was already approaching the city when the Chaldaeans[196] begged him to postpone his entry for the moment. He quoted the line *'That prophet is the best, who guesses right'*[197] but the Chaldaeans begged him a second time not to enter with his army looking towards the setting sun, but to go round and take the city while facing the rising sun. Apparently he relented at this and began to make a circuit, but when he became annoyed with the marshes and swampy ground disregarded this second warning too and made his entrance facing west. Anyway, he entered Babylon, and sailed down the Euphrates as far as the river Pallacotta which takes the water of the Euphrates away into swamps and marshes and prevents the irrigation of the Assyrian country. They say that as he was considering the damming of this river, and taking a boat to look, he poked fun at the Chaldaeans because he had safely entered and safely sailed from Babylon. Yet he was destined to die as soon as he returned there. Caesar, too, indulged in mockery of a like sort. The seer had foretold the day of his death, saying that he would not survive the Ides of March. When the day came Caesar mocked the seer and said, 'The Ides have come', but he still died that day. In this way, then, they made similar fun of the omens which related to themselves, displayed no anger with the seers who announced these omens to them, and were none the less caught according to the letter of the prophecies.

154. In the field of knowledge they were also enthusiastic lovers of wisdom, whether traditional, Greek or foreign. The Brahmans, who are considered to be the astrologers and wise men of the Indians like the Magi among the Persians, were questioned by Alexander on the subject of Indian learning, and Caesar investigated Egyptian lore when he was in Egypt establishing Cleopatra on the throne. As a result he improved much in the civilian sphere at Rome, and brought the year, which was still of variable length due to the occasional insertion of intercalary months which were calculated according to the lunar calendar, into harmony with the course of the sun, according to Egyptian observance. It turned out that none of the men who conspired against his person escaped, but were punished by his son, as they deserved, just as the killers of Philip were punished by Alexander; and the following books explain how.

BOOK III

1. In this way Gaius Caesar, who was of inestimable value to the Romans in the development of their empire, was killed by his enemies and given a funeral by the populace. All his murderers were brought to justice, and this and the following book will show how the most prominent were punished; they will also include the other Roman civil wars which took place at the same time.

2. The senate attacked Antonius over his funeral speech for Caesar, because the populace had been so strongly roused by it that they had disregarded the amnesty that had just been voted and had hurried off to set fire to the houses of the murderers. However, he turned their displeasure with him to goodwill by a single political act. There was a certain Amatius, the pseudo-Marius, who pretended to be Marius' grandson and was very popular with the crowd for Marius' sake. Having become a relative of Caesar by this imposture, he indulged in excessive mourning for his death, built an altar where the pyre had been, kept a gang of toughs, and was a constant threat to the murderers. Some of these had fled from Rome, and those of them to whom Caesar himself had given provincial governorships had gone to their provinces: Decimus Brutus to Cisalpine Gaul, Trebonius to Asia,[1] and Tillius Cimber to Bithynia. Cassius and Marcus Brutus, whose fortunes were of particular concern to the senate, had also been chosen by Caesar to be governors in the following year, Cassius of Syria and Brutus of Macedonia,[2] but so long as they were still holding urban office as praetors they were forced <*to remain in Rome*>. In this capacity they pandered to the settlers with their judicial decisions and whatever else they could think of, even agreeing that the settlers could sell the land they had been allotted, although the law prohibited this until twenty years had elapsed.

3. It was being said that Amatius, when the opportunity offered, would

actually ambush Brutus and Cassius. Antonius therefore, as consul, arrested Amatius on this rumour of an ambush and very boldly put him to death without trial. The senate were amazed at the drastic and illegal nature of his action, but were very happy to pretend it was necessary because they thought that without such firmness the position of Brutus and Cassius would never be secure. Amatius' followers, as well as the rest of the people, felt his loss keenly and were angry at what had occurred, because it had been Antonius, currently held in particular respect by the citizenry, who had carried it out. They thought it wrong that he should spurn them, and occupied the forum. They shouted and cursed him, and told the magistrates to stand in for Amatius, consecrate the altar and be the first to offer sacrifice for Caesar at it. When they were driven out of the forum by soldiers sent in by Antonius they became angrier still, and their shouts louder, and some of them drew attention to the plinths from which statues of Caesar had been removed. Then a man said that he would point out the actual workshop to which the statues had been taken. The crowd immediately followed him, and on seeing them began to set fire to the place, until Antonius sent more soldiers. Some of the rioters resisted and were killed, while others were arrested and crucified, if they were slaves, or hurled from the Tarpeian rock, if they were free men.[3]

4. The disturbance was over, but among the population of the city indescribable hatred had been aroused against Antonius in place of indescribable goodwill. The senators, on the other hand, were delighted because they could not have been relieved in any other way of the anxiety they felt for Brutus' party. Antonius then proposed to recall from Spain the son of the still universally and deeply missed Pompeius Magnus, Sextus Pompeius, who was continuing the war against Caesar's generals. Antonius also proposed that in place of his father's property, which had been confiscated, Sextus should be given fifty million denarii from public funds, and that he should now be supreme commander at sea, as his father had been, and have the immediate use of Roman ships anywhere to meet emergencies. The senate was amazed at each of these provisions, but accepted them with enthusiasm and spent the whole day blessing Antonius. They thought that no one could be more republican than Magnus, and hence no one was more greatly missed. Cassius and Brutus, who had belonged to Magnus' party and were at that time highly respected by all, imagined that they were going to be quite safe. They thought that the view which had motivated their actions would prevail, and that they would ultimately restore the

Republic, if fate continued to run their way. Antonius was constantly praised by Cicero for this, and the senators, who like Antonius realized that it was because of them that the people were scheming against him, gave him a bodyguard, which he chose for himself from veterans who were temporarily in the city.

5. Whether Antonius' whole conduct had aimed to achieve precisely this, or whether he gladly seized the happy chance, he began to enrol his guard and went on adding to it until it numbered 6,000 men. He chose them not from serving rank and file, whom he thought he would easily be able to obtain by other means when he needed them, but entirely from centurions because they had qualities of leadership and were experienced in war and were known to him from service under Caesar. From among them, to command them in proper order, he appointed military tribunes to whom he paid respect and with whom he shared his public plans. The senate were suspicious both of the number of his men and of the way they had been recruited, and recommended him to reduce the guard to the size that was appropriate, as it was causing ill-feeling. He promised that he would, when he had suppressed the disruptive elements among the people. It had also been decreed that all Caesar's past acts and as yet unimplemented decisions were to be valid. Antonius, who not only possessed the memoranda of what had been decided but also controlled Caesar's secretary Faberius (who was totally obedient to Antonius because Caesar himself, as he was about to leave Rome, had passed petitions like this over to Antonius) inserted many addenda to secure the gratitude of a large number of people, and made gifts to cities and princes and to these bodyguards of his. Although everything was headed 'Caesar's memoranda', it was to Antonius the recipients felt grateful. In the same way he also enrolled many new senators and took other steps to ingratiate himself with the senate so that they should cease to object to his guard.

6. While Antonius was busy with all this, it became apparent to Brutus and Cassius that none of the ordinary citizens or veterans was peacefully inclined to them and that it was not impossible that Amatius' ambush could be sprung on them by someone else. They were apprehensive of Antonius' inconstancy, now that he had troops, and since they observed that no action was being taken to strengthen the democratic constitution viewed Antonius with suspicion for that reason also. They placed most confidence in Decimus Brutus, who had an army of three legions on the flanks of Italy, and they sent secret instructions to Trebonius in Asia and

Tillius in Bithynia to collect money unobtrusively and look for military forces. They themselves were eager to be on their way and take possession of the provinces which had been given them by Caesar. The time for doing so had not yet come, but although they thought it would give a bad impression if they abandoned their city praetorships before their terms of office were complete, and thus attracted the suspicion that they were over-keen to enjoy power, they were nevertheless inclined to choose, as a matter of necessity, to pass the interval somehow as private citizens rather than be praetors in Rome, where they neither felt safe nor were paid the honour that they expected for their services to their country. Such was their attitude when the senate, which sympathized with their views, made them responsible for the supply of grain to Rome from as many countries as possible, until the time should arrive for them to take control of their provinces.[4] This was done to protect them from the imputation that they had at any point run away, and so great was the senate's concern and respect for them that it was chiefly on their account that it assisted the other murderers.

7. After Brutus and his companions had left the city, Antonius, who now enjoyed a monopoly of power, cast around for command of a province and an army. He particularly wanted Syria, but was well aware that he was under suspicion, and that this suspicion would increase if he made any request. He also knew that the senate was secretly setting up Dolabella, the other consul, who had always been an opponent of his, to resist him. He therefore played on Dolabella's youth and desire for status. He persuaded him to ask that he, Dolabella, should himself replace Cassius in command of Syria and fight the Parthians with the army that had been enlisted for use against them, and to make this request not of the senate (for that was impossible)[5] but of the people by means of a law. Dolabella was delighted and immediately promulgated the law. When the senate accused him of modifying Caesar's decisions he replied that, first, the war against the Parthians had not been entrusted by Caesar to anybody, and, second, Cassius, although thought fit to hold Syria, had previously himself altered some of Caesar's decisions by granting permission to men who had received allotments of land to sell them before the twenty years prescribed in the law. Furthermore, he was ashamed, being a Dolabella, to be thought unfit to take Cassius' place in Syria.[6] His opponents then persuaded Asprenas,[7] one of the tribunes, to make a false report of heavenly omens during the voting assembly. They hoped that Antonius would co-operate, because he was

consul, and an augur,[8] and was still believed to be against Dolabella. However, when Asprenas announced during the voting that an inauspicious omen had appeared in the sky, although it was the practice for others to perform this function, Antonius became very angry with him for lying and instructed the tribes to go on with the vote on Dolabella.

8. In this way Dolabella became governor of Syria and general in charge of the war with the Parthians and the army that had been enlisted for it by Caesar, together with the forces which had already proceeded to Macedonia, and people realized for the first time that Antonius was co-operating with Dolabella. Now that this had been done in the popular assembly, Antonius asked the senate for Macedonia, well knowing that after Syria had been granted to Dolabella the senate would be reluctant to deny Macedonia to himself, especially as it was denuded of troops. Unwillingly, they gave him the province. They were surprised that he had previously ceded its army to Dolabella but pleased none the less that Dolabella rather than he had the army, and seizing their opportunity asked him for other provinces to give to Cassius' party by way of compensation. They were given Crete and Cyrene, or according to another view both of these for Cassius and Bithynia for Brutus.[9]

9. Such was the state of affairs in Rome. Now Octavius, the grandson of Caesar's sister,[10] had been made his Master of Horse for a year, for the dictator had begun to pass the office round among his close associates and sometimes made it annual. He was not yet of military age, but had been sent by Caesar to Apollonia on the Adriatic to continue his education and receive military training in preparation for following Caesar on campaign. He exercised with squadrons of cavalry from Macedonia which came to him by turns at Apollonia, and some of the senior officers of the army were always visiting him because he was a relative of Caesar's. As a result the army came to know him and wish him well, for he received everyone with kindness. When he had been six months at Apollonia, he was informed one evening that Caesar had been killed in the senate by the men who were closest to him and carried most influence with him at the time. In the absence of any further news he felt fearful and wondered whether the deed had the support of the whole senate or was the private work of its perpetrators, and whether they had already met justice at the hands of the majority, or were <in fear>* of this, or whether the ordinary people also were pleased.

10. Consequently, some of his friends gave him the advice that he

should ensure his safety by sheltering with the army in Macedonia and then, when he was sure the murder was not an agreed act, be bold enough to proceed against his enemies and avenge Caesar; and there were in fact some senior officers who promised to give him protection if he came to them. But his mother and her husband Philippus wrote from Rome to say that he should not become excited or confident yet, but bear in mind the fate which Caesar, who had worsted all his enemies, suffered at the hands of his particular friends; instead he should choose the temporarily less dangerous course of behaving more like a private citizen, and come quickly and circumspectly to them in Rome.[11] Because he still did not know what had happened after Caesar's death, Octavius took their advice and made his farewells to the senior officers of the army. He then crossed the Adriatic, not to Brundisium (because he had not sounded out any of the troops there and was being extremely careful), but to another town called Lupiae which was not far from Brundisium but off the road.

11. When he received more exact information about the murder and the state of public feeling, together with copies of the will and the senatorial decrees, his relatives warned him still more solemnly to beware of Caesar's enemies, because he was Caesar's son and heir, and advised him to renounce both the inheritance and the adoption. But as he thought that this course, along with failure on his part to avenge Caesar, would be disgraceful, he made his way to Brundisium, after first sending ahead to find out if the murderers had laid any trap for him. When the troops there too came to meet him and greeted him as Caesar's son, he took heart and sacrificed and immediately assumed the name Caesar, because the Romans have a custom whereby adoptive children take the names of those who have adopted them. He did not, however, simply add it, but changed both his own name and his patronymic completely, so that he became 'Caesar, son of Caesar', instead of 'Octavius, son of Octavius', and continued to use these names. Immediately a great mass of people flocked to him, as Caesar's son, from every direction. Some came out of friendship for Caesar, and some because they were ex-slaves and slaves of Caesar's; and apart from these there were soldiers engaged in conveying either baggage or money to Macedonia, or different categories of money and tax revenue from other provinces to Brundisium.

12. Octavian was encouraged by the number of people who came to join him and by Caesar's own reputation and the universal goodwill shown to Caesar, and made his way towards Rome accompanied by a remarkable

crowd which increased every day like a torrent.[12] He was safe from any
open attack because of this crowd, but for the same reason he was very
wary of a plot, since the overwhelming majority of his companions were
men with whom his acquaintance was very recent. The attitude of the
other towns was not altogether favourable to him, but from the colonies
the men who had served as soldiers under Caesar and had been dispersed to
their new landholdings flocked to him. They were pleased to see the young
man, expressed their grief for Caesar, cursed Antonius for failing to follow
up such a monstrous deed, and said that if they had a leader they would
exact vengeance. Octavian commended them and sent them away, deferring the question for the moment. When he was at Tarracina, fifty miles
from Rome, he heard the news that Cassius and Brutus had been deprived
of Syria and Macedonia by the consuls and had as a consolation received
the smaller alternative provinces of Crete and Cyrene;[13] also that some of
the exiles had returned and Pompeius been recalled, and that Caesar's
memoranda had provided the excuse for some enrolments into the senate
and much else that was going on.

13. When he arrived in Rome, his mother and Philippus and his other
relations were again anxious.[14] They were frightened of the movement of
opinion in the senate against Caesar, and the resolution that there should be
no punishment for the murder, and the suspicion evinced towards Octavian by Antonius, who was then in power and had neither been to see
Caesar's son when he arrived nor established contact with him. Octavian,
however, again calmed the situation by saying that he, as a young man and a
private citizen, would call on Antonius, as his senior and a consul, and
would show due deference to the senate. He also said that the resolution
had been passed before anyone had yet pursued the assassins, but when
someone plucked up the courage to act against them, the people and the
senate would support him because it was the law, and the gods would support him because it was just, and Antonius would do the same. Furthermore, if he were to ignore the inheritance and the adoption, he would be
betraying Caesar and doing a wrong to the people over the distribution of
money to them. As he finished speaking, he burst out with the assertion
that it was right for him, not simply to put himself in danger, but actually to
die, if, when Caesar had chosen him above everyone else for such a great
role, he was to show himself worthy* of Caesar and Caesar's willingness to
face danger. Then he turned to his mother as though she were Thetis and
quoted the words of Achilles which were then fresh in his mind:

*Would I might die at once, a man who failed to take
Due vengeance for his slaughtered friend!* [15]

So saying, he declared that these words, and above all his deed, had brought Achilles eternal glory in the eyes of all men. He himself called Caesar not his friend, but his father, not his companion in arms, but his commander-in-chief, and not a victim of the law of war, but of godless butchery in the senate.

14. At this his mother, swept from fear to delight, saluted him as the only man worthy of Caesar, and after forbidding him to say any more wished him all good fortune and urged him to carry out his plans. None the less she advised him to proceed craftily and patiently and for the moment avoid open or over-bold action. Octavian commended her and promised to follow her advice, and immediately sent messages that evening to his friends, asking each of them to come to the forum first thing in the morning with a crowd of companions. There he presented himself to Gaius Antonius, Antonius' brother, who was urban praetor, and announced that he accepted adoption by Caesar (it being the Roman practice for adoptions to be witnessed before the praetors). When the public clerks had taken down his declaration, he went straight from the forum to Antonius, who was in the gardens of Pompeius which Caesar had given him. There was a long delay at the gate, which Octavian also put down to Antonius' aversion to him, but when he was eventually invited in they exchanged the normal greetings and made the proper enquiries about each other. When the time came to broach the subject of their business, Octavian said:

15. 'Father Antonius (for the favours Caesar conferred on you and your gratitude to him justify the claim that you are a father to me), for some of the things you did in his case I praise you and thank you, but for others I blame you. I shall speak freely, because grief drives me to do so. When he was being killed you were not there because the murderers had drawn you aside at the door, since you would either have saved him or run the risk of sharing his fate; and if the latter of these was going to happen, it was as well that you were not there. When there was an attempt to vote the murderers honours as if they had removed a despot, you strongly opposed it. I give you real thanks for that, even if you knew that the conspirators had planned to kill you along with Caesar – their reason being not that you would become, as I think you will, his avenger, but that you would perpetuate his despotism. At the same time, they would not have been tyrannicides if they

had not also been murderers, and it was for this reason they took refuge on the Capitol like suppliant criminals at a sacred precinct – or like enemies seizing a citadel. Why then were they granted an amnesty and immunity from a charge of murder, unless some senators and some of the public were bribed by them? As consul, it was your duty to have taken notice of the view of the majority. If you had wanted to act differently, your magistracy would have helped you to avenge such terrible pollution and show the misguided a better way. But you actually sent hostages, who were your very own kin, to the Capitol to guarantee the safety of the murderers.

'Let us suppose, though, that those who had been bribed forced your hand in that as well. Yet when the will was read and you yourself had delivered a worthy oration at the funeral, the ordinary people, in their vivid remembrance of Caesar, began to set fire to the assassins' houses, although they desisted for the sake of the neighbours and agreed to return armed the next day. Why did you not co-operate with the people then? Why did you not take charge of the arson or the armed attack? And seeing that you were Caesar's friend, and consul, and Antonius, why did you not at least bring a legal action against the murderers, if a legal action was necessary against manifest criminals?

16. 'On the contrary, you relied on the majesty of your office to decree the execution of Marius,[16] but you ignored the escape of the murderers and the assumption by some of them of provincial governorships which it is wrong for them to hold after killing the man who made these appointments. When the general situation had only recently been brought under control, you and Dolabella, as consuls, acted very properly in stripping them of Syria and Macedonia and taking these provinces yourselves. I would have thanked you for that, if you had not immediately voted to give them Cyrene and Crete and thought it right that fugitives should for ever be protected against me by holding provincial governorships.[17] You ignore the fact that Cisalpine Gaul is held by Decimus Brutus, a man who was one of my father's murderers just like the others. It will be maintained that this too was a decision of the senate. But it was you who put the matter to the vote, you who presided over the senate – you whom above all it suited to oppose the proposal in your own interests: granting these men an amnesty was only the act of people graciously sparing their lives, but confirming them in their provinces constituted an honour bestowed by people who were insulting Caesar and undermining your own judgement.

'My emotion has carried me to this point, perhaps further than I should have gone in view of my age and the respect I owe you. None the less, my words have been directed to you as being one of the truer friends of Caesar. He thought you deserved the highest honour and power and would perhaps have adopted you as a son if he had been sure that you would be willing to become a descendant of Aeneas instead of Heracles;[18] but <*he is supposed*> to have been doubtful about this, when he was pondering the succession.

17. 'As for the future, Antonius, I entreat you in the name of the gods who protect friendship and in the name of Caesar himself, to amend, if you wish, even measures that have already been taken (for you can, if you wish). If not, at least from now on stand beside me and help me take revenge on the murderers, with the aid of the people and these still loyal friends of my father; and if you feel constrained by some respect for the conspirators or the senate, do not act harshly against us. But enough of that. You know my personal situation and the state of my affairs; you know about the expense of the distribution which my father ordered to be made to the people; and you know the urgency there is to make it, because delay risks making me appear to be lacking in gratitude and to be causing hardship to everyone who is on the lists for colonial settlement and waiting in Rome. As to Caesar's property which was transferred to you for safety immediately after the murder, from a house that was dangerous at the time, I beg you to hold on to the valuables and all the other finery, and to accept anything else you like as a gift from me, but please hand over to me for distribution all the gold coin which Caesar had collected for his intended campaigns. That will be enough for me to share out among 300,000 recipients. The remainder of what it will cost, if I may be so bold, I might perhaps borrow from you, or from the state treasury on your authority, if you will grant it.'

18. Antonius was taken aback by this speech of Octavian's, whose degree of frankness and self-confidence struck him as unexpected, even allowing for Octavian's youth. He was irritated by the lack of the necessary politeness to himself in Octavian's words, and particularly by his demand for the money, and answered him rather severely: 'My lad, if Caesar had bequeathed you his position of leadership, as well as his inheritance and his name, it would be appropriate for you to ask me for a justification of my public acts, and for me to supply it. But Romans have never yet conferred political leadership by succession on anyone, not even the kings, at whose expulsion they swore never to endure any others – this being the principal

accusation the murderers level against your father when they allege that they killed him because he was no longer playing the leader, but the king. I need not therefore even make an answer to you on the subject of my public acts, and for the same reason I relieve you of any obligation to feel grateful to me on that score. They were done, not for your sake, but for the sake of the Roman people, except for one single act which is by far the most important for Caesar and for you. If, for the sake of my own security and popularity, I had allowed honours to be voted for the murderers as tyrannicides, Caesar would have become a tyrant, his glory and his honour lost, his decisions stripped of any validity. He would have had no will, no son, and no property, and his very body would have been denied even a private burial, because the law casts out unburied the body of a tyrant, dishonours his memory, and confiscates his property.

19. 'I was afraid of that, so I took up the fight for Caesar, to secure, not without danger and unpopularity for myself, his immortal glory and a public funeral. I faced men who were swift to act and ready to kill, and had, as you discovered, already formed a conspiracy against me as well. I faced a senate which objected to your father's rule. But I willingly preferred to run these risks and suffer anything rather than acquiesce while Caesar was deprived of burial and of honours, Caesar who was the best of his contemporaries, and the most fortunate in almost everything, and the man I esteemed most highly of all. It is thanks to these very dangers I have run that you in fact possess all the distinctions of Caesar's that you do – family, name, rank, and wealth. It would be fairer of you to thank me for these than to blame me for the concessions I made to encourage the senate, or to provide compensation for the things I needed, or to meet any other want or calculation – and you a young man and I your senior.

'No more need be said to you about that, but you imply that I also covet political mastery. This is not so, although I am regarded as not unworthy of it. You imply too that I resent not being Caesar's heir, yet you admit that my descent from Heracles is quite good enough for me.

20. 'On the subject of your needs, I would have thought that your wish to borrow money from the treasury was dissimulation, if it were not for the fact that you may quite plausibly still be unaware that the state treasury was left empty by your father. From the time he came to power the revenues were paid to him, instead of to the treasury, and they will shortly be discovered among his assets when we vote to investigate them. This will not be at all unfair to him, as he is already dead, and he would not have said it

was unfair if he had been asked for accounts while he was still alive. There are also many private individuals who dispute your claim to particular items and will make you realize that you do not enjoy uncontested ownership of this property. Of the money that was transferred to my house, there is neither the quantity you suppose, nor is any now in my hands. The reason is that the men who were in positions of authority or power, except for Dolabella and my brothers,[19] at once divided it up on the pretext that it was the property of a tyrant, although I won them round to a favourable view of our decisions about Caesar. And if you see things as I do* you yourself will give the rest of it, when you get your hands on it, not to the people of Rome but to the malcontents. These, if they have any sense,* will send the people away to their colonies, and the people, as you too ought to know, fresh from your Greek studies, *"are as unstable as the waves of the sea: one approaches, another retreats".*[20] For which reason the people are always building our own demagogues up and then knocking them over.'

21. Octavian was furious at the insulting content of much of this speech, and went away repeatedly invoking his father's name. He at once put up for sale all the property which had come to him by inheritance, hoping that this urgency would encourage the people to lend him support. After Antonius' hostility to him became apparent and the senate had decreed that there should be an immediate investigation of the state finances, the majority of Romans grew apprehensive of the young Caesar because of his father's favours to the soldiery and the populace, and his own present popularity with the mob over the money he was expected to pay out, and his enormous wealth, which had come to him in such quantity that in the eyes of most people it would prevent his status remaining that of a private citizen. They were also very nervous that Antonius might win over Octavian, young, well respected, and rich as he was, make him his junior partner, and win the race to seize the power that Caesar had held. Others were pleased at the turn of events, thinking that the two men would obstruct each other, and that when the money was investigated Octavian's wealth would immediately melt away and they would have a treasury full to overflowing from that source − their belief being that they would find most of the public funds in Caesar's estate.

22. Many of them brought legal actions against Octavian over landed property, each of them making different claims but in most cases having this in common, that the property had been acquired as a result of the proscription of persons who had been exiled, or fled the country, or been put

to death. They brought the actions before Antonius himself or the other consul Dolabella. If anyone had his case taken by another magistrate, there too the judgement was almost always given against Octavian, to keep in with Antonius, although Octavian showed that the purchases had been made by his father from the treasury and pointed to the final decree of the senate confirming all Caesar's acts. Great injustices were inflicted on him in these cases, and there was no end in sight to the damages until Pedius and Pinarius (who were Octavian's co-heirs under the will)[21] attacked Antonius on their own behalf and on Octavian's, saying that they were being unjustly treated, in breach of the resolution of the senate. In their opinion Antonius should only correct situations where power had been abused, and uphold everything else that Caesar had done.

Antonius agreed that what was currently being done did not perhaps fully conform with the resolution they had jointly passed, but said that the wording of the resolution was actually contrary to the senate's view. He argued that it was due solely to the urgent need for an amnesty that the clause 'not to upset any of the decisions that have already been taken' was written in, not for its own sake or to have universal application so much as to look good and soothe the people of Rome, who were agitating for it. It would be fairer, he said, to observe the intention and not the letter of the decree: they ought not to act in an unreasonable way against so many men who had lost their own or ancestral estates through civil war, and do so on behalf of a young man who had acquired enormous and unexpected wealth which did not belong to him or to any private individual and was being used stupidly and with opportunistic rashness by him. However, he promised to be lenient to them once they had separated Octavian's share from theirs. On receiving this answer from Antonius, Pinarius and his friends immediately divided up the inheritance to prevent their own share also from being lost in the courts. It was not in their own interests that they did this, but in Octavian's again, since they were very soon going to make him a gift of the entire amount.

23. Gaius Antonius, Antonius' brother, was attending to all the absent Brutus' duties, including the festival, now close, which he was going to stage on behalf of Brutus as the praetor responsible.[22] The preparations were lavish and hopes were high that the entertainment would break the people's resistance and induce them to recall Brutus and his companions. Octavian, on the other hand, attempted to gain the favour of the mob for himself and went on dividing out the money he received from his sale to

the officials of the tribes, for them to distribute to those who came first to collect it. He went round the salerooms and said that his agents would put the lowest possible price on everything, title to it all being still doubtful and fraught with risk because of the court actions and Octavian's own haste. All this won him the support and sympathy of the people, who thought his troubles were undeserved. To fund the distribution, he also put up for sale, on top of what he had inherited from Caesar, not only the property of his own that had come from his father Octavius and other sources, but everything owned by his mother and Philippus, and also Pedius' and Pinarius' share of the inheritance (which he asked them to give him), alleging that because of his own disgraceful treatment Caesar's estate was insufficient even for this purpose. Then the people no longer saw the gift as coming from Caesar, but from Caesar's heir as well. They pitied him deeply and gave him credit for tolerating such treatment and having such ambitions, and it was apparent that they would soon stop disregarding Antonius' insulting behaviour towards him.

24. The populace showed their feelings in the course of Brutus' festival, which was indeed magnificent. When some spectators, who had been paid to do so, shouted for the recall of Brutus and Cassius and the remainder of the audience had been overcome by pity for them, a crowd burst in and stopped the performances until the demand faded away.

As the hopes they had placed in the festival had been thwarted by Octavian, Brutus and Cassius decided to set out and take forcible possession of Syria and Macedonia on the grounds that these provinces had been theirs before being allocated to Antonius and Dolabella. Once their designs became apparent, Dolabella also hurried off to Syria, but went to Asia first in order to raise money there. Antonius, for his part, judged that in order to face the future he needed some forces. The army stationed in Macedonia was of excellent fighting quality and was very strong in numbers, consisting of six legions, plus the other troops brigaded with them such as archers, light infantry, and other light-armed, along with a large quantity of cavalry and a full quota of stores and equipment. Although it apparently belonged to Dolabella, who was in charge of Syria and the Parthian front, because Caesar himself had been going to employ it against the Parthians, Antonius was thinking of transferring it to himself, because it was so very near that it would be in Italy directly it had crossed the Adriatic.

25. A rumour suddenly broke out that the Getae, on hearing of the death of Caesar, had attacked Macedonia and were laying it waste. Antonius

asked the senate to give him the army in order to punish the Getae, pointing out that it had been assembled for Caesar to use against them before
proceeding against the Parthians, and that the Parthian front was quiet for
the moment. The senate mistrusted the rumour and sent a commission to
investigate, but Antonius laid their fear and suspicion to rest by passing a
measure that it was to be illegal on any grounds whatsoever to <*make or*>[23]
put to the vote a proposal to confer dictatorial power, or accept it if conferred, and that anyone who ignored any of these prohibitions could be
killed at sight with impunity. Thanks chiefly to this he carried his hearers
with him, and after agreeing with Dolabella's representatives that he would
give Dolabella one legion Antonius was appointed commander-in-chief of
the army in Macedonia. Having secured what he wanted, he immediately
sent his brother Gaius to communicate this decree urgently to the army.
The commission who had been sent to investigate the rumour then returned and reported that they had seen no Getae in Macedonia, but added
(whether genuinely or prompted by Antonius) that people were afraid that
if the army were transferred anywhere else the Getae might attack.

26. While all this was happening in Rome, Brutus and Cassius were collecting money and troops. Trebonius, the governor of Asia, was fortifying
towns in their interest, and would not admit Dolabella, when he arrived,[24]
into either Pergamum or Smyrna. He would only allow him, as consul, to
buy provisions outside the walls. Dolabella in anger attacked the defences,
but without result. Trebonius then said he would admit him to Ephesus,
and on his immediate departure in that direction sent troops to shadow
him at a distance. These men observed Dolabella marching away as night
was falling, and since they had as yet no reason to suspect him left a few of
their number to follow him and themselves returned to Smyrna. Dolabella
proceeded to lay an ambush for this handful, and after capturing them and
putting them to death came back to Smyrna before the night was over. He
found the defences unmanned, and took the town by scaling the walls.
Trebonius, who was still in bed, told his captors to take him to Dolabella,
saying that he was quite willing to go with them. One of the centurions
sarcastically answered, 'Go where you like, but leave your head behind; our
instructions are to bring not you, but your head.' With these words he instantly cut off Trebonius' head, and when daylight came Dolabella ordered
it to be displayed on the governor's tribunal where Trebonius had conducted business. Because he had been involved in the killing of Caesar and

at the moment of the murder had detained Antonius in conversation at the entrance to the hall, the army and its throng of camp-followers fell with fury on Trebonius' body, which they treated in various degrading ways, and on his head, which they threw like a ball from one to another across the town paving, laughing, until it was smashed to pieces. This was how Trebonius, the first of the murderers, was punished.[25]

27. Antonius was planning to bring the army from Macedonia across to Italy, and as he lacked any other excuse for doing this he asked the senate to let him exchange Macedonia for Cisalpine Gaul, of which Decimus Brutus Albinus was the governor.[26] On the one hand it was in Antonius' mind that Caesar had started from Cisalpine Gaul when he defeated Pompeius, and on the other he intended to give the impression that he was recalling the army not to Italy, but to Gaul. The senate, who thought that this fortress of Cisalpine Gaul was under their control, were resentful and then for the first time realized they had been tricked, and regretted that they had given Macedonia to Antonius. The leading senators privately sent word to Decimus advising him to keep a very firm hold on his province, and to collect another army and money in case Antonius used force against him: such was the degree of the fear and anger they felt towards Antonius. Antonius, however, intended to ask the people, instead of the senate, to confer Gaul on him by means of a law [27] – exactly as Caesar himself had obtained the same province at an earlier date, and Dolabella Syria very recently – and gave his brother Gaius orders to bring the army across the Adriatic to Brundisium at once in order to intimidate the senate.[28]

28. Gaius proceeded to do as he was instructed. Meanwhile there came the festival which Critonius as aedile was going to produce.[29] For the occasion, Octavian was making ready his father's golden throne and wreath, which it had been decreed should be displayed in his honour at all the festivals. When Critonius announced that he would not tolerate honour being paid to Caesar at his expense, Octavian brought him before Antonius as consul. Antonius said that he would refer the matter to the senate, at which Octavian became irritated and said, 'Refer it, but I shall display the throne so long as the decree is in force.' Antonius was angry, and forbade it. He also forbade it, still more unreasonably, at the subsequent festival, produced by Octavian himself. (This had been instituted by his father in honour of Venus Genetrix when he also dedicated to her the temple in his forum, along with the forum itself.)[30] Then a general feeling of enmity towards

Antonius became very apparent, because he was not so much locked in rivalry with Octavian as churlishly insulting Caesar.

Octavian himself, accompanied by a crowd like a bodyguard, solicited the ordinary people, and anyone who had received a favour from his father, and the soldiers who had served under him, and inflamed their feelings by begging them to overlook and ignore the disgraceful treatment he himself had willingly undergone, but to defend Caesar, their general and benefactor, against the dishonour being inflicted by Antonius; and they would be defending themselves as well, because nothing they had received from Caesar would be safe if even decrees passed in Caesar's personal interest had no validity. All over the city Octavian would climb up on to any elevated spot and accuse Antonius at the top of his voice: 'Don't be angry with Caesar on my account, Antonius. Don't insult the man who has turned out to be above all *your* benefactor, and your greatest benefactor. Heap as much indignity on me as you like, but stop plundering his property until the citizens have had their legacy, and then take all the rest. In my poverty I shall be content with my father's glory, if it lasts, and the legacy to the people, if you let it be paid.'

29. As a result accusations were now shouted frequently and openly against Antonius by everyone. When he threatened Octavian more sharply, and his threats became public, they attacked him still more vigorously. Then the officers of Antonius' guard, who had served with Caesar and were at that time held in the highest regard by Antonius, asked him to moderate his arrogance both for their own sakes and for his, because he had served under Caesar and owed his present good fortune to him. He realized that what they said was true, and since he respected the men who put them forward, and also stood in need of some support from Octavian himself with the people over the question of exchanging his province for Gaul, he agreed with the points they made. He swore that he had not wanted to act at all in this way but had altered his original policy because of the lad, who was most painfully conceited, in spite of being so young, and showed no deference to his elders or honour to those in authority. For this, Antonius said, the young man still needed a warning for his own good; but because his officers had made this request of him themselves, he would control his anger and return to his former self and policy, provided that Octavian also moderated his behaviour.

30. The officers welcomed these remarks and brought the two men together. After mutual criticism, they accepted each other as friends, and the law on the province of Gaul was at once promulgated, to the dread of the senators, who planned to block it in the senate, if Antonius brought it to them first, and to use the tribunes to veto it if he took it to the people without preliminary senatorial debate. Some even thought that the province should no longer have a governor at all, so great was their fear of the proximity of Gaul. Antonius counter-attacked, accusing them of entrusting it to Decimus because Decimus had killed Caesar, and of not trusting himself because he had not killed the man who had conquered Gaul and brought it to its knees. He now cast these taunts openly in their faces, saying that they were all pleased at what had happened. When the day for the voting arrived, the senate expected that the assembly would be called together by centuries, but while it was dark their opponents roped off the forum and summoned the tribal assembly, which had gathered by prior arrangement.[31] The common people, although they were irritated with Antonius, still voted in his interest because Octavian stood by the ropes and asked them to do so. His request was made chiefly to prevent Decimus, his father's murderer, having control of an army and such a strategic area, and secondly to do Antonius a favour now that they were reconciled. He certainly also expected to get something himself from Antonius in return. The tribunes were bribed by Antonius and kept quiet, the law was passed, and Antonius' army now possessed a respectable reason for crossing the Adriatic.

31. When one of the tribunes died, Octavian supported Flaminius for election as his successor. The populace, who thought Octavian wanted the office himself but had not stood because of his age, formed the idea of electing him when it came to the vote. The senate was jealous and afraid of his rise, in case he brought his father's killers before the people for trial. Antonius, disregarding his recently established friendship with Octavian, and either wishing to gratify or soothe the senate which was displeased with the law about Gaul, or for reasons of his own, issued a consular edict that if Octavian attempted anything illegal, he would use the full power of his authority against him.[32] Since this edict betrayed ingratitude to Octavian and contempt both for him and the people, the people became very angry and intended to oppose Antonius' wishes in the election, with the result that he became frightened and cancelled the election. For his part, Octavian, claiming that he was now clearly being plotted against, despatched a large number of messengers to make his plight known in his father's colonies and find out what their feelings were. He also sent bogus traders to

Antonius' army to mix with the men, establish contact with the most daring, and secretly distribute pamphlets to the rank and file.

32. While Octavian was busy with this, the military tribunes again requested an appointment with Antonius and said: 'Antonius, we and all the other men who served with you under Caesar jointly helped to establish his position of leadership and continued to support it as each day demanded. We recognize that the attitude of his murderers to us is one of loathing and intrigue, and that senatorial feeling is swinging towards them, but when the people expelled them we took heart because we saw that Caesar's cause was not utterly bereft of friends, or fading from memory, or untouched by gratitude. We placed our hopes of future safety in you: you are Caesar's friend, you are a man endowed with qualities of leadership second only to his, and you are also the current holder of power and in every way most suitable. However, our enemies are recovering. They are engaged upon an impudent and forcible seizure of Syria and Macedonia, and gathering money and troops to use against us, while the senate is grooming Decimus to resist you. Yet you are allowing your disagreement with the young Caesar to distract you, and we are not unreasonably afraid that your quarrel may become mixed up with the war which looms over us, and that the result our enemies desire may come about. Bear all this in mind, and remember your piety towards Caesar, and your concern not only for us – and we have not come to blame you in any way – but also, more importantly, for yourself and your own interests. We ask you, so long as you can, simply to give Octavian assistance, no more, in wreaking vengeance on the murderers. By taking an immediate grip on power you will free yourself from anxiety and will have taken steps to do the same for us; for we are concerned both for ourselves and for you.'

33. To this speech by the military tribunes Antonius replied: 'You campaigned alongside us and shared our experiences. You know well the extent of the friendship and support I gave Caesar, and how I was the readiest of all to undergo danger in his service; as to the gratitude and honour he always showed me, it would not be right for me to dwell on that. The murderers were equally aware of both these facts and were plotting to kill me along with Caesar, because they thought that if I remained alive they would not secure their ends. Whoever persuaded them to change their minds did so not out of concern for my safety, but to make the act of tyrannicide look plausible and allow them to appear to be killing, not a number of men because they were enemies, but one man because he was a despot. Who on

earth could imagine that I do not care about Caesar, when he was my benefactor? Or that I pay greater respect to his enemies, and willingly condone
his murder to gratify men who plotted against me, as his young heir believes? How do you think they came to enjoy an amnesty for the murder,
and hold provincial governorships? I tell you, he wants to blame me, and
not the senate, for that. Listen to how it happened.

34. 'When Caesar was suddenly butchered in the senate, I was the one
who was the most afraid of all. This was due to my friendship with Caesar
and my lack of accurate information, for I was not yet clear about the conspiracy or the number of its targets. The ordinary people were in uproar,
the assassins and their gladiators had seized and shut off the Capitol, and the
senate was on their side, as it now is more openly, and was on the point of
voting honours to the killers as tyrannicides. If Caesar had been declared a
tyrant, it was all up with us, as associates of the tyrant. So I was beset by confusion, anxiety and terror, but if you consider the matter, you will find that
at a time when it would not have been at all surprising for me not to have
known what to do, I was very daring where boldness was needed, and re-
sourceful where play-acting was required. The very first thing, from which
the rest followed, was to quash the honours which were being voted to the
conspirators; and this I did by boldly and dangerously venturing to place
myself in uncompromising opposition to the senate and the assassins, because I considered that we Caesarians could safely survive only if Caesar
were not judged a tyrant. Now our enemies and the senate itself were
gripped by a similar fear, that if Caesar were not a tyrant, then they would
be guilty of murder, and for that reason they argued violently with me. I
therefore gave way to them when the amnesty was proposed in place of the
honours, so that I could obtain the things I wanted in exchange. How
many things, and how important? That the name Caesar, sweetest of all
names to me, should not be suppressed; that his property should not be forfeit to the state; that the adoption, on which the youth now prides himself,
should not be annulled, nor the will invalidated; that his body should be
given a princely burial; that the honours that had been awarded him in the
past should be permanently commemorated; that all his acts should be
confirmed; and that his son, and we his associates, whether commanders or
soldiers, should be guaranteed a safe and honoured existence, instead of
ignominy.

35. 'Do you regard these concessions which I won from the senate in
exchange for the amnesty as few and insignificant? Or that the senate

would have granted them without the amnesty? It would have been perfectly creditable to have made this bargain in all honesty, and quite sin-
cerely spared men who were murderers, for the sake of Caesar's reputation
and the guarantee of our own safety; as it was, I made it not with this intention, but in order to postpone retribution. When I had got my way with
the senate over my immediate goals, and the assassins relaxed as though
there was nothing to worry them, I took courage and began to undermine
the amnesty, not by votes of the assembly or decrees of the senate (that was
impossible), but by unobtrusive manipulation of the mob. On the excuse of
his funeral, I brought Caesar's body into the forum. I uncovered his
wounds, pointed out how many there were, and displayed his clothing, all
blood-stained and cut to ribbons. With intense emotion I kept alluding,
there in public, to his virtues and his love for the people, and lamented for
him as a mortal slain while invoking him as a god. These actions and words
of mine inflamed the people, ignited their feelings after the amnesty, sent
them to attack the homes of our enemies, and drove the latter out of the
city. How far this happened against the opposition, and to the irritation, of
the senate, it at once made clear by accusing me of demagogic behaviour,
by sending the murderers abroad to provincial governorships, and by telling
Brutus and Cassius to hurry, under cover of a corn commission and even
before the official date, to Syria and Macedonia, which held large armies.[33]
Then another, still greater, fear took hold of me, because I had as yet no
army of my own and might find myself in a situation where, unarmed, we
had to face all this armed force. In addition, I was suspicious of my colleague in office: he had always been at odds with me, he had pretended to
be in the plot against Caesar, and he had proposed to declare the day of the
murder the birthday of the city.

36. 'While I was in this quandary, eager to disarm our enemies and transfer their military resources to us, I put Amatius to death and recalled Pompeius, in order to ensnare the senate again and win it over to my side. Even
so, I did not trust it, and I persuaded Dolabella to ask for Syria, not from the
senate, but from the people by legislation. I gave him my co-operation in
this, so that he should become an enemy instead of an ally of the assassins,
and the senate would feel it morally wrong to deny me Macedonia afterwards. But even in this situation, because of its army they would not have
given me Macedonia, not even after Dolabella's precedent, if I had not previously conceded the army to Dolabella on the grounds that Syria and the
Parthian front had been allotted to him. Furthermore, the senate would not

have taken either Macedonia or Syria from Cassius and his associates if they had not been allowed other provinces in exchange to provide these men with some security. Granted that an exchange was necessary, look what compensation they received: Cyrene and Crete, provinces innocent of soldiers. Even our enemies despise them because they will not be safe in them, and are now trying to seize by force the provinces that were taken away from them. This, then, was the way in which the military forces too were transferred from our enemies to Dolabella – by means of guile, contrivance, and exchange, because while I still lacked armed backing I had to proceed by legal means.

37. 'After this, while our enemies were collecting another army, I needed the army from Macedonia, but was short of a pretext. A rumour broke out that the Getae were plundering Macedonia. This was treated with scepticism and a delegation was sent to investigate, but meanwhile I introduced measures by which it became illegal to make or put to the vote a proposal to confer dictatorial power, or accept it if conferred. The senate, seduced by this, gave me the army. Then for the first time I felt myself to be as strong as my enemies, not these declared enemies, as Octavian imagines, but the more numerous and more powerful enemies who wish to remain unidentified. After I had achieved this, one of the murderers remained on my flank, Decimus Brutus. He too commanded strategic territory and a large military force, and I knew him to be a man of some boldness as well. I therefore proposed to take Gaul from him, promising for the sake of appearances in the senate to exchange it for Macedonia, which now lacked an army. When the senate became irritated and now realized the trap, many of them wrote at a length and in terms you are aware of to Decimus and also incited my consular successors to resistance.[34] I responded yet more boldly with my scheme of being granted the province under a law of the people instead of by the senate, and I brought the army over from Macedonia to Brundisium to have it available against emergencies. And, God willing, we shall use it as needs dictate.

38. 'In this way we have exchanged the terror which previously gripped us for positive personal safety and confidence in face of our enemies. Now that this is apparent, the sentiments of the masses towards our enemies have also become clear. You can see how much the latter regret their decrees, and how hard they are striving to take Gaul away from me although it has already been given me. You are aware of what they write to Decimus and how much pressure they are putting on my successors in the consulship to

revoke the law on the province of Gaul. But with the gods of our fathers on our side, and a policy which conforms with the demands of piety, and your bravery and nobility, which helped Caesar too to triumph, we shall avenge him, deploying all our powers of body and determination of mind to do so.

'While all this was happening, fellow-soldiers, I preferred it to remain a secret; but now it has taken place I have admitted it to you, as I consider you, in word and deed, my partners in everything. If there are others who take a different view of the matter, share this information with them — though not with Octavian, because he shows me no gratitude.'

39. After this exposition by Antonius, the military tribunes were convinced that all his actions had been informed by genuine hostility to the murderers and a desire to outwit the senate. None the less, they requested him to be reconciled with Octavian, and after gaining their point effected a second reconciliation between them on the Capitol. Not long afterwards, Antonius seconded to his friends some of his bodyguard on the grounds that they had been accomplices in a plot of Octavian's against him. Whether he was making false allegations, or really believed this was true, or had found out about the agents sent out to the army camps and transformed a stratagem aimed at his plans to one aimed at his person, the story immediately went the rounds and caused general excitement followed by great indignation. A few people, who had the ability to think a problem out, were aware that it was in Octavian's interests for Antonius to survive, even if he did Octavian some harm, because Caesar's assassins were afraid of him; while if he died the assassins, enjoying strong support from the senate, would embark with less apprehension on every venture. Although this was the view of the more intelligent, the majority, seeing the insults and losses which Octavian suffered every day, thought the slander might be true and considered it sacrilegious and intolerable that a plot had been laid against the life of the consul Antonius.[35]

Mad with anger, Octavian hurried around confronting even those who held this latter opinion, and kept declaring that he himself was the victim of a plot by Antonius to deprive him of the favour of the people, favour which was, even now, his alone. He ran to the doors of Antonius' house, shouted the same message, and called the gods to witness as he swore all kinds of oaths and challenged Antonius to bring a case in court. When no one appeared, he said, 'I agree to be judged by your friends', and with these words tried to go inside. On being stopped, he again cried out and abused Antonius, and became angry with the men at the door, *<claiming that>* * they

were preventing him from being called to account. As he went away, he
asked the people to witness that if anything happened to him, his death
would be due to Antonius' treachery. At these words, spoken with deep
emotion, the crowd began to change its attitude, and repent somewhat of
its previous opinion. Even then there were sceptics who were reluctant to
believe either side. Some levelled the charge that both men were play-
acting, because they had recently come to an agreement on sacred soil and
this was a contrivance against their enemies, while others maintained that
Antonius had thought it up as a way of increasing his bodyguard or detach-
ing the colonists from Octavian.

40. It was then reported by the agents who had been sent out secretly by
Octavian that the army at Brundisium and the settlers felt angry with Antonius because he did not care about Caesar's murder, and would lend assistance if they could. As a result Antonius left Rome for Brundisium.[36]
Octavian, who was afraid that if Antonius returned with the army he himself might be caught defenceless, took money and set off for Campania to
persuade the towns that had been founded by his father to enlist with him.
He was successful first at Calatia, and then at Casilinum, places which lie
either side of Capua. By giving each recruit 500 denarii he increased his
force to 10,000 men.[37] They were not yet properly equipped or organized
into units, but resembled a single bodyguard under one standard. The
Roman population were apprehensive of Antonius returning at the head of
an army, and when they learnt that Octavian too was approaching with
another one, some were doubly afraid while others were glad because they
intended to use Octavian against Antonius. Those, however, who had witnessed the reconciliation on the Capitol thought these events were a sham
and that the bargain had conceded power to Antonius and the lives of the
murderers to Octavian.

41. Such was the state of unrest when the tribune Cannutius,[38] who was
an enemy of Antonius and therefore friendly to Octavian, went to meet
Octavian and found out his intentions. He then announced to the people
that Octavian was advancing with open hostility to Antonius, and that if
they feared an unconstitutional seizure of power by Antonius they ought to
associate themselves with Octavian because they had no other military
force at the present moment. After saying this he brought Octavian, who
was camped two miles out in the precinct of Mars, into the city. On entry,
Octavian proceeded to the temple of Castor and Pollux, and his men

surrounded the temple openly wearing their swords.[39] Cannutius spoke first to the people, and attacked Antonius. Then Octavian reminded them of his father and of what he himself had suffered at the hands of Antonius, which was why he had assembled this military force to protect himself; and he declared that he would assist and obey his country in all things, and as for the present, was ready to face Antonius.

42. When he had finished this speech and dissolved the assembly, his troops, who thought the opposite, that they had come to support the reconciliation between Antonius and Octavian, or at least do no more than protect Octavian and take revenge on the murderers, were not pleased by the attack on Antonius, who had once been their commander and was now consul. Some of them asked permission to go back to their homes to equip themselves, saying that they were not happy with any weapons except their own, while others hinted at the truth. Octavian was at a loss, finding himself in a position that was the opposite of what he had expected, but because he hoped to get the better of them by persuasion rather than by force, he went along with their excuses and sent some of them off to fetch their arms and others simply to stay at home. He hid his disappointment, commended all who had gathered together, and presented them with further gifts;[40] he said he would reward them still more splendidly in future, and always employ them as friends of his father, and not as soldiers, to meet his pressing needs. These words induced only 1,000, or 3,000, men (the number is disputed) out of 10,000 to stay with him. At the time the remainder left Rome, but they soon remembered the toil of farming, the profits of military service, the words of Octavian, his readiness to fall in with their wishes, and the favours they had both received already and hoped to receive in the future. Like a fickle mob they changed their minds. To cover themselves they made use of their original excuse, and after they had equipped themselves came back to Octavian, who now had fresh quantities of money and was going round Ravenna and all the nearby districts, recruiting men non-stop and sending them all to Arretium.

43. Antonius was met in the middle of Brundisium by four out of the five Macedonian legions, who criticized him for failing to follow up the murder of Caesar and made him mount the platform, without applause, to explain this to them first of all. Angry at their silence, he did not restrain himself. He berated them for not being grateful to him for transferring them from the Parthian front to Italy, and for failing to mention this favour. He also blamed them for not bringing to him the emissaries sent by a rash

youth (his term for Octavian) to undermine their loyalty. None the less, he would find these men himself; the army he would take to the rich land of Gaul allotted him, and he would give 100 denarii to each man present. They laughed at his meanness and when he grew angry they became rowdier and began to disperse. Antonius then left, saying, 'You will learn to obey orders.' He asked the military tribunes to supply him with the names of the disruptive men (for in the Roman armies a note is always kept of each individual's character), and having drawn lots in military fashion[41] he put to death not every tenth man, but a proportion of this tenth, in the belief that he would very quickly terrify them. But this treatment led them to feel angry and resentful, not afraid.

44. When they saw this, the men Octavian had previously sent to tamper with the soldiers' loyalty seized the moment to scatter quantities of leaflets around the camp, urging the troops to exchange Antonius' meanness and cruelty for the memory of Caesar and the protection and lavish gifts of his heir. Antonius attempted to identify these agents by promising large rewards for information and threatening anyone who sheltered them. He failed to arrest a single one, and was furious with the army because it was sheltering them. When he was informed of what Octavian had been doing in the colonies and in Rome, he was perturbed and went before the army again to say that he was pained by the fate that had, under compulsion of military discipline, been visited on a few men, instead of on the greater number punishable by law, but that they knew quite well that he was neither mean nor cruel, 'Let us forget our ill-will, fed enough by crimes and punishments. The hundred denarii I ordered to be given you was not a bounty (not being in keeping with Antonius' fortune) but rather a little present to mark our meeting, and you ought to maintain your obedience to the laws of our country and military discipline, in this matter as in all.' Such were his words, and he did not as yet increase the bounty at all, to prevent it seeming that the general had been defeated by his troops. But they accepted it, either because they had had a change of heart or because they were apprehensive. He changed their military tribunes, perhaps from continuing anger at the mutiny, or perhaps for some other purpose, and in his present straits cheerfully condoned the behaviour of the rest and sent them ahead of him in detachments along the coast road to Ariminum.

45. He himself selected from the whole force a praetorian cohort consisting of men who had the best physique and character, and made his way to Rome with the intention of going on from there to Ariminum.[42] He

made an arrogant entry into the city, putting his troops into camp just out-side it, keeping his escort ready for action, and having the men who guard-ed his house at night armed. Passwords were given them, and guard-duty was rotated as in camp. He called the senate together to launch an attack on Octavian for what he had been doing, but heard as he was on the point of going in that one of his four legions, the one called the Martian, had switched its loyalty to Octavian *en route*.[43] As he was delaying his entry and wondering what to do, further news came that the Fourth legion, like the Martian, had changed sides. Deeply disturbed in consequence, he entered the senate, said a few words on the pretence that he had summoned them for other reasons, and immediately proceeded to the city gates, and from there to Alba Fucens to try to persuade the rebels to change their minds. When they shot at him from the walls, he turned back, and after sending 500 denarii a man to the other legions left Rome for Tibur, accompanied by his own troops and wearing the dress of a man setting out for war.[44] And there was plainly a war now, because Decimus refused to give up Gaul.

46. While he was at Tibur almost the entire senate and the majority of the equestrian order came to pay their respects, along with the most im-portant of the ordinary people. Finding Antonius engaged in swearing in both the troops already there and such of his former fellow-soldiers as had flocked to join him (a large number), they willingly joined in affirming on oath that they would never cease to give him their goodwill and loyalty, so that people were at a loss to know who had recently been cursing him in Octavian's assembly.

He thus had a fine send-off for Ariminum, where the province of Gaul begins. Apart from the new recruits, his army consisted of the three legions he had summoned from Macedonia (the last having now arrived), and one of veterans, who although they were ageing were still twice as good as the recruits. So he had four legions of trained men, with their usual auxiliaries, his own bodyguard, and the newly raised forces. Lepidus with four legions in Spain, Asinius Pollio with two, and Plancus with three in Transalpine Gaul, were believed to support Antonius.[45]

47. On Octavian's side there were two legions, both equally formidable, which had deserted to him from Antonius, one of new recruits, and two of veterans, though these were neither up to strength nor fully equipped and had their numbers made up by recruits. Having collected them all at Alba, he sent a letter to the senate. The senators then renewed their enthusiasm for him, so that once again there was a puzzle, who had given Antonius his

send-off; but they were annoyed with the legions because they had transferred their allegiance not to the senate, but to Octavian. None the less they commended them and Octavian, and declared that they would vote a little later on what they should do, when the new magistrates had entered office.[46] It was obvious that they would use the legions against Antonius, but as they had as yet no army of their own and could not enlist one without the consuls they decided to postpone everything until they had their new magistrates.

48. The army brought Octavian axes and lictors in full dress, and requested him to proclaim himself propraetor because he was their war leader and they always served under a magistrate.[47] He thanked them for the honour, but referred the decision to the senate. The soldiers wanted to set off in a body to secure it, but he stopped them and held back a delegation with the argument that the senate would confer the rank of its own accord, 'and all the more so if they see your eagerness and my reluctance'.

With difficulty they were thus dispersed, but their leaders accused Octavian of ignoring them. He explained to them that the senate was leaning his way, not because it wished him well, but because it feared Antonius and had no army of its own, 'until we bring Antonius down, and the assassins, who are friends and kinsmen of the senate, gather military forces for them. I am aware of this, and the help I offer is a pretence. Let us not be the first to expose the deception. If we snatch the magistracy, they will accuse us of high-handedness or violence, but if we show deference, perhaps they will freely bestow it for fear that I will accept it for myself from you.' This said, he went to watch the training exercises of the two legions that had deserted from Antonius, which formed up to face each other and unstintingly did all they had to do in a real battle, but kill. Delighted with the spectacle, he gladly made it the excuse for presenting them with another 500 denarii each and announced that if it came to war and they were victorious, he would give them 5,000. In this way Octavian stiffened his mercenaries by the lavishness of his gifts.

49. Such was the state of affairs in Italy. In Gaul, Antonius ordered Decimus to depart for Macedonia, in obedience to the people and for his own safety. In reply Decimus sent Antonius the letter conveyed to him from the senate, to the effect that it was inappropriate for him to give way to Antonius by resolution either of the people or even of the senate.[48] Antonius then

fixed a date after which he would treat Decimus as an enemy, and Decimus told him to fix a more distant one to avoid becoming an enemy of the senate too soon. Antonius, who would have defeated Decimus without difficulty in the open, decided to proceed against the towns, and they began to admit him. Afraid that he would no longer be able even to enter any of them, Decimus invented a letter from the senate summoning him and his army back to Rome. He loaded all his equipment and took the road for Italy. Everybody welcomed him, because he was on his way out, but when he was passing through the rich city of Mutina he shut the gates, concentrated the resources of the people living in the territory of Mutina to provide food, killed and salted down all the beasts of burden for fear of a long siege, and waited for Antonius. His army was made up of a quantity of gladiators and three regular legions, of which one was composed of recent and still untried recruits, while the other two, which had previously served under his command, were completely loyal. Antonius angrily came to attack him and encircled Mutina with ditches and walls.

50. So Decimus was under siege. At Rome Hirtius and Pansa, immediately after the sacrifice on entering office on 1 January, convoked the senate on the Capitol itself to discuss Antonius.[49] Cicero indeed, and Cicero's associates, considered that he should now be declared an enemy of the state, because he had occupied Gaul by violence and in defiance of the senate as a bastion against his country, and had brought over to Italy the army which had been given to him for use against the Thracians. They also attacked him for the other aspects of his policy after Caesar's death, for being openly escorted in the city by a large military escort of centurions, for treating his house like a fort with passwords and armed guards, and for appearing to them more overbearing in the rest of his behaviour than befitted an annual magistrate. On the other hand Lucius Piso, one of the most distinguished Romans, who was looking after Antonius' interests in his absence, and a number of other men who supported Piso (whether for himself, or because of Antonius, or for reasons of their own), thought Antonius should be given a hearing because it was not their custom to condemn a man unheard, nor decent to act in this way today towards a man who had been consul yesterday, particularly when Cicero himself, among others, had often sung his praises. At the time the senate were divided in their views, and sat until nightfall. The next morning they gathered again in the senate-house to debate the same question, and under the pressure exerted by Cicero's party Antonius would have been declared an enemy if Salvius, one of

the tribunes, had not forced them to adjourn until the next day (since the magistrate who blocks a decision always overrides the others).[50]

51. Cicero's party not only reviled Salvius and insulted him in the coarsest manner, but at once went out to inflame the people against him, and called for him to appear in front of them. Undaunted, he was about to go out until he was restrained by the senate, who were afraid that he would make the people change their minds by reminding them of Antonius. They were aware that they were condemning a distinguished man without trial and that it was the people who had given Antonius Gaul, but in their concern for the safety of the assassins they were angry with him for being the first to disturb the arrangements affecting them after the amnesty. For this reason they had already made use of Octavian against him, and Octavian, who realized this, had nevertheless also made his own choice to destroy Antonius first. Such were the reasons for the senate's anger with Antonius, and although they postponed the vote as the tribune had demanded, none the less they voted to commend Decimus for not vacating Gaul to Antonius; also that Octavian should share the command of the force he currently had with the consuls Hirtius and Pansa, that a gilded statue of him should be erected, that he should forthwith rank as an ex-consul in senatorial debate,[51] that he should be allowed to stand for the consulship ten years before the legal age,[52] and that the state should pay the legions which had defected to him from Antonius the sum which Octavian had promised them in the event of victory.

After passing these measures, the senate adjourned, so that Antonius knew that by this means he had been declared an enemy and that the tribune would raise no further opposition the next day. However, his mother, wife, and son (still only a lad), and his other relations and friends spent all night going round to the houses of the influential and pleading with them.[53] When day broke they accosted senators on their way to the meeting, threw themselves wailing and lamenting at their feet, and stood by the doors clad in black and crying out. The senators wavered under the influence of the cries, the sight, and the extent of this sudden change of fortune, and Cicero, perturbed, addressed them as follows:[54]

52. 'Yesterday we reached the decision we ought to have reached about Antonius. By the honours we conferred on his enemies we voted him an enemy of the state. Salvius, the single dissenter, must be more acute than everyone else or have acted either from friendship or in ignorance of the circumstances. One of these alternatives is highly discreditable to ourselves, if we are to suppose that we are all more stupid than a single individual; the other is highly discreditable to Salvius, if he is putting friendship above the common interest. And if he is ignorant of the current state of affairs, he ought to trust not his own judgement, but that of the consuls, the praetors, the tribunes who share his office, and the other senators. We are numerous, we have great prestige, we outdo Salvius in age and experience, and we condemn Antonius. Besides, in voting assemblies and in jury trials justice is always with the majority. However, if Salvius still wants to learn the reasons, let me give a brief résumé of the most important of them.

'After Caesar's death Antonius converted our money to his own use. We granted him Macedonia as his province, but he rushed to take Gaul without our consent. He was also given his army to use against the Thracians, but brought it over to Italy to face us instead of the Thracians. Both these things he requested of us in an attempt to ensnare us, and when he was unsuccessful he acted unilaterally. At Brundisium he mustered a praetorian cohort to guard him, and in Rome men carrying swords openly escorted him and mounted guard at night with a password. He was also in the act of bringing all the rest of his army from Brundisium to Rome, aiming more directly at what Caesar intended. But when Caesar's heir anticipated him with another army, he took fright and turned aside to Gaul, thinking it an opportune base for an attack on us because Caesar too had started out from there and made himself our master.

53. 'As a means of then striking terror into his troops, so that they would not object to any illegal behaviour of his, he had lots drawn for men to be put to death. This was not for mutiny, or quitting their watch, or abandoning their post in battle, for which alone military custom sanctions such a savage punishment (and even in such cases few have employed it, and that reluctantly and in extreme danger, when they had no choice). But Antonius has led Romans to execution for a word or a jest – execution not of men proved to have done wrong, but of men who drew the lot. That is why those who were able to do so have rejected his authority, and yesterday you decreed rewards for them because they had acted rightly. Those who could not desert are his frightened partners in injustice. They are advancing like enemies into your territory and laying siege to your army and your general, to whom you send instructions to stay in Gaul, while Antonius orders him to leave. Which is it then? Are we declaring Antonius an enemy, or is Antonius already at war with us? Is our tribune here staying "uninformed"[55] until Decimus actually perishes, and his vast province border-

ing on Italy, and his army too, go to reinforce the hopes Antonius has of success against us? That, it appears, is when the tribune will declare him an enemy, when he is stronger than us.'

54. While Cicero was still speaking his supporters broke into a continuous clamour and prevented anyone from putting the contrary view, until Piso himself came forward. The other senators then fell silent out of respect for him and the Ciceronian party restrained themselves. Piso said, 'The law, gentlemen, prescribes that a man who is called to account should himself hear the accusation, and that he should be judged after he has spoken in his own defence. And I call Cicero, our greatest orator, in support of these propositions. However, since he shrinks from accusing Antonius when he is here, but has levelled certain charges at him in his absence, alleging them to be the most important of all, and incontrovertible, I have come forward to demonstrate, with the briefest of defences, that they are false. He says that Antonius converted the public funds to his own use after Caesar's death; yet on the one hand the law does not state that a thief is a public enemy, but punishes him according to a scale of penalties, and on the other this was the very charge that Brutus, after killing Caesar, made before the people, that Caesar had plundered the money and left the treasury empty. Furthermore Antonius almost immediately proposed that the matter should be investigated, and you accepted and approved his motion and promised a reward of ten per cent to informers, which we will double if anyone has anything he can prove against Antonius in this connection.

55. 'So much for the money. As for the governorship of Gaul, Antonius was not appointed to it by us, but by the people, who gave it by a law which was passed when Cicero himself was present, in the same way as they have often conferred other powers and indeed once gave this very governorship to Caesar. One of the provisions of the law is that if Decimus does not give way to Antonius when the latter comes to claim the province he has been given, Antonius is to open hostilities against him and lead his army, not against the Thracians who are no longer a threat, but to Gaul against the man who disputes his claim. In spite of this, Cicero does not consider Decimus an enemy for resorting to arms in contravention of these provisions, but he does consider Antonius an enemy for acting in accordance with them. If it is the law that Cicero criticizes, he is criticizing the people who passed it. He should have made them change their minds, not insult them after joining them in passing it. Nor should he entrust the

province to Decimus, whom the people expelled as a result of the murder, and refuse to trust Antonius with what the people have granted him. Good counsellors do not quarrel with the people at times of great danger, nor do they forget that this very function, of deciding who is a friend and who a foe, used once to belong to the people. According to the ancient laws the people are the sole and sovereign authority in cases of peace and war.[56] I hope to God they will not find a leader and understand any of this and be angry with us.

56. 'Another charge is that Antonius put some of his soldiers to death. He was of course commander-in-chief and appointed to that office by you, and no commander-in-chief has ever yet had to justify such an action. The constitution has not judged it to be to our advantage that a general should be accountable to his troops. There is nothing worse in an army than insubordination, which has even led to the murder of victorious leaders and failure to bring the killers to book. Nor is it any person related to the present victims, but Cicero, who is flinging blame and making accusations of murder and proposing to call Antonius an "enemy of the state" instead of invoking the penalties that are prescribed for murderers. How ill-disciplined Antonius' force was, and how arrogant, is also apparent from the two legions which left him. You decreed they were to form part of his army, but when they deserted him in breach of military law and came over, not to you, but to Octavian, Cicero still commended them and paid them a reward yesterday out of public funds. I hope this precedent does not haunt you in the future. Hatred has even led Cicero into inconsistency: he accuses Antonius of tyrannizing and punishing his soldiers, when revolutionaries humour their troops, not punish them. And since he has not even flinched from branding the rest of Antonius' administration after Caesar's death as despotic – well, let me examine the items one by one.

57. 'Did Antonius, himself now in danger of being condemned without trial, behave like a despot in putting anyone to death without trial? Did he expel anyone from Rome? Did he blacken anyone's name in front of you? Or perhaps he was innocent of blame so far as individuals were concerned, but was plotting against all of us collectively? When was that, Cicero? When he secured the amnesty for what had happened? Or when no one was to be prosecuted for murder? Or when there was to be an investigation into the public finances? Or when he recalled from exile Pompeius, son of your Pompeius, and made full restitution from the treasury for his father's property? Or when he caught the pseudo-Marius plotting revolution and put him to death, and you all praised him – and because of you this is the one fact that Cicero has not twisted? Or when it was decreed that no one should make a proposal to appoint a dictator, and no one should put such a proposal to the vote, and if someone did he could be killed with impunity by anyone who liked to? For these were Antonius' public acts for us during the only two months that he remained in Rome after Caesar's death, precisely when the people drove out the murderers and you dreaded what lay ahead. What better opportunity did he have, if he was a mischief-maker?

'On the contrary, you say, he failed to exercise authority. What nonsense! Was he not in sole charge when Dolabella left Rome for Syria? Did he not have a military force that you had given him ready in the city? Did he not set guards at night in the city? Was he not guarded at night because of the designs of his enemies? Did he not have a reason in the murder of Caesar, his friend and benefactor and favourite of the people? And a personal reason too, because the conspirators plotted against his life? He did not put any of them to death or drive them into exile, but he pardoned them so far as he decently could and when governorships were granted them he did not grudge them these.

'You see, then, my fellow-Romans, the important and incontrovertible accusations brought by Cicero against Antonius.   58. And since my opponents go further and bring prophecies as well as accusations into play, by saying that Antonius intended to lead his army on Rome, but was afraid to do so because Octavian anticipated him with another army, will they tell me this: how is it that if mere intention brands a man as an enemy, someone who has come and pitched his military camp beside us with no proper identification is not considered an enemy? Why did Antonius not come here, if he did indeed want to? I suppose that with a coherent force of 30,000 men he took fright at the 3,000 ill-armed, ill-organized men Octavian had with him, who had gathered only to gain Octavian's friendship and would leave him the moment they knew he had chosen war? And if he was afraid to come with 30,000, why did he come with only 1,000? When he departed with them for Tibur, how many of us escorted him on his way, how many of us voluntarily swore to be loyal to him? What praises Cicero heaped on his policy and his virtues! And why did Antonius himself, if he contemplated such a dreadful deed,[57] leave us the hostages who are now outside the senate-house – his mother, his wife, and his young son? Their tears and terror are produced not by the constitutional behaviour of Antonius, but by the oligarchic power wielded by his enemies.

59. 'I have laid these points before you as an illustration of Antonius' defence and Cicero's change of heart, and I shall add an exhortation to men of sense not to wrong the people or Antonius, nor to imperil the common interest and indulge personal antagonisms while the state is still weak and does not know where to look for energetic defenders. You should raise an adequate force in Rome, before upsetting anything further afield, and then keep a watch on whatever emergencies develop, and pass judgement on whoever you like when you have the ability to enforce your decision. How can this be done? By allowing Antonius to keep Gaul, either using the people as an excuse or humouring them, and by recalling Decimus with his three legions.[58] Then when he arrives, we send him out to Macedonia but keep back the legions. And if the two legions that have deserted Antonius have in fact deserted to us, as Cicero claims, we should summon them to leave Octavian and come to Rome. In this way, with five legions at our disposal, we could make effective decisions, as we saw fit, without being swayed by the ambitions of any one man.

60. 'These words have been directed to those who have listened to me without malice or rivalry. I urge those who, from motives of private hatred or rivalry, are blindly and hastily throwing you into turmoil not to be rash and hasty in their judgement on important men in command of substantial forces, and provoke them to go to war against their will. They should remember Marcius Coriolanus and the very recent situation of Caesar.[59] The latter likewise had an army and offered a settlement which would have been excellent for us, but by precipitately declaring him an enemy of the state we forced him to become in actual fact an enemy. I urge you also to be careful of the people, who very recently assaulted Caesar's murderers, in case we appear to be insulting them by giving some of the murderers provincial governorships and by commending Decimus for ignoring a law passed by the people, while we judge Antonius to be a public enemy because he received Gaul from the people. For the sake of those who are still in error, men who are directing policy wisely should ponder these facts, and the consuls and tribunes should assume the role of leaders* in the face of the danger to the state.'

61. This was Piso's defence of Antonius, both censuring and alarming his opponents, and he was clearly responsible for the fact that Antonius was not declared a public enemy. Not that he succeeded in gaining agreement that Antonius should govern Gaul, because the friends and relatives of the murderers prevented it from fear that if hostilities were ended Antonius might be reconciled with Octavian and seek revenge for the murder, and they therefore tried to arrange matters so that Octavian and Antonius were permanently quarrelling. The senate decided to inform Antonius that he was to have Macedonia instead of Gaul, and whether by accident or design they gave Cicero the task of putting their other instructions in writing and giving them to the delegation. In distortion of the senate's motion he wrote as follows: Antonius was to move away from Mutina immediately, relinquish Gaul to Decimus, and on a stated day, on the hither side of the river Rubicon, which divides Gaul from Italy, submit all his activities to the authority of the senate.[60] These were the false and aggressive terms in which Cicero wrote the instructions. No great hatred underlay his action, but it would seem that the divine will was interfering with public affairs to bring about change and was intending no good to Cicero himself. Also, as soon as the remains of Trebonius had been brought back and the violence done him was more reliably known, the senate had little difficulty in decreeing Dolabella a public enemy.[61]

62. The delegates who were sent to Antonius were ashamed of the extraordinary nature of the instructions and handed them to him without any preamble.[62] Antonius was furious and burst into a long invective against the senate and Cicero. He wondered how they could think Caesar, whose contributions to the Roman Empire were unparalleled, to be a despot or a king, but did not pass the same verdict on Cicero. Caesar had taken Cicero prisoner but spared him, while Cicero valued Caesar's murderers above his own friends; he hated Decimus while he was friendly to Caesar but loved him once he turned assassin, and he took his side when he seized Gaul without authorization after Caesar's death, and wanted to make war on the man who received it from the people. 'By rewarding deserters from the legions legitimately granted me, but failing to reward the men who stay, he undermines military discipline and hurts Rome more than me. He granted amnesty to the murderers, a course in which I joined for the sake of two men who deserve the greatest respect. But he considers Antonius and Dolabella public enemies, because we hold on to what has been given us. That is the real reason: if I withdraw from Gaul I cease to be either a public enemy or an autocrat. I swear to you that these developments will put an end to our unloved amnesty.'

63. After much in this vein, Antonius wrote in response to the senatorial decree that he would obey the senate in everything as a patriot, but that the answer to Cicero who had composed the instructions was this: 'The people

granted me Gaul by a law, and I shall pursue Decimus for failing to obey the law. I shall also seek vengeance for the murder from him alone, as representative of them all, so that the senate too may finally be purged of the pollution with which it is now thoroughly tainted through Cicero's support of Decimus.' In view of these reactions of Antonius in speech and writing, the senate immediately declared him a public enemy, and also his army if it did not at once desert him.[63] Macedonia and Illyria themselves, together with the forces remaining in both provinces, were to be under the control of Marcus Brutus until republican government was re-established. Brutus already had an army of his own, to which he had added some troops of Apuleius.[64] He also possessed warships, merchantmen, about 16,000 talents in cash, and a large quantity of arms, assembled some time previously for Gaius Caesar, which he had found at Demetrias. The senate now decreed that he should use all these in the interests of his country. They also decided that Cassius should be governor of Syria and make war against Dolabella, and that all other men who held provincial governorships or commanded Roman troops, from the Adriatic eastwards, should take orders from Cassius or Brutus.[65]

64. In this way the senate, following their own inclinations, swiftly put Cassius and his party in a much better light. As he became aware of each development, Octavian had not known what to think. The amnesty, in his view, had embodied a decent appearance of common humanity and pity for men who were relatives and peers of the senators, while their rather insignificant governorships gave them protection. In confirming Decimus' tenure of Gaul against Antonius, the senate appeared to have fallen out with the latter over his autocratic behaviour, the pretext on which he himself had been brought in against him. But when they also decreed Dolabella a public enemy for killing one of the murderers, exchanged Brutus' and Cassius' governorships for those of the largest provinces, suddenly gave them quantities of troops and money, and placed under their authority all the governors east of the Adriatic – these were clearly the actions of men who wanted to build up the Pompeian party and ruin the Caesarian. In addition he reflected on the way they had treated him like a boy, offering him a statue and a front seat at the theatre and calling him propraetor, but in fact taking the army that was his own away from him, because a propraetor counted for nothing when he campaigned alongside consuls. The rewards that had been decreed, but only for soldiers who deserted Antonius, insulted the men who were serving with himself. The war brought him only disgrace, and the senate were really making use of him against Antonius until such time as they had destroyed the latter.

65. These were his reflections, but he hid them, and after performing sacrifice to mark the conferment of his command addressed his army: 'This too, my fellow-soldiers, has come about through you, not just now, but from the time when you gave me the command. It is because of you that the senate has conferred it. You must therefore realize that I owe you thanks for this also, and that if the gods grant us success I will repay you handsomely.'

In this way Octavian ingratiated himself with his troops and attached them to himself. Of the consuls, Pansa was recruiting in the country areas of Italy, while Hirtius divided the command of the army with Octavian. In accordance with secret instructions given him by the senate, Hirtius demanded as his share the two legions that had deserted from Antonius, because he knew that they were the best part of the force. Octavian agreed to everything, and when the division had been made they went into winter quarters alongside each other. As winter wore on, Decimus had begun to suffer from famine and Hirtius and Octavian advanced to Mutina to prevent his starving army falling into Antonius' hands. Antonius was keeping a tight guard on Mutina, and they did not engage with all their forces but waited for Pansa. There were frequent cavalry skirmishes but although Antonius possessed far more cavalry, the difficulty of the terrain, which was cut up by winter streams, deprived him of the advantage of numbers.

66. Such was the course of events around Mutina, while at Rome, in the absence of the consuls, Cicero acted like a popular leader. There were frequent meetings of the people, and he had arms manufactured by gathering the craftsmen together to work without pay, collected money, and exacted extremely heavy contributions from Antonius' supporters. The latter readily paid up to avoid damaging accusations, until Publius Ventidius, who had served under Caesar and was a friend of Antonius, could not endure Cicero's oppression any longer. He took himself off to Caesar's colonies, and being a well-known figure re-enlisted two legions for Antonius and made a rapid march on Rome to arrest Cicero.[66] There ensued a gigantic commotion. Most of the population expected the worst and evacuated their women and children, while Cicero himself fled the city. On hearing this, Ventidius turned away to join Antonius. His way was barred by Octavian and Hirtius, so he proceeded to Picenum, recruited another legion, and awaited further developments.

On the approach of Pansa and his army, Octavian and his advisers sent Carfulenus with Octavian's praetorian cohort and the Martian legion to help Pansa through a constricted part of the route.[67] Antonius had not bothered to occupy the narrow passage, thinking that he could do no more than check Pansa there; but he was keen for a fight, and as he was unable to score any notable success with his cavalry because the ground was too boggy and intersected by ditches, he stationed his two best legions in ambush in the marshes, hiding them in the reeds on either side of the narrow causeway.

67. Carfulenus and Pansa passed along the constricted part of the route at night, and at daybreak, as they came on to the causeway, still unoccupied by the enemy, with only the Martian legion and five other cohorts, they carefully inspected the marsh on either side. The movement of the rushes roused their suspicions, here and there a shield or a helmet glinted, and suddenly Antonius' praetorian cohort appeared straight ahead of them. The men of the Martian legion, who were surrounded and had nowhere to flee, ordered the new recruits, if they came up, not to join in the fighting in case their inexperience caused confusion. They placed Octavian's praetorian cohort opposite Antonius', split the legion into two, and advanced into the marsh on either side, one wing under Pansa, the other under Carfulenus.[68] As there were two areas of marsh, there were two battles, each cut off by the road between from information about the other, and on the road itself the praetorian cohorts were fighting another battle of their own. The Antonians were determined to punish the Martian legion for their desertion and betrayal of them, and the men of the Martian legion were determined to punish the others for condoning the executions at Brundisium.[69] Each recognized in the other the best troops of the opposing army, and they hoped to settle the campaign by this one battle. One side was spurred by the disgrace if two legions were to be worsted by one, the other by the ambition of a single legion to overcome two.

68. Thus fired by anger and ambition they fell on each other in the belief that this battle was more their own concern than their commanders'. Because of their experience, they raised no battle-cry, which would have terrified neither side, nor did any of them utter a sound as they fought, whether they were winning or losing. Since the marshes and ditches gave them no chance of making outflanking movements or charging, and they were unable to push each other back, they were locked together with their swords as if in a wrestling contest. Every blow found a target, but instead of cries there were only wounds, and men dying, and groans. If a man fell, he was immediately carried away and another took his place. They had no need of encouragement or cheering on, because each man's experience made him his own commanding officer. When they were tired, they separated for a few moments to recover as if they were engaged in training exercises, and then grappled with each other again. When the new recruits arrived they were amazed to see this going on with such discipline and silence.

69. The result of these superhuman efforts on the part of all those involved was that Octavian's praetorian cohort was wiped out, while the part of the Martian legion that was under Carfulenus got the better of their opponents, who gave way, not discreditably, little by little. The men under Pansa were pressed back in the same way, but nevertheless both sides held on with equal determination until Pansa was wounded in the side by a javelin and carried out of the battle back to Bononia. At that point the men around him began to retreat, at first a step at a time, then moving position more quickly as if in flight. When the recruits saw this they fled in noisy disorder to the earth fortification which the quaestor Torquatus,[70] suspecting that it might be needed, had completed while the battle was still being fought. The recruits crowded into it in confusion, although they were just as Italian as the men of the Martian legion: so much more difference than racial origin does training make to bravery. The Martian soldiers did not themselves go inside the fortification for fear of losing their reputation, but stood beside it, and although they were exhausted they were still angry enough, if anyone attacked, to fight to the bitter end. Antonius kept away from them as difficult targets, but attacked the recruits and killed many of them.

70. When Hirtius, eight miles away at Mutina, heard about the battle, he set out at the double with the other legion that had deserted Antonius. It was already late in the evening, and Antonius' victorious troops were on their way back, singing in triumph and keeping no sort of order, when Hirtius appeared in front of them with a complete legion that had not suffered at all.[71] Of necessity Antonius' men were drawn up again for battle, and registered many notable exploits against these opponents too, but in their exhaustion they were, as one might expect, overcome by the fresh troops. Hirtius' attack accounted for the great majority of them, even though he did not pursue them because he was wary of the marshes, and with darkness coming on allowed them to scatter. Wide areas of the bog were full of arms, dead bodies, and men who were wounded and half-dead, but those among them who were actually unhurt took no notice because of their fatigue. The cavalry of Antonius' bodyguard went round all night picking them up. They put the survivors on their horses, changing places with some and lifting others up beside them, or they made them hold the tail and encouraged them to run along with them and help themselves to reach safety. In this way, although Antonius had fought well, his force was destroyed by Hirtius' attack. He made camp for the night, without building any defences, in a village called Forum Gallorum which lies beside the plain. Octavian's entire praetorian cohort was lost, but only a few of Hirtius' men, while the other losses amounted to about half the troops on each side.

71. The next day they all moved off to their camps at Mutina. After such a reverse, Antonius' plan was no longer to engage the enemy in a set battle or face them if they advanced, but to do no more than harry them daily with his cavalry until Decimus, who was already reduced to the last stages of starvation, surrendered. On the other hand Hirtius and Octavian, for this precise reason, were anxious for a battle. When Antonius did not lead his troops out against them when they offered battle, they went round to the other side of Mutina, which was less strongly guarded because of the difficulty of approach, intending to force their way in to the town by strength of military numbers. Even then Antonius attacked them with only his cavalry, but they too used cavalry alone to defend themselves while the rest of the army proceeded towards their objective. Alarmed that he might lose the town, Antonius led two legions out to battle, and his delighted opponents turned round and engaged them. Although Antonius summoned other legions from his other camps, they came slowly, as the call was sudden and the distance considerable, and Octavian's men won the battle. Hirtius actually rode into Antonius' camp, and fell in fighting around the commander's tent. Octavian burst in, took up the body, and held the camp for a short while until he was ejected by Antonius. Both sides passed the night actually under arms.[72]

72. On meeting with this second blow, Antonius sought the advice of his associates immediately after the battle. They thought he should adhere to his previous plan of keeping Mutina under siege and declining battle, because both sides had suffered equally, Hirtius had been killed, Pansa was ill, their own side had more cavalry, and Mutina was in the final stages of starvation and would very soon surrender. This was the course his associates recommended, and it was the best one. However, Antonius' judgement

was now impaired by heaven and he was afraid that Octavian would break into Mutina, as he had attempted to do the day before, or would set about encircling them with fortifications as he had a larger body of men to do the work. 'In that case', he said, 'our cavalry will be rendered useless and Lepidus and Plancus will ignore me as I go down to defeat. But if we withdraw from Mutina, Ventidius will immediately bring his three legions from Picenum to join us, and Lepidus and Plancus will ally themselves firmly with him.'[73] So he spoke, being a man who was no coward in a dangerous situation, and with these words immediately struck camp and made off towards the Alps.

73. Decimus, now that the siege had been lifted, was in dread of Octavian instead, fearing him as a personal enemy now that the consuls were out of the way. He therefore broke down the bridges over the river before dawn and sent emissaries by boat to Octavian to acknowledge him as his saviour and request a discussion with him, with the river between them, in the hearing of the citizens.[74] He would convince Octavian that he had been stricken by <the> * divine power when he had been induced by the others to plot against Caesar. Octavian made an angry reply to the delegates and refused to accept the thanks which Decimus gave him: 'I am not here to save Decimus' life, but to make war on Antonius. With him I may rightly one day come to terms, but nature forbids me either to set eyes on or talk to Decimus. Let him seek his own safety, none the less, while that has the approval of the people in Rome.' When he heard this, Decimus stood at the edge of the river, called on Octavian by name, and read out at the top of his voice the letter from the senate which gave him the supreme authority in Gaul. He also forbade Octavian to cross the river into another man's sphere of authority independently of the consuls, or to proceed further against Antonius since he himself had quite sufficient force to pursue him. Octavian realized that Decimus had been encouraged to this effrontery by the senate, and although he could have given orders for his arrest he restrained himself for the moment and turned back to Pansa in Bononia, where he wrote a full report to the senate, as did Pansa.

74. In Rome, Cicero read out Pansa's letter to the people, as it was a communication from a consul, but read Octavian's only to the senate. He proposed a thanksgiving[75] of fifty days for the victory over Antonius, a number which the Romans had never decreed either for successes over the Gauls or for any other campaign. He wanted to give the consuls' army to

Decimus (for although Pansa was still alive he was not expected to survive) and appoint Decimus to be sole commander against Antonius. He also arranged public prayers to ask for the victory of Decimus over Antonius. Such was the intensity of the madness that drove him on against Antonius, and so deficient his sense of proportion. He again guaranteed to the two legions which had deserted Antonius, as though they had already secured victory, the reward of 5,000 denarii each that had been previously promised them from public funds if they were victorious, and the permanent right to wear a crown of olive during the festivals. There was not a word about Octavian in the senate's decrees, nor even a mention of his name, so completely was he despised, as if Antonius had been eliminated.[76] Letters were also sent to Lepidus and Plancus and Asinius, ordering them to conduct hostilities by moving towards Antonius.

75. While this was happening in Rome, Pansa, who was dying of his wound, called Octavian to his side and said, 'I loved your father as myself, but when he was killed I had no means of helping him or avoiding joining the majority, whom you too have done well to obey in spite of having an army. Although at first they were afraid of you and Antonius, who like you seemed very keen to uphold Caesar's policies, when you quarrelled they were overjoyed at the prospect that you would destroy each other. When they saw that you had also become master of an army, they tried to win you over as they would a boy with specious and trivial honours. But at that moment you had your eye on a more impressive and more powerful position, and when you declined the command which your army offered you, they were thrown into disarray and appointed you to a joint command with us. Their object was that we should divest you of the two more effective legions, and they hoped that when one of you and Antonius was defeated the other would be weaker and lacking allies. After destroying him they would then eliminate all Caesar's supporters, and restore those of Pompeius. This is the essence of their policy. 76. Hirtius and I were carrying out our orders to the point of bringing Antonius and his arrogant behaviour to heel, but once he was defeated we intended to reconcile him with you. This was a debt of gratitude to Caesar's friendship that it was in our power to repay, and the only thing that would be of real service to our party in the future. It was impossible to explain this to you earlier, but Antonius has now been defeated, Hirtius is no more, and death is gathering me in, so it is the right moment for it to be said – not to make you grateful to me after my death, but to ensure that as a man whose achievements

demonstrate that you have the divine force of destiny on your side, you appreciate what is best for yourself and also understand the course which Hirtius and I had no choice but to adopt. The troops which you yourself gave us it is perfectly reasonable to return to you, and I hand them over to you. I will give you our recruits as well, if you wish to take and keep them. But if they are completely overawed by the senate, because their officers were in fact sent to keep an eye on us, and if doing this will bring you unpopularity and make you move earlier than necessary, then my quaestor Torquatus will assume command of them.' After saying this, and handing the recruits over to his quaestor, he died. The quaestor passed the men on to Decimus, in accordance with the senate's instructions, and Octavian gave Hirtius and Pansa splendid funeral honours and sent their bodies in state to Rome.

77. The events of the same period in Syria and Macedonia were as follows. When Caesar passed through Syria,[77] he had left a legion there as he was already thinking of an invasion of Parthia. Caecilius Bassus looked after this legion,[78] but its command was held by a young man related to Caesar himself, Sextus Iulius, who had gone astray and adopted luxurious habits, and led the legion about with him in a permanently disgraceful state. On one occasion when Bassus reproved him for this, Iulius insulted him, and afterwards, when he called to Bassus and the latter was slow to pay heed, he ordered Bassus to be dragged before him. There was a commotion and blows, and the army, unable to endure Iulius' arrogant behaviour, killed him under a hail of weapons.[79] But repentance and terror of Caesar immediately overwhelmed them, and the soldiers therefore bound themselves together by oath that if they were not pardoned and regarded as loyal, they would fight to the death. They forced Bassus to do the same, and raised and trained another legion. This is one version of the Bassus affair, but Libo[80] believes that Bassus, who had been in Pompeius' army and was living quietly in Tyre after his defeat, bribed some men in the legion and they killed Sextus and put themselves under Bassus. Whichever version is right, these men made a spirited resistance to Staius Murcus, who was sent against them by Caesar with three legions, until Murcus summoned Marcius Crispus the governor of Bithynia, and Crispus came to help him with three more legions.[81] 78. While Bassus' legions were under siege from these forces, Cassius rapidly took control of the province. He immediately acquired both Bassus' two legions and the six commanded by the men who were

besieging him, who handed them over both from friendship and because they were subordinate to the proconsul as a result of the decree, which I have mentioned, that everyone was to obey Cassius and Brutus. In addition, Allienus, who had been sent by Dolabella to Egypt, was bringing back from there four legions composed of men who had been scattered after the defeats of Pompeius and Crassus or had been left behind by Caesar with Cleopatra.[82] He was not forewarned, and was caught by Cassius in Palestine and forced to join him, as he was afraid to pit his four legions against eight. In this way Cassius unexpectedly gained control of a total of twelve legions and surrounded and besieged Dolabella, who had come from Asia with two legions and been admitted into Laodiceia because it was sympathetic.[83] When the senate heard the news it was delighted.

79. In Macedonia, Gaius Antonius, Marcus Antonius' brother, challenged Brutus' authority and was conducting military operations against him with one legion of foot. After a reverse, he ambushed him; Brutus then escaped and laid a counter-ambush, but inflicted no injury on the men he trapped and simply told his own army to greet their opponents in a friendly manner. When they did not return the greetings and remained deaf to his attempt, Brutus let them go unharmed from the ambush. He then outflanked them by another route, again stopped them in a precipitous spot, and again did not attack but greeted them. Seeing that Brutus was sparing Roman lives and deserved his reputation for wisdom and clemency, they felt great admiration for him, replied to the greeting, and went over to him.[84] Gaius also surrendered to Brutus and was honourably treated by him, until after several attempts to tamper with the men's loyalty he was found out and put to death. Thus Brutus likewise acquired legions, six including his previous forces. He also raised two more from the Macedonians, of whom he had a high opinion, and trained them in the Italian way like the others.

80. Such were the developments in Syria and Macedonia. In Italy, Octavian regarded it as an insult that Decimus had been chosen instead of himself to hold the command against Antonius, but he hid his anger and requested a triumph for his achievements. When he was spurned by the senate as wanting honours beyond his years, he feared that if Antonius was destroyed he would have to endure still greater contempt, and longed for the accommodation with Antonius that Pansa on his deathbed had indicated to him. He was therefore kind to the stray officers and men of

Antonius' army, recruiting them into his own forces or sending those who wished to Antonius to show that no incurable hatred lay behind his attack.* He also camped close to Antonius' supporter Ventidius and his three legions, frightening him but making no hostile moves and giving him an equal chance to join himself or to depart unmolested with his army to join Antonius and reprove him for failing to realize their common interest. Ventidius understood and went off to Antonius. Octavian also gave respectful treatment to Decius,[85] one of Antonius' officers, who had been captured at Mutina, and released him provided he was willing to go to Antonius. When Decius enquired what Octavian's policy towards Antonius was, he replied that he had given plenty of hints to people who had their wits about them, but that more would still not be enough for the stupid.

81. This was Octavian's signal to Antonius, but he wrote still more plainly to Lepidus and Asinius about the insult to himself and the general advancement of the murderers. He wanted to frighten them with the prospect that to satisfy the Pompeian party each of Caesar's followers would individually suffer the same fate as Antonius, a fate which he had incurred through his own thoughtlessness and failure to see this danger. Octavian thought they ought, for appearances' sake, to obey the senate, but plan together for their own safety while they still could. They should reprimand Antonius for his behaviour, and imitate their own soldiers, who even when they were discharged from service did not separate and become easy targets for their enemies, but preferred settlement in a body, by force, in foreign lands, to enjoyment of their native regions as individuals. Such was Octavian's message to Lepidus and Asinius. Meanwhile Decimus' veteran troops were suffering from poor health, having over-eaten after their famine and contracted dysentery, and his recruits were still untrained. Plancus was at hand with his own army, and Decimus informed the senate that he would hunt down Antonius in his wanderings † even though some naval actions had already taken place †.[86] 82. When the Pompeians heard this it was amazing how many of them appeared, exclaiming that this was the moment their country had regained its freedom. Each of them offered sacrifice, and a commission of ten was appointed to investigate Antonius' period of office. This was a cloak for upsetting Caesar's decisions, because Antonius had made no administrative decisions, or only trivial ones, on his own authority, but had done everything on the basis of Caesar's memoranda. Well knowing this, the senate had been annulling some of them on various pretexts, but was hoping in this way to annul them all. The

commissioners gave notice that everyone should forthwith register and account for whatever they had received during Antonius' magistracy, and appended sanctions against those who did not obey. The Pompeians sought the consulship for the remainder of the year, in place of Hirtius and Pansa, as also did Octavian, who no longer communicated with the senate, but with Cicero privately. He even begged him to be his colleague, saying that Cicero with his greater age and experience could take care of the duties of the office, while he himself would simply profit from the title to lay down his arms honourably, which was, he said, the reason why he had the other day requested a triumph.[87] Cicero, fired by these words because of his hankering for office, said that he had knowledge of an intended pact between the commanders outside Italy and advised the senate to cultivate this man who had been insulted and was still master of a large army, and to put up with him as an under-age magistrate in Rome rather than as an infuriated individual under arms; but he told them that in order to prevent any action by Octavian against the interests of the senate, they should choose as his colleague a sensible senior man to provide firm guidance for his lack of years. The senate, however, laughed at Cicero's longing for office, and the relatives of the murderers in particular blocked the proposal because they were afraid that if Octavian became consul he would take his revenge on them.

83. For a variety of legitimate reasons the election was more than once put off. In the meantime Antonius crossed the Alps, after winning over Culleo whom Lepidus had posted to guard them, and came to a river where Lepidus was encamped.[88] There, as if he were really camping alongside a friend, he enclosed his camp with neither bank nor ditch. A flurry of messages was exchanged. Antonius reminded Lepidus of his friendship and a variety of favours, and pointed out that after himself all who had been friendly with Caesar would suffer the same fate one by one. Lepidus said that he was afraid of the senate, which had instructed him to fight Antonius, but none the less promised that he would not do so willingly. Lepidus' army, who were in awe of Antonius' reputation, noticing the exchange of messages, and surprised at the simplicity of his camp, fraternized with his men first secretly and then openly, as Romans and fellow-soldiers. They ignored the prohibitions of the military tribunes, and bridged the river with boats to make fraternization easier. The Tenth legion, recruited from non-Italians and led in the past by Antonius, prepared the way for him within the camp.

84. This was noticed by Laterensis,[89] one of the distinguished senators. He informed Lepidus, and told him, if he did not believe him, to divide his army into several sections and send them out for some purpose or other, to make them reveal their loyalty or disloyalty. Lepidus then divided his army into three and ordered them to go out at night to guard some nearby storehouses. The men who were on the final watch, after arming themselves as if for departure, seized the strongpoints of the camp and opened the gates to Antonius. The latter ran towards Lepidus' tent, with the whole of Lepidus' army now urging him on and asking Lepidus to proffer peace and compassion to distressed fellow-citizens. Lepidus leapt out of bed, to appear before them half-dressed, just as he was; he promised to do as they asked and offered his greetings to Antonius, excusing himself on the grounds of necessity. Some believe that, being a feeble and timid man, he fell to his knees in front of Antonius, but this does not seem credible to all historians, or plausible to me: for he had not yet taken any hostile action against Antonius which could justify his fear. In this way Antonius again attained a position of great strength and great menace to his enemies. He possessed the army which he had brought from Mutina together with its quite outstanding cavalry, while Ventidius' three legions had also joined him on the way, and Lepidus had become his ally with seven legions and many other troops and excellent equipment. Of these the nominal commander was still Lepidus, but Antonius directed everything.

85. When news of these events reached Rome, another sudden and marvellous transformation occurred. Those who shortly before had regarded Antonius with contempt became afraid, while those who had been afraid became bold. The notices of the commission of ten were insultingly torn down, and the consular elections were still further postponed. The senate was completely at a loss and feared that Octavian and Antonius would unite with each other. They unobtrusively sent two of their own number, Lucius and Pansa,[90] on the pretence of attending a festival in Greece, to Brutus and Cassius to ask them to bring help to themselves so far as they could. They also recalled two of Sextius' three legions from Africa and ordered the third to be handed over to Cornificius, governor of the other African province and a supporter of the senate. They knew that these troops too had served under Caesar, and they were suspicious of everything to do with him; but desperation drove them to take this action, since they reappointed Octavian, quite inappropriately, to the command along with Decimus, even though they were afraid that he would unite with Antonius.

86. Octavian, as the victim of continual insults, was already inciting his troops to anger, both on his own behalf and on their own, because they were being sent on a second campaign before receiving the 5,000 denarii the senate had promised them for the first. He advised them to send a deputation to ask for the money, and they sent their centurions. The senate realized that they had been put up to this, and said they would reply to them by another deputation. This they sent with instructions to see that Octavian was not present when they met the two legions which had deserted Antonius. They were then to tell the men to pin their hopes not on a single individual, but on the senate which alone possessed permanent power, and they were to instruct them to go to Decimus' camp, where they would find their money. Having given these instructions as to what to say, the senate now sent on half the bounty and appointed ten men to oversee the distribution, to whom they would not add Octavian even as an eleventh. But as the two legions would not permit the deputation to meet them unless Octavian were present, they returned with nothing achieved. Octavian then no longer expressed his views through others, nor thought he should delay any further. He appeared in person before his assembled army and told them at length of every insult he had suffered at the hands of the senate, and of the manoeuvring against all Caesar's partisans, who were being eliminated one by one. He told them they should be afraid for themselves when they were transferred to a commander who was the enemy of their party, and to one campaign after another so that they might be completely destroyed or even quarrel with each other. It was, he said, with this in view that although they had all participated in the battles at Mutina the rewards were being given to only the two legions, so as to embroil them in disagreement and contention. 87. 'You know', he said, 'the circumstances of Antonius' recent defeat, and you have become aware of the action the Pompeians have taken in Rome against people who accepted any gifts from Caesar. Why should you have any confidence that you will keep the land and money he gave you, or I that I will keep my life, when the close associates of the murderers are so powerful in the senate? For my own part, I will accept whatever fate may lie in store for me, for it is a noble thing simply to suffer in one's country's service. But for you I am afraid, so many fine men who are risking danger for my sake and my father's. You know, from the occasion when you offered to make me your commander, with the official trappings, and I

refused, that I am not ambitious for distinction; but I can now see only one salvation for both of us, which is for me to be proclaimed consul through you. In that case everything that my father gave you will be safe, and the colonial settlements still due will be founded as well, and your rewards will be paid in full. I would also bring the murderers to justice and release you from all other campaigns.'

88. The army cheered these words enthusiastically and immediately despatched the centurions to ask for the consulship for Octavian. When the senate in reply pointed out his age, the centurions repeated what they had been told to say, that not only Corvinus a long time ago, but also more recently the first and second Scipios had held consulships when too young, and the country had profited a great deal from the youth of each of these.[91] They also adduced the recent examples of Pompeius Magnus and Dolabella, and the fact that Octavian himself had already been granted the right of standing for office ten years early. The centurions delivered this with great outspokenness, and some of the senators, unable to stomach such freedom of expression on the part of men who were mere centurions, struck them on the grounds that their insolence went beyond what was proper for a soldier. When the army heard this, they became still more angry and told Octavian to lead them at once on Rome because they themselves would elect him, as Caesar's son, in a special election, and they heaped constant praise on Caesar's name. Seeing their state of eagerness, Octavian led them off directly from the assembly, eight legions of foot, and sufficient cavalry, and all the usual auxiliaries. After he had crossed the river Rubicon from Gaul into Italy, the river which his father had crossed in the same way to start the civil war, he split his force into two and ordered one division to follow without haste, but made a forced march with the better, picked, division, hurrying to catch his opponents while they were still unprepared. He encountered a convoy carrying some of the money which the senate had sent to pay the rewards to the soldiers, but afraid of the effect it might have on his mercenaries, he secretly sent a party ahead to frighten its bearers, who took to flight with the money.

89. When this news reached Rome there was uproar and a huge panic. People rushed about in confusion, and some moved their wives or children or anything else they held precious to the country or to the fortified points in the city; for since it was not yet clear that Octavian's aim was simply to gain the consulship, their fears knew no bounds when they heard that a hostile army was advancing in deadly earnest. The senate were inordinately

terrified, having no force ready at their disposal, and as is the way at times of panic, they laid the blame on each other. Some said this had happened because they had high-handedly taken the campaign against Antonius away from Octavian; some blamed their refusal to take seriously his request for a triumph, although his claim was not unjustified; some ascribed it to his resentment over the distribution of the money; and some believed it was because they had not made him even the eleventh commissioner. Others said that it was the fact that the actual rewards had not been given either promptly or in full which had made the army resort to war against them. Most of all they blamed their inopportune aggressiveness, at a time when Brutus and Cassius were too far away and still organizing themselves, while their enemies Antonius and Lepidus were hanging on their flanks; and when they thought of the possibility that these two would come to an agreement with Octavian, their fear reached a climax. Cicero, who up until now had been their leading figure, did not even appear.

90. All at once there was a complete transformation of the situation. Instead of 2,500 denarii, 5,000 were to be given, and to all eight legions instead of the two; and Octavian was to distribute the money in place of the ten commissioners, and be a candidate *in absentia* for the consulship. A deputation hurried away to communicate these decisions to him urgently. But hardly had they left the city when the senators began to change their minds and think that they ought not to be such terrified cowards, nor accept another despotic regime without a fight, nor accustom men who sought office to obtaining it by violence, or serving soldiers to dictating to their country. On the contrary, they should arm themselves from the available resources and confront their attackers with the constitution, since they did not anticipate that even these latter would use force against their country if faced with the constitution. If their opponents did persist, they themselves would endure a siege until Decimus or Plancus arrived, and they would fight to the death rather than submit to a fundamentally incurable slavery. They quoted the fine old sentiments of the Romans on freedom, and the sufferings they had endured in their uncompromising pursuit of freedom. 91. When the two legions summoned from Africa also arrived in the harbour that very day, they believed the gods were urging them on to defend their freedom. So their change of mind was confirmed, Cicero again made his appearance, and they proceeded to alter all their decisions. All men of military age were enlisted, and these two legions from Africa, with their thousand cavalry, and another legion which Pansa had left

behind in Rome, were all divided into smaller units. Some guarded the height known as the Janiculum, where they also concentrated the money, and some the bridge over the river,[92] the praetors in the city being allocated to the various commands. Others made ready the boats in the harbour and ships and money, in case they should be defeated and need to escape by sea. Their morale was high as they set about these tasks, hoping in this way to strike terror into Octavian in return, and either convince him that he should seek the consulship from them and not from his army, or repulse him firmly. They also expected that the adherents of the opposite party would at last change their position now that the struggle was for freedom. They searched for Octavian's mother and sister both publicly and privately, but could not find them.[93] As a result they were greatly disturbed again at having important hostages snatched from them, and as the Caesarians no longer made concessions to them they thought them responsible for so effectively concealing the women.

92. The news that the decrees had been revoked reached Octavian while he was still meeting the delegation, who left him and returned in embarrassment. His army was now in a yet more inflamed state, and he advanced rapidly, in fear that something might happen to the women. He sent horsemen to tell the agitated city population not to be afraid, and in the general state of amazement seized the area north of the Quirinal Hill without anyone standing their ground to fight or resist him.[94] And again there was another sudden and wonderful change, as prominent figures hurried to go and greet him. The ordinary people also hurried to him, taking the good discipline of his soldiers as a sign of peace. Leaving his troops just where they were, Octavian entered the city on the following day with an appropriate bodyguard. Even then his opponents went to meet him in separate groups all along the way, greeting him with every sign of friendliness and spineless readiness to serve. His mother and sister, in the company of the Vestal Virgins, embraced him in the sanctuary of Vesta. The three legions, taking no notice of their commanders, sent delegations to him and changed sides; of the praetors who commanded them, Cornutus committed suicide but the others were given a truce and safe-conduct.[95] Hearing of the truce, Cicero arranged through Octavian's supporters to meet him, and when he did so defended himself and made much of the proposal about the consulship which he himself had previously put forward in the senate.[96] Octavian, however, made only the mocking reply that Cicero was the last of his friends to greet him.

93. That night a rumour suddenly went round that two of Octavian's legions, the Martian and the Fourth, had come over to the city's side on the grounds that they had been tricked into being led against their country. The praetors and the senate believed it, without bothering to make any check, although the army was very close. They thought that with the help of these two legions, which were of the highest quality, they could resist Octavian's remaining troops until they received some additional forces from elsewhere. So while it was still dark they sent Manius Aquillius Crassus off to Picenum to recruit an army and gave Apuleius, one of the tribunes, the task of going quickly round and alerting the people to the good news.[97] The senate gathered hastily before dawn in the senate-house, and Cicero welcomed them at the door. However, when the rumour turned out to be false he disappeared in a sedan-chair.

94. Octavian laughed at them and brought his army nearer the city, to the Campus Martius, but did not at the time punish any of the praetors – not even Crassus who had been on his way to Picenum, although he was brought before him exactly as he had been captured, wearing slave's clothing. He let them all go to create an impression of generosity, but not much later listed them among the proscribed. He ordered the public funds which were on the Janiculum or elsewhere to be collected together, with the rest of the money which on Cicero's proposal the population had previously been registered to contribute, and he distributed 2,500 denarii a head to his army, promising that he would pay them the balance later.[98] He then withdrew from the city until the people had elected consuls of their choice. He was himself elected along with the man he wanted, Quintus Pedius, who had presented him with his share of Caesar's inheritance.[99] He again entered the city, as consul, and as he sacrificed twelve vultures appeared to him, the number said to have been seen by Romulus as he carried out the foundation of the city. After the sacrifices, he had his adoption by his father validated again by a *lex curiata*. This is when adoption takes place by act of the people, their name for the divisions of tribes or communities being *curiae*, just as the Greeks, to give a comparison, call them *phratriai*. Among the Romans, this is the most legitimate mode of adoption for the fatherless, who have full rights, exactly like the natural children, towards the relatives and ex-slaves of the persons who have adopted them. Apart from the magnificent nature of the rest of the inheritance, Caesar had many wealthy ex-slaves, and it was perhaps chiefly for this reason that Octavian needed this adoption in addition to the previous testamentary one.[100]

95. By another law Octavian revoked the declaration that Dolabella was a public enemy, and made the murder of Caesar a crime. Charges were immediately laid, with Caesar's supporters accusing some men of personally participating in the murder, and others simply of being sympathizers. This latter charge was actually formally made, even against people who had not even been in Rome when Caesar was killed. It was announced that all the cases would be heard on a single day, and all the accused were found guilty in their absence. Octavian had charge of the courts and no juror cast a vote for acquittal save for one aristocrat, who likewise was not punished at the time but was also proscribed a little later along with the others.[101] It seems that it was at this time that Quintus Gallius, who held the urban praetorship, and was the brother of Marcus Gallius, who was with Antonius, asked Octavian for the governorship of Africa, and when he obtained it plotted against Octavian.[102] His fellow-magistrates stripped him of his command, the Roman populace ransacked his house, and the senate condemned him to death. Octavian gave him orders to join his brother, and he apparently embarked, but was never seen again.

96. Having accomplished this much, Octavian planned to come to an accommodation with Antonius, because he already knew that Brutus' party had collected an army of twenty legions, and he needed Antonius to deal with them. So he left Rome for the Adriatic coast, moving on from camp to camp in a leisurely manner while he waited to see what the senate would do; for Pedius, once Octavian had removed himself, was urging them to make their peace with Lepidus and Antonius and not regard their mutual differences as irreconcilable. The senators foresaw that a reconciliation would be in the interest neither of themselves nor of their country, but was intended to give Octavian allies against Cassius and Brutus. None the less they expressed their approval and agreed to it because they had no choice. Their decrees declaring Antonius and Lepidus and the armies under their command to be enemies of the state were repealed, and others speaking of peace were despatched. Octavian wrote to express his delight at this, and even promised that he would come and assist Antonius against Decimus, if he were needed. Without delay Antonius and Lepidus made friendly replies and praised him. Antonius wrote that he would himself punish not only Decimus on Caesar's behalf, but also Plancus on his own behalf, and would join forces with Octavian. **97**. Such was the exchange of correspondence between them, while Asinius Pollio with two legions joined Antonius as he went in pursuit of Decimus. Pollio brought about an accommodation with Plancus, who went over to Antonius with three legions, so that Antonius was now at the head of a very powerful force. Decimus had ten legions, of which the four most experienced in combat had been ravaged by famine and were still not healthy, while the six of new recruits were not yet capable of enduring hardship and had no experience of it. He therefore rejected any idea of battle and decided to withdraw to join Brutus in Macedonia. He did not retreat on this side of the Alps, to Ravenna or Aquileia, since that was the way Octavian was marching, but proposed to take a longer and barely passable route, crossing the Rhine and traversing the wilder barbarian territory.* As a result, because of fatigue and the difficulty of the march, the new recruits were the first to abandon him; they went over to Octavian, and were followed by the four longer-serving legions, who left him for Antonius, together with all the rest of the troops except his bodyguard of Gallic cavalry. Even of these, he instructed any who so wished to return to their homes, and after paying them each a bounty from the gold he still had, rode on towards the Rhine with the 300 who stayed with him. It was difficult to cross the river with a small number of men, and they also deserted him, all but ten. He changed into Gallic dress, and as he already had a thorough knowledge of the language, made his escape with them as though he were a Gaul – no longer by the roundabout way, but towards Aquileia, believing he would avoid notice because his party was so small.   98. He was captured and held prisoner by bandits, and on asking what Gallic prince ruled their tribe, and hearing that it was Camilus, a man to whom he had done many favours, he told his captors to take him to Camilus, which they did. When Camilus saw Decimus, he was outwardly friendly to him and blamed the men who had held him captive for ignorantly committing an outrage against a person of his standing, but in secret he sent a message to Antonius. Antonius, not unmoved by the reversal of fortune, could not bear to set eyes on Decimus. He ordered Camilus to kill him and send him the head, and when he had seen it told his companions to give it burial. This was the end of Decimus, who had been Caesar's commander of cavalry, governed the old part of Gaul for him,[103] and had been chosen by him to be consul the following year and govern the other part of Gaul. He was the next of the murderers after Trebonius to pay the penalty, a year and a half, more or less, after the killing. At the same time Minucius Basilus, who was also one of Caesar's murderers, was killed by his slaves because by castrating some of them he spurred them to take revenge on him.

BOOK IV

1. In this way two of Caesar's murderers, Trebonius in Asia and Decimus in Gaul, met their deserts when they were attacked and defeated in their own provinces. This fourth book of the civil wars traces how retribution overtook Cassius and Brutus, who were chiefly responsible for the plot against Caesar, and were masters of all the territories from Syria to Macedonia and possessed a large fighting force of cavalry, sailors, and more than twenty legions of infantry, together with ships and money. At the same time there occurred the hunting and detection of the proscribed at Rome, whose harrowing experiences were of a severity unparalleled in men's memories of what had happened either in the internal conflicts or foreign wars of the Greeks, or in the history of the Romans themselves – except only under Sulla, who had been the first to proscribe his personal enemies. Marius tracked down and punished those he could find; but Sulla proclaimed that anyone at all could do the killing, for large rewards, and there were corresponding penalties for persons who hid the proscribed. However, the events of the period of Marius and Sulla have already been described in the chapters devoted to them,[1] and my story goes on as follows.

2. Octavian and Antonius met near Mutina, on a small low-lying island in the river Lavinius, to exchange enmity for friendship. Each had five legions, which they left drawn up facing each other while they each advanced with 300 men to the bridges over the river. Lepidus went ahead in person to search the island, and signalled with his cloak to each of them to come across. They then left their 300 men with their advisers at the bridges and went forward in full view into the space between, where the three of them sat down together, with Octavian in the centre presiding because of his office. They met for two days, from dawn until dusk, and their decisions were as follows: Octavian would resign the consulship to

Ventidius for the remainder of the year, and a new office charged with the resolution of the civil wars would be created by law for Lepidus, Antonius, and Octavian. They would hold this office for five years, and it would have an authority equal to that of the consuls. This was the title they decided to use, instead of dictators, perhaps because of Antonius' resolution abolishing the dictatorship.[2] They were to appoint immediately the annual magistrates at Rome for five years ahead, and they distributed the provincial governorships in such a way that Antonius received the whole of Gaul except for the part adjoining the Pyrenees, which they call Old Gaul; this was to be held by Lepidus, along with Spain; and Octavian was to have Africa, Sardinia, Sicily, and any other islands in that area.   3. Thus the three distributed the Roman Empire among themselves. The only territories whose allocation they postponed were those to the east of the Adriatic, because these were still controlled by Brutus and Cassius, against whom Antonius and Octavian were to campaign. Lepidus was to become consul in the following year and stay in Rome because he would be needed there. He would govern Spain through deputies, while three legions from his army would be kept by himself to meet his needs in Rome and seven would be divided between Octavian and Antonius – three to Octavian and four to Antonius, so that each of them could take twenty legions to the war. They would spur their troops on to win the rewards of victory in the war by offering them other bounties and especially by granting them eighteen Italian towns where they could settle. These towns, which were remarkable for their wealth and fine lands and houses, they intended to allocate to the army, complete with lands and houses, like a substitute for plunder taken on enemy soil. The most famous of the towns included Capua, Rhegium, Venusia, Beneventum, Nuceria, Ariminum, and Vibo. In this way they divided up the best parts of Italy among their soldiers. They also decided to put their private enemies to death early on, to prevent them causing trouble to themselves as they put these arrangements into effect while simultaneously conducting a war outside Italy. Such were their decisions, which they recorded in writing, and Octavian as consul read them out (with the exception of the list of those who were to die) to the soldiers, who raised cheers of triumph when they heard them and embraced each other to mark the rapprochement.

4. While these events were taking place, many frightening prodigies and portents occurred in Rome. Dogs howled just like wolves, a grim portent, and wolves, animals strange to the city, ran through the forum; an ox uttered with human voice; a new-born baby spoke; statues sweated, and some

even sweated blood; and loud shouts, the din of weapons, and the pounding of unseen horses were heard. There were many ill-omened signs involving the sun, there were showers of stones, and lightning constantly struck the sanctuaries and images of the gods. Thereupon the senate summoned diviners and soothsayers from Etruria, of whom the eldest, after declaring that the kingships of ancient times would return and that they would all become slaves except for himself, shut his mouth and held his breath until he died.

5. The triumvirs withdrew privately to put together a list of those who were to die. They marked down not only the powerful men they mistrusted,* but also their own private foes. In exchange, they surrendered their own relations and friends to each other, both then and later. Extra names were constantly added to the list, some from enmity, others only because they had been a nuisance, or were friends of enemies, or enemies of friends, or were notably wealthy. They needed, you understand, a great deal of money for the war. Brutus and Cassius were profiting from the taxes of Asia, both those which had already been paid and those that were still coming in, and from the support of kings and satraps, while they themselves, whose base was Europe and particularly Italy, which had been worn out by wars and financial exactions, were short of resources. For this reason the triumvirs finally imposed savage demands for money even on ordinary male citizens and women, and invented duties on sales and leases. The point was reached where a person was proscribed because he had a fine house in town or country. The total of those condemned to death and confiscation of property was about 300 senators and 2,000 equestrians. These included brothers and uncles of the men who proscribed them and of their subordinates, if they had done anything to offend the leaders or these subordinates.

6. As they came away from their meeting, the triumvirs intended to go to Rome and post up the names of the great majority of their victims there. However, there were twelve very influential men, or according to others seventeen, whom they decided to put to death first by sending orders ahead immediately. Four of these were killed at once, at dinner or on the streets. A hunt was made for the others, and temples and houses were searched. There was sudden panic, which lasted all night, and people shouted and wailed and ran to and fro as though the city was being captured. Because it was known that arrests were being made, but no names of those who had been pre-condemned had been published, everyone supposed that he was himself being hunted by the men who were hurrying about. Thus in despair for their lives some people were going to set fire to their own property, and others to the public buildings, making an illogical choice to inflict some terrible harm before suffering it; and they would have done so, had the consul Pedius not gone round with heralds to persuade them to wait until dawn and obtain precise information. As day broke, contrary to the intention of the triumvirs, Pedius posted the names of the seventeen as being those who were considered to be solely responsible for the disaster of civil war, and had alone been condemned. Not knowing what had been decided, he gave an official pledge of immunity to the others, but the stress of the night caused his death.

7. The triumvirs Octavian, Antonius, and Lepidus made their separate entrances into the city over three days, each with their praetorian cohorts and one legion of soldiers. When they had entered, the city was immediately full of weapons and military standards deployed in key places, and straight away an assembly was held in the midst of all this. The tribune Publius Titius put forward a bill setting up a new magistracy of three men, Lepidus, Antonius, and Octavian, to hold office for five years to bring order to the present situation. Their power was to be equal to that of the consuls, and their function was what a Greek might call that of harmosts, a name the Spartans in fact used to give to those currently engaged on the regulation of their subject territories. No interval was allowed for examination of the proposal, and no future date fixed for voting on it. It was passed into law on the spot. That night lists of another 130 men, in addition to the seventeen, were posted in many places in Rome, and shortly afterwards a further 150. The names of extra people who were being condemned, or who had already been put to death by mistake, were constantly being added to the notices to make it seem that they had been lawfully killed. It had been decreed that the heads of all of them should be brought to the triumvirs for a set reward; a free man was rewarded with money, a slave with his freedom and money. Everyone was to open up his property to search, and anyone who harboured or concealed one of the proscribed, or would not allow a search, was to be liable to the same penalties as the proscribed. Anyone who wished could also lay information relating to all these offences, for the same rewards.

8. The text of the proscription ran thus: 'Marcus Lepidus, Marcus Antonius, and Octavius Caesar, the men appointed to regulate the Republic and restore it to order, declare: if it were not for the treachery of criminals who

were pitied when they begged for mercy, and when they received mercy became enemies of their benefactors and subsequently conspirators against them, Gaius Caesar would not have been killed by men whom he took prisoner, spared out of pity, admitted to his friendship, and favoured *en masse* with office, honour, and gifts, nor would we have been compelled to deal *en masse* with those who have insulted us and proclaimed us enemies of the state. But as it is, we observe from the plots laid against us and from the fate of Gaius Caesar that their evil nature cannot be tamed by kindness, and we would rather arrest our enemies first than suffer at their hands. No one should consider this action unjust, or savage, or excessive, in the light of what has happened to Gaius and ourselves. Gaius, who was *imperator*[3] and chief priest, who conquered and incorporated into the Empire the peoples most dreaded by Romans, and who was the first man to venture on the un-sailed sea beyond the Pillars of Heracles to discover a land unknown to Romans, was assaulted and stabbed to death with twenty-three wounds in the middle of the supposedly sacred senate-house, under the eyes of the gods, by men whom he had captured in war but saved from death and even in some cases named in his will as heirs to his property. The others, instead of punishing the guilty for this abominable deed, sent them out to military commands and provincial governorships. Enjoying these, they have seized the public funds and are now raising an army from them against us. They are demanding another army from foreigners who have always been hostile to our power, and they have burnt, destroyed or pillaged the cities within the Roman domain which they cannot win over, while they lead the rest in terror against their country and ourselves. **9.** From some of these men we have already exacted vengeance, and the others, God willing, you will soon see punished. Now that we have succeeded in bringing under our control the most important regions, namely Spain, Gaul and these here in Italy, there is one task left to carry out, which is to mount a campaign against the assassins of Gaius overseas. As we intend to conduct a war on your behalf outside Italy, we think it endangers both our interests and yours to leave our other enemies behind us to exploit our absence and wait to seize opportunities offered by the accidents of war. On the other hand we do not believe we should delay such an urgent project because of them, but should rather eliminate them all at once – seeing that they were the ones who started the war by their official decision that we and the armies we commanded were enemies of the state. **10.** They were set on destroying tens of thousands of Romans along with ourselves, regardless of the vengeance of heaven or the hatred of men. Our own anger, however, will not extend to any member of the masses, nor will we name all the private enemies who have quarrelled with us or plotted against us, nor anyone simply for his wealth or assets or position, nor the numbers of people who were put to death by another *Imperator* before us (who also brought order to the state at a time of civil war and was called "Fortunate" by you),[4] in spite of the fact that three men must have more enemies than a single man had. We shall take our revenge only on the worst and most guilty. And this we do in your interests as much as in our own, since while our conflict lasts you are all bound to be exposed to great suffering. We must also offer some consolation to our army, which has been insulted, provoked, and declared hostile by our mutual enemies. We could simply have summarily arrested the men we have selected, but it is our choice to post their names rather than arrest them still unawares. This step too we have taken on your behalf, to prevent it being possible for the soldiers, in their fury, to go too far and act against people who bear no responsibility; instead, they will have a certain definite number of names and be under orders to touch no one else.   11. May fortune, then, bless our proclamation: that no one is to harbour or conceal any of the persons listed below in this register, or arrange to convey them anywhere else, or be induced by payment to do so. If any person is discovered to have saved, assisted, or been privy to information about them, we regard such a person as one of the proscribed, and we exclude the possibility of excuse or pardon. The killers are to bring the heads of their victims to us: for each, a free man will receive 25,000 denarii, and a slave will receive his personal freedom, 10,000 denarii, and Roman citizenship for his master.[5] The same will hold for informers, and to preserve anonymity the names of none of those who receive rewards will be noted in our records.' So ran the proscription notice of the triumvirs, so far as one can translate it from Latin into Greek.

12. The first to proscribe was Lepidus, and the first of the proscribed was his brother Paullus; and the next to proscribe was Antonius, and the next of the proscribed was his uncle Lucius.[6] This was because these men had been the first to vote them enemies of the state. The third and fourth were relatives of Plancus and Asinius, whose names were announced on another list as consuls-designate: Plotius, Plancus' brother, and Quinctius, Asinius' father-in-law.[7] And it was not so much by reason solely of their distinction that these men occupied the leading places, as to produce astonishment and render vain the hope that any individual could afford protection to anyone.

Even Toranius was among the proscribed, a man said by some to have been Octavian's guardian.[8] With the publication of the lists the gates and all other ways out of the city were closed, and also the docks, marshes and lagoons, and any other feature suspected of affording a means of escape or a secret refuge. The countryside became the responsibility of the centurions to go round and search; and all this happened simultaneously.

13. Many sudden arrests immediately ensued, both in the countryside and in Rome, wherever anyone happened to be caught; people were also murdered in all kinds of ways, and decapitated to furnish evidence for the reward. They fled in undignified fashion, and abandoned their former conspicuous dress for strange disguises. Some went down wells, some descended into the filth of the sewers, and others climbed up into the smoky rafters or sat in total silence under close-packed roof tiles. To some, just as terrifying as the executioners were wives or children with whom they were not on good terms, or ex-slaves and slaves, or creditors, or neighbouring landowners who coveted their estates. All at once there broke out all the resentment which had long been festering in secret. A shocking change occurred in the behaviour of senators, whether consuls, praetors, or tribunes, or men still seeking these offices or actually holding them, who threw themselves moaning at the feet of their own slaves and called their domestics 'lord' and 'saviour'. The most pitiable thing was that even when they had suffered this degradation they were shown no mercy.

14. The whole nature of their misfortunes was unlike that of a civil conflict or a wartime occupation. It was not the case that, as in those instances, they feared members of the other faction, or the enemy, and put themselves in the hands of their own household; on the contrary, they were more in fear of the latter than of the death squads – not because they were like opponents in war or civil conflict, but because they were members of their household who had suddenly become enemies, either from festering hatred, or because of the rewards announced, or on account of the gold and silver in the house. It was certainly for these reasons that no slave could any longer be trusted by his master, and each of them put his own personal gain above any feeling of pity for his master. Faithful or kindly slaves were afraid to give help, or provide shelter, or be an accomplice because of their liability to identical punishment. The situation was quite different from the terror associated with the action against the first seventeen. Then, no one had been publicly named, and when a few men were arrested without warning everyone feared the same fate and all stood shoulder to shoulder.

But when the lists were published, some people at once became the prey of all, while others, secure now on their own account and eager for gain, helped the executioners by hunting the others for a reward. As for the rest of the population, some looted the houses of the murdered men, and their gains distracted them from understanding the present troubles. Reasonable people, and those of greater intelligence, were terrified and aghast, and it appeared all the more extraordinary to them when they reflected that other states suffered cruelly in civil conflict and found salvation through agreement, whereas in the case of Rome first the conflicts of her magistrates ruined her and then their agreement brought these horrors.

15. Some of the proscribed died resisting their executioners. Others made no resistance, in the belief that it was not their attackers who were to blame. A few deliberately starved themselves to death, or hanged themselves, or drowned themselves, or threw themselves from the roof, or leapt into fires, or offered themselves to their executioners or even sent for them when they were slow to appear. Others tried to hide, and made abject pleas, attempting to ward or buy off death. Some lost their lives by mistake or deliberate malice, contrary to the intention of the triumvirs. It was obvious when a body was not that of one of the proscribed, because the head was still attached. The heads of the proscribed were displayed in the forum at the rostra, where those who brought them in had to claim their rewards. There was equal commitment and bravery on the part of others: wives, children, siblings, and slaves rescued the victims, helped them with numerous tricks, and died with them when their efforts failed; some even committed suicide over the dead bodies of the proscribed. Of those who made their escape, some died as a result of shipwreck and a consistently unkind fate, while others were paradoxically restored to hold office in Rome, command armies in war, and celebrate triumphs. Thus that period provided a catalogue of amazing stories.

16. Furthermore, these things occurred not in an inconsequential city-state, or in a weak little kingdom: it was the mightiest state of the world, mistress of so many nations and of land and sea, which was shaken by the divine power which had blessed her with good order from ages past until the present. Certainly, similar events took place in Rome under Sulla, and even before him under Gaius Marius (the most notable of these dreadful experiences being likewise narrated in the parts of my work which deal with these men), and in addition the proscribed were denied burial; but the present tribulations are more notable, on account of the standing of the tri-

umvirs and particularly because of the character and good fortune of one of them, who established the Empire on safe foundations and left after him a family and a name which still embodies power. I shall now recount the most outstanding and terrible examples, particularly remembered because they were the last. I shall not go through all of them (for it would not be worth telling of plain killing or escape, or of the later return of some who were pardoned by the triumvirs, or of their inconspicuous mode of life after they returned), but only those which are the most extraordinary and are likely to produce the greatest astonishment and give support to my introductory remarks. The material is plentiful, and many Romans have composed accounts of them for themselves in numerous books; but for reasons of space I shall place on record, by way of summary, only a few instances of each kind, to confirm that examples of each really occurred and to point up the happiness of the present day.

17. The bloodletting began, as it happened, with the magistrates who were still in office, and the first man killed was the tribune Salvius. The tribunate is a constitutionally sacrosanct and inviolate office with very great powers, so that tribunes have on occasion imprisoned even consuls. Salvius was the tribune who had at first prevented Antonius from being declared an enemy of the state, but had then co-operated completely with Cicero. When he heard of the agreement of the triumvirs, and their rapid move on Rome, he gave his friends a feast, because he would not be with them on many future occasions. As the legionaries burst in on the drinking-party, the revellers jumped up in fear and confusion, but the centurion told them to keep quiet and resume their places. He beheaded Salvius there and then, pulling his head over the table by his hair as far as was necessary, and repeated his instruction to those present to stay quiet, just as they were, because if they made a disturbance they would suffer the same fate. Stupefied and speechless even after the centurion had departed, the guests remained until far into the night reclining beside what was left of Salvius' body. The second man to die was the praetor Minucius, who was holding an electoral assembly in the forum.[9] When he heard that the soldiers were coming, he leapt up, and thinking even as he ran how he could elude them slipped quickly into one of the workshops, changed his clothes, and dismissed his attendants with his official insignia. But they stayed there out of respect and pity for him and made it easier, in spite of themselves, for the executioners to find the praetor.

18. Another praetor, Annalis, was escorting his son, who was a candidate for the quaestorship, and canvassing for support from the voters, when the friends accompanying him and the attendants carrying his insignia learnt that his name was on the proscription lists, and hurriedly abandoned him.[10] He took refuge with a dependant of his, whose house in the suburbs was small and shabby and thoroughly mean. He was hiding safely, until his son, who had guessed that he had fled to this dependant, led the executioners up to the house, received his father's property from the triumvirs, and was chosen to be aedile. When this son was under the influence of drink,* some soldiers quarrelled with him and killed him, and they were the same men who had killed his father.

Turranius, who was no longer in office but was now an ex-praetor, was the father of a licentious young man who none the less enjoyed some influence with Antonius.[11] He asked the centurions to delay killing him for a short time, until his son could put in a plea for him to Antonius. They laughed and said, 'He already has, but to the opposite effect.' Understanding the reason, the elder Turranius requested another very short delay so that he could see his daughter, and when he did he told her to take no share of his property, in case her brother asked Antonius for her life as well. This young man, too, came undone: he wasted his assets on dissolute pleasures, was convicted of theft, and went into exile to escape paying the fine.

19. Cicero, who after Caesar's death had held as much unchallenged power as a popular leader may, was condemned along with his son, his brother, his nephew, and all his connections, supporters, and friends. He was escaping by boat, but being unable to tolerate the roughness of the sea, returned to land, and lay low in a country place of his, which I visited while investigating this story, near the Italian town of Caieta. When the men who were tracking him down came near (and Antonius was hunting more eagerly for him than for anyone else, as were all Antonius' helpers), some crows flew into his room, squawking and rousing him from sleep, and pulling his bed-clothes from him, until his attendants divined that this was a sign from the gods, put him in a litter, and took him down to the sea again through a dense thicket which hid them. Numbers of men were running in various directions and trying to discover if Cicero had been seen anywhere. Everyone else, wishing Cicero well and pitying him, said that he had already put out to sea and his boat was under way, but a cobbler, who was a dependant of Clodius, one of Cicero's bitterest enemies, showed the path to a small party under Laenas, the officer in command. He ran along it, and when he saw that Cicero's attendants far outnumbered the men coming with him to wreak their vengeance, he very astutely shouted out, 'Centurions in the rear, up here!' Then the attendants were terror-struck, thinking that more soldiers were coming, (20) and Laenas, who had actually once won a court case with Cicero's support, pulled his head out of the litter and proceeded to cut it off.[12] It took three blows and some sawing through, because of his inexperience, and he also cut off the hand with which Cicero had composed the speeches against Antonius, portraying him as a despot, which he entitled *Philippics* in imitation of Demosthenes.[13] People immediately rushed to take the good news to Antonius, some on horseback, others by sea. Laenas found him seated in the forum and waved the head and hand at him from a long way away. Antonius was overjoyed and garlanded the officer, and gave him 250,000 denarii on top of the normal reward, on the grounds that he had removed the man who had been his greatest and most aggressive personal enemy. Cicero's head and hand were fastened for a long time to the rostra in the forum, where he had previously played the popular leader, and more came to see the sight than had listened to him. It is said that Antonius had the head placed before the table at his meals, until he was sated with looking at the vile object. This, then, was the way in which Cicero was killed and outraged after his death – a man who is renowned to this day for his literary achievements, and was of the greatest service to his country when he held the office of consul. His son had been sent away previously to Brutus in Greece, but his brother Quintus, and Quintus' son, were captured. When Quintus begged to be killed before his son, but the son pleaded to be killed before his father, the executioners said they would reconcile the two requests: each of the two was taken away by a separate party of executioners and put to death at the same time on an agreed signal.

21. The Egnatii, father and son, clung together and died with a single blow, and although their heads had been cut off, their bodies remained twined together.[14] Balbus sent his son on ahead of him to the sea to make his escape, and after a short while followed him at a distance, to avoid being noticed as they travelled together.[15] When someone, either by mistake or as a deliberate trick, gave him the news that his son had been arrested, he turned back and sent for the executioners. It happened that his son did indeed lose his life, in a shipwreck: thus did the divine power aggravate the disasters of the time. Arruntius' son would not agree to flee without his father, but Arruntius eventually persuaded him to preserve his life, because he was a young man.[16] His mother saw him off at the gates and went back home to bury her dead husband, then when she discovered that her son too had lost his life at sea she starved herself to death. Let these serve as examples of good and bad sons.

22. Two brothers, by the name of Ligarius, who were proscribed together,[17] hid themselves in an oven until their slaves found them. One was killed immediately. The other escaped, and on discovering that his brother was dead threw himself into the water from the bridge over the river.[18] Some fishermen picked him up, thinking that he had fallen, not jumped. After a protracted argument with them he tried to push himself into the current, but he lost his struggle with them and survived, saying, 'You are not saving me, but destroying yourselves together with me, because I have been proscribed.' Even then they pitied him and wanted to save him, until some of the soldiers who were watching the bridge saw him, ran up, and cut off his head. In the case of another pair of brothers, one of them threw himself into the river. His slave searched for his body for five days, and on finding it, because it was still recognisable, cut off the head for the reward. The other brother hid in a cesspit and was betrayed by another slave. The executioners thought it beneath them to plunge in, but prodded him with their spears and made him come out before cutting off his head, just as it was, without even washing it. Another man, when his brother was caught, ran up unaware of the fact that he himself had also been proscribed, and said, 'Kill me in place of him.' The centurion, who had the precise details recorded, replied, 'You're asking for the right thing – your name is down before his',[19] and so saying put them both to death in the order on his list.

23. So much for examples concerned with brothers. Ligarius' wife hid him, but let one serving-maid into the secret, and was betrayed by her.[20] She followed the woman as she carried her husband's head, crying, 'I gave this man shelter, and the penalty for those who offer shelter is the same.' As no one killed her or denounced her, she went to the magistrates and made her own deposition against herself, and when they too ignored her because of her love for her husband, she starved herself to death. (I have mentioned this woman here, because she failed in her attempt to save her husband's life, and committed suicide to accompany him. I shall write about the women whose love for their husbands achieved its aim in my section on the men whose lives were saved.) Other women committed the sin of plotting against their husbands. One of them was married to Septimius, but was seduced by a friend of Antonius. Anxious to convert adultery into mar-

riage, she made a request to Antonius through her lover, and Septimius' name was at once added to the lists of the proscribed. When he discovered this he fled to his wife's house, in ignorance of his domestic problems. Under the pretence of helping her husband, she barred the doors and kept guard over him until the executioners came; and on the same day that they murdered him she celebrated her wedding.

24. Salassus, who was on the run and did not know what to do, entered Rome at night, when he thought the danger would be least. His house had been sold, and the only person to recognize him was the doorkeeper who had been sold along with the house. The doorkeeper took him into his quarters and promised to hide him and feed him so far as he could. Salassus told him to summon his wife from her house. She pretended that although she was anxious to come, she was afraid because to do so at night would be suspicious even to her maids, and said she would come in the morning. At daybreak she went to fetch the executioners, while the doorkeeper ran back to her house to hurry her up, thinking she was simply being slow. Salassus feared that the doorkeeper had gone off to spring a trap on him and ran up on to the roof to await events. When he saw, not the doorkeeper, but his wife bringing the executioners he threw himself off the roof.

Fulvius took refuge with a serving-woman who had been his concubine, and to whom he had given her freedom and also a dowry for her marriage. Although she had been so well treated by him, she betrayed him from jealousy of the woman who married him afterwards. Let these suffice as examples of women who did wrong.

25. Statius the Samnite, who did much for the Samnites in the Social War and had been made a Roman senator on account of the fame of his deeds and his wealth and family, was already eighty years old when he was proscribed for his wealth. He threw open his house for the ordinary people and his slaves to take away whatever they wanted, and some of it he tore down himself. When it was empty, he barred the door, set the house on fire, and perished, and the flames spread to many other parts of the town.

Capito half-opened his door and for some time killed those who were trying to force their way in one by one, but when a number of them applied their weight, he died after single-handedly killing many of them.[21]

At Rhegium Vetulenus assembled a considerable force composed of the proscribed and their fellow-refugees, and also of men from the eighteen towns, which were very angry at being advertised as the prizes of victory. With these troops Vetulenus killed some of the centurions who were scouting about these parts, and even when a stronger force was sent against him he did not give up, but made the crossing to Sicily to join Pompeius, who controlled the island and welcomed any fugitives. Subsequently he fought valiantly, but after being defeated in numerous engagements he sent his son and all the other proscribed persons to Messana. He himself waited until he saw that the boat had entered the straits, and then plunged in among the enemy and was slaughtered.

26. Naso, on being betrayed by a freedman who was his lover, snatched a sword from one of the soldiers and after slaying only the traitor offered himself to the executioners. A slave who was fond of his master made him stay at the top of a hill while he himself went down to the sea to hire a boat for him. On his return he saw his master being killed, and as the latter was already expiring gave a great shout of 'Wait a minute, master', and suddenly attacked and killed the centurion. He then turned the sword on himself, and said to his master, 'Now you have some consolation.' Lucius gave money to two of his most faithful freedmen and was making his way to the sea, but when they ran away he despaired of life, turned back, and gave himself up to the executioners. Labienus, who had arrested and put to death many men in the Sullan proscriptions, thought it unworthy of him not to suffer the same fate with nobility and went out in front of his house to sit on a chair and await the executioners. Cestius was hiding in the country with friendly slaves, but as centurions constantly passed by with weapons, or heads, in their hands, he could not endure his protracted fear and persuaded the slaves to light a pyre so that they could say that they were conducting Cestius' funeral. They were tricked, and lit the pyre, and Cestius leapt into it. Aponius, who had concealed himself safely, could not endure the squalor of his existence and brought himself out for execution. Another man voluntarily waited for the executioners without concealment, and when they were slow in coming throttled himself.

27. Lucius, who was the father-in-law of Asinius, the consul of the time,[22] was escaping by sea, but was unable to stand the discomfort of the weather and threw himself overboard far from land. When Caesennius was trying to slip away from his pursuers, shouting that he had not been proscribed, but was being victimized by them for his money, they took him to the notice, made him read out his own name, and killed him as he read it. Aemilius, not knowing that he had been proscribed, saw another man being pursued and asked the centurion giving chase who the proscribed person was; the centurion, recognising Aemilius, replied, 'You and him', and killed both of them. Cillo²³ and Decius, discovering as they came out of the senate-house that their names were on the proscription lists, fled precipitately through the city gates before anyone had yet set on them, and by their act of flight betrayed themselves to the centurions whom they encountered. Silicius,²⁴ who had been a juror at the trial of Brutus and Cassius, when Octavian and his army were supervising the courts, and had been the only man to cast his vote openly for acquittal when the other members of the jury were secretly voting for condemnation, now forgot his high-principled stand for freedom and putting his shoulder under the bier joined the bearers of a corpse that was being carried out to burial. The guards at the gates noticed that there were more bearers than usual for a single body, but they did not suspect the bearers and investigated the bier in case someone was faking death. However, the bearers proved that Silicius was not a member of their profession, and he was recognized and killed by the executioners.

28. Varus, who had been betrayed by a freedman, made his escape and after moving from mountain to mountain entered the marshes of Minturnae, where he stayed quietly resting for a while. The people of Minturnae were searching the marshes in a hunt for a robbers' hideout, and the movement of the reed-tips gave Varus away. When he was captured, he said he was a robber and resigned himself to being condemned to death on these grounds, but when they were going to torture him as well to find out his accomplices he could not bear the indignity of this and said, 'I forbid you, people of Minturnae, to proceed further with the torture or killing of one who has been consul and – a thing of much greater consequence to the present government – has been proscribed; if it is impossible for me to escape, it is better to suffer at the hands of my equals.' The people of Minturnae were unconvinced and suspicious of his story, but a roving centurion identified and decapitated him, leaving the rest of his body to Minturnae.²⁵

Another party captured Largus in the country when they were on the track of someone else. They pitied him, because he had been caught when he was not being hunted, and let him escape into the woods. Others then pursued him, so he ran back to the first group and said, 'You kill me instead. You had pity on me, and you should have the reward, not these people.' This was the return that Largus made for their kindness by dying.

29. In contrast, Rufus, who owned a fine tenement block next door to property belonging to Fulvia, Antonius' wife, and had in the past refused her offer to buy it, was proscribed although he now gave it to her. When

Rufus' head was brought to him, Antonius said it was nothing to do with him and sent it to his wife, who ordered it to be displayed, not in the forum, but on the tenement. Another man had a very fine country house with a shady retreat containing a beautiful deep grotto, and perhaps it was for this reason that he was actually proscribed. He happened to be resting in the grotto, and when the executioners were closing in on him but were still some distance away, a slave sent him into the recesses of the grotto, put on his master's tunic, and pretended to be him and to be terrified. Perhaps he would have been successful, and been put to death, had not one of his fellow-slaves revealed the trick. In this way his master was killed, but the people went on making their anger apparent to the magistrates until they had the informer hanged and the protector given his freedom. A slave informed on Haterius, who was in hiding, gained his freedom immediately, and bid against Haterius' children for his property, treating them with extreme arrogance.[26] Weeping and silent, they followed him about everywhere until the people became incensed and the triumvirs re-enslaved him to the children of the proscribed man, on the grounds that he had gone too far.

30. Such were the things that happened to grown men, but the misfortunes of the time struck at orphans too, because of their wealth. One such, on his way to a lesson, was killed along with his slave attendant, who embraced the boy and would not let him go. Atilius, who had just assumed the adult toga,[27] was proceeding, as the custom is, with a crowd of friends to sacrifice in the temples. Suddenly his name was entered on the lists, and his friends and slaves ran off. He left his splendid procession to go, deserted and alone, to his mother, and when even she was afraid to shelter him he did not think it worth trying anyone after her, and fled to the mountains. Forced by hunger to come down to the plains, he was captured by a man who habitually preyed on passing travellers and put them in chains to work for him. As was natural for a boy brought up in luxury, he could not endure the toil, and still wearing his fetters made off to the main road, where he identified himself to some passing centurions and was killed.

31. While all this was happening, Lepidus celebrated his triumph over the Spaniards, and the following edict was published: 'May fortune's blessing attend this proclamation, that every man and every woman is to sacrifice and feast this day; anyone who is seen not to do so will be proscribed.' And so Lepidus conducted his triumphal procession to the sacred shrines, and the whole population escorted him, outwardly cheerful but inwardly

hostile. As for the proscribed, the belongings in their houses were looted, and the buyers of their estates were few, because people were reluctant to add to the woes of the unfortunate and considered that such property would bring bad luck on themselves, and that it was most unsafe to be seen to possess gold or silver. They also thought that additions to their wealth were dangerous at the present time, and that what they owned would be at much greater risk. The isolated individuals who were bold enough to come to the sales bought at extremely low prices, because they were the only buyers. For this reason the triumvirs, who hoped that sales would provide sufficient money for their preparations for war, were short of 200 million denarii. 32. They explained this to the people and posted a list of 1,400 particularly wealthy women, who had to have their property valued and contribute to the war expenses an amount individually assessed by the triumvirs. Penalties were imposed for undervaluation or concealing any assets, and rewards were offered for information laid by free persons and by slaves. The women decided to appeal to the female relatives of the triumvirs. They succeeded in winning support from Octavian's sister and from Antonius' mother, but were turned away from the door of Fulvia, Antonius' wife. Resentful at her rudeness, they pushed their way to the magistrates' tribunal in the forum, where the people and the military guard parted for them, and said, through their chosen spokeswoman Hortensia: 'As was appropriate for women of our rank who wished to make an appeal to you, we resorted to your womenfolk; but the treatment we have received from Fulvia has been inappropriate, and we have been driven by her to the forum. You have already taken our fathers, sons, husbands, and brothers from us on the pretext that you have been wronged by them. If you also take our property, you will reduce us to squalor unworthy of our family, character, and feminine nature. Do you allege that we, like our menfolk, have wronged you? If so, proscribe us too, as you proscribed them. But if we women have voted none of you an enemy of the state, nor torn down your houses, nor destroyed your army or put another in the field against you, nor prevented you enjoying command or honours, why do we share the punishment when we have not collaborated in the crime? 33. Why should we pay tax, when we have no share in magistracies, or honours, or military commands, or in public affairs at all, where your conflicts have brought us to this terrible state? Because, you say, there is a war? And when have there not been wars? And when have women paid taxes? Our nature exempts us in all human societies. Our mothers overstepped the bounds set by nature on one single occasion in the past, when you risked losing all our power and the city of Rome itself, in the Carthaginian troubles. Then they paid tax voluntarily, and not from land or country properties or dowry or town-houses, without which a free woman has no livelihood, but only from their ornaments at home – and not after valuation, nor under the threat of informers or accusers, but as much as they wished. So what fear now grips you for our Empire or our country? Let us have a war with the Gauls, or with the Parthians, and we shall rival our mothers when it comes to saving Rome. But may we never pay taxes for a civil war or aid you against each other. Under Caesar and Pompeius we paid no tax, nor were we forced to do so by Marius or Cinna or Sulla – and the last was a man who enjoyed absolute power over our country. You, on the other hand, claim to be re-establishing political order.'

34. After these words of Hortensia's, the triumvirs were annoyed that when men were submissive women were standing up to them, making public speeches, and questioning the actions of the government, and that although the men were serving as soldiers the women would not even contribute money. They instructed their attendants to clear the women away from the tribunal, but when the crowd beyond began to boo the attendants stopped and the triumvirs said that they were deferring the question to the following day. The next day they posted a notice that 400 women instead of 1,400 were to have their property valued, along with any man who possessed more than 100,000 denarii. This applied without exception to all alike, whether Roman citizen, foreigner, freedman, or priest, and of any nation. These people, too, were placed under the same threat of penalties and the same offer of rewards for informers, and they were to lend the government immediately two per cent of their wealth and contribute a year's tax for the war.[28]

35. Such were the misfortunes which engulfed the Romans as a result of the decrees of the triumvirs, but they were made worse by the lawlessness of the military. Because the only safety for the rulers, engaged as they were on this business, lay with their soldiers, the latter would ask sometimes for the town-house, estate, country place, or whole inheritance of the proscribed, sometimes for adoption as children of their victims.[29] Some took other action on their own initiative, killing men who had not been proscribed and plundering houses belonging to the innocent, so that the triumvirs had actually to publish an edict that one of the consuls was to reverse acts where orders had been exceeded. He was afraid to touch the

soldiers, for fear of rousing them against him, but arrested and hanged some of the slaves who had masqueraded as soldiers and participated in their crimes.

36. Such were the chief means by which the sufferings of the proscribed reached a conclusion. The surprises which befell some of them, and brought them immediate safety and subsequent renown, are not only more pleasant for me to relate, but of more service to those who hear them, as they will encourage them to hope for deliverance and never to despair. For those who could, escape lay to Cassius and Brutus, or to Cornificius in Africa, who also took the republican side. A large number went to Sicily, as it adjoined Italy, and they were very warmly received there by Pompeius, who at that time displayed remarkable concern for these unfortunates. He sent messengers out to invite them all to come to him and to announce that he would give to anyone, free man or slave, who saved the lives of any of them double the reward offered for their capture. His small boats and merchant vessels met any who came by sea; his warships patrolled the shores, made signals to help the lost, and picked up anyone they encountered. He came in person to meet new arrivals and immediately handed out clothing and equipment to them. To those worthy of it he gave military or naval command. Later, when he was offered peace by the triumvirs, he refused to take it until the terms were extended to include also these people who had taken refuge with him. In this way he did his unfortunate country the very greatest service and thereby gained on his own account a high reputation, on top of and in no way inferior to that he inherited from his father. Others of the proscribed made their escape in other ways or remained in hiding until the amnesty, some in tombs or in the countryside, some by employing pitiable expedients in Rome itself. Astonishing examples were witnessed of love by wives for their husbands, of devotion by children to their fathers, and of unnatural goodwill on the part of slaves towards their masters.

37. The centurions scrupled to kill Paullus, Lepidus' brother, because he was their general's brother, and he sailed to find safety with Brutus. After Brutus' death he went to Miletus, whence he decided not to return even when he was invited back after peace was made. Antonius' mother kept his uncle Lucius, her brother, quite openly in her house, and the centurions showed a high degree of respect to her, too, as the mother of their commander-in-chief. When force was later tried, she rushed out of the

house into the forum where Antonius was presiding with his colleagues over public business and said, 'Imperator, I inform you that I have taken Lucius into my house, still have him there, and will continue to keep him until you put both of us to death, since the same penalties have been proclaimed for the proscribed and for those who give them shelter.' Antonius criticized her, saying she was a good sister but a wrong-headed mother: 'You ought not to be saving Lucius' life now: you should have stopped him when he was voting your son an enemy of the state.' None the less he arranged for Plancus, who was consul, to rescind the decree of banishment against Lucius.

38. Messalla, a young noble,[30] fled to join Brutus, and the triumvirs, fearing his abilities, posted the following notice: 'Since his relatives have demonstrated to us that Messalla was not even in Rome when Gaius Caesar was killed, his name is to be removed from the list of the proscribed.' He would not acknowledge the pardon, but when Brutus and Cassius fell in Thrace, and their army, which was still numerous and possessed ships and money and prospects that were far from hopeless, chose him as their commander, he would not agree and persuaded them to yield to the pressure of fortune and join Antonius' troops. He was one of Antonius' closest companions until he objected to Cleopatra's control over Antonius and deserted him for Octavian. The latter proclaimed him consul in place of Antonius himself, who had been stripped of office when he was again declared an enemy of the state, and appointed him to a naval command at Actium against Antonius, and then sent him to subdue a revolt in Gaul, granting him a triumph for his victory.

Bibulus made his peace at the same time as Messalla, held naval command under Antonius, and served many times as an intermediary in negotiations between Antonius and Octavian; appointed military commander of Syria by Antonius, he died while still in office.[31]

39. Acilius escaped from Rome without being seen, but was betrayed to the soldiers by a domestic slave. By the prospect of a larger reward he induced the soldiers to send some of their number to his wife with an agreement which he gave them. When they came she showed them all her jewellery and said she would give it to them on the understanding that they would honour their side of the exchange, but did not know if they would. Her love for her husband was not, however, cheated, since the soldiers chartered a boat for Acilius and sent him off to Sicily.

Lentulus[32] was unhappy that his wife, who wanted to share his exile and was therefore keeping a close watch on him, should run the same risks as himself. So he slipped away secretly to Sicily, where he was accepted as a military commander by Pompeius, and sent word to her that he was alive and holding command. Her mother was watching her, but when she learnt where her husband had gone she imitated him and escaped with two slaves. In their company she travelled rough and cheaply like a slave woman, until one evening she reached Messana from Rhegium. She easily discovered the commanding officer's tent, where she found Lentulus not like a senior officer, but unkempt, on a little pallet-bed, and existing in a wretched way because of his longing for his wife.

40. Apuleius'[33] wife threatened to inform on him if he fled without her. Unwillingly, he took her with him, but his escape was assisted by the lack of suspicion aroused by a man travelling openly with his wife, manservants, and maidservants.

Antius' wife rolled him up in a sack of bedding, which she gave to hired bearers to carry, and took him from his house to the coast, whence he escaped to Sicily.

Reginus'[34] wife lowered him at night into a sewer, which the soldiers did not enter during the day because they could not stand the smell, and on the next night she disguised him as a charcoal-seller and gave him a donkey carrying charcoal to drive. She herself led the way, carried in a litter a little way ahead. One of the soldiers at the gates was suspicious of the litter and while he was investigating it Reginus, taking fright, ran up and as though he were any passer-by begged him not to harass women. The soldier replied angrily, thinking he was addressing a charcoal-seller, but recognized Reginus (for he had once served under him in Syria) and said, 'Go on your way, and be glad, general – for I ought to call you that even now.'

Coponius'[35] wife cajoled his life from Antonius, although she had previously been chaste, and thus remedied one misfortune with another.

41. Geta's[36] son pretended to burn his father's body in a courtyard of the house, saying that he had strangled himself; he then secretly left his father on a newly acquired estate, where the older man changed his appearance by putting a patch over one eye. When the amnesty was declared he took off the patch, but his eye had been destroyed by lack of use. ⁄

On account of his great infirmity in old age, Oppius wished to remain in Rome, but his son carried him on his back until he was clear of the gates and by leading him or carrying him took him the rest of the way to Sicily.[37] No one suspected or took advantage of these figures, in the same kind of way that Aeneas' enemies, according to the story, respected him when he was carrying his father. The people approved of the young man and later made him aedile, but because his property had been confiscated and he could not meet the expenses of his office the craftsmen made him what he needed *gratis*, and each of the spectators at the theatre threw into the orchestra coins of whatever value he liked, so that they made him a rich man.

By the terms of his will Arrianus actually had inscribed on his gravestone: 'The man who lies here was proscribed; his son, who was not proscribed, hid him, made his escape with him, and saved his life.'

42. There were two Metelli, father and son. The father was a commander under Antonius at Actium, where he was captured but not recognized, while his son was with Octavian's army and had also served as an officer in the same campaign. Octavian was passing sentence on the prisoners at Samos and the son was on the dais among his advisers when Metellus senior was brought in, unshaven, sunk in filth and misery, and with his appearance greatly changed in consequence. When he was summoned by the herald at his place in the sequence of prisoners, his son leapt up from the council, with difficulty recognized his father, embraced him, and wept over him. Eventually controlling his sobs, he said to Octavian, 'This man was your enemy, Caesar, and I your ally. He should be punished, and I should be rewarded. But I beg you either to save my father on my account or to put me to death too on his account.' Everyone felt pity, and Octavian spared Metellus' life, although he had been a most determined enemy of his and had many times turned down generous inducements to change sides.[38]

43. Marcus' slaves, with goodwill and good luck, kept him safe at home through the whole duration of the proscriptions, until on the declaration of the amnesty he emerged from his house as though he had returned from exile.

Hirtius,[39] who had escaped from Rome with his slaves, travelled about Italy freeing chained slaves and gathering up runaways. He attacked settlements, small at first, then larger, until he controlled a band strong enough to control Bruttium, and when an army was sent against him he sailed across to Pompeius with all the resources he had.

Restio[40] believed he had escaped alone, but a slave secretly followed him. This slave had been brought up by Restio himself and had previously been well treated, but was later tattooed for his failings of conduct. As Restio was taking some rest in a marsh, the slave stood in front of him, terrifying him by his sudden appearance, and said to his frightened master that he was not so much conscious of his present tattoos as mindful of the kindnesses he had formerly received. He made Restio stop in a cave, found work, and collected what food he could for him. The soldiers of the locality became suspicious that there might be some connection between Restio and the cave, and proceeded towards it. Understanding their intentions, the slave shadowed them, and ran ahead to kill and decapitate an old man who was travelling along the road in front of them. The soldiers were amazed and arrested him for murdering a traveller, but he said, 'I have killed my master Restio, who stamped me with these tattoos.' The soldiers took the head away from him for the reward and vainly hurried with it to Rome, while the slave moved his master on and crossed to Sicily.

44. Appius was resting in a farmhouse, and when the soldiers burst in a slave put on Appius' clothes, lay down in bed as though he were the master, and voluntarily died in place of his master, who stood by like a slave attendant.

When the soldiers descended on Menenius' house, a slave stepped inside his master's litter and was carried away by his co-operating fellow-slaves, until he was put to death still pretending to be Menenius, and Menenius escaped to Sicily.

Vinius had a freedman called Philemon, who owned a splendid house. This man concealed Vinius in its inmost recesses in an iron chest of the kind made for keeping money or books, and brought him food at night until the amnesty. Another freedman, who was the custodian of his master's tomb, kept his master's son, who had been proscribed, safe in the tomb along with his father.

Lucretius[41] roamed about with two faithful slaves, but was forced by lack of food to go back to his wife in Rome, carried in a litter by the slaves as a weakened man would be. One of the slaves broke his leg and Lucretius went on by supporting himself on the other man. When he reached the gates, where his own father had been arrested after being proscribed by Sulla, he saw a detachment of soldiers running out. Overwhelmed by the coincidence, he hid with the slave in a tomb. Some tomb-robbers came to rifle the tombs, and the slave allowed the robbers to strip him while Lucretius escaped to the gates. Lucretius waited for him there, and after sharing his own clothing with him reached his wife and was concealed by her between double roofs, until friends were able to secure his pardon from the proscribers. Afterwards, when peace came, he held a consulship.

45. Sergius was hidden in Antonius' own house, until the latter persuaded Plancus, who was consul, to have his 'return' approved. For this reason Sergius later, at the time of the civil war between Octavian and Antonius, was the only man to cast his vote openly against the proposal when Antonius was voted an enemy of the state by the senate.

Such was the manner in which the preceding persons were saved. Pomponius, though, disguised himself as a praetor, equipped his slaves as his attendants, and proceeded through the city like a praetor conveyed by lictors, with the attendants crowding round him so that he should not be recognized by another praetor. At the gates he mounted an official vehicle and travelled the length of Italy, welcomed and sped on his way by everyone because they thought he was a praetor sent by the triumvirs to negotiate a treaty with Pompeius, until finally he sailed across to him in a state warship.[42]

46. Apuleius and Arruntius pretended to be centurions and equipped their slaves as soldiers.[43] First they burst through the gates like centurions in pursuit of other people. Then for the rest of their journey they separated, releasing chained slaves and collecting runaways, until the strength of each man's group was sufficient to have military standards and weapons, and resemble an army. They both proceeded towards the coast, where they encamped either side of a ridge, observing each other with great apprehension. In the morning, as they peered warily from the crest, each thought the other was a military force sent against themselves and they closed and fought until eventually they realized the truth, threw aside their weapons, and with lamentations laid the blame on fortune which dogged their every step. They sailed off in different directions, one to join Brutus, the other Pompeius. The latter returned from exile along with Pompeius, the former governed Bithynia for Brutus and after Brutus' death handed the province over to Antonius and secured his return to Rome.

Immediately Ventidius[44] was proscribed a freedman tied him up as if he was going to hand him over to the executioners, but when night came he won over the slaves, dressed them as soldiers, and brought his master out in the guise of a centurion; and in completing their journey through the remainder of Italy to Sicily they often stopped for the night in the company of other centurions who were hunting for Ventidius.

47. Another man was hidden in a tomb by a freedman, but could not endure the spookiness of the place and was moved to a miserable lodging. When a soldier came to share the lodging, his fear was again too much for him. He abandoned his cowardice for an amazing boldness, had his head shorn, and conducted a school in Rome itself until the amnesty.

Volusius, who was an aedile, was proscribed, but had a friend who was an initiate of the cult of Isis. He borrowed the outfit, put on the ankle-length linen robes, added the dog's head,[45] and made his way to Pompeius dressed like this and celebrating the rites.

Sittius, who was a citizen of Cales and had made many benefactions to the town from his great wealth, was protected by the inhabitants, who took up arms on his behalf. They threatened his slaves, and kept the soldiers outside the walls, until the trouble was dying down. Then they petitioned the triumvirs for him and succeeded in winning permission for him to remain in his native town although he was barred from the rest of Italy. Thus this Sittius was the first and only man to be banished to foreign soil and enjoy his exile in his home town.

Varro was an intellectual and historian. He was a man with a fine military record, who had held the office of praetor, and was perhaps proscribed because these things would have made him hostile to autocracy.[46] The well-known thought it an honour to give him shelter, competing with each other to do so. Calenus[47] was the successful man, and accommodated him at a country property where Antonius used to stop on his journeys. However, not a single slave, either Varro's own or Calenus', gave away Varro's presence in the house.

48. Verginius was silver-tongued, and persuaded his slaves that if they killed him for a small and chancy reward they would become polluted and live in terror afterwards, but if they saved his life they would win a reputation for moral behaviour, have good prospects, and eventually receive a much larger and safer sum of money. They fled with him as one of themselves, and when he was recognized on the road they resisted the soldiers. He was captured by the soldiers but explained to them too that they would be killing him, not because they hated him, but only for money, and that it would be possible for them to earn a larger amount of less iniquitous money if they came to the coast with him, 'where', he said, 'my wife has made arrangements to meet me with a shipful of money'. They were likewise convinced by him and went down to the coast. His wife had indeed arrived at the beach as had been agreed, but as Verginius was late she thought he had already sailed to join Pompeius. So she had put out to sea again, but not without leaving a slave on the beach to explain. When the slave saw Verginius he ran up to him, as he would to his master, pointed to

the ship sailing away, and told him about his wife and the money and why he himself had been left behind. Verginius' captors now believed everything, and when he asked them to wait there until his wife could be called back, or else to accompany him to her to get the money, they embarked in a small boat and rowed manfully to convey him to Sicily. There they received what they had been promised and did not leave Verginius' service until the amnesty.

A ship's captain took Rebilus on board, on the understanding that he would ferry him across to Sicily, and demanded money by threatening to inform on him if he did not get it. But Rebilus, rather like Themistocles when he was on the run, made a counter-threat to denounce him for accepting money to carry him, until the captain became afraid and took him safe across to Pompeius.[48]

49. Marcus, who was serving as an officer with Brutus, was another man proscribed for that reason. After Brutus' defeat he was arrested, but pretended to be a slave and was purchased by Barbula. Barbula saw that he was clever, put him in charge of his fellow-slaves, and appointed him to handle the cash; and as he was good at everything and of quicker understanding than the normal slave, Barbula suspected something and encouraged him to believe that if he would admit to being one of the proscribed, Barbula would save his life. As Marcus strenuously resisted the suggestion and invented an ancestry, and a name, and former owners, Barbula took him to Rome in the expectation that a man who had been proscribed would be reluctant to go there, but even so he followed. At the gates, one of Barbula's friends who had come to meet him noticed Marcus standing beside him as a slave and quietly told Barbula, who then made a request of Octavian through Agrippa.[49] Marcus' name was removed from the lists, he became a friend of Octavian, and not long afterwards was actually one of his commanders at Actium against Antonius. Barbula, too, was one of Antonius' commanders, and the wheel of fortune came round full circle. On Antonius' defeat Barbula was captured and pretended to be a slave; Marcus bought him as if he did not know him, then told the whole story to Octavian, and succeeded with his request that he be allowed to repay Barbula in the same way. And even later the equality of fortune of these two men persisted, for they were colleagues in the consulship at Rome.[50]

50. In contrast, Balbinus, who was exiled and made his return with Sextus Pompeius, and held the consulship not long afterwards, was approached under pressure of the following circumstances by Lepidus, who had been stripped of his power by Octavian and reduced to the status of a private citizen. Maecenas was prosecuting Lepidus' son for treason against Octavian, and also his mother for complicity with her son; Lepidus himself he ignored, because of his weakness.[51] He was sending the son to Octavian at Actium, but asked the consul to obtain a bond for the mother's appearance before Octavian in order to avoid having to convey a woman under arrest. As no one undertook to give the bond, Lepidus kept waiting outside Balbinus' door and appearing when he was dispensing justice, and although for a long time the attendants pushed him away he at last managed to say 'Even the prosecution testify to my moderation. They do not allege that I sympathized with either my son or my wife. Yet though it was not I who proscribed you, I am lower than those who were proscribed. You should not ignore the mutability of human fortune, nor me as I stand here in front of you. Allow me, please, to stand surety for my wife's appearance before Octavian, or grant me my request to go there with her.' Before Lepidus had finished speaking, Balbinus was overcome by the change of fortune and released his wife from the bond.

51. Cicero's son Cicero was sent away to Greece before the proscriptions by his father, who expected that something of the sort would occur. From Greece he joined Brutus, and after Brutus' death Pompeius. He was respected by both and thought fit for command. After that, Octavian quickly gave him a priesthood by way of apology for his sacrifice of Cicero's father, and not much later made him consul and governor of Syria. When Octavian sent word of Antonius' defeat at Actium,[52] it was this Cicero, as consul, who read the letter out to the people and posted it on the rostra, where his own father's head had once been displayed.

Appius divided his goods between his slaves and sailed with them for Sicily. A storm engulfed them, and the slaves plotted to lay their hands on the money. They put Appius in a small boat, pretending that they were transferring him to give him a better chance of survival, but it turned out that he unexpectedly made a successful crossing, while they were lost when the ship broke up.

Publius,[53] Brutus' quaestor, was urged by Antonius' supporters to betray Brutus. He would not do so, and for this reason was proscribed, then was restored and became a friend of Octavian; and once when Octavian was visiting him he brought out portraits of Brutus, and was praised even for this by Octavian.

I have ignored many other cases, but these were the most extraordinary examples of danger and survival of some of the proscribed.

52. While these events were taking place in Rome, all the overseas territories were being convulsed by military conflicts caused by this civil war. The most important of these were in Africa between Cornificius and Sextius, in Syria between Cassius and Dolabella, and around Sicily against Pompeius. Cities endured many horrors when they were taken by force, but I pass over the lesser instances. The most intense and in the general estimation the most celebrated sufferings were those of the inhabitants of Laodiceia, Tarsus, Rhodes, Patara, and Xanthus. Their nature, briefly described, was as follows.

53. The Romans call the part of Africa which they took from the Carthaginians Africa Vetus; the part which Juba held and they later acquired under Gaius Caesar they call, for this reason, Africa Nova, but it could be considered part of Numidia. Sextius, who had been appointed to govern Nova for Octavian, requested Cornificius to vacate Vetus for him, because in the triumviral allocations the whole of Africa had been allotted to Octavian. Cornificius replied that he did not recognize the allocation that had been made by the triumvirs on their own initiative,* and would not surrender the province he had received from the senate to anyone else without its authority. As a result, they went to war with each other. Cornificius had a larger and more heavily armed army, Sextius a smaller and lighter-armed one, but with it he none the less traversed and raised in revolt the inland parts of Cornificius' province and repulsed Ventidius, Cornificius' commander, when he arrived with a more numerous force and besieged him. Laelius, another of Cornificius' commanders, ravaged Sextius' portion of Africa, took up a position outside Cirta, and put the town under siege. 54. All of them sent ambassadors to win the support of King Arabio and the so-called Sittians, who had acquired their name as a result of the following circumstances. Sittius had failed to defend a civil action brought against him in Rome, and had gone into exile.[54] He had collected a military force from Italy itself and from Spain, sailed over to Africa, and allied himself to various of the African kings as they fought among themselves. As those he joined always won, Sittius became famous and his army had become outstandingly well trained. He fought on Gaius Caesar's side when he was pursuing the Pompeians in Africa, and killed Saburra, Juba's cele-

brated general.[55] As a reward for these services he received from Caesar the
territory of Masinissa, not the whole of it, but the best part. Masinissa was
an ally of Juba and the father of this Arabio, and Caesar had given his land
to Bocchus, the Mauretanian king, and to this Sittius, who had distributed
his share to the men under him. Arabio then left the country to join the
sons of Pompeius in Spain, but when Gaius Caesar was killed he returned
to Africa, and by constantly sending Africans to the younger Pompeius in
Spain and getting them back trained he was able to take his land back from
Bocchus and managed to kill Sittius by deception. Although he was well-
disposed to the Pompeians because of this, he always held it against them
that fortune was pitiless to them, and so gave his support to Sextius, and
through him won the favour of Octavian. His followers also supported Sextius, in their case because of the goodwill they felt towards Octavian's
father.

55. Sextius then took heart and broke out from the siege to give battle.
Ventidius was killed, and when his army retreated in disorder, Sextius followed, killing and taking prisoners. On hearing the news Laelius raised the
siege of Cirta and went to join Cornificius. Sextius, greatly encouraged by
what had happened, was already on his way to meet Cornificius at Utica
and though inferior in numbers was taking up a position opposite him.
Cornificius sent Laelius out with the cavalry to make a reconnaissance, but
Sextius sent Arabio to make a frontal attack on Laelius with cavalry while
he himself outflanked the cavalry engagement with his light-armed troops.
When he attacked he threw the enemy into such confusion that eventually
Laelius, though not yet defeated, was afraid that his line of retreat had been
cut off and seized some high ground in the middle, and Arabio, who was
sticking close to him, killed many of his men and surrounded the rise.
When he saw this, Cornificius came out with the major part of his army to
assist Laelius, but Sextius got behind him too, attacked, and hung on his rear
until Cornificius turned about and beat him off with considerable losses.

56. Meanwhile Arabio had made an unobserved entrance into Cornificius' camp by scaling the cliffs with men who were experienced climbers.
When the palisade was taken, Roscius, who was in charge of the defence,
offered his throat to one of his armour-bearers and was killed. Cornificius,
who was in difficulties in the battle, and was still unaware of what had occurred at his camp, tried to slip quickly across to Laelius on his hill; but as
he made the move Arabio's cavalry charged and killed him. Laelius saw this
taking place as he looked down from the hill, and committed suicide. Their

leaders dead, Cornificius' army escaped in separate groups. Of the proscribed who had been with Cornificius, some crossed to Sicily, others went
where they could individually. Sextius rewarded Arabio and the Sittians
with a large quantity of spoils, and consolidated the control of Octavian
over the towns by not punishing any of them. This was the end of the war
in Africa between Sextius and Cornificius, its brevity apparently being due
to the rapidity of its action.

57. The campaign which involved Cassius and Brutus took the following course. To repeat by way of reminder a little of what has already been
said, after Gaius Caesar had been killed his murderers occupied the Capitol
but descended on the declaration of an amnesty. When Caesar's body was
brought out for burial the ordinary people in a surge of pity for Caesar
went about hunting for his murderers, who for the moment defended
themselves from the roofs of their houses, while immediately afterwards
such of them as had been appointed provincial governors by Caesar left
Rome. Cassius and Brutus were holding office as praetors in the city, and
they too had been chosen by Caesar to follow their praetorships with governorships, Cassius with that of Syria, Brutus with that of Macedonia.[56] Although they could not assume authority in their provinces before the due
date, they were too afraid to stay in Rome and intended to leave the city
while they were still praetors in office. To give them some respectability the
senate entrusted them with a commission to procure corn, to prevent them
from being regarded as refugees from the city during the intervening
period. When they had gone, in face of the strong disapproval of the senate
it was voted that Syria and Macedonia should be transferred to Dolabella
and Antonius. However, as a concession to Cassius' supporters, Cyrene and
Crete were given in exchange. Brutus and Cassius spurned these as too
small, and proceeded to collect money and military forces with the intention of invading Syria and Macedonia.   58. While they were busy with
this, Dolabella killed Trebonius in Asia and Antonius besieged Decimus
Brutus in Cisalpine Gaul. Angry, the senate voted Dolabella and Antonius
enemies of the state, restored Brutus and Cassius to their original provinces,
added Illyria to Brutus' sphere of authority, and issued instructions to every
Roman provincial governor or military commander between the Adriatic
and Syria to obey the orders of Cassius and Brutus. After this Cassius forestalled Dolabella's attack on Syria, assumed the symbols of his governorship
and took over a total of twelve legions, which had been enlisted and trained

by Gaius Caesar long before. Caesar had left one of them behind in Syria, as he was already thinking of an invasion of Parthia.[57] Caecilius Bassus had been given the job of looking after this legion, but the command was held by Sextus Iulius, a young man related to Caesar himself. Sextus Iulius had gone astray and adopted luxurious habits,* and took the legion about in a disgraceful state. On one occasion when Bassus reproved him for this, he insulted him, and later, when he called to Bassus and the latter was slow to take notice, he gave orders for Bassus to be brought before him by force. There was an unseemly commotion, blows were directed at Bassus, and the army, unable to tolerate the scene, killed Iulius under a hail of weapons. They immediately repented and became afraid of Caesar. The soldiers therefore bound themselves together by oath that if they were not pardoned and trusted they would fight to the death, and they compelled Bassus to go along with them in this. Finally they enlisted another legion, trained jointly with it, and made spirited resistance to Staius Murcus, who had been sent against them with three legions by Caesar. Marcius Crispus came to help Murcus with three further legions from Bithynia, and together they were now besieging Bassus with all six legions. 59. Cassius therefore dealt urgently with this siege. He at once took control of Bassus' army, with their consent, and then of the legions of Murcus and Marcius, who transferred them to him not only from friendship but also because by the resolution of the senate they were subordinate to him. In addition, Allienus, who had been sent by Dolabella to Egypt, was bringing back from there four legions composed of men who had been scattered after the defeats of Pompeius and Crassus or had been left behind by Caesar with Cleopatra. He was not alerted to the current situation, and was taken by surprise by Cassius in Palestine and forced to hand over his army and join Cassius, as he was afraid to fight against eight legions with four. In this way Cassius unexpectedly gained control of a total of twelve first-rate legions. Even some Parthian mounted archers also joined him on account of the reputation he enjoyed among the Parthians ever since, as quaestor to Crassus, he had appeared more sensible than his commander.

60. Dolabella had spent some time in Ionia, killing Trebonius, imposing taxes on the towns, and through the agency of Lucius Figulus gathering a mercenary fleet from the Rhodians, the Lycians, the Pamphylians, and Cilicia. When everything was ready, he invaded Syria, with himself in command of two legions on land, and Figulus in charge at sea. Informed about Cassius' army, he pressed on and reached Laodiceia, which was friendly to

him and was built on a peninsula. It was well defended on the landward side and had a harbour to seaward which he thought would give him easy access to supplies by sea and allow him to sail safely away whenever he wished. Cassius, appreciating the situation and afraid that Dolabella would escape him, blocked the neck of the peninsula, which was a quarter of a mile wide, with stone and all sorts of material which he collected from farm buildings, suburban dwellings and tombs. He also sent for ships from Phoenicia, Lycia, and Rhodes. 61. Except for Sidon, they all ignored him, but he put to sea to engage Dolabella: a fair number of ships were sunk on each side, and Dolabella captured five complete with their crews. Cassius again sent a request to those who had ignored him, and also to Cleopatra, the Queen of Egypt, and to Serapion, her military commander in Cyprus. Then Tyre, Aradus, and Serapion (without consulting Cleopatra) sent him what they had, but the queen, who offered as her excuse the famine and plague which were then simultaneously troubling Egypt, co-operated with Dolabella because of her relationship with Caesar. It was for this reason that she had previously sent him the four legions under Allienus, and she now had another expedition ready to send to his defence, but the winds kept it in harbour. As for the Rhodians and the Lycians, they declared that they would not give military assistance to either Cassius or Brutus in a civil war, when they had given Dolabella only escort vessels and had not known that they would fight alongside him.

62. Cassius therefore made further preparations with the resources available to him, and fought two naval battles with Dolabella. The first engagement was inconclusive, but Dolabella was defeated in the second, and Cassius raised a siege-mound and was on the point of breaking through the wall and entering the town. He was unable to bribe Marsus, the night commander of the wall, but succeeded with the centurions who were in charge by day; and when Marsus went off watch he entered, once it was light, by a number of posterns which were surreptitiously opened in different places. After the capture of the town, Dolabella proffered his head to his bodyguard, telling him to cut it off and take it to Cassius as the fee for his own safety. The guard decapitated him, but then killed himself. Marsus likewise committed suicide. Cassius swore Dolabella's troops into his own army, plundered the sacred and public property of Laodiceia, punished the leading townspeople, and ground the rest down with savage exactions. In this way he reduced the town to the depths of misery.

63. After Laodiceia, he started to move against Egypt. He knew that

Cleopatra was going to sail to join Octavian and Antonius with a powerful fleet, and his plan was to prevent its departure and punish the queen for her policy. Even before this he had thought it a good moment to attack Egypt, as the country was suffering from famine and had only a small mercenary army thanks to the recent departure of Allienus' men. His preparations were in train, his hopes were high, and the time was right, but Brutus summoned him urgently because Octavian and Antonius were already crossing the Adriatic. Cassius regretfully abandoned his Egyptian ambitions, and rewarded and sent home his Parthian mounted archers. He also despatched an embassy to their king to ask for a larger supporting force – which arrived in Syria after the decisive battle,[58] attacked many of the peoples in that area as far as Ionia, and went home again. Cassius himself left his nephew in Syria with one legion and sent his cavalry on in advance to Cappadocia.[59] There they surprised and killed Ariobarzanes on the grounds that he was intriguing against Cassius, and brought back to Cassius a great deal of his treasure and his other property.

64. At Tarsus, the population was in the grip of civil strife. One party had voted a golden wreath to Cassius, who was the first to arrive, while the other had voted the same to Dolabella, who followed him, and both did this claiming to represent the town.[60] And in counterpoint to Tarsus' honours to the two of them, Dolabella and Cassius each treated it badly because it was a town too ready to change its loyalties. After he had defeated Dolabella, Cassius imposed a levy of 1,500 talents on its inhabitants.[61] They did not know how to find this sum, and in face of the violent demands of the soldiery, who would not wait, they sold off all the public property and in addition turned into coin the sacred objects which they kept for processions or offerings. Even so, they were nowhere near meeting the amount, so the authorities started to sell free citizens into slavery. First were girls and boys, then women and pathetic old men, who fetched a very low price, and finally the young men. The majority of them committed suicide, but finally Cassius, returning from Syria, took pity on the plight of the population and excused them the remainder of their contribution. Such were the sufferings of Laodiceia and Tarsus.

65. Cassius and Brutus then met to confer with each other. Brutus thought they ought to concentrate their forces and set out for the greater struggle in Macedonia, because their enemies had an army of forty legions, of which eight had crossed the Adriatic. But Cassius thought they should continue to ignore their enemies, who thanks to their numbers would

suffer self-inflicted damage through shortage of supplies, and should reduce the Rhodians and the Lycians, who sympathized with their opponents and possessed a fleet, so that these people would not be in their rear during the decisive struggle. They decided on the latter course, and Brutus therefore proceeded against the Lycians and Cassius against Rhodes, where he had been brought up and educated in things Greek. Because he was about to fight against men who were outstanding sailors, he refitted his own ships at Myndos, brought their crews up to strength, and gave them training.

66. The more reputable of the Rhodians were afraid at the prospect of fighting the Romans, but the ordinary people were very confident because they recalled ancient struggles against rather different opponents. They launched their thirty-three best ships, but as they did this they none the less sent a delegation to Myndos to ask Cassius not to hold in contempt either Rhodes, which was a state that had always resisted those who looked down on her, or the treaty of non-aggression between Rhodes and Rome. If there were any complaint about providing military aid, they wished to learn of it from the senate of Rome, and they said that if the senate gave orders, they would furnish aid. This was the substance of the Rhodian position, to which Cassius replied that war, not argument, would settle the other points, but that the treaty forbade them to attack each other and the Rhodians had attacked him when they fought alongside Dolabella; the treaty bade them assist each other militarily, and when he had asked them for help they feigned ignorance with their reference to the Roman senate, which was exiled and scattered at the present time because of the despots in the capital. These despots would themselves be punished, and so would the Rhodians, for siding with them, if they did not at once obey his orders. This was Cassius' answer to them, and the saner Rhodians were still more frightened. The mob, however, were inflamed by Alexander and Mnaseas who reminded them that Mithridates had attacked Rhodes with a larger fleet, and Demetrius likewise before Mithridates.[62] After this, then, they elected Alexander to be *prytaneus*, which is their supreme office, and Mnaseas to be their admiral. **67**. Notwithstanding, they still sent an ambassador to Cassius in the shape of Archelaus, who had taught him Greek on Rhodes, to make him a more polished appeal. This he did, taking Cassius' hand in a familiar manner: 'As a man who loves Greece, do not destroy a Greek city. As a man who loves freedom, do not destroy Rhodes. Do not bring shame on the reputation of our Dorian state which has remained undefeated from its first existence, and do not forget the proud history you learnt in Rhodes and in Rome – in Rhodes, the great exploits of the Rhodian cities even against kings, above all Demetrius and Mithridates, who appeared completely irresistible, and how these exploits were performed in the name of that same liberty by which you too justify your efforts; and in Rome, where you possess inscriptions in our honour, you learnt how much we assisted you in fighting against Antiochus and others. I will say no more of our descent and reputation, or of the fact that we have never so far lost our freedom, or of our alliance and goodwill towards you, Romans.   **68**. But as for you, Cassius, you must feel a peculiar reverence towards the city and your nurture in it, towards your education, the time you passed here, the home you had, my school itself, and me. I had hoped to pride myself one day on these facts for a different purpose, but as it is I lay them out now for my city's sake. I do this both to prevent her being forced to fight you, although you were educated and brought up by her, and to stop one of two things inevitably occurring: either the total destruction of the Rhodians or the defeat of Cassius. Besides this appeal, I advise you, as you set your hand to such tasks on behalf of the Roman state, to make the gods your guides in every undertaking. You Romans swore by the gods when you recently made a treaty with us, pouring offerings as the oaths were taken, and clasping hands. Are these things, which even enemies respect, to have no force with friends and tutors? And the gods aside, do not harm the reputation you have among men. Nothing does more than the violation of a treaty to brand the guilty as for ever untrustworthy in the eyes of friend and foe.'

69. As he spoke, the old man did not let go of Cassius' hand, but let tears fall upon it, so that Cassius blushed at the sight and felt rather ashamed. However, he withdrew his hand and said: 'If you did not advise the Rhodians not to wrong me, you did me a wrong; but if your lesson has failed to persuade them, I shall protect you. Surely the first wrong is the one clearly done to me, when I requested alliance from those who taught me and brought me up, and they ignored me. The next wrong is that they put me second to Dolabella, whom they had not educated or brought up. And most abominable of all is the fact that I and Brutus and all these admirable senators you see are in exile from a tyranny and attempting to free our country, while Dolabella was reducing it to slavery in the interests of others, to whom you are sympathetic, although you make a pretence of not becoming involved in our internal struggles. It would certainly be an internal struggle, if we too were trying to seize personal power, but what is taking place is open war between democracy and autocracy. You refuse to give help to democracy, but you plead for your independence. You adduce your friendship with Rome, but you show no pity to men who have been sentenced without trial to death and confiscation of property. You pretend that you wish to have instructions from the senate, which is the victim of this treatment and has no means left of defending itself, but it has already given you its response with its decree that everyone in the east should assist Brutus and myself. 70. You count up the times you Rhodians have co-operated with us when we have been making some addition to our empire, for which services Rhodes has naturally received benefactions and rewards, but you forget that you will not fight alongside us when our lives and freedom are unjustly threatened. Even if there had existed no previous relationship between us, now at least it would have been appropriate for you to begin to fight of your own free will in support of democracy at Rome, as you are Dorians.[63] But instead of acting or thinking along such lines, you quote a treaty, a treaty furthermore which was made between yourselves and Gaius Caesar, the architect of this autocracy. The treaty nevertheless states that Romans and Rhodians are to protect each other in times of need. Therefore you must now protect Romans in extreme danger. Cassius it is who quotes this treaty and calls on you to fight alongside him, a Roman citizen and a Roman general, as is stated in the resolution of the senate in which all east of the Adriatic are instructed to obey us. Brutus also draws your attention to the same resolutions, as does Pompeius, who holds command at sea by appointment of the senate; and apart from the resolutions there are the appeals for succour made to you by all these members of the senate who have taken refuge, some with me and Brutus, some with Pompeius. The agreement, of course, is for Rhodians to help Romans, even if the request is made by single individuals. If, however, you consider us not to be Romans or generals any more, but exiles, strangers and condemned men, as those who have proscribed us allege, you Rhodians no longer have an agreement with us, but with Romans, and we, as strangers and foreigners to the treaty, will make war on you unless you obey our every order.' And with these ironical words Cassius dismissed Archelaus.

71. The Rhodian leaders, Alexander and Mnaseas, put to sea with their thirty-three ships against Cassius at Myndos, intending to be first to strike terror into their opponents with their attack. They were somewhat light of heart at the prospect, because they considered that it was their similar attack on Mithridates at Myndos which had brought them success in the final

result of that war. For show, they proceeded under oars, and bivouacked at Cnidus the first day. On the next they appeared from seaward to show themselves to Cassius' forces, who were amazed and put out to face them. The conflict was a matter of stamina and strength on each side: with their light ships the Rhodians passed swiftly through and round the enemy line and turned to attack from astern, while the Romans had heavier ships and when they came to grips used their greater momentum to overbear their opponents as in an infantry battle. Then Cassius, with his greater number of ships, surrounded the enemy fleet and the Rhodians were no longer able to sail round and through the Romans. They could only attack the Romans from ahead, and back off again, and their skill was rendered useless by the constricted space within which they had been penned. Ramming and bow-shearing were ineffective against the heavier Roman ships, which were in good shape against lighter vessels, and finally three Rhodian ships were captured complete with their crews, two were broken apart and sank, and the remainder were damaged and escaped to Rhodes. All the Roman ships returned to Myndos, and repairs were put in hand to the majority, which had also suffered damage.

72. Such was the result of the naval battle at Myndos between the Romans and the Rhodians, which Cassius watched from a mountain. When he had made his fleet seaworthy, he sailed across to Loryma, a Rhodian fort on their mainland territory opposite the island, and transported his infantry over to Rhodes in merchant ships under the command of Fannius and Lentulus.[64] He himself sailed to the attack with his eighty ships equipped in a manner calculated to inspire terror, surrounded Rhodes with his fleet and his army together, and remained inactive in the expectation that the enemy would weaken a little. On the contrary, the Rhodians again sailed out with great confidence to give battle, but lost another two ships and were blockaded. They hurried up on to the walls, stationed armed men everywhere on them, and simultaneously repulsed both Fannius' men, who were harassing them from the landward side, and Cassius, who was leading the attack on the sea walls with a fleet that was well prepared for such an assault. He had anticipated something of the sort and brought with him collapsible towers, which were now erected. Rhodes, then, laboured under a double assault and was besieged by both land and sea. Furthermore, as the crisis was sudden and unexpected, no preparations had been made to withstand a siege. It was therefore obvious that the city would very soon be taken by force or starvation. The more intelligent of

the Rhodians saw this, and Fannius and Lentulus were talking to them. **73**. Suddenly, while these negotiations were still going on, Cassius, accompanied by picked troops, appeared in the centre of the town without any apparent use of force or scaling-ladders. The ordinary people guessed, and they seem to have been right, that Cassius' sympathizers among the population secretly opened postern gates because they pitied the city and forecast famine.

Thus Rhodes fell. Cassius took his official seat on a dais inside the city, and had a spear set upright beside the dais to signify that the capture had been by force. He gave strict orders to his troops to remain quiet and announced that he would put to death any soldier who indulged in any looting or violence. Then he himself summoned by name about fifty of the Rhodians, and when they were brought he punished them with death; approximately twenty-five others, who could not be found, he sentenced to exile. He pillaged all the money and gold or silver from the sacred and public treasuries, and ordered those who possessed private wealth to produce it on a particular day. He announced that any who concealed it would be rewarded with death, while informers were to receive ten per cent, and slaves their freedom as well. At first many of them hid their treasures because they did not expect that Cassius would carry through his threats; but when the rewards were paid and the people who were denounced were punished, they became frightened. They were given another appointed day, and much larger quantities than before were produced after being unearthed from the ground, drawn up from wells, or brought out of tombs.

74. Such were the sufferings of the Rhodians, and Lucius Varus was left with a garrison to watch over them. Cassius was delighted that he had taken the place so quickly and gathered so much money, but nevertheless gave orders to all the other peoples of Asia to contribute ten years' worth of taxes. They rapidly began to raise these, but news reached him that Cleopatra was about to sail with a large and powerfully equipped fleet to join Octavian and Antonius. Even before this she had favoured their side for Caesar's sake, but now she was all the more inclined to do so because of her fear of Cassius. He sent Murcus with one of his best legions and some archers on board sixty decked ships to the Peloponnese to lie in wait off Taenarus <*for her; and so he did*>,* after taking as much booty from the Peloponnese by surprise as he could.

75. The events involving Brutus in Lycia were as follows. To recapitulate some of his actions, when he had received from Apuleius[65] such armed forces as he had, and about 16,000 talents in money which had been gathered from the taxes of Asia, he reached Boeotia. The senate then decreed that he could use the money to meet his present needs, and that he was to be governor of Macedonia and of Illyria as well. He took over the three legions in Illyria, which the previous governor Vatinius surrendered, and captured one in Macedonia from Gaius, Antonius' brother. In addition he raised four others to make a total of eight, which for the most part had served under Caesar. He also had numerous cavalry, light-armed infantry, and archers, and drilled the Macedonians, of whom he thought highly, in the Roman way. While he was engaged on gathering an army and money, he had the following stroke of luck in Thrace: Polemocratia was the wife of one of the petty rulers, who was killed by his enemies, so Polemocratia, in fear for her son who was not yet grown up, came to Brutus with him and entrusted the boy to him along with her husband's treasure. Brutus handed the son over to the people of Cyzicus to look after, until he had the time to restore him to his throne, and discovered among the treasure an astonishing quantity of gold and silver. This he struck and turned into coin. **76**. Then when Cassius came and they decided to reduce Rhodes and the Lycians before taking any other action, he attacked Xanthus before any of the other Lycian states. The Xanthians destroyed the parts of their town outside the walls to stop Brutus using them either as billets for his troops or as a source of timber, and dug a ditch all round the town. They conducted their defence from this ditch, which was more than fifty feet deep and correspondingly wide,[66] standing beside it and hurling missiles and shooting arrows as if there were an uncrossable river in between. But Brutus proceeded to fill it in, against opposition: he pushed forward mantlets to protect his men as they worked, divided his army into day and night watches, and brought material from far away, running and cheering with his men as though it were a competition, and sparing no effort or enthusiasm. The result was that a task which in the face of enemy opposition was expected either not to be completed at all, or only with difficulty after several months, was finished in a few days, and the Xanthians were shut in and besieged. **77**. Brutus pressed the assault, with some of his men using siege engines against the walls, and others attacking the gates on foot, and he constantly relieved his troops. Although the exhausted Xanthians were always being pitted against fresh opponents, and they were all wounded, they nevertheless held out as long as their battlements remained. But when these too were knocked down, and their towers were broken through, Brutus, guessing what would happen, ordered the troops conducting operations against the gates to withdraw. The Xanthians thought this was a sign of carelessness and failure to mount guard, and made a night sortie with torches against the siege engines. When the Romans, at an agreed signal, made a swift attack on them, they retreated again towards the gates. However, the guards on duty, frightened that the enemy would pour in with them, closed the gates before they were inside, and the carnage at the entrance among the Xanthians who were shut out was terrible.   **78**. Not long afterwards the remainder made another sortie in the middle of the day, when Brutus' troops had again been withdrawn, and set fire to all the siege equipment at once. The gates were left open for them on account of the previous disaster, and about 2,000 of the Romans burst in with them. Still others were pushing in through the entrance when the gates suddenly came down, either because the ropes simply broke or because they had been cut by one of the Xanthians, with the result that some of the Romans who had forced their way in were killed and others were isolated inside, unable to raise the gates now that they had no lifting mechanism. In the narrow streets they were pelted with missiles from above by the Xanthians, but eventually managed to force their way through to the nearby main square. There they had the better of those who came to grips with them, but they suffered badly from archer fire, and having no arrows or javelins with them they made their way along to the shrine of Sarpedon to avoid being encircled.[67] The Romans outside the fortifications were riled, and afraid for those inside. Brutus went round encouraging them, and they resorted to various expedients, since they were unable to break through the gates, which were sheathed with iron, and they were short of ladders and towers, because these had been burnt. Some improvised ladders, some put tree-trunks against the walls and used them like ladders, and some attached coiled ropes to sharpened hooks, which they slung on to the wall above, and when any caught fast hauled themselves up.   **79**. The neighbouring Oenoandans, who were assisting Brutus because they were enemies of the Xanthians, scaled the cliffs by rock-climbing. Seeing this, the Romans with great effort copied them. Numbers fell off, but a few surmounted the wall. They opened a postern gate which had been stockaded with a mass of sharpened stakes, and admitted the most daring of the attackers, who swung themselves up over the stakes. They were now superior in numbers and started to smash the gates, which were not iron-sheathed on the inside. At the same time others worked with them on the same task from outside by battering through in the opposite direction. The Xanthians were making a tremendous din attacking the Romans who were at the shrine of Sarpedon, and in fear for their fellows the Romans who were smashing the gates from inside and out made insane efforts to force them. Just after sunset they broke through and charged in all together, shouting as a signal to the others. **80.** Now that the town was taken, the Xanthians ran home and put their loved ones to death, a fate they willingly endured. Cries of anguish arose, and Brutus, thinking that it was pillage, had heralds order the army to stop. When he found out what was happening, he took pity on the independent spirit of the Xanthians and offered a truce, but they hurled missiles at the messengers. They took all their possessions, piled them on pyres which had been previously heaped up inside their houses, and after setting light to the pyres committed suicide on top of them. Brutus saved what he could of the sacred property, but the only prisoners he took from Xanthus were slaves and, of the free population,* a few women and not as many as 150 men in all.

This was the third occasion on which the Xanthians perished by their own hands in the name of freedom. In the time of Harpagus the Mede, commanding an army for Cyrus the Great, they destroyed themselves in a similar way rather than be enslaved: they were penned by him in the city, and it became their tomb.[68] It is said that they suffered the same fate in the time of Alexander, son of Philip, because they would not submit even to Alexander with all his territory.

81. From Xanthus Brutus descended to Patara, a town which acts as the port for Xanthus, and stationed his army around it. He ordered the inhabitants to give him total obedience or suffer the same disaster as Xanthus; and the Xanthians, grieving for their own fate, were produced and advised them to take a wiser decision. The Patarans did not make an immediate answer to the Xanthians, so Brutus gave them the rest of the day to consider the question, and withdrew, reappearing with his army at daybreak. The Patarans shouted from the walls that they would obey whatever instructions he wished to give, and opened the gates. On entering, he did not execute or exile anyone, but collected together all the gold and silver in public ownership and ordered individuals to deliver up their private wealth under similar penalties, and similar rewards for information, as Cassius had announced at Rhodes. The citizens brought in their treasure, but one slave laid information against his master for hiding gold, and showed it to the centurion who was sent for it. As it was all being taken away, the owner said not a word, but his mother, in an attempt to save her son's life, followed crying that it was she who had hidden it. The slave, without being interrogated, indicated that she was lying and that his master had hidden it. Looking favourably on the young man's silence and his mother's suffering, Brutus let them both go away unpunished with the gold, but crucified the slave for going beyond the duty laid on him in pursuing his owners.

82. At the same time Lentulus, who had been sent against Andriace, the seaport of Myra, broke the chain across the harbour and went up to Myra. The people of the town agreed to obey him, and after enriching himself in similar fashion he returned to Brutus. Also, the joint council of the Lycians sent an embassy to Brutus, promising to ally themselves with him and contribute whatever they could. He fixed contributions for them to pay, returned the freeborn Xanthians to the city, and ordered the Lycian fleet to sail with the other ships round to Abydus, whither he himself was also bringing his land forces to wait for Cassius to come from Ionia, so that they could cross to Sestus together.

Murcus had been lying in wait in Peloponnesian waters for Cleopatra, but when he heard that her fleet had been damaged by a storm off Africa, and saw the wrecks that drifted as far as Laconia, and knew that she was returning with some difficulty and in a weakened state to her own country, he was unwilling to let such a large fleet lie idle. He crossed to Brundisium, made his base on the island that lies opposite the harbour, and prevented the remainder of the enemy army and their supplies from reaching Macedonia. Antonius fought against him with the few warships he had, and also with towers erected on rafts, whenever he sent off parts of his force in merchant ships after watching out for a strong offshore wind so that they would not be caught by Murcus. But he was in difficulties, and called for help from Octavian, who was engaged in a naval campaign against Sextus Pompeius in Sicilian waters for control of the island.

83. With Pompeius, the situation was as follows. He was the younger son of Pompeius Magnus, but was at first ignored in Spain by Caesar because his youth and inexperience would prevent him achieving very much, and he roamed the sea with a handful of men, living by piracy, and avoiding identification as Pompeius. As more men joined him for the piracy, his force became powerful and he revealed who he was. Immediately, any vagabond ex-soldiers of his father and his brother flocked to him as their

natural leader, and Arabio, who had been deprived of his patrimony as I have already said, arrived from Africa.[69] In this way his forces grew large, and his exploits became more than those of a pirate. His reputation spread far and wide among the extensive peoples of Spain as he moved about, darting from place to place, and not staying to do battle with Caesar's governors. When Caesar heard this, he sent Carrinas with a larger army to reduce Pompeius. But with his greater mobility Pompeius made unexpected appearances, disappeared again, harassed his enemies, and ended up taking a number of towns, small and large. **84.** Caesar then sent Asinius Pollio to succeed Carrinas and fight against Pompeius. Honours were even in this version of a war when Caesar was murdered and the senate invited Pompeius to return. He went to Massilia, where he continued to watch developments in Rome, and when he was appointed admiral of the seas, as his father had been, he still did not go back to Rome but gathered together all the ships he found in the harbours and left Spain with this fleet. When the triumvirate supervened, he sailed to Sicily and blockaded its governor Bithynicus, who would not surrender the island to him; finally Hirtius and Fannius, proscripts in exile from Rome, persuaded Bithynicus to abandon it to Pompeius.[70]

85. In this way Pompeius gained control of Sicily. He possessed a fleet, and an island lying off Italy, and a now numerous army, which was composed of his original forces and of those brought by the refugees from Rome, whether slave or free, or sent to him by the Italian towns that had been earmarked as prizes for the soldiers. These places dreaded a victory of the triumvirs, and acted secretly against them in so far as they could. Those who were able to do so deserted their native towns as being no longer truly their native towns and took refuge with Pompeius, who was very near at hand and was regarded with great affection by everyone at that time. Also, experienced sailors from Africa and Spain were at his side, so that he derived great confidence from his commanders, his fleet, his infantry, and his money. Reports of this reached Octavian, who sent a naval force under Salvidienus to sail down the coast and destroy Pompeius, which he thought would be an easy business. Pompeius himself sailed across towards Italy intending to engage Salvidienus off Rhegium. He met Salvidienus with a great fleet, and there was a battle at Scyllaeum at the entrance to the straits, in which Pompeius' ships, which were lighter and manned by more experienced crews, had the advantage in speed and skill, while those of the Romans, which were bigger and heavier, were in trouble. When the usual sea got up in the straits and the waves were driven in different directions by the current, Pompeius' men were in less difficulty because they were used to the heavy sea, while Salvidienus' were unable to keep their feet owing to their lack of practice, or continue to lift their oars back, or steer reliably, and were in complete confusion. The result was that with the sun now about to set Salvidienus called the action off first. An equal number of ships was lost on each side, and Salvidienus repaired his remaining vessels, which were damaged and in a poor state, after withdrawing to the port of Balarus by the entrance to the straits.

86. At this point Octavian arrived. He gave the most solemn personal guarantees to the people of Rhegium and Vibo that he would remove them from the list of prizes (since their position on the straits gave him particular concern), but in response to Antonius' call sailed in haste to him at Brundisium, taking a course which left Sicily on his port hand and postponing for the moment the matter of Pompeius and Sicily. On Octavian's approach Murcus dropped back a little from Brundisium, to avoid being caught between him and Antonius, and kept a lookout for the merchantmen on passage carrying the army from Brundisium to Macedonia. These ships were escorted by triremes, but by god's grace a strong and favourable wind sprang up and they sped confidently through without any need of their escort. Murcus was irritated, but still lay in wait for them as they returned empty. However, on that occasion also, and again when they were transporting another convoy of soldiers, they sailed by under swelling canvas, with the result that the whole army, and Octavian and Antonius as well, made the crossing. Murcus regarded himself as the victim of some supernatural power, but nevertheless waited for the supplies and food and additional recruits being ferried across from Italy and did what damage he could. In addition, Domitius Ahenobarbus was sent by Cassius and his followers with a further fifty ships and another legion and some archers to assist in the same task, which was clearly of the greatest value;[71] for as food was not widely available to Octavian's side from anywhere else, it had been decided to blockade the supply route from Italy. And so they sailed across with 130 warships, more auxiliary vessels, and a large number of fighting men, and harassed their opponents.

87. Decidius and Norbanus,[72] whom Octavian and Antonius had sent on ahead to Macedonia with eight legions, advanced from there 170 miles into the mountainous region of Thrace, until they had gone beyond the

town of Philippi and occupied the passes of the Corpili and the Sapaei in
the kingdom of Rhascupolis, which is the only way of going by any recognized road from Asia to Europe.[73] This was the first check to Cassius and
his followers, who had crossed from Abydus to Sestus. Rhascupolis and
Rhascus were brothers, Thracian princes who ruled a single country. ·
Rhascus had allied himself with Antonius' side, Rhascupolis with Cassius',
and each had 300 horsemen. When Cassius' advisers asked about the roads,
Rhascupolis said that the one through Aenus and Maroneia, which was the
highway, was the usual route, and short, but it led to the pass of the Sapaei,
and if the enemy were holding this, it would be impossible to go through;
on the other hand the outflanking route was difficult, and three times as
long.   **88**. But the others, supposing that the enemy had advanced from
Macedonia into Thrace not in order to confront them and block the roads,
but because they were short of food, set off for Aenus and Maroneia from
Lysimacheia and Cardia, which cut off the Thracian Chersonese like gates,
and on the second day they came to the Black Gulf.[74] When they reviewed
their army, there were nineteen legions in all, eight of Brutus', nine of Cassius', <*and some other units*>, * none at full strength, which were nevertheless made up into some semblance of two legions, so that there were about
80,000 legionary troops. As for cavalry, Brutus had 4,000 Gauls and Lusitanians and 2,000 Thracians, some Parthini from Illyricum, and Thessalians,
while Cassius had 2,000 Iberians and Gauls, and 4,000 Arabian, Median,
and Parthian mounted archers. There followed as allies kings and tetrarchs
of the Gauls of Asia with a great number of other infantry and more than
5,000 cavalry.

89. Such was the size of the army which was reviewed by Cassius and his
associates at the Black Gulf, and such was the size of the army with which
they proceeded to the decisive encounter, leaving the rest for their needs
elsewhere. After carrying out a ritual ceremony of purification, they paid
the donatives promised and still owing to some of the soldiers. They had
been careful to provide themselves with plenty of money, because they
wanted to make gifts to conciliate their men, most of whom had served
under Caesar, and avert the possibility that they might mutiny at the sight
or sound of his heir with the identical name, when he arrived.[75] And again,
because of this, they decided to make a speech as well. So a great platform
was erected, and the commanders mounted it accompanied only by the
senators, while their army, both Roman and allied, stood around them
below. Each of the two was instantly delighted at the sight of the other's

numbers, which appeared extremely strong, and they were at once given confidence and real hope by the great size of their forces. These factors more than anything else led the troops to have faith in their commanders, for shared expectations of success generate goodwill. The noise to be expected from such a crowd was silenced by heralds and trumpeters, and when quiet was eventually secured Cassius (who was the elder) stepped forward a little from his place and spoke as follows:

90. 'First of all, it is our shared struggle which leads us to have faith in one another. Next is the fact that we have given you everything we promised, which is the best guarantee that you can trust our future promises. Our hopes lie in the excellence both of yourselves, who serve as soldiers, and of ourselves, whose distinction and number you see as we stand, senators all, upon this platform. You know, too, the extent of our preparations: food, weapons, money, ships, and allied troops both from our provinces and from kings. So what need is there of argument to exhort you to enthusiasm and unity of purpose, when our preparations and our shared enterprise draw us together? As for the slanders directed against us by two men who are our personal enemies, you understand them very well, and for this reason you are ready to fight beside us. But I think I should still explain, even now, the root cause, which very clearly demonstrates that we have a complete and noble justification for going to war.

91. 'Like you, we fought alongside Caesar in his campaigns and as his senior officers we raised him to greatness and continued to be his associates; so there can be no suspicion that hatred caused us to conspire against him. But his behaviour in civilian matters was offensive, not to us his associates, because we gained promotion in this sphere as well, but to the ordinances and constitution of the Republic, which was no longer subject to the rule of law, whether its base was aristocratic or popular. Yet all this was settled by our ancestors when they expelled the kings and took an oath solemnized by curses never to tolerate another king. This is the oath to which we, the descendants of those who swore it, were loyal. We wanted to deflect the curses from ourselves and could not endure for long the sight of a single individual transferring powers to himself, even if he was our friend and benefactor. From the people he took the treasury, the army, and the election of magistrates, and from the senate the government of the provinces. In every sphere, his word replaced that of the law, his authority that of the people, and his decree that of the senate.   92. Perhaps you did not fully realize this, and saw only his abilities on campaign. But you can easily

appreciate it now, by looking simply at an aspect which concerns your-selves. In war, you, the people, give total obedience to your commanders because we possess authority, but in peace you resume your authority over us. The senate debates matters first, to save you from mistakes, but you yourselves decide and vote by tribes or centuries, and you elect consuls, tribunes, and praetors. Apart from the voting assemblies, you sit as jurors in cases of the greatest importance, rewarding or punishing us when we govern you in a way that deserves reward or punishment. This exchange of power, my fellow-Romans, has brought our Empire to the height of pros-perity and conferred honour on the deserving, and those who have been honoured have been grateful to you. You used this power to make Scipio consul, when you expressed your approval of what he did in Africa;[76] you also used to elect tribunes of your choice annually to oppose us on your behalf, if necessary. And why do I need to list the mass of things you know already? 93. However, once Caesar seized power, you elected no further magistrates: not a single praetor, not a consul, not a tribune. You did not signify your approval of anyone, and if you did approve you had nothing to bestow to mark the fact. To put it in a nutshell, not a soul owed you thanks for anything, whether it was a magistracy or a governorship, or acceptance of accounts, or acquittal after a trial. The most lamentable development of all was your own inability to help your tribunes when they were the vic-tims of high-handedness. This magistracy you established as a permanent office of your own, and declared it sacred and inviolate; but you witnessed its inviolate holders insultingly stripped of their inviolate office and their sacred dress, by mere decree, because they were thought to have expressed your anger against those who wanted to give Caesar the actual title of king. The senate took this particularly badly, on your behalf – the office of trib-une being not the senate's, but yours. They were unable to criticize Caesar openly or bring him to trial, because of the strength of the army, which he had also made his own although it had long been the state's, and they de-termined to fend off tyranny by the means that still remained: plotting against his life. 94. This had to be a policy approved by the aristocracy but carried out by a few. When it was done, the senate immediately made it clear that the policy had general support. This was apparent when they went so far as to vote that honours appropriate to tyrannicide should be conferred; but Antonius restrained them by pretending that this would lead to public disorder, and as not even we thought it right that honours, rather than our country's interests, should prompt the help we gave to Rome, they did not take this step. They had no wish to heap insult on Caesar, but simply to be rid of despotism, so they voted for a complete amnesty and made their views still clearer by banning any prosecution for murder. Not much later, after Antonius had played the demagogue to turn the population against us, the senate gave us charge of the largest provinces, and appointed us to military commands, and declared us to have authority over the whole area from the Adriatic to Syria. Did they do this to punish us as accursed, or to deck us out as killers of Caesar with sacred purple, rods, and axes? For the same reason they summoned back from exile young Pompeius, who had no part in these actions, simply because he was a son of Pompeius Magnus who was the first to fight for the Republic, and because he was eluding detection in Spain and causing minor annoyance to the despot's regime. They decided to refund to him from the treasury the value of his paternal estate, and they appointed him admiral of the seas, so that he too, as a supporter of the Republic, might hold some office. What further action or sign do you still want from the senate that everything has been done in conformity with their wishes? All that is missing is a specific verbal acknowledgement to you, which they will indeed give you; and when they give it, when they are able to speak out and reward you, they will repay you with substantial bounties. **95**. You know their present plight. They are proscribed without trial, their property is confiscated, they are put to death uncondemned in homes, in alleyways, and on holy ground by soldiers, slaves, and personal enemies. They are dragged from their hiding-places and pursued wherever they go, in spite of the fact that the law permits voluntary exile. The heads of men who were but yesterday consuls, praetors, tribunes, aediles, and members of the equestrian order lie exposed in the forum, where we never used to bring a single enemy head, but only their weapons and the rams of their ships. Rewards have been fixed for these atrocities. This is a boiling-up of everything that has so far been festering below the surface – summary arrest of male citizens, and various sorts of horror committed against women, children, freedmen, and slaves. Such is the extent of the decay of character too that now afflicts Rome. In all this the ringleaders of evil are the triumvirs, who themselves placed their own brothers, uncles, and guardians at the head of the proscription list.[77] History has it that Rome once fell to the most savage of barbarians; yet the Gauls beheaded no one, outraged none of the dead, and did not begrudge their opponents a chance to hide or escape. Neither we Romans, nor anyone else we know of, have ever yet imposed on a captured city anything similar to the injustices suffered, not by some insignificant place, but by a master state at the hands of men appointed to regulate it and set its affairs to rights. Did Tarquin do anything of the sort? The Romans threw him out, although he was king, for assaulting one woman in the heat of desire, and because of this single act they refused to tolerate monarchy any longer.

96. 'These, fellow-citizens, are the actions of the triumvirs who call us accursed and claim to be taking revenge for Caesar when they proscribe people who were not even in Rome when he was killed. The men you see before you are the majority of these, proscribed for their wealth or their family or their preference for republican attitudes. This was why Pompeius was proscribed along with us. He was far away in Spain when we did the deed; but for this same reason, that his father was a republican, he was both recalled by the senate to become admiral, and proscribed by the triumvirs. Was any plot against Caesar hatched by the women who were listed to pay over capital? Was any offence committed by that part of the population who were ordered to value their property if it was worth more than 100,000 sesterces, threatened with penalties and informers, and had new taxes and payments to the state imposed on them? Even by these methods the triumvirs could not pay their soldiers their full bounties. But we, who have done nothing immoral, have not only given you what we promised but have other money ready to pay greater rewards. So you see we also have the power of heaven on our side, because we are acting justly. 97. And apart from the favour of heaven, you can see how matters stand with humankind when you turn your eyes upon your fellow-Romans, whom you know have often served as praetors and consuls and won your approval. You see that they have taken refuge with us because they regard us as men who are unpolluted and republican. You see that they have chosen our side and are with us in prayer and deed for the tasks that remain. The rewards that we announced for preserving their lives have far more justice than those offered by the triumvirs for ending them. Nor do they understand that although we killed Caesar when he decided to exercise sole power, our intention was to leave alone those who pretended to his power. They do not understand that we put the state not at our own disposal but at that of the people, publicly, according to our traditions. The motives of the two sides for choosing to make war are not the same. Our opponents are driven by a desire for power and absolutism, which they have already demonstrated in the proscriptions, we by nothing except a wish to free our country and live as private individuals under the law. It is not therefore surprising that these

men here have followed the lead of the gods and decided in our favour. And the greatest source of hope in war is the justice of one's cause.

98. 'If anyone here served with Caesar, second thoughts are not for him. Even at that time, we were not Caesar's soldiers, but our country's. The bounties and prizes came not from Caesar but from the public funds, just as you are now the army not so much of Cassius or Brutus as of Rome, and we, commanders of a Roman army, are your fellow-soldiers. If our enemies shared this view, it would be possible for us all to lay down our arms in safety and give all her armies back to Rome, and for her to choose what is best for her. We challenge them to accept this. But they do not accept it, nor could they now do so thanks to the proscriptions and everything else they have done; so let us march forward, my fellow-soldiers, to fight with solid loyalty and honest enthusiasm, on behalf of no one but the senate and people of Rome, in the cause of liberty.'

99. They all shouted 'Forward!' and urged Cassius to lead them on at once. Delighted with their enthusiasm, he called again for silence and resumed: 'May the gods who control just wars reward you, fellow-soldiers, for your loyalty and enthusiasm. As for our superiority over the enemy in the quantity and quality of what human planning can provide, listen. We are leading into the field against them an equal number of legions, and have left several others behind in a number of places as our needs dictate. We have a great advantage in cavalry and ships, and kings and peoples as distant as Medes and Parthians are allied with us. We only face the enemy, whereas they have behind them our sympathizer Pompeius in Sicily, and in the Adriatic Murcus and Ahenobarbus who are constantly on patrol with a large fleet, ample support, two legions, and archers; they are creating considerable problems, while the land and sea behind us is clear of the enemy. As for money, which some call the sinews of war, they have none. They have not yet paid what they promised to their army, and the proceeds of the proscriptions have fallen short of their expectations since no fair-minded person is buying such tainted property. Other sources are short, as Italy is exhausted by civil conflict and levies and proscriptions. But on our side, careful planning has ensured that our present resources are abundant, so that we can make you further gifts, and much more besides is being collected and is on its way to us from the provinces in our rear. 100. Sources of food are the most difficult thing to secure for large armies; our opponents have none, except for Macedonia, which is mountainous, and Thessaly, which is small in area, and the produce must be transported over-

land with great effort. If they bring it from Africa or Lucania or Iapygia, Pompeius and Murcus and Domitius will intercept it.[78] We on the other hand have supplies, which are being transported with ease by sea daily from every land and island from Thrace to the river Euphrates, and we do this without interference because we have no enemy behind us. We therefore have the capability of both bringing the decisive contest on quickly and of wearing the enemy down at leisure by starvation. Such is the scale and nature, my fellow-soldiers, of the factors which depend on human foresight. With your help and that of the gods, may what remains match them. We have paid you everything we promised for your previous service and rewarded your loyalty generously; and we shall also reward you for this greater conflict in a manner worthy of it, according to the decision of the gods. And now, to encourage you as you go on your way to the struggle, and to mark this gathering and these words, we shall make an additional gift from this platform of 1,500 denarii to each soldier, five times that amount to each centurion, and proportionately to each military tribune.'[79]

101. With these words Cassius dismissed the assembly, having made his army ready with practical preparation, verbal encouragement, and financial reward. But the men lingered, giving the most generous praise to him and Brutus and promising for their part to do their duty. The commanders immediately proceeded to distribute the donative, giving bonuses to the best troops on sundry pretexts. They sent each group on ahead separately to Doriscus as it was paid, and followed after a short interval themselves. Two eagles now flew down on to two silver eagles of the standards and pecked at them, or according to others screened them from view. They stayed there, and the commanders thought them worth feeding officially, until they flew away the day before the battle.

The army passed around the Black Gulf in two days and came to Aenus, then marched from Aenus to Doriscus and along the rest of the coast as far as Mount Serrium.[80] **102.** As Serrium is a promontory, Brutus and Cassius themselves went inland and sent Tillius Cimber with the fleet and a single legion and some archers to sail round along the shore. The place used to be quite deserted, although the soil is good, because the Thracians were not a seafaring people and used not to come down to the coastal areas because they were afraid of attack from the sea. Chalcidians and other Greeks then occupied it, and since they exploited the sea, trade and agriculture flourished and the Thracians too were pleased at the opportunity to barter their produce, until Philip the son of Amyntas uprooted them all, including the Chalcidians, so that nothing is to be seen there now except the sites of their temples.[81] This shore was then once more deserted. Tillius Cimber sailed along it, as he had been instructed to do by Brutus and his advisers, surveying suitable places for camps and also marking out at intervals places where ships could come in to land, so that Norbanus and his force would think that there was no longer any point in guarding the pass, and evacuate it.[82] What they expected happened: because of the show put on by the fleet, Norbanus became worried about the Sapaean pass and asked Decidius to come as quickly as possible from the Corpilan pass to help him. Decidius did so, and Brutus' force passed through the abandoned pass.   103. The ruse revealed, Norbanus and Decidius held the Sapaean pass firmly, and Brutus and his men were again in a quandary. They were despondent for fear they might now need to set out on the roundabout route they had discounted and go back upon their tracks, although time was short and the season advanced. Such was the state of affairs when Rhascupolis said that there was a route, which would take three days, along the flanks of the Sapaean range itself. Men had up till now not used it, because it was sheer, waterless, and passed through thick forest, but if they were willing to carry their own water and make a narrow but adequate path, the tree cover would hide them even from birds and on the fourth day they would reach the river Arpessus, which is a tributary of the Hermus. It needed another day from there to Philippi, and they would then have encircled the enemy in such a way as to cut them off completely and deny them any retreat. Brutus and Cassius approved the plan both because of their present impasse and because they hoped to trap such a large enemy army.   104. Accordingly they sent forward a detachment, commanded by Lucius Bibulus, to open up the route with Rhascupolis. The task was laborious, but the men performed it with energy and enthusiasm, all the more so when some scouts returned from ahead with the news that they could see the river in the distance. On the fourth day, when thirst and exertion had exhausted them, and the water which they had brought with them was showing signs of running out, they remembered being told that the waterless stretch lasted three days and they became panic-stricken with fear that they had been tricked. They did not disbelieve the report of the scouts that they had seen the river, but thought that they were being taken a different way. They lost heart, raised a clamour, and when they saw Rhascupolis riding round and encouraging them, they abused him and pelted him with missiles. Bibulus implored them to make the effort to complete the work without protest, and at evening the river came into the view of the leading party. As was natural, a huge cheer of joy arose and this cheer, after being taken up in succession by those behind, reached the rearmost. When Brutus and Cassius heard the news, they immediately set off at high speed, and led the rest of the army along the cleared path. Not that in the end they either escaped detection by the enemy, or cut them off, because Rhascus, Rhascupolis' brother, had his suspicions raised by the cheer, and investigated. When he saw what was happening he was amazed that such a large army had come along a waterless route which he considered impenetrable even to an animal because of the density of the forest, and he passed the news to Norbanus' force, who retreated in the night from the Sapaean pass to Amphipolis. Both the Thracians acquired a great reputation with the armies, one for taking them by an unrecognized route, the other for not failing to recognize it.

105. Thus by a piece of extraordinary daring Brutus' force reached Philippi, where Tillius also joined them after disembarking, and the whole army had assembled. Philippi is a town which was formerly called Daton, and The Springs[83] before that, because there are a number of springs of running water around the ridge. Philip fortified it as a convenient strongpoint against Thrace and called it Philippi after himself. The town stands on a crest that is precipitous on all sides, and its size matches the width of the crest. On its northern side are thick woods, through which Rhascupolis led Brutus and his men, and to the south lie a marsh and then the sea.[84] To the east are the Sapaean and Corpilan passes, and to the west a fine fertile plain, stretching about forty-five miles, as far as Myrcinus and Drabescus and the river Strymon. This is the place where according to the story Kore was abducted when she was picking flowers, and the river is the Zygaktes, in which they say the yoke of the god's chariot broke as he was driving across, and so gave the river its name.[85] The plain slopes away, favouring travellers going down from Philippi towards the sea, but making a journey from Amphipolis an uphill pull.

106. At Philippi there is another hill at no great distance, called the Hill of Dionysus, where there are also the gold mines known as The Refuge. Just over a mile beyond this are two other hills, a little more than two miles from Philippi itself and about a mile from each other. On these they encamped, Cassius on the southern hill and Brutus on the northern, but although Norbanus' force had retired, they did not yet advance. They knew that Antonius was approaching, after leaving Octavian behind ill at Epidamnus, and the plain was admirable for a battle and the springs excellent

for their camps. As for what lay on either side, in one direction were marshes and lakes as far as the Strymon, and in the other the passes and barren, trackless country. The mile between the hills was the way through from Europe to Asia, like a gate, and they built a fortification across from one camp's defensive earthworks to the other's, leaving a gate in the middle, so that the two camps were one. There was also a river alongside, which some call the Ganga and others the Gangites, and to their rear the sea, where they intended to keep their stores and find anchorages. In fact they located their store depot on Thasos, twelve miles away, and the anchorage for their warships at Neapolis, nine miles away. They were pleased with their position, and went on strengthening their camps.

107. Antonius was making a rapid march with his army, because he wanted to occupy Amphipolis before the enemy, to use it as a base for the battle. When he found it had been fortified for him by Norbanus' men, he was delighted and left his equipment there with one legion under Pinarius, while he himself with great daring advanced a long way and encamped in the plain only a mile from the enemy. The inferiority of one camp, and the superiority of the other, became immediately apparent. One side was positioned on high ground, the other on the plain; one side got their firewood from the mountains, the other from the marsh; one side drew their water from a river, the other from newly sunk wells; and as for supplies, one side brought them a few miles from Thasos, the other forty-five miles from Amphipolis. It appears that Antonius was forced to do this, because there was no other high ground and the rest of the plain, being more low-lying, was sometimes flooded by the river; for which reason he also discovered that the springs supplying the wells that were being dug were sweet and abundant. Anyway, this act of daring, even if it arose from lack of choice, frightened his opponents, because he had contemptuously put his camp close opposite them immediately after his arrival. He added numerous outposts and hastily fortified everything with ditches and earthworks and palisades. The enemy also fortified what they had so far neglected. Observing Antonius' frantic activity, Cassius built a fortification from his camp to the marsh across the sole remaining stretch, previously ignored because of the short distance, so that nothing was still unprotected except the precipitous ground on Brutus' flank, and on Cassius' the marsh and the sea beyond. Everything in between was divided from the enemy by ditch, palisade, wall, and gates.

108. So each side proceeded with its fortification work, and in the mean-

time their sallies against each other were confined to cavalry skirmishes and missile-throwing. When everything they had thought of was complete, and Octavian had arrived (although he was not yet well enough for battle, and was carried in a litter up to the fighting units of the army), he and his allies immediately deployed their army for battle. Brutus and his associates drew theirs up on the higher ground to face them, but did not descend, because they had taken a decision to delay battle in the hope that they would wear the enemy down through shortage of supplies. The infantry strength of each side was nineteen legions, Brutus' below strength, Octavian's actually over strength; as to cavalry, apart from the Thracians on both sides, Octavian and Antonius had 13,000, Brutus and Cassius 20,000. So that in number of men, in daring and skill of commanders, in arms and equipment, both the marshalled armies were a most splendid sight. But for many days there was no action, because Brutus' side did not wish to fight, but to wear the enemy down first from lack of supplies. They themselves had Asia to supply them and could bring everything by sea from comparatively nearby, but the enemy had nothing in abundance or within easy reach: it was impossible to get anything from Egypt through traders, since the country had been exhausted by famine, nor from Spain or Africa, because of Pompeius, nor from Italy, because of Murcus and Domitius. And Macedonia and Thessaly, their sole current sources of supply, would not suffice for very long.

109. Brutus' side were very well aware of these factors and were in no hurry. Antonius, though, was concerned about them and realized that he must force his opponents to fight. He decided to see if he could secretly make the marsh passable, so that he could get behind the enemy unawares and cut them off from the supplies being brought from Thasos. So he again offered battle, and on each occasion he brought out all the standards of his army, to give the impression that his entire force was deployed. Meanwhile a detachment worked night and day to clear a narrow path through the marsh, cutting down the reeds, making a causeway with stones on either side to prevent the earth sliding away, and putting in stakes and bridges over the deep parts, all in utter silence. The enemy had been prevented from seeing the work by the reeds still growing around the path. After ten days of this work he suddenly sent in a column of troops by night, seized the strongpoints in the country the other side, and fortified a number of posts as well. Cassius was amazed at the ingenuity and secrecy of the scheme, but adopted the counter-stratagem of cutting off Antonius from his outposts,

and for his part constructed a fortification wall at right angles across the whole width of the marsh from his camp to the sea, clearing and bridging it in a similar way and erecting his palisade on solid foundations. He intercepted the path Antonius had made, so that the men on the other side could not retreat to join Antonius, nor could he help them.

110. It was about midday when Antonius noticed this. Straight away, without further preparation, he led his own army, which was drawn up opposite, with speed and intense determination sideways towards Cassius' wall between the marsh and his camp. They carried crowbars and ladders, intending to destroy it and go through to Cassius' camp. His charge was a daring one, oblique and uphill, right across the space between the two armies, and Brutus' troops, being extremely hurt at the insult offered by their enemies running by so confidently when they themselves were ready and armed, spontaneously charged them without waiting for any order from their commanders and promptly killed those they trapped (as one would expect when they took them on the flank). Now that they had begun the battle, they also charged Octavian's army, which had been drawn up directly opposite them, routed them, and pursued them, finally taking their camp, which was shared by Antonius and Octavian. Octavian himself, thanks to a dream, was not there and was taking care that day, as he himself wrote in his memoirs.[86]

111. When Antonius saw that battle had been joined he was pleased to have forced it (being very concerned about his supplies), but decided not to turn back to the level ground, in case reversing his formation should throw it into disorder. Instead he maintained the momentum of the charge he had begun and with difficulty went on up under a hail of missiles until he forced his way into contact with Cassius' line, which had preserved its original formation and was amazed at the madness of what had happened. He broke through this line and audaciously reached the wall between the camp and the marsh. His men uprooted the palisade, filled in the ditch, undermined the structure, slaughtered the men guarding the gates, and withstood the rain of missiles from the wall, until Antonius himself forced his way through the gates and the rest came in, some through the breaches in the wall, others by actually climbing on the bodies of the fallen. This all happened so quickly that they had already captured the wall when they confronted the men who had been working in the marsh and were coming to lend support. With a powerful assault they routed these too and after pushing them down into the marsh turned back, this time to Cassius' actual

camp. Antonius had with him only those who had surmounted the wall, since all the rest of both forces were fighting each other beyond it. **112**. The camp, because it was considered strong, was defended by very few troops, and so Antonius easily had the better of them. By now Cassius' army outside was losing the struggle, and when they saw their camp being taken they scattered in disorder. And so each side enjoyed a perfect and similar conclusion to the battle: Brutus had routed the enemy left and taken their camp, and Antonius with irresistible daring had defeated Cassius and sacked his camp. The slaughter on each side was unequal, and because of the extent of the battlefield and the amount of dust raised they were not aware of what was happening to each other until eventually they found out and recalled the rest. These returned looking more like porters than soldiers, and even then they did not notice or see each other distinctly or they would have thrown aside what they were carrying and fought fiercely against their opponents, burdened as they were and in no sort of order. It is conjectured that the number of the dead on Cassius' side was about 8,000, including slave shield-bearers, and double that number on Octavian's side.

113. When he was driven back from his fortifications and was no longer able even to enter his camp, Cassius retreated quickly to the hill of Philippi and watched the progress of events. Because the dust of battle prevented him from seeing them clearly or in their entirety, apart only from the fact that his own camp had been taken, he ordered his armour-bearer Pindaros to turn his sword on him and put an end to his life. While Pindaros was still hesitating a messenger ran up to say that Brutus was victorious on the other wing and was sacking the enemy camp. Cassius merely replied, 'Tell him I wish him total victory', and turning to Pindaros said, 'Hurry up. Why won't you release me from my disgrace?' Then Pindaros despatched his master as he offered his throat. So runs one version of Cassius' death. Another is that when Brutus' cavalry approached to give the good news, Cassius thought they were enemy and sent Titinius to find out; the horsemen, who recognised him as a friend of Cassius, surrounded him and shouted with delight at meeting him, but Cassius thought that Titinius had met enemies and said, 'Were we waiting to see our friend taken prisoner?' He then withdrew with Pindaros into a tent, and Pindaros was never seen again. For this reason some think that he murdered Cassius without waiting for the order. The day Cassius' life ended was his birthday, on which the battle happened to be fought; Titinius also committed suicide, because he had taken his time.

114. Brutus mourned over the body of Cassius, calling him the last of the Romans because no one would ever match his virtues, reproaching him for the swiftness of his action and his impulsiveness, and judging him happy in his release from care and sorrow, which would be his own guides to an end he could not discern. He gave the body to his friends to bury secretly, in order not to reduce the watching army to tears, and spent the entire night putting Cassius' camp in order, without eating anything or taking any thought for himself. At daybreak the enemy drew up their army in line of battle, to avoid appearing to have been defeated, and Brutus, understanding their purpose, said, 'We too must arm, and reply with the pretence that we have suffered less.' When he had deployed his army, the enemy withdrew and Brutus said mockingly to his friends, 'They challenged us, thinking we were exhausted, but they have not even put us to the test.'

115. On the day on which the battle of Philippi took place, another great disaster also occurred in the Adriatic. Domitius Calvinus was bringing over in merchant vessels two legions of infantry, one of which was the famous Martian legion, which took its name from its reputation for valour. He was also bringing a praetorian cohort of 2,000 men, four squadrons of cavalry, and a further body of picked men, and was escorted by a handful of triremes. Murcus and Ahenobarbus met them with 130 warships. A few of the leading transports escaped under sail, but when the wind suddenly dropped the rest drifted about in the calm, delivered by the gods to the enemy, who rammed each ship and holed it. The triremes escorting them, owing to their lack of numbers, were surrounded and unable to assist. All sorts of brave deeds were done by the men in danger: on the one hand they set about hastily drawing their ships together with ropes and connecting them to each other with poles, to prevent the enemy sailing through between them; but on the other, when they succeeded in this, Murcus shot fire-arrows at them, so they quickly undid the lashings and moved away from each other to avoid the fire, and were again in a position where the triremes could sail round them and ram them. 116. The soldiers felt frustrated, and particularly the men of the Martian legion, because although their fighting quality was superior they were helpless in face of their destruction. Some committed suicide when the flames reached them, some jumped aboard the enemy warships, to do or die. Half-burnt ships sailed about for a long time with men on board who were incapacitated by burns

or by hunger and thirst. Some men even clung on to spars or planks and were washed up on deserted cliffs and beaches. There were also cases of men whose lives were unexpectedly saved; some survived for up to five days by licking pitch or chewing sails or ropes until the swell carried them to land. And there were a fair number who did indeed surrender to the enemy, their morale broken by disaster. They also surrendered seventeen of the triremes. Murcus' force swore the soldiers into their own ranks, but their commander Calvinus, whose life was believed lost, returned to Brundisium on his own ship five days later. Such was the catastrophe, whether it ought to be called a shipwreck or a naval battle, that occurred in the Adriatic on the same day as the battle at Philippi, and the coincidence of the encounters caused amazement when it was later realized.

117. Brutus summoned his army to assemble and addressed them as follows: 'There is no aspect of yesterday's engagement, my fellow-soldiers, in which you were not superior to the enemy. You began the fighting eagerly, even if you anticipated orders; you completely destroyed their famed Fourth legion, to which that wing was entrusted, and also the troops supporting it, until you reached their camp; and you took and sacked the camp itself before they took ours. These achievements far outweigh the damage done on our own left. But although you could have finished the whole job, you preferred plunder to killing the men you had defeated, for the majority of you went on past the enemy themselves and made for their property. Meanwhile the enemy in their turn sacked one of the two camps we have, but we are in possession of everything of theirs, so that here too they have suffered a double ration of damage. Such is the extent of our gains from the battle; as for our other advantages over them, you can hear from the prisoners about their difficulty in getting food, the high price of it, the hazards of its transport, and the imminence of an open breakdown in supply. It is impossible for them to get it from Sicily or Sardinia or Africa or Spain, thanks to Pompeius, Murcus and Ahenobarbus, who with their 260 ships have closed the sea to the enemy. Our opponents have already exhausted Macedonia, and Thessaly is now their sole source of supply – and how long will that last them? 118. So when you see them at their keenest to fight, reflect then that hunger is at their heels and driving them to choose death in battle. Our counter-strategy must be to make hunger our first line of attack, so that they are weaker and exhausted when it is time for us to meet them. We must not be too keen and choose the wrong moment, and no

one must mistake experience for inertia, by failing to notice the sea in our rear. This brings us plenty of reinforcements and supplies of food and gives us the chance of a risk-free victory, if you stand your ground and think no worse of yourselves if the enemy mock us and challenge us to fight. The reason will be, not that they are better men, as yesterday's battle made plain, but that they are trying to remedy a different reason for fear. But when we ask you for it, unloose all the enthusiasm that I now request you to repress. I shall pay you your complete rewards for a complete victory, whenever the gods decide to give it; but for the moment I grant each legionary an extra thousand denarii for his courage yesterday, and a proportionate sum to the officers.' With these words he at once divided out the donative among the legions, and some people believe he promised to let them plunder Thessalonike and Lacedaemon.

119. Octavian and Antonius knew that Brutus would not willingly give battle, and called their own army together. Antonius said, 'Soldiers, I know that success in yesterday's battle was in theory also shared by the enemy, because they routed some of us and sacked our camp. In fact, however, they will demonstrate that success was entirely ours, for I promise you that they will not come out to battle either tomorrow, or on any subsequent day. It is the clearest proof of their defeat yesterday, and of their terror, that they stay out of the way like beaten competitors at the athletics. It was not to do this, to settle down behind fortifications in the wilds of Thrace, that they assembled such a great force. Fear made them construct defences here while you were still approaching, and now that you are here they are staying behind them thanks to yesterday's defeat. Furthermore, after that defeat the senior and more experienced of their commanders committed suicide in utter despair, a fact which is itself the most telling indication of their disastrous situation. Therefore, when they refuse to accept our challenge or come down from their heights, but put their trust in cliffs instead of in their sword-arms, then, Romans, take heart and join me to force combat on them once again, as you forced combat on them yesterday; consider it a disgrace to be defeated by a frightened enemy, to refrain from attacking cowards, and to concede that real men are feebler than walls. Unlike them, we did not come here to pass our lives in this plain, and if men delay, they have no control over anything. Sensible people should have wars that are soon over and enjoy peace for as long as possible. 120. We shall create the right opportunities and take the necessary action,* and we do not deserve to be blamed by you for the plan of yesterday's energetic assault; you, on

the other hand, must display courage for your commanders when it is asked for. Do not for a moment take yesterday's looting to heart. The secret of wealth lies not in what we possess, but in using our strength to secure victory; this will give us back both the possessions which were taken from us yesterday and are still safe with the enemy, and the enemy's own possessions as well, when we are victorious. And if we are eager to lay our hands on them, we must be eager for battle. Even yesterday we took enough from them, perhaps more than enough, to compensate. They brought the entire proceeds of their violent looting with them from Asia, while you, coming from your own country, left the greater part of your possessions at home and brought only necessities with you. If there was an abundance of anything, it belonged to us, your commanders, and we are very ready to contribute our all to the cause of your victory. None the less, in recognition of this loss we shall give you an additional reward for victory: 5,000 denarii to each legionary, five times that sum to each centurion, and twice that again to each military tribune.'

121. After making this speech Antonius drew up his forces again for battle the next day, but even then the enemy did not come down. He was depressed, but continued to offer battle, while Brutus kept one part of his army in formation in case he was forced to fight, and with the other cut the vital supply routes. There was a hill very close to Cassius' camp, which was difficult for the enemy to take because it was within bowshot, but Cassius had still garrisoned it to guard against an assault, however unexpected. Brutus, however, abandoned it and Octavian's side seized it by night with four legions, who brought wicker screens and hides for protection against arrows. When they had it securely in their possession, they shifted the camp of another ten legions more than a thousand yards in the direction of the sea, and the camp of another two nearly a further half-mile, with the intention of proceeding in this manner to the sea and then forcing their way either along the coast, or through the marshes, or by whatever other means they could contrive, to cut off the enemy from their supplies. Brutus countered them with various moves of his own, including the placing of fortified posts opposite their camps. 122. Octavian's side were under pressure from the urgency of their task, since hunger was already apparent and magnified by the fear of what each day might bring. They no longer received sufficient supplies from Thessaly, and there was no hope from the sea, which was completely controlled by the enemy. News of the recent disaster in the Adriatic had now reached them and their opponents, and they

became more apprehensive, both for these reasons and because winter was approaching when they had taken up quarters in a muddy plain. In the light of these considerations they sent a legion off to Achaia, to collect everything they could lay their hands on and send it to them with all speed. Unable to endure the approach of such great danger, or the other plans against them, or further deployment in the plain, they came up beside the enemy fortifications and shouted a challenge to Brutus to fight, mocking and abusing him and determined to make him give battle against his will, not as though this were a siege but by their frenzied energy.

123. Brutus, however, adhered to his original decision, and still more so when he learnt about the famine and the favourable happenings in the Adriatic, and observed the desperation produced in the enemy by their difficulties. He preferred to endure a siege and all it entailed rather than engage in battle with men who were driven on by hunger and in their despair of help from any other source saw their right hands as their only hope. But his army was not intelligent enough to share his view, and resented being shut up inside like women, inactive and afraid. Their officers were also resentful, because although they approved Brutus' plan, they also thought they would secure victory more quickly with an eager army. The reason for this was Brutus' characteristic of being reasonable and friendly to all, unlike Cassius, who was harsh and imperious in everything. As a result, Cassius' orders were obeyed as orders, and men did not play the general alongside him, or learn his reasons or criticize them if they did learn them; while with Brutus, because of his politeness, they thought they were quite his fellow-commanders. Finally the army began to enquire more and more openly in their units and gatherings: 'Why has our general given judgement against us? What crime have we just committed by being victorious, pursuing the enemy, cutting them down as they faced us, and taking their camp?' Brutus deliberately disregarded them, and did not summon them to an assembly for fear that he would illogically lose the argument in a rather undignified way to the mob, and particularly to the mercenaries, whose hope of salvation is always defection to the other side, like unscrupulous slaves joining other masters. 124. Brutus was also pestered by the officers, who told him to put to immediate advantage the enthusiasm of the army, which would soon bring in a splendid result, and if something did go amiss in the battle, they could withdraw again to their defences and place the same fortifications between them and the enemy. Brutus was annoyed with them, particularly because they were his officers,

and was very hurt because although they were exposed to the same danger as himself they were being swept thoughtlessly along by the troops, who preferred an uncertain and sudden throw of chance to a safe victory. But he gave way, to his own ruin and theirs, blaming them to the extent of saying: 'I seem to be conducting my campaign like Pompeius Magnus, no longer giving the orders but receiving them.'[87] This, I think, was all he said, because he wished to conceal his greatest fear, that the army, since it had once been Caesar's, would become disaffected and desert. Both he and Cassius had their suspicions of this from the start, and in no operation had they given the men any excuse to feel mutinous against them.

125. Thus it was that Brutus also, but reluctantly, led his men out to battle.[88] He formed them up in their ranks in front of the wall, and instructed them not to advance far in front of the hill, so that it would be easy to withdraw, if necessary, and they would have a favourable position for hurling missiles at the enemy. In both armies every man encouraged his fellows. There was great spirit for the fight, along with confidence that went beyond the logic of the situation. One army was actuated by fear of starvation, the other by legitimate shame, for fear that after overriding their general, who still wanted to postpone the struggle, they should be proved unequal to their promises and inferior to their boasts, and stand accused of rashness instead of deserving praise for good advice. Brutus rode round and himself made things clear to his men before the battle. A forceful expression on his face, he reminded them of these points in the few words the occasion allowed: 'You wanted to fight, and you have forced me to do so when I had another way to victory. So do not cheat me or yourselves of your hope. You have the slope in your favour, and everything behind you is yours. The enemy are in a dangerous position, trapped between you and famine.' With these words, he trotted to and fro among them, and the men in the ranks raised his hopes and cheered him on his way. 126. Octavian and Antonius went round their own men, shaking hands with those they came near, and urged them on with even greater forcefulness than Brutus, making no concealment of the point that the famine was a most opportune spur to bravery. 'Men, we have found the enemy. We can capture our quarry outside their fortifications. None of you must disgrace your own challenge or fail to live up to your threats. None of you must prefer to face starvation, which is a helpless and painful way to die, instead of confronting the defences and the bodies of the enemy, which yield to bravery, steel, and

desperation. For us, the present situation is so urgent that nothing can be put off until tomorrow. A decision on everything has to be reached today, whether it be total victory or noble death. If you win, thanks to a single day and a single action you can seize food, money, ships, and encampments, and earn your victory bounties from us. We shall succeed if we first remember, as we attack them, what pressures we are under, and we then, after breaking their line, cut them off from their gates and force them towards the cliffs or the plain, so that the campaign does not regenerate and the enemy do not again escape to enjoy a period of rest – the only enemy in the world who, through weakness, place their hopes not in battle, but in avoiding a battle.'

127. This was the encouragement offered by Octavian and Antonius to the men they met. Every one of them felt morally bound to show themselves worthy of their commanders and to escape from their difficult situation, which had been hugely and unexpectedly exaggerated by the events in the Adriatic. They preferred to suffer, if need be, any sort of injury in action and in hope rather than be wasted away by an evil against which they had no defence.

Such were their feelings, and as each man communicated them to his neighbour, morale on both sides was greatly lifted and they were filled with a recklessness that was beyond the reach of fear. At the present moment they had not the slightest recollection that they were all Romans, and they issued threats against each other as though they were natural enemies by race. Thus their immediate fury overwhelmed their powers of reasoning and their nature, and both sides alike prophesied that that day and that battle would decide the entire fate of Rome. And decided it was.

128. These preparations had already consumed the day up to mid-afternoon, when two eagles attacked and fought each other in the space between the two armies. There was the profoundest silence, and when the eagle on Brutus' side flew off there came a piercing shout from the enemy, the standards were raised on both sides, and the charge was violent and harsh. They had little need of volleys of arrows or stones or javelins according to the custom of war, since they made no use of the other techniques and manoeuvres of battle, but came to grips with drawn swords, inflicting and receiving thrusts, and trying to push each other out of formation. One side fought for self-preservation rather than for victory, the other for victory and some consolation for the general whose decision they had overridden. Great was the slaughter and loud the groaning, and as the bodies were carried back out of the way fresh men took their place from the reserves. The commanders, riding about and visible everywhere, urged the men on in their surges forward, encouraged them, when they were under pressure, to endure yet greater pressure, and relieved those who were exhausted, so that there was always fresh spirit at the front. Finally Octavian's troops, either through fear of starvation or through his own good luck (for Brutus' men were not in the least to blame), started to dislodge the enemy line, as though they were tipping over a very heavy piece of machinery. <At first> * their opponents were pushed back foot by foot, gradually and with deliberation; but once their formation had been disrupted, they retreated more rapidly, and as the reserves of the second and third lines joined in the retreat they all became chaotically mixed up and were squeezed by their own men and by the enemy, who gave them no respite from attack, until they were in open flight. At this moment above all Octavian's men adhered firmly to their orders, and sought to gain early control of the gates – a highly dangerous operation, because they were under fire from ahead and from above. They succeeded in preventing a large number of the enemy from entering, and these escaped to the sea or to the mountains across the river Zygaktes.

129. After the rout, the commanders divided the remaining tasks. Octavian was to mount guard on the camp itself and capture any troops who broke out. Antonius rampaged everywhere and attacked everyone – those in flight, those still offering resistance, and those manning the other enemy positions and with magnificent energy swept all before him. Fearing that the leaders might escape him and again assemble another army, he sent cavalry out along the roads and exits from the battlefield to capture the fugitives. They divided their duties: some rode into the mountains with Rhascus the Thracian, who had been sent out with them because he knew the routes, and these surrounded the fortified positions and crags, hunted down men who tried to escape, and kept guard on those inside. Others pursued Brutus himself, and were galloping furiously along when Lucilius saw them and stood in their path. Pretending to be Brutus, he asked to be taken to Antonius, not to Octavian; and this was the main reason why he was believed to be Brutus, avoiding his implacable enemy. When Antonius heard he was being brought in, he went to meet him, pausing for a moment to wonder, in view of Brutus' reputation and virtue and what had happened to him, how he should receive him. As Antonius approached, Lucilius went up to him very confidently and said, 'Brutus has not been captured, nor

will virtue ever be taken prisoner by vice; I tricked these men, and here I am in front of you.' Antonius, seeing that the cavalrymen were ashamed, consoled them by saying, 'Your catch is not worse, but better than you think – as much better as a friend is better than an enemy.' For the moment he passed Lucilius on to one of his friends to look after, but later befriended him himself and trusted him completely.

130. Brutus retreated up into the mountains with a fair-sized force. He intended to return to his camp or go down to the sea when night came, but he had been completely surrounded by guard-posts and spent the night under arms with all his men. He is reported to have looked up at the stars and said:

'Forget not, Zeus, the author of these woes,'

referring of course to Antonius.[89] They say that Antonius himself later quoted the same line when he was beset by his own dangers, regretting that when he could have been numbered alongside Cassius and Brutus he had helped Octavian. At the time, though, Antonius also spent the night under arms on watch opposite Brutus, surrounding himself with a barrier heaped up from a collection of dead bodies and items of plunder. Octavian was active until midnight, but then retired feeling ill and handed the camp over to Flaccus to guard.

131. On the following day Brutus observed that the enemy detachments still remained in position. He had four under-strength legions which had come up with him, but was wary of approaching them himself and sent their officers, who were ashamed of their mistake and regretted it, to sound out the men and see if they were willing to burst through the blockading troops and recapture their own position, which was still being defended by those of their own side who had been left behind. But although they had gone out most inadvisedly to give battle, and had fought most courage-ously for the greater part of it, at this point heaven unhinged them and they told their commander that he was making discreditable plans in his own interest: they themselves, although they had often taken chances, would not spoil the hope that still remained of reaching an agreement. Brutus re-marked to his friends, 'Well then, I am no use to my country any longer, if this is the attitude even these men take', and called for Strato of Epirus, a friend of his. He ordered Strato to stab him, but Strato urged him to think again, so he summoned one of his slaves. Then Strato said, 'You will not be short of a friend, instead of slaves, to carry out your final commands, if your

decision has already been taken', and with these words plunged his sword into the flank of Brutus, who neither turned away nor flinched.

132. In this way Cassius and Brutus met their deaths. They were Romans of the highest nobility and distinction, and of unchallenged virtue, without a single stain; and although they were of Pompeius Magnus' party, Gaius Caesar turned them from personal and public enemies into friends, and from friends into virtual sons. The senate always missed them sorely and felt pity for them in their misfortunes, and for the sake of these two granted an amnesty to all. When they went into exile it bestowed military commands on them so that they should not be exiles. This was not because the senate cared nothing for Gaius Caesar, nor because it was pleased at what had happened, since when he was alive it marvelled at his character and good fortune, and when he was dead it gave him a funeral at public expense, ratified his actions for all time, and for a long while allotted provinces and commands according to his memoranda, thinking that it could make no better arrangements than those he had devised. But its enthusiasm and concern for the pair led it to be suspected of complicity in the plot, such was the respect universally accorded to these two. By the best of those who fled Italy they were accorded greater honour than Pompeius, although he was closer at hand and his cause was open to negotiation, while Brutus and Cassius were further away and would never be negotiated with. 133. When action was required, in less than two complete years they raised from contributors both willing and unwilling an army of more than twenty legions, about 20,000 cavalry, more than 200 warships, an impressive array of other equipment, and vast amounts of money, and they fought successful campaigns against peoples, cities, and several leaders of the opposite party. They became masters of the peoples from Macedonia to the Euphrates, forced those they fought against into alliance with themselves, and used the services of the strongest. They also made use of kings and princes, and even of the Parthians, in spite of their hostility, for minor operations – although in the case of the decisive conflict they did not wait for them to arrive, for fear of making this rival race of foreigners accustomed to Romans. The most extraordinary fact of all was that the greater part of their army had served under Gaius Caesar, and felt tremendous good will and enthusiasm for him, and yet these two men, who were Caesar's murderers, won them over so that the troops followed them against Caesar's son with greater loyalty than they showed to Antonius, Octavian's fellow-contestant and fellow-commander; for none of them deserted Brutus or Cassius even

when they had been defeated, although they had deserted Antonius at Brundisium before the conflict ever began. Their proclaimed reason for undertaking the struggle, as was still true of Pompeius, was not their own interest, but the cause of the Republic – a splendid but always profitless term. When they thought they could be of no further use to their country, both alike spurned their own lives. Embroiled in their concerns and exertions, Cassius was single-minded, like a solo gladiator against his opponent, and thought only of the campaign; but Brutus, wherever he might be, was fond of contemplation and of talk, as befitted one who was no mean philosopher.

134. But in spite of these characteristics of theirs, there was the crime against Caesar to counterbalance everything. This was no simple nor circumscribed crime: it was committed unexpectedly against a friend, ungenerously against a benefactor who had saved their lives in war, and unlawfully against an emperor;[90] it was committed in the senate, against a priest clothed in his priestly dress, and against a ruler like no other, whose services to his country and its empire far surpassed those of all other men. This incurred the just wrath of heaven, which gave them many forewarnings of its vengeance. When Cassius was conducting a ceremony of purification for the army the lictor placed the garland on Cassius' head upsidedown; a golden statue of Victory, which was an offering from Cassius, fell over; and a flock of birds flew down over his camp without uttering a cry, and swarms of bees continually settled there. It is said that when Brutus was celebrating his birthday in Samos, at the drinking-party (which was hardly a suitable occasion for such a thing) he inexplicably declaimed this line:

'But fell fate and Leto's son have slain me'.[91]

Also, when he was about to cross with his army from Asia to Europe, as he was lying awake at night his lamp went out and he saw a strange apparition standing over him, of which he boldly enquired what man or god he might be. The ghost replied, 'I am your evil spirit, Brutus; and you will see me at Philippi also.' And they say that the apparition was seen by Brutus before the final battle. As his army was going out to battle, a black man met him in front of the gates and the army immediately cut the man to pieces as a bad omen. These were surely supernatural signs too, when Cassius, in an evenly matched battle, illogically gave up all hope, while Brutus was forced to abandon his prudent procrastination and join battle with men hounded by famine when he himself had plenty of supplies and enjoyed control of the sea – and suffer this at the hands of his own people, not the enemy. Furthermore, they took part in many battles without ever being hurt in the fighting, whereas they both put an end to their own lives as they had put an end to Caesar's. Such, then, was the penalty paid by Cassius and Brutus.

135. When Antonius discovered Brutus he wrapped him at once in the finest purple, burnt the body, and sent the ashes to his mother Servilia. When the troops who were with Brutus learnt that he was dead, they sent a deputation to Octavian and Antonius, received pardon and were distributed among their armies; they numbered about 14,000 men. The garrisons of the fortified outposts, of which there were many, also surrendered on the same terms. The outposts themselves and the main camp were handed over to the armies of Octavian and Antonius to plunder. Of the distinguished men on Brutus' side, some died in the battles, some offered themselves for execution in the same manner as their generals, and some deliberately fought to the death. Among these were Cassius' nephew Lucius Cassius, and Cato's son Cato, the latter of whom charged time and again into the enemy and then, when they gave ground, took off his helmet so that he would be easy to recognize or easy to hit, or both. Labeo, well known for his learning, and father of the Labeo who is still celebrated for his knowledge of law, dug a pit in his tent large enough to hold his body, issued orders on remaining matters to his staff, wrote instructions to his wife and children as to his wishes, and gave the letter to his slaves to deliver. Then he took the most reliable of them by the right hand and spun him round, according to the Roman custom when conferring freedom, and as the man turned back to face him handed him a sword and proffered his throat; and so his tent became his tomb.[92] 136. Rhascus the Thracian, who brought many men in from the mountains, asked for and was granted as his reward the life of his brother Rhascupolis; and it became obvious that these Thracians had had no quarrel even at the beginning, but when two great and evenly matched armies were coming to grips with each other in their territory they split the risk, so that the winner could save the loser. On hearing of the way in which Brutus and the younger Cato had died, Porcia, the wife of the one and sister of the other,[93] in spite of being carefully watched by her household, seized the coals from a brazier which was being brought in, and swallowed them. As to the other notable men who escaped to Thasos, some of them put to sea while the others entrusted themselves and their remaining forces to their equals Messalla Corvinus and Lucius Bibulus on the understanding that whatever decision these men took for themselves

would apply to all of them.[94] They came to an agreement with Antonius' staff, and when Antonius sailed across to Thasos they handed over all the money, weapons, plentiful food supplies, and large amounts of other equipment that were on the island.

137. In this way, by boldly taking risks and by fighting two infantry battles, Octavian and Antonius brought this great conflict, which resembled no other before it, to a successful conclusion. For Roman armies of such size and quality on each side had never previously been matched in battle; they had not been recruited by the normal levy, but selected for their excellence; they were no tiros, but long trained; and they were turned against fellow-Romans, not people of other races and tongues. They spoke a single language, shared a single technique of fighting, and their training and endurance were similar. For these reasons it was very hard for each to defeat the other. Never have such drive and such bravery been displayed in war, and these by men who were fellow-citizens, relatives, and companions in arms. The proof of this is that if you take both battles into account the number of dead appears to have been no smaller even on the victorious side.   138. The army of Antonius and Octavian made the words of their generals come true, that in a single day and by a single battle they would exchange their extreme danger of starvation and fear of annihilation for generous plenty, certain safety and glorious victory. And what they forecast for Rome as they joined battle also happened: for it was this battle above all that determined their constitution, which has not yet reverted to a republic; nor has there been any need of similar internal struggles, except for the civil war between Antonius and Octavian which occurred shortly afterwards and was the last in Roman history.[95] The events which took place between the death of Brutus and that civil war, and are associated with Pompeius and those friends of Cassius and Brutus who escaped and controlled large remnants of this huge army, did not ever yield episodes of similar audacity or commitment on the part of individuals, states, or armies to their leaders. For neither the senate nor any member of the nobility still adhered to these men, nor did they enjoy the same reputation as Cassius and Brutus.

BOOK V

1. After the deaths of Cassius and Brutus, Octavian proceeded to Italy, and Antonius to Asia. Here Cleopatra Queen of Egypt met him and she won his heart the moment he set eyes on her. This passion ended in complete disaster both for themselves and for the whole of Egypt. For this reason there will be an Egyptian section in this book, though brief and not worth a mention in the title on account of the fact that it is included with the far more numerous episodes of civil war.[1] For even after the defeat of Cassius and Brutus other similar civil conflicts took place, although there was no single overall command as had been the case with them, and different leaders operated on their own. Finally Pompeius Magnus' younger son Sextus Pompeius, who still survived as a representative of that faction, was eliminated, like Brutus' followers, and Lepidus forfeited his share of power, and the whole government of Rome passed into the hands of only two men, Antonius and Octavian. The course of the individual events was as follows.

2. Cassius 'of Parma', as he was called, had been left behind by Cassius and Brutus in Asia with a fleet and soldiers, to collect money.[2] After Cassius' death, not expecting Brutus to meet a like end, he selected thirty of the Rhodian ships (the number he thought he could man) and burnt the rest, except for the sacred ship,[3] so that the Rhodians would be unable to rebel. This done, he put to sea with the thirty ships along with his own. Then Clodius, who had been sent by Brutus to Rhodes with a fleet of thirteen ships, found the Rhodians in revolt (Brutus now being dead), and after extricating the garrison of 3,000 legionaries went to join Cassius of Parma.[4] Turullius also joined them with many more ships and the money which had previously been collected from the Rhodians.[5] Because this fleet was now quite strong, any who held commissions in various districts of Asia rallied to it, and they manned the ships with what legionaries they could and with oarsmen taken from slaves and prisoners and from the inhabitants of the islands on which they descended. Cicero's son Cicero also joined them, together with the other prominent men who had escaped from Thasos. Soon they were a numerous body with a military organization worthy of their leaders, their fighting force, and their fleet. They collected Lepidus[6] with another contingent of troops, which had secured Crete for Brutus, and sailed round to the Adriatic to join Murcus and Domitius Ahenobarbus, who had a large force under their command. Some of them then sailed on to Sicily with Murcus and joined forces with Sextus Pompeius, while some stayed with Ahenobarbus and pursued a policy of their own. Such were the first groupings which emerged from the remains of the army that had been assembled by Cassius and Brutus.

3. Octavian and Antonius celebrated a magnificent sacrifice for their victory at Philippi, and heaped praise on their army. The former went back to Italy to hand out the rewards of their victory by distributing land to the soldiers and enrolling them for colonial settlements (this task being his own choice on account of his illness), while Antonius went to the overseas provinces to collect the money promised to the soldiers. They again allocated themselves the same provinces as before, and took those of Lepidus as well, both because he was accused of betraying their interests to Pompeius and because they decided, on Octavian's proposal, to make Cisalpine Gaul autonomous in accordance with the policy of Caesar; it was further agreed that if Octavian found the accusation to be false, they would give Lepidus other provinces in lieu.[7] They also discharged the men in their army who had served their full time, except for 8,000 whose request to continue in service with them was granted; these they divided between them and incorporated into their praetorian cohorts. The rest of their army, with the soldiers taken over from Brutus, numbered eleven legions of infantry and 14,000 cavalry. Antonius, because he would be abroad, kept six of these and 10,000 cavalry, and Octavian 4,000 cavalry and five legions, of which he in fact gave two to Antonius in exchange for two of those belonging to Antonius which had been left behind in Italy under Calenus.[8]   4. Octavian then departed for the Adriatic.

On his arrival in Ephesus Antonius made a splendid sacrifice to the goddess,[9] and pardoned all those who had fled as suppliants to the sanctuary after the disaster of Brutus and Cassius except for Petronius, who had been one of the conspirators against Caesar, and Quintus, who had betrayed Dolabella to Cassius at Laodiceia.[10] He called together the Greeks and such other peoples as inhabit the region of Asia around Pergamum, whose deputations were there to seek an accommodation or had been summoned to appear, and addressed them as follows: 'Greeks, your king Attalus left you to us by his will, and we immediately treated you better than Attalus had. We excused you the taxes you used to pay to Attalus, until even we acquired demagogues and needed taxes.'[11] And when we needed them, we did not impose them according to a property valuation, so that we could be certain of collecting the tax, but laid it down that you should contribute a proportion of the annual harvest, so that we should share bad years with you. But when the people who took the contract from the senate to collect the tax treated you outrageously and asked for much more, Caesar remitted a third of the amount you used to pay them and put an end to their extortion by giving you the responsibility for raising the taxes yourselves from the agricultural producers. And although this was the sort of man he was, our fine citizens called him a despot, and you paid large contributions to these men, who were the murderers of your benefactor, to oppose us, who were his avengers. 5. A just fortune has decided the war not as you wished but as was right; if you needed to be treated as active accomplices of our enemies, punishment was required, but as we are prepared to believe that you were forced into acting as you did, we shall waive more serious penalties. Nevertheless, we require money, land, and towns to reward our army for its victory. This force consists of twenty-eight legions of infantry, which number over 170,000 men, apart from the cavalry and the other elements from the rest of the army. So you can see the scale of our needs from the scale of these figures. Octavian will depart for Italy to distribute the land and the towns to them, and he will, to be blunt, evict the Italian population. We have counted on you for the money, so that you will not be evicted from your land, your towns, your homes, your shrines, and your tombs – not for all of it (since that would be beyond you), but for a part, and a very small part which I think you will welcome when you find out what it is. It will, then, suffice if we take, but in one year, simply the same amount as you furnished to our enemies in two years (and that was the taxes of ten years), for our needs are pressing. You will appreciate our leniency, and I would merely add that the penalty we have prescribed does not do justice to a single one of your offences.'

6. These were Antonius' words. I think he limited the recipients of rewards to twenty-eight legions because although the triumvirs had forty-three when they came to their agreement with each other at Mutina and

made the legions these promises, the war had reduced them to this number. While he was still speaking, the Greeks prostrated themselves on the ground, saying as they did so that Brutus and Cassius had used force and compulsion against them and that they deserved, not penalties, but pity; they would willingly contribute to their benefactors but did not know how to do so thanks to the enemy, who had exacted from them not only their money, but also implements and equipment and ornaments in lieu of money, and had converted these things into coin on their own soil. In the end their pleas were successful to the extent that they were to pay the taxes of nine years in two. As for kings and princes and free city-states, different contributions were imposed on each according to their power.

7. During Antonius' progress through the provinces, Lucius the brother of Cassius and any others who feared for their lives threw themselves on his mercy when they heard of his clemency at Ephesus. He pardoned them all except for those who had conspired to murder Caesar, to whom alone he was implacable. He also consoled the city-states which had suffered most, by freeing the Lycians from tax and encouraging them to resettle Xanthus, and by granting the Rhodians Andros, Tenos, Naxos, and Myndos, which were taken away from them not long afterwards because their administration was too oppressive. He allowed Laodiceia and Tarsus independence and immunity from taxation, and decreed that any citizens of Tarsus who had been sold into slavery were to be freed. To the Athenians, who approached him over the question of Tenos, he gave Aigina, Ikos, Keos, Skiathos, and Peparethos.[12] In passing he visited Phrygia, Mysia, Galatia, Cappadocia, Cilicia, Coele Syria, Palestine, Ituraea, and the other peoples of Syria. He imposed heavy contributions on them all, and acted as arbitrator in the affairs of cities and kings: in Cappadocia he decided between Ariarathes and Sisina, giving the throne to Sisina because he thought his mother Glaphyra was a beautiful woman, and in Syria he evicted self-appointed rulers from city after city.

8. Cleopatra also came to see him in Cilicia, and he censured her for not taking part in their struggles to avenge Caesar. She did not excuse herself so much as present a list of what she had done for him and Octavian: she had promptly despatched the four legions which were with her to Dolabella; after preparing another expeditionary force, she had been foiled by the gales and by the premature defeat of Dolabella himself; she had not made an alliance with Cassius, although he had twice threatened her; she had personally sailed for the Adriatic with a fleet loaded down with equipment to

help the triumvirs in their war campaign; she had not been terrified of Cassius and had paid no attention to Murcus' naval ambush, but finally a storm had not only ruined everything but also caused her to fall ill, for which reason she had not put to sea even afterwards, when the triumvirs had already gained their victory. The moment he saw her, Antonius lost his head to her like a young man, although he was forty years old. He is reputed to have always been prone to such behaviour, and also in the case of Cleopatra to have been provoked by the sight of her a long time previously, when she was still a girl and he was a young captain of cavalry on Gabinius' expedition to Alexandria.[13] **9.** So straight away the attention that Antonius had until now devoted to every matter was completely blunted, and whatever Cleopatra commanded was done, without consideration of what was right in the eyes of man or god. On Antonius' orders her sister Arsinoe, who had taken refuge as a suppliant at the temple of Artemis Leukophryene in Miletus,[14] was put to death, and he ordered the Tyrians to surrender Serapion to her, who as her commander in Cyprus had supported Cassius but was now a suppliant in Tyre.[15] He instructed the people of Aradus to hand over another suppliant, some man whom they were harbouring and making out to be Ptolemy, after the disappearance of Cleopatra's brother Ptolemy in the naval battle against Caesar on the Nile.[16] He also ordered the priest of Artemis at Ephesus, whom they call Megabyzos,[17] to be brought before him because he had once welcomed Arsinoe as queen, but released him when the Ephesians pleaded with Cleopatra herself. Such was the rapidity of the change in Antonius' behaviour, and this passion of his was the beginning and the end of the troubles which ensued.

After Cleopatra had sailed back to her own kingdom, Antonius sent his cavalry to plunder the city of Palmyra, which is not far from the Euphrates. He made a petty case against the Palmyrenes, that being on the border between Rome and Parthia they were showing goodwill to both sides (as they are a trading people, they bring Indian or Arabian products from Persia, and market them in Roman territory), but in fact he meant to enrich his cavalry. The Palmyrenes, having obtained advance warning of this, moved their essentials to the other side of the river and stood on the bank armed with bows, a weapon with which they are extraordinarily expert, to prevent an attack. The cavalry found the city abandoned, and sacked it without any fighting and without obtaining any booty. **10.** This act of Antonius seems to have put the match to the Parthian war which soon flared up, for many of the rulers expelled from Syria had taken refuge with the Parthians. Until the time of Antiochus Eusebes and his son Antiochus, Syria had been ruled by kings descended from Seleucus Nicator, as I have said in my account of the Syrians;[18] but after Pompeius had annexed Syria for the Romans and appointed Scaurus to govern it, the men the senate sent to succeed Scaurus included Gabinius, who led an expedition against the Alexandrians, and then Crassus, who died in Parthia, and after him Bibulus. Then at the time of Caesar's death and the internal struggles which followed, the Syrian cities came under the rule of individual autocrats. The latter were supported by the Parthians, who naturally made incursions into Syria after Crassus' disaster and co-operated with them. After expelling the autocrats, who took refuge on Parthian soil, and demanding oppressive contributions from the ordinary people, and taking this mistaken action against the Palmyrenes, Antonius did not even stay to restore order to the troubled country but sent his army to various winter quarters in the provinces, and went himself to join Cleopatra in Egypt.

11. She gave him a splendid reception. He spent the winter there, without any insignia of rank, adopting the dress and way of life of an ordinary person, whether because he was in a country not ruled by himself, in a city which had a monarchy, or because he was treating the winter period as a holiday. Certainly he had laid aside his cares and his general's escort. He wore the square Greek garment instead of his native Roman one, and his shoes were the white Attic type they call the *phaicasion*, which are also worn by the priests at Athens and Alexandria. He went out only to temples or gymnasia or scholarly discussions, and he passed his time in the company of Greeks, deferring to Cleopatra, who was the chief object of his attention during his stay.

12. So matters stood for Antonius. As for Octavian, his illness flared up again very dangerously on his way back to Rome, at Brundisium, and a rumour circulated that he was actually dead. When he had recovered, he returned to Rome and showed the letters written by Antonius to Antonius' friends, who ordered Calenus to hand over the two legions to Octavian and also wrote to Sextius in Africa to tell him to give the province up to Octavian. Both men complied, and Octavian gave Africa to Lepidus, who he thought had committed no serious misdemeanour, in exchange for his previous provinces. He also sold off the remainder of the property that had been confiscated in the proscriptions. But the task of distributing land and enrolling his soldiers in colonial settlements was very difficult. The soldiers

demanded to be given the towns which had been selected for them on grounds of quality before the war. The towns thought that the whole of Italy should share the burden or draw lots together with them, and asked men who had been granted land to pay the price of it. There was no money, and people came in groups to Rome, young men, old men, women with their children, and gathered in the forum or the temples, lamenting and declaring that they had done no wrong and that although they were Italians they were being evicted from hearth and home as if they had lost a war. At this, the inhabitants of Rome shared their grief and wept over their fate, particularly so when they reflected that it was not on behalf of Rome but as a check on themselves and to secure a change of constitution that the war had taken place, the rewards of victory had been given, and the colonies had been established with the purpose of preventing the Republic from ever again lifting its head because mercenaries ready to do the bidding of the men in power had been settled alongside them. **13**. Octavian made the excuse to the towns that he had no choice, and it appeared that even so their lands would not suffice. And thus it proved. The soldiers encroached on adjoining territory by violence, seizing more than they had been granted and picking out the better land. Although Octavian reprimanded them and made them many additional gifts, they would not stop, because they had no respect even for their rulers, who had need of them to make their power a reality. The five years of the triumvirate were going by, and each party was compelled to seek safety in the other – the rulers needing the army to guarantee their power, and the army needing the men who had given them the land to continue in power in order that they themselves could keep what they had received. And as the soldiers had no security of ownership unless the grantors enjoyed security of power, of necessity they favoured them and fought for them. Octavian also made many more gifts to those soldiers who were in difficulties, by borrowing from the funds of the temples. As a result the army transferred its loyalty to him and he received greater gratitude because he was giving them land, towns, money, and houses while the dispossessed malevolently denounced him, an onslaught he endured to win the thanks of the army.

14. Antonius' brother Lucius Antonius, who was consul at the time, observed this and plotted with Antonius' wife Fulvia and agent Manius to postpone the founding of the colonies until Antonius arrived back in Italy, so that it should not appear to be entirely the work of Octavian.[19] Thus Octavian would not be the sole beneficiary of the soldiers' gratitude, nor would Antonius be deprived of their goodwill. When this scheme appeared impracticable because of the urgency of the army's demands, they requested Octavian to take the organizers of the colonies for Antonius' legions from Antonius' partisans, although the agreement with Antonius gave the choice to Octavian alone, and they complained that action was being taken in Antonius' absence. They brought Fulvia and the children of Antonius in front of the army and maliciously begged them not to ignore the fact that Antonius was being deprived of the glory and the gratitude he was owed for his help to them. At this period in particular Antonius' reputation was at a peak in the eyes of both the army and everyone else, because they thought that the victory at Philippi was entirely his work, as Octavian had been ill at the time. So Octavian, although well aware that he was in the right by the terms of the agreement, gave way as a favour to Antonius. Antonius' supporters then appointed organizers of the colonies for Antonius' legions, and these organizers colluded with the soldiers to permit still more injustices, in order to appear to be doing them even greater favours than Octavian. There was also a large number of people from other towns which had suffered at the hands of the soldiers, because they were situated next to towns where land had been allocated for settlements. These protested vociferously against Octavian, saying that the colonies constituted a worse wrong than the proscriptions: for while the latter had been directed against personal enemies, the former operated against the innocent.

15. Octavian was aware that injustice had been done, but there was no way of solving the problem. There was no money to pay the farmers the value of their land, and it was impossible to put off granting the soldiers their rewards because there were still wars going on: Pompeius was master of the sea and was reducing Rome to famine by blockade, Ahenobarbus and Murcus were collecting an army and more ships, and the soldiers would be less willing to fight in the future unless they received the rewards of their previous victory. Also, an important factor was that the triumvirs' five-year term was already going by and they again needed the goodwill of an army. Octavian was therefore willing at the time to ignore the violence and disrespect shown by the soldiers. Certainly, once when he was present in the theatre a soldier who could not find an appropriate seat came and sat in the rows reserved for equestrians;[20] the crowd pointed him out, and when Octavian had him removed the soldiery became angry and surrounded him as he was leaving the theatre, asking him to produce the man because he was nowhere to be seen and they thought he had been killed.

When the soldier appeared, they thought he had at that moment been brought out of the prison, and although he denied this, and explained what had happened, they accused him of telling lies to order and heaped abuse on him as a traitor to the common cause. Such was the episode in the theatre, (16) and when they were summoned to the Campus Martius for the current allocation of land, their eagerness made them gather while it was still dark and they were angry with Octavian because he was late in arriving. A centurion, Nonius, reprimanded them in no uncertain manner, pointing out how subordinates ought to treat a superior and alleging that Octavian was not ignoring them, but ill. At first the soldiers mocked him as a bootlicker, but as provocation increased on both sides, they abused him, hurled missiles at him, and chased him when he fled. He jumped into the Tiber, but they dragged him out, killed him, and threw him down where Octavian was due to pass. Octavian's associates advised him not even to approach them, but to keep out of the way of their insane fury. None the less, he went, because he thought that he would exacerbate their fury if he did not go, and turned aside when he saw Nonius. He reproved them, assuming that the deed was the work of only a few of them, and encouraged them to exercise restraint towards each other in the future. He then made the allocations of land, and instructed the deserving to ask for gifts, and made unexpected gifts to some who did not deserve them. In the end the astonished crowd regretted their own intransigence; they became ashamed, accused themselves, and asked him to discover and punish the men who had committed the crime against Nonius. He replied that he was establishing who they were, and would punish them, but only after they had admitted their guilt and the army had condemned them. The soldiers, now that they had been found to deserve pardon, reward, and gifts, immediately changed their attitude and began to sing his praises.

17. Let these two instances, among many, stand as examples of the prevailing breakdown of authority. This occurred because the majority of the commanders were unelected, as happens in civil war, and their armies were recruited neither from the register according to ancestral custom, nor to meet any need of their country. Instead of serving the common interest they served only the men who had enlisted them, and even so not under compulsion of the law, but by private inducements. Nor did they fight against enemies of the state, but against private enemies, nor against foreigners, but against Romans who were their equals in status. All these factors undermined their fear of military discipline. They felt they were not so

much serving in the army as lending assistance from personal goodwill and by their own choice, and that their commanders were forced to rely on them to attain their private ends. Desertion, formerly an unpardonable of-fence for a Roman, was at that time actually rewarded by gifts, and it was practised both by armies *en masse* and by some prominent men, because they considered that changing like for like was not desertion. All parties were alike, and none of them had been officially condemned as public en-emies. The common pretext of the generals, that they were all assisting the interests of their country, made men readier to change sides since they were assisting their country wherever they were. The generals understood this and tolerated it, knowing that they ruled, not by law, but by bribes. **18.** In this way civil conflict engulfed everything, and the armies became un-manageable by the leaders in that conflict.

Rome was suffering from famine, since no supplies reached the city by sea because of Pompeius, and Italian land was not being cultivated because of the wars. In addition, what food there was was confiscated for military needs. The ordinary people took to theft at night in the city, and disturb-ances more violent than theft took place, disturbances which were so bold that suspicion fell on the soldiery. The civilian population shut the work-shops and made the magistrates leave, saying they had no need of either magistrates or crafts in a starving and plundered city.

19. Lucius, who held republican views and disapproved of the triumvir-ate, which was not thought likely to come to an end when its time came, experienced difficulties and more serious disagreements with Octavian. The farmers who had lost their land sought protection from any powerful man, but Lucius was the only one who listened to them and promised to help them, while they for their part promised to give him any assistance he might demand. Antonius' troops and Octavian therefore accused him of opposing Antonius, and Fulvia criticized him for fomenting war at the wrong time, until Manius maliciously put the matter in a different light by pointing out that if Italy remained at peace, Antonius would stay with Cleopatra, but if there was a war he would come back without delay. Then Fulvia, her woman's passions aroused, incited Lucius to pick a quarrel. When Octavian left the city to perform the foundation of the remaining colonies, she sent Antonius' children after him along with Lucius so that Octavian should not acquire undue credit with the soldiers by appearing alone.[21] And when Octavian's cavalry made a sortie along the Bruttian coast, which was being plundered by Pompeius, Lucius either thought or pretended that this squadron had been sent out to attack himself and the children of Antonius. He hurried away to the Antonian colonies and raised a bodyguard, and accused Octavian in front of the troops of disloyalty to Antonius. Octavian countered by stating that all was friendship and harmony between himself and Antonius, but that Lucius had a different policy: he was stirring up war between them because he opposed the triumvirate, which was the soldiers' guarantee of their land settlements, and as for the cavalry, they were at this moment obeying their orders in Bruttium.

20. When the officers in command of the army heard about these exchanges, they mediated between the two of them at Teanum and reconciled them to each other on these conditions: the consuls were to exercise their traditional functions without interference from the triumvirs; land was not to be allotted to anyone who had not fought at Philippi; Antonius' forces in Italy were to have an equal share of the money from confiscated estates and of the value of what was still being sold; neither man was in future to recruit in Italy; two legions of Antonius' were to assist Octavian's campaign against Pompeius; the passage through the Alps was to be opened to forces sent by Octavian to Spain, and Asinius Pollio was no longer to obstruct them;[22] and Lucius, on agreeing to these terms, was to dismiss his bodyguard and go about his civil duties without fear. These were the terms they agreed with each other through the officers of the army, but only the two last were acted on; and Salvidienus † unwillingly went round the Alps with him †.[23]

21. When the rest of the terms were either not fulfilled, or their implementation was delayed, Lucius withdrew to Praeneste, saying that he was afraid of Octavian, who held an office which gave him a bodyguard, while he himself had no protection. Fulvia also left Rome to go to Lepidus, claiming now that she was afraid for her children, for she preferred Lepidus to Octavian. Both sides wrote to Antonius about these events, and supporters accompanied the letters to explain individual episodes. Although I have made enquiries, I have failed to find out with any certainty what Antonius' replies were. The officers of the army, after making a pact to decide for their leaders whatever they thought was right, and to join in compelling any dissenters to comply, summoned Lucius' party to discuss this, but they would not agree to the terms, and Octavian attacked them viciously, both to the officers of the army and to the Roman aristocracy. The latter hurriedly came out to see Lucius and beg him to spare Italy and Rome civil war, and to accept that by common agreement the decision should rest

with themselves or with the officers. **22.** Lucius respected both what was said and who was saying it, but Manius very boldly claimed that while Antonius was merely gathering money in foreign lands, Octavian by distributing favours was pre-empting control of the army and of advantageous locations in Italy. He alleged that Octavian was deceiving Antonius by granting autonomy to Cisalpine Gaul, which had originally been given to Antonius; that he was making over land to the veterans not simply in the territory of eighteen towns but virtually throughout Italy; that he was distributing to thirty-four legions, instead of to twenty-eight, not only land but also the money from the temples which he had collected nominally to use against Pompeius (against whom he had not yet deployed any military force in spite of the famine raging in Rome), but had in fact divided up among the troops to buy their favour against Antonius; and that instead of selling confiscated property he was making a present of it to them. If he was serious about wanting peace, he ought to submit a report on the actions he had already taken, and in future do only what he and Antonius should jointly decide in consultation. Manius thus impudently claimed that Octavian could not take any action on his own authority, and that his agreement with Antonius was invalid, although it had been settled that each of them was to have full authority in his allotted tasks and the actions of either were to carry the approval of the other. From all these indications Octavian saw that his opponents were bent on war, and both sides began to prepare for it.

23. Two legions, which had been settled at Ancona, were Octavian's by inheritance from Caesar, although they had formed part of Antonius' army. They heard of the preparations each side was privately making, and out of respect for their links with both sent a delegation to Rome to ask them to resolve their dispute. When Octavian told them that he was not attacking Antonius, but was being attacked by Lucius, the delegates made an agreement with the officers of this[24] army and they all made a joint approach to Lucius to ask him to meet Octavian and have the case heard; and it was clear what they intended to do if he did not accept the decision. Lucius and his advisers agreed, and Gabii, a town halfway between Rome and Praeneste, was chosen as the place for the hearing. An auditorium was arranged for those who were to judge the case, with two rostra for speakers in the middle, as if it were a law-court. Octavian, who arrived first, sent some cavalry along the route by which Lucius was approaching, apparently to investigate if there were any signs of a trap. These men encountered another party of cavalry belonging to Lucius, who must have been either an ad-

vance guard or scouts like themselves, and killed some of them. Lucius retreated, in fear, he said, of a plot, and although the officers of the army
summoned him and promised to escort him, he no longer obeyed them.

24. Thus the negotiations came to nothing. The parties determined to
fight, and proceeded to issue bitter edicts against each other. Lucius had an
army of six legions, which he had enlisted himself when he became consul,
and the further eleven belonging to Antonius which were under the command of Calenus. All these were in Italy. Octavian had four legions at
Capua, and his own praetorian cohorts, and six other legions on their way
from Spain under Salvidienus. Lucius had money from Antonius' peaceful
provinces, but a state of war existed in all the provinces which had fallen to
Octavian, except Sardinia. Octavian therefore borrowed money from the
temples – from the Capitolium at Rome, and from Antium, Lanuvium,
Nemi, and Tibur, towns which are still famous for treasuries replete with
sacred funds – and promised that he would pay it back with interest.

25. Octavian was faced with disorder outside Italy too. As a result of the
proscriptions, the colonial foundations, and this quarrel with Lucius, Pompeius had become a person of great prestige and power. People who feared
for their lives, or were being robbed of their property, or were entirely
alienated from the political regime, turned above all to him. Others, young
men who were keen to be soldiers on account of the rewards, and thought
it made no difference under whose command they served since everywhere their comrades in arms would be Romans, preferred to join Pompeius because he represented the juster cause. He had become rich from
the booty he had gathered at sea, and he possessed a large number of ships
complete with crews. In addition, Murcus had joined him with two legions
of infantry, 500 archers, a large amount of money, and eighty ships, and was
sending for the rest of his army from Cephallenia. For these reasons some
think that if Pompeius had attacked Italy at that moment, he would easily
have won control of it, racked as it was by famine and civil war and well
disposed towards himself. But his folly was such that he decided not to
make the attempt, but merely to defend himself, until in the end he was not
even equal to this.

26. In Africa Sextius, Antonius' governor, had recently handed over his
forces, at Lucius' behest, to Octavian's representative Fango, and when he
was instructed to resume command of them again, and Fango refused to
give them back, he took up arms against Fango.[25] He assembled some of
the discharged veterans, along with a further crowd of Africans and other

troops sent by the kings. When the wings of both armies were defeated and
their camps captured, Fango, in the belief that he had been betrayed, took
his own life, and Sextius was again master of both African provinces. Also
Bocchus,[26] the king of Mauretania, was persuaded by Lucius to mount a
campaign against Carrinas, who was governing Spain for Octavian.[27] Ahenobarbus, too, was sailing the Adriatic with seventy ships and two legions,
along with some archers and slingers, light-armed troops, and gladiators,
and was ravaging regions which were subject to the triumvirs. He attacked
Brundisium from the sea, captured some of Octavian's warships, burnt
others, shut the inhabitants within their walls, and laid waste the
countryside.

27. Octavian sent one legion to Brundisium and hastily recalled Salvidienus from his march to Spain. Both Octavian and Lucius despatched officers to recruit for them all over Italy, and there were frequent ambushes
and clashes, some trivial and some more serious, between these mercenary
commanders.[28] The sympathies of the Italians were overwhelmingly with
Lucius, because he was fighting for them against the assignees of their land.
And it was no longer only the cities which had been marked down for the
soldiers that were in revolt, but practically the whole of Italy, because they
feared a like fate. They killed or expelled from the towns Octavian's agents
who were borrowing the sacred money, manned their walls, and joined
Lucius. Similarly those of the soldiers who were in course of being settled
joined Octavian, the two sides making their choice appropriately for a war
in which their own interests were at stake.

28. While these events were taking place, Octavian none the less still
summoned the senate and the equestrian order and said: 'I am well aware
that Lucius' party accuse me of weakness and lack of courage for not taking
action against them, an accusation they will now repeat because of this
meeting with you. However, my army is strong, not only the part of it that
has suffered the injury, which I share, of being robbed of their land allotments by Lucius, but also the other forces I have, and I am strong in all
other ways except in determination to fight. I dislike fighting civil wars
without grave necessity, or wasting the lives of those Romans who still survive by pitting them against each other, most of all when this civil war is
not one that will be known only by report from Macedonia or from
Thrace. It will take place in the very land of Italy, which will suffer countless agonies, quite apart from loss of life, if it becomes our cockpit of war.
For these reasons I do indeed hesitate, and I still protest that I am doing no

wrong to Antonius, nor he to me. Your part, please, is to question Lucius and his friends about these matters yourselves, and to reconcile them with me. And if at this point they still refuse, I shall not hesitate to show them that it is prudence, not cowardice, that has governed my actions so far; I also consider that, in view of Lucius' arrogance, you should rally round me and speak for me, both among yourselves and to Antonius.'

29. After this speech of Octavian's some of his listeners again hurried out to Praeneste. Lucius simply made two points: both sides had already begun hostilities, and Octavian was play-acting because he had recently sent a legion to Brundisium to prevent Antonius' return. In addition, Manius showed them a letter which may have been authentic from Antonius, giving orders to fight if anyone damaged his standing. When the senatorial delegation enquired if anyone was damaging Antonius' standing, and challenged him to a legal hearing on the matter, Manius produced many more clever arguments, until the senators went away without achieving anything. They held no meeting with Octavian to deliver the reply, whether because each of them reported individually, or because they had a different agenda, or because they were ashamed. War then broke out, and Octavian departed to conduct operations, leaving Lepidus with two legions to protect Rome. The majority of the aristocracy then made the clearest demonstration of their dissatisfaction with the triumvirate by joining Lucius.

30. The principal events of the war were as follows. Two legions of Lucius' at Alba became disaffected, threw out their commanding officers, and started to mutiny. Octavian and Lucius each hurried to reach them, but Lucius arrived first and won them back with a large donative and great promises. As Furnius was bringing another force to join Lucius, Octavian hung on his rear.[29] Furnius quickly took up a position on high ground, and pressed on at night to the town of Sentinum, which was friendly to him. Octavian did not follow in the dark because he was afraid of an ambush, but when daylight came laid siege both to Sentinum and to Furnius. Lucius moved rapidly on Rome by sending ahead three cohorts which entered the city unobserved at night, and followed himself with a large force including cavalry and gladiators. Nonius, the guard commander at the gates, admitted him and transferred the command of his own troops to him. Lepidus fled to Octavian, and Lucius addressed a public meeting in Rome, saying that Octavian and Lepidus would very soon pay for the violence of their rule, and

that his brother would willingly lay his authority aside in exchange for the consulship and take legal and traditional instead of illegal and arbitrary power.

31. Everyone was delighted by what he said and thought that the triumvirate was already finished. Lucius was given the title of commander-in-chief by the people and took the field against Octavian, raising more forces from Antonius' colonies and strengthening these places. Their sympathies were with Antonius, but Barbatius, Antonius' quaestor, who had had some disagreement with Antonius and had therefore come back to Italy, told enquirers that Antonius was angry with the people who had taken up arms against Octavian in opposition to their joint power. Some, who did not realize Barbatius' deceit, then switched their support from Lucius to Octavian. Lucius himself went to meet Salvidienus, who was returning from Gaul with a large force to join Octavian. Salvidienus was being pursued by Asinius and Ventidius,[30] other generals of Antonius, who prevented him from advancing, but Octavian's close friend Agrippa,[31] who was afraid that Salvidienus would be encircled, seized Sutrium. This place was important to Lucius, and Agrippa hoped to draw Lucius away from Salvidienus towards himself and that Salvidienus would help him, because he would be in Lucius' rear. Everything happened as Agrippa expected, and Lucius, disappointed in his plan, marched towards Asinius and Ventidius, with Salvidienus and Agrippa harassing him on either flank and watching for the best chance of trapping him in one of the passes.   **32**. Here the plan against him became obvious, and Lucius, who did not dare to engage both of them because he was between them, went on to the strongly fortified town of Perusia, and encamped outside to wait for Ventidius and his forces. Agrippa and Salvidienus and Octavian came up with their three armies, encircling Lucius and Perusia together, and Octavian urgently summoned the rest of his forces from all quarters to this, the key location of the war, where he had Lucius trapped. He also sent other troops ahead to block the advance of Ventidius and his allies, who were also reluctant for their own part to press ahead; they totally disapproved of the war, they did not know Antonius' attitude, and none of them, on grounds of rank, had surrendered the command of his army to any of the others.[32] Lucius did not emerge either to fight the besieging force, which was larger, of better quality, and well trained, with an army consisting chiefly of raw recruits, or to resume his march in the face of harassment by so many enemies at the same time. He despatched Manius to urge Ventidius and Asinius to assist him now that he was besieged, and sent out Tisienus with 4,000 cavalry to plunder Octavian's territory and make him withdraw.[33] He himself entered Perusia intending to winter there, if he had to, in a secure town until Ventidius and his allies arrived.

33. With great urgency Octavian immediately set his whole army to wall Perusia off with a ditch and rampart, creating a circuit of seven miles because of the hill on which the town stood, and extending long arms to the Tiber so that nothing could be brought in. Lucius took countermeasures by fortifying the bottom of the hill with more ramparts and ditches of a similar sort. Fulvia urged Ventidius, Asinius, Ateius, and Calenus from Gaul to help Lucius, and raised another force which she sent to Lucius under Plancus' command.[34] Plancus destroyed one of Octavian's legions which was on its way to Rome, while Asinius and Ventidius, although they hesitated, and disagreed about Antonius' intentions, none the less, thanks to Fulvia and Manius, advanced towards Lucius and had started to force their way past the troops stopping them. But Octavian left a garrison at Perusia and came with Agrippa to confront them. As they had not yet joined forces with each other, and were proceeding with little enthusiasm, one of them took refuge in Ravenna, the other in Ariminum, and Plancus in Spoletium. Octavian left a force to threaten each and prevent them from uniting, and returned to Perusia. Here he hastily added stakes to his trenches, doubled their width and depth to thirty feet, increased the height of the encircling wall, and erected 1,500 wooden towers on it at intervals of sixty feet;[35] it had battlements at frequent intervals, and all the rest of the layout was double-fronted, facing both the besieged and any attacker from outside. This was done to the accompaniment of many sorties and engagements. Octavian's men were better at throwing missiles, Lucius' gladiators at hand-to-hand combat; and when the latter came to grips with their opponents, they killed many of them.

34. When all Octavian's siege-works were completed, famine began to afflict Lucius, and this evil was savagely aggravated because neither he nor the town had taken any precautionary measures. Octavian became aware of this and intensified his blockade. On New Year's Eve, Lucius, who had waited for the festival in the belief that it would make the enemy careless, sprang a night assault on their gates with the intention of breaking through and leading another army against them, for he had plenty of support everywhere. But the legion that was on watch nearby charged up, along with Octavian himself and his praetorian cohorts, and Lucius, although he

fought very hard, was forced back. At Rome, during the same period, because grain was being reserved for men on military service, the mass of the population openly protested against the war and Octavian's victory; they burst into people's houses to look for grain, and seized whatever they found.

35. Ventidius and his allies, ashamed to stand by and watch Lucius being destroyed by famine, advanced in concert in his direction, pushing back Octavian's troops, who hung round them and harassed them. However, when Agrippa and Salvidienus met them with a still larger force, they were afraid of being encircled and turned aside to a place called Fulginium, twenty miles from Perusia. There, surrounded by Agrippa and his forces, they lit a large number of fires as a signal to Lucius. Ventidius and Asinius expressed the view that even under these circumstances they should proceed and be prepared to fight, but Plancus' opinion, that they would find themselves between Octavian and Agrippa, and ought still to wait and see what happened, prevailed in the discussion. The people in Perusia were overjoyed to see the fires, but when the relieving force failed to appear they conjectured that they too were in difficulties and, when the flames went out, that they had been destroyed. Under pressure of the famine, Lucius again made a night attack, which was fought along the entire circuit of fortifications from the first watch until dawn. He failed, withdrew again into Perusia, and after reckoning up what food was left forbade any to be given to the slaves, whom he watched to prevent their escape so that his terrible situation should not become clearer to the enemy. The slaves roamed about in crowds and threw themselves down on the ground, not only inside the town itself but as far out as their own line of fortifications, feeding on any grass or green vegetation they could find. Those who died Lucius buried in long trenches, both to avoid making the position obvious to the enemy by burning them, and to prevent the stench and disease that arises from rotting corpses.

36. Since there was no end to the famine or to the deaths, the legionary troops became unhappy with the situation and pleaded with Lucius to make another attempt on the fortifications and break right through them. He welcomed their initiative, and said, 'We recently failed to fight as our situation demanded.' He declared that they must now either surrender or, if they considered surrender worse than death, fight to the death. They all eagerly agreed and told him to mount the attack in daylight so that darkness could not serve as a cover for any failings, and Lucius led them out

before dawn, equipped with a great number of iron grappling devices and all sorts of ladders. They also had contrivances for filling up the ditches, collapsible towers to let drawbridges down on to the fortifications, all kinds of throwing weapons and stones, and wicker mats for flinging over the sharpened stakes. They launched their attack with great energy, filled in the ditch, made their way over the stakes, and reached the ramparts. Some of them started to dig these away at the base, others brought up the ladders, others the towers, and at the same time as they set about all this they defended themselves by hurling stones and lead slingshot and firing arrows in complete disregard of their own lives.[36] This was done in many sectors, and since <*they* . . . > some <. . . > the resistance of the enemy, who were drawn in many different directions, was weaker everywhere.   **37**. The struggle of Lucius' men became riskiest at the moment when the drawbridges were let down at various places on to the wall, and they fought on them with missiles and darts being shot obliquely at them from all directions. In spite of this they forced their way across and a few jumped on to the wall, to be followed by others. And their desperation would perhaps have brought them success, if the best of Octavian's reserves had not been brought into action, fresh men to assist the weary, when it was realized that Lucius did not have many such siege-engines. Then they managed to throw Lucius' men off their walls and smash the siege-engines, and were able to shoot at them from above with unconcern. Their opponents' weapons and bodies were totally broken; although they could no longer raise a shout, their commitment made them stand their ground. But when the stripped corpses of those who had lost their lives on the wall were also hurled down on them, they could not endure the insult. They turned away from the sight and stood for a little, uncertain what to do, like athletes taking a brief rest in a competition, and Lucius, taking pity on their condition, sounded the trumpet for retreat. Octavian's troops were delighted by this and clashed their weapons together as if they had won a victory. Consequently Lucius' were roused to fury, seized the ladders again (since they had no towers left), and carried them wildly to the wall, but did no damage as they no longer had the strength. Lucius went to them, begging them not to go on fighting to the last gasp, and led them away cursing and reluctant.

38. Such was the way in which this violently contested battle at the fortifications came to an end. To prevent the enemy making another daring attempt on his defences, Octavian had the part of his force which was on watch stationed hard by the wall and instructed them to man it in a number of different places at a signal from the trumpet; and they used frequently to man it of their own accord in order to train themselves and strike fear into the enemy. The morale of Lucius' men began to crumble, the guards became slack, as usually happens in such cases, and as a result of their slackness there was a large number of desertions. These included not only people of no consequence, but even some of the officer class. Lucius was now inclined to negotiate, out of compassion for such widespread loss of life, but still held back because some of Octavian's enemies feared for their lives. However, when it was observed that Octavian received the deserters in a friendly way, and everyone became much more eager to negotiate, Lucius became afraid that if he opposed negotiations he would be betrayed.

39. He therefore put forward the idea, and when he discovered that it had some chance of succeeding, he called the army together and said: 'It was my intention, fellow-soldiers, to restore the ancestral constitution for you. I saw that the triumvirate was despotism and that it was not dissolved even after the deaths of Brutus and Cassius, its ostensible object. Now that Lepidus has been stripped of his share of power and Antonius is raising money in far distant lands, this one man is arranging everything according to his own ideas while our ancestral constitution is a mere sham and a mockery. As I intend to replace this state of affairs with our previous liberty and democracy, I requested that when the rewards of victory had been distributed, this autocratic power should be dissolved. Since I met with no success, I tried to force the issue during my term of office. Octavian misrepresented me to the army, saying that I was obstructing the land settlements out of sympathy for the farmers. I did not hear of this accusation for a very long time, and even when I did hear of it I could not believe that anyone would credit it, seeing that the organizers of the settlements, who were going to distribute your allotments to you, were actually appointed by me. But the slander seduced some, and they went over to Octavian in the belief that you were to be their opponents, when in time they will realize that they have been fighting against their own interests. As for you, I bear witness that you chose the better cause and suffered beyond endurance, and that we have been overcome not by the enemy but by famine, to which we have been abandoned even by our own generals. For me, it would have been a fine thing to fight for my country to the last twist of fate, and such an end would have won high praise for my purpose. But for your sakes I shall not persevere. I value your lives above my own fame. I will communicate with the victor, and ask him to do what he likes

with me as a scapegoat for all of you, and grant you pardon in my place; for you are his fellow-citizens and have once been his soldiers, you have done him no wrong even now nor fought against him without good cause, and you have been defeated by famine rather than by war.'

40. After making this speech he immediately selected three aristocrats to send, while the crowd cried aloud and lamented, some for themselves, and some for their general, who seemed to them to have objectives that were simultaneously aristocratic and republican, but to have been defeated by the impossibility of the situation. When the three met Octavian, they reminded him of the single origin and joint campaigns of the two armies, of the friendships between the leading men, and of the virtues of their ancestors, who had not taken their disagreements past the point of repair; and they made any other points of a similar kind that seemed likely to be persuasive. Octavian, however, knew that some of the enemy were still raw recruits while the settlers were trained soldiers, and cleverly said that he would grant pardon to the men who had served under Antonius, because he was grateful to them, but the others must surrender unconditionally. This proposal was made to them all, but privately he led Furnius, one of the three, to hope that Lucius and his friends, and the others except for his private enemies, might be treated more leniently.

41. These enemies of Octavian, suspecting that Furnius' private meeting was not to their advantage, abused Furnius himself when he returned and requested Lucius either to ask for fresh terms that were the same for all, or to fight to the death, since the war was no one's private affair, but was a struggle undertaken in common for their country. Out of pity for men as distinguished as himself, Lucius agreed with their argument and said that he would send another delegation. He then explained that he had no one better for this than himself, and started off at once. He sent no herald, and the men who were to announce that he was coming down to see Octavian ran on ahead of him. Octavian at once went to meet him, and they were now in sight of each other, accompanied by their friends and conspicuous from their standards and the general's garb they both wore. Lucius dismissed his friends and came forward with only two lictors, thus revealing his intention by his demeanour. Octavian understood and imitated him, so that he could likewise demonstrate the kindness with which he was going to treat Lucius. But when he saw that Lucius was also hurrying to reach his fortifications, to give an additional indication that he was now surrendering, Octavian forestalled him by advancing outside the fortifications, so that it would still be possible for Lucius to weigh up the situation and take a free decision as to his own fate. Such were the messages conveyed by their dress and behaviour as they approached each other.   42. When they came to the ditch, they greeted each other and Lucius said, 'If I had been a foreigner fighting against you, Octavian, I would have thought this defeat shaming, and surrender even more shameful, and a simple way to escape this shame lay in my own hands. But since I have quarrelled with a fellow-Roman of equal distinction in the cause of my country, I think it no shame to be defeated by such a person for such a reason. I say this, not as a plea in mitigation of whatever fate you wish for me (and this is why I hurried towards your camp without arranging a truce), but in order to request the pardon for the others which they deserve and which also suits your interests. I must demonstrate this by distinguishing their case from mine, so that you may recognize that I bear sole responsibility for what has occurred, and direct your anger against me alone. Expect me to argue, not over-bluntly (for this is not the moment for that), but truthfully, because if I cannot speak the truth I cannot speak at all.

43. 'I went to war with you not to overthrow you and succeed to your power, but to bring back to my country the aristocratic government which the triumvirate dissolved, as not even you would deny. Indeed when you established the triumvirate, you admitted it to be illegal; but you claimed it to be necessary and appropriate, since Cassius and Brutus were still at large and you could not reach an agreement with them. When they, the core of the faction, were dead, and such survivors as remain were not at war with the state, but frightened of you, and in addition the five years of the triumvirate were slipping by, I thought it right that the powers of the magistrates should be restored to their traditional scope. I did not even put my brother before my country, but I hoped that when he returned he would be willing to accept my view, and I was eager that this restoration should happen during my period of office. If you had been the one to make the first move, you would have had the glory of it to yourself. When I failed to persuade you, I thought that I would march on Rome and actually compel you, since I was a Roman, a noble, and a consul. These are the sole reasons for which I went to war – not my brother, nor Manius, nor Fulvia, nor the grants of land to the men who fought at Philippi, nor pity for the farmers who were losing their property, since I too appointed commissioners to found colonies for my brother's legions, and these men stripped the farmers of their property and allocated it to the veterans. But that was how you

slanderously misrepresented me to the latter, shifting the blame for the war from yourself to the land allocations, and by this means in particular you carried them with you and have defeated me. They were persuaded that they were the object of my hostilities, and that they were defending themselves against injustice. Certainly, you had to employ tricks when you were fighting me; but now you are victorious, if you are an enemy of your country, you must also consider me your enemy since I wished for what I thought would profit her, though I was prevented by famine.

44. 'With these words I entrust myself, as I said, to your discretion; I have made clear my past and present opinions of you, which I still hold as I come here alone. So much for myself; as for my friends and my whole army, if you can trust my advice, I shall recommend you the most advantageous course, which is not to take any drastic measures against them on account of our rivalry. Remember you are human and subject to chance, which is fickle, and do not discourage those who may one day be willing to hazard their lives for you, when opportunity or need calls, by letting them learn from your practice that the unsuccessful have little hope of mercy. If, however, all advice offered by an enemy is suspect or untrustworthy, I do not hesitate to add a plea to you not to take vengeance on my friends for my mistakes and my bad luck, but to blame everything on me, as I am responsible for it all. This was in fact my intention in leaving them behind, to avoid giving the impression, if I said this to you in front of them, that I was making a devious move in my own interest.'

45. Such was the burden of Lucius' speech. After he had fallen silent, Octavian said, 'When I saw you making your way down to me without having arranged a truce, Lucius, I hurried to meet you while you were still outside my fortifications, to allow you to deliberate and to say and do whatever you think will be in your interests, while you remain a free agent. Since you are surrendering to us, and thus admitting to being in the wrong, I no longer need to argue with you about your clever lies against me. However, from the beginning it was your intention to harm me, and now you have actually harmed me. If you had wanted to negotiate terms with me, you would have found yourself dealing with a victor who was an injured party; but by surrendering yourself and your friends and your army to us unconditionally, you rob me not only of all the expression of my anger but also of the power you would necessarily have given me in making terms. For the question of what you deserve to suffer is bound up with the propriety of the action it is right for me to take. It is the latter consideration I shall honour, for the sake of the gods, and myself, and you yourself, Lucius, and I will not disappoint you of the expectation you have of me, which has brought you here.'

This was their exchange, so far as it is possible to judge the gist of what was said and render it from the memoirs into the capabilities of Greek.[37] They then separated, Octavian speaking highly of Lucius and admiring him because he had said nothing stupid or ignoble, as people usually do in times of disaster, and Lucius having the same feelings towards Octavian because of his character and his economy of speech. The others drew their conclusions as to what had been said from the appearance of the two men.

46. Lucius sent the military tribunes to obtain the password for the army from Octavian. They brought Octavian figures for the strength of the army, in the way that is even now the custom when the military tribune, on asking the emperor for the password, hands over the daily register of numbers present.[38] After receiving the password, the tribunes continued to arrange the posting of guards, for Octavian's own orders were that each side was to mount guard at night over its own lines. At dawn, Octavian performed a sacrifice, while Lucius sent his army to him, carrying their weapons, but equipped as for a march. The men saluted Octavian from a distance as their commander, and took up individual positions legion by legion where Octavian had ordered, the settlers separated from the new recruits. When the sacrifice was completed, Octavian, crowned with the victor's laurel, took his seat on a dais in front of them. He told them all to lay down their arms where they stood, and when this had been done ordered the settlers to come nearer, with the firm intention of accusing them of ingratitude and striking fear into them. It had become known beforehand that he was going to do this, and his own army, either deliberately, as soldiers are often coached, or moved by the sympathy evoked by men who were their kin, broke ranks. They poured in among Lucius' approaching troops, greeted them as men who had once fought alongside them, joined in their tears, and pleaded with Octavian on their behalf. They would not stop shouting or embracing, and now the new recruits as well joined in the emotion expressed by both sides, so that it was no longer easy to discriminate or distinguish between them. **47**. As a result not even Octavian kept to his intentions. After managing to quiet the clamour, he said to his own men, 'You, my fellow-soldiers, have always treated me in such a way that it is impossible for me to refuse any request of yours. My own view is that the new recruits were forced to serve under Lucius, but I intended to ask these men here in front, who often served alongside you and have now been saved by you, why they took up arms against me, and against you, and against themselves. What wrong did I do them? What reward were they denied? What more did they expect from someone else? My difficulties all resulted from the land settlements, in which they too had their share. With your agreement, I shall still ask them this.' When they would not let him do so, and continually clamoured for mercy, he said, 'I grant your wishes. Let them go free of punishment for their crimes, provided they agree with you in future.' Promises were given on both sides, and Octavian was cheered and thanked. He arranged for some of Lucius' men to be looked after by particular individuals, and ordered the common soldiery to camp under canvas where they stood, away from his own men, until he could allot them towns to winter in and appoint officers to lead them away to the towns.

48. Then, seated on his dais, he summoned Lucius from Perusia, together with the Romans who were in positions of authority. There came down a large number of senators and equestrians, their bitter change of fortune a pitiable sight, and as soon as they had made their exit from the town, a guard was thrown round it. When they arrived, Octavian made Lucius stand beside himself, while the others were distributed between Octavian's associates and the military tribunes, who had all been previously instructed to take them and treat them as honoured guests under discreet arrest. As for the inhabitants of Perusia, who were begging for mercy from the walls, he told them to approach, excepting only their town council, and then pardoned them. The members of the council were held in custody at the time, but were executed not long afterwards, apart from Lucius Aemilius, who when serving as one of the jurors at Rome at the trial of Caesar's murderers had openly cast his vote for condemnation, and encouraged all the others to do the same in order to expiate pollution. **49**. Perusia itself Octavian had decided to hand over to his soldiers to plunder, but one of the inhabitants, a certain Cestius, who was slightly mad and called himself 'Macedonicus' because he had fought in Macedonia, set fire to his house and threw himself on the blaze. The wind caught the flames and spread them through the town, which was completely burnt down except for the temple of Vulcan. Such was the end of Perusia, renowned for its antiquity and importance. They say that in the past, under the Etruscans, it became one of the twelve leading cities of Italy, and that is why the people used to worship Hera, in the manner of the Etruscans;[39] but at the time of which I write the people who were settled on the remains of the town chose Vulcan as their patron deity in place of Hera. On the following day Octavian solemnized peace with everyone, but the army continued to demand action against certain persons, until they were put to death; these were Octavian's particular enemies, Cannutius, Gaius Flavius, Clodius Bithynicus, and others.[40]

This then was the end of the siege of Lucius in Perusia, and thus the war was concluded, a war which was expected to be long and ruinous for Italy. **50.** The reason was that although they possessed a formidable army consisting of thirteen trained legions and 6,500 cavalry, Asinius, Plancus, Ventidius, Crassus, Ateius, and all the other commanders of that party considered that Lucius had become the key figure in the war, and they immediately marched away to the coast by different routes.[41] Some made for Brundisium, and others for Ravenna or Tarentum; some went to join Murcus or Ahenobarbus, others Antonius. They were pursued by Octavian's associates, who offered them terms and when they refused applied pressure to their infantry in particular. However, only two of Plancus' legions, which were cut off at Camerinum, were persuaded by Agrippa to change sides. Fulvia also fled with her children to Puteoli and thence to Brundisium, in the company of 3,000 cavalry who had been sent by the generals to escort her. At Brundisium she embarked on the five ships that had been summoned from Macedonia for her, and put to sea. Plancus sailed with her, abandoning out of cowardice the surviving elements of his army, who chose to put themselves under Ventidius' command. Asinius came to an agreement with Ahenobarbus to adopt friendly relations with Antonius, and both of them wrote to inform Antonius of these events and prepared disembarkation points and supplies for him at various locations in Italy, anticipating that he would come at once.

51. Antonius possessed another large army, commanded by Fufius Calenus, in the region of the Alps. Octavian had designs on this: on the one hand he did not trust Antonius, and on the other he hoped either to look after this army for him if he remained friendly, or to acquire a powerful additional force if hostilities broke out. However, while he was still procrastinating and looking about for a respectable reason, Calenus died. Then Octavian, having found his pretext for both actions, went and took over not only the army but also Gaul and Spain (which were likewise Antonius'), since Calenus' son Fufius was terrified of him and handed everything over without putting up any resistance. Having thus by this single stroke gained control of eleven legions and large amounts of territory, Octavian relieved the governors of their authority, installed his own men, and returned to Rome.

52. While it was still winter, Antonius detained the delegation that had come to him from the settlers and kept his intentions to himself; but when the spring came he travelled by land from Alexandria to Tyre, and then, as he sailed by way of Cyprus, Rhodes and Asia, heard of the events at Perusia and laid the blame on his brother and Fulvia, but chiefly on Manius. Fulvia he found at Athens after her flight from Brundisium, along with his mother Julia, who had escaped to Pompeius and had now been sent on by him from Sicily on board one of a convoy of warships.[42] She was escorted by the highest-ranking of Pompeius' entourage, including Saturninus and Pompeius' father-in-law Lucius Libo.[43] These men, who needed Antonius and his capacity for great deeds, asked him to be reconciled with Pompeius and take the latter as an ally against Octavian. He replied that he was grateful to Pompeius for sending him his mother and would repay him in due course; as for himself, if he went to war with Octavian he would treat Pompeius as an ally, but if Octavian observed the terms of their agreement, he would attempt to reconcile Octavian with Pompeius as well.

53. This was Antonius' answer. When Octavian returned to Rome from Gaul, he heard of the embassy that had sailed to Athens, but had no accurate information about the reply. So, as the greater number of the farmers had fled to Pompeius, he stirred the settlers up against Antonius by alleging that the latter was restoring Pompeius along with the farmers whose lands they were themselves occupying. This was a persuasive piece of provocation, but even so the settlers were not eager to take the field against Antonius, so popular had he become as a result of the reputation he had won at Philippi. Octavian reckoned to be superior to Antonius, Pompeius, and Ahenobarbus in legionary numbers (for he had command of more than forty legions), but since he possessed not a single ship, and had no time to build any, and they had 500, he was much afraid that they would blockade Italy by sea and reduce the country to famine. With this in mind (and he had received many offers of marriage), he gave instructions to Maecenas to arrange an engagement to Scribonia, the sister of Libo, Pompeius' father-in-law, in order to have this as a basis for a settlement, if it proved necessary. When he heard this, Libo instructed his relatives to betroth his sister to Octavian without demur. Octavian also posted to various destinations the

supporters and military forces of Antonius that he did not trust, and sent Lepidus to his official province of Africa with the six most suspect of Antonius' legions.   54. He sent for Lucius and praised him for his loyalty to his brother if in carrying out Antonius' policy he had taken the blame upon himself, but abused him for his lack of gratitude if, after being so generously treated by himself, he would not confess to him about Antonius even now, when his brother was already openly said to have reached an understanding with Pompeius. 'I trusted you', he said, 'and when Calenus died, through friends of my own I took charge not only of his army, to prevent it being leaderless, but also of the provinces under his control, on behalf of Antonius. But now that this plot has come to light, I claim them all as mine, and if you wish to go and join your brother I give you permission to do so unmolested.' He spoke in this way perhaps to test Lucius, perhaps because he wanted what he said to reach Antonius. Lucius' reply was as before: 'I saw that Fulvia was in favour of autocratic rule, but I joined her in using my brother's troops in an attempt to bring you all down. And now, if my brother comes to overthrow the autocracy, I shall go to join him, whether that be openly or secretly, in order to renew my struggle against you on behalf of my country, although you have now become my benefactor. On the other hand, if he is picking and choosing allies to share autocratic power with him, I shall fight beside you against him, so long as I believe that you are not establishing an autocracy yourself. I shall always place the interests of my country above personal obligations or family ties.' Such were Lucius' words, and Octavian, who admired him even before this, said he would not recruit him as an ally against his brother even if he were willing, but in view of his character would entrust the whole of Spain and the army stationed there to him, and make the current governors Peducaeus and Lucius his subordinates.[44] In this way Octavian removed Lucius with honour and kept a discreet check on him through these subordinates.

55. Antonius left Fulvia lying ill at Sicyon, and sailed from Corcyra into the Adriatic with only a small number of troops, but with 200 ships which he had built in Asia. He discovered that Ahenobarbus was coming to meet him with his ships and a strong military force. Some believed that Ahenobarbus might not observe the terms of the agreement that had been exchanged between them (for not merely was he one of the men who had been condemned for the murder of Caesar, but after his condemnation he had also been proscribed and had fought against Antonius and Octavian at Philippi), but Antonius none the less sailed on with five of his best ships, to

show his trust, and ordered the rest to follow at a distance. When Ahenobarbus came in sight with his whole fleet and all his troops, rowing towards
them at full speed, Plancus, who was standing beside Antonius, was frightened and asked him to take way off the ship and send someone ahead to investigate this ambiguous behaviour. Antonius replied that he would rather
die as a result of a breach of treaty than be recognized as a coward and live,
and sailed on. They were now close to each other, and the flagships were
identifiable from their ensigns and rowing towards each other. Then Antonius' chief lictor, standing in the bows, as is the custom, and either forgetting
that the man who was approaching was of ambiguous loyalty and also
commanded troops of his own, or else acting from a somewhat aristocratic
attitude of mind, as though subjects or inferiors were coming to meet him,
ordered them to lower their ensign. They did so, and turned their ship to
bring it alongside Antonius'. When the principals caught sight of each
other they exchanged greetings, and Ahenobarbus' army saluted Antonius
as commander. Plancus managed to recover his nerve, and Antonius received Ahenobarbus on board his own ship. They then sailed to Paloeis,[45]
where Ahenobarbus had his infantry, and there Ahenobarbus gave up his
own tent to Antonius.

56. From Paloeis they sailed to Brundisium, which was garrisoned by
five cohorts of Octavian's troops. The inhabitants shut their gates against
them, Ahenobarbus because he was an old enemy and Antonius because he
was bringing an enemy with him. Antonius was annoyed, suspecting that
these were sophistries and that in reality Octavian's garrison had barred the
gates by Octavian's own wish. He therefore dug a ditch across the isthmus
and walled off the town. Because this lies on a peninsula in a crescent-
shaped harbour, it was no longer possible to reach it from the mainland up a
slope across which ran a ditch and ramparts. Antonius also encircled the
harbour, which was large, and the islets in it,[46] with closely spaced guard-
posts, and sent troops off around the coastal regions of Italy with orders to
seize strategic positions. In addition he instructed Pompeius to make naval
attacks on Italy and do whatever he could. Pompeius, nothing loth, immediately sent Menodorus with a large fleet and a force of four legions to
Sardinia, which was held by Octavian, and won over the island and its two
legions, who were demoralized by Antonius' co-operation with Pompeius.[47] On the mainland, Antonius' forces took Sipontum in Ausonia
while Pompeius laid siege to Thurii and Consentia and grazed his cavalry
on their territory.[48]

57. As the attacks were widespread and fierce, Octavian sent Agrippa to Ausonia to relieve the places under pressure. Agrippa mobilized the veterans settled along his route, who followed at a distance in the belief that they were going to fight Pompeius; but when they learnt that Antonius was responsible for what had happened, they surreptitiously turned back. This particularly alarmed Octavian. None the less, he himself took the road to Brundisium with another force, and when he met the settlers again, made them see things in a different light and took along with him the veterans who had been settled by himself. They were embarrassed, and came to a secret decision that they would reconcile Antonius and Octavian, but fight for Octavian if Antonius refused to comply and opened hostilities. At Canusium Octavian lay sick for several days, and although he still possessed numerical superiority over Antonius in every respect, he found Brundisium cut off by fortifications and simply camped opposite and awaited events.

58. Thanks to his strong fortifications Antonius succeeded, for a man who was much outnumbered, in defending himself safely. He summoned his forces urgently from Macedonia, and played a trick: in the evening he would send ordinary civilians out to sea on board both warships and merchant vessels, and when daylight came they would sail in, detachment after detachment, equipped as though they had come across from Macedonia, while Octavian watched them arrive. Antonius now had siege-engines, and he was about to start the assault on the town, to Octavian's fury because he could do nothing to help. That evening news came that Agrippa had regained Sipontum, and that Pompeius had been driven back from Thurii although he still had Consentia under siege. This riled Antonius, and when it was also reported that Servilius was on his way to Octavian with 1,500 cavalry, Antonius could not repress his impatience. He rose at once from dinner, and with 400 cavalry and the companions he could find who were ready, dashed out with enormous boldness and fell on the 1,500 who were still asleep at the town of Hyria. He terrified them into surrendering without a fight and brought them back the same day to Brundisium. Such was the extent to which they had been demoralized by the reputation for invincibility he had won at Philippi. 59. His praetorian cohorts were encouraged by this same reputation to approach Octavian's defences in small groups and blame the men who had been their comrades in arms for coming to fight against Antonius, who had saved them all at Philippi. Octavian's men replied with accusations that Antonius' had likewise come to

fight against themselves, and both sides stood there arguing and accusing each other; one side cited the barring of Brundisium against them and the theft of Calenus' army, the other the investment and siege of Brundisium, the attack on Ausonia, and the two agreements, the one with Ahenobarbus, one of Caesar's assassins, and the other with their joint enemy Pompeius. Finally, Octavian's men revealed their plan to the others, that they had accompanied Octavian not because they had forgotten Antonius' virtues, but because they intended either to impose a reconciliation on the pair, or, if Antonius refused, to fight him if he chose war. And they in their turn came up close to Antonius' fortifications and announced this openly.

While these events were taking place, news arrived that Fulvia had died. It was said that she had become depressed and fallen ill as a result of Antonius' reproaches, but she was also believed to have aggravated the illness deliberately because she was angry with Antonius for leaving her when she was sick and not coming to see her even when he was on the point of departure. Both men thought her death highly convenient, as they were rid of an interfering woman whose jealousy of Cleopatra had made her fan the flames of such a serious war. None the less Antonius was much affected by her death, since he considered himself partly to blame for it.

60. One Lucius Cocceius, who was a friend of both men, and had been sent by Octavian with Caecina the previous summer to Antonius in Phoenicia, had remained behind with Antonius when Caecina went back.[49] This Cocceius did not now let the moment slip, but pretended that Octavian had asked him to come and pay his respects. After obtaining permission to go, he sounded Antonius out by asking if he was sending any letter to Octavian, seeing that he, Antonius, was in receipt of one brought by himself. Antonius said 'At the moment we are enemies, so why would we write to each other except to insult each other? I sent my answers to his old accusations back with Caecina; if you like, take the copies.' So he sneered, but Cocceius refused to let him call Octavian his enemy yet, because of Octavian's treatment of Lucius and his other friends. To this Antonius replied, 'He has shut me out of Brundisium, stolen my provinces and Calenus' army from me, and remains well-disposed only to my friends. Nor, apparently, is he saving their lives for me, but turning them against me by his favours.' Then Cocceius, having learnt what Antonius' complaints were, irritated his irascible temperament no further, but went to Octavian. 61. On seeing Cocceius, Octavian expressed his surprise that he had not come sooner: 'I did not save the life of *your* brother, too, in order to

have you as an enemy.'[50] To which Cocceius replied, 'What is the reason that you make friends of your enemies, but call your friends enemies and steal their military forces and their provinces?' 'I did it', Octavian said, 'because after Calenus' death it was wrong for young Calenus to have access to such considerable resources while Antonius was still away. It was these resources which encouraged Lucius to lose his senses, and Asinius and Ahenobarbus, who were at hand, were busy employing them against us.[51] For the same reason I also hurriedly took possession of Plancus' legions, to prevent him joining Pompeius. Their cavalry have in fact crossed to Sicily.' Cocceius replied, 'Other versions of this business were in circulation, but not even Antonius believed them until he was shut out of Brundisium like an enemy.' Whereupon Octavian denied that he had given any order to this effect, since he had neither received advance warning that Antonius was coming, nor expected him to arrive in enemy company, and said that the Brundisians themselves and the military tribune stationed there on account of Ahenobarbus' attacks had barred the gates against him on their own initiative. 'They did so because he allied himself with our joint enemy Pompeius, and brought with him Ahenobarbus, who was one of my father's assassins and has been condemned by vote, by legal judgement and by proscription. This man not only laid siege to Brundisium after Philippi, and is still conducting siege operations all round the Adriatic, but has also burnt ships of mine and plundered Italy for booty.' 62. 'You agreed between you', Cocceius said, 'that you could make terms with anyone you liked; and Antonius has made terms with none of the murderers and has paid no less honour than you to your father. Ahenobarbus was not one of the murderers, and the vote against him was due to ill-feeling: he had no part in the plot at that stage. If we were to refuse to pardon him, on the grounds that he was a friend of Brutus, would we not be the first to have reached the point of being at enmity with virtually everyone? As to Pompeius, Antonius did not agree to join him in fighting you, but said that if he found himself at war he would take him as an ally or include him too in any settlement with you, as not even he had done anything irreparable. You are in fact responsible for this state of affairs, because if there had been no war in Italy, those men would not have been encouraged to make these approaches to Antonius.' Persisting with his accusations, Octavian said, 'It was against Italy, and against myself along with Italy, that Manius, Fulvia, and Lucius made war; and Pompeius, who has not previously made any attacks on the coast, is doing so now because he is confident of Antonius' support.'

'Not "confident of Antonius' support",' Cocceius said, 'but "instructed by Antonius". I will not conceal the fact that he will descend with a large fleet on the rest of Italy, which has no fleet to defend it, if you two do not resolve your quarrel.' Octavian, hesitating a little (for the import of this gambit was not lost on him), replied, 'But Pompeius will not get away with it. He has just been ignominiously driven off from Thurii.' Then Cocceius, having identified all the points in dispute, brought up Fulvia's death and the manner of it. He told how she had fallen ill out of resentment at Antonius' anger, and how her illness had been aggravated by her depression because Antonius had not come to see her even when she was sick, so that he bore the blame for his wife's death. He pointed out: 'Now that she too is out of the way, there is nothing you need do but speak frankly to each other about your suspicions.'

63. In this way Cocceius won Octavian's trust, and he spent that day as Octavian's guest and begged him, as the younger man, to write to Antonius as his senior. But Octavian refused to do so because Antonius was still conducting hostilities, and argued that Antonius had not written either. However, he intended to complain to Antonius' mother, because although she was related to himself and had enjoyed the highest place in his esteem, she had fled from Italy as though he would not grant her everything like a son.[52] Thus Octavian also laid plans, and wrote to Julia. As Cocceius was leaving the camp a considerable number of the senior officers made the view of the soldiers known to him, and he conveyed this, along with his other information, to Antonius, to make him realize that if he did not come to an agreement they would fight against him. He accordingly advised Antonius to order Pompeius back to Sicily from the areas which he was devastating and to send Ahenobarbus somewhere else until agreement had been reached. When his mother (who by birth was a member of the Julian family) also made pleas to the same effect, Antonius felt ashamed to ask Pompeius to support him again militarily if an accommodation did not result. In the face of his mother's confidence that it would, and Cocceius' insistence on it and expectation that he would want to continue negotiations, Antonius relented. He told Pompeius to withdraw to Sicily, on the grounds that he himself would take care of their agreed interests, and sent Ahenobarbus to be governor of Bithynia.

64. When they heard this, Octavian's army selected representatives, the same men in each case, to approach both leaders. The delegation refused to listen to their accusations against each other, regarding themselves as having

been chosen not to judge between the two men, but simply to bring about a reconciliation. They co-opted Cocceius, because he was an intimate of both, along with Pollio from Antonius' supporters and Maecenas from Octavian's, and they decided that there should be an amnesty between Octavian and Antonius in respect of past acts, and friendship in the future. Marcellus, the husband of Octavian's sister Octavia, had recently died, and the negotiators recommended that Octavian should betroth her to Antonius.[53] He immediately did so, and after the two men had embraced each other, cheers and congratulations from the troops for each of them went on all day and continued right through the night.   65. Octavian and Antonius made a new division of the Roman Empire, fixing as the boundary between them the Illyrian town of Scodra, which was believed to be the place nearest to the middle of the Adriatic gulf. Antonius was to have all the provinces and islands to the east of this as far as the river Euphrates, Octavian everything to the west as far as the Atlantic, and Lepidus was to have Africa, in accordance with Octavian's grant. Octavian was to go to war against Pompeius, unless terms were made, and Antonius against the Parthians, to punish them for their breach of faith in attacking Crassus. Ahenobarbus was to enjoy the same agreement with Octavian as had been made with Antonius. Both principals were to have the right to recruit equal numbers of additional troops in Italy without hindrance.

These were the final arrangements agreed between Octavian and Antonius.[54] Each of them immediately sent his friends off to deal with urgent business. Antonius despatched Ventidius to Asia to drive out some Parthians, along with Labienus son of Labienus, who during this period of turmoil had made an incursion in concert with the Parthians into Syria and an area stretching as far as Ionia.[55] However, the exploits and the fate of Labienus and the Parthians will be treated in my Parthian history.[56]   66. Helenus, Octavian's commander, who had made a sudden attack on Sardinia and gained possession of it, was driven out again by Menodorus, the Pompeian commander, and Octavian became particularly indignant at this and refused to countenance Antonius' attempts to include Pompeius in the peace. They then went to Rome and celebrated the marriage. Antonius also put Manius to death on the grounds that he had incited Fulvia with his slanders against Cleopatra and was responsible for the enormity of the consequences. In addition, he admitted to Octavian that Salvidienus, the commander of Octavian's army on the Rhône, was secretly plotting to defect and had sent him a message to this effect while he was besieging

Brundisium. Antonius did not win general approval for making this admission, but surely acted in this way because he had an honest disposition and was quick to do a kindness. Octavian immediately issued an urgent summons to Salvidienus, pretending he wanted to see him alone for some purpose and would send him back to the army directly afterwards. On his arrival Octavian established his guilt and put him to death; the army under his command he gave to Antonius, as he was doubtful of its loyalty.

67. Rome was in the grip of famine, because the traders from the east were too afraid of Pompeius in Sicily to sail for Italy. Nor did the traders from the west come, because Pompeius' lieutenants held Sardinia and Corsica, nor those from Africa opposite, because these same men controlled the sea to both sides of them. The price of all goods had risen, and the population, who ascribed this to the quarrelling of the leaders, cursed them and urged them to make peace with Pompeius. Since even under these circumstances Octavian would not agree, Antonius advised him at least to expedite the war because of the shortage of food. As there was no money to fund a war, an edict was posted by which property-owners were to contribute half of the twenty-five denarii per slave that had been required for the war against Brutus and Cassius, and also anyone who benefited under a will was to contribute a proportion. In mad fury the people tore down the notice, seething because the triumvirs, having exhausted the public treasury, pillaged the provinces, and oppressed Italy itself with exactions, taxes, and confiscations – and these not for foreign wars or to extend the Empire, but to use against their personal enemies over the private exercise of power, the pursuit of which had brought proscriptions, slaughter, and now this terrible famine – were going on to strip them of their remaining possessions. Crowds gathered and shouted protests, and stoned those who refused to join them, threatening to ransack and burn their houses.   **68**. Finally when the whole mass of the city population had been roused to anger, Octavian made a public appearance with his associates and a few bodyguards, because he wanted to meet them and explain why they were wrong to blame him. As soon as the crowd saw him, they bombarded him with missiles and were not ashamed of themselves even though he was being injured as he stood his ground, putting himself in their hands. When Antonius discovered what was happening, he went to help as quickly he could. As he came down the Sacred Way, the crowd did not throw anything at him, because he was ready to make peace with Pompeius, but they told him to go back. He refused, and they then began to stone him. He summoned more legionaries, who were outside the city walls. Even then the crowd did not give way to him, so the legionaries split up, went off to either side of the route, and began to make their attack on the forum down the alleyways, killing anyone they met. Their opponents, who were blocked by the crowd and were now unable to run through it, could no longer even make an easy escape. People were being killed and injured, and from the rooftops came screams and shouts. With difficulty Antonius reached Octavian, rescued him from danger – never in a more spectacular way – and saved his life by taking him home. The common people eventually dispersed, and to avoid provoking them the dead bodies were thrown into the river. A further source of grief was the sight of the bodies floating in the current, and being stripped by the soldiers and the petty criminals with them who carried away the better-dressed ones as if they were their own relatives. An end was put to these disturbances, and the triumvirs became the focus of fear and loathing; the famine, however, grew more intense, and the population complained bitterly, but remained passive.

69. Antonius suggested to Libo's relatives that they should invite Libo to come over from Sicily to celebrate with his brother-in-law and also achieve something rather more important, and offered to take personal responsibility for his safety. Libo's relatives wrote at once, and Pompeius agreed that he should come. On arrival he put into port on the island of Pithecoussa, which is now Aenaria,⁵⁷ and when the people of Rome heard about it, crowds again gathered and pathetically entreated Octavian to offer Libo a safe-conduct as the latter wanted to open peace negotiations with him. Octavian unwillingly did so, and Pompeius' mother Mucia, under threat of having her house burnt down, was also sent south by the people with the object of bringing about a settlement.⁵⁸ Then Libo, realizing that his enemies were dropping their resistance, recommended that the principals themselves should meet to make whatever concessions they thought fit to each other; and as the people also were forcing them to this, Octavian and Antonius left Rome for Baiae.⁵⁹

70. Although everyone else was unanimous in urging Pompeius to make peace, Menodorus wrote from Sardinia saying that he should either make war wholeheartedly or go on procrastinating, because the famine was his ally and if he waited for further developments he would obtain better terms. He also warned Pompeius to beware of Murcus, if he opposed an agreement, alleging that he was seeking to acquire power for himself. As a

result Pompeius, who even before this had found Murcus' prestige and strong views difficult, kept him still more at arm's length, and excluded him from all confidences. Finally Murcus retired in resentment to Syracuse, where on noticing that he was being followed by some men sent by Pompeius to watch him he heaped open abuse on Pompeius in front of them. Pompeius then bribed Murcus' own military tribune and centurion and sent them to kill him and say the murder had been committed by slaves. To lend plausibility to the deception he also crucified the slaves. However, since he had previously perpetrated the same atrocity against Bithynicus, he failed to elude detection when he repeated it against a man who was a soldier of distinction, had supported the party unwaveringly from the beginning, and had not only been Pompeius' personal benefactor in Spain but had willingly joined him in Sicily.[60]

71. Murcus, then, was dead, but Pompeius' other supporters pressed him to make peace and accused Menodorus of hankering after power, saying that it was not so much a concern for his patron as a desire for his own military and territorial authority that was responsible for his opposition to a treaty. So Pompeius gave in, and made the voyage over to Aenaria on board a splendid 'six' accompanied by a large fleet of fine ships.[61] He sailed proudly past Puteoli with these in the evening under the eyes of his enemies. Wooden platforms had been laid on piles that had been driven close together in the sea, and in the morning Octavian and Antonius went to the more landward platform, and Pompeius and Libo to the more seaward. A narrow strip of water lay between which prevented them hearing what the others were saying unless they shouted. Pompeius put the view that he should take Lepidus' place and share power with Antonius and Octavian, but they would only concede his return from exile. So they separated for the moment without achieving anything, but constant negotiation took place between their associates on all sorts of proposals from both sides. Pompeius demanded, for the proscribed and those who had been accomplices in the plot against Caesar, a safe exile, and for the others, restoration of their rights as citizens and of the property they had lost. So under pressure from the famine and from the people to reach an agreement, Octavian and Antonius reluctantly conceded that they would buy back up to a quarter of the property from its current holders, and wrote directly to the proscribed about this in the expectation that they would be very well pleased with it. The latter accepted all the terms, since now they were even afraid of Pompeius, thanks to the foul murder of Murcus. They went to Pompeius

and begged him to agree, whereupon he rent his clothes, crying that even those whose cause he had championed were betraying him, and repeatedly invoked Menodorus as a gifted commander and his only friend. **72.** Through the intervention of Mucia, Pompeius' mother, and Julia, his wife,[62] the three men met again on the mole at Puteoli, with the sea on both sides of them and guard-ships anchored alongside, and came to the following agreement: the war between them was at an end, both on land and sea, and commerce was to go unhindered everywhere; Pompeius was to withdraw any outposts stationed on the mainland, and was no longer to give sanctuary to runaway slaves or maintain a naval blockade of the Italian coast; he was to have authority over Sardinia, Sicily, Corsica, and any other islands he controlled at this time, for as long as Antonius and Octavian had authority over other areas; he was to supply the Romans with the grain which these places had long been required to provide; he was, in addition, to have the Peloponnese; and he was to hold the consulship *in absentia* through his own nominee and be co-opted as one of the priests of the most important priesthood.[63] These were the terms which applied to Pompeius. Also any of the aristocracy who were still in exile could return, except for those who been condemned by political and judicial process for the murder of Caesar; the possessions of the remainder, if they had left Italy from fear and their property had been seized by force, would be restored to them in full, apart from moveables, but a quarter only to those who had suffered proscription. As for men serving in Pompeius' forces, slaves were to have their freedom, while free persons, when they were discharged, were to be given the same rewards as those who had served with Octavian and Antonius.

73. Such were the conditions agreed, which were drawn up in a document and signed and sent to Rome for safe-keeping by the Vestals. The principals at once entertained each other, drawing lots to decide the order. Pompeius acted as host first, on board his flagship moored alongside the mole, and on the following days Antonius and Octavian erected tents, also on the mole, on the pretext that they should all feast each other beside the sea, but perhaps in order to avoid any suspicion of a plot. Not that they were unwary even so: their ships were moored close by, guards were stationed around, and those actually attending the dinner carried daggers concealed beneath their clothing. It is said that while they were banqueting on the ship Menodorus sent a message to Pompeius advising him to attack his guests and exact vengeance for the wrong done to his father and brother, and seize back his father's power by the swiftest of coups; for as he, Menodorus, was with the ships he would see that no one escaped. Pompeius' answer was worthy of his ancestry and his situation: 'How I wish Menodorus had acted without asking me!', for it was acceptable for Menodorus to break an oath, but not Pompeius. At this dinner Pompeius' daughter, Libo's granddaughter, was betrothed to Marcellus, Antonius' stepson and Octavian's nephew.[64] On the following day they announced the consuls for the next four years, first Antonius and Libo (Antonius nevertheless substituting whom he liked), after them Octavian and Pompeius, next Ahenobarbus and Sosius, and finally Antonius and Octavian again, who would then be about to hold the consulship for the third time and were also expected to make it the occasion for restoring the democracy.[65]

74. After this business had been completed, they parted, and Pompeius sailed for Sicily while Octavian and Antonius took the road to Rome. On hearing the news, the whole of Rome and Italy immediately praised them to the skies for bringing peace: men were rid of war in their own country and of the conscription of their sons, rid of the violence of military outposts and of the desertion of their slaves, rid of the plundering of farmland and of the interruption to agriculture, and rid above all of the famine which had brought them to the limits of their endurance. As a result they sacrificed to the triumvirs along their way as if to saviour gods. Rome was ready to give them a splendid welcome, if they had not slipped into the city by night to avoid the common crowd. The only group who were discontented were those who had been allotted land belonging to people who were about to arrive back with Pompeius; they believed that the landowners, living alongside them, would be their undying enemies and would attack them if ever they could. The majority of the refugees in Pompeius' following immediately (with a few exceptions) bid farewell to Pompeius at Puteoli and sailed back to Rome, and there was further rejoicing and shouting and cheering on the part of the common people at the unexpected salvation in this way of so many of the aristocracy.

75. After this they set out, Octavian for Gaul, which was disturbed, and Antonius for the war against the Parthians. Since the senate had voted to ratify all his past and future acts, Antonius again appointed governors everywhere and made any other administrative arrangements according to his own wishes. In some places he established kings of whom he approved, on payment of set amounts of tribute: in Pontus, Darius, who was the son

of Pharnaces and grandson of Mithridates; in Idumaea and Samaria, Herod; in Pisidia, Amyntas; Polemon in part of Cilicia; and others in other regions. Since he wanted to train and enrich that portion of his army which was going to go into winter quarters with him, he sent some of them against the Parthini, an Illyrian people living around Epidamnus who had been enthusiastic supporters of Brutus, and some against the Dardani, another Illyrian people who were always making incursions into Macedonia.[66] Others he ordered to remain in Epirus, so that he should have his forces all round him, his intention being to pass the winter himself in Athens. He also sent Furnius to Africa to fetch the four legions which were under Sextius' command for the campaign against the Parthians, since he was as yet unaware that Lepidus had taken them from Sextius.

76. After making these arrangements he wintered in Athens with Octavia just as he had in Alexandria with Cleopatra.[67] He paid attention to military matters only in so far as they were referred to him by letter, and he again laid aside the role of commander to assume the simplicity, Greek clothes, Attic shoes, and quiet front door of a private citizen. Likewise there was no pomp when he went out, with a couple of friends and a couple of attendants, to the schools of the teachers or to lectures. He dined in the Greek manner, took exercise with Greeks, and attended festivals in Octavia's company, in which he took great delight. With her, too, he was very much in love, because he was easily attracted by women. But when the winter was over he was like a different man. He changed his dress again, and with his dress his image. Straight away a mass of military standards, officers, and guards appeared at his door, and fear and awe were omnipresent; embassies which had been summoned and had so far waited in vain were admitted, legal decisions were given, ships were launched, and every other sort of preparation was put in hand.

77. While Antonius was busy with these activities, the accord reached between Octavian and Pompeius collapsed, for reasons, it was suspected, other than those publicly alleged by Octavian, which were as follows. Antonius was ready to cede the Peloponnese to Pompeius on condition that he either took it over after paying him, Antonius, the taxes that were still owed him by the Peloponnesians, or guaranteeing to pay them himself, or else he must wait until they had been collected. Pompeius was unwilling to accept the territory on these terms, because he considered that it had been given to him along with its arrears of tax. Being dissatisfied, according to Octavian, either for this reason, or because his policies were treacherous,

or because he was jealous of the large armies possessed by the others, or because Menodorus incited him to think that he was enjoying not so much a permanent accord as a pause in hostilities, he built some more ships, collected crews, and on one occasion made a speech to his troops saying they ought to be prepared to meet any eventuality. Clandestine raiding vessels again disturbed the seas, and the population of Rome enjoyed little or no relief from the famine, leading to public protests that the peace had brought them, not relief from their distress, but a fourth tyrant on top of the other three. Octavian captured some of these vessels, and after the crews had admitted under torture that Pompeius had sent them to make the attacks, he put these facts to the population and wrote to Pompeius himself, who repudiated any involvement in the matter but made counter-accusations on the subject of the Peloponnese.

78. Those of the aristocracy who were still with Pompeius saw that he always took the advice of the ex-slaves, so either on their own initiative or to do Octavian a favour, they bribed some of the ex-slaves to turn their master against Menodorus, who still held authority in Corsica and Sardinia. Since they were themselves jealous of Menodorus' power, the ex-slaves willingly did so. Thus Pompeius was being alienated from Menodorus at the same time as Philadelphus, an ex-slave of Octavian's, sailed over to contact Menodorus in connection with the grain supply, and Micylion, the most reliable of Menodorus' attendants, sailed in the opposite direction to raise with Octavian the possibility of Menodorus' desertion, promising that he would put into Octavian's hands Sardinia, Corsica, three legions, and a further force of light-armed troops.[68] Whether it was the work of Philadelphus, or the result of the blackening of Menodorus in Pompeius' eyes, Octavian accepted the offer – not at once, but in due course, regarding the peace as having been in practice broken. He also asked Antonius to come from Athens to meet him at Brundisium on a certain day and confer with him about this war, and he sent orders for warships from Ravenna, and an army from Gaul, and other necessities of war to be assembled quickly at Brundisium and Puteoli, with the intention of making a naval attack on Sicily from both directions, if Antonius agreed. **79.** The latter came with a small escort on the appointed day, but did not find Octavian and refused to wait for him, either because he disapproved of the plan to go to war as contrary to the terms of agreement, or because he observed the scale of Octavian's preparations (for the lust to enjoy sole power prevented them ever enjoying a respite from fear),[69] or because he took fright at an omen.

This was, that one of the guards who was sleeping beside Antonius' tent was found eaten by wild animals, all except his face, which had been left as though to identify him; he had uttered no cry, and none of his fellow-sleepers had seen anything. The people of the town indeed maintained that a wolf had been sighted at dawn running away from the encampment. At any rate, Antonius wrote to Octavian not to break their agreement and threatened to drag Menodorus off for punishment as his own runaway slave, because he had been owned by Pompeius Magnus, whose property Antonius had purchased when by law it had been put up for sale as belonging to an enemy of the state.

80. Octavian sent men to Sardinia and Corsica to take over the areas which Menodorus was handing over to him, and strengthened the Italian coasts with a large number of fortified posts in case Pompeius attacked them again. He gave orders that more triremes were to be built at Rome and Ravenna and sent for a large army from Illyria. When Menodorus arrived he immediately deemed him free-born, not an ex-slave, and put him in charge of the ships he had brought, under the command of Calvisius as admiral.[70] In making these arrangements and assembling still more extensive resources for the war, he fell behind schedule. He criticized Antonius for not waiting for him, and ordered Cornificius to move the forces he had already made ready from Ravenna to Tarentum.[71] As Cornificius was making the passage he encountered a storm, and the only ship lost was the flagship which was meant for Octavian. This seemed to be an omen for what was to come. And because the suspicion still prevailed that this war amounted to a breach of treaty, Octavian tried to quell it by writing to Rome, and himself telling the troops, that Pompeius had broken the treaty by acts of piracy at sea, as his pirates had confessed in detail, that in addition Menodorus had revealed his whole plan, and that Antonius was also aware of this and had therefore not surrendered the Peloponnese.

81. When all his preparations were complete, Octavian sailed to attack Sicily, himself from Tarentum and Calvisius Sabinus and Menodorus from the Tyrrhenian side. The land forces also advanced to Rhegium, and haste was the order of the day. Pompeius heard about the desertion of Menodorus when Octavian was already on his way, and met the two-pronged attack by waiting himself for Octavian at Messana and ordering Menecrates, who of all his ex-slaves was by far the most hostile to Menodorus, to go and meet Calvisius and Menodorus with a substantial fleet. This Menecrates was sighted by the enemy in the late afternoon, to seaward

of them. They took shelter in the bay of Cumae and stopped there for the night, while Menecrates went on to Aenaria. At first light they sailed along the bay in crescent formation, hugging the land, to stop the enemy breaking through and spinning round to attack them. Menecrates again appeared and immediately came to close quarters in a furious rush, but as he could do them little harm while they refused to sail out towards open water, he pressed close on them and forced them towards the shore. They put their ships aground close together and fought off his ramming attacks. The situation was such that one side could withdraw to seaward and attack again whenever it liked, and substitute fresh ships by turns, while the others were in difficulties due to the rocks on which they had run aground and the impossibility of moving their ships, so that they were like infantry fighting a naval attack, with no chance either of pursuit or retreat.

82. In the course of this struggle, Menodorus and Menecrates caught sight of each other. Ignoring the rest of the fighting, they immediately drove their ships angrily at each other with loud cries, thinking that victory depended on this encounter, which constituted the critical moment of the campaign in which one of them was going to be victorious. The ships collided with force, and Menodorus' lost her ram while Menecrates' had her oars broken; but when grappling-irons were thrown from both, they lay side by side and nautical manoeuvres had no further part to play. On the other hand the men on board could not have displayed greater bravery and endurance if they had been fighting on land. They directed a constant hail of javelins, stones and arrows against each other and threw gangplanks down on to the other vessel to give a means of access. Menodorus' ship being the higher, the gangplanks were easier for his own daring spirits to cross, and his missiles had more force as they were thrown from a greater height. Many men had already been killed and the remainder badly injured when Menodorus was wounded in the arm by a dart, which was removed, and Menecrates in the thigh by a multi-barbed Spanish javelin of solid iron which was impossible to extract quickly. Menecrates thus became unable to fight, but even so he remained present and urged on the others until, as his ship was being captured, he threw himself into the sea. Menodorus bound his own ship together with ropes and sailed off landwards, even he unable to do any more. **83.** Such was the outcome of the battle on the left wing. On the right, Calvisius, as he made for the left, cut off some of Menecrates' ships and pursued them as they fled seaward, and Demochares, Menecrates' lieutenant and fellow ex-slave, engaged the remainder of

Calvisius' squadron. He put some ships to flight and wrecked others on the rocks, burning the hulls after the crews had leapt off, until Calvisius returned from the chase bringing back with him his own runaway ships, and prevented the fires spreading. Darkness overtook them, and they all spent the night in the same places as before. This was the end of the sea-battle, in which Pompeius' side came off far better. However, Demochares was as depressed by Menecrates' death as if it had been a major defeat (for it was these two, Menecrates and Menodorus, who were Pompeius' chief sea-captains), and sailed at once for Sicily, letting everything slip from his grasp as if he had lost not simply Menecrates' body and one ship, but his whole fleet.

84. So long as Calvisius expected an attack from Demochares he stayed where he had anchored, because it was impossible for him to fight after losing the best of his ships, with the others in no state to do battle; but when he learnt that Demochares had left for Sicily, he refitted his ships and proceeded along the coast, following the shoreline of the bays. Octavian had sailed from Tarentum to Rhegium with a large fleet and a considerable number of troops, and off Messana had come across Pompeius with only forty ships. His associates advised him to take advantage of the opportunity and use his superiority in numbers to attack Pompeius and his handful of ships while the rest of the enemy fleet was absent, but Octavian rejected the advice and waited for Calvisius, observing that it was not wise to court danger when he could expect further reinforcement. When Demochares reached Messana, Pompeius appointed him and Apollophanes, another of his own ex-slaves, as his admirals in place of Menodorus and Menecrates.

85. At the news of what had happened at Cumae, Octavian sailed from the Straits to go and meet Calvisius, but when he had cleared the major part of the narrows and was already passing Stylis and altering course for Scyllaeum, Pompeius dashed out from Messana, harassed the rearmost ships, gave chase to the leaders, attacked everywhere, and challenged them to battle. Although Octavian's ships were in difficulties, they did not turn round to fight because he would not allow it, either because he was afraid to fight in constricted waters or because he was sticking to what he had originally decided, not to give battle without Calvisius; and by his decision they all drew back close to the shore, rode at anchor, and fought off their assailants from the bows. But Demochares set two ships to attack each of them, and they were then thrown into disorder as they were smashed on the rocks and against each other and filled with water. So this fleet was also

being destroyed without putting up any resistance, like the one at Cumae, lying at anchor and being attacked by an enemy who alternately moved in and withdrew again. 86. Octavian scrambled out of his ship on to the rocks, pulled out of the water the men who were swimming to shore, and escorted them up into the mountains. However, Cornificius and the other senior officers present encouraged each other and on their own initiative cut their anchor ropes and moved out against the enemy, feeling that they ought to be active in defeat rather than wait there, open to attack, without retaliating. First Cornificius, in an unexpected act of daring, rammed and took Demochares' flagship. Demochares himself then leapt across to another ship, but at this point in the progress of the struggle and the slaughter, Calvisius and Menodorus appeared, approaching from the open sea. Octavian's forces did not sight them either from the land or from the water, but Pompeius', who were further out to sea, did so, and consequently withdrew, because the light was already starting to fade and they lacked the confidence, in their exhausted state, to engage in battle against fresh forces.

This was a fortunate coincidence for the survivors after the misfortunes they had so far experienced. 87. When darkness fell some of them abandoned their ships, took refuge in the mountains, lit numerous fires as signals to those who were still afloat, and so passed the night, without food or attention or any necessities at all. Octavian, who was in a similar situation, went round to the various groups and encouraged them to endure their sufferings until the morning. Although in distress under these circumstances, he was still not aware that Calvisius had arrived, nor did any help come from the ships, which were fully occupied with the wrecks;[72] but by another stroke of luck the Thirteenth legion came near them on its march through the mountains and after hearing about the disaster hurried across the precipitous terrain, using the fires as indications of the way to go. Finding their commander-in-chief and his fellow refugees in this poor state, they treated them for lack of rest and food by distributing them among their own messes, while their commander was conducted to an improvised tent by the military tribunes – none of his own slave attendants being present because they had become separated from him in the darkness and desperate confusion. Octavian immediately sent messengers out everywhere to say he was safe, and on hearing of Calvisius' arrival with the advance guard of his fleet, permitted himself some rest on the strength of two unexpected but favourable events.

88. At daybreak, as he looked out over the sea, his gaze was met by ships

that had been set on fire, ships that were still half-ablaze or half-burnt, and ships that had been smashed; the sea was covered with sails and rudders and tackle, and the greater part of what was still being recovered was damaged. So, behind the protection of Calvisius' fleet, he moved down the coast and carried out the most urgent repairs. The enemy did not interfere, either because of Calvisius or because they had decided to attack when the fleet put to sea again. Such was the position on each side, when in the afternoon a gale began to blow from the south and kicked up a vicious sea in the narrow strait with its strong current. Pompeius was at Messana inside the harbour, but Octavian's ships were again driven on to a rugged shore without much shelter and were pounded against the rocks and each other, not even having crews sufficiently up to strength to master the conditions. **89**. For his part Menodorus, who expected when the storm began that it would intensify, went further out to sea and lay to anchor; and although the waves were less rough in the deeper water he nevertheless rowed vigorously into them to avoid the anchors dragging. Some of the others followed his example, but the bulk of the fleet, thinking that the wind would soon drop because it was spring, moored their ships by warps from bow and stern to anchors in the sea and on land, and used poles to fend each other off. But the wind became more violent, and total confusion ensued, with the ships breaking away from their anchors and being pounded against the shore or each other. There was a babel of shouts from men terrified or crying or making exhortations to each other that fell on deaf ears. Orders no longer reached the hearer, and neither technical knowledge nor authority served to distinguish a ship's captain from an ordinary seaman. A similar death awaited a man, whether he stayed on the ships themselves or went overboard as they broke up under the blows of the waves and the surf and pieces of wood, the sea being full of sails and timber and men alive and dead. And if any of them managed to avoid these dangers and swim away to the shore, they too were smashed against the rocks by the waves. When in addition to all this the sea became violently convulsed, as normally happens in these straits, this not only struck terror into the men, who were unused to it, but also tossed their vessels about more violently than ever and threw them against each other. With sunset the gale intensified, so that destruction no longer came in daylight, but in the dark. **90**. Cries of distress arose all night long. Men ran along on land, calling out by name to their friends and relatives in the water and lamenting for them, in the belief that they were dead, when they did not hear; conversely, others in the water lifted their heads above the waves and begged those on shore to help them. But nothing could help either party. Nor was it simply the sea which offered no escape either to those who had plunged into it or to any who were still on board the ships. The land posed a threat no less great than that of the surf, that their bodies would be smashed to pieces against the rocks by the waves. They were struggling in a storm of unprecedented strangeness: they were very close to land, yet they were afraid of that land and had no means to escape from it, whether out to the open sea or far enough offshore to be clear of each other. The constricted nature of the place, the natural difficulty of exit from it, the pounding of the breakers, the wind swirling in violent squalls off the surrounding mountains, and the convulsion of the deep water boiling up in all directions permitted them neither to stay nor to escape, and the darkness of a pitch-black night made matters worse. And so they went to their deaths unable to see each other any longer, some agitated and crying out, others quietly surrendering and accepting their doom, and a few hastening it on in the belief that their end was quite inevitable. The disaster, by surpassing anything they could conceive, even robbed them of the hope of some miraculous salvation, until eventually, as day was breaking, the wind suddenly started to go down and after sunrise fell completely calm. Even then the sea continued to be rough for a long time after the wind had dropped. Not even the local people could remember such a severe storm; and its severity, in exceeding all normal bounds, destroyed the majority of Octavian's ships and men.

91. Having suffered serious losses in the fighting on the previous day and met with two such disasters simultaneously, Octavian immediately made his way in great haste that very night through the mountains to Vibo, since he was unable to recover from the catastrophe in a situation where he had no means of assistance. He sent orders to all his supporters and military commanders to be on the alert, in case his misfortunes provoked a plot against him from some quite different quarter. He also stationed the available infantry around the whole coast of Italy, in case Pompeius' good fortune encouraged him to try attacking the land as well. Pompeius, however, did not think about the mainland, nor did he take any action against the survivors of the wrecked fleet either while they were still present or as they slipped away after the swell had subsided. He took no notice as they bound the hulls up with ropes as best they could and drifted with the wind to Vibo, either because he thought the disaster suffered by the enemy was enough for him, or because he had no experience in following up a victory, or (as I have remarked elsewhere also)[73] he was thoroughly feeble in taking the initiative and had determined to do no more than repel anyone who came to attack him.

92. Less than half Octavian's ships had survived, and these were badly damaged. Nevertheless he left some people behind to supervise repairs, and proceeded to Campania in low spirits. He had no other ships, although he needed a large number, and he had no time to build any, because he was under pressure from the famine and from the city population, who were again agitating for an agreement and deriding the war as a breach of treaty. He needed money and was short of it, because the Romans were neither paying their taxes nor allowing him to raise money in the ways he had devised. Always clever at seeing where his advantage lay, he sent Maecenas to Antonius to persuade him to change his mind about the matters over which they had recently exchanged harsh words, and to enlist his aid in the war. If he failed to win Antonius over, he was planning to embark his legionaries on transport ships, cross to Sicily, forget about the sea, and conduct the war by land. While he was in this state of depression he received the news that Antonius had agreed to give him military help, and that under the leadership of Agrippa a magnificent victory had been won over the Gauls of Aquitania. Also his friends and some of the towns promised him ships, and began to build. So he recovered his spirits and proceeded to put together a force more splendid than his previous one.

93. At the beginning of spring[74] Antonius sailed from Athens to Tarentum with 300 ships to fight alongside Octavian, as he had promised, but the latter had changed his plan and was waiting for the ships which were still in the course of being built for him. On being invited a second time to join Antonius' forces, because they were ready and sufficient for the task, he pleaded other engagements and it was obvious that he was either again blaming Antonius for something or disregarding his military support because he had plenty of his own. Although Antonius was irritated, he none the less waited and sent another invitation to Octavian. He found the maintenance of the fleet a burden and needed Italian soldiers against the Parthians, and so he thought he would give Octavian ships in exchange for them – for although it was part of their agreement that either could recruit in Italy, it was going to be difficult for him to do so as the country had fallen to Octavian to govern. Octavia therefore went to Octavian to mediate between the two men. Her brother said that he had been left in the lurch when the catastrophe struck him in the Straits, to which she replied that Maecenas had received an explanation on that point. He alleged that Antonius had also sent the ex-slave Callias to make a pact with Lepidus against him, but she said that she knew that Callias had been sent to arrange a marriage, because Antonius wanted his daughter to be betrothed to Lepidus' son, as had been agreed, before the Parthian campaign.[75] This was Octavia's explanation, and Antonius was also ready to send Callias for Octavian to question under torture; but Octavian refused the offer and agreed to come and meet Antonius between Metapontum and Tarentum, with the river which gives its name to the town between them.[76]   94. By chance they both approached the stream at the same time. Antonius sprang down from his carriage, jumped unaccompanied into one of the small boats moored alongside, and started to cross to Octavian, trusting him as a friend. When Octavian saw this, he imitated Antonius' example, and they met on the water and had an argument, because each of them wanted to disembark on the other's bank. Octavian won, since if he went to Tarentum he would also be going to Octavia; he sat beside Antonius in his carriage, arrived unescorted in Antonius' quarters in Tarentum, and likewise slept there that night without any armed guards beside him. The same trust was displayed by Antonius on the following day. Thus their behaviour constantly swung between suspicion, arising from their desire for power, and trust, arising from their current needs.

95. Octavian wanted to put off the expedition against Pompeius to the following year, but Antonius was unable to stay on account of the Parthians. Nevertheless they made an exchange of forces, Antonius giving Octavian 120 ships, which he sent immediately and handed over at Tarentum, and Octavian giving Antonius 20,000 Italian legionaries, whom he promised to send later. In addition Octavia begged from Antonius and presented to her brother ten light triremes of a hybrid type between merchantmen and warships, and Octavian gave his sister 1,000 picked praetorians, chosen by Antonius.[77] Also, since the triumviral authority voted to them had expired, they gave themselves another five-year period without seeking any further approval from the people.[78] On these terms they parted, and Antonius at once hastened to Syria, leaving Octavia, and the daughter who had already been born to them, with her brother.[79]

96. Whether because repeated treachery was in Menodorus' nature, or because he was afraid of the threat uttered by Antonius to drag him off to punishment as a captured slave who had provoked a war, or because he

considered that he was being less well rewarded than he expected, or because Pompeius' other ex-slaves constantly reproached him for his disloyalty to his master and begged him to return now that Menecrates was dead, he asked for, and received, a promise of personal immunity, and deserted to Pompeius with seven ships, unnoticed by Octavian's admiral Calvisius. Whereupon Octavian removed Calvisius from his command and replaced him with Agrippa.[80]

When the fleet was ready, Octavian purified it in the following manner. The altars are in contact with the water, and the crews stand around them, by ships, in total silence; those performing the ceremony make sacrifice standing at the water's edge and carry the purificatory offerings three times around the fleet by boat, accompanied by the senior officers who pray that evil has been turned on to these offerings instead of the fleet.[81] They then divide them, throwing part into the sea and placing part on the altars and burning them, and the crowd shouts its assent. This is the Roman way of purifying their fleets.

97. Octavian was going to sail from Puteoli, Lepidus from Africa, and Taurus from Tarentum against Sicily, in order to surround the island from the east, west and south simultaneously.[82] The day on which Octavian intended to put to sea had been notified to all. This was the tenth day after the summer solstice, which for the Romans is the first day of the month which in honour of the first Caesar they call July instead of Quintilis, and in fixing on this day, Octavian perhaps regarded it as a good omen because his father was always victorious. Meanwhile Pompeius stationed Plinius[83] at Lilybaeum with a force of legionaries and a quantity of light-armed troops to counter Lepidus, and guarded the whole east and west coasts of Sicily, particularly the islands of Lipara and Cossyra, so that Cossyra should not furnish Lepidus, nor Lipara Octavian, with harbours or roadsteads convenient to Sicily.[84] The pick of his fleet he kept at Messana, on the watch for where it might be needed.

98. Thus both sides made their preparations. When the first of the month arrived they all put to sea at first light – Lepidus from Africa with 1,000 transport ships, seventy warships, twelve legions, 5,000 Numidian cavalry, and a great deal else; Taurus from Tarentum with only 102 of Antonius' 130 ships, because the rowers of the rest had died during the winter; and Octavian from Puteoli, sacrificing and pouring libations into the sea from his flagship to Gentle Winds and Saviour Neptune and Calm Sea, to win their support against his father's enemies. Some ships went ahead to

reconnoitre the indentations of the coastline, while Appius acted as rear-guard with a sizeable squadron. On the third day of their voyage a southerly gale struck them. Many of Lepidus' transports capsized, but he nevertheless reached the shelter of Sicily, put Plinius under siege in Lilybaeum, and won over some of the towns and took others by force. Taurus ran back to Tarentum as the wind began to rise. Appius had just rounded the Cape of Minerva,[85] and some of his ships were battered against the rocks, others were driven aground on mud-flats by the force of the waves, and others were scattered, not without loss. Octavian had taken refuge at the onset of the storm in the well-protected bay of Velia, though he lost one 'six' wrecked on the headland;[86] but as the wind veered to the south-west the gulf, being open to the west, became very rough. It was no longer possible to sail out of the bay into the teeth of the wind, nor could oars or anchors hold the ships in position. They smashed into each other or against the rocks, and night made their predicament still more extraordinary.

99. When the storm eventually abated Octavian proceeded to bury the dead, tend the wounded, clothe and provide with fresh equipment those who had swum to safety, and repair the whole fleet as best he could under the circumstances. He had lost six heavy ships, twenty-six lighter ones, and a still greater number of Liburnians.[87] It was going to take thirty days to set matters straight, and since the end of summer was already in sight, it would have been better for him to have put off the campaign until the following year. However, the people of Rome were suffering because of the shortages, and he began hauling his ships out of the water and refitting them with great urgency, and sent the crews of the vessels he had lost to the unmanned ships at Tarentum. Fearing a greater disaster, he despatched Maecenas to Rome because there were people who were still greatly moved by the memory of Pompeius Magnus, whose glory had not faded from their minds, and he himself went round Italy speaking to the settler veterans and soothing the fear induced in them by what had happened. He also hurried to Tarentum where he inspected the fleet under Taurus, and visited Vibo where he encouraged the infantry and hastened on the repair of the ships. The second assault on Sicily was now imminent.

100. Not even after such a stroke of good luck did Pompeius consider it necessary to take any action over the large number of wrecks, but simply sacrificed to the sea and to Neptune and promised to call himself their son[88] because he believed that only by divine power could the enemy have been thwarted twice in summertime. It is said that he became so conceited

as a result of these events that he changed the colour of his military cloak from the normal purple of a commander-in-chief to dark blue, thus signifying that he was Neptune's adoptive son. He expected that Octavian would call off the attack, but when he heard that his opponent had put the shipwrights to work and was going to launch another invasion that very summer, he became nervous of fighting against such overwhelming determination and military preparation, and sent Menodorus with the seven ships he had brought with him to reconnoitre Octavian's shipyards and do what damage he could. Menodorus, however, who was already irritated because he had not had the command at sea restored to him, now realized that he was not fully trusted even with the handful of ships he had brought, and plotted another desertion.

101. His plan was first to perform some notable exploits, because this would profit him in any eventuality. He distributed all the money he had among the men who sailed with him, and in three days covered 190 miles under oars. He fell like a thunderbolt from nowhere on the detachment guarding Octavian's ships which were being repaired and reconstructed, and disappeared into nowhere after capturing the ships of the guard squadron in twos and threes. He also sank, took in tow, or set fire to the merchant ships carrying grain as they lay in harbour or made their passage along the coast. He caused disruption everywhere, because Octavian and Agrippa were still away, the latter having gone off to acquire timber. He was so proud of himself that on one occasion he deliberately and contemptuously went aground on a soft shoal and pretended that his ship was held fast by the mud. The enemy dashed down from the hills, thinking to make easy prey of him, but he then backed his ship off and vanished laughing, leaving Octavian's army overcome by chagrin and amazement.

He had now given a convincing demonstration of the kind of friend or foe he would be, and with an eye to the future he released Rebilus, a senator he had captured.[89]   102. He also told his own entourage that Mindius Marcellus, one of Octavian's companions, with whom he had become friendly during the period of his previous desertion, was planning to betray Octavian and desert, and he approached the other side to request a meeting with Mindius on a small island for a discussion that would be to their advantage. When Mindius met him he said, out of earshot of everyone else, that he had fled to Pompeius because he had been badly treated by the then admiral Calvisius; but now that Agrippa had taken over the command he would return to Octavian, who had done him no wrong, if Mindius could bring him a promise of immunity from Messalla, who was acting as commander in Agrippa's absence. He added that on his return he would make up for his mistake with some spectacular exploits, but until he received the promise he would continue to inflict damage on parts of Octavian's force in order not to arouse suspicion. He then resumed his offensive operations, and Messalla, though he hesitated over such a discreditable bargain, gave in, either thinking that such was the necessity of war, or because he already knew or had divined something about Octavian's intentions. So Menodorus changed sides again, and on Octavian's arrival fell at his feet and asked for forgiveness without saying why he had left him. Octavian granted him his life, because of the guarantees given, and had him secretly watched; the captains of his ships he allowed to depart and go wherever they wished.

103. When the fleet was ready, Octavian again put to sea and sailed along the coast to Vibo. He ordered Messalla to cross to Sicily with two legions to join Lepidus' army, and when he had crossed establish a base in the bay facing Tauromenium. He also sent three legions to Stylis at the end of the Straits to await developments. Taurus he instructed to sail round from Tarentum to the high ground at Scolacium, which lies across from Tauromenium.[90] Taurus obeyed, prepared both for battle and for progress under oars; the infantry marched parallel with him, and reconnaissance was done by cavalry on land and by Liburnians at sea. While he was proceeding in this fashion, Octavian rode over from Vibo, made his appearance at Scolacium, and returned to Vibo after having assured himself of the good order of the troops. Meanwhile Pompeius, as I have already said, was guarding all the landing-places on the island and keeping his ships together at Messana in order to provide help wherever it might be required.

104. Such was the state of the preparations on this front. Meanwhile Lepidus' transport ships were making a second voyage from Africa to bring him the four remaining legions of his army. While still out at sea, they encountered a squadron under Papias sent out by Pompeius, which they supposed to be Lepidus' ships come to meet them and took to be friendly, and were destroyed.[91] Lepidus' ships were not only launched too late, but when they eventually made their approach the transports kept out of their way thinking they were other enemy vessels, until some were burnt out, some captured, some capsized, and some sailed back to Africa. Of the soldiers, two legions were lost in the water, of whom the few who escaped by swimming also died at the hands of Pompeius' commander Tisienus as they

emerged on shore;[92] the remainder landed and joined Lepidus, some at once and some later. Papias then rejoined Pompeius.

105. Octavian sailed across with his whole fleet from Vibo to Strongyle, one of the five Aeolian islands, after first making a naval reconnaissance. Seeing that the forces on the Sicilian coast opposite him, at Pelorus, Mylae, and Tyndaris, were rather large, he thought it probable that Pompeius himself was present. So he handed over the direction of operations there to Agrippa, and himself sailed back to Vibo. From there, accompanied by Messalla with three legions, he hurried on to Taurus' army with the intention of capturing Tauromenium in Pompeius' absence and threatening him with two separate thrusts. Agrippa, consequently, sailed from Strongyle to Hiera and took it in face of limited resistance from the Pompeian garrison. He intended to make an attack the next day on Pompeius' lieutenant Demochares and his forty ships at Mylae, but Pompeius, foreseeing Agrippa's assault, sent his ex-slave Apollophanes from Messana with another forty-five ships and followed with a further seventy himself.

106. While it was still dark Agrippa left Hiera with half his fleet, expecting to do battle with Papias alone.[93] When he saw Apollophanes' ships as well, and also the seventy on his other hand, he immediately sent a message to Octavian that Pompeius was at Mylae with the larger part of his fleet, and himself placed his heavy ships in the centre and summoned the rest of his fleet urgently from Hiera. Both sides were magnificently equipped and had towers on their ships at both bow and stern. When the appropriate exhortations had been made, and the flags had been hoisted on each ship, they came forward to the attack, either head on, or by outflanking each other, to the accompaniment of shouts and spray thrown up by the ships, and all sorts of feelings of fear. Pompeius' craft were smaller, light and quick to attack and to row round an opponent, while Octavian's were bigger and heavier and consequently also slower, but on the other hand more powerful when ramming and more difficult to damage. As for the crews, Pompeius' men were better sailors than Octavian's, but Octavian's were stronger; accordingly the former tried to gain the advantage not by ramming but simply by superior manoeuvring, and they broke the oar-blades or rudders of the bigger ships, or knocked out their oars, or isolated them completely and did them as much damage as if they had rammed them. Octavian's side used their rams to disable Pompeius' ships, as they were smaller, or to spring their timbers, or to break them apart; and when they came to close quarters, because their opponents were below them they could hurl missiles

down from above and were more easily able to throw grappling-irons or hooks aboard them. If the Pompeians were being overpowered, they would jump into the sea and Pompeius' smaller craft would sail round and pick them up. 107. Agrippa went straight for Papias, striking his ship by the cat-heads, splintering it apart, and breaking into the main hull. The men in the towers were shaken off, and the sea poured in everywhere. The rowers on the lowest bank of oars were all lost by drowning, but the others broke through the deck and swam away. Papias himself was taken on board the ship lying alongside and resumed the attack on the enemy.

Pompeius, watching from a hill, saw that his own ships were of little assistance and were losing their marines when they fought at close quarters, while the rest of Agrippa's fleet was sailing to his assistance from Hiera. He therefore made a signal to disengage in good order, and they broke off the engagement by attacking and then always withdrawing a little further. With Agrippa in close pursuit, they escaped not towards the beaches but to places where the rivers had created shoals. 108. Agrippa's captains told him not to take large ships into shallow water, so he lay to anchor offshore in readiness to blockade the enemy and fight by night if necessary. His companions, however, begged him not to be carried away by rash enthusiasm, nor to wear out his men by depriving them of sleep and rest, nor to trust a sea so liable to frequent storms, and at evening he reluctantly drew off. The Pompeians coasted along to their harbours, having lost thirty of their ships, sunk five of the enemy's, and damaged a quantity of others while suffering similar damage themselves. Pompeius praised them for standing up to such enormous vessels and said that they had been assaulting walls, not ships. He rewarded them as though they had won a victory and encouraged them to hope that in the strait, because of the current, the lightness of their ships would give them superiority, and said himself that he would increase the height of the ships. Such was the conclusion of the naval battle at Mylae between Agrippa and Papias.

109. Pompeius, who correctly supposed that Octavian was on his way to Taurus' army and would make an attack on Tauromenium, sailed immediately after supper to Messana, leaving a detachment behind at Mylae to make Agrippa think he was still there. Agrippa gave his forces as much rest as his haste allowed and sailed to Tyndaris, which was on the point of surrender. He actually penetrated into the town, but was driven out by magnificent efforts on the part of its garrison. Other towns came over to him and accepted his garrisons, and he returned to Hiera. Octavian had by now

sailed along from Scolacium to Leucopetra on positive confirmation of the intelligence that Pompeius was on his way from Messana to Mylae because of Agrippa. He intended to make a crossing of the strait between Leucopetra and Tauromenium in the dark, but when he heard the news of the naval battle he decided, as victor, no longer to steal over like a thief in the night but to cross in daylight with a confident army. He remained certain that Pompeius was still close to Agrippa. So when day came and his survey from the heights showed the sea to be clear of the enemy, he sailed with as many troops as his ships could carry, leaving Messalla in charge of the remainder until the ships returned. When he reached Tauromenium, he sent a message to demand its surrender, but the garrison rejected it. So he coasted along past the river Onobalas and the shrine of Aphrodite and tied up at the Archegetes,* intending to fortify a camp there and make an attack on Tauromenium. (The Archegetes is a statue of Apollo, the first to be set up by the Naxians who came to settle in Sicily.)   110. At this spot Octavian slipped and fell as he disembarked from his ship, but sprang to his feet unaided. As he was still making camp Pompeius sailed up with a large fleet – a complete surprise to Octavian, who thought that he had been drawn into combat by Agrippa. Riding along parallel with Pompeius were his cavalry, who strove to rival the fleet in speed; his infantry appeared from the other side; and caught like this between three enemy forces, everyone was afraid, as also was Octavian, because he was unable to send for Messalla. Pompeius' cavalry at once began to harass those of Octavian's men who were still at work on the fortifications, and if the infantry and the fleet had joined the cavalry in their attack, perhaps something more would have been achieved by Pompeius. But as it was, like men inexperienced in war, and because they knew nothing of the disarray of Octavian's men and shrank from starting a battle late in the day, the one part of Pompeius' force found an anchorage by the headland of Coccynus, while the infantry did not dare to make camp near the enemy and withdrew to the town of Phoenix.[94] That night they rested, while Octavian's men finished their defences but were rendered unfit for battle by exhaustion and lack of sleep. Octavian had three legions, 500 cavalrymen without their horses, 1,000 light-armed troops, and 2,000 veteran settlers who had come as volunteers to fight with him, plus his naval force.

111. He therefore handed over command of all the foot to Cornificius, instructing him to repel the enemy land forces and take whatever emergency action might be necessary, and himself put out to sea with his fleet

before it was yet light in order to prevent the enemy blockading him here too. He entrusted the right wing to Titinius and the left to Carisius,[95] and himself went aboard a Liburnian and sailed round the fleet giving general encouragement. After making his exhortations he stowed away his admiral's standard, as if he was in extreme danger. Pompeius then put out from shore and they twice attacked each other in a battle which lasted until nightfall. As Octavian's ships were being captured and set on fire, some of them hoisted reduced sail and made for the Italian mainland, in disregard of their orders. Pompeius' ships pursued them for a short distance and then turned back to the remainder and continued to capture or burn them. Some of the crew members from these ships who swam to shore were killed or taken prisoner by Pompeius' cavalry, and others scrambled up to Cornificius' camp. As the latter ran towards the camp they were given help* by the light-armed troops, whom Cornificius sent out unsupported, because he thought it a bad moment to disturb a despondent legionary battle-line facing troops whose morale was high at the likely prospect of victory.

112. Octavian spent most of the night among his auxiliary craft deliberating whether to make his way back to Cornificius through the middle of so many wrecks or to escape and join Messalla, and was brought by providence to the harbour of Abala, accompanied by a single armour-bearer, without any companions or bodyguards or servants.[96] Some people from the mountains who had hurried down to find out what had happened found him physically and mentally exhausted, and by transferring him from one small boat to another to escape detection brought him to Messalla, who was not far away. Straight away, before receiving any attention, he despatched a Liburnian to Cornificius and sent a message around the mountains that he was safe; he also ordered everyone to help Cornificius and wrote that he himself would send assistance immediately. He then attended to his own physical needs and took a little rest before setting out by night, escorted by Messalla, for Stylis where Carrinas had three legions ready to sail. He gave orders to Carrinas to cross to the opposite shore, to the point where he himself intended to cross, and wrote to Agrippa requesting him to send a force under Laronius to Cornificius since he was in danger[97]. Once again he sent Maecenas to Rome in response to revolutionary stirrings, and some agitators were punished. He also sent Messalla to Puteoli to fetch the First legion to Vibo. 113. This was the Messalla whom the triumvirs had proscribed at Rome and whose killer had been

promised money and freedom; he had fled to Brutus and Cassius, and when they had died had negotiated the surrender of their fleet to Antonius. I think it right to recall this here as a model of Roman virtue, that Messalla, when he had the man who proscribed him alone and between the jaws of disaster, cared for him as his commander-in-chief and saved his life.

Cornificius was easily able to repel the enemy from his fortifications, but since he was threatened by a shortage of supplies he drew his forces up for battle and invited combat; but Pompeius, who expected that they would surrender from starvation, would not close with men whose sole hope lay in fighting. Cornificius therefore placed the unarmed fugitives from the ships in the middle of his force and began a difficult march, under bombardment from the cavalry when they were on level ground and from the light-armed troops when the road was rough; the latter were Numidians from Africa who hurled their javelins from long range and gave the slip to the men who ran out to pursue them.   **114.** On the fourth day the force managed to reach the waterless district which is said to be a stream of lava which on its descent at some time in the past towards the sea swamped and sealed up the springs in the area.[98] The locals travel across this region only at night, because it is full of an ash-like dust from the lava which is liable to choke them. Cornificius and his party were not confident enough to cross it at night, particularly as there was no moon, because they were ignorant of the route and afraid of an ambush. On the other hand they could not stand the conditions by day, and the soles of their feet, especially those of the men who were barefoot, became burnt as a result of the fierce summer heat. Tormented by thirst and unable to go more slowly, they stopped making sorties against their assailants and accepted injuries without being able to offer any defence. When they discovered that another enemy force was in control of the exit, too, from the scorched region, the men who were fit left the weak and the barefoot to look after themselves and charged with remarkable boldness up into the throat of the pass, where they overpowered the enemy with what remained of their strength. But when the next pass too was held against them, they started to lose hope and succumb to thirst, heat, and exhaustion. Cornificius then encouraged them on and pointed out that a spring was near, and they broke through a second time, with considerable losses; but because further enemy troops were holding the spring, they completely lost heart and were on the point of giving up.   **115.** Such was their condition when Laronius, who had been sent by Agrippa with three legions, appeared in the distance. It was not yet clear that he was a friend, but since hope induced the constant expectation that he would turn out to be one, they recovered themselves. And when they also saw the enemy withdrawing from the water, to avoid being trapped between two hostile forces, they shouted for joy as loudly as their strength allowed. Laronius shouted in answer, and they ran to take possession of the spring. They were ordered by their officers not to slake their thirst all at once; but some took no notice, and died as they drank. In this way Cornificius and the part of his army which managed to elude the enemy unexpectedly reached safety with Agrippa at Mylae.[99]

116. Agrippa had just taken Tyndaris, a place which was plentifully stocked with food and well situated for a war of invasion from seaward, and Octavian ferried his infantry and cavalry across to it. The total of his forces in Sicily was twenty-one legions, 20,000 cavalry, and more than 5,000 light-armed. Mylae and the whole coast from Mylae to Naulochus and Cape Pelorus was still held by Pompeius' garrisons, who were particularly afraid of Agrippa and kept fires continuously alight with the intention of torching any naval force that might attack. Pompeius also controlled the passes at either side.[100] Around Tauromenium and in the neighbourhood of Mylae he sealed off the mountain by-ways with fortifications and harassed Octavian as he advanced from Tyndaris, but without giving battle. In the belief that Agrippa was making an assault, he quickly moved over to Pelorus and abandoned the pass at Mylae, which Octavian seized along with Mylae and Artemisium, a little town where they say the cattle of the sun lived and Odysseus fell asleep.[101] 117. When the report about Agrippa proved false, Pompeius was stung* by losing the pass and sent for Tisienus and his forces.[102] Octavian went to confront Tisienus, but lost his way in the area of Mount Myconium, where he spent the night in the open; and when a great thunderstorm broke out, as they do in autumn, members of his bodyguard held a Gaulish shield over him all night.[103] In addition, from Etna there came harsh roars, protracted rumblings, and flames which lit up the army, so that the Germans leapt up from their beds in terror, and the others, who had heard the stories about Etna, were convinced that such extraordinary phenomena meant that streams of lava were also about to engulf them. After this, Octavian ravaged the territory of Palaiste, and when Lepidus had met him with supplies of food they both encamped outside Messana.

118. Because a large number of skirmishes were taking place all over Sicily, but no decisive battle, Octavian sent Taurus to intercept Pompeius'

commissariat and forestall him in occupying the towns which were supplying him. This caused Pompeius great difficulties, and he decided to stake all
on a major engagement. He feared Octavian's infantry, but felt confident in
his own fleet, so he sent a message to ask if Octavian would agree to settle
matters by a naval battle. Octavian on the other hand was afraid of anything
to do with the sea, since until now he had enjoyed no luck on it, but he accepted the challenge because he thought it cowardly to refuse. A day was
fixed, for which 300 ships were got ready by each side in secret, fitted with
every kind of missile, and fighting-towers, and whatever mechanical con-
traptions they could devise. Agrippa in fact devised the 'grab', a piece of
wood two-and-a-half metres long, shod with iron, with a ring at each end;
to one of the rings was attached the grab, which was an iron claw, and to the
other several ropes for winching in the grab when, after being fired from a
catapult, it had hooked an enemy ship.[104]

119. When the day arrived,[105] first came the struggle for advantage and
the shouts of the oarsmen, and then the volleys of missiles such as stones,
flaming arrows, and ordinary arrows, hurled by hand and by catapult. Next,
the ships rammed each other, some amidships, some by the catheads, and
some at the ram, where the shock has the greatest effect in upsetting the
marines and disabling the ship.[106] Some rowed through the enemy lines,
firing missiles and hurling javelins, and the smaller craft picked up men
who fell overboard. Hand-to-hand combat took place; oarsmen displayed
their strength, and helmsmen their skill; cries arose, commanders exhorted
their men, and every mechanical contrivance came into play. The grab was
particularly highly valued: it fell on the ships from long range, because it
was light, and became firmly fixed as soon as it was hauled back by its ropes;
it could not easily be cut by its victims because of the iron sheathing, and its
length made it extremely difficult for anyone cutting the ropes to reach
them; and because the device had never been known before, they had not
fitted sickles to poles. In this unexpected situation they could think of but
one answer, to pull in the opposite direction by rowing astern. But as the
same was done by the enemy, the force exerted by the crews was equal, and
the grab did its work.

120. When the ships lay at close quarters with each other, the crews
fought in all kinds of ways, even leaping across to the opposing vessel. It was
no longer so easy to distinguish the enemy, because for the most part they
used the same arms and equipment and they almost all spoke Latin. The
passwords had been given away as they became mixed up with each other,

and therefore all sorts of traps were sprung by both sides. They ceased to believe men who uttered the passwords, and none of them knew friend from foe as the battle raged and the sea was filled with corpses and weapons and wrecked ships. Nothing was left untried, except fire, which they avoided after the first volleys because ships lay alongside each other. From the land, the infantry of each side looked out to sea, apprehensive and deeply involved, since for them too that was where hope of their own salvation lay. They contributed nothing to the decision, nor could they, however keenly they gazed at the vast deployment of 600 ships and listened to the cries of despair that came in turn from either side.

121. The only thing which distinguished the ships was the colour of their towers, and from this fact Agrippa eventually realized, not without difficulty, that more of Pompeius' ships than of his own had been destroyed. He encouraged the men who were with him with the news that they were now winning and fell again on the enemy with a sustained assault until those directly in his path gave way. These pulled down their towers, turned their ships about, and fled for the straits. Seventeen succeeded in reaching them first, but the rest were cut off by Agrippa. Some ran aground on being pursued to land, and the pursuers in their enthusiasm ran aground with them, or hauled them off as they were being moored, or set fire to them. As for those that were still fighting out at sea, they surrendered when they saw what was happening around them. Octavian's men chanted a paean of victory on the water, and were answered by the infantry on land. Pompeius' men, on the other hand, uttered despondent cries, and Pompeius himself quickly left Naulochus and hurried to Messana. He was so stunned that he gave not a single order concerning his infantry, with the result that Tisienus surrendered and Octavian took over on agreed terms, not only these troops, but also the cavalry when their commanding officers surrendered. Three ships of Octavian's were sunk in the battle, and twenty-eight of Pompeius'; the remainder went up in flames, or were captured, or broke up after running ashore, and only the seventeen escaped to safety.

122. When Pompeius learnt on the road of his infantry's switch of loyalty, he exchanged his commander-in-chief's dress for that of a private person and sent a message ahead to Messana to load everything practicable into the ships, for it had all been made ready a long time previously. He also ordered Plinius to make all speed from Lilybaeum with his eight legions, because he intended to escape with them. Plinius was hurrying on

his way, but when other supporters, garrisons, and military units began to desert, and the enemy started to sail into the straits, Pompeius did not wait even for Plinius; although Messana was well fortified, he took his seventeen ships and fled to Antonius, remembering that he had saved the life of the latter's mother under similar circumstances. In spite of missing him, Plinius reached Messana and took possession of the town. Octavian himself remained in his camp at Naulochus, and ordered Agrippa to take up a position outside Messana; which he did, in company with Lepidus. When Plinius opened negotiations for a truce, Agrippa thought they should wait until the morning for Octavian to arrive, but Lepidus was in favour of granting the truce, and in order to ingratiate himself with Plinius' force made an agreement for them to join the rest of the army in plundering the town. So Plinius' men got an unexpected bonus on top of the personal safety which was the only thing they had actually appealed for, and after pillaging Messana all night in company with Lepidus' soldiers they went into camp with Lepidus.   123. Including these men, Lepidus commanded twenty-two legions and a large number of cavalry. He therefore became very confident and thought he would make himself master of Sicily, on the pretext that he had made the first landing on the island and had received the surrender of more towns. He immediately sent orders to the garrisons not to admit anyone who might come from Octavian, and took possession of all the passes. The next day Octavian arrived and took Lepidus to task through friends, who claimed that he had come to Sicily as Octavian's ally, not to take the island as his own possession; Lepidus' retort was that he had been stripped of his previous authority, which Octavian now exercised alone, and that he would now, if Octavian wished, exchange Africa and Sicily for it. Octavian was angry, and in his fury appeared in person to accuse Lepidus of ingratitude. The two men parted after issuing threats against each other, and at once their guards were differentiated and the ships put out to ride at anchor, because it was rumoured that Lepidus planned to set fire to them.[107]

124. The soldiers were exasperated at the prospect of fighting another civil war and never being rid of internal conflicts. Even the men in Lepidus' army did not regard Octavian and Lepidus as comparable; on the contrary they admired Octavian's courage and were well aware of Lepidus' laziness. They also criticized Lepidus over the sack of Messana, when they had found themselves on the same footing as the troops they had defeated. When Octavian heard this, he sent out agents to explain secretly to indi-

viduals what was in their best interests, and undermined the loyalty of a considerable number of men, particularly the ex-Pompeians who feared that their terms of surrender would not be secure until Octavian approved them. Thanks to his own inertia, Lepidus was still unaware of the situation when Octavian arrived at his camp, escorted by a large group of cavalry, which he left by the outer defences, and entered with a few companions. Passing along the lines, he swore to everyone that he did not wish to be at war. As those who saw him saluted him as their commander-in-chief, the Pompeians whose loyalty had been tampered with were the first to converge on him and beg him to pardon them. He replied that he was amazed at the fact that men who were asking for pardon were not yet acting according to their own interests. Understanding what he meant, they immediately snatched up their standards and went over to his side, and others began to take their tents down. 125. Alerted by the uproar, Lepidus rushed out of his tent to take up arms. Weapons were then thrown, one of Octavian's bodyguards was killed, and Octavian himself was hit on the breastplate; but the weapon failed to penetrate to the skin, and he escaped by running to his cavalry. The men in one of Lepidus' outposts jeered at him as he ran, and his anger was not satisfied until he had captured and destroyed the post. The commanders of other outposts went over from Lepidus to Octavian, some immediately, others when it was dark, some without being approached, others on the pretence of being harassed (though not seriously) by the cavalry. A few continued to resist the attacks and beat them off, for Lepidus had sent reinforcements out to all of them. When the reinforcements themselves changed sides, the remainder of Lepidus' troops, even any who still remained loyal, began to change their views. Again it was those Pompeians still with him who were the first to desert, a few at a time; and when Lepidus gave the others arms to stop them, the men who had been armed for this purpose collected their own standards and departed to join Octavian along with the others. As they went off, Lepidus threatened them, pleaded with them, and caught hold of the standards, saying he would not let go, until one of the standard-bearers said he would let go when he was dead, and Lepidus was frightened and let go. 126. The last to go were the cavalry, who sent a messenger to Octavian to enquire if they should kill Lepidus, as he was no longer their commander-in-chief; but Octavian forbade it. In this way Lepidus, through unexpectedly encountering a general resistance to orders, was rapidly deprived of a magnificent opportunity and a magnificent army. He changed his dress and ran to

Octavian, with the spectators running along beside him as if they were at a show. Octavian stood up to meet him as he approached, prevented him abasing himself although he wished to do so, and sent him to Rome dressed just as he was, a commander-in-chief no longer, but a private individual and a nobody, except for the chief priesthood he held.[108] And so a man who had many times commanded armies, and held the office of triumvir, and appointed others to magistracies, and condemned so many of his peers to death by proscription, passed the rest of his life as a private citizen and begged favours from some of the men he had once proscribed, who subsequently became magistrates.

127. As for Pompeius, Octavian neither pursued him nor ordered others to do so. Perhaps he was wary of invading a sphere of authority that belonged not to him but to Antonius; or else he wanted to see what would happen and what action Antonius would take towards Pompeius, so that he would have grounds for a quarrel if the action were unjustified (it having long been suspected that because of their love of power he and Antonius would fall out with each other once they had eliminated third parties); or else it was, as Octavian himself afterwards said, that Pompeius was not one of his father's murderers.

When Octavian gathered his army together, he had forty-five legions, 25,000 cavalry, half as many light-armed troops again as cavalry, and 600 warships. The great mass of cargo vessels he sent back to their owners, although there was a huge number of them. He rewarded the army for their victory, paying part of the money now and promising the rest later, and he distributed crowns and honours and pardoned Pompeius' officers. 128. As a result he was full of pride; but heaven showed its jealousy of his pride, and his army mutinied, particularly his own soldiers, insisting on immediate discharge and the enjoyment of the same rewards as had been paid to the veterans of Philippi. Although Octavian knew that the two struggles could not be compared, he nevertheless promised that he would reward them fairly, along with the men serving under Antonius, when the latter returned. As for their refusal to serve, he reminded them in a threatening way of the traditional laws, oaths, and punishments. When they gave him a sceptical hearing he moderated his tone, to avoid any trouble from the troops he had recently subdued, and said that he would act in concert with Antonius to discharge them at a suitable moment. For the present, he would lead them not in further civil wars, for these had fortunately ended, but against the Illyrians and other foreign tribes who were disturbing the hard-won peace, and make them rich from that source. But they again refused to serve until they had received the rewards and honours due from their earlier campaigns. Octavian denied that he was putting off giving honours, even as things were, and said that although he had made many awards he would grant additional crowns to the legions, and to the centurions and military tribunes the purple-bordered toga and the status of decurion in their home towns.[109] As he was continuing to make more awards of this sort, a military tribune, Ofillius, called out that crowns and purple were toys for children, but that soldiers' rewards were land and money. The gathering shouted that he was right, and Octavian left the platform in anger while the soldiers thronged around the tribune congratulating him and heaping abuse on anyone who would not stand beside him. Ofillius said he needed no supporters in such a just cause, but by the next morning he had disappeared and it was never known what had happened. 129. The soldiers were frightened and no longer spoke out individually, but formed groups to call collectively for their discharge. Octavian conciliated their leaders in various ways, and granted their discharge, if they wished, to any who had served at Philippi and Mutina, because they were overdue for it. These numbered 2,000, and he immediately discharged them and sent them away from the island to prevent the spread of disaffection, saying only to the veterans of Mutina that he would give them what he had promised them at that time, although they had now been discharged in this way. Then he went to the rest of the army and called them to witness that the mutineers had broken their oaths by being released from service against the wishes of their commander-in-chief. He commended those who remained with him, encouraged them with the hope that he would soon discharge them, so that none of them changed his mind,* and promised that when they were discharged he would make them wealthy, but for the moment would give them each an extra 500 denarii. He then imposed a levy of 1,600 talents on Sicily[110]. He also appointed governors for Africa and Sicily, to both of which he allocated troops, and sent Antonius' ships over to Tarentum. As for the remainder of the army, he despatched part ahead to Italy by sea and brought the rest across from Sicily under his own command.

130. While he was still on his way back to Rome, the senate voted him countless honours and gave him the choice of whether to accept them all or only those he approved of. Senate and people, garlanded, went to meet him a long way from the city and escorted him to the temples and from there to his house. On the following day, he gave addresses to the senate

and to the people, detailing his achievements and his administration from the beginning until that time; he also published a pamphlet containing a written-up version of what he had said. He proclaimed peace and contentment now that the civil wars were finally ended, and remitted unpaid instalments of the special taxes and cancelled debts owed by the collectors and contractors of regular taxes. From among the honours that had been voted him, he accepted an ovation, and the institution of an annual festival on the anniversary of his victory, and in the forum a golden statue of himself, dressed as he was when he had entered Rome, standing on top of a column decorated with the rams of ships.[111] The statue is still there, bearing the inscription PEACE, LONG DISRUPTED BY CIVIL DISCORD, HE RESTORED ON LAND AND SEA. 131. The people wished to transfer the high priesthood, which one man customarily holds for life, from Lepidus to himself, but he would not accept it or listen to any request to put Lepidus to death. He sent sealed letters to every military camp, with orders that they were all to be opened on the same day and the instructions carried out. These concerned the slaves who had absconded and enlisted as soldiers during the time of conflict. Pompeius had asked for them to be given their freedom, and although the senate and the terms of the treaty had conceded this, they were arrested on a single day and brought to Rome.[112] Octavian returned to their owners, or to the owners' heirs, the slaves who belonged to Romans or Italians, and likewise in the case of Sicilians, but he had those who were not claimed put to death in the towns from which they had actually absconded.

132. This was apparently the end of the civil conflicts of the period, and Octavian, who was then in his twenty-eighth year, was given a place among their gods by the towns. Both Rome itself and the rest of Italy were suffering from a high degree of organized brigandage, and what was occurring was more like open raiding than furtive robbery. Sabinus was therefore appointed by Octavian to deal with the problem.[113] He put to death a large number of those he caught and within a year brought all districts a peace that needed no armed force to maintain it. It is said that the institution and organization of the corps of *vigiles* go back to this operation.[114] Octavian was much admired for such a swift and unexpected restoration of order. He handed over much state business to the annual magistrates to administer in the traditional way, and began to burn documents relating to the civil conflict. He also maintained that he would surrender all his special powers when Antonius came back from the Parthian campaign, in the belief, he

said, that the latter was also willing to lay down his office now that the civil wars were over.[115] The Romans acclaimed him for this and made him tribune for life, encouraging him by the gift of the permanent office to give up his previous one.[116] But he took it in addition to the other, and wrote independently to Antonius about their power. The latter gave his instructions to Bibulus, who was leaving him to meet Octavian; he also appointed provincial governors in a similar way himself, and planned to join in the campaign against the Illyrians.[117]

133. On leaving Sicily to take refuge with Antonius, Pompeius touched at the Lacinian promontory and plundered the sanctuary of Hera, which was rich in offerings. He put in to harbour at Mytilene and spent some time there, where his father had left him and his mother for safety, when he was still a boy, at the time of the war with Gaius Caesar, and had collected him after his defeat.[118] Antonius was campaigning in Media against the Medes and the Parthians, and Pompeius' intention was to surrender to him on his return. When he heard of Antonius' defeat, its extent exaggerated by rumour, his hopes rose again and he thought he might either succeed to Antonius, if he were dead, or share power with him on his return; and Labienus, who had recently overrun Asia, was constantly in his mind.[119] Such were his thoughts, when news came that Antonius had returned to Alexandria. Keeping both schemes in view, he sent intermediaries to him, entrusting himself to him and making out that he was a friend and ally while in reality he was spying on Antonius' affairs. To the rulers of Thrace and Pontus he secretly sent other agents, with the idea that he would escape through Pontus to Armenia if these plans failed. He also established contact with the Parthians, in the hope that they would eagerly welcome a Roman general, and particularly the son of Magnus, for the remainder of the war against Antonius. He refitted his ships and drilled the troops he had on board them, making a pretence that he was either afraid of Octavian or preparing to help Antonius.

134. As soon as Antonius heard about Pompeius, he appointed Titius[120] to the command against him, and told him to take a fleet and soldiers from Syria: if Pompeius offered resistance Titius was to conduct all-out war against him, but if he surrendered Titius was to bring him with due respect to Antonius. When the delegation from Pompeius arrived Antonius gave them an audience, and they delivered this message: 'Pompeius has sent us when it was quite possible for him, if he had decided on war, to sail to

Spain, which is well disposed to him for his father's sake and is currently inviting him to do this; but he prefers to join you in keeping the peace and to fight under you, should that be necessary. This is not the first time he has made this offer. He made it while he still controlled Sicily and plundered Italy, at the time when he saved your mother's life and sent her to you. If you had accepted it, he would not have lost Sicily (because you would not have provided Octavian with the ships to use against him), nor would you have been defeated in the Parthian war thanks to Octavian's failure to send you the troops he raised; and you would now be master of Italy as well as the territory you then possessed. But although you failed to accept his offer, which would have been most opportune at the time, he now begs you not to be ensnared again and again by Octavian's words and the family tie you have contracted with him, and to remember that Octavian went to war with Pompeius without any pretext in spite of having a treaty and a family connection with him, that he stripped Lepidus, his partner in office, of his portion of power, and that he did not share the fruits of either success with you.   135. You are now the only remaining obstacle to Octavian's acquisition of the sole power he so much desires. He would already be locked in struggle with you if Pompeius were not still in the way. Of course you too can probably foresee these developments for yourself, but goodwill makes Pompeius draw them to your attention, because he prefers an innocent and generous-minded man to one who is devious, scheming, and inwardly rotten. Nor does he make any criticism of you for lending the ships which you were forced to give Octavian to use against him, because you needed to exchange them for troops for your Parthian campaign; but he recalls the fact to remind you that the troops were never sent. In short, Pompeius places himself in your hands, together with the ships he still has and his soldiers, who are extremely loyal and have not deserted him even in his flight. If you keep the peace, you will earn great credit for having saved the life of Magnus' son; and if you fight, you will acquire significant resources for the war which is to come.'

136. When the envoys had finished, Antonius revealed to them the instructions he had given Titius, and said that if Pompeius was sincere, he would come to him escorted by Titius. While these negotiations were going on, Pompeius' ambassadors to the Parthians were captured by Antonius' commanders and brought to Alexandria. After he had heard the details, Antonius summoned Pompeius' envoys and showed them the captives. Even then, the envoys pleaded for indulgence towards a young man in

desperate straits who was forced by his fear that Antonius might not treat him as a friend into making advances to Rome's deadliest enemies; and they promised that when he knew Antonius' intentions, he would demonstrate that he had no further need to probe or scheme. Antonius believed them, because in every sphere of behaviour his character was straightforward, generous, and innocent.

137. Meanwhile Furnius,[121] the governor of Asia, allowed Pompeius, who caused no trouble after his arrival, into his province, because he was not strong enough to stop him by force and he did not yet know Antonius' decision; but when he saw Pompeius drilling his men he conscripted some of the provincials and sent urgently for Ahenobarbus, who as governor of the neighbouring province had an army, and for Amyntas from the other direction.[122] They came immediately, but Pompeius reproached them for thinking he could be an enemy when he had sent envoys to Antonius and was waiting for his answer. Even as he said this he was planning to capture Ahenobarbus through the treachery of one Curius, a member of Ahenobarbus' entourage, in the expectation that Ahenobarbus would be a bargaining counter of some value to himself. However, the conspiracy was discovered. Curius was put to death after trial by the Romans present, and Pompeius executed Theodorus, an ex-slave who alone was privy to the plan, for having divulged it. Since he no longer expected to outwit Furnius and his companions, he captured Lampsacus by treachery. This town contained many Italians from Gaius Caesar's colonial settlement, whom he immediately enlisted on generous terms. He now possessed 200 cavalry and three legions of foot, and mounted an assault on Cyzicus by land and sea. The townspeople beat him back on both fronts, for there was in fact a small force of Antonius' soldiers in Cyzicus, who were guarding some gladiators being kept there for him, and Pompeius withdrew to the Harbour of the Achaeans to reprovision.[123] 138. Furnius refused to give battle, but kept shadowing Pompeius with a large force of cavalry and preventing him from getting supplies or winning over any towns. Pompeius, lacking cavalry, therefore made a frontal assault on Furnius' camp accompanied by a surprise attack from the rear after an outflanking move. The result was that Furnius, who was facing Pompeius, was driven out of his camp by the attack from behind. His men fled across the plain of the Scamander, where many of them were killed as they were pursued by Pompeius, since the plain was waterlogged after rainstorms. The survivors withdrew for the moment, since they were in no condition to fight. Pompeius was

welcomed by people from Mysia, the Propontis, and regions on either side, who had been impoverished by the constant exactions and gladly enlisted in his service as mercenaries, particularly because of the reputation he had won by his victory at the Harbour of the Achaeans, but he was short of cavalry and consequently experienced difficulty in foraging. At this point he heard that a squadron of Italian horse, which had been sent by Octavia who was wintering in Athens, was on its way to Antonius. He immediately despatched some men with money to bribe them, but they were arrested by Antonius' governor of Macedonia and the money divided out among the cavalry. **139**. None the less, he captured Nicaea and Nicomedia, which spectacularly improved his finances, and great prospects suddenly and unexpectedly opened up for him. But Furnius, who had taken up a position not far from Pompeius, was first of all reinforced at the beginning of spring by the seventy ships which survived from those which Antonius had lent to Octavian to use against Pompeius (Octavian having released them after his victory in Sicily), and then by a force from Syria under Titius, comprising another 120 ships and a substantial number of soldiers. This whole fleet swooped on Proconnesus, and Pompeius in fear burnt his own ships and armed the rowers, thinking that they would all do better as a unified force on land. But Cassius of Parma, Nasidius, Saturninus, Thermus, Antistius, and the other prominent men who still supported Pompeius, including the most prestigious of them, Fannius, and Pompeius' father-in-law Libo, saw that even after the arrival of Titius, whom Antonius had placed in charge of the operations against him, Pompeius refused to abandon the struggle against superior forces; so they despaired of him and after negotiating terms for themselves left to join Antonius.[124]

140. Now bereft of supporters, Pompeius began to retreat to the interior of Bithynia, reportedly making for Armenia. He had stealthily broken camp in the dark and was being pursued by Furnius and Titius, and Amyntas as well. By making a tremendous effort, they caught up with him in the evening and encamped around a hill, each separately, without entrenchments or palisades, because it was late and they were exhausted. That night Pompeius attacked them in this state with 3,000 light-armed troops. Many of them were killed while they were still asleep or as they sprang up from the ground, and some even ran away without their arms in a quite disgraceful manner. I think that if at that moment Pompeius had made a night attack with his entire force, or at least followed up after the rout, he might have won a decisive victory over them. But as it was heaven blinded him and he ignored this chance too, gaining nothing more from such a notable success than the ability to continue his march to the interior. His opponents, having collected themselves, followed him and interfered with his food supplies, until he was in danger of starving and made a request to talk to Furnius, who had been a friend of Magnus, and enjoyed greater prestige than the others and was of a more trustworthy character. 141. Selecting a place with a river between them, Pompeius stated that he had sent an embassy to Antonius, and went on to say that since he needed provisions for this considerable time, and enjoyed no help from them, he had taken this course of action. 'If it is by Antonius' decision that you are in the field against me, he is blind to the impending war and is taking poor counsel for his own interests; but if you are pre-empting that decision, I appeal to you and implore you to await the return of the embassy I sent to him, or to receive me now and take me to him. I will surrender to you alone, Furnius, and I ask you to give me your word on this, that you will bring me alive to Antonius.' He said this because he trusted Antonius' good nature and was afraid only of the stages between. Furnius replied, 'Someone who wanted to surrender to Antonius would have gone to him straight away, or awaited his reply quietly at Mytilene, but someone who wanted to make war would have done exactly what you did. Why do you need to tell me what I know already? If you have changed your mind, you ought not to set us commanders against each other; you should surrender to Titius, because it was Titius whom Antonius put in charge of the operation against you. As for the promise you ask of me, you can perfectly well ask Titius for it. Antonius' orders are to put you to death if you fight against us, but to send you to him with honour if you place yourself in our hands.' 142. Pompeius expressed anger with Titius for his ingratitude in agreeing to undertake this military campaign against him, because he had saved Titius' life when Titius had been taken prisoner. As well as being angry, he also thought it demeaning that he, Pompeius, should be a suppliant before Titius, a man of insufficient distinction, and he was wary of him, both because he suspected him of possessing an untrustworthy character and because he was aware of an old injury he had done him before the act of kindness. He made another attempt to surrender to Furnius, begging him to receive him. When Furnius refused, he even threatened to surrender to Amyntas, but Furnius said that not even Amyntas would countenance an act so insulting to the man who had been placed in overall charge by Antonius, and they parted. It was the view of Furnius' entourage that shortage would force Pompeius to surrender himself to Titius the next day. That night, however, Pompeius left the customary fires burning, with the trumpeters sounding the watches of the night as usual, and slipped out of the camp together with his crack troops, without previously telling even them where he intended to go. His plan was to reach the sea and set fire to Titius' fleet. He might have succeeded had Scaurus not deserted, and in spite of being ignorant of the plan revealed Pompeius' departure and the route he took. Then Amyntas, with 1,500 cavalry, set off in pursuit of Pompeius, with none. On Amyntas' approach, Pompeius' men deserted, some of them slipping away and others openly changing sides. And so Pompeius, isolated and afraid now of his own side, a man who had thought it beneath him to surrender on terms to Titius, surrendered unconditionally to Amyntas.[125]

143. In this way Sextus Pompeius was captured, Pompeius Magnus' remaining son. He had lost his father while still not yet of age, and his brother when a young man, and after that had concealed himself for a long time and taken to clandestine piracy in Spain until it was realized that he was Pompeius' son and numbers of people flocked to him. He then carried out his raids more openly, and after Gaius Caesar's death mounted a vigorous campaign: he assembled a large force, captured ships, money, and islands, became master of the western sea, and caused Italy to know starvation and his enemies to come to an agreement with him on his own terms. His greatest achievement was to be the saviour of Rome at the time of the proscriptions, when she suffered comprehensive ruin, by rescuing many of her finest citizens, who at the time of his death were living in their native land. But the malevolence of heaven saw to it that although chance gave him plenty of admirable opportunities, he never took the offensive against his enemies, but simply continued to defend himself.[126]

144. Such was Pompeius. After his capture, Titius absorbed his troops into Antonius' army and put him to death at Miletus aged thirty-nine, either on his own initiative because he was angry over the old wrong and felt no gratitude for Pompeius' subsequent act of kindness, or in fact on Antonius' orders. There are those who say that Plancus, the governor of Syria, and not Antonius, gave the orders, because he had been authorized in urgent cases to sign letters for Antonius and use his seal. And of these, some think that Plancus wrote with Antonius' knowledge, Antonius being ashamed to write himself because of Pompeius' name and Cleopatra's sympathy with him on account of his father Magnus; but others hold that Plancus acted independently with exactly these considerations in mind, in

order to guard against the possibility that Pompeius, acting in concert with Cleopatra, might disturb the auspicious respect which Antonius and Octavian had for each other.

145. After Pompeius' death Antonius set out on a second expedition against Armenia. Octavian proceeded against the Illyrians, since Italy was being raided not only by those of them who had never been subject to Rome but also by those who had rebelled during the civil wars. I have no detailed knowledge of the Illyrian wars, and as their length does not justify separate treatment and there is nowhere else to relate them, I have thought it best to insert their history, down to the time when the capture of Illyria brought them to completion, in an earlier book and append them to that of neighbouring Macedonia.

NOTES

1. Fragment 19, to be found in Appianus, *Historia Romana*, vol I, ed. Viereck–Roos, pp. 534–5 (trans. and discussed by Gowing, *The Triumviral Narratives of Appian and Cassius Dio*, Michigan University Press, 1992, 13–16).

2. The letter: *ad Antoninum Pium*, 10.2 (van Hout); discussed by C. R. Haines, *Classical Quarterly* 8 (1914), 119, and see also E. Champlin, *Fronto and Antonine Rome* (Cambridge, Mass., 1980), 98–100.

3. *Scriptores Historiae Augustae, Vita Marci* 11.6.

4. Preface, 2.

5. See H.-G. Pflaum, *Les Procurateurs equestres sous le Haut-empire romain* (Paris, 1950), 204–5.

6. *Biblioth. cod.* 57, pp. 15, 21b–17, 21a, Bekker.

7. E. Gabba, *Appiani Bellorum Civilium Liber Primus* (2nd ed., Florence, 1967), Introduction, xiii.

8. Caesar's ghost, in Shakespeare's *Julius Caesar*; Appian, *Civil Wars* IV.134; Plutarch, *Brutus* 36.

9. Such comparisons (*synkriseis*) were a regular feature of history and biography: see, e.g., Livy (9.17–19) on Alexander and the Roman generals of his age, Sallust (*Catiline* 54) on Caesar and Cato, and above all the Prefaces of Plutarch's *Parallel Lives*.

10. *Cicero's Letters to His Friends*, trans. D. R. Shackleton-Bailey (Penguin Books, 1978), no. 22 (=*ad Familiares* 5.12). None of Lucceius' works has survived.

11. Names particularly associated with this type of history are those of Douris of Samos, Timaeus, and Phylarchus.

12. *Histories* 1.1 (= *Rise of the Roman Empire,* trans. Ian Scott-Kilvert (Penguin Books, 1979) 41).

13. Preface, 8.

14. ibid., 8.

15. ibid., 12.

16. ibid., 8.

17. Appian says elsewhere that *theoblabeia* 'destroys reasoning powers' (*Syriaca* 28).

18. Preface, 13.

19. I.3 and 9.

20. Examples are IV.38 (on Bibulus) and IV.49.

21. J. L. Moles, 'Fate, Apollo, and M. Junius Brutus', *American Journal of Philology* 104 (1983), 249–56. Cf. Plutarch, *Brutus* 24.4–7, Valerius Maximus 1.5.7.

22. Hermogenes 16.22 (2nd–3rd century AD)

23. The essay on the subject by Appian's younger contemporary Lucian of Samosata survives ('How History Should be Written').

24. D. Magnino, in W. Haase and H. Temporini (eds.), *Aufstieg und Niedergang der römischen Welt, II: Prinzipät*, vol. 34.1 (1993), 546.

BOOK I

1. This 'secession of the *plebs*', as it is usually called, is traditionally dated to 494 BC (there were others in 450 and 287 BC). It represents a kind of strike by the class of citizenry (evidently not the most impoverished) who were wealthy enough to own effective fighting equipment. They thus formed the (part-time) army of the infant Republic, which would have been defenceless without them.

2. The seceding citizens formed themselves into an impromptu assembly to elect leaders (the tribunes) and vote on other questions, though this assembly and its decisions occupied an ambiguous place in Roman political life until the third century BC. See further Appendix (*A*), on the *comitia tributa*.

3. Appian operates with the time-honoured schema, canonized by the great history of Livy, of the 'struggle of the orders', that is, the structuring of Roman history in terms of the opposition between the under-privileged *plebs*, or common people, and the socially, politically, and economically privileged upper class to which senators belonged and whose interests they defended.

4. In 491 BC.

5. In 133 BC.

6. Proscription was introduced by Sulla in 82 BC (see ch. 95). Lists of names were posted in public declaring that the persons specified were outlaws (and their property therefore forfeit), and that a price would be paid for their heads. The object was simultaneously to exact political revenge and fill the coffers of the state.

7. The latter half of this chapter refers principally to the period between 90 and 82 BC, when the Social War was immediately followed by the civil war between Sulla and the supporters of Marius.

8. At the end of 82 BC. See chs. 98–9 for the dictatorship, and Sulla's election to it.

9. At the end of 50 BC.

10. The battle of Pharsalus, 48 BC. See Book II, chs. 29–90 for the events here alluded to.

11. Caesar's dictatorship was not conferred on him for life until early in 44 BC, but he had in fact held the office for ten days at the end of 49, for a year from late 48 to late 47, and then continuously, with annual renewal, from the spring of 46.

12. Caesar was murdered on 15 March 44 BC.

13. Appian, here and in many other places, speaks of 'the so-called knights' to

distinguish the members of the non-senatorial upper class at Rome from ordinary cavalry troopers in the army. The latter had, by the time of the late Republic, ceased to be recruited from Roman citizens and were provided as auxiliary troops from nations such as the Numidians and Gauls. I have used the expression 'equestrian class' (or 'order') to avoid the connotations of the word 'knight' in English.

14. Octavius is the future emperor Augustus. Appian henceforth, like all historians in antiquity, calls him Caesar. This edition adheres to the modern convention of calling him Octavian before 27 BC (when he took the name Augustus) in order not to confuse him with his great-uncle, whom Appian calls either 'the earlier Caesar' or 'Gaius Caesar' and whom we know as Julius Caesar (see n. 12 to Book III, ch. 12).

15. In 31 BC.

16. Egypt was captured in 30 BC.

17. Book I in fact ends in 70 BC, eight years after Sulla's death, the events of 78–70 being treated as a postscript to Sulla's actions.

18. Appian conforms with the official Augustan line that the war against Antonius was a foreign war waged against the Egyptian queen and her renegade Roman consort. The *Civil Wars* ends with the death of Sextus Pompeius in 35 BC. The *Egyptian History* itself (in four books) does not survive.

19. Such new towns or formal additions to existing towns were called 'colonies' (*coloniae*), from the Latin *colonus*, which means a farmer or settler. It was from the fourth century onwards, above all between 340 and 170 BC, that the Romans systematically practised this means of exploiting the conquests they made in Italy.

20. The second half of this sentence (after the semicolon) applies to the period following the end of the Second Punic War, as a result of which the Romans found themselves in possession of large quantities of confiscated land, particularly in the south of Italy, which they could neither occupy by the traditional means just referred to by Appian, nor set up a workable system to lease properly. The problems described by Appian from this point on are those of the second century BC.

21. On the problem of what Appian means by 'Italians' in Book I, see Appendix (G).

22. The demands of military service, which the Romans required of their allies as well as of their own citizens, created great difficulties for the smallholder, and accelerated the drift from the country to the towns and to Rome. It has been estimated that the wars of the second century regularly kept between 25,000 and 75,000 Italians, mainly of the peasant class, on military service abroad. Meanwhile the slave labour force had been greatly increased by an influx of prisoners-of-war and the Mediterranean slave trade had been enabled to expand.

23. The law which limited individual ownership of land to 500 *iugera* (125 hectares) was most probably an updating, in the earlier second century, of the provisions of the Lex Licinia of 367 BC. This limit was certainly in force by 167 BC, since it was referred to by the elder Cato in that year in terms which imply that it was topical.

24. Tiberius Gracchus became tribune in 133 BC.

25. In 135 BC an uprising of slaves had taken place in Sicily, where there were many large estates. The rebels numbered some 60,000 and were ably led by Eunus, a Syrian, and Cleon, a Cilician: their aim was to occupy and hold Sicily. The war was not brought to an end until 132 BC.

26. For an explanation of 'colonies' see n. 19.

27. According to Plutarch, Octavius' replacement was Mucius.

28. Gaius Sempronius Gracchus was only twenty years old and not yet the holder of even the most junior elected office; on the other hand Ap. Claudius was a very senior man who had held the offices of consul in 143 and censor in 136 BC.

29. Repeated election to the other magistracies, except after a substantial interval, had been barred by the Lex Villia of 180 BC, but it appears that it was custom alone which had prevented repeated or consecutive tribunates since the semi-legendary ten-year occupancy of the office by C. Licinius Stolo and L. Sextius from 376 to 367 BC.

30. It is not clear how Gracchus, who clearly was not presiding, could have adjourned the assembly. Perhaps he used his veto to stop the proceedings.

31. See chs. 98–9.

32. Appian does not advance the most likely explanation of Nasica's garb, that he was adopting the ritual dress (*caput velatum* or *cinctus Gabinus*) appropriate on certain occasions to one who was about to make a sacrifice, and was in this way attempting to sanctify his action.

33. The elder Tiberius Sempronius Gracchus had been consul in 177 and 163 and had distinguished himself in Spain, where he had been an excellent commander and governor, much trusted by the Spaniards. He had died soon after 153, so that his sons Tiberius (b. 163 BC) and Gaius (b. 153 BC) were brought up by his widow Cornelia, daughter of P. Scipio Africanus (236–184 BC), who defeated Hannibal at Zama in 202 BC.

34. In 133 BC Attalus III, the ruler of Pergamum, bequeathed his kingdom to Rome. Aristonicus, the illegitimate son of Attalus' predecessor Eumenes II, refused to acquiesce and raised a revolt against Rome which was not finally quelled until 129 BC.

35. Appian omits to note that Tiberius Gracchus had already been replaced by P. Licinius Crassus, who became consul in 131 and died fighting against Aristonicus in Asia at the very end of that year. Appius died soon after, in 130. C. Papirius Carbo was tribune in 131 or 130.

36. P. Cornelius Scipio Africanus the younger (185–129 BC) sacked and obliterated Carthage in 146 BC. He is usually known in modern writings as Scipio Aemilianus to distinguish him from his adoptive grandfather of the same name, who defeated Hannibal. Cornelia, the mother of the Gracchi, was his (adoptive) aunt, and Tiberius and Gaius themselves were not only his adoptive cousins, but also his brothers-in-law by his marriage to their sister Sempronia (see ch. 20).

37. C. Sempronius Tuditanus was consul in 129 BC.

38. In 147 (his first consulship) Aemilianus had been under age, and by 134 (his second) it had been made illegal, by a law of 151, to hold a second consulship.

39. This was in 125 BC.

40. To hold office in 123 BC.

41. It is inconceivable that Gracchus' opponents could not field ten *candidates* for the tribunate; but to be elected at all a man had to secure the votes of at least eighteen of the thirty-five voting units (the tribes; see Appendix, *A* ii) and so the Gracchans, who were obviously in a majority in the tribes, could prevent the *election* of more than nine tribunes. The way would then be open to accept another candidate, Gaius Gracchus.

42. It is unlikely that Appian means that everything that now follows belongs after Gaius' re-election in the autumn of 123 BC. Rather, he proceeds by explaining first how it was that Gaius secured re-election, then with that fact out of the way embarks on an account of his whole period as tribune. Our other main source, Plutarch, for analogous reasons gives the impression of placing almost all Gaius' legislation in his *first* tribunate.

43. The standing court in question (and probably no others existed at this date in spite of Appian's plural) was that which dealt with charges of extortion made against provincial governors. By 'transfer' of the court Appian means that the jury, which had previously been composed of senators, that is the very group from which governors were drawn, would now be selected from the equestrian class. Large fragments of Gracchus' actual law survive. (For the equestrian order, see Appendix, *B*.)

44. For the meaning of 'Italians', see Appendix (*G*).

45. In fact, the equestrian jurors simply profited from the legal accident whereby only senatorial jurors could be arraigned for bribery (see ch. 35) – the relevant law presumably dating from before 123 BC and therefore not envisaging the possibility of jurors who were not senators.

46. See n. 19.

47. Latins who happened to be in Rome had the right to vote in the Roman assemblies, in a single tribe determined by the presiding magistrate on the day. For the broader picture, see Appendix (*D*).

48. Flaccus was the only ex-consul in Roman history to hold the office of tribune (as distinct from the tribunician *power* held by Augustus and his imperial successors).

49. See n. 36. The new colony was to be named Junonia.

50. This was in 121 BC, when Gracchus, having failed to win a third term as tribune, had become a private citizen.

51. This temple, at the south-east corner of the republican forum, stood on a high podium and was a building useful to control in a riot.

52. The Greek says 'evict them by force on these pretexts', but this cannot be right and I have adopted an easy correction.

53. The manuscripts of Appian give this man's name as 'Borius' or 'Bourius'. The correction to 'Thorius' rests on two passages of Cicero (*Brutus* 136; *de Oratore* II, 284). His tribunate is to be dated between 114 and 111 BC.

54. This third law is probably to be identified with the surviving but fragmentary Lex Agraria of 111 BC, whose main thrust is to convert public land occupied by individuals into fully private, rent-free, land. Its author is unknown.

55. Some words must have been lost from the text towards the end of this sentence: it is impossible that the decline of the Roman population (etc.) was caused, even in Appian's view, by mere suspension of court hearings, as the text would have it. (There exists an inscription from the site of Carthage which has been held to show that the land commission ceased to function about 118 BC, but it is not clear which Gracchus Appian means.)

56. The best manuscripts of Appian give the consul's name as Caepio, though all modern editors follow the Renaissance correction to Scipio. I accept the view of J. A. North ('Deconstructing stone theatres', *Apodosis: Essays in honour of Dr W. W. Cruickshank,* London, St Paul's School, (1992), 75–83) that the protagonists of this episode, which is not recorded elsewhere, are L. Cassius Longinus, the consul of 107 BC, and Q. Servilius Caepio, the consul of 106 BC. The usual theory (reading 'Scipio' for 'Caepio') holds that Appian has erroneously transferred to 111 BC, when one of the consuls was a Scipio Nasica Serapio and one of the praetors the same Lucius Cassius Longinus, somewhat similar events which occurred in or soon after 154 BC and involved another Scipio Nasica (Corculum), who was *not* consul at the time, and a Gaius Cassius Longinus (see Livy, *Periochae* XLVIII; Velleius I, 15.3 (with the emendation of Caepio to Scipio!); Valerius Maximus II, 4.2).

57. Q. Caecilius Metellus, normally referred to as Metellus Numidicus, became consul in 109 BC and censor in 102. His unco-operative colleague was his first cousin C. Metellus Caprarius, who had been consul in 113. L. Appuleius Saturninus held the office of tribune (for the first time) in 103 BC. 'Glaucia' is C. Servilius Glaucia.

58. Appian is in error, as only a tribune could preside over tribunician elections. In fact, Glaucia was tribune in 101, and thus could preside over the elections for the following year, when Saturninus became tribune for the second time. However, since Glaucia was already praetor-designate for 100 (contrary to normal practice, which allowed for at least one year's interval between offices), Appian's confusion is explicable.

59. In 100 BC.

60. i.e. Cisalpine Gaul, the Po valley.

61. Such clauses were not unusual in legislation of this period (see the Latin law from Bantia, and the so-called 'piracy law' from Delphi), and it is unlikely that this was the first occasion on which such a clause had been inserted in a law.

62. The identification of 'the Italians' with the 'rural population' of the preceding sentence appears complete. See Appendix (G).

63. This was the normal formula of banishment.

64. That is to say, he became tribune-elect for 99.

65. His name was L. Equitius.

66. C. Memmius had held the offices of tribune in 111 and praetor by 102 BC.

67. The tribunes entered office on 10 December, but there is a difficulty with the date, because at that time of year interrupting the water supply to the Capitol was not likely to have been such an effective stratagem. Cicero and Velleius suggest that the false Gracchus was only tribune-designate when he was killed. It is therefore possible that Appian has simply misinterpreted his source and that this was in fact the first (or, allowing for a little rhetorical licence, nearly the first) day after the false Gracchus' *election* to the tribunate.

68. 98 BC.

69. The war began at the end of 91 BC.

70. See ch. 21.

71. This M. Livius Drusus was the son of Gaius Gracchus' opponent (ch. 23). He was tribune in 91 BC.

72. These were probably colonies set up by the legislation of Drusus' father (see ch. 23 above), the need for the implementation of which vanished with the downfall of Gracchus. Less attractive, because of the lack of family connection, is the possibility that they were Saturninus' colonies, approved by law but never founded because of his death.

73. The Gracchan judiciary law (see n. 42) had set up a panel of 450 members of the equestrian order from whose number a jury of fifty was to be selected for any particular trial.

74. Appian is confused here: his account only makes sense if the 300 equestrian jurors did *not* become senators. In particular, the provision that bribe-taking was to be made a criminal offence would have been quite unnecessary if Drusus' equestrian jurors were actually to become senators, since senators had always been liable to prosecution on this score.

75. Since Gaius Gracchus' judiciary law of 123 BC (with the exception of the years 106–101, when jury service was shared with the senate) the equestrian order had provided the jurors both for the extortion court and for other standing courts which had been set up after its pattern in subsequent years. The workings of the extortion court were the most liable to abuse, exemplified by the famous case of Drusus' uncle, the ex-consul Rutilius Rufus, in the late nineties: as assistant, and then acting, governor of the province of Asia in 97–96 BC, Rutilius favoured the inhabitants of the province and the interests of justice by checking the profiteering activities of the equestrian tax companies, only to be vindictively condemned by an equestrian jury, after his return to Rome, for *extortion*. (See also Book II, ch. 13, n. 32.)

76. Cf. chs. 18–19. The trouble to the Italian allies' own land would be caused by the difficulty of establishing which land was properly Roman and could legitimately be taken back and used for Roman colonial settlements.

77. Tribune in 90 BC.

78. Appian actually writes 'Mummius who took Greece', evidently misinterpreting, and paraphrasing into Greek, the *cognomen* 'Achaicus' which he found in his source. The famous Mummius, of whom this man must have been the son or grandson, took his name Achaicus from the campaign of 146 BC in which, as consul, he brought to an end a war in southern Greece (= Achaea) and destroyed Corinth. The other two men mentioned here are C. Aurelius Cotta, who was to become consul in 75 BC, and (probably) L. Calpurnius Bestia, consul in 111 BC.

79. Asculum was a town in Picenum, the Adriatic region north-east of Rome. In spite of what Appian says, it was not a routine practice in the Republic to send proconsuls (that is, men entrusted with power of military command) to oversee parts of the Italian peninsula. Q. Servilius was one of the praetors of 91 BC and his presence in the region is to be explained by Roman awareness that trouble was brewing. It is not at all impossible that he was given this responsibility even before the end of his praetorship, and so one may date the outbreak of the Social War to very late in 91 or early in 90 BC.

80. There is no other evidence that the Liris (modern *Liri/Garigliano*) was ever called the Liternus, a river which in fact debouched at Liternum, not far south of the mouth of the Volturnus (*Volturno*); but both apparently had the alternative name of Clanis, which may explain Appian's mistake. The direction taken by Appian's imaginary traveller must be around the coast of Italy anti-clockwise from Campania.

81. The consul of 90 BC was *Lucius* Iulius Caesar, whom Appian has consistently confused, here and in chs. 41, 42, and 45 (but not 48), with the consul of the previous year, *Sextus* Iulius Caesar.

82. These men are, in order: Cn. Pompeius Strabo, who became consul in 89 BC; Q. Servilius Caepio, probably praetor in 91 (not the man whose murder at Asculum is related in ch. 38); the brother (probably) of M. Perperna, the consul of 92 BC; the famous Marius; and Marcus (or Manius) Valerius Messalla, presumably an ex-praetor.

83. These men are: (probably) the P. Lentulus mentioned at the opening of ch. 72 (but since he is not otherwise known to be a relation of Lucius Caesar, the text may be corrupt, as the consul certainly numbered among his senior officers his indubitable half-brother Q. Lutatius Catulus (consul in 102 BC), who is missing from Appian's list); the consul of 98 BC; P. Licinius Crassus, consul in 97 BC; L. Cornelius Sulla, the future dictator, praetor in 93 BC; and M. Claudius Marcellus, perhaps curule aedile in 91 BC.

84. The nationalities and full names, where known, of these men are: Lafrenius, a Picene or Marsian; Pontilius (or Pontidius), probably a Vestinian; Egnatius, probably a Samnite or from the Frentani; Q. Poppaedius Silo, a Marsian, commander-in-chief of the northern theatre of war, facing Rutilius; C. Papius Mutilus, a Samnite, commander-in-chief of the southern theatre, facing Lucius Caesar; Lamponius, a Lucanian; Vidacilius, a Picene from Asculum (ch. 48); Asinius, from the Marrucini; and P. Vettius Scato, a Paelignian.

85. See n. 81.

86. This was at Alba Fucens in the Marsic country.

87. Respectively, the modern *Castellamare di Stabia* and *Sorrento* on the Sorrentine peninsula, and *Salerno* at its southern base.

88. See n. 81.

89. 118–105 BC, for the latter part of which time he was at war with Rome.

90. The region on the eastern side of Italy south of Apulia.

91. Actually the Tolenus, the modern *Turano*, which flows north to Reate (*Rieti*) through the mountains north-east of Rome (Ovid, *Fasti* VI, 565–8, dating the disaster to 11 June).

92. See n. 81.

93. Poppaedius Silo had been a close friend of the murdered tribune Drusus. This may explain how he was able to carry through his treacherous ruse, and why he chose Caepio as his victim: Caepio had been a violent opponent of Drusus.

94. See n. 81.

95. Perhaps the consul was attempting to cross Mons Tifernus (*Monte Matese*) towards Allifae.

96. Teanum Sidicinum, in Campania.

97. In view of the sequel, either this 'Cornelius Sulla' along with 'Sulla' in the next sentence, must be a mistake (perhaps for Valerius Messalla?), or the following 'Cornelius Sulla' is.

98. Appian is at last (see n. 81) correct in naming *Sextus* Caesar, who had been consul in 91. At this point of the narrative we are still in 90 BC and *Lucius* Caesar is therefore still consul.

99. Some time in the first half of 90 BC. Some hard fighting took place before the settlement, in spite of Appian's silence.

100. According to Livy, ex-slaves had previously been conscripted in the Hannibalic War (XXII, 11.8; 57.11) and even in the Samnite Wars of the early third century (X, 21.4).

101. In the tribal voting assembly (*comitia tributa*; see Appendix, *A* ii), a candidate was elected, or a measure carried, when he or it had obtained an absolute majority of the available votes (one per tribe, cast in an order determined by lot). It would not often be necessary, under this system, to take account of the votes of the last ten of the new total of forty-five tribes.

102. The winter is that of 90–89 BC. The consuls Pompeius and Cato entered office on 1 January 89.

103. Q. Caecilius Metellus Pius, praetor in 89, son of Numidicus (see ch. 34 above).

104. See ch. 49 above.

105. A. Sempronius Asellio was urban praetor (in charge of civil cases between Roman citizens) in 89 BC.

106. Appian refers to Book XII of his *Roman History*; see Introduction sect. I*b*. For the past twenty-five years, Mithridates had practised a systematic policy of aggrandizement in eastern and central Anatolia by diplomatic, dynastic, or military means, but had always backed down in the face of Roman threats or actual armed intervention. In 89 he once more humoured Rome by withdrawing peaceably from Bithynia, which he had attempted, not for the first time, to annex. However, he was then goaded beyond endurance by the greed of the Roman diplomatic mission, led by M'. Aquillius (consul in 101 BC), who encouraged the Bithynian king Nicomedes to recoup the handsome fee they demanded from him for his restoration by invading and plundering Pontus in 89. The news of Mithridates' victory over the forces of Rome's allies on the River Amnias in spring 88 BC (Plutarch, *Marius* 34.5, with Appian, *Mithridatica* 18), and his subsequent defeat of M'. Aquillius and violent incursion into her protectorate in Asia Minor probably reached the capital in April or May of that year. He went on to attack Rhodes, and his army under his general Archelaus crossed the Aegean and 'liberated' the southern part of the Greek mainland at the invitation of the democratic party in Athens. All Romans and Italians in the province of Asia, slave and free, men and women, are said to have been massacred on a single day on Mithridates' orders, and more by Archelaus at Delos.

107. Possibly L. Licinius Lucullus.

108. The name of the first gate is corrupt in the Greek (Kloilia). Esquilina is the correction commonly accepted, but another possibility (see Gabba's edition), is Caeli-montana, the southern of the two gates on the Caelian hill.

109. This was the principal street leading into the forum.

110. That is, all measures had to go before the *comitia centuriata*, whereas it had become the practice for legislation to go before the *comitia tributa*, where the voting procedure was less complicated. For the nature of these assemblies, see Appendix (A). The senate's power to block legislation had been removed in 287 BC.

111. This seems to be an anticipation of Sulla's reform in 82.

112. Plutarch (*Marius* 40) identifies this island as Aenaria (modern *Ischia*).

113. 'Africa' is the Roman province of that name, roughly co-extensive (at times) with modern *Tunisia*.

114 Appian is probably mistaken here. Even if we did not have the statement of Valerius Maximus (IX.7) that Q. Pompeius was appointed to this task by the *senate*, the consular commands for 88, which had by law to be allotted by the senate in mid-89, can only have been the northern and southern fronts of the desperate war in Italy. The Mithridatic emergency then caused Sulla's province to be changed, but not Q. Pompeius', whose departure for the north was delayed by the Sulpician troubles until the present time.

115. L. Cornelius Cinna.

116. The sum named represents several million pounds at present-day prices: a talent was 6,000 denarii (= 24,000 sesterces, for the value of which see Book II, ch. 8, n. 24).

117. This was evidently prior to the assembly which was to vote on Cinna's proposal. One of the tribunes will have acted as Cinna's mouthpiece.

118. See n. 51.

119. Milonius was probably a tribune at this time; he later died in battle on the Janiculum (cf. ch. 71) when Cinna re-took Rome. Quintus Sertorius was of Sabine origin and was an able and experienced soldier, but had been thwarted of a tribunate in 87 by Sulla's interference in the elections in 88. Gaius Marius cannot be Marius' son, who was in Africa (ch. 62), but is probably a mistake for *Marcus* Marius (Gratidianus), a more distant relation of the great Marius.

120. Certain priests at Rome, including some of the most important, were called *flamen*: L. Cornelius Merula, as priest of Jupiter, was *Flamen Dialis*. The ceremonial

cap (the *apex*) referred to was highly distinctive: tight-fitting, with a strap under the chin and a short spike on top.

121. These forces were those deployed against the remnants of the Social War insurgents (cf. ch. 68, Metellus' command).

122. Marius had evidently adopted the rags, dirt, and lack of a shave and haircut (collectively known as *squalor*) affected by Romans who wished to arouse the compassion of their neighbours for alleged ill-treatment or injustice.

123. Cn. Papirius Carbo, who had been praetor during the Social War and probably held a command in Lucania.

124. Crassus is probably P. Licinius Crassus (see ch. 72 and n. 128).

125. Appian probably expects his readers to understand that this was unconstitutional, because at least seventeen days' public notice had to be given of legislative proposals.

126. The officer is probably C. Marcius Censorinus, who reappears in the narrative (as Marcius) in chs. 88–93.

127. The brothers are Gaius Iulius Caesar Strabo (consular candidate in 88 BC) and Lucius Iulius Caesar (consul in 90 BC); C. Atilius Serranus was consul in 106 BC; for Lentulus, see n. 83.

128. This is P. Licinius Crassus (consul in 97 BC). Cicero (*de Oratore* III, 10) says he died by his own hand.

129. This is the M. Antonius who was consul in 99 BC.

130. Probably the ex-praetor M. Caecilius Cornutus, who had held a command during the Social War.

131. Ancharius was another ex-praetor.

132. See ch. 65.

133. 86 BC.

134. L. Valerius Flaccus was the brother of the consul of 93 BC, and possibly a cousin of the consul of 100 BC who was described by the Sullan supporter Rutilius Rufus as 'more Marius' shadow than his colleague'. He was not in fact killed until January 85, by which time Carbo (for whom see n. 123) had been elected consul for that year in the normal way.

135. The three years were 86–84 BC. Appian described these events in the *Mithridatica* (see Introduction, sect. I*b*).

136. In 105 BC, while serving as (pro)quaestor under Marius, Sulla had personally captured Jugurtha at considerable risk to himself. In the Cimbric war, he served under Marius in 104 and 103 BC and under Catulus in 102 and 101 BC. As governor of Cilicia in 92 BC, he restored the Cappadocian king Ariobarzanes to his throne against the opposition of Mithridates and his ally Tigranes, the king of Armenia, and established friendly diplomatic relations with the Parthian king Arsaces.

137. Cinna and Carbo were self-proclaimed consuls for 84 BC. Dalmatia is not a plausible base for operations against an army coming by sea from Asia Minor to Italy. It is more likely, in view of the identical action of Octavian when preparing for his showdown with Antonius in the late thirties BC, that Cinna wished to give his relatively green troops some battle practice against Dalmatian tribesmen before they had to face Sulla's veterans.

138. For 'in Africa', which is a correction based on Plutarch, *Crassus* 6.2, the manuscripts read 'in Liguria'.

139. See ch. 68.

140. Pompeius was only twenty-four or twenty-five years old at the time (he was sent to Africa at the end of 82, but it is uncertain whether his triumph, 12 March, took place in 81 or 80), nor was he yet a senator. There was in fact no minimum age set by law for the award of a triumph, but a condition was that one had to be fighting 'under one's own auspices', that is not under the command of, or exercising authority delegated by, anyone else. This would normally mean that one had been elected to a magistracy which conferred *imperium* (the legal right to command), namely praetorship or consulship. The minimum permitted ages for these, by the Lex Villia of 180 BC, were thirty-nine and forty-two respectively. It was thus outrageous for Pompeius, who had never held elected office at all, to demand a triumph. Sulla could obviously have crushed him if it had come to a fight, but must have felt that this was a quarrel which would bring him more trouble than profit, and therefore yielded.

141. See ch. 60.

142. The year is 83 BC. L. Scipio had the *cognomen* Asiaticus or Asiagenus.

143. This was the equivalent of twenty legions.

144. Earthquakes were popularly ascribed to the agency of the god Poseidon (Neptune).

145. This Olympiad ran from 84 to 81 BC. Sulla landed at Brundisium some time during the winter of 84–83.

146. Sulla was elected dictator towards the end of 82 BC. Appian's strange tally of three years may possibly be explained by supposing that he refers to the Olympic years 84/3, 83/2, and 82/1.

147. All other sources identify this Marius as Marius' son. His age is mentioned because no one under forty-two could legally hold the consulship.

148. C. Carrinas, praetor in 82 BC.

149. Sena Gallica was on the Adriatic coast south of modern *Rimini*.

150. These men are, respectively: L. Iunius Brutus Damasippus; P. Antistius, once a supporter of Sulpicius and presently father-in-law of Pompeius (Magnus); C. Papirius Carbo Arvina, who had held a tribunate in 90 BC; L. Domitius Ahenobarbus, consul in 94 BC; and Q. Mucius Scaevola, consul in 95 BC.

151. Appian calls the territory 'Viritane', transliterating the Latin *viritanus*, which means 'assigned to settlers on an individual basis', and seems to refer (cf. ch. 91) to the area adjacent to Faventia (*Faenza*), which was so assigned in 173 BC.

152. C. Marcius Censorinus.

153. 'Arretium' is an emendation of the senseless 'Arregium' of the manuscripts.

154. This commander is P. Albinovanus, one of the twelve men proscribed by Sulla in 88 (see ch. 60).

155. 'Africa' means the Roman province of Africa, i.e. modern *Tunisia*.

156. Aristophanes, *Knights* 542.

157. See ch. 85.

158. Midway between Sicily and North Africa, the present *Pantelleria*.

159. This was late in 82 BC.

160. By 'sortition' Appian appears to be referring to the fact that the regular procedures for constituting the juries in the criminal courts (which was done by drawing lots) were suspended, i.e. that no normal system of justice was in operation.

161. Appian's comments apply simply to the word here rendered 'Favoured of the Gods' (*Eutyches* in Greek, *Felix* in Latin). The other title, *Hegemon* ('Leader'), may perhaps be intended as a translation of the Latin *Imperator* ('Victorious General'), which was bestowed by the acclamation of his army on a commander who had won a notable victory and constituted *prima facie* evidence for the granting of a triumph by the senate; but *imperator* is usually rendered by *autokrator* in Greek. A contemporary gold coin depicting the statue bears the legend L. SULLA FELIX DIC(TATOR).

162. Faustus was the highly unusual name Sulla gave his son, but that does not mean that the epithet was not applied to the dictator himself.

163. A name for Aphrodite (Venus), the mother of Aeneas.

164. Aphrodisias.

165. Actually only 120 years, the last previous dictator, C. Servilius Geminus, having held office in 202 BC. Appian's mistake may derive from a careless reading of Dionysius of Halicarnassus, who says (*Roman Antiquities* V.77) that there were about 400 years between Rome's *first* dictator and Sulla.

166. The dictatorship, which was essentially a device for coping with an emergency whether military or administrative, was supposed to be laid down after six months. The office was 'despotic' because, unlike all other Roman magistracies, its holder had no equal colleague and was therefore not subject to veto. The consuls continued in office, but were subject to the superior authority of the dictator until he laid down his power.

167. A reference to the first celebration, apparently in 80 BC (the first year of the four-year cycle of the 175th Olympiad), of the new permanent addition to the calendar known as the 'Festival of Sulla's Victory' (*Ludi Victoriae Sullanae*), which lasted from 26 October to 1 November, the date of the Battle of the Colline Gate (ch. 93). Such Roman festivals consisted largely of theatrical and other shows, including athletic and sometimes gladiatorial contests.

168. M. Tullius Decula and Cn. Cornelius Dolabella, consuls for 81 BC.

169. The kings in fact had only twelve *fasces*, as Appian himself elsewhere (*Syriaca* 15) and all other sources state.

170. The change is no earlier than AD 15, when the election of other magistrates was 'transferred to the senate', i.e. this body now produced a list of candidates, equal in number to the offices to be filled, for rubber-stamping by the popular assembly.

171. When slaves were granted their freedom, they had to take a Roman name, normally that of their ex-master, who as their patron still retained a right to obedience and certain services from them. In the case of this particular group Sulla had usurped the place of patron, and *faute de mieux* they took his name.

172. 27 and 28 January, 81 BC.

173. The father (Ptolemy X Alexander I) had died in 87 after being deposed in the previous year by his elder brother Ptolemy IX Soter II (Lathyrus), who then unwisely refused to support Sulla against Mithridates. On Lathyrus' death in 80 BC the son married Lathyrus' daughter Berenice III, who was also his own stepmother, and became (briefly) Ptolemy XI Alexander II. His death at the hands of the Alexandrians followed his own murder of Berenice.

174. The year is 80 BC.

175. Ptolemy I Soter abdicated in 285 BC, Ariobarzanes in 63 BC, and Seleucus I Nicator in 294 BC, all in favour of their sons.

176. Q. Lutatius Catulus and M. Aemilius Lepidus, consuls for 78 BC.

177. Lepidus had gone, not to Gaul, but to Etruria to suppress an uprising, of which he ended up becoming the leader.

178. M. Perperna Vento, who had attained the praetorship and been the (Marian) governor of Sicily in 82 BC.

179. See ch. 85.

180. The year is now 75 BC. The main war area, lying between the contestants, was the Celtiberian uplands and the valley of the Ebro which flanks them to the north; Metellus and Pompeius were based on the coast and the north side of the Ebro, Sertorius on Lusitania, running up to the headwaters of the Douro and the Tagus.

181. Nicomedes IV of Bithynia died in 74 BC (the 176th Olympiad ran from 76 to 73 BC). Ptolemy Apion, who died in 96 BC, was the illegitimate son of Ptolemy VIII Euergetes II (Physkon) and had inherited the kingdom of Cyrene in 116 BC under his father's will.

182. The year is 73 BC.

183. Appian has amalgamated two of the praetors of 73 BC, C. Claudius Glaber, who suffered the first defeat at the hands of Spartacus, and P. Varinius, who suffered the second. 'Publius Valerius', a man otherwise unknown, is probably a related mistake for the missing P. Varinius.

184. The consuls for 72 BC were L. Gellius Publicola and Cn. Cornelius Lentulus Claudianus, of whom Gellius defeated Crixus and Lentulus intercepted Spartacus. Plutarch (*Crassus* 9.7) says that after defeating the consuls (probably somewhere between the Po and Ariminum) Spartacus also defeated C. Cassius Longinus, the proconsul of Cisalpine Gaul, who tried to stop him near Mutina (*Modena*).

185. This may be the defeat suffered in 72 BC by the praetor Cn. Manlius (Livy, *Periochae* XCVI).

186. Appian is here referring, not to fresh popular elections, but to the appointment by the senate of an existing magistrate to a new area of responsibility – in this case, to replace the disgraced consuls in command of the army. Crassus was probably one of the serving praetors of 72, who had been elected in late 73 to perform normal administrative duties in the capital, leaving Spartacus to P. Varinius and the new consuls. An alternative view is that Crassus had held a praetorship in 73 and at the end of that year had chosen (somewhat improbably in view of the number of wars the Romans currently had on their hands) to retire from office directly instead of assuming a promagistracy, so that he was in Rome and free to take up the command against Spartacus in the latter part of 72.

187. This was a recognized punishment in the Roman army (cf. Polybius VI.38).

188. Appian has confused the more famous Lucius Lucullus (consul of 74 BC), who fought against Mithridates from 74 and did not return to Italy until 66, with his brother Marcus (consul of 73 BC), referred to here, who was proconsul of Macedonia in 72–71 and was recalled by the senate to help deal with Spartacus.

189. A distance of approximately 115 miles. If the number of captives is correctly recorded, there would have been a cross every thirty to thirty-five yards.

190. Pompeius was in fact born on 28 or 29 September 106 BC; for Sulla's law governing qualifications for office, see ch. 100. As for the tribunate, one of Sulla's most important restrictions, the ban on holding further office, had already been removed in 75 BC.

BOOK II

1. Appian resumes his narrative in 64 BC. During the seventies and early sixties BC the pirates had extended their raids from the eastern Mediterranean to the coasts of Italy and Sicily and were even threatening the food supplies of the capital. Pompeius employed twenty legions and 270 ships in his campaign. Starting from the west, he cleared the whole Mediterranean and finally reduced the pirates' strongholds in Cilicia. The entire operation was completed in three months in 67 BC. The popularity he derived from this exploit led to the immediate conferment on him, in 66, of the command against Mithridates, whom he drove from his kingdom. He was also active in Armenia, the Caucasus, Syria, and Palestine, the effect of his interventions being to change fundamentally the political geography of this entire area and antagonize the Parthians. Although military action was over by 63 BC, Pompeius remained for a further year in the east, engaged in diplomatic tidying-up, and did not reach Italy until late in 62 BC

2. Caesar, born in 100 BC, was only six years younger than Pompeius.

3. Caesar was aedile in 65 BC and praetor in 62 BC.

4. The shows at the great public festivals ('games', *ludi*) of Rome were laid on by the aediles or the praetors. Providing a good show by spending lavishly in these magistracies was therefore a way of becoming popular and ensuring support for one's next candidacy for public office.

5. His full name is correctly *Lucius* Sergius Catilina.

6. In 63 BC.

7. Cicero was a Tullius, one of the leading families of Arpinum. This town, famous as the home of the great C. Marius, lay some sixty miles south-east of Rome, and its inhabitants had possessed full Roman citizenship since 188 BC. Cicero and his brother were the first members of his family to make a career in metropolitan politics, but if he was a 'lodger', so were many other members of the Roman aristocracy who had similar origins.

8. Roman marriages were seldom made for love, but rather for social, economic or political reasons. In the late Republic a widow could expect to inherit a not inconsiderable portion of her late husband's estate and enjoy in practice a legal and financial independence which was denied to other Roman women, even if in theory her father or male guardian held control.

9. P. Cornelius Lentulus Sura had held the praetorship in 74 and the consulship in 71, but had been expelled from the senate in 70 and was now rehabilitating himself by repeating the career path. No other source supports Appian's assertion that C. Cornelius Cethegus, certainly a senator (Sallust, *Catiline* 17.3), was a praetor.

10. Manlius had served as a centurion under Sulla.

11. These actions were taken after the meeting of the senate on 21 October at which Cicero persuaded it, in the light of his information that the plot was planned for 28 October, to pass the decree known as the *senatus consultum ultimum* which in effect declared a state of emergency.

12. Catilina left Rome on the night of 8 November.

13. The plan here described by Appian seems to have been scheduled for 17 December. The new tribunes, among whom was L. Calpurnius Bestia, assumed office on 10 December.

14. L. Statilius, a member of the equestrian order.

15. L. Cassius Longinus, a senator.

16. A town in southern Italy.

17. Q. Fabius (Maximus?) Sanga was a descendant of that Q. Fabius Maximus who had conquered the Allobroges, a tribe of south-eastern Gaul, in 121 BC, and taken the name Allobrogicus as a result.

18. D. Iunius Silanus.

19. Ti. Claudius Nero, who must have held a praetorship before this year. He was the grandfather of the future emperor Tiberius.

20. M. Porcius Cato, a tribune-elect for 62, later to become famous as Caesar's most determined opponent.

21. Cicero is supposed to have uttered the single word '*Vixerunt*' ('They have lived').

22. In fact, at Pistoria (modern *Pistoia*) at the south side of the Apennine chain, north-west of Florence.

23. The Romans (and their subjects) frequently referred to the governor of a province, who was in most cases technically an ex-praetor holding the rank of proconsul, as 'the praetor'. This was particularly the case in older provinces like Spain and Sicily where the governors had for many years indeed been serving praetors. Caesar was praetor (in Rome) during 62 and went to Spain as proconsul in 61.

24. Presumably 25 million sesterces (HS), this being the Roman unit of account (4

HS = 1 denarius, the silver coin). As to the real value of this sum, Caesar doubled a legionary's pay to 900 HS p.a.; a moderate year's rent in Rome in the late Republic might perhaps be 2,000 HS (P. A. Brunt, *Past and Present* 35 (1966), 13); entrance to a cheap bath-house was a *quadrans* ($\frac{1}{16}$ HS); and in 5 BC an Egyptian wet-nurse received 10 drachmae (= 10 denarii or 40 HS) per month to suckle a slave infant. Say 1 HS = £1 at present (1995) values?

25. If he entered the city of Rome (see n. 79 below), a provincial governor had to lay down his power of command *(imperium)*, yet he needed to retain it to celebrate a triumph. Hence a governor who had been voted a triumph by the senate was technically required to remain outside the formal boundary of the city until he entered in triumphal procession with his army. However, as Appian notes below, the senate had often agreed exceptions, and the requirement that a man declare his candidacy in person, in the city, to the appropriate magistrate was equally capable of being waived. Caesar's dilemma was entirely manufactured by his enemies, who were to pay dearly for this piece of petty spite.

26. Bibulus' correct name was *Marcus* Calpurnius Bibulus. He was married to Cato's daughter, and had already been Caesar's colleague as aedile (in 65 BC) and praetor (in 62 BC). Appian has lapsed into the terminology of the imperial age in saying that the *senate* elected Bibulus to the consulship. He may possibly have been the candidate supported by a majority of senators, but it was the Roman people in the *comitia centuriata* (see Appendix, *A* i) who elected him.

27. That is, Caesar spoke himself at one of the public meetings *(contiones)* which preceded the voting on a bill. Since 287 BC, with the exception of the Sullan years, there had been no constitutional requirement for any bill to go to the senate for debate or approval before it went to the people for a vote; however, convenience and convention dictated that this was normally done.

28. That is, one consul could not call a senate in a month when the other 'had the *fasces*', i.e. took precedence, and had responsibility for summoning and presiding over the senate. The consuls presided in alternate months, beginning with the one first elected. The events Appian goes on to describe will therefore have taken place in January, when Caesar had precedence.

29. See Book I, ch. 29, n. 61. However, the idea that the *people* needed to swear to obey a law that they themselves had just passed is out of place.

30. Approved, that is, by the popular assembly.

31. The lictors were the consul's attendants, who carried the *fasces*.

32. Under the system devised by C. Gracchus (and relevant to Book I, ch. 22), the state auctioned to contractors (who could not be senators) the potentially lucrative right to collect the taxes of Asia, but the yield depended to a large extent on the harvest and was unpredictable. In this case the successful syndicate of equestrians (*societas publicanorum*) had overbid and stood to make a loss.

33. The Lex Vatinia, passed in May through the agency of the friendly tribune P. Vatinius, gave Caesar the proconsulship of Cisalpine Gaul and Illyria until some time in 54 which was apparently not clearly specified, as the sequel shows; later in the year the proconsulship of Transalpine Gaul fell vacant through the death of Metellus Celer, and was also given to Caesar.

34. Q.(?) Servilius Caepio, uncle and adoptive father of Brutus the tyrannicide, and half-brother of Cato.

35. P. Vatinius was in fact tribune for the current year, 59. P. Clodius Pulcher was born a patrician Claudius, the son of the consul of 79 BC, but became (by adoption) a plebeian in order to be able to hold the politically attractive office of tribune of the *plebs*, and took to using the plebeian spelling of his family name.

36. The sacrilege took place in December 62 BC in Caesar's own house, where the ceremony of the Bona Dea was being held *ex officio*. This was the occasion when Caesar remarked that his wife (at that time Pompeia) must be above suspicion. At the trial in May 61 BC Cicero was a key witness and incurred Clodius' enmity by disproving his alibi. However, the jurors were bribed (according to Cicero) and Clodius was acquitted.

37. Appian is wrong: Vatinius, in 59, was the agent of the Gallic command.

38. It was in fact an accepted Roman custom for an accused to behave in this way, as a means of exciting public sympathy and advertising his predicament. Cf. Marius' behaviour: Book I, ch. 67, n. 122.

39. This appears to be a garbled version of Demosthenes' flight into exile in 324 BC. He was found guilty (in court) of accepting a bribe, and fled to avoid imprisonment for non-payment of the enormous fine imposed.

40. A consul was accompanied by twelve lictors, a praetor by six, and a promagistrate by five (his own ration at the time).

41. This meeting took place at Luca (modern *Lucca*), which was (just) within Caesar's province of Cisalpine Gaul, at the end of April 56 BC. It was prompted by attacks on Caesar's legislation and the threat by Domitius Ahenobarbus, if he won his expected consulship in the following year, to deprive Caesar of his Gallic command. There was also tension between Crassus and Pompeius. (In spite of what Appian says at the start of this chapter, Caesar had not yet invaded Britain.)

42. L. Domitius Ahenobarbus (father of the character in Shakespeare's *Antony and Cleopatra* and great-great-grandfather of the emperor Nero) was one of Caesar's most determined opponents.

43. For 55 BC.

44. The appointments of both Pompeius and Crassus (under the Lex Trebonia) were for five years. Appian is probably wrong to give Africa to Pompeius.

45. Crassus was defeated in the desert near Carrhae, to the east of the Euphrates, on 9 June 53 BC.

46. For the Parthian history, see Book V, ch. 65, n. 56.

47. In 57 BC Pompeius was given proconsular power for five years, with the right to appoint fifteen assistants (*legati*). Appian is the only source to give their number as twenty.

48. In August 54 BC.

49. This *may* refer to the electoral scandal of September 54 BC (see Cicero, *Letters to*

Atticus IV, 17.2), when two of the candidates made a corrupt pact with the consuls in office to secure their own election; if they defaulted on their part of the bargain they were to pay the consuls 4 million sesterces (=166 talents, but the figure is uncertain and should perhaps be ten times that amount, making each candidate liable for 800 talents).

50. 53 BC Consuls were finally elected about the end of July. In spite of what Appian goes on to say, Pompeius, who was a proconsul, was constitutionally powerless to intervene inside the city of Rome except by authority of the senate.

51. It was the violence orchestrated by two of the candidates themselves, Milo (standing for the consulship, as he had intended ever since 54 BC) and Clodius (standing for the praetorship), which made it impossible to hold the elections for 52 before the end of 53. Thus 52, like 53, opened without consuls or praetors in office. It was not until Milo murdered Clodius (as described in ch. 21 below) that public disorder reached such a height that Pompeius was called in to restore order and appointed consul without a colleague.

52. The murder took place on 18 January 52 BC.

53. Marcus Caelius Rufus, a friend of Cicero, who had defended him (in a speech still extant) on a charge of attempting to poison his lover, Clodius' sister Clodia, in 56 BC.

54. Members of the equestrian order enjoyed the privilege of wearing a gold ring.

55. Spain was divided into two provinces (but cf. ch. 18).

56. This Ptolemy, who never reigned in Egypt, was a brother of the then current occupant of the Egyptian throne, Ptolemy XII Auletes. Appian is in error over the date of Cato's mission, which took place in 58 on Clodius' initiative.

57. In particular, a new law against public violence (*de vi*).

58. 70–52 BC.

59. Aulus Gabinius (consul in 58 BC) was in fact tried (in person) at the end of 54. As proconsul of Syria from 57 to 55, he had invaded Egypt in the latter year to restore Ptolemy XII Auletes to his throne (for a vast price). The Sibylline books had yielded an oracle that Ptolemy was not to be restored 'with a host', and the senate had in any case given the commission to Lentulus Spinther, proconsul of Cilicia and Cyprus. He was none the less acquitted of *maiestas* (treason, Appian's 'flouting the law') but was condemned at a subsequent trial for extortion.

60. Hypsaeus is P. Plautius Hypsaeus (praetor by 55 BC), one of Milo's rivals for the consulship of 52. Memmius is C. Memmius, one of the consular candidates involved in the corrupt bargain referred to in ch. 19 (see n. 49). 'Sextus', which is a *praenomen* (first name), is probably a manuscript error for the *nomen* (family name) 'Sextius' or 'Sestius'; if the former, he has not been identified, but if the latter, a plausible candidate is P. Sestius (tribune in 57 BC) who had already been successfully defended in 56 BC by Cicero (whose speech is extant) on a charge of electoral bribery.

61. M. Aemilius Scaurus had been successfully defended on an extortion charge in 54 BC by Cicero, who could not repeat the trick this time. Scaurus had held the praetorship in 56 and was a consular candidate for 53. Trials were held in the forum, in the open air, and often attracted a large crowd, which explains the events here described.

62. Correctly, and in full, *Quintus* Caecilius Metellus Pius Scipio Nasica, usually referred to as Metellus Scipio, whose daughter Cornelia (widow of Crassus' younger son, killed at Carrhae) Pompeius had married earlier that year.

63. That is, they adopted the soiled clothing and unkempt appearance *(squalor)* of the suppliant; cf. n. 38.

64. 'The exiles' were the people condemned in Pompeius' judicial purge.

65. i.e. *imperium*, which protected its holder against almost all legal action.

66. M. Claudius Marcellus.

67. This town is modern *Como*. For the 'Latin right', see Appendix *(D)*.

68. Flogging counted as a capital punishment and could not be summarily inflicted on a Roman citizen (except on military service).

69. See n. 33 and ch. 18.

70. See Appendix *(F)* for the whole question of Caesar's Gallic command.

71. L. Aemilius Lepidus Paullus and C. Claudius Marcellus, consuls for 50 BC.

72. C. Scribonius Curio, son of a Sullan stalwart, the consul of 76 BC.

73. In Campania, in June 50 BC.

74. Pompeius had built himself a new house near his theatre on the Campus Martius. It was more luxurious than his inner-city house (Plutarch, *Pompey* 40), which he had to forsake for constitutional reasons (see n. 79 below). He also had a house in the Alban Hills near Rome.

75. See Book I, ch. 121.

76. Q. Titurius Sabinus and L. Aurunculeius Cotta were both killed, with the loss of a legion and a half, in the revolt of the Eburones at the very end of 54.

77. A year's pay for an ordinary legionary was 225 denarii (= 225 drachmae).

78. Claudius was on perfectly sound constitutional ground here: the formal status of the senate was that of an advisory council to the consuls. See Appendix *(B)*.

79. Pompeius, as a holder of proconsular power, could not enter 'the city', i.e. the central part enclosed by the ancient ritual boundary known as the *pomoerium*, without laying down that power. When he attended a senate in these years (other than as consul in 55 and 52) it had to be held outside the *pomoerium*, for example in one of the temples on the Campus Martius. See also n. 74.

80. The tribunes' authority extended one mile beyond the *pomoerium* (see n. 79).

81. Caesar left Britain in the autumn of 54 BC.

82. This was the Thirteenth legion with its support.

83. The consuls for 49 were C. Claudius Marcellus, cousin of his predecessor and brother of the consul of 51, and L. Cornelius Lentulus Crus. Caesar's own account of the civil war starts at this point.

84. This is L. Domitius Ahenobarbus, who had been consul in 54 BC.

85. M. Antonius ('Mark Antony') and Q. Cassius, a relation of Caesar's murderer. They entered office on 10 December 50 BC.

86. According to Caesar himself, whose figure is confirmed in Pompeius' letters (in

Cicero, *Letters to Atticus* VIII, 11A and 12A), Domitius had eighteen or twenty cohorts (say 6–10,000 men) in Corfinium, with seven at neighbouring Sulmo and six at Alba Fucens. Caesar also says it was Domitius' own men, not the inhabitants of Corfinium, who arrested him.

87. Erytheia was the island somewhere in the west where the triple-bodied monster Geryon was slain by Heracles.

88. The Briges (or Brigae) are called Brygi by Strabo.

89. The usual modern view of this matter is that there was one town, colonized by Greeks from Corcyra and originally called Epidamnus. Dyrrachium (probably the name of the peninsula on which the town stood) came into use in the period of Roman supremacy because of the ill-omened character, to a Latin speaker, of the '-damn-' element in Epidamnus.

90. These were booby-traps, containing upward-pointing spikes and lightly covered over (Caesar, *Civil War* I,27).

91. Q. Valerius Orca, who had been praetor in 57 BC.

92. L. Caecilius Metellus.

93. M. Aemilius Lepidus (the future triumvir) was one of the praetors of 49 BC.

94. Q. Valerius Orca (see ch. 40).

95. Brother of Marcus.

96. M. Licinius Crassus, elder son of Caesar's erstwhile associate killed at Carrhae.

97. Q. Hortensius and P. Cornelius Dolabella (Cicero's son-in-law).

98. The word simply means 'commander'.

99. Scipio Africanus, the conqueror of Hannibal, had encamped for a time near Utica on a promontory which was thenceforth known as 'Scipio's Camp' (*Castra Cornelia*).

100. The persons named are Gaius Antonius and P. Dolabella (see ch. 41), and M. Octavius.

101. A dictator was normally named by one of the consuls. Caesar himself says that while he was still at Massilia he was named dictator by the praetor Lepidus (*Civil War* II, 21).

102. P. Servilius Vatia Isauricus.

103. For Lepidus, see n. 93; Decimus Junius Brutus had already been in charge of the siege of Massilia throughout the summer of 49 while Caesar was in Spain. This siege is not mentioned by Appian, perhaps because Massilia was an independent state.

104. This was the first time in Roman history (with the dubious exception of C. Flaminius in 217 BC) that a consul had not entered office in Rome.

105. See n. 59.

106. Caesar probably intended to land considerably further north. The wild, rocky, and harbourless Ceraunian coast was a notorious graveyard for ships, and was not far from the main Pompeian fleet base at Corcyra.

107. The commander was L. Manlius Torquatus.

108. Q. Lucretius Vespillo and (–). Minucius Rufus, subordinate commanders (*praefecti*) under the squadron admiral D. Laelius.

109. Called the Apsus by Caesar.

110. Postumius is probably A. Postumius Albinus; Gabinius, A. Gabinius, the consul of 58 BC; Antonius, M. Antonius; and Calenus, Q. Fufius Calenus, who was to be consul in 47 BC.

111. Appian has misdated this episode by a year; it happened in the winter of 48–47 BC.

112. This was just south of Dyrrachium, where Caesar succeeded in encircling Pompeius with his fortifications. Pompeius had easy access to the sea and supplies, but water, and fodder for his cavalry, became a problem, while Caesar's men were desperately short of food.

113. There is a gap in the text at this point. By a strange coincidence, Caesar's own narrative of the campaign has also lost the account of his night attack on Dyrrachium (*Civil War* III, 50–51).

114. Appian seems to have confused C. Calvisius Sabinus, who was operating with a small force in central Greece on Caesar's behalf, with Cn. Domitius Calvinus, who with two whole legions blocked Scipio on the river Haliacmon between Thessaly and Macedonia. Caesar himself says nothing about the loss of a legion.

115. The figure, which equals 140 miles, is probably corrupt and certainly wrong. Caesar himself gives the length of his circumvallation as 17 Roman miles, or 15½ statute miles (*Civil War* III, 63). However, Appian's whole account from here on to the battle of Pharsalus is muddled and bears only a distorted resemblance to Caesar's own, which, however slanted its presentation, is much clearer and makes far better tactical sense.

116. Each legion had an eagle as its standard, and to lose it was regarded as the ultimate disgrace.

117. Apparently a reference to the judgements expressed at the ends of chs. 58 and 62, and perhaps also to those in chs. 64 and 65.

118. Appian's readers could be expected to know that Venus (Aphrodite) was the mother of Aeneas. 'Ilus' is usually called Iulus (or Ascanius) in Latin authors.

119. These 'authorities' include Caesar himself, whose figures, and omissions, are exactly those reported by Appian. By 'troops from Italy' Appian means the legions, that is heavy infantry, of which Pompeius put eleven into battle and Caesar eight, but he is mistaken about the origins of the cavalry (and indeed correctly states the nationality of Caesar's just below).

120. Appian may be in error here, as Spartan coins of the forties BC attest 'republican' forms of government, or it may be that since for most of the history of Sparta the army had been commanded by the kings, Appian means no more than that the Spartans at Pharsalus were under their own chosen commanders.

121. I retain Appian's version of this name, although it is an error: the king of Greater Armenia at this time (55–34 BC) was called Artavasdes.

122. In this, Pompeius was adopting the normal practice of his day, when the main line of battle was always composed of legionaries, who were by definition Roman citizens ('Italians').

123. I have omitted one word of Viereck's text here to avoid having Appian state that the cavalry were stationed on the wings of *each* division, a formation which was neither practical nor actually adopted by either commander.

124. An alternative translation is 'Afranius and Pompeius guarded the camp', but can Appian really have believed, against all previous accounts including Caesar's own, that Pompeius, along with his most experienced general, stayed in his camp on this of all occasions? The word for 'camp' (*stratopedon*) is also commonly used to mean 'army'.

125. These men are P. Cornelius Sulla, nephew of the dictator and son-in-law of Pompeius; M. Antonius ('Mark Antony'); and Cn. Domitius Calvinus. Appian here agrees exactly with Caesar.

126. This is nonsense. The only spears a legionary carried were his two throwing spears (*pila*), which were useless for hand-to-hand combat because they had special heads designed to bend or break off at the neck on impact, so that the enemy could not throw them back. Note also that Appian's description at this point implies that Pompeius' army was stationary, waiting (as in Caesar's account of the battle) for the enemy to charge, while in the previous chapter he has both the armies advancing to meet each other. (His version of the battle seems to be a mixture of authentic detail and colourful invention.)

127. If Caesar himself is to be believed, he actually spent the night on a hillside (probably some five miles away), cutting off from any water the remnants of Pompeius' army, who surrendered the following morning.

128. Cornelia had been the wife of the triumvir's son, who like his father had fallen at Carrhae (see ch. 18 above).

129. Juba was King of Numidia (and see chs. 45–6 above).

130. Ptolemy XII Auletes ('the oboist') had died in 51 BC, owing his occupation of the Egyptian throne to Pompeius' support in 58–55 BC. His son and heir Ptolemy XIII was now thirteen, while his daughter Cleopatra, Ptolemy XIII's consort, joint ruler, and present enemy, was twenty-one or twenty-two.

131. Fragment 873 (Radt), from an unidentified play.

132. 'Rich in temples' refers to the fact that Pompeius (like Hellenistic kings, and indeed some other Romans of the late Republic) received cult worship in many places in the eastern provinces.

133. The sanctuary referred to must be that of the principal temple of the settlement of Mount Casius. A sacred building's *adyton* (the closed part entered only by the priests) was commonly used to store publicly owned valuables and money.

134. AD 130–131.

135. L. Cassius, not to be confused either with C. Cassius (the later murderer of Caesar), who was already commanding a Pompeian fleet which was active around southern Italy and Sicily before the battle of Pharsalus took place, or with the latter's brother, also L. Cassius, who was on Caesar's side.

136. Cn. Pompeius the younger.

137. T. Quinctius Scapula, an equestrian.

138. Appian has confused two different men: see n. 135.

139. In AD 117 Trajan's governor of Egypt, Q. Marcius Turbo, suppressed the Jewish rising which had been gathering strength since its outbreak in 115.

140. Pharnaces defeated Domitius Calvinus near Nicopolis.

141. This is the battle of Zela (2 August 45 BC).

142. None of the attested volumes of the *Roman History* fits this description (see Introduction, sect. I*b*).

143. The title of a Roman dictator's second-in-command was *magister equitum*.

144. This battle took place outside the town of Thapsus on 6 April 46 BC. If Appian had read our main surviving source for the campaign in north Africa, the *Bellum Africanum* (probably written by one of Caesar's officers), his sketchy narrative does not betray the fact.

145. To dine sitting, like a slave or a child, rather than reclining, like a free adult, was a sign of austerity. Our equivalent might be to dine standing up. Plutarch (*Cato Minor* 53, 67) tells us that from the day he left Rome in January 49 BC Cato went into mourning for the Republic by refusing to shave, or have his hair cut, or wear a garland (usual at dinner), and that after Pharsalus he always sat for meals, lying down only to sleep.

146. The *Phaedo*.

147. Marcia's father was L. Marcius Philippus (consul 56 BC), whose current wife Atia (not the mother of Marcia) was Julius Caesar's niece and the future emperor Augustus' mother by her previous husband.

148. i.e. of pardon.

149. This man is the historian Sallust.

150. See ch. 87 above.

151. These triumphs were celebrated in September 46 BC, after Caesar's return to Rome at the end of July.

152. Appian gives the sums in Attic currency, but their Roman equivalents have been used here. Suetonius (*Divus Julius* 38) agrees with the figure of 100 denarii for the distribution to the *plebs*, but says that Caesar distributed 24,000 sestertii (= 6,000 denarii) to each ordinary soldier. (The Attic silver drachma (nominal weight 4.3g) is generally used loosely by Greek writers as an equivalent for the Roman denarius (nominal weight, from *c.* 200 BC to Nero, 3.98g.) In practice, weights of individual coins fluctuated quite widely, and there is also evidence that under the Empire the drachma of the eastern provinces was tariffed at *less* than the full sixteen *asses* which made up the denarius.)

153. See ch. 68 above.

154. 45 BC.

155. As he had done at Pharsalus; see ch. 76.

156. Appian's generic word (*agones*) embraces musical, dramatic, athletic, and even gladiatorial contests or shows. The Latin word *ludi*, usually and in this context misleadingly translated 'games', covers the first three.

157. In Latin, PATER PATRIAE or PARENS PATRIAE; the latter has better support from contemporary documents.

158. See Book I, chs. 98–9 and notes.

159. i.e. 44 BC.

160. The diadem worn by Hellenistic kings was of this form, with the ends of the ribbon falling down the back of the neck.

161. King (*Rex*) is found as a surname in Latin, just as it is in English.

162. Appian is obscure here. He is, I think, trying to manufacture a paradox by contrasting kingly (traditionally autocratic) power, defended by Caesar when he should have condemned it, with tribunician (traditionally democratic) power, violated by Caesar when he should have defended it. Note that here and elsewhere I have preferred to translate the Greek term *tyrannos*, which indicates something like a modern dictator, by 'despot' rather than 'tyrant', because the connotations of the latter in English are over-negative.

163. The Lupercalia was an ancient festival, held on 15 February each year, connected with the Lupercal, a cave below the Palatine where Romulus and Remus were supposed to have been suckled by the she-wolf. The priests, the Luperci, were drawn from the best families of Rome.

164. Brutus was born Marcus Iunius Brutus, but after his father's death was adopted into his mother's family, the Servilii Caepiones, and became officially Q. Servilius Caepio Brutus, although he continued to be generally known as M. Brutus; his father had supported the rising of Lepidus (see Book I, ch. 107) and was put to death by Pompeius after surrendering to him in Mutina in 77 BC. For Cassius, see n. 135 above. Decimus Iunius Brutus Albinus (only very distantly connected with M. Brutus) was one of Caesar's most competent and trusted officers in Gaul, and was in command of naval operations at the siege of Massilia in 49 BC.

165. This is a ridiculous though not biologically impossible tale. The well-attested liaison of Caesar with Servilia belongs to the fifties and forties BC (when she was a widow), while Brutus was born in 85, when Caesar was fifteen. Servilia was Cato's half-sister.

166. 'Decimus' is Decimus Brutus (see ch. 111), and 'Trebonius' is C. Trebonius, praetor in 48 and consul (suffect) in 45.

167. Apart from Brutus and Cassius, Sextius Naso, named in ch. 113 above, was also a praetor (assuming him to be the P. Naso mentioned by Cicero in *Philippic* III, 25). The legal functions of the praetors, particularly Brutus and Cassius as urban and peregrine praetors respectively, meant that they had to make themselves available to the public on a regular basis.

168. In Roman divination, 'head' (*caput*) was the technical term for a projecting part of the liver, which was an organ of great significance in Roman divination.

169. The roofs of ancient Mediterranean houses were mostly flat.

170. In fact, the authority of a dictator's Master of Horse lapsed if there ceased to be a dictator.

171. A felt skullcap was headgear worn by ex-slaves to signify their acquisition of freedom. The same symbol, flanked by two daggers and accompanied by the legend EID. MART. (*The Ides of March*), appears on coins later issued by Brutus.

172. These men, all senators, are P. Cornelius Lentulus Spinther (consul in 57), M. Favonius (praetor in 49), M. Aquinus, P. Cornelius Dolabella (tribune in 47), L. Staius Murcus (praetor in ?45), and Q. Patiscus. The former three had fought on Pompeius' side in the civil war, the latter three on Caesar's.

173. Cf. Caesar's behaviour in 59 BC, at the end of ch. 10 above.

174. L. Cornelius Cinna was the brother of Caesar's first wife.

175. Appian appears to be referring to the *toga praetexta* and lictors.

176. Cisalpine Gaul.

177. The meeting took place on 17 March, not 16 March as might appear from Appian's narrative.

178. Appian means the Curia Hostilia, the senate-house in the Roman forum. This had been rebuilt by Sulla's son Faustus after it had been burnt down in the demonstration at Clodius' impromptu funeral (see ch. 21 above).

179. Under the constitution of the late Republic, the minimum age at which a man could become consul was forty-two.

180. It is unclear whether Appian (who confusingly writes throughout of both sides as 'they') means that pro-Caesar praetors tried to reinforce the belief of the opposition that they (the opposition) really could control the elections when in fact they could not (and would be wiped out, to the advantage of the Caesarians); or that pro-Cassius praetors tried to dupe Caesar's supporters into going along with a process which the opposition was well aware that it could not control (in spite of its statement to the contrary) but hoped would lead to the failure of Caesarians to be re-elected to their present offices.

181. Pontifex Maximus.

182. According to Suetonius (*Divus Iulius* 83), Caesar had entrusted his will to the senior Vestal Virgin, but it was opened and read at the request of Piso, who was Calpurnia's father.

183. See ch. 41.

184. Antonius would have been wearing a toga, which fell nearly to the ground and as normally worn left only the right arm tolerably free.

185. According to Suetonius (*Divus Iulius* 84), this was a quotation from a play about Ajax by the old Roman tragedian Pacuvius (*Men servasse, ut essent qui me perderent?*).

186. Appian has confused the senate-house in the forum, where the funeral was taking place, with the hall adjoining the Theatre of Pompey where Caesar was actually killed (cf. ch. 115 above).

187. Crowns (wreaths made of precious metal) were given as military decorations. Caesar's veterans doubtless took a leading part in the events here described.

188. 15 March. Anthesterion is a month in the Ionic Greek calendar.

189. At the oasis of Siwa, in the desert west of Cairo.

190. That is, the western part of what we call Asia Minor.

191. See ch. 57 above.

192. L. Aurunculeius Cotta and Q. Titurius Sabinus, together with fifteen Roman cohorts, were wiped out by a revolt of the Eburones in north-eastern Gaul in the late autumn of 54 BC.

193. For these four incidents, see chs. 42, 61, 95 and 104.

194. See n. 168.

195. Hephaistion was the most honoured, and the closest to Alexander, of all the king's companions.

196. The Chaldaeans were the Babylonian priests who specialized in divination, astrology, and so forth.

197. From a lost play by Euripides.

BOOK III

1. Appian says 'Ionian Asia', by which he means the Roman province of Asia. This was the western part of what we call Asia Minor, to the whole of which area it would appear that Appian and his contemporaries had incorrectly extended the name 'Asia'.

2. No other source (except the highly compressed and rhetorically coloured account by Florus) supports Appian on this point. Cicero's numerous letters of these months never mention it, even though they have much to say about the predicament of Brutus and Cassius, to which the fact, if true, would have been highly relevant. Most decisive is the evidence of Cicero's *Eleventh Philippic*, delivered at about the end of February 43. In this speech, the orator (at §§ 27–30) is urging the senate to legitimize retrospectively the unauthorized seizure of Macedonia and Syria by Brutus and Cassius at the end of the previous year. If Caesar had indeed allocated them these provinces, Cicero would have been able to argue that the step he was proposing was completely legal, being in perfect conformity with Caesar's known wishes and the agreement following Caesar's death. However, he does not do so, and is forced instead to use much more questionable arguments based on the 'higher legality' of true patriotism. The conclusion that Appian is mistaken is reinforced by the fact that Caesar appears to have assigned provinces to none of the other praetors of 44 before his death, and there is no discernible reason why he should have made an exception for Brutus and Cassius.

3. Cicero's correspondence makes clear that it was Dolabella who took this drastic action about the end of April, during Antonius' absence from Rome (from about mid-April to mid-May).

4. This commission was granted to Brutus and Cassius on 5 June, to give them a respectable reason for absenting themselves from Rome.

5. 'Impossible' not in constitutional terms, for the senate normally allotted provincial governorships, but for practical reasons: in the present political climate the senate would clearly not take Syria from Cassius (accepting Appian's mistake; see n. 2).

6. The Cornelii Dolabellae were not only patrician, but of more ancient consular lineage (first consul in the family, 283 BC) than the plebeian Cassii Longini (first consul 171 BC).

7. This Asprenas (presumably a Nonius Asprenas) is otherwise unknown.

8. Antonius was a member of the priestly college of augurs, whose business was to interpret omens and recommend the action to be taken.

9. The grant of Syria to Dolabella (and presumably of Macedonia to Antonius) had been made by 17 April at the latest (Cicero, *Letters to Atticus* XIV, 9.3). On the other hand the grant to Cassius of Cyrene (or Bithynia, or according to Dio Illyricum), and to Brutus of Crete (Cicero, *Philippic* II, 97) was made no earlier than 5 June (when the face-saving corn commission referred to in ch. 6 was conferred) and no later than 17 September, most probably in the second half of July.

10. Octavian's mother Atia was the daughter of M. Atius Balbus, a non-senator who had married Caesar's sister.

11. Atia married L. Marcius Philippus (consul in 56 BC) after the death of her first husband C. Octavius (praetor in 61 BC) early in 58.

12. In the interests of clarity, this translation uses the convenient but inaccurate modern convention which calls Caesar's heir 'Octavian' until 27 BC and 'Augustus' thereafter. By the normal rules of Roman nomenclature C. Octavius, after his adoption by a C. Iulius Caesar, should have become C. Iulius Caesar Octavianus, but neither he, nor (with rare and politically motivated exceptions) anyone else, ever used the last of these names, because it very clearly indicated that he had been adopted. From March 44, he was simply 'Caesar' to his contemporaries and to antiquity generally.

13. See nn. 2 and 9.

14. Octavian entered Rome about the end of April.

15. Homer, *Iliad* XVIII, 98.

16. i.e. Amatius, the false Marius (see ch. 3).

17. A provincial governor was immune from prosecution until his tenure of office was over.

18. The Antonii claimed descent from Heracles through one of the hero's sons, Anton; see Plutarch, *Antony*, ch. 4.

19. Gaius Antonius was a praetor, and Lucius (the youngest of the three brothers) a tribune, in 44 BC.

20. Quoted from Demosthenes (*de Falsa Legatione* 136).

21. Q. Pedius (who had been proconsul of Spain in 45 BC) and L. Pinarius <Scarpus?> were, like Octavian, nephews or great-nephews of Caesar. Octavian took three-quarters of the inheritance, while Pedius and Pinarius shared the remaining quarter (Suetonius, *Divus Iulius* 83).

22. These major 'games' (so usually but misleadingly translated, consisting primarily of theatrical performances and other displays) were those in honour of Apollo, the *Ludi Apollinares*, which took place from 7 July to 13 July. It was the responsibility of the urban praetor to make the arrangements. In the present case, Gaius Antonius' role would simply have been to preside officially over a show which was organized by Brutus' friends.

23. Words inserted by analogy with the otherwise identical claim in ch. 37 below.

24. Dolabella was still in Italy on 25 October, but had not ceased to be consul when he passed through Macedonia. He probably reached Asia at the end of the year.

25. Trebonius died about mid-January 43 BC.

26. Appian now jumps back some eight months from the death of Trebonius, to May 44 BC.

27. Provinces were normally allocated by the senate, but the decision (like any senatorial decision) could always be overridden or bypassed through a vote taken in the popular assembly, which then became a 'law' (more akin to our notion of a parliamentary Act). Note that from this point onwards Appian ceases to identify Decimus Brutus' province explicitly as 'Cisalpine' Gaul.

28. Gaius Antonius stood in for Brutus as urban praetor after the latter departed from Rome (see n. 22). There is no evidence that he left Italy before he was allotted the province of Macedonia at the emergency senate meeting of 28 November, by which time the legions there had already crossed to Brundisium.

29. The 'games' in honour of Mars, the *Ludi Martiales*, which took place on 12 May.

30. The Forum Iulium, which lay alongside the old Republican forum. Temple and Forum were dedicated on (pre-Julian) 26 September 46 BC but as a result of Caesar's calendar reform at the end of that year, with its insertion of sixty-seven days, the commemorative festival of the *Ludi Victoriae Caesaris* fell thereafter on (Julian) 20–30 July.

31. Appian's account remains constitutionally implausible, even though editors have improved it by the transposition (accepted here) of centuries and tribes. For the difference between the two assemblies, see Appendix (*A*). According to Cicero the law was proposed by a tribune and would therefore have had to come before the tribal assembly. Furthermore, the centuriate assembly did not meet in the forum. The date was either 2 June or 3 June.

32. Octavian was not only too young to be a tribune, but was also a patrician and thus permanently ineligible.

33. See n. 2 and the end of ch. 6.

34. The consuls for 43, already designated by Caesar, were A. Hirtius and C. Vibius Pansa.

35. The report (which was believed by Cicero) of the attempt on Antonius' life became known about the end of September.

36. On 9 October.

37. This occurred at the very end of October 44 BC, as Cicero's correspondence shows. Five hundred denarii was the equivalent of rather more than two years' pay for an ordinary soldier.

38. Tib. Cannutius.

39. Octavian must have entered Rome in the second or third week of November. It was contrary to constitutional practice for soldiers to appear armed in the city.

40. Certainly cash gifts, or donatives, are meant.

41. See Book I, ch. 118 and note.

42. A praetorian cohort was one selected to fight under, and guard, the commander personally. Cicero, in Campania, heard initial reports that Antonius was accompanied by a whole legion, *V Alaudae*, and was expected to stay the night of 9 November at Casilinum, on his way to Rome; however, he later says that much of what he had previously heard about Antonius was untrue.

43. The contemporary evidence of Cicero's *Third Philippic* (delivered on 20 December) shows that Appian has telescoped the meeting of the senate which was called for 24 November, and had to be postponed because of the desertion of the Martian legion, with the meeting held (by night) on 28 November at which the news of the desertion of the Fourth arrived.

44. i.e. Antonius exchanged his toga for military dress and the commander's cloak (*paludamentum*).

45. C. Asinius Pollio was governor of Further Spain, M. Aemilius Lepidus (see Book II, ch. 118) of Nearer Spain and Narbonese (southern) Gaul, and L. Munatius Plancus of the rest of Transalpine Gaul.

46. The new consuls, A. Hirtius and C. Vibius Pansa, entered office on 1 January.

47. The only historical precedent for such a grant of *imperium* (see Appendix, Ai) to a man who had not held any elective magistracy was the case of Pompeius Magnus in 82–80 (retrospectively) and 77–71 BC. Without *imperium*, which was a power possessed in full only by consuls, proconsuls, praetors and propraetors (and by a dictator and his Master of Horse), a commander had no constitutional authority to issue orders.

48. Presumably because all Caesar's decisions were to be valid, and it was by Caesar's decision that Decimus held the governorship of Cisalpine Gaul.

49. The first act of the new consuls was always to sacrifice to Jupiter on the Capitol.

50. Salvius' other names are not known. For his fate, see Book IV, ch. 17.

51. Opinions were sought in order of seniority in the senate. Ex-consuls ranked immediately after serving magistrates and magistrates-elect, and could always expect to speak. Cicero proposed that Octavian should be granted propraetorian *imperium* and have the status of an ex-praetor. These resolutions were passed on 3 January.

52. The minimum legal age for the consulship under the Republic was forty-two.

53. Antonius' mother was a Julia, and his current wife, his third, was Fulvia. His elder son by the latter was at most three, so it is possible that the lad here mentioned is an otherwise unrecorded son of his previous marriage to his cousin Antonia (see Book V, ch. 19, n. 21).

54. Appian made virtually no use of Cicero's *Fifth Philippic*, delivered on 1 January, in composing this speech, which corresponds to none of the extant *Philippics* (see Introduction, IVd).

55. The grounds on which Salvius secured a postponement of any senatorial

condemnation of Antonius (ch. 50–51) must have included the lack of any reliable information from Cisalpine Gaul.

56. Theory and practice were out of step by the late Republic. The popular assembly is known to have declared war on only eight occasions between 264 and 31 BC, all against other states. Many dozens of wars must have been started in this period on the authority of the senate or by personal decision of a provincial governor.

57. That is, armed attack on Italy.

58. Or 'with three of his legions'. Decimus certainly had four legions in Mutina (see ch. 97), but ch. 49 shows that the fourth must have been raised at the last minute and the sense of Piso's proposal, if accurately reported by Appian, was probably to withdraw *all* the forces under Decimus' command, since Antonius had at least as many.

59. Coriolanus was an exiled Roman patrician who is said to have led a Volscian army on Rome in 489 and 488 BC.

60. Cicero's *Sixth Philippic*, delivered to a public meeting in Rome on 4 January, reveals many of the terms of the senate's resolution: Antonius was to cease attacking Decimus, lift the siege of Mutina, stop plundering the province and raising troops, and submit to the authority of the senate and people of Rome by withdrawing south of the Rubicon but remaining more than 200 miles from Rome. The embassy was also to enter Mutina and thank Decimus and his troops for their loyalty. The *Seventh Philippic* (late January, before the return of the embassy), by alleging that Antonius will negotiate to be confirmed in Further Gaul or ask for Macedonia, shows that the senate had not in fact agreed to give him Macedonia in exchange for Gaul, as Appian asserts. The *Sixth Philippic* also reveals Cicero's implacable hostility to Antonius as he argues passionately for immediate military action on the grounds that the embassy is bound to fail and sending it is a waste of time.

61. Piso's speech was delivered on 3 January. The news about Trebonius came in late February or early March. See ch. 26 and notes thereto.

62. The delegation consisted of Piso himself, Octavian's stepfather Philippus, and Ser. Sulpicius Rufus (consul in 51 BC). All could be described as moderates in politics.

63. The embassy (minus Sulpicius who had died *en route*) returned from Antonius on 2 February, but in spite of Cicero's efforts more moderate counsels prevailed and Antonius was not declared a public enemy (*hostis*) until the news of the second battle of Mutina (ch. 71) reached Rome on 26 April. What was declared on 3 or 4 February was a state of emergency.

64. M. Ap(p)uleius, the retiring proquaestor of Asia, delivered public funds from the province to Brutus in Euboea late in 44 BC, and assisted him in raising troops.

65. Although Cicero proposed at about the beginning of March that Cassius be given the governorship of Syria, it was not actually conferred on him until the end of April, by which time reasonably reliable reports of what was happening in the eastern provinces had reached Rome.

66. P. Ventidius had served as tribune of the *plebs* in 45 BC and became one of the praetors for 43 BC. Born in Picenum of local stock, he had been a child in Asculum when the town fell in the Social War, and walked as a captive in the triumph of Pompeius Magnus' father in 89 BC. There is no further evidence for the tale related here of his march on Rome.

67. D. Carfulenus, whose name has become corrupted in the MSS of Appian to Carsuleius, had been a violently anti-Antonian tribune of the *plebs* in 44 BC and was currently a military tribune. The purpose of his mission was to provide veteran stiffening for Pansa's four legions of new recruits in case Antonius should decide (as he did) to attack them before they reached Mutina.

68. In fact the right wing, consisting of eight cohorts of the Martian legion, was commanded by Carfulenus' superior, the legion's usual commanding officer Ser. Sulpicius Galba, who was already with Pansa after having been sent back earlier by Hirtius to hurry him up. The battle took place near Forum Gallorum (modern *Castelfranco*), a settlement on the Aemilian Way about eight miles south-east of Mutina. Galba's eye-witness account of the battle (in Cicero, *Letters to his Friends* X, 30), written on the following day, 15 April, differs in many important respects from Appian's.

69. See ch. 43 above.

70. –. Manlius Torquatus (*praenomen* unknown) was the consul Pansa's quaestor, and was *ex-officio* his second-in-command. After Pansa's subsequent death from his wound he arrested the physician Glyco on suspicion of having administered poison.

71. According to Cicero, speaking a few days later after receiving reports of the battle, Hirtius had two legions, the Fourth and Seventh (*Philippic* XIV, 27).

72. This battle took place on 21 April.

73. For Lepidus and Plancus, see ch. 46 and n. 45, and for Ventidius ch. 66.

74. 'Citizens' probably means 'Roman citizens' – i.e. not only the relatively unimportant and powerless population of Mutina, but the armies on both sides, whose views on Decimus' case would be crucial in determining what action Octavian might feel able to take.

75. Latin *supplicatio*, a mixture of holiday and religious ceremonies in celebration of victory.

76. Cicero's *Fourteenth Philippic*, delivered on receipt of the news of the battle(s) at Forum Gallorum on 14 April, proposes a *supplicatio* of fifty days for the achievement of all three commanders, reiterates the promises already made of rewards to the veterans, and commissions the erection of a public memorial to the men who died in battle.

77. In the spring of 47 BC.

78. It is not clear what function Appian intended to indicate by this phrase. Q. Caecilius Bassus was of equestrian rank and if he was in service with the legion may have been the *praefectus fabrum*, in charge of the camp itself. Alternatively, Appian may have thought he was the chief civilian contractor for its supplies. (The bulk of this and the following chapter is repeated almost verbatim in Book IV, chs. 58–9.)

79. Sextus Iulius Caesar was appointed to command the forces in Syria about July 47 BC, and met his death approximately a year later.

80. 'Libo' is possibly an error or corruption for 'Livy'. Otherwise, a Libo is on record as the author of an annalistic history published by 45 BC, but it is quite uncertain whether Appian's 'Libo' is the same man or whether either of them could be L. Scribonius Libo, father-in-law of Sex. Pompeius, and consul in 34 BC.

81. L. Staius Murcus (praetor in ?45) had been appointed proconsul of Syria for 44, but was still in Rome when Caesar was murdered. He then associated himself with the conspirators, but on arrival in Syria still proceeded to take action against the Pompeian Bassus, whom he besieged in Apamea. Q. Marcius Crispus (praetor in ?46) governed Bithynia in 45 and 44.

82. A. Allienus (praetor in 49 BC) served as a senior officer (*legatus*) in Asia, first under Trebonius and then under Dolabella. For Crassus, see Book II, ch. 18.

83. This is the Laodiceia on the Syrian coast some fifty miles south of Antioch. According to Dio, its inhabitants were well-disposed to Caesar.

84. Other sources, including Cicero, indicate that G. Antonius was deserted by his soldiers after being besieged in Apollonia.

85. P. Decius <Mus?>, mocked by Cicero in the *Philippics*; rank unknown, perhaps a military tribune.

86. The words between the daggers are certainly corrupt but no agreement exists on their correction.

87. A triumph could in theory only be celebrated by a general whose victory was significant enough to allow him to return to Rome and discharge his army.

88. Culleo was perhaps the son of Q. Terentius Culleo, one of the tribunes of 58 BC.

89. M. Iuventius Laterensis, praetor in 51 BC.

90. These two men are not identifiable, but may indeed have been the official bearers of the terms of a (public) senatorial decree, referred to by Cicero in his private correspondence with M. Brutus, which summoned him to bring his army back to Italy.

91. M. Valerius Maximus Corvus (often called Corvinus) held six consulships between 348 and 299 BC, the first at the age of twenty-three. P. Cornelius Scipio Africanus attained the consulship in 205 BC at the age of about thirty, but perhaps more to the point is his proconsular command in Spain from 210 to 206 BC. At neither period had a minimum age for holding the consulship yet been enshrined in law, though forty-two had been prescribed by the time P. Cornelius Scipio Aemilianus (the second Africanus) was elected by popular pressure in 147 BC at the age of thirty-eight. From 180 BC until the end of the republic, forty-two remained the legal minimum age.

92. There were several bridges within the walls, so perhaps Appian means the Milvian Bridge a little way out of the city, where the Flaminian Way crossed the Tiber.

93. Octavian had a full sister, Octavia minor, who was about three years older than himself, and a half-sister, Octavia major, older again. Presumably the former is referred to here. For his mother Atia, see nn. 10 and 11.

94. It seems that Octavian approached from the north by the Milvian Bridge and the

Flaminian Way, halting in the general area of the Campus Martius and the Pincian Hill before he reached the city proper.

95. M. Caecilius Cornutus was urban praetor, and therefore the senior magistrate after the deaths of the consuls Hirtius and Pansa.

96. See ch. 82.

97. M'. Aquillius Crassus was one of the current praetors. The tribune P. Ap-(p)uleius, a committed supporter of Cicero's policies, is to be distinguished from the M. Ap(p)uleius of ch. 63.

98. Up to the 5,000 denarii voted in ch. 90.

99. For Pedius, see ch. 22. He and Octavian entered office on 19 August 43 BC.

100. Before the constitutional reforms ascribed to King Servius Tullius in the sixth century BC, which instituted new territorial tribes based on domicile, the Roman people were divided into three tribes, each composed of ten *curiae* (probably meaning 'groups of men'), whose basis appears to have been at least partly one of kinship. The earliest Roman assembly (the *comitia curiata*) comprised these thirty *curiae* meeting together, but after the Servian reforms the only functions which it retained were the official conferment of *imperium* on magistrates and some acts connected with the validation of wills and adoptions – especially the adoption of one (like Octavian) who by virtue of his father's death had become an independent person no longer subject to the legal control (*patria potestas*) of another, and who would as a result of the adoption (normally) be losing that legal independence to his new 'father'. By the time of the late Republic these acts had become so formal that each *curia* was represented by a single lictor. In the present case, in spite of what Appian says, Octavian's purpose must have been to put the fact of his adoption as far beyond doubt as was possible under the circumstances, since both the genuineness of Caesar's will and the validity of the testamentary adoption were open to question. Octavian's claim, as Caesar's heir, on the services of Caesar's ex-slaves ('freedmen') was not affected by the method of his adoption, so long as that adoption was recognized.

101. This man was P. Silicius Corona; see Book IV, ch. 27.

102. Appian is in error either over Gallius' office or over the date of this episode (see n. 95 above).

103. Appian means not Cisalpine but Narbonese Gaul, that southern part of Transalpine Gaul which was already a Roman province before Caesar embarked on his conquests. This information seems to conflict with that at Book II, ch. 48, where Decimus is said to have been appointed to govern 'newly-conquered' Gaul, but perhaps in the present passage Appian is thinking of the scope of Decimus' immediately preceding command during the siege of Massilia in 49 BC.

BOOK IV

1. Book I, chs. 71–3, 95–6, 103.

2. For Antonius' abolition of the office of dictator, see Book III, ch. 25. The official title used by Lepidus, Antonius, and Octavian was *Tresviri rei publicae constituendae* (Board of Three (triumvirate) for the Ordering of State). Although Appian is correct to state that they possessed consular *imperium*, this was not, it seems, part of their title, and he has expressed himself very loosely. He means that they called themselves, not dictators, but triumvirs. (Apart from the objection he mentions to the title of dictator, there was another, namely that the essence of the Roman dictatorship, and the feature which gave it its unique power, was that, unlike all other magistracies, it was *not* collegiate: see Book I, ch. 99 and n. 166.)

3. See Book I, ch. 97, n. 161.

4. See Book I, ch. 97, n. 161. Antonius and Octavian had both been saluted '*Imperator*' by their armies for successes during the campaign of Mutina, and Lepidus for victories in Spain for which he subsequently triumphed (on 31 December 43 BC).

5. If a slave's master was not a Roman (or Latin) citizen, Roman law had no power to free his slave. For the relative value of these sums, see n. 24 to Book II.

6. L. Aemilius Paullus was consul in 50 BC, L. Iulius Caesar (Antonius' uncle, a distant relation of the dictator) consul in 64 BC.

7. L. Plotius Plancus, one of the praetors of the current year, and L. Quinctius. The latter is almost certainly not the celebrated tribune of 74 BC, praetor in 68 BC, but another man of the same name who is recorded as an ex-praetor in an undated late republican inscription from Tenos; for his fate, see ch. 27.

8. C. Toranius, colleague of Octavian's real father in the aedileship of (probably) 64 BC.

9. No further identification of this Minucius can be made.

10. This man is probably L. Villius Annalis, praetor by 58 BC at the latest. It would be very unlikely for a praetor in office to have a son old enough to stand for the quaestorship.

11. Appian's manuscripts spell the name 'Thouranios'. This man should not be identified with the 'Thoranios' of ch. 12, who is certainly the C. Toranius mentioned by Suetonius as the guardian of Octavian, but with C. Turranius, one of the praetors of 44 BC.

12. Plutarch, in his rather different account of the death of Cicero, describes Popillius Laenas as a military tribune (*chiliarchos*), says that the charge on which Cicero defended him was one of parricide, and ascribes the actual killing to the centurion Herennius. Laenas must have been a member of the family which produced four consuls in the second century, but had subsequently slipped from prominence.

13. These were the fourteen speeches, still extant, which Cicero delivered (except for the Second, which was circulated) between 2 September 44 BC and mid-April 43 BC. Demosthenes' four *Philippics*, urging the Athenians to act against the expansionist Philip II of Macedon, were delivered between 350 and 341 BC.

14. A certain L. Egnatius Rufus was a banker and business agent of Cicero's in the fifties and forties BC, and he and his son could therefore plausibly be the pair here mentioned; but proof is lacking, and the family name is common. In particular, there

is a senatorial family of Egnatii Maximi who are perhaps just as likely to have been victims of the triumvirs.

15. 'Balbus' is C. Octavius Balbus, who joined the conspirators immediately after the murder of Caesar.

16. These Arruntii are unidentified, but are probably related to the L. Arruntius who commanded a wing of Octavian's fleet at the battle of Actium in 31 BC and attained the consulship in 22 BC. The family came from Atina in northern Samnium.

17. These were probably the brothers Quintus (a conspirator against Caesar; see Book II, ch. 113) and Titus, who were both senators. There is known to have been a third brother (conceivably the Gaius Ligarius recorded as a friend of Marcus Brutus), and he *may* be the Ligarius mentioned in ch. 23, below, as the name is uncommon.

18. In the context, this river is almost certainly the Tiber.

19. The Greek puns on the preposition *pro* which means both 'instead of' and 'before'.

20. See n. 17.

21. Capito is possibly Cicero's friend C. Ateius Capito. A one-time Pompeian, he was given a post by Caesar, assisting L. Plotius Plancus (L. Munatius Plancus' brother) to distribute land to settlers in Epirus in 45 or 44 BC. Plotius Plancus became one of the praetors of 43 BC, but was proscribed (see ch. 12 above).

22. C. Asinius Pollio, historian and soldier, was consul in 40 BC, but Appian probably does not mean to use the consulship as a date so much as a means of identifying Pollio. His father-in-law was L. Quinctius; see ch. 12.

23. Perhaps L. Flaminius C(h)ilo, candidate for a suffect tribunate in 44, and a moneyer in 43 BC.

24. Appian's MSS give Icelius, but the correct name, Silicius Corona, is preserved by Dio Cassius (XLVI, 49.5).

25. We know of no ex-consul alive in 43 BC who was called Varus (a not uncommon name), but Appian leaves the truth or otherwise of his assertion quite open. Of the ex-consuls who were proscribed, L. Iulius Caesar and L. Aemilius Paullus escaped and only Cicero died.

26. The property of the proscribed was forfeit to the state, and was therefore auctioned to raise money for the triumvirs.

27. At the age of fourteen or fifteen, to mark their entry on manhood, Roman boys of good class exchanged the purple-bordered child's toga for a plain white one.

28. According to Dio (XLVII, 14.2) the rich who received rents upon property had to contribute a whole year's worth of such income, plus half a year's worth of the notional rent of property which they occupied themselves. 100,000 denarii = 400,000 sesterces, which was the property qualification for membership of the equestrian order.

29. In order to inherit their property.

30. M. Valerius Messalla Corvinus, son of the consul of 61 BC.

31. L. Calpurnius Bibulus, son of Caesar's great enemy and consular colleague

M. Bibulus (see Book II, ch. 10ff.). He became proconsul of Syria in 34 or 33 and died before 31 BC.

32. (L.?) Cornelius Lentulus Cruscellio, who subsequently (38 BC?) became praetor.

33. This *may* be the pro-Ciceronian tribune of 43 BC.

34. (C.?) Antistius Reginus, perhaps the man mentioned as a partisan of Sextus Pompeius in Book V, ch. 139. A G. Antistius Reginus served as an officer under Caesar in Gaul from 53 to 50 BC.

35. This is probably C. Coponius, praetor in 49 BC. He survived until at least 32 BC, when, perhaps significantly, he is found opposing Antonius.

36. Perhaps C. Hosidius Geta.

37. The son is M. Oppius, aedile in 37 BC. The father cannot be identified.

38. These Metelli, in spite of the prominence of the family in late republican history, are not identifiable. The tale, whose authenticity must be suspect, has nothing to do with the proscriptions and appears to have crept in here by virtue of similarity of subject-matter.

39. Some historians believe this name to be a mistake for (C. Lucilius) Hirrus, tribune in 53 BC, Pompeius Magnus' cousin and a great landowner. Hirrus is certainly unlikely to have escaped proscription, on account of his wealth and his political sympathies, but there is no other evidence.

40. Possibly C. Antius Restio, who was tribune in or before 68 BC and passed a sumptuary law, or his son, who was a moneyer in 47 BC.

41. Q. Lucretius Vespillo, consul in 19 BC.

42. Pomponius cannot be further identified. Valerius Maximus ascribes the exploit to one Sentius Saturninus Vetulo.

43. These men are M. Ap(p)uleius and L. Arruntius, who both later held consulships. It was Apuleius who governed Bithynia, Arruntius who sought refuge with Sextus Pompeius.

44. This Ventidius is not be be confused with the P. Ventidius mentioned in Book III, ch. 66.

45. According to Diodorus Siculus (I, 87), dogs helped Isis to find Osiris, and the dog-headed god Anubis is represented as guarding the company of Isis and Osiris. Ovid (*Amores* II, 13.11) associates the (dog?-) face of Anubis with the cult of Isis, and the emperors Commodus and Caracalla, who were both initiates, are said *portare Anubim*, a phrase which in the light of this passage and the other evidence presumably means to wear the mask of the dog-headed god (*Scriptores Historiae Augustae, Commodus* 9.4–6 and *Caracalla* 9.11).

46. This is the same M. Terentius Varro who wrote (among much else) the satirical attack on the 'First Triumvirate' of Caesar, Pompeius, and Crassus (see Book II, ch. 9, end). He was born in 116 BC, attained the praetorship between 74 and 70 BC, and was governing Lusitania for Pompeius at the outbreak of the civil war in 49 BC. He survived just long enough to see the monarchy he opposed established in 27 BC.

47. Q. Fufius Calenus (consul in 47 BC), a distinguished officer of Caesar's and prominent supporter of Antonius.

48. Themistocles, exiled from Athens *c.* 472 BC, was crossing the Aegean in a merchant ship when a storm drove it to Naxos. The island was at the time under siege from an Athenian fleet, to which the ship's captain threatened to betray the refugee.

49. M. Vipsanius Agrippa, Octavian's contemporary, and his best general, most loyal supporter, and right-hand man from the very beginning, held both official and unofficial positions of great power during the revolutionary period and eventually became his son-in-law and held a constitutional position only slightly less dominating than his own.

50. It has been conjectured that the protagonists of this tale are the consuls of 21 BC, Marcus Lollius (who commanded part of Octavian's fleet at Actium), and Q. Aemilius Lepidus (one of whose ancestors certainly used the *cognomen* Barbula: Livy IX, 20.7), but the identification must remain doubtful. The tale seems too neat to be true.

51. Lepidus had been stripped of his triumviral power in 36 BC and sent to finish his days quietly at Circeii, south of Rome. For the circumstances of his fall, see Book V, ch. 123ff. If 'Balbinus' is L. Saenius, consul in the second half of 30 BC, as believed by R. Syme (*The Augustan Aristocracy,* Oxford, 1986, p. 35), we have a firm date for young Lepidus' plot, which could otherwise belong to any time between mid-31 and mid-29 BC. In 29 BC, on his way back from the eastern Mediterranean, Octavian called in at Actium to dedicate the memorial of the battle. The triumvir's wife was Junia, sister to M. Brutus, the tyrannicide.

52. As the younger Cicero was consul in the second half of 30 BC, it was the news of Antonius' defeat and death at *Alexandria* which he read out.

53. Actually *Lucius* Sestius Quirinalis, suffect consul in 23 BC.

54. This is P. Sittius of Nuceria (very probably a relation of the man mentioned in ch. 47 above), who was already in Mauretania with his mercenaries in 63 BC.

55. See Book II, ch. 45.

56. See note to Book III, ch. 2.

57. The bulk of this and the following chapter are repeated almost verbatim from Book III, chs. 77–8.

58. i.e. the battle of Philippi (ch. 108ff. below).

59. This 'nephew' would appear to be the Lucius Cassius who surrendered to Antonius in the east after Philippi and is described as Cassius' brother (*adelphos*) in Book V, ch. 7. Another Lucius Cassius, said to be Cassius' nephew (*adelphidous*, as here), was killed at Philippi. One or other of these men (who *could* be father and son) is probably to be identified with the L. Cassius Longinus who was tribune of the *plebs* in 44 BC. It is likely that Appian has (understandably) become confused (see Book II, n. 135).

60. In the Greek world, a golden wreath or 'crown' was often bestowed for outstanding military or political services.

61. One talent was worth 6,000 drachmae (= denarii; see Book II, n. 152). For the purchasing power of money, see Book II, n. 24.

62. Mithridates VI, King of Pontus, attacked Rhodes in 88 BC, Demetrius Poliorcetes ('The Besieger'), son of Alexander the Great's marshal Antigonos, in 305–4 BC. The Rhodian success in withstanding the latter was commemorated by the erection of the famous Colossus.

63. The arch-Dorians, the Spartans, had in earlier times made it a deliberate policy to overthrow autocratic regimes ('tyrannies'). Paradoxically, they themselves had kings, but these were constitutional figureheads and only rarely exerted political power.

64. P. Cornelius Lentulus Spinther, son of Caesar's opponent of the same name, had been quaestor to Trebonius in Asia in 44 BC, and after the latter's death at the hands of Dolabella (see Book III, ch. 26) had joined Brutus and Cassius. Fannius is probably the well-known Pompeian C. Fannius, praetor in or before 50 BC, who appears to have survived Pharsalus and after the defeat of Brutus and Cassius at Philippi went on to join Sextus Pompeius in Sicily (see ch. 84 below).

65. See Book III, ch. 63.

66. A depth (though not a width) of fifty feet is virtually impossible, and certainly unexampled in siege warfare of the period. The numeral must be corrupt and should perhaps read *fifteen*.

67. Sarpedon was the Lycian hero who fell at Troy. His shrine must have abutted the perimeter wall of the town.

68. See Herodotus I, 176.

69. Ch. 54 above.

70. See n. 64.

71. This Domitius was the son of Caesar's great opponent L. Domitius, who had died at Pharsalus.

72. L. Decidius Saxa and C. Norbanus Flaccus.

73. The Corpili are said by Strabo, writing in the reign of Augustus, to live along the valley of the Hebrus, which enters the sea at Aenus. It appears from the stratagem described in ch. 102 below that the Corpilan pass was some way to the east of the Sapaean, and both lay on the route of the Via Flaminia.

74. The text is corrupt, and I have adopted an easy emendation to make Cardia and Lysimacheia lie on the correct (eastern) side of Aenus and Maroneia. The two former towns are in fact near the head of the Black Gulf (which divides the Thracian Chersonese from the land to the north-west), and Appian's 'second day' ought to mean the second day from Sestus, the start of the march.

75. See Book III, ch. 12, n. 12.

76. P. Scipio Africanus the younger ('Scipio Aemilianus') was elected consul for 147 BC, although technically too young, in recognition of his outstanding service as an officer at the siege of Carthage and his perceived fitness to command the whole operation.

77. See ch. 12.

78. Domitius is Ahenobarbus.

79. For these proportions, see ch. 120, end.

80. Strabo places Serrium between Doriscus and Maroneia, i.e. directly opposite the island of Samothrace.

81. Philip is Philip II of Macedonia, father of Alexander the Great. He annexed western Thrace in 356–355 BC.

82. See ch. 87.

83. In Greek, *Krenides*. Strabo (7.36,41) identifies Daton as a separate place, on or very near the coast.

84. Philippi is about eight miles from the sea at the nearest point (the port of Neapolis, modern *Kavalla*).

85. *Zygon* means 'yoke', and *-aktes* is from the verb-stem *ag-* meaning 'to break'. The myth referred to is that of the abduction of Demeter's daughter Kore (or Persephone) by the god of the underworld, Dis or Hades.

86. Suetonius tells us that Octavian wrote his autobiography down to the end of the Cantabrian war (25 BC). This has not survived, but the extant *Life* of Octavian by his contemporary and acquaintance Nicolaus of Damascus appears to draw heavily on it.

87. See Book II, ch. 69.

88. The date of the second battle, some three weeks after the first, was 23 October, according to official Roman calendars.

89. Euripides, *Medea*, 332. Plutarch (*Brutus*, 48, 51) makes it clear that this detail comes from an account, now lost, of the battle written by one P. Volumnius, probably the same man (Volumnius Flaccus) who had acted as an emissary to the senate on Decimus Brutus' behalf in 43.

90. The word for 'emperor' (in Latin, *imperator*) is the word which denotes 'supreme commander' in the Republic. Here, Appian seems to be thinking anachronistically of Caesar rather as emperor, and therefore by the customs of Appian's own age due especial respect and protection, than as a military commander about to leave Rome to assume the leadership of his projected expedition against the Parthians. Note that Suetonius, writing his imperial biographies (*The Twelve Caesars*) a generation before Appian, begins the sequence with Julius Caesar.

91. Homer, *Iliad* XVI, 849: the dying words of Patroclus, killed by Hector. 'Leto's son' is the god Apollo.

92. This man was Pacuvius Antistius Labeo, one of the conspirators against Caesar. His son Marcus Antistius Labeo, though also of fiercely independent spirit as befitted a Samnite (cf. Book I, ch. 87, end), survived as a senator and indeed held a praetorship under Augustus; he was one of the most famous and influential of the Roman jurists.

93. Porcia had previously been married to M. Calpurnius Bibulus, Caesar's enemy and colleague in the consulship of 59 BC, and Brutus to the daughter of Ap. Claudius Pulcher, consul in 54 BC and an equally extreme opponent of Caesar. The 'younger Cato' is the man referred to just above as 'Cato's son Cato', who courted death in battle. For his father's suicide, see Book II, chs. 98–9.

94. For Messalla, see ch. 38, and for L. Calpurnius Bibulus, ch. 104. The latter was one of the sons of Caesar's great enemy M. Bibulus (consul in 59 BC), and grandson of Cato.

95. Appian seems to have forgotten the civil wars of AD 68–9.

BOOK V

1. This book in fact contains very little about Egypt, but perhaps when Appian started to put it together he was proposing to lay some foundations for his treatment of the conflict between Antonius and Octavian in the subsequent *Egyptian History*. (See also Introduction, sect. I*b*, and Book I, ch. 6.)

2. C. Cassius Parmensis, so called to distinguish him from his erstwhile leader, the more famous C. Cassius, was one of the murderers of Caesar. He had been quaestor (or at least given the title) in Asia in 43 and had commanded a fleet which fought that of Dolabella in June of that year. He later joined Sextus Pompeius in Sicily, and after Sextus' defeat transferred his allegiance to Antonius. He fought on the losing side at Actium and was subsequently put to death.

3. Greek city-states often kept one or more ships especially for ceremonies or missions of a religious nature.

4. The identity of this Clodius is unclear, but it is possible that he was the lieutenant to whom Brutus gave the duty of guarding Gaius Antonius at Apollonia earlier in 42 BC (see Book III, ch. 79, with Dio XLVII, 24.2).

5. D. Turullius (quaestor in 44 BC) was another of the murderers of Caesar, and shared with Cassius of Parma (see n. 2 above) the distinction of being the last of them to die.

6. P. Aemilius Lepidus, whose local Cretan coinage terms him proquaestor (*pro praetore*?). His family relationship to the triumvir is unknown.

7. For Lepidus' provinces, see Book IV, chs. 2–3.

8. Q. Fufius Calenus had been one of Caesar's senior officers in the civil war in 49–48 BC, and became consul in 47. The anecdote involving Varro told in Book IV, ch. 47 indicates his standing at this time. For his command in Italy, see ch. 24 below.

9. Artemis ('Diana of the Ephesians').

10. See Book IV, ch. 62.

11. For Attalus, see Book I, ch. 18, n. 34. 'Demagogues' means Gaius Gracchus, for whose system see Book II, ch. 13, n. 32.

12. Ancient Peparethos is modern *Skopelos*, and ancient Ikos modern *Chiliodromia* or *Alonnisos*.

13. In the spring of 55 BC Gabinius, then proconsul of Syria, led a Roman force into Egypt to restore the exiled king Ptolemy XII Auletes, Cleopatra's father. At the time Antonius was twenty-seven and Cleopatra sixteen.

14. Appian has garbled something: the temple of Artemis Leukophryene was at Magnesia-on-the-Maeander, while Dio and Josephus make Arsinoe a suppliant at the more famous temple of Artemis at Ephesus.

15. See Book IV, ch. 61.

16. In the winter of 48–47 BC, when Caesar supported Cleopatra in her dynastic struggle with her sister Arsinoe and her young brother Ptolemy, later Ptolemy XIII.

17. This was the hereditary name of the eunuch priests at Ephesus.

18. The Syrian and Parthian wars form Book XI of Appian's *Roman History* (see Introduction, sect. I*b*).

19. Fulvia, Antonius' third wife, married him in 47 or 46 BC, having previously been married to Publius Clodius (see Book II, chs. 14–15, 20–21) and then C. Scribonius Curio (see Book II, chs. 26–31, 44–5). She bore him two children, M. Antonius ('Antyllus') in 46 or 45 BC, and Iullus Antonius in 42 BC. Lucius Antonius became consul at the start of 41 BC, in virtue of the arrangements made at Mutina in November 43 BC (Book IV, ch. 2). 'Manius' is presumably not the *praenomen*, but a family name, as it is attested in inscriptions at both Praeneste and Tibur; his history and other name(s) are unknown, but as Antonius' private agent in Italy he is certain to have been a wealthy and important member of the equestrian class.

20. By a law (the Lex Roscia) passed in 67 BC the front fourteen rows of the theatre were reserved for men of equestrian rank.

21. For Antonius' children, see n. 19. He also had a daughter by his second wife, his cousin Antonia. This girl was betrothed as a child in 44 BC to Lepidus' son, but eventually married Pythodorus of Tralles in 34 BC.

22. C. Asinius Pollio commanded Antonian forces in Transpadane Gaul, and was engaged in the establishment of colonies and the distribution of land to veterans there.

23. Text between daggers corrupt. Probably some reference to Pollio is intended, but note that Dio (XLVIII, 10.1) makes Calenus and Ventidius, Antonius' governors in Transalpine Gaul, responsible for blocking Salvidienus' march. Q. Salvidienus Rufus was one of Octavian's generals who was on his way to Spain but was very soon recalled (see chs. 24, 27). It is quite unclear to whom 'him' refers.

24. 'This' is possibly corrupt. If correct, it seems to refer to Lucius' army.

25. For Sextius, see ch. 12 and Book IV, chs. 53–6, where he is called Octavian's governor, but this appears to mean merely that he was the triumviral appointee in a province which was Octavian's by the division agreed at Mutina (IV, ch. 2). At any rate by this time, if not earlier, he was a follower of Antonius. C. Fuficius Fango was an ex-centurion from the colony of Acerrae who had been admitted to the senate by Caesar; his present command was a portent of the revolutionary age.

26. Dio (XLVIII, 45.1–2) ascribes this expedition to Bogud, the king of western Mauretania, which is more probable. The error (if it is one) may be Appian's or may be due to textual corruption of the name.

27. C. Carrinas, son of Marius' supporter who held a praetorship in 82 BC, had been appointed governor of Spain by Caesar in 45, held a consulship in 43, and was back in Spain by the winter of 42–41 BC, when the present disturbances were occurring.

28. By using the derogatory term 'mercenary' Appian seems to mean that this recruiting, though very probably of Roman citizens, was not carried out by the proper constitutional machinery of the levy, but on an *ad hoc* basis by offering cash inducements.

29. C. Furnius (praetor in 42, later governor of Asia in 36–35 BC) was evidently bringing these troops south when he was intercepted. Sentinum is the modern *Sassoferrato*, north-east of Perusia (*Perugia*).

30. On P. Ventidius, see Book III, ch. 66, n. 66. He had become suffect consul for a short period at the end of 43 BC, abdicating his praetorship to do so, and was almost certainly governor of one of Antonius' Gallic provinces in 42–41 BC. For Asinius Pollio, see n. 22.

31. On M. Agrippa, see Book IV, ch. 49, n. 49.

32. Plancus (see n. 34) and Ventidius had both held consulships, while Pollio had been designated consul for 40 BC. In addition, Plancus despised Ventidius (calling him a 'muleteer' in a letter to Cicero of 43 BC).

33. Tisienus Gallus had previously defended Nursia against an attack by Octavian. After the fall of Perusia he joined Sextus Pompeius in Sicily.

34. Q. Fufius Calenus was governor in Transalpine Gaul, and Ateius (Capito?) apparently held some kind of command in Cisalpine Gaul. L. Munatius Plancus (consul in 42 BC) had been making colonial settlements of veterans in the area of Beneventum.

35. The closeness to each other of the towers is paralleled a dozen years earlier in Caesar's siege-works at Alesia, where the distance between the towers was eighty feet (*Gallic War* VII.72). As for the stakes, Caesar (ibid., 73) makes it clear that these were sharpened at the top and set in the ground in various configurations, both in the bottom of the ditch and elsewhere.

36. Some examples of the lead slingshot (the so-called *glandes Perusinae*) survive, inscribed with the names of, or insults to, the principals in the war.

37. By 'the memoirs' (*hypomnemata*, notes or summaries serving as 'reminders') Appian seems to mean Octavian's own autobiography, which he drew on elsewhere in his work and refers to in the same way. On the other hand, the speeches as reported by Appian make Octavian give a good press to his opponent while denying himself a perfect opportunity to state his own case in refutation. Gabba therefore suggested (at pp. xvii–xxii of his commentary on this Book) that *hypomnemata*, which has a well-attested sense as 'minutes', might refer to the *Acta Diurna*, a daily record of public business published at Rome; but this requires that a speech by a defeated leader, who was no longer consul and had already been incommunicado for some weeks, was recorded, transmitted to Rome, and published at the precise moment when his opponent had re-established his supreme authority in Italy. This seems extremly unlikely. It is more plausible to suppose that Octavian's memoirs contained, not speeches, but a brief summary of the arguments on either side, which Appian worked up and slanted in a way appropriate to the rest of his very individual depiction of Lucius. However, *some* Octavianic influence is clearly present, because Appian's version of the surrender and its sequel is a great deal more favourable than that of Cassius Dio (XLVIII, 14) to Octavian.

38. The reference must be to the officer commanding the duty cohort(s) of the praetorian guard.

39. Before their conquest by Rome, which occurred piecemeal between the fourth and second centuries B C, the principal political organization of the Etruscans collectively was a league of the twelve leading peoples (perhaps the city-states of Veii, Caere, Tarquinii, Vulci, Rusellae, Vetulonia, Volsinii, Volaterrae, Clusium, Cortona, Perusia, and Arretium). Appian's statement here seems to be an inaccurate recollection of this fact.

40. Cannutius *may* be Gaius Cannutius, on record as an orator who was an enemy of Antonius and Octavian, since the known political figure, the tribune of 44 B C, Tiberius Cannutius, was (i) an ally of Octavian against Antonius, though he may subsequently have changed his allegiance, and (ii) dead by this time, if Velleius is correct to say that he was killed in the proscriptions. It is impossible to identify the other two men with even this limited degree of likelihood.

41. For Ateius, see n. 34. P. Canidius Crassus had probably been a commander with Antonius' forces in Gaul or the north of Italy, like Ateius, and was to become suffect consul later in the year.

42. Julia was the daughter of the consul of 90 B C, L. Iulius Caesar, who was great-uncle to the dictator. Antonius was thus the dictator's second cousin.

43. L. Scribonius Libo had been a prominent supporter of Pompeius Magnus in the civil war of 49–48 B C. 'Saturninus' is probably (–). Sentius Saturninus Vetulo, who was one of the proscribed and father of the staunch Augustan supporter who became consul in 19 B C, C. Sentius Saturninus.

44. Spain was normally administered as two separate provinces. Peducaeus *may* be the T. Peducaeus who was rewarded with a suffect consulship in 35 B C, but 'Lucius' (= Livius?) defies firm identification.

45. On the island of Cephallenia. The usual form of the name is Pale.

46. The crescent of the inner harbour, embracing the peninsula on which the town stands, is connected by a narrow entrance to the much larger outer harbour, where the islands are.

47. Menodorus, also called Menas, was one of Sextus' two leading admirals (the other being Menecrates). He had once been a slave, and had been freed either by Pompeius Magnus or by Sextus. If the description of him by other authors as a pirate has anything more to it than mere abuse, it is possible that he was taken captive by Pompeius Magnus in his campaign against the pirates in 67 B C (see Book II, ch. 1, and Antonius' threats against him, ch. 96 below).

48. Ausonia means northern Apulia. Thurii was on the Gulf of Taranto, while Consentia is modern *Cosenza*, lying to the west of the Sila massif, a little further to the south.

49. L. Cocceius Nerva was also to mediate between Antonius and Octavian in 37 B C. Nothing else is known of Caecina.

50. Cocceius' brother M. Cocceius Nerva presumably fought at Perusia. He later governed Asia for Antonius, in 38–37 B C.

51. 'Ahenobarbus' appears to be a slip for Ventidius, since the latter's name is frequently coupled with that of Asinius in the context of the Perusine war (see especially chs. 32–5), in which Ahenobarbus plays no part.

52. For Julia's relationship to Octavian, see n. 42.

53. C. Claudius Marcellus, consul in 50 BC, died early in the present year (40 BC). He had been a passionate anti-Caesarian (see Book II, chs. 26–31) but remained neutral during the war of 49–48 BC. His marriage to Octavia, who was perhaps five years older than her brother, took place in or before 53 BC. There were three children, two girls and the boy (42–23 BC) briefly destined to be Augustus' successor, who was so memorably mourned by Virgil in the *Aeneid* (VI. 860–86).

54. The date of this agreement, the so-called 'pact of Brundisium', was late September or early October, 40 BC.

55. Q. Labienus, son of Caesar's officer T. Labienus who deserted to Pompeius at the outbreak of the civil war, had been sent by Cassius in the summer of 42 BC to ask the Parthian king Orodes for assistance. The king had still not given his answer when the news of Philippi arrived, and Labienus stayed on at Orodes' court. In the winter of 41–40 BC he and the king's son Pacorus made a two-pronged attack on Syria and the southern parts of Asia Minor.

56. The work which survives under this title in the company of Appian's genuine works is a compilation from other authors, chiefly Plutarch, and is generally believed to be spurious.

57. Modern *Ischia*, on the Bay of Naples.

58. Mucia, daughter of the great Q. Mucius Scaevola, Pontifex Maximus and jurist (for whose death see Book I, ch. 88), was Pompeius Magnus' third wife and mother of both his sons. She was married to him from *c.* 80 to 62 BC, when he divorced her, according to one story for adultery with Caesar. She subsequently married M. Aemilius Scaurus, Sulla's stepson and a notable figure of the fifties BC, but was now a widow.

59. Baiae (modern *Baia*), a luxury resort, lay on the peninsula of Misenum opposite Ischia.

60. A. Pompeius Bithynicus, governor of Sicily in 44 and 43 BC, threw in his lot with Sextus Pompeius (no relation) in 43 (see Book IV, ch. 84) and was murdered in 42 BC.

61. Ancient warships were classified by the number of rowers in each vertical block of oars. A 'six' could have had three banks of oars with two men on each oar, or vice versa. The standard warship of this time, the 'five' (quinquereme) had either three banks of oars of which two were pulled by two men each and the third by one, or else (more probably, in view of the greater difficulty of managing three banks) two banks with three men on one oar and two on the other. The trireme of Athens' heyday had three banks of oars, each pulled by a single man.

62. Apparently Appian's mistake for Scribonia, Sextus' actual wife, whose aunt of the same name was now married to Octavian. Although Antonius' mother Julia *might* be meant, this seems less probable; ch. 52 above, where she is referred to in connection with Sextus, may well have caused Appian's slip.

63. Sextus became a member of the college of augurs, of which his father had also been a member.

64. At this time Marcellus was about three, and Pompeius' daughter likewise an infant.

65. This list of future consuls corresponds to those who actually held, or should have held, office in the years 34–31 BC (note that the Sex. Pompeius who appears as consul in 35 BC is documented as being son of *Sextus*, and therefore is not our Sextus). Sextus Pompeius, son of Gnaeus (Magnus), was dead by 33 BC and his place is occupied by L. Volcacius Tullus. In 31 BC the official record claims that Octavian's colleague was not Antonius (for the third time), but M. Valerius Messalla, but this is because war had by then broken out between Octavian and Antonius: Antonius' own coins testify to the fact that he at any rate still regarded himself as consul in that year. Appian's error in ascribing these consuls to the wrong run of years may be palliated by supposing that the triumvirs had already designated the consuls as far ahead as 35 BC, and that his fault lies simply in his failure to indicate that these four years were the first *available* four years after the present date (39 BC). This otherwise neat solution to the difficulty is unfortunately at odds with the reference to the restoration of the democracy, a phrase most plausibly interpreted as meaning the ending of triumviral rule. This in fact happened at the end of 33 or at the latest in the course of 32 BC, after a five-year extension retrospectively agreed in 37 BC (ch. 95), but in 39 BC must have been expected to happen at the end of the five-year period laid down in the law, i.e. in late 38 BC.

66. Epidamnus is Dyrrachium (*Durazzo, Dürres*) on the Albanian coast. The Dardani lived in the upper valley of the river Axius (*Vardar*), more or less due north of Thessalonike.

67. The winters concerned are those of 39–38 BC (Athens) and 41–40 BC (Alexandria).

68. Neither Philadelphus nor Micylion is otherwise known to history.

69. Appian seems to mean that Antonius suspected Octavian of having prepared a large force in order to overpower him if he did not consent to the war against Pompeius – this being the sort of thing autocrats do to maintain or secure personal power, and therefore suspect others of planning to do.

70. C. Calvisius Sabinus, who had been consul the previous year (39 BC). He was one of the two senators, the other being L. Marcius Censorinus, who attempted to defend Caesar on the Ides of March.

71. L. Cornificius, a partisan of Octavian who held the tribunate in 43 BC, was 'the astute careerist who undertook to prosecute the absent Brutus under the Lex Pedia' (R. Syme, *The Roman Revolution*, 236; for the trials, see Book III, ch. 95 above). He went on to become consul in 35 BC.

72. After being holed ancient warships, being made largely of wood, tended to float in a waterlogged state rather than sink.

73. Ch. 25 above.

74. 37 BC.

75. The elder Antonia, the immediate fruit of the union between Antonius and Octavia, was born in 39 BC.

76. The river Taras (which is also the Greek name for Tarentum).

77. These men corresponded to a legion's double-strength first cohort, which normally accompanied the legionary commander. From this practice developed the imperial praetorian guard, always in attendance on the emperor.

78. The political events of the beginning of the year 32 BC leave little doubt that this second period of triumviral power ran from 1 January 37 BC to 31 December 33 BC, i.e. that it was renewed retrospectively in order to legitimize acts performed between the expiry of the first period (31 December 38 BC?) and the date of this meeting (commonly referred to as the 'Treaty of Tarentum'), which is uncertain but may have been as late as September 37 BC.

79. Octavia was also pregnant with the younger Antonia, born on 31 January 36 BC, and had the care of Antonius' two sons by Fulvia (M. Antonius 'Antyllus' and Iullus Antonius) as well as her own three children by C. Marcellus (see n. 53).

80. Menodorus' second desertion took place in the winter of 37–36 BC, and Octavian's second campaign against Sextus belongs to 36 BC.

81. This naval ceremony of purification (*lustratio*) was adapted by the Romans, when they first went to war by sea in the First Punic War, from their habitual practice at the beginning of a campaign on land.

82. T. Statilius Taurus, who was probably of Lucanian origin and certainly the first member of his family to become a Roman senator, was according to Velleius second only to Agrippa among Octavian's supporters. He had held a suffect consulship in 37 BC, and like Agrippa was spectacularly rewarded for his loyalty and military ability during this age of revolution.

83. L. Plinius Rufus, praetor designate, as revealed by a contemporary inscription from Lilybaeum.

84. Appian is not at his best here: Lipara is off the north coast of Sicily, Cossyra off the south and also considerably nearer to Africa than to Sicily.

85. The cape (*Punta Campanella*) west of Surrentum (modern *Sorrento*).

86. Octavian seems to have taken refuge either in the lee of Cape Palinurus, south of Velia, or in the northern of the two ancient harbours of Velia, now silted up. For explanation of the term 'six' (*hexeres*), see n. 61.

87. Liburnians were light, fast, and highly manoeuvrable warships.

88. Neptune's consort Amphitrite is regarded as equivalent to the sea.

89. Probably either the consul of 45 BC or, more plausibly in view of his curt description as 'a senator', his son.

90. Tauromenium is the modern *Taormina*, a little south of the entrance to the Straits of Messina; Scolacium (earlier Scylletium), which a modern geographer would surely hesitate to describe as 'across from' Tauromenium, is the modern *Squillace*, lying on the eastern side of the isthmus of Calabria, opposite Vibo.

91. Papias is almost certainly another name of the man usually called Demochares; see chs. 105–6 and Dio XLIX, 8.2.

92. For Tisienus Gallus, see ch. 32.

93. On Papias-Demochares, see n. 91.

94. Perhaps a town called Palma (in Greek, *phoenix* means palm-tree).

95. Carisius may be the P. Carisius who was one of Augustus' generals in the Spanish campaigns of 26–23 BC. Of Titinius nothing else is known.

96. Abala is unidentifiable, but must be somewhere on the Italian side of the strait between Rhegium and Leucopetra.

97. C. Carrinas, son of the Marian leader mentioned in Book I, ch. 87, had been a follower of Julius Caesar and became suffect consul in 43 BC. Q. Laronius, otherwise barely known, went on to hold a suffect consulship in 33 BC.

98. Cornificius was marching north-west from Tauromenium (*Taormina*) towards Tyndaris across the ridges and lava flows on the northern flanks of Etna. For a detailed discussion of the topography, see Gabba's commentary on this passage.

99. 'At Mylae' is an error (whether of a copyist or of Appian himself), to judge from the events narrated in the following chapter.

100. Appian seems to mean that Pompeius controlled the way in to the north-eastern triangle of the island, both on the east coast around Tauromenium (*Taormina*) and on the north around Mylae (*Milazzo*).

101. See Homer, *Odyssey* XII, 260ff.: Odysseus prevented his companions from eating the cattle of the sun-god but when he fell asleep they disobeyed him, with calamitous consequences.

102. Tisienus Gallus had been at the western end of the island confronting Lepidus: see ch. 104.

103. Mount Myconium (unidentified) must lie somewhere near *Montalbano d'Elicona*, not far from the region crossed by Cornificius (ch. 114).

104. The Latin word for this grab was *harpago*. Caesar, describing a naval battle in 49 BC, speaks of the preparation of 'iron claws and *harpagones*' (*Civil War* I, 57). Agrippa's innovation consisted in adapting the existing manual grappling device by armouring it and enabling it to be used at long range.

105. 3 September 36 BC. According to Suetonius (*Divus Augustus* 16.1) the battle took place between Mylae and Naulochus. It is generally called the battle of Naulochus, the earlier engagement described in chs. 106–8 being known as the battle of Mylae.

106. By 'at the ram' Appian must mean ramming from abeam, which would dislodge or even shear off the victim's ram, rather than from ahead, when the shock would be equal for the two ships and there would be no advantage to the attacker. For the shaking-off of marines, see the opening sentences of ch. 107.

107. Warships were as far as possible kept in dockyards or ashore, since the timber of their hulls took up water when afloat and they rapidly became heavier and therefore slower.

108. See Book II, ch. 132. Henceforth Lepidus was allowed to live quietly at Circeii, south of Rome. He did not die until 12 BC, whereupon Augustus could at last emulate his 'father' Caesar by becoming Pontifex Maximus (see ch. 131 below).

109. Members of the local senates (town councils) were called decurions. It was a privilege of the equestrian order to wear a toga with a narrow purple stripe (the broad stripe being reserved for senators of Rome, and well-born children), and many decurions, though by no means all, would have been equestrians. It seems, from the sequel, that Octavian was attempting to avoid also giving the officers in question the money necessary to raise their personal wealth to the 400,000 sesterces which was normally a condition of membership of the order.

110. At 6,000 denarii to the talent, 1,600 talents would pay a bonus of 500 denarii to 19,200 men.

111. Octavian had to be content with an ovation, a sort of minor triumph (held on 13 November 36 BC), because to claim a full triumph it would have been necessary to maintain that the foe in Sicily was a foreigner, not the son of one of the most famous of all Romans. The festival for Naulochus (3 September) is documented in the official calendars, while the 'rostral column', as it is known, appears on coins issued by Augustus.

112. The treaty is that of Misenum, of 39 BC; see ch. 72.

113. C. Calvisius Sabinus, consul in 39 BC.

114. The *vigiles* combined the functions of night-watch and police and were instituted by Augustus in AD 6.

115. In 36 BC Antonius had embarked on a campaign against Parthia and Media, which took him through Armenia to the gates of Phraaspa (south of modern *Tabriz*, in north-western Iran). He was still incommunicado in Media at the time of the battle of Naulochus.

116. It is generally believed that at this date Octavian can have been granted at most *some* of the powers and privileges of a tribune (probably no more than the personal sacrosanctity which the office conferred, as Cassius Dio says), since others were given in 30 BC and it was not until 23 BC that he received the full powers.

117. L. Calpurnius Bibulus is attested as commander of the Antonian fleet that had helped Octavian against Sextus Pompeius. If the Greek is correct (and there are difficulties with the usual translation, adopted here *faute de mieux*), Bibulus must have returned to Syria without the ships (see ch. 139) and been sent back to Italy almost at once.

118. The 'mother' was not Mucia, but Sextus' stepmother Cornelia.

119. For Labienus, see ch. 65.

120. M. Titius, nephew of L. Munatius Plancus, who was governor of Syria at this time (the winter of 36–35 BC).

121. C. Furnius (see chs. 30, 40, 75).

122. Ahenobarbus was governor of Bithynia and Amyntas was king of Galatia.

123. The Harbour of the Achaeans was where the Homeric Greeks were supposed to have camped when besieging Troy, near the mouth of the river Xanthus in the Troad.

124. For Cassius of Parma, see ch. 2; Q. Nasidius (probably son of L. Nasidius, a Pompeian fleet commander in 49–46 BC) had served under Sex. Pompeius since at least early in 43 BC, when he issued coinage for him; for Saturninus, see ch. 52; Q. Minucius Thermus, praetor in 58(?) BC, and C. Fannius, praetor in 55 BC, had both negotiated with Sextus on behalf of the senate in 43 BC and sought safety with him from the proscriptions at the end of that year; for Antistius Reginus, see Book IV, ch. 40.

125. By Roman standards, it was a disgrace to surrender to any non-Roman (even a king) rather than to a fellow-Roman.

126. See chs. 25, 91, 110, 140.

APPENDIX

The following is an attempt to supply essential background to a number of topics which underlie or crop up in Appian's narrative but are too complicated to explain in a footnote. Many matters are controversial, particularly in detail, and the approach has perforce to be dogmatic. The statements are intended to be correct for the very late Republic (80–50 BC) but should not necessarily be taken as true of earlier periods.

A. THE ROMAN ASSEMBLIES IN THE LATE REPUBLIC

The source of sovereignty was the assembly of citizens (all free, i.e. non-slave, males over seventeen). This elected the annual magistrates, passed laws, and declared (or, later, ratified) war and peace. It had once constituted the court for capital offences, but during our period this function became devolved to inappellable standing courts set up by law, which therefore acted as committees, so to speak, of the sovereign people. It met in two chief guises:

(i) The Comitia Centuriata

The more ancient (though not *the* most ancient; see n. 100 to Book III, ch. 94), was called the *comitia centuriata* ('the assembly meeting by centuries'). It was composed of a number of voting units called 'centuries' (regardless of the number of men in them), which each had a single vote determined within the century by a majority of those present. The centuries were subdivisions of the five property classes into which the censors distributed all citizens except the very poor, who were classed as *infra classem* ('below class') and were lumped into a single century for voting. The subdivision of the five classes into centuries was arranged in such a way that the few rich were distributed into far more centuries, and therefore had vastly more voting power, than the many poor and relatively poor. Out of 193 centuries in all, seventy belonged to the first class and another eighteen to the 'knights' (see *B*, below), who were in effect the cream of the class. Voting started with the centuries of Class I and continued down the classes until the required total of ninety-seven affirmative votes was reached. The result was that the *comitia centuriata* was much more conservative than the tribal assembly (see below, on the *comitia tributa*) and tended to represent the interests of the rich. Such a system can hardly be called democratic, but the only real business of this assembly in our period, with one or two famous exceptions like the bill to recall Cicero from exile in 57 BC, was to elect the higher magistrates. And these, it has been observed, were 'fiercely competitive contests *within the ruling class*' (A. Yakobson, *Journal of Roman Studies* 82 (1992), p. 45). In any hard-fought election, where there was a fairly even split in Class I, it would be the centuries of the lower classes which would deliver the deciding votes. This explains why it was necessary for consular candidates to compete for the favour of the Roman *plebs* by giving them entertainment, food, privileges, and money. The votes of the poor might not be required; but if they were, they were vital.

Every year the *comitia centuriata* elected the two consuls, who had charge of the state and in theory (and quite often in practice) commanded its armies, and the six (after 80 BC, eight) praetors, whose main duty in this era was to preside over one of the standing courts, but could assume the functions of consuls if there were a need. From time to time (but not between 70 and 28 BC) censors were elected, who let the state contracts and saw to the revision of the register of citizens which determined liability for military service and membership of a class in the assembly.

By the last decades of the Republic it had become normal for the consuls to remain in Rome for the duration of their year of office, presiding over the deliberations of the senate and attending to routine and ceremonial duties; whereas earlier a consul would if possible take the field with an army and strive to enhance his reputation with military victories. Once their year of office was over, consuls and praetors alike would normally expect to be sent out to provinces as governors. In this capacity a man might find himself performing exclusively administrative and legal duties, or commanding legions engaged on more or less serious war, or any combination of the two. The importance of a provincial governorship in the late Republic was that (depending of course on the province) it gave the holder a position which he could exploit to line his own pocket, and/or command of an army which owed its first loyalty to him. For this purpose the constitutional authority (*imperium*, the power to give binding orders) which had been conferred on him by his initial election was extended by senatorial decree for as long as was necessary, and he was termed (normally) proconsul. So long as he held *imperium* he was immune from prosecution (except for a very limited number of offences, mostly relating to his election) and retained the right to command troops and issue valid legal judgements. The *imperium* of proconsuls was fully valid only in their designated provinces and had to be laid down on entry into Rome.

(ii) *The* Comitia Tributa

The other main assembly was known as the *comitia tributa* ('assembly meeting by tribes') or *concilium plebis* ('plebeian assembly'); these two forms were technically different, but Roman authors themselves confuse them and for all practical purposes they may be taken as the same. Here the voting units were the thirty-five tribes, which were not kinship groups, but territorial areas. They each delivered a single vote, determined by a majority of members present, in the same way as the centuries of the other assembly. Thus a magistrate was elected, or a law passed, as soon as eighteen affirmative votes had been secured (cf. I.12). Membership of a tribe depended on owning property in its area, but once determined appears to have been hereditary until the censors noticed, or were told, that it was no longer appropriate for a man to be registered in a particular tribe. Many Roman citizens lived long distances from Rome and could not easily journey in to vote. Thus at most assemblies many of the thirty-one 'rural' tribes were represented by a very small number of voters, and a man who belonged to such a tribe but happened to live in Rome possessed a vote that was worth very much more than that of the thousands of his fellow-citizens (including all ex-slaves) who were registered in one of the four urban tribes. It was also easier, in these tribes, for the candidate or the proposer of legislation to activate the systems of patronage and mutual obligation characteristic of Roman society in order to secure the vote he desired.

This assembly elected the junior magistrates and its own presidents, the tribunes of the *plebs*. The latter could call it together and put legislation to it; they also presided at elections and trials conducted by it; they had the right, in the unlikely case that they were not already senators, to attend meetings of the senate and could even summon that body and put business before it; and they had the power to forbid (Latin *veto*) an action not only of an ordinary citizen, but also of any magistrate including a consul or another tribune. When exploited to the full, as they were by some tribunes of the late Republic, these powers were an explosive and potentially anarchic element in the constitution. But the tribunes of the late Republic were in no sense men of the people. The office had become a normal rung on the exclusively senatorial ladder of public office which led eventually, for the fortunate few, to the consulship. Relatively few men employed the powers of the tribunate to become political figures of consequence, and even fewer employed them demagogically, but those who did played a crucial part in the collapse of the Republic into ungovernability. Particularly potent at the end of the Republic was the alliance, first adumbrated by Marius and Saturninus in 103 BC, of a (pro)consul with an army who was prepared to act in concert with a demagogic tribune to bring before the assembly, without reference to the senate, legislation favourable to the interests of the coalition. Had the assembly been properly representative, this might not have mattered; but as it was, the contentious assemblies of the sixties and fifties BC were violent and unrepresentative, being attended, if we can believe Cicero, by thugs, brawlers, bribed voters, and all too few honest citizens.

B. SENATE AND EQUESTRIAN ORDER ('KNIGHTS')

Although the senate was at the heart of the way the Roman state actually worked, and senators had great status and influence, it had very little constitutional power and found itself on the defensive when faced by troublesome tribunes. A man became a senator (in this period) by securing election to one of the twenty annual quaestorships; and once a senator, always a senator, unless he committed a misdemeanour serious enough to warrant expulsion by the censors or condemnation in the courts. Senators were public figures and to them, almost exclusively, were entrusted all the important posts and duties which ensured that the state could function. None but senators were elected to any of the higher magistracies, so that the senate was in fact composed of all serving and ex-magistrates and its composition was determined by popular election. After Sulla it numbered about 600. Sons of consuls and censors had to submit themselves to the Roman people for approval just as their fathers had done, and there was no hereditary or automatic right of entry. None the less, things were a great deal easier for men who could boast consular, or at least senatorial, ancestors than for someone like Cicero who was the first member of his family to enter the senate, and there was considerable continuity amongst the Roman political élite.

The formal function of the senate was to be the consuls' advisory council. The consuls presided alternately, a month at a time. The method of debate was for the consul to ask senators in order, starting with the most senior, to give their opinion on the question at issue. Standards of relevance were lax, and as important men liked to talk, it seems that debate seldom proceeded much beyond the ex-consuls and magistrates-elect. The senate could pass decrees (*senatus consulta*), which were authoritative and gave *prima facie* backing for executive action by the magistrates, but in the Republic they did not have the force of law unless they were translated into formal legislative instruments and passed by the *comitia*. In practice, some *senatus consulta*, usually of an administrative or legal nature, came to acquire the force of law by virtue of simple acceptance, and there were large areas of Roman public life where the senate was accepted as the right body to make decisions: amongst them provincial administration, diplomatic relations, internal security, and finance. But in principle, any decree of the senate could be challenged and overturned by a decision of the assembly. Furthermore, a tribune could veto a decree in the senate, however large the majority that supported it, as Antonius and Cassius did just before Caesar crossed the Rubicon (cf. II.33, though Appian does not explain that this was the case).

The *equites* (members of the equestrian order, 'knights') were no more true cavalry than the boardroom Knights of the City of London. The qualifications for membership of the order, which must have numbered several thousand after the Social War, were respectable birth, possession of property worth more than 400,000 sesterces (for comparison, note that a soldier was paid 900 sesterces per annum after Julius Caesar's doubling of the rate), and some cavalry (i.e. officer) service in the army – and this last became a token, or was even completely ignored, in the late Republic. The *equites* thus represented the cream of society, forming in effect a special census class above the first class. From it were drawn the senators, but senatorial status was purely personal (like that of a life peer in our day). There was no distinct senatorial order until it was brought into being by the legislation of Augustus, and senators' sons remained *equites* unless and until they too succeeded in being elected to a quaestorship and therefore membership of the senate. Although in our period (but not for most of the Republic) a man relinquished his membership of the equestrian order on becoming a senator, and the *equites'* role in public life went no further than their membership of the juries of the standing criminal courts, the two classes were indissolubly interconnected by ties of blood, marriage, and friendship. The wealthiest *equites* were heavily involved in finance and in state contracts (especially tax collection), which in a few celebrated contexts (e.g. II.13) brought their interests into collision with those of the government (an analogy might be a clash between the City of London and a Tory government on, say, a regulatory issue). Lesser men included the local aristocracies of the towns of Italy – such places as Arpinum, home to Marius and Cicero – and the sort of comfortably-off Roman who lacked the desire for a public career and preferred to live a gentlemanly life attending to the family estates. In general senators and *equites* together formed the Roman élite, having an identical economic base and a shared social background. Both depended for their basic wealth on the ownership of land and the exploitation of an agricultural surplus obtained from tenants or slaves. To this might be added various land-related enterprises such as the working of quarries or clay-pits, shipping to get produce to the market, and letting of urban property. Senators were debarred from taking the great state contracts like those for tax collection or army supplies, and were not supposed to indulge openly in money-lending or large-scale trade; but they in fact did so by way of intermediaries and men of straw, so that by far the largest financial operations known to us from the late Republic are those which were conducted on behalf of mighty political figures like Pompeius Magnus and Crassus. The picture that emerges from some of our sources of two classes locked in ongoing political combat with each other is very largely false.

C. THE ROMAN PROLETARIAT

Rome grew in the last hundred and fifty years of the Republic from a city of perhaps 200,000 inhabitants to one of nearly a million. The actual figures are debatable, the fact and the order of magnitude of the growth are not. The problems of feeding, draining, watering, and controlling such a city were immense, and it is hardly surprising that a free corn ration had to be introduced, that political bribery and corruption were rife, that violence frequently broke out, and that much political capital could be made out of the provision of splendid public facilities to offset what must have been the squalor of a good deal of ordinary domestic life. Many people lived in jerry-built tenement blocks without sanitation or water, many others, one presumes, in huts and shanty accommodation on the outskirts. The immense growth distorted the city-state political institutions of Rome and changed the character of the sovereign assemblies, a process fiercely resisted by the traditional upper class as they felt themselves losing control of the system. The origin of the new inhabitants was twofold: some were peasants who had been forced off their land by the process described by Appian at the beginning of his narrative (I.7), while others were (ex-)-slaves or their descendants, whose presence was the result of the enormous importation of slave labour into Italy which had gone on from the beginning of the second century BC, and of the humane and remarkable Roman habit of freeing large numbers of slaves and making citizens out of them. Add to this the natural growth of the population (though one cannot be certain about this), and the attraction of a great metropolis to traders, tricksters, and entrepreneurs of all kinds, and one begins to have a faint idea of what late republican Rome was like. It bore very little relationship to the more modest city of the early and middle Republic for which the constitution had been designed, and from whose political life and military achievements the aristocracy still derived their notions of public service. One of the great men of the second century BC, Scipio Aemilianus, addressing a gathering of Roman citizens shortly after the death of Tiberius Gracchus, expressed his feelings brutally and memorably by daring to tell the crowd that Rome was 'but their step-mother' (Velleius II.4.4).

D. THE LATINS AND THE ROMAN CITIZENSHIP

Except for a few old Latin-speaking towns near Rome, such as Tibur and Praeneste, the Latin communities were new foundations above all of the fourth and third centuries, planted as 'little Romes' to secure and consolidate the Roman conquest of central Italy. All shared with Rome a common language and common basic political institutions, including a large measure of civil law, but were quite independent sovereign states. They were allied with Rome and regularly contributed troops to the joint army. Citizenship was originally interchangeable, as it used to be in the old British Commonwealth. However, as Rome grew in size and strength, and her armies operated even farther from home, she came to regard the other Latins as her satellites. During the course of the second century the Romans derived much more benefit from their conquest of large parts of the Mediterranean world than did their Latin (and other Italian) allies, but continued to demand military contributions from them and treat them almost as though they were part of the Roman state. The Romans also attempted to control migration to Rome (and so prevent reduction of the Latin military manpower available to the Roman authorities) by taking away the right of any Latin to become a citizen of Rome by moving to the city and declaring his new domicile at the next census. Some compensation was given by allowing men who attained the chief magistracy in the Latin towns to become Roman citizens (cf. II.26), so that in time, since citizenship was hereditary, the local élites would become Roman, presiding over a Latin proletariat. Thus the Latins, with the exception of their upper class who enjoyed this limited privilege, became increasingly disadvantaged and were treated more and more like Rome's other Italian allies, most of whom had been conquered in war and lacked the bond of common language and ethnic origin. For the ordinary citizen of a Latin community, the Latin rights (*ius Latinum*) meant little more than access to the Roman system of civil law, particularly that concerned with contract and marriage. But the distinction between the two classes of Rome's allies in Italy was still sufficiently strong for Gaius Gracchus to use it as a means of tempering his radical policy of extending membership of the Roman state to all the Italians. According to the most likely interpretation of *Civil Wars* I.23, he proposed that existing Latins become Roman, and the other allies Latin – thus allowing *their* upper class to become slowly Roman, and not admitting huge numbers of new voters at a stroke to the citizen body. The Latins (with the single exception of isolated Beneventum) were also conspicuously loyal to Rome when the Social War eventually broke out over this very question, though one suspects that their loyalty may not have been unrelated to the fact that a high proportion of their upper class would already have possessed the Roman citizenship by this time.

E. THE ARMIES OF THE LATE REPUBLIC

The Roman army had originally been a citizen militia recruited each campaigning season and disbanded at the end of it. To enable this system to work every adult Roman male, except the very poor who possessed so little property that they fell below the minimum for enrolment in the five census classes (see *A* above), had the obligation to serve a certain number of campaigns (sixteen in the third century) before he could claim exemption from further service. But as Rome's power and military needs grew, the army gradually turned into a permanent force, with legions serving overseas for numbers of years continuously. The requirement to serve sixteen campaigns seems to have been mitigated, but none the less to take a peasant farmer from his land for (say) five whole years, during which the working of his land and maintenance of his family fell upon wife, children, or relatives, was capable of ruining him (even if he survived disease and battle). There is other evidence than that of Appian (*Civil Wars* I.7) that one of the effects of this burden of military service, from the second century onwards, was the dispossession of the traditional peasantry by larger landowners employing slaves. The state's need for military manpower was such that the lower limit for membership of the five census classes (see *A (i)* above), and hence the obligation to serve in the army, was eventually dropped to a point little above bare subsistence level. By the late second century military service was highly unpopular, because Rome had already looted most of the wealthiest areas and campaigns were apt to be against tough opponents who afforded the or-

dinary soldier little prospect of returning home laden with booty. Ther
pears to have been a genuine shortage of men. But the need for soldiers
(and in fact without the contribution of her allies Rome would have been v
iously weakened).

The obvious solution was found by Marius, who cut the knot by accepting ᴀꜱ recruits into his army in 107 BC men who were technically not qualified because they
were outside the five census classes. Such near-destitutes saw military service as at
worst a dangerous and uncomfortable way of getting meals, clothes, and a bed, and
at best a means of becoming rich. A Roman ex-peasant's idea of riches was his own
smallholding, and the Roman state had in the past rewarded its citizen-soldiery by
making grants of land at the conclusion of successful campaigns. There is no evidence that Marius actually promised his new recruits land when he enlisted them,
but by means of his alliance with Saturninus (see I.29) he set about providing it.
Thus, although it is unlikely to have been obvious at the time, the foundations of the
Roman 'professional' army were laid. It was now worth a man's while to serve for
long periods in the expectation that when he was finally discharged he would receive a reasonable reward. The state provided no pension, gratuity, or compensation
other than a miserable level of pay to its troops, and it was up to a commander to
reward them – out of booty or, from Marius onwards, with the hope or reality of
land settlements. Under these circumstances the loyalty of an army became transferred from the state to its general, who alone was in a position to see that the necessary legislation was put through. Because soldiers were also citizens, and therefore
voters when they could get to Rome, they constituted a formidable political
weapon even before being persuaded to unsheathe their swords in defence of their
commander's interests or dignity.

Sulla was the first man to exploit to the full the changed character of the army,
and after him the power struggle at Rome was always bound up with the control of
provinces, and therefore of armies. Commitment by the soldiery to any political or
religious cause is conspicuously absent. Although the troops swore a personal oath
of loyalty to their general, it was only Caesar, and to a certain extent M. Brutus, who
inspired much personal devotion amongst their men. In particular, the story of the
civil wars after the death of Caesar often involves desertion, selling of services, or
mutinous demands for improved rewards. The soldiers were indeed taking their revenge on society for the way in which they, who had created the Roman Empire,
had been largely excluded from its profits.

F. THE TERMINAL DATE OF CAESAR'S COMMAND IN GAUL

This question, which is of some importance to any analysis of the outbreak of the
civil war in 49 BC, has been endlessly discussed, and in German scholarship even
dignified with its own title, *die Rechtsfrage*. It is, unfortunately, complicated.

By a bill of May 59 BC proposed by the tribune Vatinius, Caesar was appointed proconsul of Cisalpine Gaul and Illyria, to which Transalpine Gaul was very soon added by the senate. Caesar was to govern these provinces, with a substantial army, for five years: it seems that the date of 1 March 54 was in some way relevant – whether because that was the date before which he could not be superseded, or because no discussion about his successor could take place until then. But events overtook this first terminal date. As a result of the Conference of Luca (II.17) his command was in effect extended (in 55) for a further five years by a law of Pompeius and Crassus which forbade discussion of a successor to him until 1 March 50. By the legal procedures governing provincial appointments as they then stood, this meant that Caesar would not have to give place to another governor until early in 48. The reason for this was that the first consuls to whom Caesar's provinces could be assigned were those of 49, since Gaius Gracchus had passed a law which forced the senate to nominate provincial commands for the consuls before they were elected. Thus consuls elected in the autumn of 50 would, under the usual procedures of the fifties, serve their year of office (49) in Rome and only then proceed to a province early the next year (48). By this time Caesar hoped to be holding his second consulship, having waited the prescribed ten-year interval since his first.

It was important to Caesar that he passed straight from a proconsular command to his anticipated second consulship without an interval in which he became a private citizen and could therefore be prosecuted by his political enemies for the illegalities of his first consulship. To ensure that he was protected, Pompeius Magnus in 52 supported a law proposed by all ten tribunes which permitted Caesar to stand in absence for the consulship instead of canvassing in person, a procedure which would have entailed laying down his magisterial authority. This was fair. But Pompeius also changed the ground rules of the system of provincial appointments, by providing that a five-year interval must elapse between the holding of a city magistracy (consulship or praetorship) and the tenure of a province. This meant that Caesar could now be replaced by someone other than a consul of 49, and it was theoretically possible for the senate to decide on 1 March 50 that Caesar be superseded immediately by a legally named successor. The only reason why this did not happen is that Pompeius had omitted to make his new law immune to tribunician veto, as appointments under Gaius Gracchus' law had been. Caesar promptly bought one of the tribunes, young Curio, the heavily indebted son of one of his opponents, by paying off his debts. Curio, without revealing his change of allegiance, was successful in preventing any decision being taken on a successor to Caesar until the end of the year. His role was then taken over by Antonius and Q. Cassius, who entered office as tribunes on 10 December 50 BC. Negotiations meanwhile proceeded to try and reach a compromise whereby both Pompeius and Caesar would lay down their military commands in whole or in part, and Caesar would be protected from the pent-up wrath of his die-hard opponents (who included both the consuls of 49). These negotiations broke down, as Appian relates, and when Antonius and Cassius dared to veto the senate's decision to appoint Domitius Ahenobarbus to succeed Caesar forthwith, the reaction of the consuls and Caesar's enemies was such that they feared for their lives. They fled by night to Caesar, who it is clear had already decided to invade Italy, but was glad to have a convenient pretext for war – namely the defence of the ancient inviolability and sacrosanctity of the tribunes of the Roman people.

G. 'THE ITALIANS' IN BOOK I

Appian first draws a picture of social and economic crisis afflicting Italy, and then uses the term 'Italians' to describe the beneficiaries of Tiberius' land law. None of our other authorities write as if the law was designed to benefit any class of person other than Roman citizens. Can Appian really mean that a Roman tribune, enthusiastically supported by the Roman populace (and the agricultural part of it at that; see I.13–14), was proposing to give away to non-Romans large areas of Roman public land: and if so, why did an upper class who bitterly opposed the measure fail to whip up opposition among the mass of ordinary voters by the obvious tactic of appealing to their selfishness (cf. I.36)?

The most attractive solution to this much-discussed problem is to suppose that Appian is using 'Italians' (*Italiotai* in the Greek, or sometimes *Italoi* or *Italikon genos*) anachronistically to mean, as in his own day, non-metropolitan Roman citizens of Italian origin living in (or occasionally outside) Italy. This interpretation will more or less square with the account he gives (I.7) of Rome's exploitation of her conquest of Italy, especially if the Latin colonies are counted for these purposes as Roman (see *D* above). It is also consistent with his apparent identification of 'the Italians' with the country voters (who must by definition be Roman citizens) who supported Appuleius Saturninus' land law in 100 BC (I.30–31). However, it will clearly not square with his usage in I.21, where 'the Italians' prefer the acquisition of Roman citizenship to the retention of their estates, nor with the narrative from I.34 onwards, leading up to the Social War, where 'the Italians' rebel against Rome precisely in order to gain the Roman citizenship.

Appian is, manifestly, inconsistent in his usage. My own view is based on J. Bleicken's argument ('Tiberius Gracchus und die italischen Bundesgenossen', *Palingenesia* XXXII (1990), 101–31) that he was probably confused by the terminology of his sources as well as by that of his own day. Two facts are of particular relevance. One is that 'Italy' was apparently a name first invested with *political* significance by the Italian peoples who rebelled against Rome in 90 BC and gave their capital Corfinium the name Italica or Italia. Previously it had been a purely geographical term which originally denoted modern Calabria, but spread until by the very end of the third century BC it had come to describe the whole peninsula south of the Apennines. Thus in the written sources of the late second century BC, on which Appian's narrative must ultimately depend, 'Italians' simply means 'people who live in the peninsula'. The other fact is that between 133 and 70 BC the whole free population of the peninsula south of the Po acquired Roman citizenship, whereas at the outset only about a third of them had possessed it. At the beginning of the period metropolitan Roman citizens can be logically distinguished from their rural brethren, some of whom lived large distances from the capital, and both can be legally distinguished from citizens of all the other independent states and cities of Italy (although some of these, like Tibur or Praeneste, were much nearer to Rome than the more far-flung pieces of Roman territory). But in practice, largely thanks to the way the Romans exploited their alliances with these other states and cities in the second century BC, the interests of rural Romans were often closer to those of the non-Romans than to those of their urban fellow-citizens; and once all had become Roman citizens, only one distinction came to obtain, the one familiar to Appian and his contemporaries, namely that between Romans living in Rome and Romans living in the rest of Italy.

It has been argued that however inaccurate a historian Appian may sometimes be, in a matter of such importance to his narrative he cannot simply have been careless. Yet this remains the best explanation, and constitutional niceties are clearly not his forte. For example, he mentions Latins but once in the whole of Book I (ch. 23), in spite of the fact that Latins were an extremely important and privileged category of 'almost-Romans': they were deeply involved in the turbulent politics of 123–80 BC and possessed a peculiar status which furnished a powerful political tool which has to be understood by any historian of the period (see *D* above). It seems, then, reasonable to conclude that Appian's unique account of Tiberius Gracchus' legislation results not from any use of a variant and possibly superior source, but from his own failure to use consistent terminology or to explain clearly the juridical differences between the various interest groups.

MAPS

A. *Northern and Central Italy*

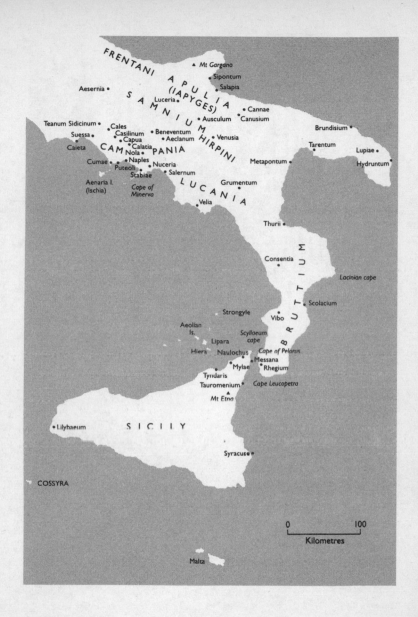

FRENTANI

APULIA
(IAPYGES)

SAMNIUM

HIRPINI

CAMPANIA

LUCANIA

BRUTTIUM

SICILY

▲ Mt Gargano

Sipontum •
Salapia •

Aesernia •

Luceria •

Teanum Sidicinum •

Cales •
Casilinum •
Capua •
Calatia •
Nola •

Suessa •

Caieta •

Cumae •
Puteoli •
Stabiae •

Aenaria I.
(Ischia)

Cape of
Minerva

Beneventum •
Aeclanum •

Ausculum •
Canusium •

Cannae •

Venusia •

Brundisium •

Tarentum •

Lupiae •
Hydruntum •

Metapontum •

Naples •
Nuceria •
Salernum •

Grumentum •

Velia •

Thurii •

Consentia •

Lacinian cape

Scolacium •

Strongyle •

Aeolian
Is.

Lipara •

Hiera •

Vibo •

Scyllaeum
cape

Naulochus •

Mylae •

Tyndaris •

Tauromenium •

Messana •
Rhegium •

Cape of Pelorus

Cape Leucopetra

Mt Etna ▲

• Lilybaeum

Syracuse •

COSSYRA

0   100

Kilometres

Malta

B. *Southern Italy and Sicily*

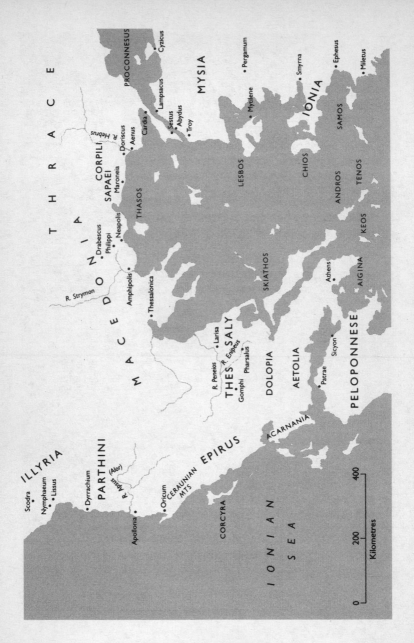

C. *Greece and the Aegean Basin*

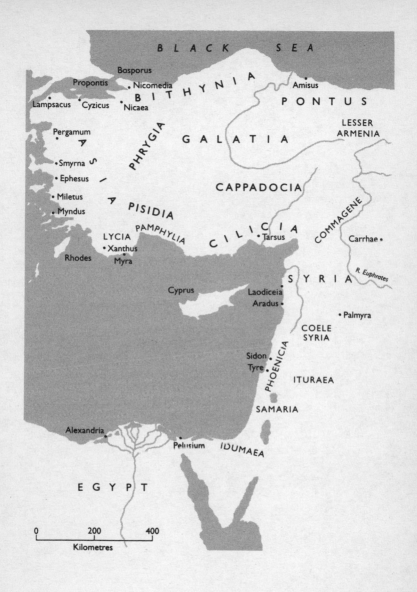

D. *Provinces and Kingdoms of the East*

INDEX

What follows is chiefly an index of proper names, but a few subjects have also been included. Roman magistrates are as far as possible further identified by a date of office, in most but not all cases the highest held (cos. = consul; pr. = praetor; aed. = aedile; qu. = quaestor; suff = suffectus (replacement); tr. pl. = tribune of the plebs). All dates are BC unless otherwise indicated. Where known, full names have been given, even though these seldom appear in Appian's text, and some persons described but not actually named by Appian (e.g. 'the consuls', 'the triumvirs') have been indexed under their names. Not indexed: Italy, Rome, Sicily in Book V, and some references serving as dates or identification (e.g. 'after the death of Caesar', 'one of Pompeius' party').

Ilerda II.42

Illyria(ns) I.19; II.32, 39, 41, 47, 59;
III.63; IV.58, 75, 88; V.75, 80, 128,
132, 145; *Map C*

Ilus II.68

Imperator II.44; IV.8, 10, 37

India II.149, 153, 154; V.9

interrex I.98

Ionia(ns) I.76; II.49, 71, 89; IV.63, 82;
V.65; *Map C*

Ionian Sea I.109; *Map C*

Ionius II.39

Isauricus *see* Servilius

Isis IV.47

Ituraea V.7; *Map D*

Iuba (*King of Numidia*) II.44-6, 83, 87,
95, 96, 100, 101; IV.53, 54

Iuba (*son of foregoing*) II.101

Iugurtha (*King of Numidia*) I.42, 77

Iulia (*d. of cos. 59*) II.14, 19

Iulia (*sister of cos. 59*) III.9

Iulia (*mother of M. Antonius*) III.51, 58;
IV.32, 37; V.52, 63

Iulia (*?error for Scribonia*) V.72

Iulius Caesar, C. (*cos. 59, 48, 46-44*) I.4,
6, 104; II.1, 6, 8-19 passim, 23-36
passim, 38, 40-43, 47 9, 52-154
passim; III.1-35, 40, 55, 60-63
passim, 73-87 passim, 94, 95, 98;
IV.8, 33, 38, 53, 54, 57, 58, 61, 70,
74, 75, 83, 84, 89-98 passim, 124,
132-4; V.3, 4, 7, 23, 55, 72, 97, 137

Iulius Caesar (Augustus), Imp. C. *see*
Octavius, C.

Iulius Caesar, L. (*misnamed Sex. by
Appian, cos. 90*) I.40, 41, 42, 43, 45,
72

Iulius Caesar, L. (*cos. 64*) IV.12, 37

Iulius Caesar, Sex. (*cos. 91*) I.48

Iulius Caesar, Sex. (*qu. 48*) III.77;
IV.58

Iulius Caesar Strabo, C. (*curule aed.
90*) I.72

Iunius Brutus, L. (*cos. 509*) II.112, 120

Iunius Brutus, M. (Q. Servilius Caepio
Brutus) (*pr. 44*) I.4; II.111-23,
136, 137-42; III.2-8, 12, 23, 24, 35,
54, 63, 64, 78, 79, 85, 89, 96, 97;
IV.1, 3, 5, 20, 27, 36-8, 46, 49, 51,
57, 58, 61, 63, 65, 69, 70, 75-82, 88,
89, 98, 101-14, 117-38; V.2, 6, 43,
67, 75, 112

Iunius Brutus, M. (*pr. 88*) I.60

Iunius Brutus Albinus, D. (*pr. 45*) II.48,
111, 113, 115, 122, 124, 143, 146;
III.2, 6; 16, 27, 30, 32, 37, 38, 45,
49-51, 53, 55, 59-65, 71, 73, 74, 76,
80, 81, 85, 86, 90, 96-8; IV.1, 58

Iunius Brutus Damasippus, L. (*pr.
82*) I.88, 92

Iunius Silanus, D. (*cos. 62*) II.5

Iuppiter Stator, temple of II.11

Iuventius Laterensis, M. (*pr. 53*) III.84

Jews II.71, 90

Keos, *island* V.7; *Map C*

Kore (Persephone) IV.105

Labeo *see* Antistius

Labienus IV.26

Labienus, T. (*pr. by 59?*) II.62, 87, 95,
105

Labienus, Q. (*son of foregoing*) V.65, 133

Laelius Balbus, D. (*qu. 42*) IV.53, 55,
56

Laenas *see* Popillius

Laetorius, M. I.60, 62

Lafrenius, T. I.40, 47

Lamponius, M. I.40, 41, 90, 93

Lampsacus V.137; *Map C*

Lanuvium I.69; II.20; V.24; *Map A*

Laodiceia III.78; IV.52, 60, 62; V.4, 7;
Map D

Largus IV.28

Larinum I.52